Praise for Werner & Jones!

"I felt that the author was talking to me. . . . The writing style is clear and effective and supports effective teaching. The use of well-known companies throughout gives more credibility to the reading. **I have used many introductory texts and I feel that this is one of the best presentations."**

— *A. J. Potts, University of Southern Maine*

"I believe there are two topics that present the greatest difficulty for students. First is the cash versus accrual bases of accounting. The second is the process of recording transactions via debits and credits, normalization, and posting to the ledger. **The Werner/Jones text handles both of these issues better than my current text."**

— *Marshall Pitman, University of Texas–San Antonio*

"The entire book is very clearly written at a presentation level appropriate for an introductory course. The clarity and effectiveness of presentation is excellent, and I have enjoyed using this text. **My students typically give me unsolicited positive feedback on the text, particularly its readability."**

— *Connie Groer, Frostburg State University*

"Chapter 11 is excellent! It gives a very good description of where to look for information of a nonfinancial nature. This is an unusual asset in a beginning accounting text, and the authors should be congratulated. **This one chapter is enough to justify buying the book."**

— *Harold Wyman, Florida International University*

"I am currently using the Second Edition of this text and have found the chapters to be consistently strong in content, examples, and writing style."

— *Michael Welker, Drexel University*

"The 'Accounting for Inventory' [chapter] did an excellent job of comparing periodic inventory to perpetual inventory systems. **Overall, Werner/Jones have done a better job of presenting the data on inventory in a more concise and understandable manner than [current text in use]."**

— *Ken Couvillion, San Joaquin Delta College*

"Werner/Jones lays out the inventory chapter (Chapter 8) in a way that is easier for the student to understand than does my present book."

— *David Caslan, Bethune-Cookman College*

" 'Statement of Cash Flows' is a difficult chapter . . . [and it] always challenges students. The discussion of the cash flow statement is clear, the example that walks us through the preparation is uncomplicated, and the discussion of the direct method included in the appendix is fine. **The best way to understand this topic is through actually preparing a statement of cash flows, and the chapter does a good job of doing so."**

— *Mark Bettini, University of California–Berkeley*

"It is my personal belief that the 'Analyzing of Financial Statements' chapter is the most important chapter in the course. After all, what's it all about if a student doesn't know how to use the financial statements to make important business decisions about a company. . . . **Trying to be objective, I must tell you that Werner/Jones have done an excellent job in this chapter."**

— *Ken Couvillion, San Joaquin Delta College*

Introduction to Financial Accounting

A User Perspective

THIRD EDITION

Michael L. Werner

University of Miami

Kumen H. Jones

Arizona State University, Retired

PEARSON

Prentice Hall

Upper Saddle River, NJ 07458

Dedication

To Frank Collins and Oscar J. Holtzmann, in appreciation of their friendship, guidance and encouragement.

–Michael Werner

To Kenneth A. Smith, my mentor and friend, without whom none of this would have happened.

–Kumen Jones

Library of Congress Cataloging-in-Publication Data

Werner, Michael L.
    Introduction to financial accounting : a user perspective / Michael L. Werner, Kumen H. Jones.— 3rd ed.
        p. cm.
    Rev. ed. of: Introduction to financial accounting / Kumen H. Jones . . . [et al.]. 2nd ed. c2000.
    Includes bibliographical references and index.
    ISBN 0-13-032759-X
        1. Managerial accounting. I. Jones, Kumen H. II. Introduction to financial accounting. III. Title.

HF5635.I657 2003
657—dc21   2002044962

Executive Editor: Mac Mendelsohn
Editor-in-Chief: P. J. Boardman
Assistant Editor: Sam Goffinet
Senior Editorial Assistant: Jane Avery
Development Editor: Amy Whitaker
Senior Media Project Manager: Nancy Welcher
Executive Marketing Manager: Beth Toland
Marketing Assistant: Patrick Danzuso
Managing Editor (Production): John Roberts
Production Editor: Kelly Warsak

Production Assistant: Joe DeProspero
Permissions Supervisor: Suzanne Grappi
Manufacturing Buyer: Michelle Klein
Art Director: Jayne Conte
Cover Illustration: Getty Images, Inc.
Composition: Rainbow Graphics
Full-Service Project Management: Linda Begley/Rainbow Graphics
Printer/Binder: Courier–Westford
Cover Printer: Phoenix Color Corp.

Credits and acknowledgments borrowed from other sources and reproduced, with permission, in this textbook appear on appropriate page within text.

Pearson Prentice Hall™ is a trademark of Pearson Education, Inc.
Pearson® is a registered trademark of Pearson plc
Prentice Hall® is a registered trademark of Pearson Education, Inc.
Pearson Education LTD.
Pearson Education Australia PTY, Limited

Pearson Education Singapore, Pte. Ltd
Pearson Education North Asia Ltd
Pearson Education, Canada, Ltd

Pearson Educación de Mexico, S.A. de C.V.
Pearson Education—Japan
Pearson Education Malaysia, Pte. Ltd

10 9 8 7 6 5 4 3 2 1
ISBN 0-13-032759-X

ontents

Preface

The world is changing, accounting education is changing, and so are accounting textbooks. Our book is no exception. In this edition, we have incorporated a number of changes that we believe will make this book an even better teaching resource than previous editions. In addition to rewriting much of the material for improved clarity, we have integrated coverage of the statement of cash flows and key financial ratios throughout the text. We also consolidated the two balance sheet chapters into one. In this edition, we added significantly to the assignment material and improved its alignment with the topics covered in each chapter. We have revised the chapter opening vignettes to increase student interest and to suggest the need for the accounting applications covered in the chapters. You will find that these changes, along with many others, help make this text an easy-to-use tool to teach beginning accounting students.

◆ BASIC PHILOSOPHY

Businesspeople must be prepared to perform tasks that only *people* can perform; in particular, they must be able to communicate, to think, and to make solid, well-informed decisions. Decision making is *the* critical skill in today's business world, and *Introduction to Financial Accounting: A User Perspective,* Third Edition, helps students to better use accounting information to improve their decision making skills.

This text provides an introduction to accounting within the context of business and business decisions. Readers will explore accounting information's role in the decision making process and learn how to use the accounting information found in financial statements and annual reports. Seeing how accounting information can be used to make better business decisions will benefit all students, regardless of their major course of study or chosen career.

We agree with the recommendations made by the Accounting Education Change Commission in its Position Statement No. Two: The First Course in Accounting. We believe the course should be a broad introduction to accounting, rather than introductory accounting as it has traditionally been taught. It should emphasize what accounting information is, why it is important, and how it is used by economic decision makers.

This text is purposely written so students will find it easy to read and understand. In this edition, many passages have been rewritten to further enhance readability and student understanding. In addition, we include the exhibits necessary to get important points across, but we very intentionally do not include the array of glitz and graphics that can break up the flow and distract student attention. We do not generally segregate material into special presentation boxes that might be skipped by students attempting to focus on the most relevant points. All of the points of interest and examples we present are woven into the body of the text.

◆ SUPPORT FOR THE INTERACTIVE CLASSROOM

We believe this text provides tools to actively involve students in their learning processes. The conversational tone of the text, its user perspective, and the logical presentation of topics all contribute to the ability of this text to meet that goal. However, several features are particularly important in developing a classroom atmosphere in which students share ideas, ask questions, and relate their learning to the world around them.

Throughout each chapter of the text, you will find Discussion Questions (DQs) that challenge students to reach beyond the surface of the written text to determine answers. Far from typical review questions, for which the students can scan a few pages of the text to locate an answer, many of the DQs provide relevant learning by relating students' personal experiences to the knowledge they gain through the text.

The DQs provide a variety of classroom experiences:

- Many DQs provide the basis for lively classroom discussions, requiring students to think about issues and formulate or defend their opinions.
- Some DQs are springboards for group assignments (in or out of the classroom) to put cooperative learning into practice.
- DQs may be assigned as individual writing assignments to allow students to practice and develop their writing skills.
- Combining individually written DQ responses with follow-up group discussions can spark lively debate!
- Having students keep a journal of their responses to all DQs (regardless of whether they are used in another way) encourages contemplation of accounting concepts.

The DQs comprise an important part of the text's pedagogy designed to emphasize important points that students may skim across in their initial reading. Even if they are not formally part of the required work for your course, students will gain a greater understanding of the concepts discussed when they take time to consider each question as part of the text.

Students get enthused about accounting when working with real companies. Chapter F1 and its appendix provide students with the knowledge they need to use library and Internet resources to research real companies. The chapter also introduces students to the annual report and Form 10-K. We included the 2002 *Pier 1 Imports, Inc.,* annual report with our text with the hope that instructors will find it a helpful resource for class examples. We also use *Pier 1*'s annual report for selected assignment material and to demonstrate financial analysis in Chapter F11.

Aside from its support for the interactive classroom, a major distinction of this text is its total separation of the use of accounting information and its preparation.

◆ SEPARATION OF ACCOUNTING AND BOOKKEEPING

Coverage of recording procedures differs from school to school. Some schools choose to have all students learn basic accounting procedures; others require only accounting majors to acquire these skills. Our text offers institutions the flexibility to cover accounting procedures to a significant degree, to cover just the basics, or to omit the coverage of accounting procedures entirely. In this text, we do not use debits and credits or journal entries to demonstrate or explain characteristics and uses of accounting information. In fact, except in the accounting procedures chapter itself (Chapter F6), no references are made to the recording process except in chapter appendices. To facilitate the separation of accounting and bookkeeping, we introduce the accounting cycle in Chapter F6 and complete its coverage in appendices to Chapters F7, F8, and F9. We hold off coverage of accounting procedures until Chapter F6 to give students the chance to acquire the basic accounting background that will help make accounting procedures easier to comprehend and learn.

Institutions that desire to omit recording procedures entirely would simply skip Chapter F6 and these appendices from their course coverage.

For those institutions that would like to include accounting procedures in their introductory accounting curriculum, Chapter F6 and the appendices in Chapter F7 through F9 cover the complete accounting cycle from analyzing transactions through post-closing trial balance. Coverage includes debits and credits, journal entries, adjusting entries, posting to the general ledger, trial balance preparation, the worksheet, and financial statement preparation. Chapter F6 assignment material includes short, medium, and long accounting procedure problems. In addition, the chapter includes three mini practice sets that take a student from the beginnings of a company all the way through the preparation of financial statements.

◆ IMPROVED AND EXPANDED ASSIGNMENT MATERIAL

In this edition, we added significantly to the assignment material and improved the alignment of assignment material with the topics coved in each chapter.

- *Discussion Questions.* As we have already mentioned, throughout each chapter of the text, you will find Discussion Questions (DQs) that challenge students to reach beyond the surface of the written text to determine answers.
- *Review the Facts.* Students can use these basic, definitional questions to review the key points of each chapter. The questions are in a sequence reflecting the coverage of topics in the chapter.
- *Annual Report Project.* The text includes a completely revised annual report project that begins in Chapter F1 and continues throughout the text. Adventures into real information about real companies always raise student interest! In addition it can foster an open, interactive environment in the classroom. In Chapter F1, the annual report project assignment requires students to select a publicly traded company and to obtain the company's Form 10-K and annual report. Instructors should not be concerned that they will need to spend valuable class time to tell students how to accomplish the assignment. The text and the material included in the assignment itself provide enough guidance so that students should be able to obtain the Form 10-K and annual report by themselves. The annual report project requirements in later chapters are similarly supported by the text. In Chapter F3, students use key financial ratios to analyze their company, and in Chapter F6, students select a peer company to use as a comparison throughout the remainder of the project. Instructors should note that even if they omit coverage of Chapter F6, the annual report project for Chapter F6 should be assigned as it is vital to the continuity of the project.
- *Apply What You Have Learned.* These end-of-chapter assignment materials include a mix of traditional types of homework problems and innovative assignments requiring critical thinking and writing. Many of the requirements can be used as the basis for classroom discussions. You will find matching problems, short essay questions, and calculations. Assignments dealing directly with the use of financial statements are also included. Many of these applications also work well as group assignments.

  There are three versions of most problems—one to use as an example in class, one for homework, and one extra.
- *Financial Reporting Exercises.* Financial Reporting Exercises included in the assignment material for each chapter encourage students to use the Internet including the SEC's EDGAR system.

◆ TOPICS COVERED

We carefully considered the inclusion or exclusion of topics and feel that our coverage has resulted in a balanced text consistent with our pedagogical goals of building a foundation that supports effective student learning. As we considered individual topics, we continually explored whether their inclusion would enhance a student's ability to interpret and use accounting information throughout his or her personal and professional life. The result is that *Introduction to Financial Accounting: A User Perspective,* Third

Edition, covers those topics that every accounting student should leave the course understanding well. For example, we cover the calculations of only two depreciation methods—straight-line and double-declining-balance. By limiting the coverage of detailed depreciation calculations, we have the opportunity to focus on the concepts of cost allocation, expense recognition, financial statement differences between the two methods, and the distinction between gains and revenues and losses and expenses. Students will not only know how to calculate depreciation expense, but will also understand why they are calculating it and how to use those calculations in making business decisions. In the chapter, students learn how to properly interpret gains and losses. Most of them are surprised to find out that two companies buying identical assets for the same price can sell them later for the same amount and have different results—one company can have a gain and the other experience a loss.

We have carefully chosen the sequence of coverage so the material flows from one topic to the next. Not only does this make accounting easier to teach, but it is more understandable as well. To effectively present the user perspective, we developed a logical flow of topics so that each chapter builds on what the student has already learned. Students can easily understand how the topics fit together logically and how they are used together to make good decisions. Moreover, students can see that accounting and the information it provides is not merely something that exists unto itself, but rather it is something developed in response to the needs of economic decision makers.

If you could read the entire text before using it in your classroom, you would have a very clear picture of the experience awaiting your students. However, even a short tour through the material covered in each chapter will show you how we have structured our presentation of the topics to maximize student learning.

◆ CHAPTER HIGHLIGHTS

Chapter F1 provides a brief overview of business and the role of accounting in the business world, setting the stage for the introduction of accounting information. Without the world of business, there would be no need for accounting information or the accounting profession. We also introduce the balance sheet, the income statement, the statement of owners' equity, and the statement of cash flows. The standard-setting process and outside assurance is also covered including the roles of the SEC, the FASB, and the external auditor. In the appendix, we provide students with information they can use to access accounting and other information for publicly traded companies.

Chapter F2 presents an introduction to economic decision making. Because the purpose of financial accounting information is to provide information to be used in making decisions, we believe an understanding of the decision making process is essential. In today's business environment, an understanding of ethics is essential. We cover ethics and personal values and discuss how they impact business decisions. We explore the qualitative characteristics crucial to making accounting information useful in that process.

Chapter F3 covers the balance sheet. In this chapter, we focus on how equity and debt financing affects businesses and how its results are reflected on balance sheets. We also cover using cash to acquire assets, the statement of cash flows and how it is impacted by the financing and investing activities covered in the chapter, and key financial ratios that relate to the balance sheet.

Chapter F4 covers the income statement and statement of owners' equity. The chapter also covers financial statement articulation and how the financial statements relate to one another. We also cover the statement of cash flows and how it is affected by the operating activities covered in the chapter, and seven key financial ratios that relate profitability.

Chapter F5 compares the cash basis and accrual basis of accounting. The coverage helps students understand that accrual accounting is one basis of measurement and not *the* measurement basis. The material in this chapter helps students understand the weaknesses of cash basis accounting and makes the logic of accrual accounting much easier to grasp.

Chapter F6 is an optional chapter covering the accounting system and recording process. As we mentioned earlier, we hold off coverage of accounting procedures until Chapter F6 to give students the chance to acquire the basic accounting background that will help make accounting procedures easier to grasp. To afford maximum teaching flexibility and to make the material easier to understand, we present the chapter in two parts.

Part I introduces students to the accounting bookkeeping system and the accounting cycle. This part of the chapter introduces and describes the concept of analyzing transactions, journal entries, posting to the general ledger, the trial balance, adjusting entries, preparing financial statements from the adjusted trial balance or worksheet, and closing entries and the post-closing trial balance.

Part II covers the details of the application of accounting procedures. This part of the chapter begins with a presentation to help students learn and remember how debits and credits work. Then, each part of the accounting cycle is explained and demonstrated in a step-by-step fashion. We cover everything from analyzing transactions and preparing journal entries, to preparing a bank reconciliation and adjusting entries, through preparing trial balances, the worksheet, and financial statements. Finally, Part II concludes with a step-by-step procedure to prepare closing entries and the post-closing trial balance.

We understand that some schools will choose to omit this chapter entirely while others will cover only Part I, and still others will include the entire chapter in their curriculum.

Chapter F7 explores issues surrounding the acquisition, depreciation, and disposal of long-lived assets under accrual accounting. This chapter examines the effects of depreciation method choice, using straight-line and double-declining-balance as examples. We also show students how to properly interpret gains and losses and depreciation's impact on cash. The appendix demonstrates how to record the acquisition, depreciation, and disposal of assets.

Chapter F8 explores accounting for inventory. The periodic and perpetual inventory methods are introduced. Students learn how to calculate amounts under LIFO, FIFO, and average cost methods for the perpetual inventory system. They also learn how the choice of cost flow method affects the accounting information that income statements and balance sheets provide. The chapter also covers the impact of inventory transactions on the statement of cash flows and financial ratios dealing with inventory turnover. This chapter has two appendices. The first appendix covers some inventory purchasing issues and presents a discussion of freight terms and cash discounts and how they alter the cost of inventory. The second appendix presents the recording procedures for inventory using the perpetual inventory system.

Chapter F9 takes a closer look at the way the balance sheet and income statement are organized. We explore each of the balance sheet's classifications. In addition, we explore the income statement in detail including nonrecurring items (discontinued operations, extraordinary items, and changes in accounting principles). Income tax disclosure relative to nonrecurring items and an introduction to basic and diluted earnings per share are included. The chapter concludes with coverage of several key financial ratios.

Chapter F10 takes an up-close look at the statement of cash flows. The chapter reviews operating, investing, and financing activities and provides step-by-step coverage of the statement's preparation using the indirect method. Students also learn how to read and interpret the information provided on the statement of cash flows and how to use two key financial ratios relating to cash flows. The appendix to this chapter provides step-by-step coverage of preparing the operating section of the statement using the direct method.

Chapter F11 covers financial statement analysis. The chapter reviews the 17 ratios presented throughout the earlier chapters of the text. The chapter covers industry classification codes and peer company and industry comparisons. In addition, the chapter discusses general economic conditions, political events and political climate, and the industry outlook. For each of the 17 ratios, the chapter presents charts comparing ***Pier 1 Imports, Inc.***, to two peer companies and discusses ***Pier 1***'s ratios relative to its peers and to industry averages.

◆ OTHER IMPORTANT FEATURES OF THIS TEXT

In addition to the Discussion Questions and the inclusion of the ***Pier 1 Imports, Inc.***, annual report, our text offers other features that will enhance the learning process:

- *Learning Objectives*. Previewing each chapter with these objectives allows students to see what direction the chapter is taking, which makes the journey through the material a bit easier.
- *Marginal Glossary*. Students often find the process of learning accounting terminology to be a challenge. As each new key word is introduced in the text, it is shown in bold and also defined in the margin. This feature offers students an easy way to review the key terms and locate their introduction in the text.
- *Summary*. This concise summary of each chapter provides an overview of the main points, but is in no way a substitute for reading the chapter.
- *Key Terms*. At the end of each chapter, a list of the new key words directs students to the page on which the key word or phrase was introduced.
- *Review the Facts*. Students can use these basic, definitional questions to review the key points of each chapter. The questions are in a sequence reflecting the coverage of topics in the chapter.
- *Apply What You Have Learned*. Our end-of-chapter assignment materials include a mix of traditional types of homework problems and innovative assignments requiring critical thinking and writing. Many of the requirements can be used as the basis for classroom discussions. You will find matching problems, short essay questions, and calculations. Assignments dealing directly with the use of financial statements are also included. Many of these applications also work well as group assignments. There are three versions of most problems—one to use as an example in class, one for homework, and one extra.
- *Glossary of Accounting Terms*. An alphabetical listing of important accounting terms, including all of the key terms plus additional terms.
- *Company Index*. A listing of the companies used in the text as examples or in assignment material.

◆ SUPPLEMENTS FOR USE BY THE INSTRUCTOR

Additional support for your efforts in the classroom is provided by our group of supplements.

Instructor's Resource Manual, Connie Groer (Frostburg State University)

Substantially revised, this resource manual provides insightful and useful tips on how to best manage course content when using Werner/Jones in class. Chapter-by-chapter explanations and pedagogical philosophies are clearly delineated and oriented to greatly aid the teaching process. Also included are chapter outlines organized by objectives, lecture suggestions, teaching tips, group activities, and suggested readings, as well as suggested solutions to text discussion questions. Available online at *www.prenhall.com/werner*.

Solutions Manual, Mike Werner (University of Miami)

Solutions for all end-of-chapter material. Available online at *www.prenhall.com/werner*.

Test Item File, Tim Carse (CPA)

A ready-to-use bank of testing material. Each chapter includes a variety of types of questions, including true/false, multiple choice, essay and critical thinking problems. Intended for ease-of-use, each question is linked to chapter objectives, and also provides suggested difficulty level and reference to text pages where answers can be found. Available online at *www.prenhall.com/werner.*

PowerPoint, Olga Quintana (University of Miami)

Complete PowerPoint presentations for each chapter. Instructors may download and use each presentation as is or customize the slides to create a tailor-made slide show. Each presentation allows instructors to offer a more interactive experience using colorful graphics, outlines of chapter material, and graphical explanations of difficult topics. Available online at *www.prenhall.com/werner.*

Course Web site at *www.prenhall.com/werner*

A complete online resource that offers a variety of Internet-based teaching and learning support. Our Web site provides a wealth of resources for students and faculty. These resources include:

- An online study guide
- Downloadable supplements, including PowerPoint and General Ledger Software for student use
- Learning assessment sections
- Practice tests with immediate feedback for self-study use.

◆ **ACKNOWLEDGMENTS**

This project would not have been possible without the support and encouragement from a number of people, the faith in the concept's value from Prentice Hall, and the suggestions for improvements from our colleagues.

In particular, we thank executive editor Debbie Hoffman for her patience, determination, and faith in the project. She was always there for us. We also express our debt of gratitude to Amy Whitaker, our development editor, for her significant contributions to this edition. We appreciate the support of Prentice Hall team members P. J. Boardman, Stephen Deitmer, Mac Mendelsohn, Alana Bradley, Jane Avery, Beth Toland, Kelly Warsak, and Elena Picinic for their help and contributions.

We are also grateful to Annie Todd, Katherene P. Terrell, and Robert L. Terrell for all their support in the past and for truly making this project possible. We also thank Linda Begley and the rest of the staff at Rainbow Graphics for their help in transforming our manuscript into a book.

Sincere thanks, too, to Thomas R. Robinson and Oscar J. Holzmann, both of the University of Miami, for their help with the financial statement analysis material. We are grateful to Cam Matheis and Steve Speace, who gave us valuable editorial help and guidance, and to Stacy Sexton, who contributed editorial help and assignment material.

We thank our colleagues for their intellectual contributions and friendship that have helped to enrich this book. Martha Doran, San Diego State University, good friend and teacher, shared her wisdom with us about learning and teaching, and our students are better off because of it. Connie Groer, Frostburg State University, reviewed the first six chapters with extraordinary care. Thank you. Many other colleagues tested our ideas, were brave enough to offer constructive criticism, and gave us friendship through the difficult times. They include: Gary J. Weber and Kay C. Carnes, Gonzaga University; Connie D. Weaver, University of Texas–Austin; Thomas R. Robinson, Oscar J. Holzmann, Paul Munter, Frank Collins, Olga Quintana, Mark

Friedman, Seth Levine, Kay Tatum, Larry Phillips, Juan M. Rodriguez, DeWayne Searcy, William Belski, Carlos Garcia, Guillermo Arguello, Teresita Miglio, Ray Placid, Sergio Varona, Manny Sicre, and Diane Clifford, University of Miami; Richard E. Flaherty, Harriet MacCracken, Patrick B. McKenzie, and Karen Gieger, Arizona State University; Lorren H. Beavers, Charles R. Pursifull, Mary F. Sheets, Bambi A. Hora, Thomas K. Miller, Ura Lee Denson, David J. Harris, Joan Stone, Karen Price, and Jane Calvert, University of Central Oklahoma; Alfonso R. Oddo, Niagara University; Marilyn T. Zarzeski, University of Central Florida; Joanne Sheridan, Montana State University–Billings; Aileen Ormiston and Charles Lewis, Mesa Community College; Allison L. Drews-Bryan, Clemson University; George R. Violette, University of Southern Maine; A. J. Potts, University of Southern Maine; Marshall K. Pitman, University of Texas–San Antonio; David Caslan, Bethune-Cookman College; Michael Welker, Drexel University; Kenneth Couvillion, San Joaquin Delta College; Mark E. Bettini, University of California–Berkeley Extension; and Tim Carse.

We would also like to thank the following third edition reviewers for their recommendations:

Mark E. Bettini, University of California–Berkeley
David F. Caslan, Bethune-Cookman College
Kenneth P. Couvillion, San Joaquin Delta College
Connie J. Groer, Frostburg State University
Sally Nelson, Northeast Iowa Community College
Marshall K. Pitman, University of Texas–San Antonio
A. J. Potts, University of Southern Maine
Suzanne S. Roe, University of Wyoming
Robert W. Rouse, College of Charleston
Jerry D. Siebel, University of South Florida
Judith Walery, Grossmont College
Michael G. Welker, Drexel University
Harold E. Wyman, Florida International University

Other colleagues who have provided suggestions as adopters, as focus group members, or as reviewers of previous editions:

Gerald Ashley, Grossmont College
Sheila Bradford, Tulsa Community College
Carol E. Buehl, Northern Michigan University
Mary D. Maury, St. John's University
Mary Ann M. Prater, Clemson University
John C. Robison, California Polytechnic State University–San Luis Obispo
Sheldon R. Smith, Brigham Young University–Hawaii
George R. Violette, University of Southern Maine

We believe the approach we have taken will help students see how accounting fits into the "big picture of business." We hope students will find that what they learn from this text and in their introductory accounting class relates directly to them, regardless of their career path.

Please feel free to contact us at *mwerner@miami.edu* with your comments or suggestions.

Michael L. Werner
Kumen H. Jones

CHAPTER 1

Introduction to Business in the United States

People make decisions every day. Information makes decisions easier to make. For example, let's say you are in the market for a new cellular phone and service. First, you must choose a phone. Many companies—***Nokia, Ericsson,*** and ***Motorola***—manufacture cell phones with various and often different features. In addition, you must select a service plan from the assortment that ***Sprint PCS, AT&T, Verizon, Nextel,*** and other cell phone service providers offer. You have a myriad of choices. How will you decide? Well, you could just buy the first phone you find, but you may be disappointed if you later determine that the phone doesn't have all the features you like and the service plan does not suit your needs. In contrast, you could begin your quest for a phone by gathering information about cellular phones and cellular service plans. Once you had the information, your decision would become much easier to make. The information wouldn't make the decision for you—you would still have to weigh various factors—but it would help you make a better decision. Whether you are making a personal decision such as which cellular phone to buy or a business decision such as which investment to make, useful information won't make the decision for you, but it sure makes it easier to make better choices.

So, we make decisions, and solid information makes decisions easier to make. But what does all this have to do with accounting? The purpose of accounting is to provide useful economic information to decision makers. Accounting is simply a mechanism to provide useful information by recording, classifying, and reporting economic activities. Company managers use accounting information to help them make decisions about how to operate their business. People outside a company such as investors, creditors, and customers also use accounting information to help make decisions concerning the company. Often, the decisions made in business have a ripple effect throughout society. Because these business decisions are based on accounting information, accounting impacts each of us even though most of us have little or no direct contact with it. Accounting is often called the language of business. To help you better understand this language, we begin by exploring business in its many different forms.

The business of America is business.

—CALVIN COOLIDGE
30th President of the United States

The word *business* means different things to different people. For some, the word conjures up a dream of excitement and opportunity; for others, it represents a nightmare of greed and exploitation. *Webster's New World Dictionary* gives several definitions of business:

> **Busi-ness** (biz'nis) n. **1:** One's work or occupation. **2:** A special task or duty. **3:** A matter or affair. **4:** Commerce or trade. **5:** A commercial or industrial establishment.[1]

---

[1]*Webster's New World Dictionary* (New York: Prentice Hall, 1939), 59.

As you can see, not only do people have different impressions of business, but the word itself has different meanings in different contexts. The last two definitions are particularly relevant for this book. It is important to understand that at times *business* is used to describe the entirety of commerce and trade and at other times it is used to describe an individual company. In fact, in the economic world, and in books about the world of business (including this one), the words *company* and *business* are often used interchangeably. So whenever you see the word *business,* make sure you understand the context in which it is used.

Accounting information is one of the key ingredients for making wise business decisions. This chapter will provide you with the background necessary to put the accounting concepts presented throughout this text into the proper business context.

Learning Objectives

After completing your work on this chapter, you should be able to do the following:

1. Describe the four factors of production.
2. Explain the basic concepts of capitalism and how they relate to the profit motive.
3. Distinguish between gross and net income. Be able to calculate each.
4. Distinguish among the three basic forms of business organization—the proprietorship, the partnership, and the corporation—and describe the advantages and disadvantages of each.
5. Distinguish among the three major types of business activities and define hybrid-type businesses.
6. Explain the basic need for international business trade and the complications involved in this activity.
7. Describe what is shown in each of the four financial statements.
8. Discuss the SEC's and FASB's authority over accounting reporting standards and describe the current standard-setting process in the United States.
9. Describe the basic objectives of financial reporting.
10. Explain the purpose of an independent financial audit and describe the four basic types of audit opinions.
11. Gather information about a company and obtain an annual report. (Appendix)
12. Describe the information found in a typical annual report and Form 10-K. (Appendix)

◆ WHAT IS BUSINESS?

business Depending on the context, the area of commerce or trade, an individual company, or the process of producing and distributing goods and services.

Essentially, **business** is the process of producing goods (manufacturing) and providing services and then distributing them (selling) to those who want or need them. This process sounds simple enough, but it is actually quite complex.

Although we cannot present an in-depth study of all of the aspects of business, we must talk about a few basics at the outset to present accounting in its proper context. We begin with the factors of production.

FACTORS OF PRODUCTION

factors of production The four major items needed to support economic activity: natural resources, labor, capital, and entrepreneurship.

The **factors of production** are the key ingredients needed to support economic activity (see Exhibit 1–1). Economists classify the factors of production into four categories:

1. **Natural resources**—land and the materials that come from the land, such as timber, mineral deposits, oil deposits, and water.
2. **Labor**—the mental and physical efforts of all workers, regardless of their skill or education, who perform the tasks required to produce and sell goods and services. Labor is sometimes called the human resource factor.

natural resources
Land and the materials that come from the land, such as timber, mineral deposits, oil deposits, and water. One of the factors of production.

labor The mental and physical efforts of all workers performing tasks required to produce and sell goods and services. This factor of production is also called the human resource factor.

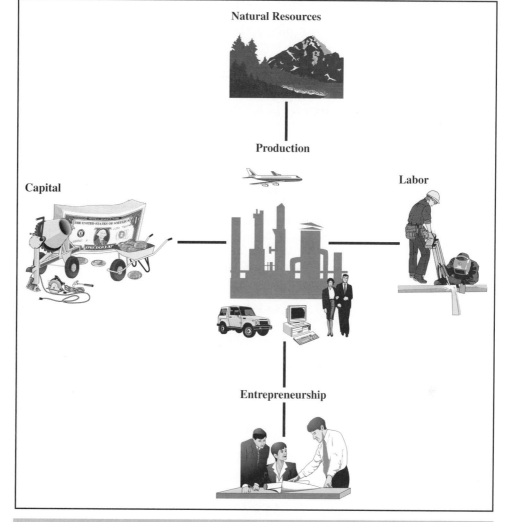

Natural Resources

Production

Capital

Labor

Entrepreneurship

EXHIBIT 1–1 Factors of Production

capital A factor of production that includes the buildings, machinery, and tools used to produce goods and services. Also, sometimes used to refer to the money used to buy those items.

entrepreneurship The factor of production that brings the other three factors—natural resources, labor, and capital—together to form a business.

communism An example of a planned economy. A *planned economy* is one with a strong centralized government that controls all or most of the natural resources, labor, and capital used to produce goods and services.

capitalism An example of a market economy. A *market economy* is one that relies on competition to determine the most efficient way to allocate the economy's resources.

3. **Capital**—the buildings, machinery, and tools used to produce goods and services. The word *capital* has many meanings. Sometimes it refers to the *money* that buys the buildings, machinery, and tools used in production. Because this double usage can be confusing, be careful to note the context in which the word *capital* is being used.

4. **Entrepreneurship**—the activity that brings the first three factors together to form a business. *Entrepreneurs* are the people willing to accept the opportunities and risks of starting and running businesses. They provide or acquire the capital, assemble the labor force, and utilize available natural resources to produce and sell goods and services.

The way these four factors of production combine to produce goods and services depends on the type of economic system that organizes a society.

In a *planned economy*, a strong centralized government controls all or most of the natural resources, labor, and capital used to produce goods and services, replacing the entrepreneur. **Communism** is an example of a planned economy. In contrast, a *market economy* relies on competition in the marketplace to determine the most efficient way to allocate the economy's resources. **Capitalism** is an example of a market economy. Capitalism, also known as the *free enterprise, free market,* or *private enterprise system,* is the economic system used to conduct business in the United States.

THE PROFIT MOTIVE

The *profit motive* stimulates a person to do something when the *benefit* derived from doing it is greater than the *sacrifice* required to do it. A rational person desires the greatest benefit with the least amount of sacrifice. When this natural desire in one person is pitted against the same desire in another person, competition results.

To illustrate the profit motive, let's say that Steve needs a new pair of pants. Because he is a rational person, Steve desires the best pair of pants he can buy for the lowest possible price. Tanner owns a clothing store. Being a rational person, Tanner desires to sell his clothes for the highest price he can. Steve goes to Tanner's clothing store and looks at a pair of pants Tanner has priced at $50. Assuming he likes the pants and can afford to pay $50, Steve will buy them if he feels they provide him with the most benefit for the least sacrifice.

Now, let's add one other ingredient to the situation—competition. Enter Chelsea, who also owns a clothing store. She sells pants identical to the pair Steve is considering buying at Tanner's. The difference is that she is selling them for $45.

Discussion Questions ●

1–1. What do you think caused Tanner and Chelsea to establish different selling prices for an identical pair of pants?

1–2. Assuming Steve decides to buy the pants, what do you think will determine where he buys them?

In this example, Steve's self-interest pits the self-interests of Tanner and Chelsea against each other because Steve's desire to pay the lowest price possible for the pants will make Tanner and Chelsea compete for his business. If Tanner loses enough sales to Chelsea because she is selling pants for less than he is, he will be forced to lower his selling price. In fact, he may want to lower his price for the pants Steve likes to $40 in order to attract sales away from Chelsea. She will then be forced to lower her selling price. No one forces Tanner and Chelsea to reduce their prices; the force comes from competition in the market. Adam Smith (1723–1790), the great Scottish philosopher and economist, called this phenomenon *the invisible hand*.

If competitors lower their selling prices too much, losses will occur. For example, if Tanner and Chelsea pay $30 for the pants, they obviously don't want to resell those pants for less than that. **Profit** is the excess of benefit over sacrifice. Steve decides to buy the pants from Tanner for $50, so Tanner's gross profit can be calculated as:

Amount received from Steve (BENEFIT)	$ 50
Less what Tanner paid for the pants (SACRIFICE)	− 30
Equals GROSS PROFIT on the sale of pants	$ 20

The $20 profit that Tanner earned on the pair of pants is called *gross profit* or *gross margin*. However, it does not represent his actual profit from operating the clothing store. In addition to the cost of the merchandise he buys to sell, he has other costs such as rent on the store, utilities, and wages paid to employees. All these items must be taken into account before he can calculate his real profit, which businesspeople generally call **net income** or **net profit.**

If Tanner does not earn a sufficient profit in the clothing store business, he will be forced to close it and go into another line of work. The same, of course, holds true for Chelsea. In a capitalistic economy, businesses (except for charities and other not-for-profit organizations) that do not earn profits eventually cease to exist.

PROFITS VERSUS SOCIAL RESPONSIBILITY

People feel many ways about business. Some believe that "profit" is a dirty word and that society would be better off if companies were motivated by something other than the "Almighty Dollar." These people think that business should strike a balance between profit and social responsibility. On the other side of the spectrum are those who believe that businesses have no obligation beyond earning profits and contend that companies have no social responsibility at all.

profit   The excess of benefit over sacrifice. A less formal name for net income or net profit.

net income   The amount of profit that remains after all costs have been considered. The net reward of doing business for a specific time period.

net profit   Same as net income.

We live in a society that often measures success by whether someone "beats" someone else. It is what has been described as a zero-sum game, meaning that for every winner, there must be a loser. The following quotation from Vince Lombardi, legendary coach of the Green Bay Packers, seems to more accurately capture the workings of our economy than the quotation by sportswriter Grantland Rice:

Winning is not everything, it is the only thing!

— VINCE LOMBARDI

It matters not whether you win or lose, but how you play the game.

— GRANTLAND RICE

Recently, however, society is renewing its concern over how the game of business is played. An increasing number of investors, creditors, and other economic decision makers are interested not only in "the bottom line" (making money), but also in the way companies conduct themselves as citizens in the community. In other words, there is a movement in business toward a win–win rather than a win–lose situation.

A growing number of people refuse to invest in or do business with companies they believe are insensitive to social and environmental concerns. For example, many investors, both individuals and companies, refuse to invest in alcohol or tobacco companies, or in firms known to pollute the environment. In response to this trend, many companies are now committed to responsible and ethical business practices and make a point of communicating that commitment to their stakeholders. A **stakeholder** is anyone to whom a company owes a responsibility; anyone who has a *stake* in the way a company is run.

One of the great challenges facing any business today is determining exactly who its stakeholders are and just what responsibility it has to each of them. Stakeholders include present and potential investors, customers, employees, the community at large, and governmental bodies. To improve stakeholder confidence in the company's good citizenship, many companies now include a section in their annual report about social responsibility. For example, ***Wendy's International*** lists community involvement as one of its eight core values. It appears that the era of conducting business without regard to anything but making a profit is very likely gone forever.

stakeholder Anyone who is affected by the way a company conducts its business.

Discussion Questions

1–3. Make a list of those to whom you think a chemical manufacturing company owes responsibility. What are the specific responsibilities it has to each of these stakeholders? How do you think the company could best go about fulfilling each of those responsibilities?

1–4. Make a list of those to whom you think a retail clothing company owes a responsibility. What are the stakes that each group has? How can the company fulfill each responsibility?

1–5. Can you think of any companies that have fulfilled the responsibilities you outlined in your answers to question 1–3 or 1–4 and yet managed to remain profitable?

◆ FORMS OF BUSINESS ORGANIZATION

Generally, there are three forms of business organization in the United States: sole proprietorships, partnerships, and corporations. Each has certain advantages and disadvantages in relation to the others.

sole proprietorship An unincorporated business that is owned by one person. Also called a proprietorship.

proprietorship Same thing as a sole proprietorship.

SOLE PROPRIETORSHIPS

A **sole proprietorship,** or **proprietorship,** is a business that is owned by one individual. A common misconception about this form of business is that it is always small. While the majority of sole proprietorships *are* small, the classification suggests nothing about the size of the business, only that it has a single owner.

ADVANTAGES OF SOLE PROPRIETORSHIPS

1. *Easy and inexpensive to establish.* There are no special legal requirements associated with starting a sole proprietorship. All a person must do is decide what kind of business he or she wants to establish, obtain the necessary licenses and permits, and that person may begin doing business.

2. *Total control.* This is probably the number one reason people start their own companies. Virtually everyone who works for someone else sometimes feels stifled by having to "answer to the boss." A sole proprietor answers to no one when making decisions about how to run the business (as long as it's legal).

3. *Independence.* This is closely related to having total control, but it has a broader meaning than simply being in control of how the company is run. Think of independence as the freedom to choose one's lifestyle. There is no set number of "vacation days" for sole proprietors. Rather, the proprietor is free to take days off whenever he wants to, if he feels he can spare the time from the business. A proprietor can work his own hours.

4. *No sharing of profits.* A single owner shares profits only with the government in the form of taxes. Whatever the business earns after taxes belongs solely to the owner.

5. *No separate income taxes.* From a legal standpoint, a sole proprietorship is simply an extension of its owner. Therefore, a proprietorship pays no separate income tax. The earnings of the company are considered the earnings of the owner and become a part of his or her personal taxable income.

6. *Few government regulations.* There are no special government requirements that must be satisfied to form a proprietorship. Once formed, as long as the company conforms to business regulations and the owner pays his or her taxes, a proprietorship is reasonably free of government intervention.

7. *Easy and inexpensive to dissolve.* Sole proprietorships are about as easy to end as they are to start. If the owner decides to shut the company down, all he or she must do is notify the state and local government agencies and pay off remaining debts.

DISADVANTAGES OF SOLE PROPRIETORSHIPS

1. *Unlimited liability.* Because from a legal standpoint a sole proprietorship is simply an extension of its owner, all business obligations become the owner's legal obligations. Therefore, if the company fails to pay its debts, the creditors can sue the owner for the owner's personal property, including his or her investments, house, car, boat, or other holdings.

2. *Limited access to capital.* All businesses must have money and other assets to operate. Economists refer to these assets as *capital.* The amount of capital available to a sole proprietorship is limited to the amount of personal assets the owner can contribute to the business or the amount he or she can borrow on a personal loan. Legally, a proprietorship is not distinguished from its owner; therefore, when the business borrows money, it is the owner who is actually borrowing.

3. *Limited management expertise.* No one is an expert in everything (although we're sure you know people who think they are), and a sole proprietorship is limited to whatever management expertise the proprietor possesses. Many proprietorships fail because the owner lacks skills or expertise in areas critical to the survival of the company. Even though a proprietorship can hire individuals who possess the needed talents, the hired employees may lack the drive and motivation to employ these talents as enthusiastically as an owner would.

4. *Personal time commitment.* Running a business is hard work, and most sole proprietors work very long hours—probably longer hours than if they worked for someone else. Most sole proprietors, however, consider the time well spent because it benefits them personally. But make no mistake about it, it takes a tremendous amount of time to run your own business.

5. *Limited life.* Unless the company is sold to another entity or is passed on to the owner's heirs, the life of the business cannot exceed the life of the owner.

Notwithstanding the disadvantages of proprietorships, many people dream of owning their own business, and nearly 72 percent of companies in the United States are sole proprietorships. Because most of them are small businesses, only about five percent of all business revenues come from this form of business.

PARTNERSHIPS

partnership   A business form similar to a proprietorship, but having two or more owners.

Think of a **partnership** as a proprietorship with two or more owners sharing in the risks and rewards of the business. A common misconception is that all partnerships are small businesses. In fact, some partnerships are quite large. For example, ***Pricewaterhouse-Coopers,*** a large public accounting firm, has 9,000 partners and 160,000 partners and staff.

ADVANTAGES OF PARTNERSHIPS

1. *Easy to establish.* From a legal standpoint, partnerships are about as easy to form as proprietorships. Once the partners obtain the appropriate licenses and permits, a partnership is in business. Although not required by law, partners are wise to commit the ownership and profit-sharing structure of the partnership to a formal written partnership agreement, signed by each partner, to clarify their understanding of these issues. A well-written partnership agreement anticipates future problems and helps to resolve conflicts before they arise.
2. *Increased management expertise.* Partnerships are often formed because each partner has skills in a critical area of business that complement the skills of the others. Combining those areas of expertise into a partnership enhances the business's chances of success.
3. *Access to more capital.* Having more than one person involved in the ownership of the business usually increases access to capital (money and other assets). In fact, many partnerships are formed for this very reason.
4. *Few government regulations.* Like proprietorships, partnerships are subject to fewer government regulations than corporations. There are no special government requirements that must be satisfied to form a partnership. Once formed, as long as the partnership conforms to business regulations, and each partner pays his or her individual taxes, there is little government intervention.
5. *No separate income taxes.* A partnership is not legally separate from its owners and therefore does not pay separate income taxes. Rather, the partnership tax return is an information report that allocates the partnership profits among the partners according to the partnership profit-sharing agreement. Each partner pays personal income tax on his or her share of the partnership profits, regardless of whether or not these profits are withdrawn from the business.
6. *Greater business continuity.* Because more people are involved, partnerships are more likely to have longer lives than are sole proprietorships. When a partner dies or withdraws from the partnership, the legal life of the partnership ends. The heirs do not inherit the right to be partners in the firm. For all practical purposes, however, the business generally need not stop its operations. The partnership agreement may allow the remaining partner or partners to either continue with one less partner or admit another partner to the firm.

DISADVANTAGES OF PARTNERSHIPS

1. *Unlimited liability.* Because partnerships are not legally separate from their owners, the partners are personally liable for all obligations of the business. In fact, in most instances, each partner is personally liable for the *total* obligations of the partnership. Therefore, if any partner makes a decision that obligates the partnership, all the other partners become responsible, even if they knew nothing about the decision.
2. *Sharing of profits.* When a partnership is formed, the partners should prepare an agreement that outlines how to divide company profits. The profit-sharing arrangement usually takes into account the amount of capital each partner invests in the partnership, how much time each partner commits on a regular basis, and

any special expertise a partner may contribute. Regardless of whether the agreement is fair and equitable, once a partnership has been formed, partners will share profits with each other.

3. *Potential conflicts between partners.* Suppose one partner wants the company to begin selling a new product and another partner disagrees. If the two partners have equal power, a gridlock may result. The bases for conflicts among partners range from personal habits to overall business philosophy. Most conflicts are minor, but there may be no other way to resolve severe conflicts than to dissolve the partnership.

4. *Difficulty in dissolving.* Ending a partnership can often be a devastating emotional experience; it may result in conflicts that sever personal and professional ties. If individuals forming a partnership are wise, they will include specific provisions for dissolution in the original partnership agreement when all the partners have positive attitudes toward one another. Think of this as the business version of a prenuptial agreement: The parties forming the business agree on how the business "marriage" will end.

While there are advantages to the partnership form of business, many people believe the disadvantages outweigh them. Only about 6 percent of all businesses in the United States are partnerships, and they account for just about 7 percent of all business revenues.

SEPARATE ENTITY ASSUMPTION

In our discussion of the proprietorship and partnership forms of business, we stressed that in both cases there is no legal distinction between a company and its owner or owners. Only in the corporate form is a company considered a separate legal entity from its owners. From a record-keeping and accounting standpoint, however, proprietorships, partnerships, and corporations are considered to be completely separate from their owners. This is called the **separate entity assumption,** and reflects the notion that economic activity can be identified with a particular economic entity whether it is an individual, proprietorship, corporation, or even a division of a business.

separate entity assumption   The assumption that economic activity can be identified with a particular economic entity and that the results of activities for each entity will be recorded separately.

CORPORATIONS

In 1819, Chief Justice John Marshall of the United States Supreme Court made this statement:

> *A corporation is an artificial being, invisible, intangible, and existing only in contemplation of law.*

This ruling changed the course of business in the United States forever. As a separate legal entity, a **corporation** has many of the rights and obligations of a person, including the right to enter into contracts and the right to buy, own, and sell property. The law requires a corporation to discharge its obligations lawfully, and creditors can sue the corporation itself for recovery if it does not. A corporation can be taken to court if it breaks the law, and it is obligated to pay taxes like an individual. In addition to the legal obligations of corporations, the moral obligation of corporations to be socially responsible is currently a topic of widespread discussion. Virtually all of the large publicly traded companies like ***Target, Texaco, Intel,*** and ***Walt Disney,*** for example, are corporations. For various reasons, not the least of which is that corporations are separate legal entities, there are several distinct advantages and disadvantages to the corporate form.

corporation   A business that is a separate legal entity from its stockholders (owners).

ADVANTAGES OF CORPORATIONS

1. *Limited liability.* Because a corporation is a separate legal entity from its stockholders (owners), the owners are not personally liable for the corporation's obligations. The maximum amount a stockholder can lose is the amount of his or her investment. However, the limited liability feature of corporations is not a universal truth. Many owners of small corporations sometimes forfeit their limited liability rights by signing a *personal guarantee* to obtain business credit. When an owner

signs a personal guarantee, she or he agrees to be personally liable if the corporation fails to pay.

2. *Greater access to capital.* By dividing the ownership of the firm into relatively low-cost shares of stock, corporations can often attract a great number of investors. Although a corporation can be owned by just one individual, some corporations in the United States have more than a million stockholders.

3. *Greater management expertise.* Corporations generally have a more formal management structure than proprietorships and partnerships. Corporate stockholders elect a board of directors who have the ultimate responsibility of managing the firm. The board of directors, in turn, hires professional managers to run the company. These managers then staff the organization with people possessing the skills and expertise required to run the day-to-day operations of the business.

4. *Easy transferability of ownership.* Because shares of ownership in corporations are usually relatively low in cost, they can be purchased or sold by individual investors much more easily than can an ownership interest in either of the other two forms of business. Additionally, in contrast to the approval required to accept a new partner into a partnership, generally no approval or permission is required for buying and selling corporate stock.

5. *Continuity of life.* Because a corporation is legally separate and distinct from its owner or owners, it continues to exist even when a complete change in ownership occurs. For example, ***DuPont*** has been in existence since the early 1900s, and although the company continues to thrive, virtually none of its original owners are still alive.

DISADVANTAGES OF CORPORATIONS

1. *Greater tax burden.* All businesses, regardless of form, must pay property taxes and payroll taxes. In addition to these taxes, corporations must pay a federal income tax, and in many states must also pay state and local income taxes on the profits they earn. Corporations often distribute at least part of the firm's after-tax profit to their shareholders as dividends. The stockholders then must consider these dividends as personal income and pay personal income taxes on them. This situation is referred to as double taxation, and it has been the subject of fierce debate for many years in the United States. We should mention here that double taxation does not exist for all corporations. Small, privately held corporations (usually with 75 or fewer stockholders) may elect a special tax classification, called an *S Corporation*, so they are treated very much like partnerships for federal income tax purposes. In this case, the corporation itself does not pay income tax. Rather, the individual stockholders include their proportional share of the company's profits as part of their personal taxable income, thus avoiding double taxation.

2. *Greater government regulation.* Corporations are subject to significantly more government control than either sole proprietorships or partnerships. Many corporations, especially publicly traded ones like ***Hewlett Packard, Gap,*** and ***Union Carbide,*** must file reports with both federal and state regulatory bodies.

3. *Absentee ownership.* In almost all proprietorships and in most partnerships, the owners manage their business themselves. In many corporations, especially those that are publicly traded, few of the stockholders participate in the day-to-day operations of the business. The board of directors hires professional managers to operate the company on behalf of the owners. Professional managers sometimes operate the company in their own best interest, rather than in the owners' best interest.

Although corporations represent a small percentage of the total number of businesses in the United States, they transact approximately six times as much business as all proprietorships and partnerships combined. Corporations also control the majority of business resources in the United States. Exhibit 1–2 summarizes the advantages and disadvantages of the three forms of business.

OTHER BUSINESS FORMS

Evolutionary changes in business have prompted the creation of new forms of business organizations that combine characteristics of partnerships and corporations. A

	Advantages	Disadvantages
Proprietorship	Easy and inexpensive to form No sharing of profits Owner has total control Independence Few government regulations No separate income taxes Easy and inexpensive to dissolve	Unlimited liability Limited access to capital Limited management expertise Personal time commitment Limited life
Partnership	Easy to form Increased management expertise Access to more capital Few government regulations No separate income taxes Greater business continuity	Unlimited liability Sharing of profits Potential conflicts between partners Difficulty in dissolving
Corporation	Limited liability Greater access to capital Easy transferability of ownership Continuity of life Greater management expertise	Greater tax burden Greater government regulation Absentee ownership

EXHIBIT 1–2   Advantages and Disadvantages of the Three Forms of Business Organization

limited partnership (LP) consists of at least one general partner and one or more limited partners. The general partners have unlimited liability and operate the partnership. The limited partners enjoy limited liability (like corporate stockholders), but are precluded from a decision making role in the organization. In a *limited liability partnership (LLP)*, the liability of a general partner is limited to his or her own negligence or misconduct, or the conduct of persons he or she controls. In a regular partnership, each partner is liable for all partnership debts and the conduct of all partners and employees. In a *limited liability corporation (LLC)*, stockholders enjoy the limited liability status of a corporation but are taxed as partners in a partnership, thus avoiding double taxation.

Discussion Question

1–6. If you had the opportunity to start your own company, would you prefer to own (or be part owner) of a proprietorship, partnership, or corporation? Give specific reasons for your choice.

◆ TYPES OF BUSINESS ACTIVITIES

Companies in the United States are classified not only according to organizational form (proprietorship, partnership, or corporation), but also according to the type of business activity in which they engage. The three broad classifications are *manufacturing, merchandising*, and *service*. Although a single company can be involved in all three of these business activities, usually one of the three constitutes the company's major area of business.

MANUFACTURING COMPANIES

manufacturing The business activity that converts purchased raw materials into some tangible, physical product.

A **manufacturing** company purchases raw materials and converts them into some tangible, physical product. Raw materials consist of both unprocessed natural resources (one of the factors of production) and completely finished products manufactured by others. For example, **Boeing** purchases many items, such as electronics from **Honeywell** and tires from **Goodyear,** which it uses to produce its jetliners. The electronics and tires—raw materials to **Boeing**—are manufactured finished products of **Honeywell** and **Goodyear.**

MERCHANDISING COMPANIES

merchandising The business activity involving the selling of finished goods produced by other businesses.

Like a manufacturer, a **merchandising** company sells tangible, physical products, called *merchandise*, as its major business activity. Instead of manufacturing the product it sells, a merchandising company buys it in a finished form. There are two kinds of merchandisers:

- *Wholesale merchandiser.* A wholesaler buys its product from the manufacturer (or another wholesaler) and then sells that product to another business that eventually sells it to the final consumer. Examples of wholesale merchandisers are ***Brandess-Kalt-Aetna Corporation,*** a photo equipment wholesaler, and ***W. W. Grainger,*** a major wholesale merchandiser of electric motors and small tools. These names may be unfamiliar to you because, as a consumer, you most often deal directly with a retailer rather than with a wholesaler. Wholesalers provide a valuable service to manufacturers by creating more efficient channels of distribution, and to retailers by making the retailers' purchasing convenient and cost effective.
- *Retail merchandiser.* A retailer buys its product from a wholesaler or manufacturer and sells the product to the final consumer. Examples of major national retailers are ***Home Depot, Banana Republic, Pier 1 Imports,*** and ***Gap.*** Other retail chains focus on specific regions of the country. Still other successful retailers have one location, such as gift shops and specialty stores.

SERVICE COMPANIES

service company A business that performs a service as its major business activity.

A **service company** does not sell tangible products, but performs a service as its major business activity. For example, doctors, lawyers, accountants, plumbers, and auto mechanics provide services instead of tangible products. Examples of service companies are ***Bank of America*** and ***FedEx.***

HYBRID COMPANIES

hybrid companies Those companies involved in more than one type of activity (manufacturing, merchandising, service).

As we said earlier, some businesses participate in more than one type of activity. These are known as **hybrid companies.** For example, ***General Motors Corporation*** (GM) manufactures automobiles and trucks and is therefore classified as a manufacturer. Recently, however, ***GM*** became involved in activities that are classified as services. ***GM*** created ***General Motors Acceptance Corporation*** (GMAC) to provide financing for customers purchasing ***GM*** cars and trucks. Even more recently, it began to issue credit cards (***Visa*** and ***MasterCard***).

We can expect the distinction among manufacturing, merchandising, and service companies to become even more blurred. As the struggle for survival in the global marketplace becomes more intense, many companies find it beneficial to become involved in a wide variety of business activities.

Discussion Question

1-7. In what type of business activity (manufacturing, merchandising, or service) would you like to be involved? Describe the type of operation that most interests you. What characteristics of this type of business do you find appealing?

◆ GLOBAL NATURE OF BUSINESS IN THE 21ST CENTURY

U.S. businesses simply cannot produce all the goods and services demanded in the U.S. marketplace. On the other hand, certain items produced in the United States either have no U.S. market or are produced in greater quantities than can be sold here. These factors are the forces that drive international business. ***Ford Motor Company*** sold an average of 7.1 million cars per year during the five-year period between 1997 and 2001. Of these cars, 41.4 percent were sold outside the United States. Clearly, international trade is important to the financial health of ***Ford,*** as it is to many other firms.

imports   Foreign products brought into a country.

exports   Goods produced in a country but sold outside that country.

Foreign products brought into a country are called **imports.** Goods produced in a country but sold outside that country are called **exports.** Most countries' economic health depends on the importing and exporting of goods; however, conducting business across national borders causes economic and political complications.

ECONOMIC COMPLICATIONS

Complications can arise when a firm from a country with a market economy does business with a firm from a country with a planned economy, because the aims of these two types of economic systems are so different. Complications are also caused by countries using different currencies. For example, the United States uses the dollar, Europe uses the euro, and Japan uses the yen. When companies in different countries transact business, their contract establishes the currency they will use. One or both companies then must translate its funds into the specified currency. In business, *translation* means converting or exchanging the currency of one country (e.g., yen) into its equivalent in another country's currency (e.g., dollar).

POLITICAL COMPLICATIONS

Politics plays an important role in international trade. Even countries with the same economic system experience difficulties in economic dealings with each other. Because each country seeks to protect its own self-interest, it wants to export a larger quantity of products than it imports. When a product is exported, money comes into the country's economy. When a product is imported, money leaves the country's economy (it goes to the country where the product was manufactured). As an extreme example, assume that all of France's merchandisers decide to import all the products they sell in France, because the imported merchandise costs less than French-produced products. Before long, all the French manufacturing companies would close, the French manufacturing jobs would disappear, and an essential part of France's economic base would cease to exist. To provide protection for their own economic bases and to prevent this kind of scenario, countries create trade agreements.

quotas   A limit on the quantities of particular items that can be imported.

tariffs   Taxes that raise the price of imported products to about the same as similar domestic products.

Trade agreements are formal treaties between two or more countries that are designed to control imports and exports. These agreements generally establish quotas and/or tariffs on imported products. **Quotas** limit the quantities of particular items that can be imported. For example, a limit may be placed on the number of Japanese cars brought into and sold in the United States. **Tariffs** are taxes that raise the price of imported products to about the same as similar domestic products. Several years ago, for example, the U.S. government became concerned about the number of inexpensive Japanese automobiles being sold in the United States. Because these imported cars were less expensive than cars produced in the United States, American auto makers were losing sales. In an effort to make the domestically produced cars more attractive to consumers, the U.S. government imposed a tariff on the Japanese cars. This raised the consumer's price of these imported cars to about the same price as the domestically produced cars.

Trade agreements are an important aspect of world politics because of the enormous economic impact they can have on the countries involved. Shortly after World War II, for example, 92 countries signed the General Agreement on Tariffs and Trade (GATT). President Clinton renegotiated this agreement in 1994. Other recent treaties are the United States–Canada Free Trade Pact of 1989, which eliminated most trade barriers between the two countries, and the North American Free Trade Agreement (NAFTA) signed by the United States, Canada, and Mexico in 1993.

The problem with all these international trade agreements is the same as the problem with all treaties—getting the parties involved to abide by them. Even after the agreements have been formally ratified, there is no effective way to enforce them, so compliance essentially depends on the good faith of the treaty members.

◆ **BUSINESS AND ACCOUNTING**

Business is about making decisions—decisions about what business form to take (proprietorship, partnership, corporation), decisions about what type of business activity to engage in (manufacturing, merchandising, service), and decisions about whether to engage in international business, to name just a few. Accounting information, in one form or another, plays a significant role in these decisions and in many other business decisions as well.

This is an accounting text. Its emphasis, however, is not so much on how accounting information is *prepared* as on how accounting information is *used*. To illustrate the relationship between accounting and business decisions, let's return to the example involving Tanner, Steve, and Chelsea. Remember that Tanner paid $30 for the pair of pants he later sold to Steve for $50. We calculated the gross profit on the sale of these pants as:

Amount received from Steve (BENEFIT)	$ 50
Less what Tanner paid for the pants (SACRIFICE)	– 30
Equals GROSS PROFIT on the sale of pants	$ 20

We pointed out that the $20 does not represent Tanner's real profit because he has other costs associated with his clothing store that must be taken into account before he can calculate his real profit. Think about the phrase "taken into account": This is accounting. The function of accounting is to provide information to Tanner, Chelsea, and the clothing manufacturers so they can make sound business decisions. Every day, literally millions of business decisions are made around the world. Every one of those decisions has an economic impact on someone, and few of those decisions are made without considering some kind of accounting information.

Discussion Questions •••

1–8. If rent and other costs associated with his clothing store amount to $3,000 a month, how many pairs of pants must Tanner sell at $50 a pair before he earns a profit?

1–9. What should Tanner do if his competitor, Chelsea, begins to take sales away by selling identical pairs of pants for $45?

1–10. What if Tanner finds out he can buy the identical pair of pants from a manufacturer in Mexico for only $25 instead of the $30 he is paying the U.S. manufacturer?

1–11. What should the U.S. clothing manufacturer do if it begins to lose sales to the Mexican clothing manufacturer that is selling these identical pants at the cheaper price?

We live in the information age. Advances in technology give us almost instant access to information on almost any subject. Every advance, however, has its price. We sometimes find ourselves in "information overload." Trying to find the optimal amount of information specific to your needs sometimes feels like trying to empty the ocean with a teaspoon to get to the treasure you seek on the sea floor.

The purpose of this book is to provide you with the tools, knowledge, and skills you need to sift through and use the accounting information available to you.

◆ INTRODUCTION TO FINANCIAL ACCOUNTING REPORTS

internal decision makers
Economic decision makers within a company who make decisions for the company. They have access to much or all of the accounting information generated within the company.

We can classify economic decision makers broadly as either *internal* or *external*. **Internal decision makers** are individuals within a company who make decisions for the company, while **external decision makers** are individuals or organizations outside a company who make decisions about that company. The accounting information internal decision makers use is called **management accounting,** while the information external decision makers use is called **financial accounting.** Our coverage here focuses primarily on financial accounting information and the accounting reports prepared from that information. There are four of them: the *Balance Sheet,* the *Income Statement,* the *Statement of Owners' Equity,* and the *Statement of Cash Flows.* We will introduce them briefly here and in much greater detail throughout the remainder of the text.

external decision makers
Economic decision makers outside a company who make decisions about the company. The accounting information they use to make those decisions is limited to what the company provides them.

management accounting
The branch of accounting developed to meet the informational needs of internal decision makers.

financial accounting   The branch of accounting developed to meet the informational needs of external decision makers.

THE BALANCE SHEET

The balance sheet presents the present condition of a business by showing the valuables the business has, the debts the business owes, and the owners' holdings in the company. The statement is based on the following equation:

$$\text{Assets} = \text{Liabilities} + \text{Owners' equity}$$

Basically, *assets* are the things of value a company owns or controls. Examples include cash, equipment, land, buildings, and merchandise. *Liabilities* are debts and obligations a company has. Examples include amounts owed for purchases made on charge accounts and for loans from the bank. Most commonly, these obligations must be paid in money. Sometimes, however, the transfer of an asset other than money will settle the indebtedness, or in some cases, it is an obligation to provide services. *Owners' Equity* represents the owners' holdings in the company. The formal name of the balance sheet is the *Statement of Financial Position*. It is a financial snapshot of a company at a specific date in time. Like any other snapshot, it shows only what existed on the day it was taken. It does not show what existed on the day before it was taken or what might exist on the day after. For example, Exhibit 1–3 shows a very condensed balance sheet for **Microsoft** as of June 30, 2001. The balance sheet will be covered in much more detail later in the text beginning with Chapter 3.

THE INCOME STATEMENT

The income statement presents the past performance of a business by showing the amount the company charged to its customers (revenues) and the costs that were required to earn that revenue (expenses). The statement is based on the following equation:

$$\text{Revenue} - \text{Expenses} = \text{Net income}$$

The income statement is prepared for some specific period of time. Although the statement can be prepared for any period of time, most commonly it is prepared for a month, a quarter, or a year. Basically, *revenues* are what a business charges for its goods and services during the time period covered by the income statement from selling whatever it is the company sells. *Expenses* are the economic sacrifices that were required to generate the revenue during that same time period. Exhibit 1–4 shows a very condensed income statement for **Microsoft** for the year ended June 30, 2001. The formal name of the income statement is the *Statement of Results of Operations* and will be the subject of extensive coverage beginning with Chapter 4.

THE STATEMENT OF OWNERS' EQUITY

The statement of owners' equity traces the ownership interest in the company from the beginning of a specific time period to the end of the period. The time period is the same as the period covered by the income statement we just talked about. The statement is based on the following equation:

$$\text{Beginning equity} + \text{Investments by owners} + \text{Net income} - \text{Distributions to owners} = \text{Ending equity}$$

EXHIBIT 1–3   *Microsoft* Condensed Balance Sheet as of June 30, 2001

Microsoft
Balance Sheet
June 30, 2001
(In millions)

Assets	$59,257	Liabilities	$11,968
		Stockholders' equity	47,289
		Total liabilities and stockholders' equity	$59,257

Microsoft Income Statement For the Year Ended June 30, 2001 (In millions)	
Revenue	$25,296
Expenses	(17,950)
Net income	$ 7,346

EXHIBIT 1–4 *Microsoft* Condensed Income Statement

The main components of owners' equity are investments by owners, net income for the period (from the income statement), and distributions to owners. The statement of owners' equity begins with the initial amount of owners' equity for the accounting period. Next, additional investments by owners that were made during the period are added. Then net income from the income statement for the period is added (or a net loss is subtracted), and, finally, distributions or payments to owners are subtracted to arrive at owners' equity as of the end of the period. We will discuss this statement in greater detail beginning in Chapter 4.

THE STATEMENT OF CASH FLOWS

The statement of cash flows depicts the sources and uses of cash in a company during a particular period of time. The time period is the same as that of the income statement. The statement is based on the following equation:

$$\text{Cash inflow} - \text{Cash outflow} + \text{Beginning cash} = \text{Ending cash}$$

The statement of cash flows is organized around three principal business activities: operating, investing, and financing. The operating activities section of the statements shows the inflows and outflows of cash that relate to a company's primary business activity. The investing activities section shows cash flows for investments in property, plant, and equipment used in the business, as well as in investments in stocks, bonds, or other securities. The financing activities section shows the company's cash flows associated with obtaining and repaying the funds it needs to conduct business as well as distributions to owners. Exhibit 1–5 shows a condensed statement of cash flows for *Microsoft* for the year ended June 30, 2001.

Many businesspeople consider the statement of cash flows to be the most important of the four financial statements. Therefore, in addition to devoting a full chapter to this financial statement, we will explore facets of the statement of cash flows as we examine the other three financial statements beginning in Chapter 3.

EXHIBIT 1–5 *Microsoft* Condensed Statement of Cash Flows

Microsoft Statement of Cash Flows For the Year Ended June 30, 2001 (In millions)	
Cash from operating activities	$13,422
Cash used for investing activities	(8,734)
Cash used for financing activities	(5,612)
Net change in cash	(924)
Cash, beginning of year	4,846
Cash, end of year	$ 3,922

FINANCIAL STATEMENT ANALYSIS

If you look at the financial statements of the ***Pier 1 Imports, Inc.*** annual report accompanying this text, you will get an idea of what we meant by "information overload." To be truly useful to decision makers, the statements must be analyzed. For example, many financial statement users consider the relationship between assets and liabilities on a balance sheet to be extremely important. This relationship is called the *debt ratio,* and it reveals the proportion of assets financed by debt. The debt ratio is one of many financial ratios developed over time to help financial statement users analyze the reports they receive.

Chapter 11 of this text is devoted entirely to financial statement analysis. In addition, where appropriate in earlier chapters we will present a section on the use of financial statements including some pertinent facets of financial statement analysis.

AUTHORITY OVER ACCOUNTING REPORTS

generally accepted accounting principles (GAAP) Guidelines for presentation of financial accounting information designed to serve external decision makers' need for consistent and comparable information.

Over time, the accounting profession has developed a set of standards to be used for financial reporting. These standards are known as **generally accepted accounting principles (GAAP).** GAAP provides assurance to outsiders (external decision makers) that the information available in a given decision situation was prepared in accordance with a well-defined set of rules and guidelines.

THE SECURITIES AND EXCHANGE COMMISSION (SEC)

Securities and Exchange Commission (SEC) The government agency empowered to regulate the buying and selling of stocks and bonds and to establish accounting rules, standards, and procedures, and the form and content of published financial reporting.

Prior to the stock market crash of 1929 and the resulting Great Depression, there was not a set of accounting standards to be used in preparing financial reports. In fact, a great many people believe that the absence of such standards was at least partially responsible for the crash. Be that as it may, not long after the stock market crash, the U.S. Congress, in an attempt to protect investors and financial statement users, created the **Securities and Exchange Commission (SEC)** and gave it explicit authority to mandate for publicly traded companies:

> ... the items or details to be shown in the balance sheet and earning statement, and the methods to be followed in the preparation of accounts, in the appraisal or valuation of assets and liabilities, in the determination of depreciation and depletion ... and in the preparation ... of consolidated balance sheets or income accounts.[2]

The SEC was given the authority to establish (1) the rules, standards, and procedures used to account for transactions and events and (2) the form and content of published financial reporting.

Many thought the creation of the SEC meant that the government would establish accounting rules and standards. In 1938, however, the SEC decided to allow the accounting profession to establish standards of accounting, as long as there was "substantial authoritative support" for those standards (ASR 4, subparagraph 101). The SEC viewed its principal objective as overseeing adequate disclosure in financial reporting.

The decision to leave the setting of accounting standards to the accounting profession was a profoundly important one. Had the SEC decided differently, U.S. accounting rules today would likely be established by the federal government. Instead, for over 60 years, a series of professional committees and boards, currently the **Financial Accounting Standards Board (FASB),** has determined the accounting standards.

Financial Accounting Standards Board (FASB) The organization that is principally responsible for establishing accounting guidelines and rules in the United States at the present time.

Recently, the relationship among business, the accounting profession, and the SEC is being closely scrutinized. The collapse of ***Enron*** and the serious problems at ***Global Crossing*** and ***WorldCom*** have caused the U.S. Congress to reevaluate the role of the federal government in the standard-setting and enforcement processes.

---

[2]Securities Act of 1933, Section 19.

Discussion Questions •••

1–12. What are the pros and cons of having accounting rules established by the federal government?

1–13. What are the pros and cons of having accounting rules established by the accounting profession?

1–14. If the choice were yours, would you prefer to have accounting standards determined by a government agency or by the accounting profession? Explain your decision.

FINANCIAL ACCOUNTING STANDARDS BOARD (FASB)

The express mission of the Financial Accounting Standards Board (FASB) is

> . . . *to establish and improve standards of financial accounting and reporting for the guidance and education of the public, including issuers, auditors, and users of financial information.*[3]

Because of the FASB's structure and operating methods, it has wide acceptance in both the accounting profession and the business community. The FASB is an independent body composed of seven full-time members, who are required to resign from any other employment during their FASB service. Not all members are accountants. Members come from diverse backgrounds, though they must know accounting, finance, and business in general. This diversity gives the FASB a broad perspective of the public interest in matters of financial accounting and reporting.

Discussion Question •••

1–15. If FASB members are not required to be accountants, from what other professional backgrounds are members likely to be drawn?

One of the first things the FASB did after it was established was to assess the state of the standard-setting process. They discovered that nobody had ever formally decided what the accounting standards were attempting to accomplish. That may sound odd to you, but it can be readily explained. Accounting standards always have been, and remain, responses to specific needs. By that we mean that a situation arises and a standard is established to deal with that situation. What this can lead to, over time, is a labyrinth of standards, often confusing, and often conflicting.

Early on, the FASB developed a **Conceptual Framework of Accounting** from which to approach the process of setting standards. We will refer to this often throughout the remaining chapters of this text; from here on we will usually refer to it simply as the *Conceptual Framework*. The *Conceptual Framework* is contained in six *Statements of Financial Accounting Concepts*. These six statements establish the objectives of financial reporting and the qualitative characteristics of useful accounting information, and they define the accounting elements, assumptions, principles, and constraints. Think of the *Conceptual Framework* as an arch (see Exhibit 1–6). The top of the arch (objectives) is what accounting information attempts to provide. The base of the arch (assumptions, principles, and constraints) outlines the environment in which accounting operates. On the base, supporting the top of the arch, are columns containing the qualitative characteristics accounting information must possess to be useful, and the accounting elements used to produce accounting information. We will discuss the qualitative characteristics in Chapter 2. Our discussion of the 10 accounting elements begins in Chapter 3 and continues throughout the remainder of the text. Because all of the assumptions, principles, and constraints relate to the qualitative characteristics and the accounting elements, we will discuss them as we present the characteristics and elements in later chapters. Our discussion of the *Conceptual Framework* in this chapter will focus on the objectives of financial reporting. As we discuss each of these items, we will give the actual FASB wording in italics followed by a brief explanation of certain terms.

Conceptual Framework of Accounting A framework created by the FASB to establish the objectives of financial reporting and the qualitative characteristics of useful accounting information, and to define the accounting elements, assumptions, principles, and constraints.

---

[3]Robert S. Kay and D. Gerald Searfoss (eds.), *Handbook of Accounting and Auditing*, 2nd ed. (Boston: Warren, Gorham & Lamont, 1989), 46–48.

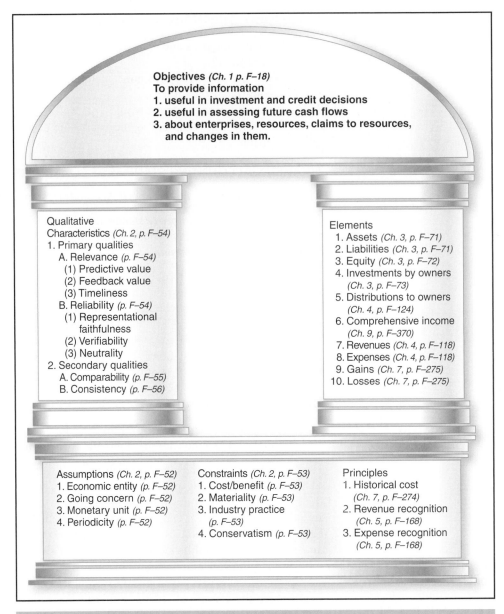

Objectives *(Ch. 1 p. F–18)*
To provide information
1. useful in investment and credit decisions
2. useful in assessing future cash flows
3. about enterprises, resources, claims to resources, and changes in them.

Qualitative
Characteristics *(Ch. 2, p. F–54)*
1. Primary qualities
   A. Relevance *(p. F–54)*
      (1) Predictive value
      (2) Feedback value
      (3) Timeliness
   B. Reliability *(p. F–54)*
      (1) Representational faithfulness
      (2) Verifiability
      (3) Neutrality
2. Secondary qualities
   A. Comparability *(p. F–55)*
   B. Consistency *(p. F–56)*

Elements
1. Assets *(Ch. 3, p. F–71)*
2. Liabilities *(Ch. 3, p. F–71)*
3. Equity *(Ch. 3, p. F–72)*
4. Investments by owners *(Ch. 3, p. F–73)*
5. Distributions to owners *(Ch. 4, p. F–124)*
6. Comprehensive income *(Ch. 9, p. F–370)*
7. Revenues *(Ch. 4, p. F–118)*
8. Expenses *(Ch. 4, p. F–118)*
9. Gains *(Ch. 7, p. F–275)*
10. Losses *(Ch. 7, p. F–275)*

Assumptions *(Ch. 2, p. F–52)*
1. Economic entity *(p. F–52)*
2. Going concern *(p. F–52)*
3. Monetary unit *(p. F–52)*
4. Periodicity *(p. F–52)*

Constraints *(Ch. 2, p. F–53)*
1. Cost/benefit *(p. F–53)*
2. Materiality *(p. F–53)*
3. Industry practice *(p. F–53)*
4. Conservatism *(p. F–53)*

Principles
1. Historical cost *(Ch. 7, p. F–274)*
2. Revenue recognition *(Ch. 5, p. F–168)*
3. Expense recognition *(Ch. 5, p. F–168)*

EXHIBIT 1–6 The Conceptual Framework of Accounting

OBJECTIVES OF FINANCIAL REPORTING

1. Information useful in investment and credit decisions—*Financial reporting should provide information that is useful to present and potential investors and creditors and other users in making rational investment, credit, and similar decisions. The information should be comprehensible to those who have a reasonable understanding of business and economic activities and are willing to study the information with reasonable diligence.* (Statement of Financial Accounting Concepts No. 1, paragraph 34) In the first sentence, *investors* include both those who buy a company's equity securities (stock) and those who buy a company's debt securities (bonds). *Creditors* include suppliers of goods and services, customers, and lending institutions. The *other users* include security analysts, brokers, lawyers, and regulatory agencies. The second sentence of this quotation describes responsibilities for both the users and the accounting profession. In order to use accounting information effectively, the various users must have a reasonable understanding of business *and* they must be willing to study the information with reasonable diligence. Users must fulfill their responsibility, and accountants are responsible to give them information that is comprehensible to them.

2. Information useful in assessing cash flows—*Financial reporting should provide information that is useful to present and potential investors and creditors and other users in assessing the amounts, timing, and uncertainty of prospective cash receipts from dividends or interest and the proceeds from the sale, redemption, or maturity of securities or loans.* (Statement of Financial Accounting Concepts No. 1, paragraph 37) Think back to the first objective for just a minute. Why do investors invest or creditors lend money? They do it primarily to ultimately increase their own cash resources. These investors and creditors need information to help them form rational expectations about whether the prospective receipt of cash is sufficient to warrant the investment or loan. We will discuss this concept in greater detail in Chapter 2 when we cover economic decision making.

3. Information about enterprise resources, claims to resources, and changes in them—*Financial reporting should provide information about the economic resources of an enterprise, the claims to those resources (obligations of the enterprise to transfer resources to other entities and owners' equity), and the effects of transactions, events, and circumstances that change resources and claims to those resources.* (Statement of Financial Accounting Concepts No. 1, paragraph 40) The term *economic resources* refers to assets owned or controlled by the enterprise. *Claims to resources* means debts owed by the company. These debts will be paid by transferring assets (usually cash) to whoever has the claim.

THE STANDARD-SETTING PROCESS TODAY

From its beginning, the FASB has employed a due process approach to setting standards. A due process approach focuses on the protection of individual rights. From the time the FASB identifies an issue that may require a new (or revised) standard to the time a standard is set, interested parties have an opportunity to express their opinions on the matter to FASB. Under the guidance of the FASB, setting standards follows a 10-step circular process emphasizing due process:

1. **Identifying issues.** The FASB, the American Institute of Certified Public Accountants (AICPA), public accounting firms, business organizations, and the U.S. Congress identify accounting issues and problems. The FASB attempts to treat seriously all issues these parties raise.
2. **Setting an agenda.** The FASB selects issues it will consider in the standard-setting process. In selecting an issue, the FASB takes account of its own resources, the perceived urgency of the matter, and any interrelationship with other projects already under consideration.
3. **Appointing a task force.** Once it places an item on the agenda, the FASB appoints a task force to see the project through to its conclusion—either the creation of a new standard or the elimination of the project. Task forces usually include FASB members and outside experts in related areas with diverse views to obtain as many different perspectives as possible.
4. **Creating a discussion memorandum.** The appointed task force prepares a discussion memorandum, which defines the problem, explains the issues, describes the scope of the project, and includes several alternative solutions. All interested parties may respond to the memorandum.
5. **Holding public hearings.** The FASB holds public hearings on major projects under consideration and announces the hearings in the financial press, inviting interested parties to make an oral presentation of their views.
6. **Inviting comment letters.** Those unable to attend the public hearings may write comment letters. The FASB considers every letter.
7. **Deliberating.** After considering the comments from the public hearings, comment letters, FASB's technical staff, and the task force, the FASB decides whether to issue an exposure draft or drop the issue.
8. **Writing an exposure draft.** The FASB prepares a draft version of the proposed standard and exposes it to public comment for at least 60 days. Comments received at this stage often bring about significant changes in the exposure draft.

9. **Issuing a Statement of Financial Accounting Standards.** After a proposed standard goes through the first eight steps of the process, FASB members vote on whether to issue a new standard. When a majority of the seven members approves the new rule, a new *Statement of Financial Accounting Standards (SFAS)* becomes part of GAAP.

10. **Conducting a post-enactment review.** Because financial accounting and reporting are dynamic areas, the FASB constantly reconsiders, refines, or amends the standards.

The FASB has issued well over 100 official pronouncements establishing standards that constitute GAAP. If a company is required to conform to GAAP, these standards are applied in preparing its financial statements and related financial information.

Only companies whose stocks or bonds are traded on an organized exchange are legally required to follow GAAP because they are regulated by the SEC. Companies not subject to SEC regulation may use whatever accounting principles they desire, unless external financial statement users demand that GAAP be followed. For instance, banks and other lending institutions often require financial information that conforms to GAAP from its borrowers. Also, any company a certified public accountant (CPA) firm audits will likely need to follow GAAP in the preparation of its financial statements whether it is regulated by the SEC or not. We will discuss the importance of independent audits in the next section.

Discussion Question ●

1–16. Why do you think a company might be opposed to adopting GAAP?

◆ OUTSIDE ASSURANCE ON FINANCIAL STATEMENTS

Common sense dictates that external decision makers cannot rely solely on the integrity of a company's management, because it is usually in management's best interests to present financial statements that reflect as favorably as possible on the company's performance. There is a need for some assurance from outside the company as to the fairness of its financial statement presentation. That outside assurance is provided by independent audits.

WHAT EXACTLY IS AN AUDIT?

Financial statement users rely on an independent auditor's opinion to assure them that they can trust what they read in the financial statements. The auditor must be independent. That is, the auditor must not have a real or perceived vested interest in the success or failure of the company being audited. Accordingly, the auditor cannot be an employee of the company being audited. He or she must be an independent contractor hired in accordance with a strict set of state legislated rules of conduct. The *independence* of an independent audit is the principal source of the audit's value. What was obviously a lack of independence between **Enron** and **Andersen** (the company's auditor) contributed significantly to **Enron** top management's ability to get away with fraudulent practices for as long as it did. This and other examples, like **WorldCom** (**Andersen** was its auditor, as well), points out the importance of the need for independence. We should note here, however, that thousands of audits are conducted in the United States every year by thousands of auditors that maintain the independence required to provide an audit opinion external parties can rely on.

The auditor examines the client's financial statements and supporting documentation to determine whether the financial statements present a fair picture of the client's financial condition and results of its operations, and to ensure that the financial statements have been presented in accordance with GAAP. It is not feasible for the auditor to examine all the client's records because to do so would make the audits so expensive that companies would not be able to afford them. Auditors examine enough of the records to satisfy themselves as to the fairness of the financial statement numbers. An auditor does not prepare the financial statements—the company's management prepares them and the auditor has no authority to make changes in the statements without the client's consent.

In addition to examining financial records, auditors also evaluate the policies and procedures that are in place to safeguard company assets. This safeguarding of company assets is called internal control.

Generally accepted accounting principles were developed to improve the usefulness of financial accounting. The independent audit is a mechanism to provide assurance to external parties that the financial statements they use have been prepared in accordance with established standards.

Discussion Questions

1–17. How would you decide which and how many records to examine to determine whether your social club's treasurer's report portrays a fair picture of the club's financial activity for the past year?
1–18. How might your answer to question 1–17 change if you were to look at your local Wal-Mart's records for the year?

Auditing standards require auditors to have an extensive knowledge of the economy, the relevant industry, and the client's business. Auditors make inquiries of company personnel, review company financial records, and conduct numerous audit procedures to achieve reasonable assurance that there are no material misstatements in the financial statements. "Reasonable assurance" is what a rational person would consider sufficient. In an accounting context, something is *material* when it would influence the judgment of a reasonable person. A "material misstatement" is one that is significant enough that it could possibly change a reasonable person's decision about a company's financial condition.

WHO PERFORMS AUDITS?

In the United States, only licensed CPAs are permitted to perform independent audits, but not all CPAs are auditors. Auditing is a highly specialized accounting function governed by a set of standards called *generally accepted auditing standards (GAAS)*. The American Institute of Certified Public Accountants (AICPA) details the procedures that CPAs must follow during audits through pronouncements called *Statements on Auditing Standards (SAS)*.

Auditors walk a curious tightrope in our society. Lawyers have one responsibility: to represent their clients who pay them to fulfill that responsibility. Doctors have one responsibility: to care for their patients who pay them to fulfill that responsibility. Auditors, on the other hand, have a dual responsibility: They are responsible to the clients who pay them, but they also have a responsibility to all the users of audited financial statements. Auditors must be independent of the entity they are auditing and objective in their assessment of the financial statements' fairness. It is a difficult balancing act, and auditors face a rising level of litigation from statement users who relied on financial statements and then suffered losses.

Discussion Question

1–19. What potential problems do you think can arise from the auditor's dual responsibility?

THE AUDIT OPINION

At the conclusion of an audit, the auditor issues an *opinion* as to the fairness of the financial statement presentation. GAAS allows the CPA to issue one of several different opinions, depending on the findings of the audit. Most firms receive an *unqualified* opinion, in which the CPA attests that the financial statements "present fairly, in all material respects, the financial position . . . and the results of operations and its cash flows . . . in conformity with generally accepted accounting principles." Also commonly called a *clean* opinion, all firms seek to have this opinion rendered on their financial

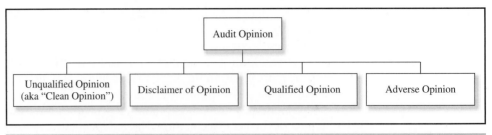

EXHIBIT 1–7   Four Possible Audit Opinions

statements. A financial statement user should be concerned about financial statements that do not receive an unqualified opinion.

Auditors may issue several other opinions. If an auditor is unable to achieve reasonable assurance because the company has not provided enough evidence or has not allowed the auditor to perform enough audit tests, the auditor may be unable to achieve reasonable assurance and will therefore issue a *disclaimer of opinion.* The financial statement user has no assurance from the auditor of fairness or conformity with GAAP when the auditor issues a disclaimer of opinion. Auditors have the option of issuing a *qualified* opinion in which they state an exception to the general fairness of presentation of the financial statements or to their lack of conformity with GAAP. Obviously, financial statement users should carefully consider the exception(s) the auditor raises. The most devastating opinion an auditor can render is the *adverse* opinion, in which the auditor states that the financial statements are not fairly presented or that they do not conform to GAAP. Readers should not rely on such financial statements. A financial statement user should examine the audit opinion to determine the auditor's level of assurance before reading the financial statements. Exhibit 1–7 illustrates the four possible audit opinions.

Discussion Question

1–20. Find the audit opinion in the annual report of Pier 1 Imports, Inc. contained in the company's 2002 annual report. Who are the auditors? What type of opinion did the auditors issue?

Earlier in this chapter we said that external decision makers use financial accounting information. There are two major sources of financial accounting information available to external decision makers, the *annual report,* and the *Form 10-K.* See the appendix to this chapter for a discussion of these two important financial reports.

Summary

The word business has several different meanings, but in the context of this book, it means either commerce or trade as a whole or a specific company involved in commerce or trade. All economic activity revolves around the four factors of production: natural resources, labor, capital, and entrepreneurship. In a planned economy, a strong centralized government controls most or all of the factors. In a market economy, most of the factors are privately owned.

Capitalism, like the market economy in the United States, relies on a profit motive that spurs competition, drives the allocation of resources, and forces business to operate efficiently. Modern U.S. business practice balances companies' profit motive with their social responsibilities to various stakeholders.

The three basic forms of business organizations are the proprietorship (one owner), the partnership (two or more owners), and the corporation (a legal entity separate from its owner or owners). Most business activity can be categorized as manufacturing, merchandising, or service. Hybrid businesses are those that conduct more than one of these types of activities.

Economic decision makers are classified broadly as either internal or external to an entity. The information designed for use by external parties is called financial accounting information and is contained in four general-purpose financial statements: the balance sheet, the income statement, the statement of owners' equity, and the statement of cash flows.

In response to the users' need for relevant, reliable financial information, accountants developed standards called generally accepted accounting principles (GAAP). The Securities and Exchange Commission (SEC) has the legal authority to regulate the accounting profession. However, under the SEC's watchful eye, the Financial Accounting Standards Board (FASB), a private body created in 1973, establishes most of the GAAP in the United States. The FASB uses a due process approach, whereby anyone who wishes to express his or her opinion has an opportunity to do so as the FASB creates new accounting standards. Early on, the FASB created the *Conceptual Framework of Accounting* and works to ensure that new accounting standards are consistent with this framework.

External users of financial statements need some form of assurance that the financial statements are fairly presented and are prepared according to GAAP. In large part, this assurance is achieved through independent audits, whereby independent CPAs examine enough of a company's records to determine whether the company's financial statements fairly present the company's economic position and that they are prepared in accordance with GAAP. The auditor then issues an audit opinion to express his or her findings.

Corporate Reporting and the Annual Report

Every publicly traded corporation has various stakeholders and potential stakeholders. These include shareholders and potential shareholders, creditors, customers, and employees and potential employees. To make sound decisions, these stakeholders must have access to financial information about the company. Two major sources of financial information in the United States are the corporate *annual report* and the SEC's *Form 10-K*. The **annual report** includes a variety of information including financial statements and a host of general information about the company and its management. The **Form 10-K,** which is required by the SEC, is much less glamorous than the annual report, but it includes financial and nonfinancial details that are not included in the annual report. Both documents provide invaluable information to external decision makers.

annual report   A corporate document that provides interested parties with a variety of information including financial statements and a host of general information about the company and its management.

Form 10-K   Less glamorous than the annual report, this corporate document includes additional financial and nonfinancial details that are invaluable to external decision makers.

HOW TO GET AN ANNUAL REPORT

The SEC requires that each publicly traded firm prepare an annual report to communicate important information about the company. As part of the SEC requirement, if you own shares of stock in a corporation, you will automatically receive a copy of its annual report. But how should you go about getting an annual report if you are not a shareholder? There are several ways to get a copy of an annual report. In addition to calling the company directly to request a copy, you can find annual report information on the Internet, in the *Wall Street Journal* Annual Report Service, and at most libraries.

- Almost all companies maintain a Web site on the Internet. Company Web sites often include a cyber version of the annual report or at least financial statements and other information taken directly from the annual report. You can download or print the annual report or, if you would rather, you can make an online request for a copy of the annual report itself.

  It may take some trial and error to find a particular company's Web site, but as the following examples show, in almost all cases the Web site address is just a modified form of the company name.

Company Name	Internet Address
Gap Inc.	*www.gap.com*
Sears	*www.sears.com*
Hallmark	*www.hallmark.com*
JCPenney	*www.jcpenney.com*

- The ***Wall Street Journal*** provides an Annual Report Service for selected companies. The ***Wall Street Journal*** listing for some companies includes a small cloverleaf. This cloverleaf signifies that the *Journal*'s annual report service can provide a copy of the company's annual report. Call 1-800-654-2582 to request an annual report.

- Many libraries provide computers and access to various CD-ROM sources for company information. Some of the most popular are:
  - ***Infotrac.*** Infotrac contains company profiles, investment reports, and article citations.
  - ***Proquest.*** Proquest is the CD-ROM version of ABI/Inform, the premier source of business articles. Proquest contains citations and the full text of articles, including photos and graphical images.
  - ***Mergent's*** (formerly ***Moody's***). Mergent's provides full-text annual reports of U.S. and international operations.

  Online systems that search databases provide access to extensive information. Among the most widely used databases for company information are:
  - ***DIALOG.*** DIALOG provides access to over 400 databases covering a wide range of topics, not all of which are business related. Available information includes annual reports and articles (both full text and citations).
  - ***LEXIS/NEXIS.*** LEXIS/NEXIS provides full text of all SEC-required filings (such as the Form 10-K) and various business articles and newsletters.

  In addition to the annual report sources listed already, you can always contact the company directly. Do not hesitate to ask a company for its annual report. Corporations know that public image is a critical factor in a company's success or failure so they are generally happy to provide a copy of their annual report upon request. To order an annual report directly from a company, first locate the corporate headquarters address, phone number, or fax number on their Web site, in telephone listings, or in some other library reference source, then simply phone, write, or fax your request to the company's public relations or investor relations department.

INFORMATION PROVIDED IN ANNUAL REPORTS

Annual reports from various companies contain much the same categories of information, mainly because the SEC requires that most of it be included. The table of contents for ***Pier 1 Imports, Inc.***'s 2002 annual report shown below represents the type of information found in most corporate annual reports. An asterisk indicates that the SEC requires the information.

> Financial Highlights
> Letter to Stockholders
> Key Financial Statistics
> *Five-Year Selected Financial Data
> *Management Discussion and Analysis
> *Independent Auditors' Report
> *Report of Management
> *Consolidated Statements of Operations
> *Consolidated Balance Sheets
> *Consolidated Statements of Cash Flows
> *Consolidated Statements of Shareholders' Equity
> *Notes to Consolidated Financial Statements
> *Shareholder Information
> *Directors and Officers

Discussion Question •

1–21. What other information would you want to know about Pier 1 Imports? Would you feel comfortable enough to call, e-mail, or write to the company with a specific question? Where can you find the address and phone number for Pier 1 in the annual report?

FORM 10-K

A Form 10-K looks very different from an annual report. The annual report is an expensive public relations brochure with high-quality glossy pages, color photos, and eye-catching graphics. The 10-K is printed on thin paper with no pictures and no color graphics. It contains a wealth of information about the company, much of which is also included in the annual report. This is not surprising because the SEC regulates disclosure requirements for both documents. That said, the annual report may be "included by reference" in the Form 10-K to avoid duplication of various required items. Exhibit 1–8 lists the required contents of the 10-K.

EXHIBIT 1–8 Outline of the Contents of Form 10-K

Part I
  Item 1. Business
  Item 2. Properties
  Item 3. Legal Proceedings
  Item 4. Submission of Matters to a Vote of Security Holders
Part II
  Item 5. Market for the Company's Common Equity and Related Stockholder Matters
  Item 6. Selected Financial Data
  Item 7. Management's Discussion and Analysis of Financial Condition and Results of Operations
  Item 8. Financial Statements and Supplementary Data
  Item 9. Changes in and Disagreements with Accountants on Accounting and Financial Disclosure
Part III
  Item 10. Directors and Executive Officers of the Company
  Item 11. Executive Compensation
  Item 12. Security Ownership of Certain Beneficial Owners and Management
  Item 13. Certain Relationships and Related Transactions
Part IV
  Item 14. Exhibits, Financial Statements, and Schedules and Reports on Form 8-K

Electronic Data Gathering, Analysis. and Retrieval (EDGAR)
A system operated by the SEC to facilitate the collection, and more importantly, the dissemination of corporate information to all interested parties. Access to EDGAR is available over the Internet at www.sec.gov.

The SEC prescribes the contents of Form 10-K in Regulation S-X and Regulation S-K, as revised in 1982. Those revisions created the SEC's Integrated Disclosure System, which simplified and improved the quality of disclosures and reduced its cost, in part by eliminating duplicate reports. The SEC's **Electronic Data Gathering, Analysis, and Retrieval (EDGAR)** system is an important component of the integrated disclosure system. Each publicly traded domestic company reporting to the SEC is required to file its Form 10-K and many other disclosure documents and schedules on EDGAR. So what does this mean to you? Well, EDGAR was specifically designed to help collect, and more importantly to disseminate, corporate information to interested parties (that is, to anyone who wants it). This means that if a document is filed on EDGAR, you have easy access to that document via the Internet. For example, all you have to do to get a Form 10-K for any publicly traded company is to log on to the SEC's Web site at www.sec.gov and click on the EDGAR link. What's more, EDGAR puts a wealth of other information about the company at your fingertips. Whether you want to obtain general information about a company, a company's financial information, or information about a particular company's industry, EDGAR at www.sec.gov can help you get it. Remember that you can log on to the EDGAR system Web site to obtain a copy of a Form 10-K for virtually any publicly traded company.

GATHERING ADDITIONAL INFORMATION ABOUT A COMPANY

If you would like more information about a company than its annual report and Form 10-K provides, try the following sources:

- The company's Web site usually contains current press releases about company accomplishments, problems, financial results, and other important news.
- You can conduct a search for news about the company with any of the Web search engines.
- Libraries generally have a wide variety of resources available, including handbooks and periodicals. Examples are:
  - *Hoover's Handbook of American Business* offers information about each of the companies it profiles. Exhibit 1–9 shows the Hoover's profile for *Pier 1 Imports, Inc.* Most of the information it provides about a company is not available in the company's annual report, and background details provided in the sections titled "Overview" and "History" are particularly relevant to potential employees. Visit: www.hoovers.com.
  - *Standard and Poor's Stock Reports* details recent news about companies. This loose-leaf publication is updated monthly and contains various types of information. Visit: www2.standardandpoors.com.
  - *Mergent's Industrial Manual* (formerly *Moody's Industrial Manual*) offers extensive company histories and more detailed financial information than can be found in *Hoover's Handbook of American Business* and *Standard and Poor's Stock Reports*. Visit: www.mergent.com.
  - *Investor's Business Daily* provides critical information previously available only to institutional investors (pension and mutual funds, banks, insurance companies, and government organizations). Features include corporate ratings that provide fundamental and technical evaluations on stocks traded on the NASDAQ and the American and New York exchanges. Visit: www.investors.com.
  - Periodical indexes help you find articles about the company. Usually available in hardback or CD-ROM, the Business Periodicals Index or the *Wall Street Journal* Index can be helpful in locating information about a particular company. The most trustworthy sources for information in the press are the *Wall Street Journal, BusinessWeek, Fortune,* and *Forbes.*

SUMMARY OF APPENDIX

The most comprehensive presentation of financial reporting to stockholders is the annual report. The SEC has specific disclosure requirements for information provided in the annual report and the Form 10-K, required annually for publicly traded companies. The SEC prescribes the rules for the form and content of the financial statements and other information included in the 10-K under Regulations S-X and S-K. The SEC's Integrated Disclosure System encourages companies to eliminate duplication between the annual report and Form 10-K through "incorporation by reference."

You can gather additional information about publicly traded companies on the Internet, in the library, or from news sources.

PIER 1 IMPORTS, INC.

Overview

Wicker World? Rattans 'R' Us? How about Pier 1 Imports? The Fort Worth, Texas-based company sells about 5,000 home furnishings items imported from more than 50 countries—mostly Asia—in almost 800 US stores. In addition to its growing US operations, Pier 1 has about 35 stores in Canada, and it also operates about 25 The Pier stores in the UK.

Pier 1 gradually has changed its merchandise from the exotic knickknacks the baby boomers used to decorate their dorm rooms to the more upscale, but still exotic, household furnishings they buy today. The product line favors natural materials (rattan, wood) and handcrafted goods. Furniture accounts for more than a third of sales, and decorative items such as lamps, vases, and baskets account for another quarter. The stores also sell bed and bath products, housewares, and seasonal items. With more than a million active holders, Pier 1's private-label credit card is used to charge almost 30% of sales.

Pier 1 started selling online in 2000 and has hinted that it might create or buy high-end and low-end home furnishings chains (a la The Gap's upscale Banana Republic and lower-priced Old Navy chains). In 2001 it acquired the Cargo Furniture chain from home furnishings manufacturer Tandycrafts.

History

Attracted by a Fisherman's Wharf import outlet called Cost Plus, marketing guru Charles Tandy (founder of RadioShack) made a loan to its owner and obtained the right to open other Cost Plus stores. Opening his first Cost Plus store in 1962 in San Francisco, Tandy leveraged the strength of the US dollar against weaker foreign currencies. He bought inexpensive wicker furniture, brass candle-sticks, and other items from countries like India, Mexico, and Thailand and gave them healthy markups, yet still managed to price them attractively for US customers.

The store was a hit with the peace and free-love generation of the 1960s, who dug its beads, incense, and wicker furniture. In 1965, with 16 locations, the company changed its name to Pier 1 Imports. Pressed by RadioShack, Tandy sold Pier 1 the next year. In 1969, with 42 stores, including its first store in Canada, the company went public on the American Stock Exchange.

By 1971 Pier 1 had 123 stores and was celebrating 100% sales gains for four consecutive years. It expanded its international presence, adding locations in Australia and Europe, and moved to the NYSE the next year. The chain experimented with alternative retail formats, including art supply, rug outlets, and fabric stores, but had abandoned them, as well as its foreign stores, by the mid-1970s. Pier 1 boasted nearly 270 locations by 1975.

Baby boomers, key to the chain's success, grew up and acquired different tastes, however. The dollar had also weakened, increasing costs. Performance faltered, and in 1980 the company brought in Robert Camp, who had successfully operated his own Pier 1 stores in Canada, to give it a makeover. Camp closed poorly performing stores, opened larger stores in more profitable areas, and began changing the merchandise mix from novelties to higher-quality goods.

In 1983 investment group Intermark bought more than a third of the company. The next year Pier 1 acquired 36 Nurseryland Garden Centers from Intermark (boosting Intermark's stake in Pier 1 to about 50%) and merged the stores with its Wolfe's Nursery to form Sunbelt Nursery Group, which was spun off in 1985. That year Pier 1 named Clark Johnson its CEO. At the time it operated nearly 265 locations, showing little growth in store count in a decade.

Johnson initiated an ambitious plan to double the number of Pier 1 stores, which reached 500 in early 1989. With Intermark struggling, Pier 1 bought back Sunbelt (including a 50% stake in Sunbelt from Intermark) in 1990. The following year Intermark sold its stake in Pier 1 to pay back debt. That year Pier 1 took Sunbelt public, keeping a 57% stake (Sunbelt has since been dissolved). In 1993 the company launched The Pier, a chain of stores in the UK, and opened boutiques in Sears stores in Mexico.

Having spruced up stores, the chain continued to adjust the merchandise mix, dumping apparel in 1997 in favor of higher-margin goods. Also in 1997 Pier 1 purchased a national bank charter from Texaco to standardize the interest rates and fees on its private-label credit card. Marvin Girouard replaced Johnson as CEO in 1998 and as chairman in 1999. Pier 1 began selling online with the launch of its Web site in June 2000.

In February 2001 the company acquired the 21-store Cargo Furniture chain from home furnishings manufacturer Tandycrafts.

Officers

Chairman and CEO: Marvin J. Girouard, age 61, $2,132,000 pay
SVP of Finance, CFO, and Treasurer: Charles H. Turner, age 44, $580,250 pay
SVP of Stores: Robert A. Arlauskas, age 46
SVP of Merchandising: Jay R. Jacobs, age 46, $580,250 pay
SVP of Legal Affairs: J. Rodney Lawrence, age 55, $424,000 pay
SVP of Marketing: Phil E. Schneider, age 49
SVP of Logistics and Allocations: David A. Walker, age 50
SVP of Human Resources: E. Mitchell Weatherly, age 53, $404,000 pay
Auditors: Ernst & Young LLP

Locations

HQ: 301 Commerce St., Ste. 600, Fort Worth, TX 76102
Phone: 817-252-8000   **Fax:** 817-252-8028
Web: www.pier1.com

Pier 1 Imports has about 800 stores in 48 states, plus 35 in Canada. It also owns 23 The Pier stores in the UK and 21 Cargo Furniture stores in the US. It also owns or franchises about 30 stores in Japan, Mexico, and Puerto Rico.

Products/Operations

2001 North American Sales

	% of sales
Furniture	40
Decorative accessories	22
Bed & bath	17
Housewares	12
Seasonal	9
Total	100

Selected Merchandise
Baskets
Bed and bath accessories
Candles
Ceramics
Dinnerware
Dried and silk flowers
Fragrance products
Furniture
Lamps
Seasonal products
Vases
Wall decor

EXHIBIT 1–9 *Pier 1 Imports, Inc.* Entry in *Hoover's Handbook of American Business* (*Continued*)

Competitors

Bed Bath & Beyond	Lechters
Bombay Company	Linens 'n Things
Container Store	Michaels Stores
Cost Plus	MJDesigns
Euromarket Designs	Spiegel
Garden Ridge	Williams-Sonoma
IKEA	

Historical Financials & Employees

NYSE: PSR FYE: Sat. nearest last day in Feb.	Annual Growth	2/92	2/93	2/94	2/95	2/96	2/97	2/98	2/99	2/00	2/01
Sales ($ mil.)	10.2%	587	629	685	712	811	947	1,075	1,139	1,231	1,412
Net income ($ mil.)	15.3%	26	23	6	25	10	44	78	80	75	95
Income as % of sales	—	4.5%	3.7%	0.9%	3.5%	1.2%	4.7%	7.3%	7.1%	6.1%	6.7%
Earnings per share ($)	13.9%	0.30	0.26	0.07	0.27	0.11	0.43	0.72	0.77	0.75	0.97
Stock price - FY high ($)	—	5.14	5.56	5.19	4.29	5.95	8.31	18.84	20.76	12.38	14.50
Stock price - FY low ($)	—	1.91	2.81	3.49	3.02	3.45	5.28	7.23	6.06	5.25	7.94
Stock price - FY close ($)	13.3%	4.24	4.92	3.71	4.18	5.84	7.73	17.84	8.63	8.75	13.00
P/E - high	—	17	21	74	16	54	17	24	25	16	15
P/E - low	—	6	11	50	11	31	11	9	7	7	8
Dividends per share ($)	—	0.00	0.03	0.05	0.05	0.06	0.07	0.07	0.12	0.12	0.15
Book value per share ($)	11.7%	2.04	2.27	2.27	2.53	2.56	3.19	3.87	4.14	4.70	5.53
Employees	7.5%	7,600	7,500	7,850	8,671	9,399	11,255	12,571	12,600	13,600	14,600

Stock Price History

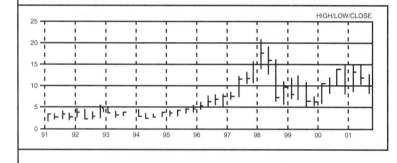

2001 Fiscal Year-End

Debt ratio: 4.5%
Return on equity: 19.5%
Cash ($ mil.): 47
Current ratio: 3.31
Long-term debt (5 mil.): 23
No. of shares (mil.): 96
Dividends
   Yield: 1.2%
   Payout: 15.5%
Market value ($ mil.): 1.250

Courtesy of *Hoover's Online* (www.hoovers.com)

Key Terms

- annual report, F–24
- business, F–2
- capital, F–3
- capitalism, F–3
- communism, F–3
- Conceptual Framework of Accounting, F–17
- corporation, F–8
- Electronic Data Gathering, Analysis, and Retrieval (EDGAR), F–26
- entrepreneurship, F–3
- exports, F–12
- external decision makers, F–14
- factors of production, F–2

- financial accounting, F–14
- Financial Accounting Standards Board (FASB), F–16
- Form 10-K, F–24
- generally accepted accounting principles (GAAP), F–16
- hybrid companies, F–11
- imports, F–12
- internal decision makers, F–13
- labor, F–3
- management accounting, F–14
- manufacturing, F–10
- merchandising, F–11
- natural resources, F–3

- net income, F–4
- net profit, F–4
- partnership, F–7
- profit, F–4
- proprietorship, F–5
- quotas, F–12
- Securities and Exchange Commission (SEC), F–16
- separate entity assumption, F–8
- service company, F–11
- sole proprietorship, F–5
- stakeholder, F–5
- tariffs, F–12

Review the Facts ●

   A. What are the four factors of production? Define each.
   B. Describe the primary difference between a planned economy and a market economy.
   C. Explain what is meant by the profit motive.
   D. What is gross profit?
   E. How does net income differ from gross profit?
   F. Explain the meaning of stakeholder.
   G. Name the three basic forms of business organization and describe the advantages and disadvantages of each.
   H. Describe the separate entity assumption.
   I. Name and describe the three major types of businesses.
   J. In the context of business activity, what is a hybrid company?
   K. Define quotas and tariffs. Explain the purpose of each.
   L. Describe the relationship between business and accounting.
   M. What information does a balance sheet provide?
   N. What information does an income statement provide?
   O. What are the three business activities listed on the statement of cash flows?
   P. Broadly define GAAP.
   Q. Explain the role of the SEC in the regulation of accounting practice.
   R. What is the FASB, and what does the acronym FASB stand for?
   S. Briefly describe the purpose of the *Conceptual Framework of Accounting*.
   T. What are the main objectives of financial reporting?
   U. List the 10 steps of the FASB's due process for standard setting.
   V. What is the purpose of an independent audit, and who can perform one?
   W. What is an audit opinion?
   X. Name and describe the four types of audit report an auditor can issue.
   Y. Identify the two major financial reports that publicly traded corporations must prepare annually.
   Z. *What is the primary purpose of the SEC's EDGAR system?
  AA. *Why are corporations generally cooperative when individuals request their annual reports?
  BB. What are the required sections of a company's annual report? Briefly describe each.

Apply What You Have Learned ●

LO 1 & 2: TERMINOLOGY

1–22. Below are items relating to some of the concepts in this chapter, followed by the definitions of those items in scrambled order.

   a. Entrepreneurship   e. Factors of production
   b. Labor   f. Natural resources
   c. Planned economy   g. Capital
   d. Capitalism   h. Profit motive

   1. _____ The human resource factor
   2. _____ Land and materials that come from land
   3. _____ The factor of production that brings all the other factors of production together
   4. _____ The motivation to do something when the benefits exceed the sacrifice of doing it
   5. _____ A type of market economy
   6. _____ The four major items needed to support economic activity
   7. _____ Buildings, machinery, tools, and money used to produce goods and services
   8. _____ A strong, centralized government controls all or most of the factors of production

Required: Match the letter next to each item on the list with the appropriate definition. Use each letter only once.

*Based on material in the Appendix.

LO 2, 4, & 5: BUSINESS TERMINOLOGY

1–23. Below are items relating to some of the concepts in this chapter, followed by the definitions of those items in scrambled order.

a. Hybrid company
b. Wholesaler
c. Imports
d. Exports
e. Tariffs
f. Manufacturing company
g. Merchandising company
h. Retailer
i. Translation
j. Quota

1. _____ Goods sold outside the country in which they were produced
2. _____ A business that converts purchased raw materials into some tangible, physical product
3. _____ A company involved in more than one type of business activity
4. _____ A type of business operated by either a wholesaler or a retailer
5. _____ A quantity limitation placed on imported goods
6. _____ A business known as a middleman
7. _____ The conversion of the currency of one country into its equivalent in another country's currency
8. _____ Taxes that raise the price of imported products
9. _____ A business that sells products to the final consumer
10. _____ Goods brought into a country that were produced in another country

Required: Match the letter next to each item on the list with the appropriate definition. Use each letter only once.

LO 3: COMPUTATION OF GROSS PROFIT AND NET INCOME

1–24. Larry Melman owns and operates a retail clothing store. Last month clothing sales totaled $5,200. Melman paid $2,800 for the clothing sold last month. He also paid rent of $300 and wages to employees totaling $900.

Required:

a. Calculate the gross profit on sales for last month.
b. Identify the expenses incurred during the month and explain whether they should be used to compute gross profit or net income.
c. Calculate the net income for last month.

LO 3: COMPUTATION OF GROSS PROFIT AND NET INCOME

1–25. James Marks sells fine imported cigars. During the month of December, James sold 3,000 cigars at a total price of $15,000. James paid $9,000 for the cigars that he sold in December.

Required: Determine the gross profit for James in December.

LO 3: COMPUTATION OF GROSS PROFIT AND NET INCOME

1–26. Carol Levine owns and operates a retail hardware store. In June her sales were $18,000. The items sold cost Ms. Levine $12,600. Ms. Levine spent $1,000 for store rent, $300 for utilities expense, and $1,500 for employee wages.

Required:

a. Calculate the gross profit on sales for June.
b. Identify the expenses incurred during the month and explain whether they should be used to compute gross profit or net income.
c. Calculate the net income for June.

LO 3: COMPUTATION OF GROSS PROFIT AND NET INCOME

1–27. In August, Mary bought 24 quilts for $100 each.

Required:

a. If Mary sells the quilts for $150 each, what is her gross profit for each quilt?
b. If she sells all of the quilts in August, what is her total gross profit?
c. If Mary rents an office for $200 and pays utilities expense of $75, advertising expense of $150, and bank charges of $15, calculate her net income for August.

LO 3 & 4: COMPUTATION OF GROSS PROFIT AND NET INCOME FOR DIFFERENT BUSINESS TYPES

1–28. The Computer Center of America manufactures and sells computers. During the month of October the center produced and sold 1,000 computers. The sale of the computers generated $1,000,000. The cost of the computers sold included $300,000 for the parts to build the computers, $200,000 for the labor to assemble the computers, and $100,000 for all other costs (overhead) necessary to make the computers. Aside from the cost of the computers themselves, the Computer Center spent $50,000 on selling and administrative expenses.

Required:

a. What type of business does the Computer Center operate (i.e., manufacturing, merchandising, service, or hybrid)?
b. Calculate the gross profit for the month of October.
c. Calculate the net income for the month of October.

LO 4: STOCKHOLDER VERSUS STAKEHOLDER

1–29. Explain the concept behind the term *stakeholder,* and contrast it with the definition of the term *stockholder.*

LO 4: FORMS OF BUSINESS ORGANIZATION

1–30. Below are the three basic forms of business in the United States, followed by some of the advantages relating to those forms of business:

a. Proprietorship   b. Partnership   c. Corporation

1. _____ Owner has total control
2. _____ Greater business continuity
3. _____ Easy transfer of ownership
4. _____ Limited liability
5. _____ Greater access to capital
6. _____ Easy and inexpensive to establish
7. _____ Few government regulations
8. _____ Easy to dissolve
9. _____ No special income taxes
10. _____ No sharing of profits
11. _____ Greater management expertise

Required: Match the letter next to each form of business with the appropriate advantage. Each letter will be used more than once and it is possible that a particular advantage applies to more than one of the business forms.

LO 4: FORMS OF BUSINESS ORGANIZATION

1–31. Below are the three basic forms of business in the United States, followed by some of the disadvantages relating to those forms of business:

a. Proprietorship   b. Partnership   c. Corporation

1. _____ Usually has less access to capital than the other two forms
2. _____ Greater tax burden
3. _____ Limited management expertise
4. _____ Unlimited liability
5. _____ Absentee ownership
6. _____ Must share profits
7. _____ Greater government regulation
8. _____ Often difficult to dissolve
9. _____ Potential ownership conflicts

Required: Match the letter (or letters) next to each form of business with the appropriate disadvantage. Each letter will be used more than once and it is possible that a particular disadvantage applies to more than one of the business forms.

LO 4: FORMS OF BUSINESSES

1–32. Professor Seth Levine is opening the Levine Publishing Company to publish and distribute travel books throughout the United States. Levine has invited all his friends to invest in his new business. He is offering shares of stock for a mere $10 each.

Required:

    a. What form of business is Professor Levine opening?
    b. Briefly explain four advantages of doing business in this form.

LO 5: DISTINGUISHING AMONG TYPES OF BUSINESSES ACTIVITIES

1–33. Phil Jackson owns and operates a jewelry store. During the past month, he sold a necklace to a customer for $2,500. Phil had purchased the necklace for $1,800.

Required:

    a. What type of business does Phil own (manufacturer, wholesaler, retailer, etc.)? Explain how you determined your response.
    b. Calculate Phil's gross margin on the sale of the necklace.
    c. Identify four costs besides the $1,800 cost of the necklace that Phil might incur in the operation of his jewelry store.
    d. If Phil's operating costs are $900 per month, what is his net income (or loss) for the month?

LO 5: TYPES OF BUSINESS ACTIVITIES

1–34. This chapter discusses five types of business in the United States, namely:

    1. Manufacturing
    2. Wholesale merchandising
    3. Retail merchandising
    4. Service
    5. Hybrid

Required:

    a. In your own words, describe the characteristics of each type of business.
    b. Discuss how each of these five types of business is different from the other four.
    c. Without citing any of the examples from the chapter, provide two examples of each type of business and explain how you determined your answers.

LO 8: REPORTING STANDARDS

1–35. Following are the 10 steps in the standard-setting process used by the Financial Accounting Standards Board:

    1. Identifying issues
    2. Placing the issue on the FASB's agenda
    3. Appointing a task force
    4. Creating a discussion memorandum
    5. Holding public hearings
    6. Inviting comment letters
    7. Deliberating
    8. Writing an exposure draft
    9. Issuing a Statement of Financial Accounting Standards
    10. Conducting a post-enactment review

Required:

    a. In your own words, explain what happens in each of the 10 steps of the standard-setting process.
    b. What is meant by a "due process approach" to setting accounting standards?

LO 8: REPORTING STANDARDS

1–36. Generally accepted accounting principles have been developed over time to aid in comparability among the financial statements of different companies. They are also intended to maintain consistency in the way a firm accounts for transactions and events from period to period.

An audit is intended to provide some assurance to external parties that the financial statements examined are reasonably presented.

Required:

a. What determines whether a company in the United States is required to prepare its financial statements according to GAAP?

b. Why are some companies forced to adhere to GAAP even though they are not required by law to do so?

LO 11 & 12: REPORTING STANDARDS (APPENDIX)

1–37. Below are some of the items discussed in this chapter's appendix, followed by the definitions of those items in scrambled order.

a. Financial reporting

b. Financial statements

c. SEC Integrated Disclosure System

d. Annual report

e. SEC Form l0-K

f. Notes to financial statements

1. _____ One of its objectives is to simplify and improve the quality of disclosures provided to investors and other users of financial information.

2. _____ Disclosures provided to economic decision makers that include not only quantitative information but also descriptive information.

3. _____ Intended to provide important information that should be considered by financial statement users when reading financial statements.

4. _____ Its content is prescribed by the SEC.

5. _____ The balance sheets for two years and statements of income, cash flows, and stockholders' equity for three years are presented as a part of the annual report.

6. _____ Originally intended to be used only by stockholders but now is broadly used by a variety of other economic decision makers.

Required: Match the letter next to each item on the list with the appropriate definition. Use each letter only once.

LO 10: FINANCIAL REPORTING

1–38. Below are some items related to the issue of outside assurance discussed in this chapter, followed by the definitions of those items in scrambled order.

a. Audit

b. Unqualified opinion

c. Adverse opinion

d. Qualified opinion

e. Disclaimer

1. _____ Caused by a material uncertainty the auditor does not feel can be adequately communicated, or by the placing of a significant restriction on the auditor as to what records may be examined.

2. _____ The process of examining a company's records to determine whether the financial statements have been prepared in accordance with GAAP standards.

3. _____ Rendered when there are departures from GAAP so pervasive that a reasonable person cannot rely on the financial statements.

4. _____ Unofficially referred to as a "clean" opinion.

5. _____ An auditor states an exception in the audit report.

Required: Match the letter next to each item with the appropriate definition. Use each letter only once.

LO 10: FINANCIAL REPORTING

1–39. Your uncle, who owns a small business, knows that you are taking a course in accounting. He tells you that his banker is requiring him to provide an audited set of financial statements for the last fiscal year. He does not understand why the bank is making this request and he asks you why they would want an audit of his financial statements. How do you respond to his question?

LO 12: ANNUAL REPORTS (APPENDIX)

1–40. Listed below are the items required by the SEC to be included in the annual report, along with some items not required but normally included:

1. _____ Audited financial statements
2. _____ The principal market in which the securities of the firm are traded
3. _____ Industry segment disclosures for the last three fiscal years
4. _____ The management report
5. _____ Offer to provide a free copy of Form 10-K to shareholders upon written request, unless the annual report complies with Form 10-K disclosure requirements
6. _____ Report on corporate citizenship
7. _____ Management's discussion and analysis of financial condition and results of operations
8. _____ Five-year selected financial data
9. _____ Brief description of the business
10. _____ Letter to the stockholders
11. _____ Identification of directors and executive officers, with the principal occupation and employer of each
12. _____ High and low market prices of the company's common stock for each quarter of the two most recent fiscal years and dividends paid on common stock during those years

Required: Identify each of the items as either required (R) or optional (O).

Financial Reporting Exercises ●

LO 11 & 12: ANNUAL REPORTS (APPENDIX)

1–41. Use the information contained in the 2002 annual report of *Pier 1 Imports* on page F–503 to answer the following:

Required:

a. What is the name of the CPA firm who audited the financial statements?
b. What type of opinion was rendered by the audit firm?
c. Which paragraph of the audit report identifies the party responsible for the financial statements?
d. Which paragraph of the audit report identifies who is responsible for the audit of the financial statements?
e. Which paragraph of the audit report actually reports the expression of an opinion?

LO 12: ANNUAL REPORTS (APPENDIX)

1–42. Use the information contained in the 2002 annual report of *Pier 1 Imports* on page F–503 to answer the following:

Required:

a. List the title and the time period covered by each financial statement included in the annual report.
b. The assets, liabilities, and stockholders' equity are listed in which of the financial statements?
c. The sales, cost of goods sold, and the operating expenses are reported in which financial statement?

LO 12: ANNUAL REPORTS (APPENDIX)

1–43. Use the information contained in the 2002 annual report of *Pier 1 Imports* on page F–503 to answer the following:

Required:

a. Who wrote the letter to the stockholders? In your opinion, what were the three most important messages in the letter?
b. What are the divisions of Pier 1? For each division, list the following information:

(1) Name
(2) Major markets

(3) Distinction in the marketplace

(4) Goals for the current year

    c. How does the information in parts a and b help a potential investor, creditor, or employee?

LO 12: ANNUAL REPORTS (APPENDIX)

1–44. The following is the 2001 letter to the stockholders from Craig R. Barrett, CEO of ***Intel Corporation.***

Education is a critical focus for Intel and for our employees around the world. In 2001 Intel Corporation and the Intel Foundation contributed over $103 million to help improve education. Through our Intel® Innovation in Education Initiative, teachers developed the skills to integrate technology into their classrooms and young people in underserved communities gained access to technology to develop new skills through neighborhood centers. In addition, we continued to reward and encourage our future scientists and engineers both at the high school and university level with scholarships, research opportunities, and curriculum support. Finally, we explored new ways to use the Internet as a means of providing content and resources for educators.

As a global community, we have witnessed some terrible events this past year. In February, India was hit with a devastating earthquake. Intel employees and the Intel Foundation responded with a donation of over $1.6 million to relief efforts. In response to the events of September 11th, the Intel Foundation immediately donated $1 million to the American Red Cross and promised to match employee donations, which eventually reached $1.2 million—for a total Intel contribution of $3.4 million from the Intel Foundation and Intel employees to help victims of the disaster. Through Operation Unity, Intel employees responded to meet immediate needs in New York by providing humanitarian aid and assistance to emergency services agencies, small businesses, and non-profit organizations.

Each of our Intel locations is actively involved in a variety of efforts that directly support their local communities with both funding and volunteer efforts. With all of our programs, our strength lies in our employees. In 2001, employees volunteered hundreds of thousands of hours at schools, community projects, and relief efforts around the world. These Intel employee "ambassadors" ensure that Intel can play a positive role in our communities—and truly make Intel a Great Place to Work.

As we all know, 2001 was a difficult year for our industry and for the economy in general. Intel will continue to support our education efforts and our communities for the same reason we continue to spend on our research and development programs—they are long-term investments in our future and the future of our world.

CR Barrett

Craig R. Barrett

Chief Executive Officer

Intel Corporation

Required:

    a. In what types of community projects does ***Intel Corporation*** participate?

    b. What does this tell you about the culture of this company?

    c. Is this the type of company in which you would seek a career? Why?

    d. Suppose there was a company equal to ***Intel Corporation*** in every way except they didn't have any community service. Would you think any less of the company? Would you be less likely to invest in or seek a career in that company?

LO 12: ANNUAL REPORTS (APPENDIX)

1–45. The following is an excerpt from the 2001 Annual Report of ***UPS.***

SERVING THE COMMUNITY

UPS serves more than its customers; we also serve our communities. Because we drive through neighborhoods and knock on the doors of homes and businesses around the world, we see first-hand the problems facing today's society. At UPS, we are committed to providing both our time and money to help strengthen the communities where our employees and customers live and work.

THE UPS FOUNDATION/CORPORATE RELATIONS

Celebrating its 50th anniversary, The UPS Foundation has a long history of enriching lives and strengthening communities through its various initiatives and programs. The Foundation supports major initiatives in the fields of volunteerism, literacy, and hunger relief, but offers its time, money, and expertise to other causes as well.

In 2001 alone, The UPS Foundation contributed $40.3 million to charitable organizations addressing education and urgent human needs through grants, scholarships, employee gift-matching, and support of United Way.

Through its Corporate Relations programs, UPS manages to match its financial resources to its human resources. UPS has long partnered with other national organizations committed to equal justice, equal opportunity, and building stronger communities. The synergy between Corporate Relations and The UPS Foundation extends the reach of UPS's philanthropy and strengthens the impact of its social investments.

UNITED WAY

Since UPS's first United Way campaign in 1982, the company and its employees have contributed more than $500 million to support a broad range of human care services. UPS is the first company in United Way's history to exceed $50 million in annual giving, and in 2001, it was the largest corporate contributor for the second consecutive year.

THE UPS COMMUNITY INTERNSHIP PROGRAM

The UPS Community Internship Program is a unique executive training program designed to attune UPS managers to the increasingly complex needs of a diverse workforce and customer base. Each year, a select group of managers immerse themselves in community service for one month at one of four internship sites, which helps create awareness, promotes understanding, heightens sensitivity, and encourages involvement.

Such community service builds better managers and more well rounded individuals. It also bridges the gap between corporations and communities. Since 1968, UPS has dedicated more than $12 million to its Community Internship Program, with more than 1,100 senior level managers having participated in the training experience.

EMPLOYMENT INITIATIVES

UPS also helps the community through its various employment initiatives, which include:

Earn & Learn Program, which offers education assistance at participating UPS locations to part-time employees who are attending a college, university, or approved trade or technical school.

School to Work Program, which provides high school students aged 17 and older with the opportunity to earn college credit while gaining work experience with UPS. The program is available in several large cities such as Chicago, Dallas, Louisville, Philadelphia, and Washington, DC.

Supplier Diversity Process, which offers minority- and women-owned businesses the opportunity to compete equally with other UPS suppliers. More than 25,000 small, minority- and women-owned businesses across America are partners in the UPS supplier network.

Welfare to Work Partnership, which works with government agencies, faith-based groups, and nonprofit organizations to develop, train, and mentor qualified candidates for positions at UPS and other area businesses.

ENVIRONMENTAL INITIATIVES

At UPS, environmental stewardship has long been recognized both as a responsibility and as a good business practice. Some significant initiatives include:

- UPS's industry-leading research into alternative fuels, designed to reduce emissions and maximize fuel economy.
- UPS's re-engineered express packaging, which eliminates bleach and reduces production waste by up to 50 percent. The Reusable Next Day Air Letter is made of 100 percent recycled fiber, saving more than 12,000 trees per year and more than $1 million in production costs.
- UPS's Electronic Equipment Recycling Program, through which the company recycled almost 3 million pounds of outdated electronic equipment in 2001.

- UPS's Automatic Return Service (ARS), through which the company assists customers in returning their used toner cartridges, automotive parts, computer and medical equipment, etc. These products are disassembled for reuse or disposed of in a responsible manner.
- UPS's delivery notices are made from recycled paper, saving more than 1,500 trees annually. To learn more about UPS's community involvement, visit www.community.ups.com.

Required:

    a. In what types of community projects does *UPS* participate?
    b. What does this tell you about the culture of this company?
    c. Is this the type of company in which you would seek a career? Why?
    d. Which company (UPS or Intel) seems to be more involved in the community? Which seems to involve more of its employees in its program? Would this make you more or less interested in becoming a part of these companies?

LO 12: ANNUAL REPORTS (APPENDIX)

1–46. The following is the opening section of the 2001 letter to shareholders from Kenneth I. Chenault, Chairman and Chief Executive Officer of *American Express Company*:

> 2001 was a year unlike any other in American Express Company's history. The nature and magnitude of the challenges we faced were unprecedented. As we have throughout our history, we are resolving these challenges with resilience and strength. We did not meet our long-term financial objectives. We did, however, make a number of fundamental changes in our businesses that will enable us to emerge from this extraordinary period a far stronger, more focused company.

Required:

    a. Summarize the main points of the CEO's message.
    b. How do you believe that a CEO should give bad news to stockholders? Why?
    c. Do you think the way Chenault gives bad news is effective? Why or why not? Do you think he instills confidence in the future?

ANNUAL REPORT PROJECT

1–47. General Information

The purpose of this project is to introduce you to the financial reporting information published by publicly traded companies. The assignment in this chapter is the first of a continuing 11-part project. Our hope is that you will learn about the various sources and uses of the valuable information available to you via a company's Form 10K, its annual report, the Internet, the financial press, and through stock market reports.

    By the time you have completed the project, you should be in a position to draw conclusions and form an opinion regarding whether the company you selected to analyze is a good investment candidate. You may also form an opinion regarding the employment prospect with the company.

    When it is complete, your annual report project will include the following sections (unless modified by your instructor):

Section 1—Selecting a Company and Obtaining an Annual Report
Section 2—General Information
Section 3—Basic Balance Sheet Information
Section 4—Basic Income Statement and Statement of Stockholders' Equity
Section 5—Strengths, Weaknesses, Opportunities and Threats (SWOT)
Section 6—Finding a Peer Company and Peer Company Comparisons
Section 7—Long-Lived Assets
Section 8—Inventories and Cost of Goods Sold
Section 9—Financial Statements—A Closer Look
Section 10—The Statement of Cash Flows
Section 11—Summary, Conclusions, and Recommendations

Organize your annual report project. Use a pocket folder to hold your company's annual report and other documents, and a binder to accommodate the three-hole punched pages you will generate to fulfill the requirements of each assignment.

Section 1—Selecting a Company and Obtaining an Annual Report

In this section, you will select a company for your project and obtain its Form 10-K and Annual Report.

Required:

a. List several publicly traded companies that interest you. They might interest you as investment candidates or employment prospects, or simply because you are familiar with their products.

b. From your list of companies, select a publicly traded United States company that sells a tangible product. It can be either a manufacturer or a merchandiser, but for purposes of this annual report project, do not select an insurance company, a stock brokerage firm, a bank, a utility company or another type of service company.

c. Once you select a company, download a copy of its Form 10-K through the SEC's EDGAR system. If you are working in a group, each member of the group should secure his or her own copy of the Form 10-K. The Form 10-K will provide you with a wealth of information about the company you have selected.

  Below are the step-by-step instructions to help you find and obtain a copy of your company's Form 10-K by using the SEC's EDGAR system.

  1. Go to the SEC's home page at www.sec.gov.
  2. Click on *Search for Company Filings* (listed under "Filings & Forms (EDGAR)").
  3. Click on *Search Companies and Filings*.
  4. Enter your company's name in the appropriate place and click *Find Companies*.
  5. Find the latest version of your company's Form 10-K. (All publicly traded companies must file a Form 10-K annually so you will want to be sure you select the latest one.) Click on the appropriate place next to the latest Form 10-K. The "text" version loads more quickly and is easier to save and print than the HTML version.

d. Obtain a copy of the company's annual report. In most cases, you can download the annual report from the company's Web site. If you are unable to obtain an annual report for your company this way, you can contact the company and ask that one be sent to you. If you are working in a group, each member of the group should secure his or her own copy of the report.

e. If you are using a downloaded copy of the company's annual report, contact your company to request an actual hardcopy of the company's printed annual report in addition to the copy you downloaded. It may take some time to receive it, so make your request as soon as possible.

CHAPTER 2

Economic Decision Making

Suppose you and some friends decide to go on a spring break vacation. Where will you go? Lots of places come to mind—Cancun, the Bahamas, Daytona Beach—but which destination will you choose? Will you just blindly pick one? Of course not. Before making a final selection, you'll gather information about each vacation spot from various sources. You'll want to know about the destination city itself, airline fares and schedules, car rentals, and hotels. Then, based on that information, you and your friends will compare the various destinations before making a final selection.

This spring break "decision" is quite complex because it is really a series of decisions. What's more, some of the decisions will be group decisions, while others will be made individually. Once all the decisions and reservations are made, the vacation's outcome is still uncertain. This uncertainty adds a dimension of adventure to the whole experience.

Life entails making thousands of decisions, some very complex and others relatively simple. Because we cannot know the future, the outcomes of the decisions we make are uncertain. While in our spring break example we were able to tolerate a bit of uncertainty because it added intrigue, uncertainty in business is something we strive to reduce. By collecting and using as much relevant, reliable information as possible, we can work to reduce the uncertainty that threatens the outcome of the decisions we make.

Regardless of the form of organization or the business activity, success—and sometimes even survival—in the world of business depends on making wise economic decisions. A key ingredient is an understanding of the decision making process itself. We designed this chapter to help you learn a logical decision making process.

Learning Objectives

After completing your work on this chapter, you should be able to do the following:

1. Explain the concepts of extrinsic and intrinsic rewards, sacrifices, and opportunity costs as they pertain to routine and nonroutine decision situations.
2. Use a cognitive problem-solving model to make decisions.
3. Explain how information processing styles affect decision making and be able to identify examples of systematic and intuitive styles.
4. Explain the importance of creativity and the role of values and ethics in the decision making process.
5. Describe the advantages and disadvantages of individual and group decision making.
6. Explain the basic differences between management accounting and financial accounting.
7. List the three questions all economic decision makers attempt to answer and explain why these questions are so important.

8. Describe the importance of cash as a measure of business success or failure.

9. Describe the basic assumptions and constraints underlying accounting information and distinguish accounting information from accounting data.

10. Describe the qualitative characteristics of useful accounting information and apply them in decision making situations.

11. Identify, discuss, and contrast information found in typical annual reports.

◆ WHAT IS DECISION MAKING?

Decision making is the process of identifying alternative courses of action and selecting an appropriate alternative in a given decision situation. This definition presents two important parts:

1. *Identifying alternative courses of action.* This does not mean that an ideal solution exists or can be identified.
2. *Selecting an appropriate alternative.* This implies that there may be a number of appropriate alternatives and that inappropriate alternatives are to be evaluated and rejected. Thus, judgment is fundamental to decision making.

Choice is implicit in our definition of decision making. We may not like the alternatives available to us, but we are seldom left without choices.

REWARDS AND SACRIFICES: THE TRADE-OFF

In general, the aim of all decisions is to obtain some type of reward, either economic or personal. Reward requires sacrifice. When you made the decision to attend college, for example, you certainly desired a reward. What was the sacrifice?

Discussion Questions ●

2–1. What rewards do you hope to obtain by attending college?

2–2. What sacrifices are you personally making to attend college?

Think of some things that you can't do because you are attending college. Some sacrifices cannot be measured in dollars, for example, the loss of leisure time while you do homework for your accounting class. Some, however, can be measured in dollars. Suppose that instead of attending college you could work full time and earn $25,000 a year. In a very real sense, then, attending college costs you that $25,000 in addition to what you pay for tuition and books. We call the $25,000 an **opportunity cost** of making the decision to attend college. An opportunity cost is the reward we give up because we choose a particular alternative instead of another. It is the amount of benefit we *would* have received if we had made a different choice. Most decisions include opportunity costs.

Decision makers strive to maximize the rewards or benefits from a decision and to minimize the sacrifice or cost required (see Exhibit 2–1). Examining the relationship between rewards and sacrifices is known as *cost/benefit analysis.* In a condition of absolute certainty, where we know the outcome of a decision without doubt, determining the cost/benefit is no problem. Unfortunately, absolute certainty rarely, if ever, exists.

In the examples we use to describe the trade-off between rewards and sacrifices, money is usually the reward. Money is an example of what we call an *extrinsic reward,* meaning that it comes from outside ourselves. An *intrinsic reward* is one that comes from inside us. When you accomplish a difficult task, the intrinsic reward comes from the sense of satisfaction you feel. An old adage says, "The best things in life are free." Not necessarily so! Many things worth having require sacrifice.

opportunity cost The benefit or benefits forgone by not selecting a particular alternative. Once an alternative is selected in a decision situation, the benefits of all rejected alternatives become part of the opportunity cost of the alternative selected.

Discussion Questions ●

2–3. What is the one thing you desire most from life? What sacrifices must you make to obtain it?

2–4. What sacrifices do you make when you buy a graphing calculator for your math class?

2–5. What benefit do you derive from purchasing the calculator?

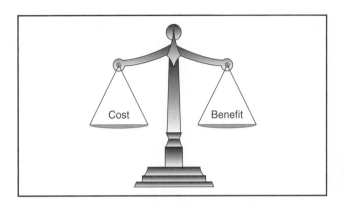

EXHIBIT 2–1   Cost versus Benefit

COPING WITH UNCERTAINTY AND RISK

Uncertainty in any given decision situation increases the chances of making the wrong choice. The higher the degree of uncertainty, the greater the risk. In decision making, we can't eliminate uncertainty completely, so we must learn to cope with it. The relationship between uncertainty and reward is called the **risk/reward trade-off.** Financial decision makers recognize the relationship in the risk/reward trade-off and therefore demand greater rewards when the risk is high. For example, banks such as ***First Union*** and ***Bank of America*** set interest rates based on the credit risk of each borrower. The higher the risk of default on a loan, the higher the interest rate charged by the bank.

So how do you cope with uncertainty, knowing that it can never be entirely eliminated? You gather as much relevant information as you can and use it to gain insight into the decision alternatives. Knowing more about each alternative helps reduce the amount of risk involved and increases your level of comfort in making the decision. This is a valuable strategy no matter what type of decision you are making.

risk/reward trade-off
The relationship between uncertainty and reward. It indicates that the higher the risk, the higher the reward required to induce the risk taking.

Discussion Question ●

2–6. How would you judge the risk of loaning a friend the graphing calculator you bought for your math class?

ROUTINE AND NONROUTINE DECISIONS

We make some decisions so frequently that our choice is automatic or routine. We need to solve such recurring problems only once, and our decision then becomes a rule or standard. Whenever the situation recurs, such as choosing the route to drive from home to work, we implement the rule.

Not all *routine decisions* arise in simple situations. Landing a jet aircraft at a busy airport with 300 people on board may be routine, but it is still complex. Whether a decision is routine depends not on its complexity, but rather on whether the situation recurs.

When a decision we make concerns a new and unfamiliar circumstance, we are making a *nonroutine decision*. Whether intricate or simple, an unfamiliar problem is considered nonroutine by its infrequency—not by its complexity. The decision to attend college certainly is a nonroutine decision. Another example is the vacation scenario we presented in the opening vignette to this chapter.

It is important that we identify the decisions we make as routine or nonroutine, because routine problems have rule-based solutions while nonroutine decisions do not. If we apply routine decision rules to nonroutine situations, we can worsen the situation by applying a solution that doesn't fit the problem.

Discussion Questions ●●●●●●●●●●●●●●●●●●●●●●●●●●●●●●●●●●●●●●

2–7. Think of a decision you consider routine. Can you remember the first time you had to make that particular decision? How did you go about making it?

2–8. Can you think of a nonroutine decision you faced? How did you go about making that decision?

2–9. Describe a situation in which you or someone else applied a decision rule developed for a routine decision to a nonroutine situation and experienced unexpected results.

◆ HOW WE MAKE DECISIONS

We think constantly, yet we rarely stop to analyze our thinking in a methodical, orderly way. It may sound silly, but we really should spend some time thinking about the way we think, because the way we process information relates directly to the quality of our decisions.

INFORMATION PROCESSING STYLES

There has been a great deal of research into how people use their brains to process information. Psychological researchers have identified two general information processing styles—the *intuitive style* and the *systematic style* (see Exhibit 2–2).[1]

Intuitive thinkers prefer to solve problems by looking at the overall situation, exploring many possible solutions, and making a decision based on their hunches or gut reaction. Intuitive thinkers tend to prefer nonroutine situations. They enjoy rapidly changing environments, dealing with broad issues, and general policy options; they are "big-picture" people.

Conversely, systematic thinkers prefer to solve problems by careful analysis, breaking the problem into component parts. They prefer working in an environment that allows them to think methodically; they are "detail" people.

Everyone uses both styles to some degree, but all of us prefer to employ one style over the other. Each style has advantages and disadvantages and each can be effective. For example, some investment analysts use primarily an intuitive style and others tend to use a systematic style. The job of a Wall Street investment analyst at *Lehman*

EXHIBIT 2–2 Information Processing Styles

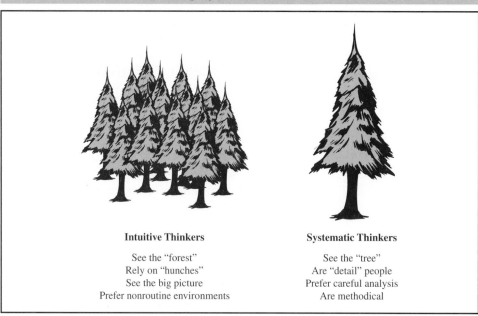

Intuitive Thinkers	Systematic Thinkers
See the "forest"	See the "tree"
Rely on "hunches"	Are "detail" people
See the big picture	Prefer careful analysis
Prefer nonroutine environments	Are methodical

---

[1]Weston H. Agor, "Managing Brain Skills: The Last Frontier," *Personnel Administrator* (October 1987): 55–56.

Brothers or **Merrill Lynch** is to pick stocks that will earn dividends and go up in price rather than down. Some analysts systematically study an extensive amount of information about a company, carefully sifting the numbers through a computer and analyzing statistics before making a decision. Other analysts do a little analysis but mainly rely on their intuition. Some of the most successful investors on Wall Street claim to "feel" what is going to happen to the price of a particular stock. Although it is difficult if not impossible to learn to be more intuitive, one can learn to be a more systematic thinker.

Discussion Questions

2–10. To which careers do you think intuitive people are most attracted?

2–11. To which careers do you think systematic people are most attracted?

2–12. Which of the two information-processing styles do you believe you use more often?

2–13. What problems and benefits could arise when you work with someone using an information-processing style that differs from your own?

REASONED DECISION MAKING

Reasoned decision making, also called *cognitive* or *rational* decision making, involves considering various aspects of a situation before deciding on a course of action. This approach to decision making can be used with both intuitive and systematic information processing. Systematic thinkers will feel comfortable with this approach, and intuitive thinkers will become more disciplined thinkers, which may improve their intuitive skills. Reasoned decision making can be described as a seven-step process (see Exhibit 2–3).

EXHIBIT 2–3 The Seven-Step Decision Model

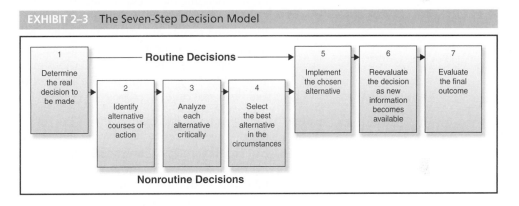

Step 1: *Determine the real decision to be made.*

The key to successful reasoned decision making is identifying the real problem. This is frequently the most difficult task in the decision process. Too often, we concentrate on a symptom of the problem and not on the problem itself. This step is so important that firms sometimes hire consultants to identify the real problems and to determine the decisions to be made.

Step 2: *Identify alternative courses of action.*

Before identifying alternative courses of action, we should first determine whether the decision we are making is routine or nonroutine. If the decision is routine, we simply apply the appropriate decision rule and skip steps 2, 3, and 4 of this decision model. For nonroutine decisions, we must work to identify alternatives. Some alternatives will emerge quickly, but these often treat symptoms, not problems. We may be comfortable choosing an obvious course of action, but the obvious course may not be the best.

In order to make sound nonroutine decisions, you must think creatively to uncover as many decision alternatives as possible. Eliminate only impossible potential solutions and consider everything else, however improbable. Sherlock Holmes, the great master sleuth, offered this explanation as to why Dr. Watson had been unable to unravel a particular mystery:

Once again, Watson, you have confused the impossible with the improbable.
—SIR ARTHUR CONAN DOYLE

Fictional characters like Sherlock Holmes can always make correct decisions, but real-life decision making is more difficult. Because it is an important topic, following this presentation of the seven-step decision making process, we will discuss creative decision making in greater detail.

Step 3: *Analyze each alternative critically.*
Critical analysis of each decision alternative requires us to trace the alternatives into the future and consider the possible outcomes of each. In most cases, a completely accurate assessment is impossible because there are too many variables. We often must select a few critical factors, such as cost, completion time, and risk, and evaluate the strengths and weaknesses of each alternative relative to those factors.

Step 4: *Select the best alternative in the circumstances.*
Russell Ackoff, a noted scholar in the field of problem solving, identified three types of alternatives that occur in any decision situation:

Those that will resolve the problem,
Those that will solve the problem, and
Those that will dissolve the problem.[2]

Resolving a problem means finding an acceptable alternative. *Solving* a problem means finding the absolute best solution. *Dissolving* a problem means changing the circumstances that caused the problem, thereby not only eliminating the problem but also ensuring that it will not happen again. Ideally, the results of a decision making process will produce an alternative that dissolves the problem, but realistically, this occurs only occasionally. In fact, Ackoff suggests that most decisions merely resolve problems by finding acceptable, stopgap solutions. For this reason, one decision may create the need to make other decisions.

Step 5: *Implement the chosen alternative.*
On the surface, this appears to be the easiest of all the steps in this process. Not so! Regardless of how methodical and analytical our approach to making the decision, we know we have not considered everything, and we hesitate. This hesitation is called *cognitive dissonance*,[3] or "second thoughts." When cognitive dissonance sets in, all the alternatives you have rejected begin to look better and better. There is no easy remedy for this hesitation except to understand that second thoughts are a part of life and that there comes a point when we must find the courage to implement the chosen alternative.

Step 6: *Reevaluate the decision as new information becomes available.*
After overcoming second thoughts, decision makers become very committed to their decision. In fact, most of us will go out of our way to avoid new information after implementing a decision. Why? Because it puts us back in the position of questioning the soundness of our decision, which can make us extremely uncomfortable. It may sound odd, but to become good at making tough decisions, you must become comfortable with being uncomfortable. You should not be afraid to revisit a decision in light of new and better information, even after you implement the decision.

---

[2]Russell L. Ackoff, "The Art and Science of Mess Management," *Interfaces* 11, No. 1 (February 1981): 20–21.
[3]Leon Festinger, *A Theory of Cognitive Dissonance* (Stanford, CA: Stanford University Press, 1975).

Step 7: *Evaluate the final outcome.*

It may be a long time before we can determine whether our decision was a good one, and factors outside our control may influence the outcome. Nevertheless, evaluation is an important step in the process if we are to continue refining our decision making skills.

This basic decision model, in one form or another, is found in numerous textbooks for various courses. The one we presented here is not the only correct way to make decisions; however, it does offer you a reasoned, cognitive approach to decision making.

Discussion Questions

2–14. If you had used the seven-step decision model when you were selecting your university, would you have made the same choice? Explain.

2–15. Think again about your decision to attend your particular college. At what point will you be able to apply step 7 to your decision making process?

CREATIVE DECISION MAKING

The second step of the decision making model stresses the importance of being creative in identifying possible courses of action. Going beyond the obvious alternatives reduces your chances of overlooking the best possible solution.

Anyone can become a more creative decision maker. Sidney J. Parnes, a professor of creative studies at Buffalo State University, states that creativity increases when the problem solver progresses from "what is" (awareness of the facts surrounding the present situation), to "what might be" (free-thinking consideration of many possible alternatives), to "what can be" (elimination of impossible and unacceptable alternatives), to "what will be" (choice of the best alternative in the circumstances), and finally to an action that creates a new "what is."[4] For example, sales representatives used to go door-to-door selling sets of *World Book Encyclopedias*. Today, you can simply log on to *www.worldbookonline.com* and subscribe to **World Book**'s encyclopedia service!

Discussion Questions

2–16. Think of a daily irritation that you currently endure. Use Professor Parnes's creative process to create at least three feasible alternatives under "what might be."

2–17. If you could change one other "what is" into a new "what is," what would it be? How would you do it?

◆ PERSONAL VALUES AND DECISION MAKING

The most important influence on the decisions we make is the set of personal values we hold. *Personal values* are just that—personal. Yours are different, even if only slightly, from those of every other person. What is important in relation to personal values and decision making is that each of us examines critically what is truly important to us.

ETHICS AND PERSONAL VALUES

There are two very different approaches to ethics (see Exhibit 2–4). The first approach is *virtues ethics*, or *character ethics*. This approach to ethics, called classical ethics because it is derived from the teachings of Socrates, Plato, and Aristotle, comes from within a person. It requires you to contemplate what kind of person you want to be. Once you have identified the virtues and character traits required to be that kind of person, they determine your reaction to any situation. Virtues ethics presumes that the virtues and character traits the individual identifies as desirable will include respect for others.

---

[4]Sidney J. Parnes, "Learning Creative Behavior," *The Futurist* (August 1984): 30.

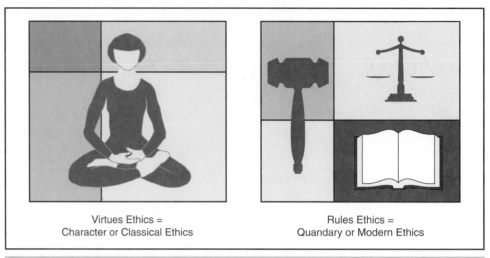

Virtues Ethics =
Character or Classical Ethics

Rules Ethics =
Quandary or Modern Ethics

EXHIBIT 2–4   Two Approaches to Ethics

The second approach is *rules ethics*, or *quandary ethics*. This approach, also called modern ethics, traces its roots to organized religion and law. It imposes rules that dictate how to react to given problems. Successful application of rules ethics depends on the individual's ability to apply the appropriate rule in a given situation and on society's acceptance of the rules and those who establish them. An inability to apply the appropriate rule or a loss of respect for the rules or rule makers leads to moral confusion and uncertainty.

Most businesspeople have discovered that "good ethics is good business." Historically, ethical companies that hire ethical management eventually rise above less ethical firms. Businesspeople constantly face ethical dilemmas. For example, should a U.S. shoe manufacturer open a plant in Southeast Asia, where workers are paid only 50 cents an hour? We might argue that the company is exploiting those workers. On the other hand, 50 cents an hour might be double the going wage in that country, providing employment for those who otherwise have no jobs. It's a tough decision, without any clear-cut "right" answer.

Discussion Questions

2–18. Do you agree with the statement, "Good ethics is good business?" Explain your position.

2–19. Do U.S. companies exploit workers in other countries when they pay them less than the U.S. minimum wage?

2–20. Should U.S. companies follow U.S. labor laws for their foreign operations or the less stringent local labor laws?

2–21. Do you believe it is ethical to buy products manufactured by a U.S. company in a foreign country with less restrictive labor laws than the United States?

2–22. What is your responsibility as a consumer to determine whether products are made under fair labor practices?

◆ INDIVIDUAL VERSUS GROUP DECISION MAKING

Thus far, we have discussed the challenges in decision making caused by uncertainty and different information-processing styles. We've also looked at routine versus non-routine decision situations, the need for creativity in decision making, and the influence of personal values on the decision making process. We now consider *individual decision making* versus *group decision making*. If the old saying that two heads are better than one is true, does involving more people in the decision process improve the chances of making the right decision? Not always.

Individual decision making has some distinct advantages over group decision making. First, you do not spend a lot of time organizing meetings. Second, you do not have to consider others' comments and suggestions that you know for a fact are no good. Finally, compromise is unnecessary because you are a committee of one. However, your decision will be only as good as your individual judgment and grasp of the circumstances. This becomes the most significant drawback to making decisions on your own. This limitation is the reason that when we make important, nonroutine decisions by ourselves, most of us need to bounce the decision off someone else. We know, or at least fear, that we may have failed to consider all of the important factors.

Groups bring a greater knowledge base to the decision making process simply because more people are involved. Viewing the problem from various perspectives usually generates more alternative solutions. Groups take the pressure of responsibility for decisions off individuals. Also, groups tend to be confident that the decision alternative chosen to solve the problem is a reasonable solution.

On the surface, it would seem that group decision making is superior to individual decision making; however, some serious problems are associated with working in groups. Some of these have to do with the actual functioning of groups, and others with the quality of decisions made by groups.

At one time or another, each of us is called on to work as part of a group. Knowing about and being able to recognize the classic problems associated with working in groups will not only reduce your level of frustration, but it will also make your work in groups more effective and rewarding.

PROBLEMS WITH GROUP DECISIONS

- *Information-processing styles*. If all members of the group are intuitive types, the group may have many grandiose ideas but wind up short on specifics. If all members are systematic types, the group may never get past deciding on a seating arrangement at the first meeting. Ideally, the group should be a mix of the two types, but working together will be a challenge. The group must be able to utilize the best aspects of each style, or the group can become paralyzed.
- *Domineering members*. In any group situation, there will be members that are more domineering than others. This is a natural occurrence. The quality of group decision making usually suffers when some members of the group cave in to other members simply because those other members talk louder and longer. Now that you know this, don't allow yourself to steamroll over other group members and don't let others roll over you. Keep in mind that just because a person has an ability to be persuasive does not mean they know more and are more capable than the other members of the group.
- *Social pressure*. The pressure to conform to the views of other members of the group, coupled with the natural desire to not look foolish, can stifle an individual's creative contributions. Group members should work to keep this from happening.
- *Goal replacement*. The goal of the group should always be to accomplish the purpose for which it was formed. Secondary considerations, such as winning an argument, proving a point, or taking revenge on a fellow group member, sometimes become more important to some members of the group.
- *Differing personal values*. Each member of the group will bring a different set of personal values to the process. From time to time, those values may conflict, making resolution difficult or impossible.
- *Unequal effort*. This phenomenon occurs in virtually all groups. And, with the vast differences in personalities, drive, abilities, and interests of group members, it is completely understandable that the problem of unequal effort occurs so often. Groups are certainly more effective when all members do their share of the work. It is best to somehow even the workload because, in addition to negatively affecting the morale of the other group members, underperformers also tend to reduce the overall effectiveness of the group.
- *Groupthink*. Many people consider groupthink to be the most dangerous threat to good group decision making. Group members may ignore their own sound judg-

ments in evaluating alternatives to allow the group to achieve consensus. A group member may not feel good about the decision being made but *thinks* everyone else in the group does, and so he or she goes along with the decision. Disaster occurs when several group members go along with an apparent consensus only to find later that few, if any, in the group actually agreed with the decision. Have you ever heard one friend say to another, "What do you mean you didn't even want to come here? I only agreed to come here because I thought you wanted to come here." In such a case, both parties *agree* to something, each erroneously thinking she or he is going along with the wishes of the other person.

Discussion Questions •••••••••••••••••••••••••••••••••••

2–23. Which of the group decision making problems have you encountered at work or in school? Was the problem resolved? If so, how?

2–24. If you were an instructor in a course that required students to work in groups, what policies would you institute to avoid the classic problems associated with group work?

◆ ECONOMIC DECISION MAKING

The term *economic decision making*, as used in this book, refers to the process of making business decisions involving money. All economic decisions of any consequence require the use of some sort of accounting information, often in the form of financial reports. Anyone using accounting information to make economic decisions must understand the business and economic environment in which accounting information is generated, and they must also be willing to devote the necessary time and energy to make sense of the accounting reports.

Economic decision makers are either internal or external. **Internal decision makers** are individuals within a company who make decisions on behalf of the company, while **external decision makers** are individuals or organizations outside a company who make decisions that affect the company. For example, people that work for *General Mills,* such as company managers, supervisors, and other employees, are internal decision makers. Those that do not work for *General Mills,* such as bankers, investors and potential investors, and customers, are external decision makers even if they have a close relationship with the company.

INTERNAL DECISION MAKERS

Internal decision makers decide such things as whether the company should sell a particular product, whether it should enter a new market, or whether it should hire or fire employees. Note that in all these matters, the internal decision maker makes the decision not for himself or herself, but rather *for* the company.

Depending on their position within the company, internal decision makers may have access to much, or even all, of the company's financial information. Even so, they do not have complete information, because all decisions relate to the future and the future always involves unknowns.

EXTERNAL DECISION MAKERS

External decision makers make decisions *about* a company. External decision makers decide such things as whether to invest in the company, whether to sell to or buy from the company, and whether to lend money to the company.

Unlike internal decision makers, external decision makers have limited financial information on which to base their decisions about the company. In fact, they have only the information the company gives them—which is never all the information the company possesses. Exhibit 2–5 lists examples of external and internal decision makers.

internal decision makers
Economic decision makers within a company who make decisions for the company. They have access to much or all of the accounting information generated within the company.

external decision makers
Economic decision makers outside a company who make decisions about the company. The accounting information they use to make those decisions is limited to what the company provides them.

External Decision Makers	Internal Decision Makers
Make decisions *about* the company	Make decisions *for* the company
Use **Financial Accounting**	Use **Managerial Accounting**
Available information is limited to what the company supplies to external users	Available information is limited only by time and the user's position within the company
• Stockholders (Present and Potential) • Bankers and Other Lending Institutions • Bondholders (Present and Potential) • Suppliers • Customers	• Marketing Managers • Salespersons • Production Managers • Strategic Planners • Company President • Engineers • Financial Officers

EXHIBIT 2–5   Economic Decision Makers

Discussion Questions

2–25. Why would a company withhold certain financial information from external parties?

2–26. Do you think it is entirely ethical for company managers to limit the information available to their own internal decision makers?

2–27. Is it ethical for a company to limit the information it provides to external decision makers?

The decisions made by internal and external decision makers are similar in some ways but very different in others—so different, in fact, that over time, two separate branches of accounting evolved to meet the needs of the two categories of users. **Management accounting** generates information for use by internal decision makers, whereas **financial accounting** generates information for use by external parties. Exhibit 2–6 contrasts financial accounting and management accounting.

management accounting
The branch of accounting developed to meet the informational needs of internal decision makers.

financial accounting
The branch of accounting developed to meet the informational needs of external decision makers.

EXHIBIT 2–6   Contrast of Financial and Management Accounting

Feature	Financial Accounting	Management Accounting
Principal users	External parties for decisions *about* firm	Internal parties for decisions *for* firm
Rules and regulations	Governed by GAAP	Company policy. Need not conform to GAAP
Level of detail	Little detail. Deals with the company as a whole	Quite detailed. Deals with various parts of the company
Timeliness	Quarterly and annually	As needed by users
Future/past orientation	Depicts the present condition and past results. Does not generally include future projections	Includes future projections in addition to present condition and past results

WHAT ALL ECONOMIC DECISION MAKERS WANT TO KNOW

Virtually all economic decision makers, whether internal or external, are trying to make decisions in light of what might happen in the future. Specifically, economic decision makers attempt to predict future cash flow—the movement of cash in and out of a company. These decision makers need information that can help them predict what future cash flows will be. Accordingly, one of the major objectives of financial reporting is to provide helpful information to those trying to predict cash flows.

Thus, financial reporting should provide information to help investors, creditors, and others assess the amounts, timing, and uncertainty of prospective net cash inflows to the related enterprise.[5]

net cash flow
The difference between cash inflows and cash outflows; it can be either positive or negative.

The mathematical difference between cash inflows and cash outflows is: **net cash flow.** Positive net cash flow occurs when the amount of cash flowing into the company exceeds the amount flowing out of the company during a particular period. For example, a company that collects $1 million during a period when it pays out $950,000 has a positive cash flow of $50,000. Negative net cash flow occurs when the amount of cash flowing out of the company exceeds the amount flowing into the company during a particular period (see Exhibit 2–7).

EXHIBIT 2–7   Cash Flow

	Positive	*Negative*
Cash Inflow	1,000,000	500,000
Cash Outflow	950,000	575,000
Net Cash Flow	50,000	(75,000)

All economic decisions involve attempts to predict the future of cash flows by searching for the answers to the following three questions:

1. Will I be paid?
This question refers to the *uncertainty* of cash flows.
2. When will I be paid?
This question refers to the *timing* of cash flows.
3. How much will I be paid?
This question refers to the *amounts* of cash flows.

The answer to each question contains two parts: return *on* investment and return *of* investment. *Return on investment* consists of the earnings and profits an investment returns to the investor. *Return of investment* is the ultimate return of the principal invested. Exhibit 2–8 shows the conceptual link between the three major questions posed by economic decision makers and the resulting cash flows using the following example. Assume you wish to invest in a $1,000 certificate of deposit (CD) at your bank, which will earn 10 percent interest per year, payable every three months, over the course of two years. If you invest in this CD, you must hold it for two years, after which the bank will return your $1,000.

---

[5]Statement of Financial Accounting Concepts No. 1, paragraph 39.

	Concepts	Return on Investment	Return of Investment
1. Will I be paid?	Uncertainty	Interest	CD Maturity
2. When will I be paid?	Timing	Every quarter	At the end of two years
3. How much will I be paid?	Amount	$25 per quarter; Total of $200	$1,000

EXHIBIT 2–8   Three Big Questions for Economic Decision Makers

Before you make this economic decision, you must attempt to answer the three questions:

1. *Will you be paid?* Because it is impossible to know the future, making an economic decision always involves risk. However, assuming the economy does not collapse and the bank stays in business, you will be paid both your return on investment and your return of investment.
2. *When will you be paid?* You will receive an interest payment every three months for two years (return on investment), and then at the end of two years, you will receive your initial $1,000 investment back (return of investment).
3. *How much will you be paid?* The return on your investment is the interest you receive quarterly $25 ($1,000 × 10 percent × 3/12), and the return of your investment is the $1,000 the bank gives you back. The total received in interest in two years is $200 (8 × $25).

Interest: Return on Investment	$ 200
Principal: Return of Investment	1,000
Total Return	1,200
Less: Initial Investment	1,000
Profit on Investment	$ 200

We can answer these questions easily for a government-insured certificate of deposit. In the vast majority of economic decision situations, however, the answers to the three questions are much less certain. We will show you how to use accounting information to answer them in various economic decision situations throughout this text.

Discussion Questions

2–28. Describe how you would apply the seven-step decision model in deciding whether to invest in a certificate of deposit.
2–29. Assume that you have $10,000 you will lend to only one of three loan applicants. What information would you require of each applicant to help you answer the three questions?

CASH IS THE "BALL" OF BUSINESS

In games such as baseball, football, or soccer, players must keep their eye on the ball if they want to win. Well, in the game of business, cash is the ball. Because the business game is so complex, businesspeople can easily become distracted and lose sight of the ball—cash. Various measures of performance such as gross profit, net income, net worth, and equity help those in business to make economic decisions. These are important measures of financial performance, *but they are not cash!* Never allow yourself to become so focused on any of them that you lose sight of cash, because when a company runs out of cash, it dies. Remember that the three questions we talked about in the previous section—Will I be paid? When will I be paid? How much will I be paid?—are all centered on cash. The secret to becoming a street-smart user of accounting information is learning to balance the complexity of business with the simple rule of keeping your eye on cash flow.

◆ ACCOUNTING INFORMATION

accounting   A service activity that has the function of providing quantitative information, primarily financial in nature, about economic entities that is intended to be useful in making economic decisions.

accounting information   Raw data concerning transactions that have been transformed into financial numbers that can be used by economic decision makers.

data   The raw results of transactions. Facts and figures that are not organized enough to be useful to decision makers.

information   Facts and figures that are sorted, arranged, and summarized and otherwise put into a form that is useful to decision makers.

economic entity   The assumption that economic activities can be identified with a particular enterprise.

going concern   The assumption that unless there is persuasive evidence otherwise, a particular business enterprise will stay in business indefinitely.

monetary unit   The assumption that all economic transactions and events can be measured by some monetary unit. In the United States, for example, the dollar is used.

periodicity   The assumption that the economic activities of an entity can be traced to some specific time period and results of those activities can be reported for any arbitrary time period chosen.

The dictionary defines **accounting** as a reckoning of financial matters, and *information* as knowledge or news. Putting the two together, we see that **accounting information** is knowledge or news about a reckoning of financial matters. The accounting profession's definition of accounting is as follows:

> Accounting is a service activity. Its function is to provide quantitative information, primarily financial in nature, about economic entities that is intended to be useful in making economic decisions.[6]

A company or a person generates accounting data with every business transaction. You generate a number of transactions each month when you pay your rent, buy groceries, make car payments, lend money to a friend, and so on. In business, the volume of accounting data can be staggering.

DATA VERSUS INFORMATION

Accounting data and *accounting information* are not interchangeable terms. **Data** are the raw results of transactions: Data become **information** only when they are put into some useful form. Clearly, the correct data items must be gathered and converted into useful information before they are of any help to economic decision makers. Suppose you are the credit manager for a major electronics supplier and you are trying to decide whether to extend credit to a particular customer. You have learned that the customer's sales are $15 million annually and that it just paid various suppliers $800,000 for goods and services. Do you extend the credit? Although you know two bits of data, they provide insufficient information on which to base a credit decision. You need to know more facts and figures than the two already presented, and they must be organized so that they are useful.

USEFUL ACCOUNTING INFORMATION

In Chapter 1, we introduced you to the Financial Accounting Standards Board's (FASB's) *Conceptual Framework of Accounting*. Recall that we described the framework as an arch, which we have reproduced as Exhibit 2–9.

The top of the arch outlines the objective of financial reporting, which we discussed in Chapter 1. In this chapter, we will discuss the qualitative characteristics accounting information must possess to be useful to economic decision makers (the left pillar of the arch). Before we do that, however, we need to talk about the base of the arch. As we stated in Chapter 1, these assumptions, constraints, and accounting principles make up the environment in which accounting information is produced. Our treatment here will focus on the assumptions and constraints. We will wait to cover the accounting principles in later chapters when we discuss the accounting elements to which they relate.

Assumptions Underlying Accounting Information

1. **Economic entity**—All economic activities can be identified with a particular enterprise. This means that the accounting information produced for a particular company is associated with that company and no other company or individual.
2. **Going concern**—Unless there is persuasive evidence otherwise, a particular business enterprise will stay in business indefinitely. This means that unless there is persuasive evidence to the contrary, a company will be around to continue its business and to fulfill its obligations and commitments in the future.
3. **Monetary unit**—All economic transactions and events can be measured by some monetary unit. This means that companies in the United States use the dollar, in Europe they use the euro, in Japan they use the yen, and so on.
4. **Periodicity**—An entity's economic activities can be reasonably divided into specific time periods. This means that when a company produces accounting reports for a specific time period (month, quarter, year, etc.), those reports contain information related to that specific time period.

---

[6]Statement of the Accounting Principles Board #4, 1970, p. 6.

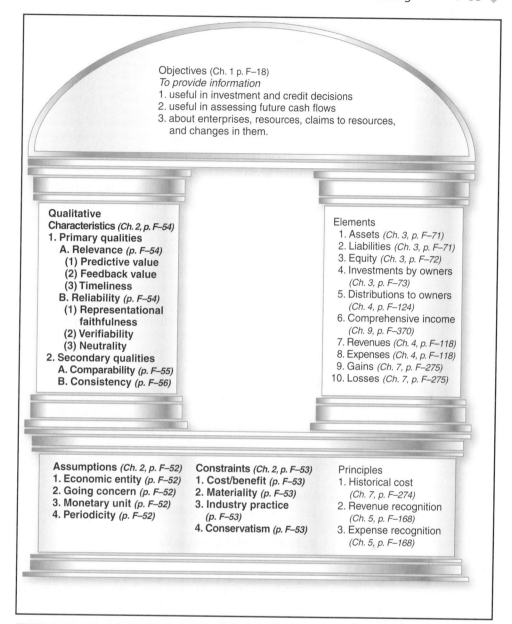

Objectives (Ch. 1 p. F–18)
To provide information
1. useful in investment and credit decisions
2. useful in assessing future cash flows
3. about enterprises, resources, claims to resources, and changes in them.

Qualitative Characteristics *(Ch. 2, p. F–54)*
1. Primary qualities
   A. Relevance *(p. F–54)*
      (1) Predictive value
      (2) Feedback value
      (3) Timeliness
   B. Reliability *(p. F–54)*
      (1) Representational faithfulness
      (2) Verifiability
      (3) Neutrality
2. Secondary qualities
   A. Comparability *(p. F–55)*
   B. Consistency *(p. F–56)*

Elements
1. Assets *(Ch. 3, p. F–71)*
2. Liabilities *(Ch. 3, p. F–71)*
3. Equity *(Ch. 3, p. F–72)*
4. Investments by owners *(Ch. 3, p. F–73)*
5. Distributions to owners *(Ch. 4, p. F–124)*
6. Comprehensive income *(Ch. 9, p. F–370)*
7. Revenues *(Ch. 4, p. F–118)*
8. Expenses *(Ch. 4, p. F–118)*
9. Gains *(Ch. 7, p. F–275)*
10. Losses *(Ch. 7, p. F–275)*

Assumptions *(Ch. 2, p. F–52)*
1. Economic entity *(p. F–52)*
2. Going concern *(p. F–52)*
3. Monetary unit *(p. F–52)*
4. Periodicity *(p. F–52)*

Constraints *(Ch. 2, p. F–53)*
1. Cost/benefit *(p. F–53)*
2. Materiality *(p. F–53)*
3. Industry practice *(p. F–53)*
4. Conservatism *(p. F–53)*

Principles
1. Historical cost *(Ch. 7, p. F–274)*
2. Revenue recognition *(Ch. 5, p. F–168)*
3. Expense recognition *(Ch. 5, p. F–168)*

EXHIBIT 2–9   The Conceptual Framework

cost/benefit   Deals with the trade-off between the rewards of selecting a given alternative and the sacrifices required to obtain those rewards.

materiality   Something that will influence the judgment of a reasonable person.

industry practice   The notion that the peculiar nature of some industries actually causes adherence to GAAP to have misleading results, and therefore, these industries have developed accounting treatments for certain items that depart from GAAP.

conservatism   Provides a guideline in difficult valuation or measurement situations. Accountants should guard against accounting treatments that unjustly overstate financial position or earnings.

Constraints to Consider in Generating Accounting Information

1. **Cost/benefit**—The trade-off between the benefit received and the cost to obtain that benefit. For example, a certain level of detail in accounting information costs a certain amount. The benefit received from that level of detail should outweigh the cost. If that level of detail makes little or no difference, then the detail may not be worth its cost. We referred to this constraint earlier in this chapter when we discussed decision making.

2. **Materiality**—Relates to whether particular information is significant enough to influence the judgment of a reasonably prudent person. If it is, it is material. If not, it is immaterial.

3. **Industry practice**—The peculiar nature of some industries actually causes adherence to generally accepted accounting principles (GAAP) to have misleading results. Therefore, these industries have developed accounting treatments for certain items that depart from GAAP. Because all companies in the industry account for these items the same way, however, their accounting treatment is permissible.

4. **Conservatism**—Provides a guideline in difficult valuation or measurement situations. Accountants should guard against accounting treatments that unjustly overstate financial position or earnings.

Now that we have considered the assumptions and constraints under which accounting information is produced, we can proceed to our discussion of the qualitative characteristics of useful accounting information. As we did in Chapter 1, we will give the actual FASB wording in italics followed by a brief explanation of certain terms.

◆ QUALITATIVE CHARACTERISTICS OF USEFUL ACCOUNTING INFORMATION

In the *Conceptual Framework*'s discussion of the characteristics of useful accounting information, the FASB made it plain that the interrelationship among the various characteristics makes consideration of them individually extremely difficult. As a consequence, the FASB treatment of the characteristics is quite complex, and in fact covers 66 pages. As the arch in Exhibit 2–8 shows, however, the characteristics can be boiled down to two major categories: primary and secondary.

PRIMARY CHARACTERISTICS

The qualities that distinguish "better" (more useful) information from "inferior" (less useful) information are primarily the qualities of relevance and reliability, with some other characteristics that those qualities imply (Statement of Financial Accounting Concepts No. 2, paragraph 15). The *other characteristics* to which the FASB refers are timeliness, predictive or feedback value, verifiability, representational faithfulness, and neutrality. If accounting information lacks relevance or reliability (with the other related qualities), it is not useful.

Relevance

To be relevant to investors, creditors, and others for investment, credit, and similar decisions, accounting information must be capable of making a difference in a decision by helping users to form predictions about the outcomes of past, present, and future events or to confirm or correct expectations (Statement of Financial Accounting Concepts No. 2, paragraph 47). To be considered **relevant,** then, accounting information must have a bearing on the particular decision situation. That is, it must make a difference to decision makers. The accuracy of the information does not matter if its content does not pertain to the decision being made. To be relevant, accounting information possesses at least two characteristics:

relevance Pertinent to the decision at hand. The capability of making a difference in a decision by helping users to form predictions or to adjust their expectations.

predictive value A primary characteristic of relevance. To be useful, accounting must provide information to decision makers that can be used to predict the future and timing of cash flows.

feedback value A primary characteristic of relevance. To be useful, accounting must provide decision makers with information that allows them to assess the progress of an investment.

timeliness A primary characteristic of relevance. To be useful, accounting information must be provided in time to influence a particular decision.

1. **Predictive value and/or feedback value.** Before economic decision makers commit resources to one alternative instead of another, they must be satisfied that a reasonable expectation of a return *on* investment and a return *of* investment exists. Accounting information that helps reduce the uncertainty of that expectation has predictive value. This is not to say that financial accounting information itself is a prediction. Rather, by meaningfully reflecting past and present events, accounting helps the information user to predict future outcomes. Just as information about someone's past driving record is useful in helping to predict future driving tendencies, information about a company's present condition and past financial performance can be an excellent indicator of the company's financial future.

    After making an investment decision, the decision maker must have information to assess the progress of that investment. Recall the seven-step decision model. Step 6 is a reevaluation of the decision as new information becomes available, and step 7 is an evaluation of the final outcome of the decision. If accounting information provides input for those evaluations, it has feedback value.

2. **Timeliness.** Predictive value and/or feedback value alone do not make information relevant. If information providers delay making information available until every number is perfectly accurate, it may be too late to be of any value. That is, it becomes irrelevant. This does not mean that accuracy does not matter. But if accounting information is not timely, it has no value.

Reliability

That information should be reliable as well as relevant is a notion that is central to accounting. It is, therefore, important to be clear about the nature of the claim that is being made for an accounting number that is described as reliable.

The reliability of a measure rests on the faithfulness with which it represents what it purports to represent, coupled with an assurance for the user, which comes through verification, that it has that representational quality (Statement of Financial Accounting Concepts No. 2, paragraphs 58 and 59). This statement says, then, that to be **reliable,** accounting information must possess the qualities of representational faithfulness and verifiability. Not mentioned in the quotation, but implicit, is the characteristic of neutrality.

reliability   A characteristic of information whereby decision makers can depend on information actually depicting the reality of a given situation.

representational faithfulness   A primary characteristic of reliability. To be useful, accounting information must reasonably report what actually happened.

verifiability   A primary characteristic of reliability. Information is considered verifiable if several individuals, working independently, would arrive at similar conclusions using the same data.

neutrality   A primary characteristic of reliability. To be useful, accounting information must be free of bias.

1. **Representational faithfulness.** There must be agreement between what the accounting information says and what really happened. If a company's accounting information reports sales revenue of $1,000 and the company really had sales revenue of $1,000, the accounting information is representationally faithful. However, if a company's accounting information reports sales revenue of $1,000 and the company really had sales revenue of only $800, then the accounting information lacks representational faithfulness.
2. **Verifiability.** We consider accounting information verifiable if several qualified persons, working independently of one another, would arrive at similar conclusions using the same data. For example, if we asked two people to independently determine the amount of an employee's wages last year, they should come to the same conclusion; using the canceled paychecks and other payroll documents for that employee, each should arrive at the same annual wage. If however, payroll documents were unavailable or incomplete, the employee's wages may not be verifiable.
3. **Neutrality.** To be useful, accounting information must be free of bias, which means accountants should not omit details simply because the information is unpleasant. We have stressed how difficult it is to make good decisions. Good decision making is even more difficult when information is suppressed or slanted, either positively or negatively. Accounting information should not unduly glorify or downplay the transactions and events it depicts. The need to remain neutral is one of the most difficult challenges facing the accounting profession.

Discussion Questions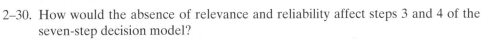

2–30. How would the absence of relevance and reliability affect steps 3 and 4 of the seven-step decision model?

2–31. Do you think these qualities should apply to nonaccounting information? Explain.

Besides the primary qualities of relevance and reliability, the *Conceptual Framework* also discussed two secondary qualities of useful accounting information: comparability and consistency.

SECONDARY CHARACTERISTICS

Information about an enterprise gains greatly in usefulness if it can be compared with similar information about other enterprises and with similar information about the same enterprise for some other period or some other point in time (Statement of Financial Accounting Concepts No. 2, paragraph 111).

Comparability

Economic decision makers evaluate alternatives. Accounting information for one alternative must therefore be *comparable* to accounting information for the others. For example, assume you intend to make an investment in one of two companies. If each company used completely different accounting methods, you would find it very difficult to make a useful comparison.

comparability   A quality needed to meaningfully assess the relative performance on *two different entities*. The requirement that every company provide accounting information in conformity with a fairly uniform structure enables decision makers to compare one company to another.

To achieve **comparability,** accounting rules require that every company provide accounting information that conforms to a fairly uniform structure. This is useful when an accounting information user is comparing one company to another. Under GAAP, every company uses the same basic classification and valuation structure and issues the same basic set of financial reports. That said, companies may choose from alternative accounting techniques and formats so the information from one company will not be exactly the same as that of the next, but it will be close enough to be comparable.

consistency A quality that is needed to meaningfully assess the performance of a *single entity* over time. Consistent application of accounting rules enables us to track a single company's performance over time.

Consistency

To achieve **consistency,** accounting rules require that once a company chooses an accounting technique, it should continue to use the technique. This is helpful when an accounting information user is trying to track the financial progress of a particular entity over time. We said in the preceding paragraph that companies may choose from alternative accounting techniques and formats, but once they decide, they should continue to use the chosen accounting treatment. Otherwise, information users who are trying to plot the financial progress of a company may be confused or distracted by changes in accounting information that are due solely to a change in the accounting methods the company uses rather than due to a change in the company's situation.

Accounting students often confuse comparability and consistency. Comparability is a quality needed to meaningfully assess the relative performance on *two different entities.* Comparability enables us to compare one company to another. On the other hand, consistency is a quality that is needed to meaningfully assess the performance of a *single entity.* Consistent application of accounting rules enables us to track a single company's performance over time.

Discussion Question ●

2–32. How would the absence of comparability and consistency affect steps 4 and 6 of the seven-step decision model?

◆ DECISION MAKERS AND UNDERSTANDABILITY

Now that you understand the qualities required to make accounting information useful, you can appreciate the fact that, as a decision maker and user of accounting information, you must evaluate financial information to assess its usefulness. You must also recognize that the information presented in the financial statements you receive from accountants constitutes only a part of the information you need to make sound economic decisions. It is an important part, to be sure, but only a part. As various financial statements are introduced and discussed throughout the rest of this text, keep in mind that each has its limitations and imperfections. After working with the material provided here and the remainder of the text, however, you should be able to use the information contained in each of the financial statements to its fullest potential.

Summary ●

In general, the aim of all decisions is to obtain some type of reward, either extrinsic or intrinsic. To obtain that reward, some sacrifice must be made. Good decisions are those that result in situations where the rewards outweigh the sacrifice even in the context of uncertainty.

Decisions can be classified as either routine (recurring) or nonroutine (those that must be made in new and unfamiliar circumstances). A key to good decision making is the ability to distinguish between routine and nonroutine decision situations. Neither style is necessarily better than the other; each is useful in certain decision situations.

However, another key to good decision making is establishing a cognitive approach to the decision process, such as the seven-step model presented in this chapter.

A third key to good decision making is to develop a more creative approach to the process. A creative thinker has the ability to consider alternatives that are not readily apparent.

Economic decisions are those involving money. For our purposes, they are decisions within the context of business transactions. These decisions are made by internal decision makers (individuals within a company) or external decision makers (individuals or organizations outside a company). Management accounting information is prepared for use by internal parties, and financial accounting information is prepared for use by external parties (but is also used by internal parties).

Both internal and external parties attempt to predict the future and timing of cash flows. Essentially, they are all trying to determine whether they will be paid, when they will be paid, and how much they will be paid. Cash flow, then, is an important criterion to evaluate business success or failure, along with other accounting measures of performance.

Accounting information is a key ingredient of good decision making. Business activity produces data. These data are of no value to decision makers until they are put into a useful form and become information. Accounting information must possess certain qualitative characteristics: (1) relevance, including timeliness and either predictive value or feedback value; and (2) reliability, including verifiability, representational faithfulness, and neutrality. Useful accounting information should also possess comparability and consistency and be understandable to economic decision makers.

Key Terms

- accounting, F–52
- accounting information, F–52
- comparability, F–55
- conservatism, F–53
- consistency, F–56
- cost/benefit, F–53
- data, F–52
- economic entity, F–52
- external decision makers, F–48
- feedback value, F–54

- financial accounting, F–49
- going concern, F–52
- industry practice, F–53
- information, F–52
- internal decision makers, F–48
- management accounting, F–49
- materiality, F–53
- monetary unit, F–52
- net cash flow, F–50
- neutrality, F–55

- opportunity cost, F–40
- periodicity, F–52
- predictive value, F–54
- relevance, F–54
- reliability, F–55
- representational faithfulness, F–55
- risk/reward trade-off, F–41
- timeliness, F–54
- verifiability, F–55

Review the Facts

A. Define cost/benefit analysis.
B. Describe the difference between an extrinsic reward and an intrinsic reward.
C. What is the relationship between risk and reward?
D. What is the difference between routine and nonroutine decisions?
E. Describe the two major information-processing styles.
F. Explain the term *reasoned decision making*.
G. Describe the seven steps of the decision model presented in this chapter.
H. What is creative decision making and why is it important?
I. What is the role of personal values in the decision making process?
J. Name and describe the two different approaches to ethics.
K. Describe the advantages and disadvantages of both individual and group decision making.
L. What is economic decision making?
M. Name the two broad categories of economic decision makers, and explain the differences between them.
N. List the two major branches of accounting mentioned in the chapter and describe how they differ from one another.
O. List the three major questions asked by economic decision makers.
P. What is accounting information?
Q. Explain the difference between data and information.
R. List and define the four accounting assumptions.
S. List and define the four accounting constraints.
T. Name the two primary qualitative characteristics of useful accounting information.
U. What characteristics are necessary for accounting information to be relevant?
V. List the characteristics necessary for accounting information to be reliable.
W. Name and describe the secondary qualities of useful accounting information.

Apply What You Have Learned

LO 1: INTRINSIC VS. EXTRINSIC REWARDS

2–33. Fred Payne, a college senior, has just gotten a part-time job working with developmentally challenged children making $10 per hour. Fred has always wanted to work with such children and thinks he may pursue this work as a career.

Required:

    a. From the facts given in the problem, what would you consider to be the extrinsic and intrinsic rewards Fred will receive from his new job?

    b. Which do you think will be more valuable to Fred, the extrinsic rewards or the intrinsic rewards? Explain your reasoning.

LO 1: ROUTINE VS. NONROUTINE DECISIONS

2–34. Some situations occur routinely in business, and management has standard operating procedures to apply when they happen. Below are a number of situations.

    1. _____ An employee calls in sick.
    2. _____ An employee makes a mistake in adding his travel claim.
    3. _____ Five dollars is missing from the petty cash fund.
    4. _____ The petty cash fund and the petty cashier are missing.
    5. _____ A vendor bills the company for 25 items and only 24 are received.
    6. _____ A vendor bills the company for 25 items that are neither ordered nor received.
    7. _____ The company's delivery person taps the bumper of a car while parking.
    8. _____ The company's driver totals the delivery van in a one-vehicle accident.
    9. _____ The building loses its roof in a tornado.
    10. _____ The building suffers extensive hail damage in a storm.
    11. _____ An employee fails to return from lunch.

Required: Identify whether these situations should invoke a routine (R) or nonroutine (N) decision.

LO 3: INTUITIVE VS. SYSTEMATIC INFORMATION PROCESSING

2–35. Briefly describe the intuitive and the systematic information-processing styles. Include in your answer ways in which these two styles are similar and ways in which they differ.

LO 3: INTUITIVE VS. SYSTEMATIC INFORMATION PROCESSING

2–36. Most people have a predominate style of processing information that is either systematic or intuitive. In a given situation, you may prefer to have one style of thinker over another.

    1. _____ You need a designer for your dream home.
    2. _____ You need a contractor to build a warehouse.
    3. _____ You need an engineer to plan a highway system in a wilderness area.
    4. _____ You need an engineer to design a five-mile expansion bridge.
    5. _____ Two employees have a serious, ongoing conflict. You need to refer them to a mediator.
    6. _____ Your business has serious financial problems that must be solved within one week. You need to hire a consultant.
    7. _____ You are a systematic thinker and you need a partner.
    8. _____ You need an advertising consultant to promote a new product.

Required: Identify whether you prefer to have an intuitive (I) thinker or a systematic (S) thinker in each of these situations and state your reasons why.

LO 2: APPLICATION OF SEVEN-STEP DECISION MODEL

2–37. Kathy Stumpe is in trouble! She has been in Paris on business for the past week. This morning, she was supposed to fly to New York for a very important dinner meeting. Unfortunately, Kathy overslept and missed her flight. As she hurries to shower and get dressed, she is trying to decide what to do next. "If only I had not slept through my alarm," she says to herself over and over. "That's the real problem."

Required:

    a. Do you think Kathy has determined her real problem? If not, help her identify it.

    b. Now that the real problem has been determined, identify two alternative courses of action Kathy might take to solve her problem. Then analyze each of them critically.

LO 2: APPLICATION OF SEVEN-STEP DECISION MODEL

2–38. You are presented with the responsibility of choosing the new copy machine for your office. Using the seven-step decision model, describe how you would approach this decision.

LO 2: APPLICATION OF SEVEN-STEP DECISION MODEL

2–39. Upon graduation from college, you receive three different job offers. Identify the various factors that you might consider to make your decision and illustrate how you would apply the seven-step decision model.

LO 2: APPLICATION OF SEVEN-STEP DECISION MODEL

2–40. Your employer offers two different types of retirement plans to all eligible employees. You may select only one of the plans. Plan A requires you to contribute 10 percent of your monthly salary, which your employer matches equally. You may not withdraw or borrow from the plan until you reach age 60. Plan B requires you to contribute 10 percent of your salary but is matched by your employer with an additional 5 percent. This plan allows you to borrow against the balance at any time without penalty.

Required: Using the seven-step decision model, discuss how you would choose between the plans assuming:

    a. You are a single individual 23 years of age.
    b. You are a married individual 40 years of age with two teenage children.

LO 2: APPLICATION OF SEVEN-STEP DECISION MODEL

2–41. As the chief lending officer for the bank, you received loan requests from three different clients for $150,000 each. Assume you may only make one of the loans. The following information is available to you:

    1. The first applicant is 21 years old and needs the loan for four years of Harvard Medical School.
    2. The second applicant is a 45-year-old businessman who wants to start his own manufacturing business. He needs the loan for equipment and start-up expenses.
    3. The third applicant is a 30-year-old dental school graduate who wishes to start her own practice. She needs the loan for equipment and to cover some operating expenses.

Required:

    a. Use the seven-step decision model to decide who should receive the loan.
    b. Now assume that you can make the loan to all three candidates and that the interest rates you can assess range between 3 percent and 12 percent. Using the concepts of risk and uncertainty, discuss the factors that would influence the interest rate you would select for each loan candidate.

LO 2: APPLICATION OF SEVEN-STEP DECISION MODEL

2–42. Let's say that you would like to begin investing in the stock market. After your preliminary research, you have decided that you will invest in pharmaceutical companies, airlines, and computer technology companies.

Required:

    a. List 10 pieces of information that you would like to have for each company in each of the three industries. Be specific and make sure the information that you request is relevant to your decision. Remember that the 10 pieces of information should allow you to make comparisons of each company within the industries.
    b. Now that you have your list of 10 pieces of relevant information, where do you think you might look to find this information?

LO 2: APPLICATION OF SEVEN-STEP DECISION MODEL

2–43. Compare and contrast the seven-step decision model presented in this chapter with the process outlined in Chapter 1 that demonstrates how the Financial Accounting Standards Board approaches the problem of standard setting. Do you think that the FASB follows the seven-step decision model?

LO 2 & 3: APPLICATION OF SEVEN-STEP DECISION MODEL

2–44. The semester break is approaching and Seth Levine, a college student, is trying to decide how he will spend the week. He has narrowed his options to these three:

Option 1: He could go to Vail, Colorado, and ski for the week (he is an avid skier). He estimates the total cost of the trip—airfare, lodging, food, and lift tickets—to be $1,700. If he selects this option, he will have to cut the last day of classes before the break. He will also have to take time off from his part-time restaurant job. He earns $10 per hour and could work as many as 60 hours over the break.

Option 2: He could drive to his parents' home for the week. They live only 140 miles from Seth's school, so he would not have to leave until after his last class. This option requires no out-of-pocket cost because he will be staying with his parents and his father has offered to pay for the gas. He would, however, have to take time off from work, just as in Option 1.

Option 3: He can remain at school for the week and devote his time to studying and working at the restaurant.

The final decision, of course, is Seth's. However, he has come to you for advice because he believes you are a person of sound judgment.

Required:

a. Tell Seth what you think are the most important factors he needs to consider when making his decision. Some of these factors may involve money, others will not. Identify the factor you consider to be most important, and explain why you think it is crucial.

b. Prepare an analysis for Seth of what you perceive to be the potential benefits and costs of each of his three alternatives. Although economic benefits and costs are always important, do not restrict yourself to the financial considerations for either benefits or costs.

c. Assume that about a month before semester break, Seth decides to go skiing in Vail (Option 1). Identify three relevant pieces of new information Seth might receive before he leaves on his ski trip and explain how each of them might cause him to rethink his decision.

LO 4: PERSONAL VALUES AND ETHICS

2–45. The chapter states that the most important influences on the decisions we make are the personal values we hold.

Required:

a. Explain in your own words the relationship between personal values and ethics.

b. How do you think that a person's values and ethics change over time? What will cause a person's values and ethics to change?

LO 5: PERSONAL VALUES AND ETHICS

2–46. Charles Rickman, an employee of Failsafe, Inc., has been away on business in Bedford Falls, Pennsylvania, for the past two weeks. Bedford Falls happens to be his hometown, and Charles stayed the entire two weeks with his mother. Wilbur Parker, Charles's boyhood pal, owns the local motel and offered to provide Charles with receipts for a two-week stay at the motel. Charles could submit the receipts and be reimbursed by his company. Failsafe generally expects to reimburse its employees for out-of-town lodging, so the company would not be out of any unexpected costs.

Required:

a. Explain how Charles would approach this decision situation using virtues ethics.

b. Explain how Charles would approach this decision situation using rules ethics.

c. Which approach do you think would serve Charles better in all such decision situations? Explain your reasoning.

LO 5: PERSONAL VALUES AND ETHICS

2–47. Assume that you have been working as a staff accountant for Fox Manufacturing Company for the past six months. Your boss needs you to increase the current year's profit by $25,000 and has asked for your help. He tells you of certain accounting entries and how you could make them to make it seem like the company earned the additional profit. Even though he is the boss, based on your knowledge, you believe what he is asking you to do is not really proper.

Required:

    a. Using the concept of virtues ethics, how would you respond in this situation?

    b. How would you apply rules ethics in this situation, and would that change your overall response?

    c. Assuming that the method your boss wishes you to use to increase profits is technically legal, how do you reconcile his request with your personal values?

LO 5: GROUP DECISION MAKING

2–48. Listed below are the disadvantages of group decision making presented in the chapter, followed by the definitions of those disadvantages in scrambled order:

    a. Different information-processing styles
    b. Domineering members of the group
    c. Social pressure
    d. Goal replacement
    e. Differing personal values
    f. Unequal effort
    g. Groupthink

    1. _____ Some members of the group may not work as hard as others.
    2. _____ Not everyone believes the same way.
    3. _____ The group may contain both intuitive types and systematic types.
    4. _____ The natural desire to not look foolish may stifle a group member's creative contribution.
    5. _____ Group members are often tempted to ignore their own judgment to achieve consensus.
    6. _____ Winning an argument, proving a point, or taking revenge can become more important than accomplishing the task at hand.
    7. _____ The work of the group suffers simply because some members can talk louder and longer than others.

Required: Match the letter next to each disadvantage with the appropriate definition. Use each letter only once.

LO 5: GROUP DECISION MAKING

2–49. Explain in your own words the advantages and disadvantages of group decision making in relation to individual decision making.

LO 7 & 8: ECONOMIC DECISION MAKING

2–50. Tommy Hoag is a commercial artist and sign painter by trade. He received a $15,000 order from Bill Bates, Inc. for *1,500* signs to be displayed in Bates's retail outlets. This is a very large job for Tommy's new business. He has concerns because he estimates it will take him a month working full time to complete the signs and Bates proposes to pay him the full contract amount 30 days after he delivers the signs. These are Bates's standard payment terms. Tommy did a small job for Bates last year ($1,500) and received payment 50 days after completing the work.

    Tommy estimates the materials (sign board, paint, brushes, etc.) will cost $9,500, which he can buy on 30-day terms from Long's Art Supply Company.

    Tommy remembers from his first accounting course that any economic decision entails attempting to answer the following three questions:

- Will I be paid?
- When will I be paid?
- How much will I be paid?

Required:

    a. If Tommy can satisfy himself as to the first question (Will I be paid?), what are the answers to the other two questions? Remember the last question (How much?) has two parts.

    b. The problem states that Tommy has concerns. What do you think is troubling him about the order from Bill Bates, Inc.?

    c. Based on your answer to the previous requirement, identify three things Tommy could do to solve his dilemma.

LO 7 & 8: ECONOMIC DECISION MAKING

2–51. Jon Smythe is a trained automobile engine mechanic. He has received a $25,000 contract from David Watts and Company to replace 25 automobile engines for Watts' taxi cabs. Jon has concerns about the terms of the contract. He estimates it will take him a month working full time to complete the engine changes and Watts has agreed to pay him 30 days after he completes the work. These are Watts's standard payment terms, and Watts has paid Jon on average after 40 days in the past.

    Jon estimates the parts will cost $13,000, which he can buy on a 30-day charge account from Sam's Auto Supply Company. Jon has the typical questions that any economic decision maker has:

- Will I be paid?
- When will I be paid?
- How much will I be paid?

Required:

    a. Jon believes that Watts will pay him based on their prior dealings. What are the answers to the other two questions? Remember the last question (How much?) has two parts.

    b. The problem states that Jon is concerned about the contract terms. Why do you think he is concerned?

    c. Based on your answer to the previous requirement, identify three things Jon could do to lessen his concerns.

LO 7 & 8: ECONOMIC DECISION MAKING

2–52. Rob Schwinn is a furniture manufacturer who specializes in high-quality wooden tables and chairs. He received a $50,000 contract from Dillon Corporation to build 100 uphol-stered sofas, to be sold in Dillon's stores. Rob believes he needs two months to complete the sofas. He must purchase an industrial sewing machine for the fabric work on the sofas at a cost of $10,000 for the machine and training, which will equal the profit that he will make on this contract. Dillon has agreed to pay Rob Schwinn 30 days after delivery of the sofas.

    Rob knows that he can buy the sewing machine on a 90-day plan from Dan's Sewing Machine Company. Rob knows that any economic decision entails attempting to answer the following three questions:

- Will I be paid?
- When will I be paid?
- How much will I be paid?

Required:

    a. Assuming Rob can be satisfied as to the first question (Will I be paid?), what are the answers to the other two questions? Remember the last question (How much?) has two parts.

    b. List the pros and cons of Rob's accepting this contract.

LO 8: CASH CONCEPTS

2–53. In sports, you often hear the expressions, "keep your eye on the ball." Interpret the following statement: "cash is the 'ball' of business."

LO 9 & 10: QUALITATIVE CHARACTERISTICS OF ACCOUNTING INFORMATION

2–54. Below are the qualitative characteristics of useful accounting information as discussed in the chapter, followed by definitions of those items in scrambled order:

a. Relevance
b. Timeliness
c. Predictive value
d. Feedback value
e. Reliability

f. Verifiability
g. Representational faithfulness
h. Neutrality
i. Comparability
j. Consistency

1. _____ The same measurement application methods are used over time.
2. _____ The accounting information is free of bias.
3. _____ The information provides input to evaluate a previously made decision.
4. _____ The information allows the evaluation of one alternative against another alternative.
5. _____ In assessing the information, qualified persons working independently would arrive at similar conclusions.
6. _____ The information helps reduce the uncertainty of the future.
7. _____ The information has a bearing on a particular decision situation.
8. _____ The information is available soon enough to be of value.
9. _____ The information is dependable.
10. _____ There must be agreement between what the information says and what really happened.

Required: Match the letter next to each item with the appropriate definition. Each letter will be used only once.

LO 9 & 10: CHAPTER TERMS AND CONCEPTS

2–55. Presented below are items relating to the concepts discussed in this chapter, followed by the definitions of those items in scrambled order:

a. Cash flow
b. Comparability
c. Data
d. Financial accounting

e. Information
f. Management accounting
g. Net cash flow
h. Economic decision making

1. _____ The raw results of transactions and events
2. _____ A branch of accounting developed to meet the information needs of internal decision makers
3. _____ Data transformed so they are useful in the decision making process
4. _____ The movement of cash in and out of a company
5. _____ Any decisions involving money
6. _____ Reports generated for one entity may be compared with reports generated for other entities
7. _____ The difference between the cash coming into a company and the cash going out of a company
8. _____ A branch of accounting developed to meet the information needs of external decision makers

Required: Match the letter next to each item with the appropriate definition. Use each letter only once.

LO 10: QUALITATIVE CHARACTERISTICS OF ACCOUNTING INFORMATION

2–56. Emma Peel is the chief accountant of Venture Company. She is trying to decide whether to extend credit to Freed Company, a new customer. Venture does most of its business on credit but is very strict in granting credit terms. Frank Freed, the owner and president of Freed Company, has sent the following items for Emma to examine as she performs her evaluation.

1. All company bank statements for the past seven years (a total of 84 bank statements)
2. A detailed analysis showing the amount of sales the company expects to have in the coming year and its estimated profit
3. Another, less detailed analysis outlining projected company growth over the next 20 years

4. A biographical sketch of each of the company's officers and a description of the function each performs in the company
5. Ten letters of reference from close friends and relatives of the company's officers
6. A report of the company's credit history prepared by company employees on Freed Company letterhead
7. A letter signed by all company officers expressing their willingness to personally guarantee the credit Venture extends to Freed. (Assume this is a legally binding document.)

Required:

a. As she evaluates Freed Company's application for credit, is Emma Peel an internal decision maker or an external decision maker? Explain your reasoning.
b. Analyze each item Freed sent in light of the primary qualitative characteristics of relevance (including timeliness, predictive value, and feedback value) and reliability (including verifiability, representational faithfulness, and neutrality). Explain how each item either possesses or does not possess these characteristics.

LO 10: QUALITATIVE CHARACTERISTICS OF ACCOUNTING INFORMATION

2–57. You are in the market for a used car. You notice a promising advertisement in the local newspaper and make an appointment to meet with the seller, whose name is Chet. During your meeting, you obtain the following information:

- The car is a 1996 model.
- Chet said he has used the car only for commuting to and from work.
- You notice the car has out-of-state license tags.
- The odometer reading is 65,319 miles.
- Chet reports that he has had the oil changed every 3,000 miles since he bought the car new.
- Chet says this is the greatest car he has ever owned.
- The glove box contains a maintenance record prepared by a licensed mechanic.

Required:

a. Evaluate each item from the list above in terms of its relevance (specifically, predictive value and timeliness) to your decision about whether to buy Chet's car.
b. Evaluate each item from the list above in terms of its reliability (verifiability, representational faithfulness, and neutrality) for deciding whether to buy Chet's car.

LO 10: QUALITATIVE CHARACTERISTICS OF ACCOUNTING INFORMATION

2–58. The chapter states that to be useful, accounting information must possess the primary qualitative characteristics of relevance (timeliness and predictive value or feedback value) and reliability (verifiability, representational faithfulness, and neutrality). These characteristics are also applicable to other types of information.

Suppose that prior to taking your midterm exam in this course, your instructor gives you two options:

Option 1: One week before the midterm exam, you will be given a rough idea of what is going to be on the exam.

or

Option 2: On the day following the exam, you will be given a copy of the actual midterm exam with an answer key.

Assume further that you have two goals:

Goal 1: To prepare for the midterm exam.
Goal 2: To evaluate your performance on the midterm exam.

Required: Within the context of each of your two goals, evaluate both options using the primary qualitative characteristics. Be sure to explain how the primary characteristics are present or absent and how such presence or absence affects you as a rational decision maker.

LO 10: QUALITATIVE CHARACTERISTICS OF ACCOUNTING INFORMATION

2–59. Suppose you are about to buy a new car. The car you want is a **Nissan** Maxima. You have enough money in the bank, ready to spend on the new car. You obtain the following items of information:

1. On your first visit to **Quality Nissan,** a salesperson casually tells you that the price of a new **Nissan** Maxima is about $25,500.
2. A friend tells you he heard that someone was selling a three-year-old Maxima for $17,000.
3. Another friend just bought a new **Chevy** pickup truck for $23,500.
4. The sticker price of a Maxima with the options you want is $27,188.
5. A **Nissan** dealer in the area is advertising a new Maxima with the options you want for $25,000.
6. A friend tells you she heard that someone bought a new Maxima a couple months ago for around $24,000.

Assume that you are about to visit another **Nissan** dealership and your goal is to buy a new Maxima for the best price. You intend to use the previous information to evaluate whether or not the price you get is a good deal.

Required:

a. Evaluate each item from the list above in terms of its relevance (feedback value, predictive value, and timeliness). Explain how the presence or absence of the characteristics affects your ability to use the information to determine if you are getting a good deal.
b. Evaluate each item from the list above in terms of its reliability (verifiability, representational faithfulness, and neutrality). Explain how the presence or absence of these characteristics affects your ability to use the information to determine if you are getting a good deal.

LO 10: QUALITATIVE CHARACTERISTICS OF ACCOUNTING INFORMATION

2–60. Your accounting midterm exam is in about two weeks. You can't figure out exactly how you should prepare for the exam. As you are walking across campus, you see the following notice pinned to a bulletin board:

Worried About the Accounting Mid-Term???
I CAN HELP!
WILL TUTOR FOR $15 PER HOUR

I GUARANTEE AN "A" OR "B"

Qualifications:

1. Got an "A" in the course myself.
2. Have outlines of all chapters of the text.
3. Have over 120 satisfied customers from previous semesters.
4. Know the professor personally.
5. Know the authors of the text personally.
6. Working on a graduate degree in Biology.

CALL BILL AUSTIN AT 555-5555

Required: Evaluate each of Bill's claimed qualifications in relation to the primary characteristics of:

a. Relevance (including timeliness and predictive value or feedback value).
b. Reliability (including verifiability, representational faithfulness, and neutrality).

Financial Reporting Exercises •

LO 9 & 10: QUALITATIVE CHARACTERISTICS OF ACCOUNTING INFORMATION

2–61. Presented below are the qualitative characteristics of useful accounting information.

a. Relevance	f. Verifiability
b. Timeliness	g. Representational faithfulness
c. Predictive value	h. Neutrality
d. Feedback value	i. Comparability
e. Reliability	j. Consistency

In 2001, **WorldCom** allegedly published misleading financial statements that made it appear as though the company had billions of dollars more in profits and billions of dollars more in assets than the company really had.

Required:

a. Which four of the qualitative characteristics of accounting information listed above were most directly violated by **WorldCom**'s actions?

b. What impact does such a major misrepresentation have on the credibility of **WorldCom**'s published financial information?

c. What impact does this particular misrepresentation have on the credibility of all financial information?

LO 11: IDENTIFY SPECIFIC ANNUAL REPORT INFORMATION

2–62. Look at **Pier 1**'s annual report and answer the following questions.

a. List the three divisions of stores that **Pier 1 Imports** accounts for in their annual reports.

b. Name five cities in North America where **Pier 1** opened a new store in the fiscal year.

c. List the five types of products **Pier 1** sells.

d. Name and briefly describe the relationships of **Pier 1** with all of its subsidiaries.

e. Which of the subsidiaries is an example of a situation that resulted in the closing of that part of the company? Explain why. What is another way in which this might happen with another one of the subsidiaries?

LO 11: IDENTIFY AND CONTRAST INFORMATION FROM ANNUAL REPORTS

2–63. **Williams Sonoma Inc.** is a competitor of **Pier 1 Imports.** Visit its Web site by clicking on **Williams Sonoma**'s link at the PHLIP Web site to find its annual report information.

Required:

a. What are the two reportable segments that **Williams Sonoma** uses?

b. List some of the types of products that **Williams Sonoma** sells.

c. How many stores did **Williams Sonoma** open in 2001? How many did it close?

d. List the subsidiaries of **Williams Sonoma.** Which of these names has the most stores?

e. Did you know that **Williams Sonoma** owned all these subsidiaries? Why do you think the corporation keeps all of these names separate?

f. Which company (**Williams Sonoma** or **Pier 1 Imports**) do you consider to be involved in more types of business? Do you consider this to be more of an asset or a liability to this company?

LO 11: IDENTIFY AND DISCUSS SPECIFIC ANNUAL REPORT INFORMATION

2–64. **JCPenney** operated the **Thrift Drug** store chain profitably for 28 years. **Penney's** purchased **Kerr Drug** in 1995 and **Fay's** in 1996. In February 1997, **Penney's** completed the purchase of **Eckerd Drug** to have the fourth-largest drug store chain in the United States. (For more information on **JCPenney,** visit the PHLIP Web site and click on the **JCPenney** link.)

Required:

a. Why would a mall-centered retail department store acquire large chains of pharmacies?

b. Why do you think **JCPenney** operates all of the drug stores under the **Eckerd** name instead of the **JCPenney** name?

c. Name a couple of the services other than clothes, shoes, and the like that **JCPenney's** has within their stores. Why would they want to provide these services under their own name as opposed to opening n stores under different names to provide them?

ANNUAL REPORT PROJECT

2–65. Section 2—General Information

By now, you should have a copy of the annual report for the company you selected for your annual report project. In this assignment, you will prepare a report based on general information found in your company's annual report.

Required: Prepare a report that includes the following information:

a. A listing of the contents of the company's annual report. Preparing this list will help you become familiar with the annual report. If you are working in a group, it would be best if each member made his or her own list of the report's contents. Your list should include each major section of the report and its page number. Among other things, your list should include the following:

Five-Year Selected Financial Data	Page ?
Management Discussion and Analysis	Page ?
Independent Auditor's Report	Page ?
Report of Management	Page ?
Consolidated Statements of Operations	Page ?
Consolidated Balance Sheets	Page ?
Consolidated Statements of Cash Flows	Page ?
Consolidated Statements of Shareholders' Equity	Page ?
Notes to Consolidated Financial Statements	Page ?
Shareholder Information	Page ?
Directors and Officers Information	Page ?

b. The name of your company's auditing firm. You can find this in the auditor's report, which usually follows the financial statements in the company's annual report.

c. Your company's Standard Industry Code (SIC) or North American Industry Classification System (NAICS) code and a description of that industry. You can find one or both of these codes in several ways. We have listed step-by-step instructions to help you find your company's SIC code using the Securities and Exchange Commission's (SEC's) Electronic Data Gathering, Analysis, and Retrieval (EDGAR) system.

Step-by-step instructions to find a company's SIC using the SEC's Web site:

a. Go to the SEC's home page at *www.sec.gov.*
b. Click on *Search for Company Filings* (listed under *"Filings and Form (EDGAR)"*).
c. Click on *Search Companies and Filings.*

d. Enter your company's name in the appropriate place and click *Find Companies.*
e. The company's SIC code and a description of the company's industry will appear just under the company's name in the upper left area of the page. For example, for ***Pier 1 Imports, Inc.,*** the following information appears on the Web page just under the SEC's logo and seal:

```
PIER 1 IMPORTS INC
SIC: 5700-Retail-Home Furniture, Furnishings & Equipment
Stores
```

Company SIC codes are also available on the front page of the company's Form 10Q SEC filings. You can find this form and many other filings by logging on to the SEC's EDGAR system.

f. A statement regarding how you feel the description of the industry pertaining to your company's SIC code compares to the company's actual business as described in its annual report.
g. A brief summary of the president's (or CEO's) message included in your company's annual report.
h. A brief summary of the general information and promotional material included in your company's annual report. Your summary should include a general description of your company's business and a summary of the firm's views on social responsibility, marketing strategy, direction for the future, environmental issues, and so forth.
i. An outline of the major points covered in the letter to stockholders.
j. With respect to the report of the independent auditors:

1. What does the opinion say about the division of responsibility between the auditor and management?
2. What does it mean when the auditor's report says something similar to "present

fairly, in all material respects"?

3. What does it mean when the auditor's report says something similar to "in accordance with generally accepted accounting principles"?

4. What does the audit report say about auditing standards?

5. In the context of the auditor's report, what does "on a test basis" mean?

k. Following the presentation of the company's financial statements, there is a series of notes. The first note presents information about significant accounting policies. Summarize the kind of information the note includes. Explain how the information in this note would help a decision maker understand the company's financial statements.

CHAPTER 3

The Balance Sheet and External Financing

Last night you woke up at 2:30 A.M. and simply could not get back to sleep, so you turned on the TV and began surfing through the channels. As is typical for middle-of-the-night broadcasting, nearly every channel was showing an infomercial of one kind or another. Most of them had to do with either making a fortune in real estate with no money down or losing weight by eating more. Neither topic held much interest for you. Then you stumbled on a channel that was showing *The New Yankee Workshop*. Norm, the host of this popular woodworking show, can build just about anything you can imagine and makes even the most intricate project look easy. In this episode, Norm was crafting a bedroom dresser. What luck! You've needed a dresser for quite some time. You tune in, thinking you may get some tips about what to look for in a dresser. The longer you watch, the more excited you get. Although you've never built a piece of furniture before and don't even own any tools, you find yourself thinking, "I could build that dresser," and indeed this is what you decided to do.

This morning, you set off for **Home Depot** to buy the supplies you'll need to build your dresser. You haven't made a list of the tools Norm used, as you're sure you'll recognize them when you see them on the shelves. But when you reach the tool department, you're shocked to realize it covers about 30 acres and brims with tools of all types and description. In the area displaying saws, for example, you see hand saws (crosscut and rip), power circular saws, table saws, jigsaws, miter saws, and coping saws, to name just a few. "What in the world?", you ask yourself. "Isn't there just one saw I can buy that will do everything I need to do to build my dresser?"

The answer, unfortunately, is no. No single saw will serve every need. And what's true for saws is true for every other tool, as well. Tools are developed to solve specific problems; they are responses to specific needs. Well-developed tools, properly used, produce satisfactory results. Inadequate or improperly used tools result in difficulties at best and disaster at worst. Consider the following parable:

> *The Problem* developed. So, somebody analyzed *The Problem* and, having figured out what needed to be done to solve it, invented *The Tool*. Soon, people began using *The Tool* to solve *The Problem*. Eventually, no one would even consider using anything else.
>
> For many years *The Tool* was used with great success. There came a time, however, when it no longer solved *The Problem*, but nobody realized it. Whenever confronted with *The Problem*, folks instinctively reached for *The Tool*. Even when results were devastating, no one ever questioned the use of *The Tool*.

There are at least three possible explanations for what happened in the situation described above:

1. The nature of *The Problem* had changed. If this were the case, it's no wonder *The Tool* would no longer solve the problem.
2. Those using *The Tool* thought they were applying it to *The Problem*, when in fact they were attempting to use it to solve *Another Problem*, which, on the surface, looked like *The Problem*.

3. *The Tool* never really did solve *The Problem*, but merely appeared to, and reality finally caught up with it.

Think of financial information as a tool developed to solve economic problems. People have been using financial tools for hundreds of years, but their use has not always met with favorable results. In fact, the inadequacy of financial tools in the late 1920s was at least partially responsible for the stock market crash of 1929 and the resulting Great Depression. Fortunately, since then, the Securities and Exchange Commission (SEC), the Financial Accounting Standards Board (FASB), and other organizations have worked to improve the quality of the financial tools available to us. But it is our responsibility to know what tools are available, what those tools can do, and what they cannot do. In the words of the FASB's *Conceptual Framework*:

> *Financial information is a tool and, like most tools, cannot be of much direct help to those who are unable or unwilling to use it or who misuse it. Its use can be learned, however, and financial reporting should provide information that can be used by all—nonprofessionals as well as professionals—who are willing to learn to use it properly.*[1]

We must update the financial tools we use so they keep up with changing circumstances. We must bear in mind that a financial tool that addresses a particular financial problem may not necessarily help solve other financial problems. And, before reaching for a tool to solve a financial problem, we must be sure we have properly identified the problem. Then, we can select the appropriate tool for that problem.

Although there is a substantial number of financial schedules and reports, many of them are used only by company managers and are not available to company outsiders. Financial accounting, the focus of this book, deals with the financial tools that are available to these outsiders (external parties). General purpose financial statements—and the related financial information that accompanies them—are the primary tools available to external parties. Like all tools, these statements were developed in response to specific needs.

In this chapter, we will focus primarily on one of these financial statements—the balance sheet. Near the end of the chapter, we will also show the effects of certain investing and financing transactions on another financial statement—the statement of cash flows. We will discuss the other financial statements in the chapters that follow.

No matter which organizational form companies take (proprietorship, partnership, or corporation) or which type of business (service, merchandising, or manufacturing), all companies have one thing in common: They must obtain capital (money) to support their operations. In the long run, a company must finance its activities with the profits it generates. We call this **internal financing.** However, when either starting out or in a time of expansion, companies must obtain capital from sources other than the profits. This is called **external financing.**

The two external sources of capital are equity financing and debt financing. **Equity financing** exchanges an ownership interest in the company for the needed cash. Virtually every business begins its life using cash invested by its owner or owners. In many cases, however, the company needs more cash than can be raised from investments by owners. Consequently, almost all companies at one time or another need to obtain financing by borrowing money. Borrowing funds to support a business is called **debt financing.** In this chapter, we will discuss external financing and illustrate its impact on the balance sheets of proprietorships, partnerships, and corporations.

Learning Objectives

After completing your work on this chapter, you should be able to do the following:

1. Identify and explain the meaning of the accounting elements shown on the balance sheet.

2. Prepare a basic balance sheet for a proprietorship, a partnership, and a corporation and demonstrate how the balance sheet provides information about the financial position of a business.

internal financing
Providing funds for the operation of a company through the earnings process of that company.

external financing
Acquiring funds from outside the company. Equity and debt financing are the two major types of external financing.

equity financing
Acquiring funds for business operations by giving up ownership interest in the company. For a corporation, this means issuing capital stock. Equity financing is one type of external financing.

debt financing Acquiring funds for business operations by borrowing. Debt financing is one type of external financing.

---

[1]Statement of Financial Accounting Concepts No. 1, paragraph 36.

3. Describe how a corporation is formed and how the equity of a corporate balance sheet is structured.

4. Describe various forms of debt and equity financing and their effects on the balance sheet.

5. Perform basic interest calculations.

6. Compare and contrast two investment alternatives—equity investments and debt investments, including return on and return of investments for each alternative.

7. Read and understand a basic statement of cash flows and describe the information it includes.

8. Perform basic financial analysis relating to financing activities.

◆ INTRODUCTION TO THE BALANCE SHEET

balance sheet   The financial tool that focuses on the present condition of a business.

In Chapter 2, we said decision makers must evaluate alternative investment opportunities to determine whether they will be paid and, if so, when the payments will occur and how much the payments will be. This evaluation begins by assessing an investment's present condition and its past performance. Remember, however, that the present and the past are useful only if they have predictive value or feedback value. Over time, accountants developed financial tools to convey information about the present condition and past performance of an entity. The **balance sheet** is the financial tool that focuses on the present condition of a business.

Discussion Questions ●

3–1. Assume you are locked in a room that has no windows and only one door. To get out of the room, you must request one tool and explain how you will use it to get out. You may not request a key or any lock-picking equipment. Choose the one tool you request and describe its features. Then explain in detail how you will use it to get out of the room.

3–2. Assume your uncle's will stipulates that you and your cousin (with whom you have always competed) will each inherit one of his two businesses. You get first choice, and you may ask 10 questions to determine the present condition of each company. Lawyers for the estate will provide the answers. List your 10 questions.

THE ACCOUNTING ELEMENTS

As you recall from Chapter 1, the FASB's *Conceptual Framework of Accounting* includes 10 accounting elements. (See Exhibit 3–1.) These accounting elements are really nothing more than broad classifications. We can use these elements, or classifications, to categorize the results of every economic transaction or event a company has. In this chapter, we will discuss the elements associated with the balance sheet.

The main accounting elements that make up the balance sheet are assets, liabilities, and equity. As we discuss each of these elements, we will give the actual FASB definition in italics followed by a less technical explanation.

assets   An accounting element that is one of the three components of a balance sheet. Assets are probable future economic benefits controlled by an entity as a result of previous transactions or events—that is, what a company has.

- **Assets**—*Probable future economic benefits obtained or controlled by a particular entity as a result of past transactions or events* (Statement of Financial Accounting Concepts No. 6, paragraph 25). Assets are the things of value a company owns or controls. Generally, companies *own* their assets, but technically, a company would include certain assets it *controls* by virtue of long-term leases. The key here is that, to be an asset, the item must have probable future value. Examples of assets include cash, land, buildings, equipment, vehicles, and stocks of merchandise or supplies. Assets listed on **Office Depot**'s balance sheet for example include cash, short-term investments, receivables, merchandise inventories, and property, plant, and equipment.

liabilities   An accounting element that is one of the three components of a balance sheet. Liabilities are probable future sacrifices of assets arising from present obligations of an entity as a result of past transactions or events—that is, what a company owes.

- **Liabilities**—*Probable future sacrifices of economic benefits arising from present obligations of a particular entity to transfer assets or provide services to other entities in the future as a result of past transactions or events* (Statement of Financial Accounting Concepts No. 6, paragraph 35). Liabilities are the debts a company

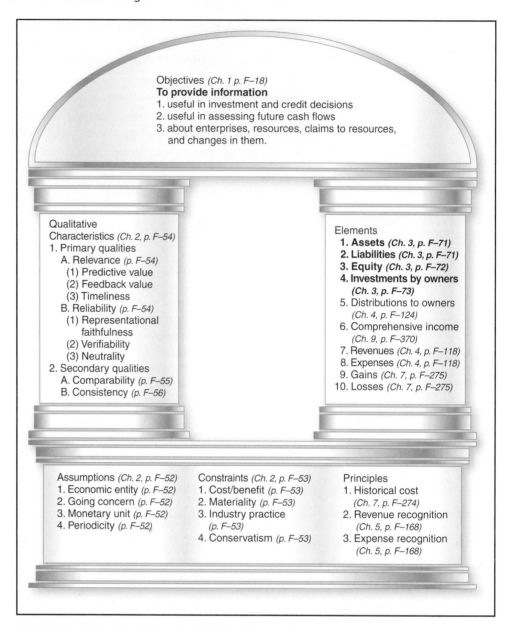

Objectives *(Ch. 1 p. F–18)*
To provide information
1. useful in investment and credit decisions
2. useful in assessing future cash flows
3. about enterprises, resources, claims to resources, and changes in them.

Qualitative
Characteristics *(Ch. 2, p. F–54)*
1. Primary qualities
   A. Relevance *(p. F–54)*
      (1) Predictive value
      (2) Feedback value
      (3) Timeliness
   B. Reliability *(p. F–54)*
      (1) Representational faithfulness
      (2) Verifiability
      (3) Neutrality
2. Secondary qualities
   A. Comparability *(p. F–55)*
   B. Consistency *(p. F–56)*

Elements
1. **Assets** *(Ch. 3, p. F–71)*
2. **Liabilities** *(Ch. 3, p. F–71)*
3. **Equity** *(Ch. 3, p. F–72)*
4. **Investments by owners** *(Ch. 3, p. F–73)*
5. Distributions to owners *(Ch. 4, p. F–124)*
6. Comprehensive income *(Ch. 9, p. F–370)*
7. Revenues *(Ch. 4, p. F–118)*
8. Expenses *(Ch. 4, p. F–118)*
9. Gains *(Ch. 7, p. F–275)*
10. Losses *(Ch. 7, p. F–275)*

Assumptions *(Ch. 2, p. F–52)*
1. Economic entity *(p. F–52)*
2. Going concern *(p. F–52)*
3. Monetary unit *(p. F–52)*
4. Periodicity *(p. F–52)*

Constraints *(Ch. 2, p. F–53)*
1. Cost/benefit *(p. F–53)*
2. Materiality *(p. F–53)*
3. Industry practice *(p. F–53)*
4. Conservatism *(p. F–53)*

Principles
1. Historical cost *(Ch. 7, p. F–274)*
2. Revenue recognition *(Ch. 5, p. F–168)*
3. Expense recognition *(Ch. 5, p. F–168)*

EXHIBIT 3–1 The Conceptual Framework of Accounting—Accounting Elements Highlighted

owes. Liabilities include obligations to transfer cash or other assets to pay off debt, as well as obligations to provide goods or services when the company receives payment in advance. The key consideration is that the company must owe something for a liability to exist. Liabilities arise from past transactions; they are debts that an entity must settle (pay) some time in the future. Liabilities listed on *Coca-Cola*'s balance sheet, for example, include accounts payable, notes payable, payables for income taxes, and long-term debt. The word *payable* is used to describe many liabilities because they are amounts to be paid.

- **Equity**—*The residual interest in the assets of an entity that remains after deducting its liabilities* (Statement of Financial Accounting Concepts No. 6, paragraph 44). Equity is the ownership interest in a company. It is the difference between the company's assets and its liabilities on those assets. The result represents the portion of the assets that the owner(s) owns free and clear. Consequently, the FASB also refers to equity as *net assets*. In practice, this element is usually referred to as *owners' equity*, and by some as *net worth*.

equity An accounting element that is one of the three components of a balance sheet. Equity is the residual interest in the assets of an entity that remains after deducting liabilities. Also called net assets.

Discussion Questions

3–3. Assume you are applying for a car loan. As part of the loan application, you are required to prepare a list of your assets. What assets would you list?

3–4. Assume that as part of the loan application you are required to prepare a list of your liabilities. What liabilities would you list?

Although we said the balance sheet shows three main accounting elements, one of these elements—equity—consists of two parts. As we will soon learn, one of these parts is itself an accounting element, according to the FASB. The two parts or sources of equity are:

investments by owners That part of owners' equity generated by the receipt of cash (or other assets) from the owners.

- **Investments by owners.** The *Conceptual Framework* lists investments by owners as a separate element, but it really is a subset of equity. The FASB defines investments by owners as *increases in equity of a particular business enterprise resulting from transfers to it from other entities of something valuable to obtain or increase ownership interests (or equity) in it* (Statement of Financial Accounting Concepts No. 6, paragraph 66). Investment by owners is the amount the owners have contributed to the company in exchange for their ownership interest. Think of it as the amount of "seed money" the owners put into the company to get it started or to finance its expansion.

earned equity   The total amount a company has earned since its beginning, less any amounts distributed to the owner(s). In a corporation, this amount is called retained earnings.

- **Earned equity.** This is the total amount a company has earned since it was first started, less the earnings the company has distributed to its owners. Earned equity comes from the profitable operation of the company over time. Think of it as the portion of income that the company keeps to plow back into the business. While earned equity is not itself considered an accounting element according to the FASB, it is composed of the remaining six elements (distributions to owners, comprehensive income, revenues, expenses, gains, and losses). Earned equity is our major focus in Chapter 4.

ORGANIZATION OF THE BALANCE SHEET

A constant relationship exists among the three main elements on the balance sheet (assets, liabilities, and equity). Logically, what a company has (assets) will be equal to the claims that are made on those assets: the creditors' claims (liabilities) or the owners' claims (equity). The following equation expresses this relationship mathematically:

$$\text{Assets} = \text{Liabilities} + \text{Owners' Equity}$$

This equation is called the *accounting equation*. We might also call it the *business equation* because it sums up an important reality of business. Accounting uses this equation to measure that reality. The rules of mathematics allow us to rearrange the accounting equation as follows:

$$\text{Assets} - \text{Liabilities} = \text{Owners' Equity}$$

This presentation of the equation shows the reality of equity as the owners' residual interest in the company. In most cases, both creditors and owners share claims to the assets (see Exhibit 3–2).

EXHIBIT 3–2   Accounting Equation

If you were to buy an automobile for $8,000, paying $3,000 in cash and borrowing $5,000 from the bank, both you and the bank would have a claim against the car.

Assets	=	Liabilities	+	Equity
Car	=	Bank Loan	+	Your Ownership Interest
$8,000	=	$5,000	+	$3,000

By rearranging the equation in the following way, you can more clearly see that in this example you would have a car valued at $8,000, the bank would have a $5,000 claim against the car, and your equity in the car would be $3,000.

Assets – Liabilities	= Equity
$8,000 – $5,000	= $3,000

Equity
Liabilities

To understand the balance sheet, you must understand the accounting equation. The term *balance sheet* comes from the need to keep the two sides of the equation in balance. The financial statement's formal name is the *statement of financial position* or *statement of financial condition*, both of which are more descriptive of the true purpose of the statement than balance sheet. Common usage in the business world, however, remains the balance sheet, so we will use it throughout our discussions of the statement. Exhibit 3–3 shows *Best Buy*'s 2001 balance sheet.

At this point, don't get caught up in trying to understand each and every asset, liability, and equity *Best Buy* lists. That will come later. But you should take note of the general format of the balance sheet and the fact that *Best Buy*'s total assets are equal

EXHIBIT 3–3 Balance Sheet for *Best Buy*

Best Buy Co., Inc.
Consolidated Balance Sheets
$ in thousands, except per share amounts

Assets	March 3 2001	Feb. 26 2000
Current Assets		
Cash and cash equivalents	$ 746,879	$ 750,723
Receivables	209,031	189,301
Recoverable costs from developed properties	103,846	72,770
Merchandise inventories	1,766,934	1,183,681
Other current assets	101,973	41,985
Total current assets	2,928,663	2,238,460
Property and Equipment		
Land and buildings	170,978	76,228
Leasehold improvements	556,534	254,767
Fixtures and equipment	1,259,880	762,476
	1,987,392	1,093,471
Less accumulated depreciation and amortization	543,220	395,387
Net property and equipment	1,444,172	698,084
Goodwill, Net	385,355	—
Other Assets	81,397	58,798
Total Assets	$4,839,587	$2,995,342
Liabilities and Shareholders' Equity	2001	2000
Current Liabilities		
Accounts payable	$1,772,722	$1,313,940
Accrued compensation and related expenses	154,159	102,065
Accrued liabilities	545,590	287,888
Accrued income taxes	127,287	65,366
Current portion of long-term debt	114,940	5,790
Total current liabilities	2,714,698	1,785,049
Long-Term Liabilities	121,952	99,448
Long-Term Debt	181,009	14,860
Shareholders' Equity		
Preferred stock, $1.00 par value: Authorized – 400,000 shares; Issued and outstanding – none	—	—
Common stock, $.10 par value: Authorized – 1,000,000,000 shares; Issued and outstanding – 208,138,000 and 200,379,000 shares, respectively	20,814	20,038
Additional paid-in capital	576,818	247,490
Retained earnings	1,224,296	828,457
Total shareholders' equity	1,821,928	1,095,985
Total Liabilities and Shareholders' Equity	$ 4,839,587	$2,995,342

to its total liabilities and equity. In other words, ***Best Buy***'s accounting equation balances as we show below.

$$Assets = Liabilities + Equity$$
$$\$4,839,587 = \$3,017,659 + \$1,821,928$$

$$\$4,839,587 = \qquad \$4,839,587$$

Companies present their balance sheets in either of two acceptable formats: the account form or the report form. As you can see in Exhibit 3–4, the account form balance sheet places assets on the left side of the page and the liabilities and owners' equity on the right.

EXHIBIT 3–4   Account Form Balance Sheet

The Toland Company
Balance Sheet
December 31, 2003

Assets:		Liabilities:	
Asset one	$$$	Liability one	$$$
Asset two	$$$	Liability two	$$$
Asset three	$$	Total liabilities	$$$$
Asset four	$$		
Asset five	$$	Owners' equity	$$$
Total assets	$$$$$	Total liabilities and owners' equity	$$$$$

THESE AMOUNTS MUST BE EQUAL

The report form, shown in Exhibit 3–5, depicts the same information in a vertical format. Although the report form of the balance sheet presents the statement's balancing feature less graphically, it is more popular than the account form, simply because it is easier to fit the balance sheet on a single page using the report form.

EXHIBIT 3–5   Report Form Balance Sheet

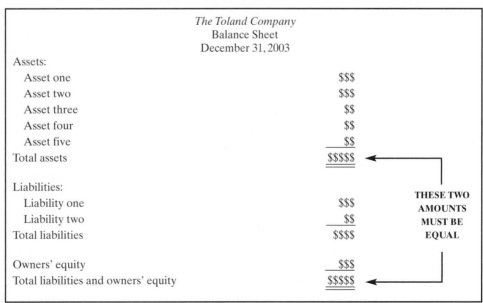

The Toland Company
Balance Sheet
December 31, 2003

Assets:	
Asset one	$$$
Asset two	$$$
Asset three	$$
Asset four	$$
Asset five	$$
Total assets	$$$$$
Liabilities:	
Liability one	$$$
Liability two	$$
Total liabilities	$$$$
Owners' equity	$$$
Total liabilities and owners' equity	$$$$$

THESE TWO AMOUNTS MUST BE EQUAL

Discussion Question ●

3–5. Prepare a personal balance sheet for yourself in accounting and report formats using the assets and liabilities you listed for Discussion Questions 3–3 and 3–4.

The balance sheet is a financial "snapshot" of a company. It represents the assets the company possessed and who had claim to those assets on the day the snapshot was taken. Now we will explore the balance sheets of proprietorships, partnerships, and corporations.

◆ STARTING A PROPRIETORSHIP OR PARTNERSHIP: INVESTMENTS BY OWNERS

Jessica Lynne has worked in the cosmetics industry for several years and would like to start a business distributing health and beauty aids to retail outlets. What does she need to do? Well, she will have to establish relationships with suppliers and carve out a market for the products she will sell. And, she will also need to buy the desks, computers, and the other business equipment she needs to begin her business, even if she works out of her house. If she wants to start bigger, she may need to rent office space and hire employees, among other things.

Even the smallest company has start-up costs. Therefore, Jessica's new operation needs cash! The business will need cash to buy equipment, merchandise, and to cover other costs. Any entrepreneur's first task in starting a new company is to get cash into the business so the business can get under way, and the initial funding almost always comes directly from the owner. In Jessica's case, she will have to transfer funds from her personal holdings to the business. Writing a personal check to the business and using it to open a business bank account under the company name most easily accomplishes this. Let's assume Jessica writes a personal check for $10,000 and deposits it into a business bank account for Jessica's Beauty Supply. Now, *the company's* records should reflect an increase in cash of $10,000 and an increase in owner's equity of $10,000, and the accounting equation would look like this:

$$\text{Assets} = \text{Liabilities} + \text{Owners' Equity}$$

$$\$10,000 = \quad \$0 \quad + \quad \$10,000$$

BALANCE SHEET FOR A PROPRIETORSHIP

If we assume that Jessica's Beauty Supply began operations on January 1, 2003, with a $10,000 cash investment from Jessica, the company's first balance sheet would look like the one in Exhibit 3–6.

EXHIBIT 3–6	Balance Sheet for a Proprietorship

Jessica's Beauty Supply
Balance Sheet
January 1, 2003

Assets:		Liabilities:	$ 0
Cash	$10,000		
		Owners' equity:	
		Jessica, capital	**10,000**
Total assets	$10,000	Total liabilities and	
		owners' equity	$10,000

We use the word *capital* to represent the owner's claim to the assets held by a sole proprietorship. Since the capital in our simple example company includes no earned equity yet, capital in this case is made up entirely of investments by the owner. In a proprietorship, there is only one owner so there will be only one capital amount.

If we now assume that Jessica had started the business with another individual, the business would be a partnership instead of a proprietorship. The balance sheet for a partnership is slightly different from that of a proprietorship because the equity section reflects more than one owner and perhaps a different company name.

BALANCE SHEET FOR A PARTNERSHIP

Partnerships, you recall from Chapter 1, are similar to proprietorships, except that they have more than one owner. If we assume that Jessica invests $6,000 and a partner, Stephanie Meadows, invests $4,000, the first balance sheet for the company would look like the one in Exhibit 3–7.

EXHIBIT 3–7   Balance Sheet for a Partnership

Jessica and Stephanie's Beauty Supply
Balance Sheet
January 1, 2003

Assets:		Liabilities:	$ 0
Cash	$10,000		
		Owners' equity:	
		Jessica, capital	**$ 6,000**
		Stephanie, capital	**4,000**
		Total liabilities and	
Total assets	$10,000	owners' equity	$10,000

When we compare the balance sheet for this partnership with that for the proprietorship (Exhibit 3–6), we notice that they are very similar except that the company names are different and equity section of the partnership's balance sheet shows a separate capital amount for each partner.

◆   STARTING A CORPORATION

Unlike proprietorships and partnerships, corporations are legal entities, separate from their owners. With very few exceptions, such as national banks that must be incorporated under federal law, incorporators obtain a corporate charter from one of the 50 states to create a corporation. This charter is a legal agreement between the corporation and the state allowing the company to conduct business as a distinct, separate legal entity with many of the same rights as individuals.

CORPORATE ORGANIZATIONAL STRUCTURE

To form a corporation, the *incorporators* must submit a formal application for a *corporate charter* to an appropriate state agency. The application, called the *articles of incorporation*, generally must include (1) basic information about the corporation and its purpose; (2) details concerning the types of stock the corporation will issue; and (3) the names and addresses of the individuals responsible for the corporation.

If the state agency approves the application, it issues a *charter* that entitles the corporation to begin operations. The incorporators then meet to formulate the *corporate bylaws*. These bylaws serve as basic rules for management to use in conducting the corporation's business. Next, the corporation raises capital by issuing stock, thereby exchanging ownership interests in the corporation for cash or other assets. Once the stock has been issued, the stockholders elect a *board of directors* that will be responsible for overall policy and strategic direction. The directors meet and appoint a *president*, who will be responsible for day-to-day operations and management, and other *officers*, as they deem necessary to manage the company.

CORPORATE CAPITAL STRUCTURE

As part of the formal application to create a corporation, the incorporators must include information regarding their plans to sell shares of stock. They request the authority to issue (sell) a certain number of shares of stock, called **authorized shares.** Authorized shares are the maximum number of shares a corporation can legally issue under its corporate charter. These authorized shares do not really exist until they are issued, however, and ownership of the corporation is based on issued, not authorized, shares. For example, even though ***Best Buy*** has 1 billion authorized shares, as of March 2001, only about one fifth of those shares have been issued. **Issued shares** are the shares of stock a corporation has already distributed to stockholders in exchange for cash or other assets. **Outstanding shares** are the shares of stock currently being held by stockholders. In many instances, the number of shares issued will equal the number of shares outstanding, but not always. Occasionally, a corporation reacquires shares of stock it has previously issued by purchasing them in the open market. This reacquired stock, called **treasury stock,** will cause the numbers of shares outstanding to be fewer than the number of shares issued. For example, assume a corporation has issued 100,000 shares of its stock and then later reacquires 2,000 of those shares. The company still has 100,000 shares issued but now has only 98,000 outstanding shares. The cash paid to reacquire the treasury stock is deducted from both cash and total stockholders' equity, which keeps the accounting equation in balance. In most instances, the number of shares companies reacquire as treasury stock is comparatively small relative to the number of shares issued. In the late 1990s, however, ***Honeywell, Inc.*** reacquired 60 million of its 180 million issued shares.

Discussion Question ●

3–6. What do you think would motivate a company to reacquire shares of its own stock in the open market?

For corporations, owners' equity is called *stockholders' equity* (sometimes *shareholders'* or *shareowners' equity*) and it is the excess of assets over liabilities, just as it is for proprietorships and partnerships. There are, however, some differences in the way equity items are classified on the balance sheet of a corporation.

On a corporation's balance sheet, common stock replaces the owners' capital designation. By law, most states require stockholders' equity to be divided into the portion invested by the owners and the portion of earnings the company retains. The amount the corporation receives in exchange for shares of stock is called **paid-in capital** or **contributed capital,** and a classification called **retained earnings** is used to reflect earnings kept in the company rather than distributed to the owners. When the corporate earnings are distributed to the owners, such a distribution is called **dividends.** Although not generally used in practice, a more descriptive term for retained earnings would be *reinvested earnings.* Total stockholders' equity is a combination of contributed capital and retained earnings.

Because corporations often have many stockholders, some into the thousands or even millions, the individual ownership interest of each stockholder is not disclosed on the face of the balance sheet. Instead, only totals of the ownership interests represented by each class of stock are shown. The two basic classes of stock are *common stock* and *preferred stock.*

Common Stock

Generally, **common stock** is the voting stock of the corporation, because each share of common stock represents a share of the corporation's ownership. If a company has 10,000 shares of common stock outstanding, for example, each of those shares represents 1/10,000th ownership of the company. If you own 1,500 of those shares, you own 15 percent of the company. Regularly (usually at least annually), all those who own shares of common stock—the owners—are invited to a shareholders meeting where they vote on matters of importance to the company. These matters might include approving the amount of dividends the company plans to give to the stockholders or approving plans to expand into new markets. The point is, common stockholders are the owners of the company, and (theoretically, at least) company management must

---

authorized shares The maximum number of shares of stock a corporation has been given permission to issue under its corporate charter.

issued shares Stock that has been distributed to the owners of the corporation in exchange for cash or other assets.

outstanding shares Shares of stock actually held by shareholders. The number may be different than that for issued shares because a corporation may reacquire its own stock (treasury stock).

treasury stock Corporate stock that has been issued and then reacquired by the corporation.

paid-in capital Total amount invested in a corporation by its shareholders.

contributed capital Another name for paid-in capital.

retained earnings The sum of all earnings of a corporation minus the amount of dividends declared.

dividends A distribution of earnings from a corporation to its owners. Dividends are most commonly distributed in the form of cash.

common stock A share of ownership in a corporation. Each share represents one vote in the election of the board of directors and other pertinent corporate matters.

obtain approval from those stockholders before it can take significant steps involving the owners' investment. The stockholders' equity section of a corporate balance sheet shows information about common stock, such as the number of shares authorized, the number of shares issued (and the dollar amount the company received from the sale of those shares), and any shares that have been repurchased (treasury stock), including the dollar amount paid for those shares.

par value (stock)   An arbitrary amount assigned to each share of stock by the incorporators at the time of incorporation.

Common stock may or may not have a par value. **Par value** is an arbitrary dollar amount assigned to the stock by the incorporators at the time they apply for the corporate charter. It has nothing to do with the market value of the stock, which is determined by the stock market. The legal reasons for having a par value no longer exist, and all 50 states have removed the par value requirement. So why do we discuss par value if it is no longer required? Because most of the large corporations in the United States were formed before the requirement was eliminated, so their stocks carry a par value. Also, for reasons that defy understanding, many incorporators elect to issue par value stock in newly formed corporations even though there is no longer any requirement to do so.

Discussion Question

3–7. If you were setting up a new corporation, would you establish a par value for your common stock? Why or why not?

Most corporations set the par value of their stock considerably below its actual value because, historically, most states did not allow stock to be sold for less than its par. It is not unusual to see par values of $1 per share or even lower. *Pfizer Inc.*, for example, has a par value on its stock of five cents per share and some have even lower par. Exhibit 3–8 shows a comparison of par and market values for some major corporate common stock.

EXHIBIT 3–8	Examples of Par Value Versus Market Value of Common Stock (August 18, 2002)	
Company	*Par Value*	*Market Value (August 18, 2002)*
GM	1 2/3¢	$25.00
IBM	20¢	79.35
GE	6¢	31.55
Philip Morris	33 1/3¢	50.95
Chevron	75¢	76.92
Boeing	$5.00	37.50
PepsiCo	.01 2/3¢	44.39

Instead of a par value, some companies have a *stated value* for their common stock, which for all practical purposes is the same thing as a par value. For example, *Wendy's* common stock has a stated value of $.10 per share.

Preferred Stock

preferred stock   A share of ownership in a corporation that has preference over common stock as to dividends and as to assets upon liquidation of the corporation. Usually non-voting stock.

Preferred stock, also called *preference stock*, is another type of stock some companies issue. It has different features than common stock. Preferred stockholders do not have voting rights (and are therefore not owners of the corporation), but they receive a variety of other benefits. Although these benefits differ somewhat from one preferred stock issue to another, two ownership benefits normally found in preferred stock agreements are:

- Preferred stockholders must receive their dividend before any dividend can be paid to common stockholders.
- In the event of a corporation's liquidation, preferred stockholders receive their distribution of assets before any assets can be distributed to common stockholders. Liquidation refers to the process of going out of business.

The stockholders' equity section of a corporate balance sheet shows information about preferred stock, such as the number of shares authorized and the number of shares issued (including the dollar amount the company received from the sale of those shares). Usually, preferred stock precedes common in the balance sheet presentation.

Preferred stock may have a par value. Although par value has little meaning for common stock, the par value of preferred stock may be important because dividends are often stated as a percentage of the stock's par value. For example, if a corporation issued 8 percent preferred stock with a par value of $100 per share, the annual dividend would be $8 per share ($100 × 8% = $8). Among other things, corporations must offer a reasonable dividend to encourage investors to buy their preferred stock. When the dividends are stated as a percentage of par, preferred stock usually has a par value of $50 to $100. Investors in preferred stock tend to be conservative investors, and they frequently buy preferred stock to earn a guaranteed rate of return through the stated dividend.

Sometimes preferred stock dividends are not expressed as a percentage of par, but rather as a specific dollar amount per share. In such a case, the stock is described by the dollar amount of the dividend per share. For example, *Colgate* designates a dividend of $4.25 per share for its preferred stock. In its annual report, *Colgate* describes this stock as its $4.25 Preferred Stock.

CONSTRUCTING THE CORPORATE BALANCE SHEET

To demonstrate how to construct a corporate balance sheet, let's return to Jessica and her beauty supply company, and assume that Jessica selects the corporate form organization for her new company. Further assume that Jessica, acting as the incorporator, has received a corporate charter from the State of Florida for her new business, aptly named Jessica's Beauty Supply, Inc.

To provide the initial financing for the operation, Jessica intends to invest $40,000 in the new venture and would like to maintain complete control of the company. Stephanie, Jessica's lifelong friend, does not want to participate actively in the company but has great faith in Jessica's abilities and wants to invest about $20,000 in the corporation.

After hours of discussion, Jessica and Stephanie agree that Jessica will purchase 4,000 shares of the company's one-dollar par common stock for $40,000 and Stephanie will purchase 200 shares of the company's 8 percent, $100 par preferred stock for $105 per share or $21,000.

As we prepare the new company's balance sheet, we must keep in mind that we are looking at this situation from the corporation's point of view, not the point of view of the stockholders. The corporation receives a total of $61,000 in cash from Jessica and Stephanie so the corporation's assets, cash in this case, increase by that amount. The transaction also affects the stockholders' equity because the corporation must show that Jessica has a $40,000 common stock ownership interest and Stephanie has a $21,000 preferred stock ownership interest in the corporation.

additional paid-in capital
The amount in excess of the stock's par value received by the corporation when par value stock is issued.

paid-in capital in excess of par   Same thing as additional paid-in capital.

If a stock carries a par value, only the par value of the stock multiplied by the number of shares issued is classified as stock. Any amount received in excess of the stock's par value is classified on the balance sheet as **additional paid-in capital,** sometimes called **paid-in capital in excess of par** or a similarly descriptive title. At one time, the laws governing corporations in all states required this accounting treatment, and even though this requirement no longer exists in most states, companies still show stock this way on the balance sheet. What this means in our example is that of the $40,000 the company received from Jessica in exchange for the $1 par value common stock, $4,000 (4,000 shares × $1 par value) is classified as Common Stock and the remaining $36,000 is classified as Additional Paid-In Capital—Common. For the sale of the $100 par preferred stock to Stephanie, $20,000 (200 shares × $100 par value) is classified as preferred stock and the remaining $1,000 is classified as Additional Paid-In Capital—Preferred. Exhibit 3–9 shows a balance sheet for Jessica's Beauty Supply, Inc., immediately following the sale of the preferred and common stock.

Jessica's Beauty Supply, Inc.
Balance Sheet
January 1, 2003

Assets:		Liabilities:	
Cash	$61,000		$ 0
		Stockholders' equity:	
		Preferred stock	**$20,000**
		Additional paid-in capital—preferred	**1,000**
		Common stock	**4,000**
		Additional paid-in capital—common	**36,000**
		Total stockholders' equity	61,000
Total assets	$61,000	Total liabilities and stockholders' equity	$61,000

EXHIBIT 3–9   Corporate Balance Sheet with Preferred and Common Stock

The total dollar amount the balance sheet shows for the preferred and common stock is simply the amounts the company received for the stock. As time goes on, the value of these stocks will likely fluctuate as conditions in the company and in the economy change. To use a balance sheet effectively, you must understand what it *can* and *cannot* tell you. A company's balance sheet does not keep track of a stock's current value because it does not reflect the changes in a stock's market value. It can only tell you the amount the company received when it originally sold the stock. In other words, the balance sheet tells you how much the company sold the stock for, but it does not tell you how much the stock is currently worth. Although this practice makes the balance sheet less relevant, it prevents manipulation so the balance sheet amounts are more reliable.

Discussion Question ●●●●●●●●●●●●●●●●●●●●●●●●●●●●●●●●●●●●

3–8. If you were to look at the balance sheet for **Harley-Davidson, Inc.,** it would not show the current market value of its shares of stock. Where can an investor find this information?

We should mention that if Jessica had been wise enough not to have a par value for her corporation's common stock, the company would have classified the entire $40,000 received from issuing the stock as common stock. There would be no need for a classification for additional paid-in capital—common.

We mentioned at the beginning of this chapter that businesses obtain external financing from two sources, equity financing and debt financing. We have illustrated the impact of equity financing on the balance sheet and will now turn our attention to debt financing.

◆ DEBT FINANCING

Neither a borrower nor a lender be!

—WILLIAM SHAKESPEARE

Although Shakespeare's advice may serve you well in your personal life, most companies could not survive without borrowing. Borrowing and lending have become an integral part of today's business world. It is truly a win–win situation. The borrower is happy to get the needed cash and the lender is happy to put cash to work earning interest.

Companies borrow funds for various reasons, and the need for external funding is *not* necessarily a sign of weakness. For example, some very strong companies, including **Goodyear, Dow Chemical,** and **Coca-Cola,** regularly finance their operations by borrowing. In fact, many very successful companies need to borrow cash because they are growing so fast that the cash provided from their business operations just can't keep up. In this section, you will learn about two debt-financing options: borrowing from financial institutions and borrowing by issuing bonds.

BORROWING FROM FINANCIAL INSTITUTIONS—PROMISSORY NOTES

For most of us, there will come a time when we want something but we just don't have enough money to pay for it, such as when we want to buy a house or a car. We don't want to wait until we have saved enough money to pay for it; we want it now. Lucky for us, we can borrow the money we need from a financial institution, such as a bank. By borrowing the money we need to buy a house, a car, or some other asset, we have the benefit of using the asset while we pay for it. Companies do much the same thing, except as they use the asset, they actually use it to earn a profit that will meet or exceed the amount they need for the loan payments.

Banks and other financial institutions must meet the borrowing needs of both individuals and businesses. If the purpose of a loan is personal, that is to say that the loan is for a nonbusiness purpose, the loan is called **consumer borrowing.** When a loan is to a business for a business purpose, the loan is called **commercial borrowing.**

Several distinct types of financial institutions serve the needs of consumer and commercial borrowers. Some, such as *savings and loan associations (S&Ls), mutual savings banks (MSBs)*, and *credit unions (CUs)*, originated to satisfy the need for consumer loans but have since begun to branch into commercial lending. Others, most notably *commercial banks*, were established specifically to meet the financing needs of businesses.

As the name implies, commercial banks are heavily involved in commercial lending, although they also offer consumer financing. At *Citibank,* the earnings from its consumer banking are about equal to that from its commercial banking services.

Whenever a company borrows money, most lenders require it to sign a promissory note. A **promissory note** is a written agreement or debt instrument between a lender and a borrower that sets forth the terms of the liability and the stipulations for the borrower to repay both principal and interest. Borrowers reflect the debt associated with a promissory note as a *note payable* in the liabilities section of their balance sheets. The reason it is called a note payable is that, after all, it is a promissory *note*, and it is an amount *payable* by the company. Borrowing cash by signing a promissory note adds to the assets of the company (cash), but at the same time creates a liability.

In addition to signing a promissory note, the lender may require the borrower to put up collateral to secure the loan. Such a loan is called a *secured loan*, whereas if no collateral is pledged to secure the loan, the loan is called an *unsecured loan*. **Collateral** is something of value that the borrower would forfeit to the lender if the borrower fails to make payments as agreed. For example, when a company borrows money from *Citibank* to buy real estate, the bank may require that the real estate serve as collateral for the loan. If the company fails to make the payments, *Citibank* will repossess the real estate and sell it to get its money back. Although it is very common for small and medium-sized companies to secure their borrowing with collateral, most of the borrowing by large companies is unsecured.

When the loan is backed by collateral, the lender has less risk, so companies can borrow more money for a greater length of time at a lower interest rate. The loan document that identifies the collateral and specifies other legal aspects of the loan agreement is called a **mortgage.** When a company uses a mortgage to borrow, the loan appears on the balance sheet as a *mortgage payable*. The difference between a notes payable and a mortgage payable is the absence or presence of collateral, respectively.

THE COST OF BORROWING

You can't use someone else's money for free. There is a cost, and that cost is called interest. The difference between the amount one borrows and the amount one repays is the cost of borrowing, or interest. The cost of borrowing can be determined once we

---

consumer borrowing Loans obtained by individuals to buy homes, cars, or other personal property.

commercial borrowing The process that businesses go through to obtain financing.

promissory note A written promise to repay a loan.

collateral Something of value that will be forfeited if a borrower fails to make payments as agreed.

mortgage A document that states the agreement between a lender and a borrower who has secured the loan by offering something of value as collateral.

know three things—the amount borrowed, the interest rate, and the loan period. Consider the following example:

> *Boston Brothers borrowed $5,000 on January 2, 2003, by signing an 8 percent, three-month note.*

Because interest rates are almost always stated as an annual percentage, the 8 percent refers to the amount of interest the lender would require for one full year, regardless of the length of time of the loan. Interest is based on the amount borrowed, called the **principal.** The formula to determine the interest amount is:

principal In the case of notes and mortgages, the amount of funds actually borrowed.

$$\text{Principal} \times \text{Rate} \times \text{Time} = \text{Interest}$$
$$P \quad \times \quad R \quad \times \quad T \quad = \quad I$$

In the above equation, *principal* refers to the outstanding balance of the loan, *rate* refers to the annual interest percentage, and *time* refers to the period of time for which we are calculating interest. If the interest period is for less than a whole year, as it is in our example, time is expressed as the fractional part of a year. For example, if we are calculating interest for one month, the fraction would be 1/12. In our example, the loan is for three months, so the time period equals 3/12. If the interest calculation is for a whole year, the time period is equal to one, so it is generally not even shown in the equation. As we have said, in our example, since the funds are borrowed for three months, time is represented by 3/12, indicating three of the 12 months in a year. The amount of interest due at the end of the three-month period for our example is:

$$P \quad \times R \times \quad T \quad = \quad I$$
$$\$5{,}000 \times .08 \times 3/12 = \$100$$

(Notice that for purposes of calculations, we converted the percentage rates to decimals.)

If the loan had been for an entire year, the interest would be calculated as follows:

$$P \quad \times R \times T = \quad I$$
$$\$5{,}000 \times .08 \times 1 = \$400$$

Or simply:

$$P \quad \times R = \quad I$$
$$\$5{,}000 \times .08 = \$400$$

Remember that the difference between the amount borrowed and the amount paid back represents the cost of borrowing. For the one-year example, the cost of borrowing is $400. It is calculated as follows:

Amount repaid over the life of a loan:

Interest **($5,000 × 8%)**	$ 400
Principal	5,000
Total cash outflow to pay lender	$ 5,400
Less: Original amount borrowed	(5,000)
Cost of borrowing (interest)	$ 400

Discussion Questions •

3–9. In the example of the Boston Brothers' three-month loan, what is the lender's return of investment and what is their return on investment?

The next two Discussion Questions require that you look up the current interest rates in the business section of your local newspaper.

3–10. List the different rates a local bank is paying on various certificates of deposit (CDs). Explain why the bank is offering these various rates.

3–11. What are the current rates banks are charging for mortgages in your area? What are the current credit card rates? Why are there differences between these two rates?

BORROWING BY ISSUING BONDS

bond An interest-bearing debt instrument that allows corporations to borrow large amounts of funds for long periods of time and creates a liability for the borrower.

A **bond** is a type of promissory note, usually a $1,000 interest-bearing debt instrument. The main differences between borrowing with bonds and borrowing with other promissory notes are the length of the loan and the amount of money borrowed and the number of lenders involved. Other promissory notes are usually up to 10 years in duration and are often limited to the amount of money a single lender feels it can lend to one customer. Bonds can have very long terms, say, 40 years or more. By selling bonds to many different investors, the total amount the company borrows can exceed what one bank could (or would) lend. Most often, bonds are sold without a pledge of collateral. These bonds are called **debenture bonds.**

debenture bond An unsecured bond payable.

Bonds are issued in set denominations, generally $1,000 for each bond. That set denomination is printed right on the face of the bond and is called the bond's **par value,** also called the *face value* or the *maturity value.* What this means is that when the par value is $1,000, the borrower repays $1,000 when the bond matures. Companies must provide information in their annual report for each bond issue including its par value, its interest rate, the timing of interest payments, and the bond's maturity date. The legal document that details the bond agreement and all the pertinent details is called an **indenture.** See Exhibit 3–10 for examples of corporate bonds.

par value (bonds) The amount that must be paid back upon maturity of a bond. Also called face value or maturity value.

indenture The legal agreement made between a bond issuer and a bondholder that states repayment terms and other details.

| EXHIBIT 3–10 | Examples of Corporate Bonds |

Source: The Bond Market Association

nominal interest rate The interest rate set by the issuers of bonds, stated as a percentage of the par value of the bonds. Also called the contract rate.

The **nominal interest rate** is the interest rate printed on the bond and used to calculate the bond's interest payments. It is always stated as a percentage of the par value of the bond. In other words, it is the interest rate the issuing company (the borrower) has agreed to pay on the face value of the bond. The nominal rate is also called the *contract rate*, *coupon rate*, or *stated rate*, and these terms are used interchangeably.

effective interest rate The rate of interest actually earned by a lender. This amount will be different from the nominal interest rate if a bond is bought at a discount or premium, or a note is discounted. Also called yield rate or market interest rate.

In contrast to the nominal interest rate, which is printed right on the bond and therefore remains constant, the effective interest rate fluctuates with market conditions. The **effective interest rate** is the actual interest rate the bondholder will earn over the life of the bond. Unlike the nominal rate, which is determined by the issuing company, the effective rate is determined by the financial markets and may cause a bond to sell for more or less than its par value. That's right, the rate printed on the bond cannot be changed, and so to *effectively* change the rate of interest the bondholder will earn, the *selling price* of the bond is adjusted. The effective rate is also called the *yield rate* or *market interest rate*, and these terms are used interchangeably.

market price (of bonds) The amount that investors are actually willing to pay for a bond. A bond's selling price.

A bond's **market price,** also called the bond's *selling price*, is the amount that investors are actually willing to pay for the bond. The effective interest rate that investors demand for a particular bond determines its selling price. Bond prices are stated in terms of their par value. A bond selling "at 100" means that it is selling at 100 percent of its par value. Likewise, a bond selling "at 102" is selling for 102 percent of its par value and a bond selling "at 97" is selling at 97 percent of its par value. If the bond is selling for more than its par value, it is selling at a **premium;** if it is selling for less than its par value, it is

premium If a bond's selling price is above its par value, the bond is being sold at a premium.

discount   If a bond's selling price is below its par value, the bond is being sold at a discount.

selling at a **discount.** Now, as we said, the effective interest rate that investors demand for a particular bond will determine whether the bond sells at par, at a premium, or at a discount. If the effective interest rate and the nominal interest rate are the same, the bond will sell at par or at 100. If the effective interest rate that investors demand is higher than the bond's nominal interest rate, investors will not buy the bonds at par. If you think about it, you will realize why bonds sell for more or less than their par values. Imagine that you are trying to sell a bond at its face value when the bond has a nominal interest rate of 8 percent, in a market where investors are getting 9 percent on similar bonds. Would anyone buy your bond? Probably not, unless you do what any department store does when its merchandise is not selling. You reduce the selling price. In other words, you discount the price of the bond until it sells. At that magical selling price, the effective interest rate on the bond will equal the rate the market demands for such an investment.

For example, assume Yoko Industries issues 1,000, 12 percent, 10-year, $1,000 bonds at 95. The bonds sell below par because investors in the market require a higher rate of return than the bond's 12 percent nominal rate. The total cost of borrowing is calculated as follows:

Interest **($1,000,000 × 12% × 10 years)**	$1,200,000
Principal **(1,000 bonds × $1,000 face)**	1,000,000
Total cash outflow from issuer of bonds	$2,200,000
Less: Original bond proceeds from investors **($1,000,000 × 95%)**	(950,000)
Net cost to the issuer and return on investment to the investors	$1,250,000

As you can see, the total cost of borrowing ($1,250,000) for 10 years exceeds the cash payments for interest ($1,200,000). This $50,000 difference is due to the lower selling price of the bond and is technically considered part of interest cost. Therefore, the effective interest rate is higher than the 12 percent nominal interest rate. Because bond terms exceed one year, the effective interest rate must be computed using present value techniques. These calculations are beyond the scope of this text.

As we have mentioned, bonds may also sell at a premium, or for more than their par value. This happens when a bond's stated interest rate is more than the market interest rate. For instance, assume that Matson Industries is trying to sell its bond issue of 1,000, 12 percent, 10-year, $1,000 bonds. Assume further that the market interest rate for similar securities is less than 12 percent. If Matson sells the bonds at par, investors would clamor to buy them because they pay 12 percent when other bonds in the market pay less than that. With such an outpouring of demand, Matson would soon realize that it can increase the selling price of the bonds to a point that they still sell, but at a normal pace. Let's say that this would occur when the company prices the bonds at 104. Although the calculations to determine this exact selling price for the bonds are beyond the scope of this course, we can see by the calculations below that if the bonds sell at 104, the total cost of borrowing is less than 12 percent interest.

Interest **($1,000,000 × 12% × 10 years)**	$1,200,000
Principal **(1,000 bonds × $1,000 face)**	1,000,000
Total cash outflow from issuer of bonds	$2,200,000
Less: Original bond proceeds from investors **($1,000,000 × 104%)**	(1,040,000)
Net cost to the issuer and return on investment to the investors	$1,160,000

The total cost of borrowing for 10 years is less than the cash interest paid, indicating that the bonds yield less than the cash interest paid, and therefore, the market interest rate required is less than the nominal interest rate.

CONSTRUCTING THE BALANCE SHEET REFLECTING DEBT

Building upon the example of Jessica's Beauty Supply, Inc., introduced earlier, assume that on January 1, 2003, the corporation borrowed $50,000 on a 9 percent, one-year promissory note and has issued 200, $1,000 ,10-year, 8 percent bonds at par ($200,000). The company's cash would increase by the amount of the borrowing ($250,000), and the two debts would be listed in the liability section of the balance sheet. Exhibit 3–11

```
                        Jessica's Beauty Supply, Inc.
                              Balance Sheet
                             January 1, 2003

Assets:                         Liabilities:
  Cash          $311,000          Notes payable                        $ 50,000
                                  Bonds payable                         200,000
                                Total liabilities                       250,000
                                Stockholders' equity:
                                  Preferred stock                        20,000
                                  Additional paid-in capital—preferred    1,000
                                  Common stock                            4,000
                                  Additional paid-in capital—common      36,000
                                Total stockholders' equity               61,000
Total assets    $311,000        Total liabilities and stockholders' equity $311,000
```

EXHIBIT 3–11   Corporate Balance Sheet with Notes and Bonds Payable

shows the balance sheet for Jessica's Beauty Supply, Inc., immediately after the company borrowed the $250,000.

The balance sheet information indicates that the company has borrowed $50,000 on a promissory note and $200,000 by issuing bonds. The borrowing provided the company with $250,000 additional cash, so total assets rose to $311,000. Jessica's Beauty Supply, Inc., now owes the bank $50,000 and bondholders $200,000. Notice that even with this change, the business equation still holds true:

	Assets	=	Liabilities	+	Owners' Equity
Sale of stock:					
Common	$ 40,000	=	00	+	$40,000
Preferred	$ 21,000	=	00	+	$21,000
Borrowing:					
Promissory note	$ 50,000	=	$ 50,000	+	00
Bond issue	$200,000	=	$200,000	+	00
Totals	$311,000	=	$250,000	+	$61,000

We should point out that in real life it would be highly unlikely for a fledgling company such as the one in our example to actually issue $200,000 in bonds to the general public. It would be difficult, if not impossible, for the company to meet the SEC requirements for such a bond issue, and further, it is very unlikely that anyone in the investing public would buy the bonds of a new, unknown company.

◆ USING CASH TO ACQUIRE ASSETS

Once a company secures the financing it needs, it can use the cash to purchase the various assets it will need for its business operation. Let's assume, for example, that Jessica's Beauty Supply, Inc., uses the cash it has obtained to purchase land for $50,000, a building for $120,000, computer equipment for $35,000, and a small truck for $25,000. Even after these assets have been purchased, the following presentation shows that the accounting equation still holds true.

	Assets	=	Liabilities	+	Owners' Equity
Sale of stock:					
Common	$ 40,000	=	00	+	$40,000
Preferred	21,000	=	00	+	21,000
Borrowing:					
Promissory note	50,000	=	50,000	+	00
Bond issue	200,000	=	200,000	+	00

Purchase of assets

Cash	(230,000)
Land	50,000
Building	120,000
Computer equipment	35,000
Truck	25,000

Total $311,000 = $250,000 + $61,000

Exhibit 3–12 shows the balance sheet for Jessica's Beauty Supply, Inc., immediately following the acquisition of these assets.

EXHIBIT 3–12   Corporate Balance Sheet with Various Assets

Jessica's Beauty Supply, Inc.
Balance Sheet
January 1, 2003

Assets:		Liabilities:	
Cash	$ 81,000	Notes payable	$ 50,000
Land	50,000	Bonds payable	200,000
Building	120,000	Total liabilities	250,000
Computer equipment	35,000	Stockholders' equity:	
Truck	25,000	Preferred stock	$ 20,000
		Additional paid-in capital—preferred	1,000
		Common stock	4,000
		Additional paid-in capital—common	36,000
		Total stockholders' equity	61,000
Total assets	$311,000	Total liabilities and stockholders' equity	$311,000

◆ EQUITY AND DEBT INVESTMENTS COMPARED

We presented equity and debt financing in this chapter from the standpoint of the company receiving the proceeds from the sale of stocks and bonds. We will now look at the same subject from the standpoint of the investor. Let's say you were trying to decide where to invest your money. Does it make more sense for you to buy stock (an equity investment) or to buy bonds (a debt investment)? Before you can decide, you need to ask how the two investment alternatives answer the three questions that should be posed by all economic decision makers:

1. Will I be paid?
2. When will I be paid?
3. How much will I be paid?

Remember that these three questions inherently consider a return *on* the investment and a return *of* the investment.

EQUITY INVESTMENTS

Question 1: *Will I Be Paid?* With equity investments, there is no way we can answer this question with absolute certainty; it is dependent on the present condition and future financial performance of the company in question. If it is a solid company with a good market for its products, if the economy is (and stays) strong, and if the industry is (and stays) healthy, you will probably receive both a return on and a return of your investment.

Question 2: *When Will I Be Paid?* We cannot answer this question with absolute certainty either. Payments on a stock investment are of two types. First, you may receive a periodic dividend on each share of stock you own. Remember, however, that corporations are not *required* to pay dividends. The company in which you invest may or may not pay dividends to its stockholders. Second, you can sell your stock, if other investors are willing to buy it. In any event, the company itself is under no obligation to return your investment. When you buy stock, you have contributed an amount to the company and must find a third party to buy your shares if you desire to sell them.

Question 3: *How Much Will I Be Paid?* Like the first two questions, we cannot answer this with absolute certainty. To answer it at all, we need to fully understand the two components of return on investment for an equity investment.

   a. *Dividends.* The dividend component is easy to understand. A company may pay no dividend, or if, for example, the company pays a $2.00 dividend, all we would have to do is to multiply the number of shares you own, say 1,000, by the $2.00 per share and we are able to readily determine that the dividend you would receive is $2,000. The dividend, if one is paid at all, would constitute a part of the return on your investment.

   b. *Stock Appreciation.* In most instances, stock appreciation represents the greater part of return on an equity investment. If the company performs well in the future, the price of each share of its common stock should increase. The stock appreciates in value because as the company earns profits, more and more investors will desire to own shares of its stock. They will, in effect, bid up the price. For example, suppose you purchased 1,000 shares of a particular stock for $22 per share. Assume further the company earns record profits and the stock's price rises to $34 per share. If you sell your 1,000 shares, you will have earned a return on investment of $12 per share, or a total of $12,000, calculated as follows:

	Per Share	Total
What you sold the stock for	$34	$34,000
What you paid for the stock	22	22,000
Your return on investment	$12	$12,000

Note that when you sell the stock, you received not only a return *on* your investment, but also a return *of* your investment as well.

In the final analysis, the equity investment alternative yields rather vague answers to the three questions. Now let us see how the debt investment alternative answers the same three questions.

DEBT INVESTMENTS

Question 1: *Will I Be Paid?* The answer to this first question is essentially the same for the debt investment alternative as it was for the equity investment alternative. That is, it is dependent on how the company in which you invest performs in the future. If it is a solid company with a good market for its products and/or services, if the economy is (and stays) strong, and if the industry is (and stays) healthy, you will probably receive both a return on and a return of your investment.

As a creditor of the company rather than a stockholder, you will have absolutely no voice in how the company conducts its business, as long as it makes the periodic interest payments on the bonds and accumulates a sufficient amount of cash to retire the bonds when they mature. If the company *does not* service the debt as it has agreed, it is technically in *default*, and if you and the other bondholders choose (the bondholders vote on this), you can actually take over the company. We might also note that, by law, companies must make their periodic interest payments before they can pay any dividends to shareholders.

Question 2: *When Will I Be Paid?* Assuming the company performs well enough to make the interest payments on the bonds and to retire them upon maturity, the answer to this question would be absolutely certain. The company would make interest payments and would pay off the bond in accordance with the terms of the bond.

Question 3: *How Much Will I Be Paid?* The answer to this question, too, is absolutely certain assuming the company performs well enough to meet the financial obligations created by issuing the bonds. Over the life of the bonds, you would earn a return on your investment in the form of interest adjusted for any bond premium or discount and, upon maturity of the bond, you would receive the return of your investment.

In the final analysis, if we can satisfy ourselves as to the answer to Question 1, the answers to the last two questions are very certain for the debt investment alternative.

WHICH IS BETTER, EQUITY INVESTMENTS OR DEBT INVESTMENTS?

Take a few minutes to ponder the way the two investment alternatives answered the three questions. Which investment would you rather make? On the surface, it appears to be no contest. Although the answer to Question 1 was essentially the same for both alternatives, the debt investment alternative is much more certain in its answers to Questions 2 and 3 than is the equity investment alternative. So why would anyone even consider the equity investment as an alternative? The one-word answer to that question is POTENTIAL!

Although risk is associated with any investment, equity investments are inherently riskier than debt investments. Oddly enough, the thing that provides bondholders with the answers to our Questions 2 and 3 in large part limits the potential return the bondholders will receive. This is because the return the bondholders will receive is stipulated in the terms of the bond. No such limitation accompanies common stock investments. The return that equity investors can potentially receive is dependent on the success of the company, not the stipulations in an agreement with the company. So with the additional risk associated with equity investments, comes the potential for greater reward. In other words, the potential associated with the equity investment alternative is theoretically unlimited.

Thus far, we have discussed equity and debt financing and how they affect the balance sheet. The balance sheet provides information about the assets of a company and the claims to those assets. Another financial statement, the statement of cash flows, serves a different purpose but is just as important. The statement of cash flows focuses on just one asset, cash, and it presents information about the changes in cash over time. Regardless of how much potential a business may have, without cash, it will never be able to realize that potential.

◆ STATEMENT OF CASH FLOWS

statement of cash flows
A financial statement that provides information about the causes of a change in the company's cash balance from the beginning to the end of a specific period.

The **statement of cash flows** shows a company's sources and uses of cash during a particular period of time. Unlike the balance sheet, which shows a particular point in time, the statement organizes cash flows based on three principal business activities: operating, investing, and financing. The statement of cash flows for ***Best Buy*** appears in Exhibit 3–13 on page F–90.

At this point, don't try to understand each and every item on the statement, just take note of the statement of cash flow's general format and use it as a reference as we describe it below.

OPERATING ACTIVITIES

operating activities
Activities that result in cash inflows and outflows generated from the normal course of business.

The **operating activities** section of the statement of cash flows includes cash inflows and outflows for revenues and expenses associated with a company's ongoing business operations. As we said at the beginning of this chapter, over the long term, the primary source of financing for a business should come from internal sources. Operating activities *are* those internal sources. We will discuss cash flows from operating activities in Chapter 4.

Best Buy Co., Inc. Consolidated Statements of Cash Flows $ in thousands			
For the Fiscal Years Ended	*March 3* *2001*	*Feb. 26* *2000*	*Feb. 27* *1999*
Operating Activities			
Net earnings	$ 395,839	$ 347,070	$ 216,282
Adjustments to reconcile net earnings to net cash provided by operating activities:			
Depreciation	167,369	103,709	73,627
Deferred income taxes	42,793	29,233	(749)
Other	20,609	5,832	4,740
Changes in operating assets and liabilities, net of acquired assets and liabilities:			
Receivables	(7,434)	(56,900)	(36,699)
Merchandise inventories	(143,969)	(137,315)	14,422
Other assets	(16,018)	(6,904)	(19,090)
Accounts payable	16,186	302,194	249,094
Other liabilities	198,721	91,715	89,639
Accrued income taxes	134,108	97,814	62,672
Total cash provided by operating activities	808,204	776,448	653,938
Investing Activities			
Additions to property and equipment	(657,706)	(361,024)	(165,698)
Acquisitions of businesses, net of cash acquired	(326,077)	—	—
Increase in recoverable costs from developed properties	(31,076)	(21,009)	(65,741)
Increase in other assets	(14,943)	(34,301)	(9,635)
Total cash used in investing activities	(1,029,802)	(416,334)	(241,074)
Financing Activities			
Long-term debt payments	(17,625)	(29,946)	(165,396)
Issuance of common stock	235,379	32,229	20,644
Repurchase of common stock	—	(397,451)	(2,462)
Total cash provided by (used in) financing activities	217,754	(395,168)	(147,214)
(Decrease) Increase in Cash and Cash Equivalents	(3,844)	(35,054)	265,650
Cash and Cash Equivalents at Beginning of Period	750,723	785,777	520,127
Cash and Cash Equivalents at End of Period	$ 746,879	$ 750,723	$ 785,777

EXHIBIT 3-13   ***Best Buy*'s** Statement of Cash Flows

INVESTING ACTIVITIES

investing activities
Business activities related to long-term assets. Examples are the purchase and sale of property, plant, and equipment.

The **investing activities** section of the statement of cash flows shows cash inflows and outflows for investments purchased or sold. In this context, *investments* include not only investments in securities such as stocks and bonds, but also investments in land, buildings, equipment, and other assets purchased for use by the business. In fact, if you look at recent statements of cash flows of such companies as **Wal-Mart, Royal Caribbean Cruises,** and **Best Buy,** the overwhelming majority of their cash outflow from investing activities was to purchase property, plant, and equipment.

Recall that our example company in this chapter, Jessica's Beauty Supply, Inc., used cash to purchase land, buildings, computer equipment, and a truck. All of these transactions are cash flows for investing activities.

FINANCING ACTIVITIES

financing activities
Business activities, such as the issuance of debt or equity and the payment of dividends, that focus on the external financing of the company.

The **financing activities** section of the statement of cash flows shows a firm's cash inflows and outflows from *external* financing. It includes cash inflows from borrowing and amounts received from the sale of company stock. Cash outflows from financing activities include debt repayments, distributions to owners to reduce (or eliminate) their investment, and profit distributions to owners. In the financing activities section of its most recent statement of cash flows, for example, **Best Buy** shows cash inflow from the sale of common stock and cash outflow for debt repayments. For example, Jessica's Beauty Supply, Inc., financed its operation by selling stock for $61,000, borrowing $50,000 on a promissory note, and issuing bonds totaling $200,000.

To prepare the statement of cash flows, the operating activities, investing activities, and financing activities cash flows are listed and totaled and then added to the beginning cash balance to arrive at the ending cash balance. A statement of cash flows for Jessica's Beauty Supply, Inc., showing both the investing activities and financing activities section is illustrated in Exhibit 3–14.

EXHIBIT 3–14   Statement of Cash Flows for Jessica's Beauty Supply, Inc.

Jessica's Beauty Supply, Inc.
Statement of Cash Flows
For the Month Ended January 31, 2003

Cash flows from operating activities:		
None	$ 0	
Net cash flows from operating activities		$ 0
Cash flows from investing activities:		
Purchase of land	$ (50,000)	
Purchase of building	(120,000)	
Purchase of computer equipment	(35,000)	
Purchase of truck	(25,000)	
Net cash flows from investing activities		$(230,000)
Cash flows from financing activities:		
Sale of common stock	40,000	
Sale of preferred stock	21,000	
Borrowing on note payable	50,000	
Sale of bonds	200,000	
Net cash flows from financing activities		311,000
Net change in cash		81,000
Cash at the beginning of the period		0
Cash at the end of the period		$ 81,000

As we said in Chapter 1, many people in business feel that the statement of cash flows is the most important financial statement. In addition to the extensive coverage of the statement in Chapter 10, we will further explore the facets of the statement of cash flows as we examine the income statement in Chapter 4.

◆ USING FINANCIAL INFORMATION

Charlene's Aunt Tillie recently passed away and left Charlene $1 million. After all the inheritance taxes were paid, Charlene received $750,000. Upon mature reflection, she decides to blow $250,000 on cars, world cruises, and other such extravagant items. She plans to invest the remaining $500,000. How should Charlene invest the $500,000?

Charlene should evaluate investment opportunities carefully, but how can she determine whether she will be paid at all, not to mention how much she will be paid and when she will be paid? The key to evaluating any investment alternative is reducing the uncertainty surrounding the prospects for receiving cash in the future. So, how can she accomplish this? You already know the answer. She can reduce uncertainty by using information—in this case financial information—to gain insight into the present condition and past performance of potential investments to help her form an opinion about the potential for future success of each investment.

To fully benefit from the financial information companies provide, decision makers should be able to analyze the information and draw conclusions that are relevant to the decisions that they are making. For example, the balance sheet and statement of cash flows for Jessica's Beauty Supply, Inc., seem to paint a bright picture with lots of cash coming in and a host of new assets for the company to use. With all the money in the bank, assets for its operation, the company is off to a good start, right? Well probably, but it is difficult to tell just by looking at individual items and amounts on the financial statements. Instead we need to analyze the financial statements.

financial statement analysis The process of looking beyond the face of the financial statements to gather more information.

Financial statement analysis entails looking closely at financial statements to scrutinize how the various financial statement items and amounts relate to one another and how they relate to those of other companies and industry averages. For example, we would probably all agree that it is a good thing to have assets totaling $311,000, but we would probably also all agree that it is not such a good thing if nearly all of the assets are financed by debt. In Jessica's case, the debt is $250,000. Is this too much? Well, for a major corporation, $250,000 in debt is nothing, but for an start-up company like Jessica's, it could be too much.

In the following section, we will look at the financial ratios that relate to the portion of the balance sheet we have covered thus far.

RATIO ANALYSIS

ratio analysis A technique for analyzing the relationship between two items from a company's financial statements for a given period.

The key concept of **ratio analysis** is that the *relationship* of one number to another may be just as important as the absolute dollar amounts of those numbers. For example, liabilities for Jessica's Beauty Supply, Inc., are only $250,000, a relatively small amount for a typical business. But when the amount is viewed in proportion to equity, $61,000, the amount for liabilities may seem disproportionately large by comparison.

Ratio analysis uses a series of calculations (ratios) to depict the relationships among financial statement amounts. Over the years, financial analysts have developed (invented) more and more ratios to accommodate their need for information. This has resulted in a myriad of ratios, many of which address the same or very similar areas of analysis. In this book, we will limit our calculations to 17 popular ratios. Lending institutions use financial ratios not only to evaluate potential loan candidates, but also as performance benchmarks. For example, the terms of *The Wet Seal, Inc.*'s borrowing require the company to maintain certain financial ratios and to achieve certain levels of annual income.

Keep in mind that the ratios in this text are not intended to be an all-inclusive list of ratios or even a list of what everyone believes are the best ratios. Our selection of ratios is intended to give adequate basic coverage of four main concerns—profitability, efficiency, liquidity, and solvency. Profitability has to do with a company's ability to generate income. Efficiency has to do with the amount of business a company conducts relative to its investment in assets. Liquidity has to do with a company's cash position and its ability to pay its near-term bills. We will discuss these topics in later chapters. Solvency has to do with how a company is financed and the company's prospects for making payments to creditors and owners over the long term. The two solvency ratios we will cover in this chapter are debt ratio and the total liabilities to net worth ratio.

Debt Ratio

debt ratio A solvency ratio that indicates what proportion of a company's assets is financed by debt.

The **debt ratio** measures the proportion of a company's assets financed by debt. Remember, either its creditors or its owners have claim to a company's assets. The debt ratio indicates the proportion of assets claimed by creditors. Like most ratios, the specifics for calculating the debt ratio vary somewhat, but generally the calculation looks something like this:

$$\text{Debt ratio} = \frac{\text{Total liabilities}}{\text{Total assets}}$$

Based on the balance sheet for Jessica's Beauty Supply, Inc., in Exhibit 3–12, the debt ratio is calculated as follows:

$$\frac{\$250,000}{\$311,000} = 0.80386 \text{ or } 80.4\%$$

The debt ratio for Jessica's Beauty Supply, Inc., indicates that 80.4 percent of the company's assets are financed by debt. By extension then, 19.6 percent of the company's assets are financed by equity. There is no consensus regarding how much of a company's assets should be financed by debt, and acceptable levels of debt may vary significantly among different industries. Generally, however, creditors feel more secure when debt financing is relatively light compared to financing from equity. The creditors feel more secure when the owners' risk of loss in the company is substantial enough that the owners will do what it takes to keep the company successful. From the owners' point of view, although a high debt ratio may help them avoid the risk of a substantial loss, they may want to keep debt to a minimum for another reason. For every dollar borrowed, the company must pay some amount of interest. The more interest the company must pay, the more the company is required to earn. Equity investors may want to keep debt to a minimum to avoid the risk of the company being unable to earn enough profits to make its interest payments.

Debt-to-Equity Ratio

debt-to-equity ratio A financial ratio that expresses the proportional relationship between liabilities and equity.

The **debt-to-equity ratio** expresses the proportional relationship between liabilities and equity. Many financial publications call this ratio the *total liabilities to net worth* ratio. You must remember this, because many of these publications do not include a ratio called the debt-to-equity ratio. They have the ratio but call it something else. The formula for this ratio is:

$$\text{Debt-to-equity ratio} = \frac{\text{Total liabilities}}{\text{Total equity}}$$

Both the items necessary to calculate the debt-to-equity ratio come from the balance sheet. As you can see, the numerator, total liabilities, is the same as it is for the debt ratio, and for the denominator, we use total equity. Based on the balance sheet for Jessica's Beauty Supply, Inc., in Exhibit 3–12, the debt-to-equity ratio is calculated as follows:

$$\frac{\$250,000}{\$61,000} = 4.1 \text{ to } 1$$

This ratio reveals essentially the same information as the debt ratio but presents it slightly differently. The lower the debt-to-equity ratio, the lower total debt is relative to total equity.

The debt-to-equity ratio for Jessica's Beauty Supply, Inc., indicates the total liabilities are a whopping 4.1 times larger than equity. That is, there is $4.10 of debt for every $1 of equity. As was the case with the debt ratio, there is no consensus regarding how much a company's liabilities should be relative to equity. Even so, the debt-to-equity ratio for Jessica's Beauty Supply, Inc., seems excessive. What do you think?

In this chapter, we began our look at the financial tools available to economic decision makers. Our focus was on the balance sheet, and we also began our discussion of the statement of cash flows. Chapter 4 will introduce you to two additional financial tools—the income statement and the statement of owners' equity.

Summary •

In many ways, *financial statements* are the primary tools available to company outsiders for solving economic problems. Like all tools, financial statements were developed in response to a specific need—the need for useful information for economic decision makers.

All companies must obtain capital (money) to support their operations. In the long run, companies must finance their activities with the profits they generate. This is called internal financing. However, at times, all companies must also obtain capital from sources other than the profits. This is called external financing. The two external sources of capital are equity financing and debt financing. Equity financing offers an ownership interest in the company in exchange for needed cash. Companies can also obtain additional financing through borrowing, called debt financing.

The balance sheet, which focuses on the present condition of a business, shows a financial snapshot of the company and the relationship of three accounting elements: assets, liabilities, and owners' equity. ASSETS = LIABILITIES + OWNERS' EQUITY. Assets are the things of value a company owns or controls. Liabilities are the debts a company owes. Equity is the ownership interest in a company. It is the difference between the company's assets and its liabilities on those assets. Corporate equity is comprised of paid-in capital and earned equity.

Stockholders provide cash or other assets to the corporation in exchange for ownership shares—shares of stock—in the company. Amounts received by the corporation in exchange for shares of stock are called contributed capital or paid-in capital. There are two basic classes of stock. Common stock is the voting stock of the corporation. Preferred stock, also called preference stock, does not vote but has certain preference features that common stock does not.

Another major source of external financing is debt financing, or borrowing. Whenever a company borrows funds from a bank, the bank requires it to sign a promissory note. Borrowing adds to the company's assets but also creates a liability. Interest is the "rent" lenders charge borrowers for the use of money.

Bonds are interest-bearing securities companies sell to borrow large amounts of money from many lenders. A bond's nominal interest rate is the interest rate printed on the bond, and it is used to calculate the bond's interest payments. A bond's effective interest rate is the actual interest rate the bondholder will earn over the life of the bond based on the selling price of the bond. Bond selling prices are stated in relation to their par value. A bond selling at a price above its par value is selling at a premium, and a bond selling for less than its par value is selling at a discount. The effective interest rate that investors demand and other market conditions determine bond selling prices.

When comparing investment opportunities, investors need the answers to three important questions: (1) Will I be paid? (2) When will I be paid? and (3) How much will I be paid? In large part, the trade-off between risks and potential rewards will determine the type of investments a person chooses. The key to evaluating investment alternatives is reducing the uncertainty surrounding the question: Will I be paid?

The statement of cash flows shows cash flows from operating, investing, and financing activities. The operating activities section of the statement shows cash flows for revenues and expenses and a company's ongoing business operations. The investing activities section of the statement shows cash flows for the purchase and sale of securities and certain other assets used in the company's operations. The financing activities section of the statement shows the cash flows associated with a firm's external financing activities.

Financial statement analysis entails looking closely at a financial statement to scrutinize how the various financial statement items and amounts relate to one another and how they relate to those of other companies and industry averages. Ratio analysis uses a series of calculations (ratios) to depict the relationship between two amounts from a company's financial statements of a given period. Ratio analysis focuses on four main areas—profitability, efficiency, liquidity, and solvency. Profitability has to do with a company's ability to generate income. Liquidity has to do with a company's cash position and its ability to pay its near-term bills. Solvency has to do with a company's financial well-being and its prospects for making payments to its owners and creditors over the long term. The debt ratio measures the proportion of company assets financed by debt. The debt-to-equity ratio indicates the relative size of liabilities, stated in terms of a proportion to equity.

Key Terms

- additional paid-in capital, F–80
- assets, F–71
- authorized shares, F–78
- balance sheet, F–71
- bond, F–84
- collateral, F–82
- commercial borrowing, F–82
- common stock, F–78
- consumer borrowing, F–82
- contract rate. *See* nominal interest rate
- contributed capital, F–78
- coupon rate. *See* nominal interest rate
- debenture bond, F–84
- debt financing, F–70
- debt ratio, F–92
- debt-to-equity ratio, F–93
- discount, F–85
- dividends, F–78

- earned equity, F–73
- effective interest rate, F–84
- equity, F–72
- equity financing, F–70
- external financing, F–70
- financial statement analysis, F–92
- financing activities, F–90
- indenture, F–84
- internal financing, F–70
- investing activities, F–90
- investments by owners, F–73
- issued shares, F–78
- liabilities, F–71
- market interest rate. *See* effective interest rate
- market price (of bonds), F–84
- mortgage, F–82
- net assets. *See* equity
- net worth. *See* equity

- nominal interest rate, F–84
- operating activities, F–89
- outstanding shares, F–78
- paid-in capital, F–78
- paid-in capital in excess of par, F–80
- par value (bonds), F–84
- par value (stock), F–79
- preferred stock, F–79
- premium, F–84
- principal, F–83
- promissory note, F–82
- ratio analysis, F–92
- retained earnings, F–78
- selling price (of bonds). *See* market price (of bonds)
- stated rate. *See* nominal interest rate
- statement of cash flows, F–89
- treasury stock, F–78
- yield rate. *See* effective interest rate

Review the Facts

A. Explain the difference between internal and external financing.
B. What are the two major sources of external financing?
C. List and define the three main balance sheet accounting elements.
D. Describe the two components of equity.
E. State the accounting equation.
F. Name and describe the two formats of the balance sheet.
G. How do the balance sheets of proprietorships differ from those of partnerships?
H. Explain the differences among authorized, issued, and outstanding shares of stock.
 I. Define the term *treasury stock*.
J. What are the two major classes of corporate stock and how do they differ?
K. What is meant by the par value of stock and what significance does it have?
L. What is interest on debt?
M. What is collateral? How can it help a borrower?
N. Explain the formula used to determine the amount of interest owed for a particular time period.
O. Why are bonds sometimes necessary to meet the borrowing needs of businesses?
P. Explain the terms *par value* and *stated rate* as they pertain to bonds.
Q. How do the nominal rate and the market rate of bonds differ?
R. Explain what causes a bond to sell for a premium or a discount.
S. Describe the effects of borrowing on the balance sheet of a business.
T. How does the statement of cash flows differ from the balance sheet?
U. Describe the purpose of operating, investing, and financing activities sections of the statement of cash flows.
V. What is financial statement analysis?
W. What is the key concept of ratio analysis?
X. What does the debt ratio measure?
Y. What does the debt-to-equity ratio indicate?

Apply What You Have Learned ●

LO 1: ACCOUNTING ELEMENTS

3–12. Below is a list of three accounting elements, followed by partial definitions of those items in scrambled order:

a. Assets   b. Liabilities   c. Equity

1. _____ Debts of the company
2. _____ Probable future economic benefits
3. _____ "Things" of value a company has
4. _____ The residual interest in the assets of an entity that remains after deducting its liabilities
5. _____ Probable future sacrifices of economic benefits
6. _____ What the company owes
7. _____ What the company has less what it owes
8. _____ The owner's interest in the company

Required: For each partial definition, identify the element (a, b, or c) to which it refers. Each letter will be used more than once.

LO 1: ACCOUNTING ELEMENTS

3–13. Below is a list of three accounting elements, followed by list of items in scrambled order:

a. Assets   b. Liabilities   c. Equity

1. _____ Cash
2. _____ Additional paid-in capital
3. _____ Bonds payable
4. _____ Land
5. _____ Common stock
6. _____ Retained earnings
7. _____ Notes payable
8. _____ Withdrawals
9. _____ Partners' capital
10. _____ Preferred stock

Required: For each item in the list, identify the element (a, b, or c) to which it refers. Each letter will be used more than once.

LO 1: ACCOUNTING EQUATION

3–14. a. Write the basic accounting equation.
　　　b. Define each element of the equation in your own words.
　　　c. Provide examples of each element of the basic accounting equation.

LO 3: TERMINOLOGY OF THE CORPORATE BUSINESS FORM

3–15. Below is a list of items relating to the corporate form of business, followed by definitions of those items in scrambled order:

a. Incorporators　　　f. Board of directors
b. Charter　　　　　　g. Corporate officers
c. Bylaws　　　　　　h. Par value
d. Stockholders　　　i. Additional paid-in capital
e. Stock certificate　j. Market value

1. _____ An arbitrary value placed on either common stock or preferred stock at the time a corporation is formed
2. _____ The group of men and women who have the ultimate responsibility for managing a corporation
3. _____ The owners of a corporation
4. _____ Any amount received by a corporation when it issues stock that is greater than the par value of the stock issued

5. _____ The formal document that legally allows a corporation to begin operations
6. _____ The group of men and women who manage the day-to-day operations of a corporation
7. _____ The person or persons who submit a formal application with the appropriate government agencies to form a corporation
8. _____ A legal document providing evidence of ownership in a corporation
9. _____ Rules established to conduct the business of a corporation
10. _____ The amount at which common stock sells

Required: Match the letter next to each item on the list with the appropriate definition. Use each letter only once.

LO 3: TERMINOLOGY OF THE CORPORATE FORM OF ORGANIZATION

3–16. a. Identify the various officers of a corporation and describe their individual duties.
   b. Explain the difference between authorized shares, issued shares, outstanding shares, and treasury stock.

LO 3: DIFFERENCES BETWEEN COMMON AND PREFERRED STOCK

3–17. A corporation is going out of business and has liquidated all of its assets and is about to distribute the limited proceeds to its preferred and common stockholders. Some of the preferred shareholders are worried that once a distribution is made to common shareholders, there won't be enough left for them. Are the preferred shareholders' concerns valid? Explain your answer.

LO 3: DIFFERENCES BETWEEN COMMON AND PREFERRED STOCK

3–18. Assume you have $20,000 to invest and you are trying to decide between investing in either the preferred stock or the common stock of Alpha Company.

Required:
   a. List and briefly explain at least two reasons why you would invest in the preferred stock rather than the common stock of Alpha Company.
   b. List and briefly explain at least two reasons why you would invest in the common stock rather than the preferred stock of Alpha Company.

LO 3: DIFFERENCES BETWEEN COMMON AND PREFERRED STOCK

3–19. For each characteristic listed below, determine if the characteristic applies to common stock (C), preferred stock (P), both (B), or neither (N).

   _____ Often has a par value
   _____ Must have a par value
   _____ Usually has voting rights
   _____ Usually does not have voting rights
   _____ Has preference in dividends
   _____ Has preference in liquidation
   _____ Is preferred by all investors

LO 3: DIFFERENCES BETWEEN COMMON AND PREFERRED STOCK

3–20. Discuss the characteristics of investors who invest in:

   a. Common stock
   b. Preferred stock

   Include in your discussion willingness to take risk, desire for current income, and desire for capital appreciation in addition to other factors.

LO 4: EFFECT OF INTEREST ON BANKS

3–21. Explain in your own words how banks make a profit when you borrow money to buy a new car.

LO 4: TERMINOLOGY

3–22. Below are some items related to notes payable and bonds payable, followed by definitions of those items in scrambled order.

a. Interest   f. Premium
b. Nominal interest rate   g. Principal
c. Effective interest rate   h. Defaulting
d. Maturity value   i. Notes payable
e. Discount   j. Bonds payable

1. _____ The amount above par value for which a bond is sold
2. _____ The amount of funds actually borrowed
3. _____ The rate of interest actually earned by a bondholder
4. _____ Failing to repay a loan as agreed
5. _____ Liabilities that allow corporations to borrow large amounts of money for long periods of time
6. _____ The cost of using someone else's money
7. _____ The amount below par value for which a bond is sold
8. _____ An agreement between a lender (usually a bank) and borrower that creates a liability for the borrower
9. _____ The interest rate set by the issuers of bonds, stated as a percentage of the par value of the bonds
10. _____ The amount that is payable at the end of a borrowing arrangement

Required: Match the letter next to each item on the list with the appropriate definition. Use each letter only once.

LO 4: TERMINOLOGY

3–23. Below are two definitions of items related to interest on bonds payable, followed by a list of terms used to describe bond interest.

a. The rate of interest actually earned by the bondholder
b. The interest rate set by the issuer of the bond, printed on the bond, and stated as a percentage of the par value of the bond

1. _____ Nominal interest rate
2. _____ Effective interest rate
3. _____ Stated interest rate
4. _____ Coupon rate
5. _____ The interest rate printed on the actual bond
6. _____ Market interest rate
7. _____ Contract rate
8. _____ Yield rate

Required: For each of the eight items above, indicate to which definition ("a" or "b") it refers. Each will be used more than once.

LO 2: CORPORATE BALANCE SHEET PREPARATION—STOCK ISSUANCES ONLY

3–24. Gaylord Corporation began operations on July 10, 2002, by issuing 10,000 shares of $5 par value common stock and 2,000 shares of $100 par value preferred stock. The common stock sold for $10 per share and the preferred stock sold for $130 per share.

Required: Prepare a balance sheet for Gaylord Corporation at July 10, 2002, immediately after the common stock and preferred stock were issued.

LO 2: CORPORATE BALANCE SHEET PREPARATION—STOCK ISSUANCES ONLY

3–25. Sheets Corporation began operations on May 5, 2003, by issuing 150,000 shares of $2 par value common stock and 25,000 shares of $100 par value preferred stock. The common stock sold for $10 per share and the preferred stock sold for $150 per share.

Required: Prepare a balance sheet for Sheets Corporation at May 5, 2003, immediately after the common stock and preferred stock were issued.

LO 2: CORPORATE BALANCE SHEET PREPARATION—STOCK ISSUANCES ONLY

3–26. Mayes Corporation began operations on April 15, 2003, by issuing 200,000 shares of no-par value common stock and 20,000 shares of $50 par value preferred stock. The common stock sold for $25 per share and the preferred stock sold for $125 per share.

Required: Prepare a balance sheet for Mayes Corporation at April 15, 2003, immediately after the common stock and preferred stock were issued.

LO 2: BALANCE SHEET PREPARATION WITH COMMON STOCK AND BORROWING ONLY

3–27. John Kenyon formed Offshore Racing Engines, Inc., on January 2, 2003. The company was established when it sold 1,200 shares of Offshore Racing Engines, Inc., common stock to John for $24,000. The common stock has a par value of $1 per share.

On January 3, 2003, the company borrowed $12,000 from APBA National Bank by signing a one-year, 9 percent note. The principal and interest on the note must be paid to the bank on January 2, 2004.

Required:

a. Prepare a balance sheet as of January 2, 2003, immediately following the $24,000 stock sale to John Kenyon, that is, before the company borrowed money.

b. Prepare a balance sheet as of January 3, 2003, that reflects both the $24,000 stock sale to John Kenyon and the $12,000 borrowed from the bank.

c. Calculate the amount of interest Offshore Racing Engines, Inc,. must pay on January 3, 2004.

d. Assume that the note was for six months rather than one year, so it must be repaid on July 3, 2003. Calculate the amount of interest Offshore Racing Engines, Inc., must pay on July 3, 2003.

LO 2 & 4: BALANCE SHEET PREPARATION WITH COMMON STOCK AND BOND FINANCING ONLY

3–28. Bobbye Miller formed Offshore Public Relations, Inc., on January 2, 2003. The company was established when it sold 3,000 shares of Offshore Public Relations, Inc., common stock to Bobbye for $30,000 cash. The common stock has a par value of $5 per share.

On January 3, 2003, Offshore Public Relations, Inc,. sold 100 of its $1,000, five-year, 9 percent bonds at par. Interest is to be paid semiannually on July 2 and January 2. The bonds must be repaid when they mature on January 2, 2008.

Required:

a. Prepare a balance sheet for Offshore Public Relations, Inc., as of January 2, 2003, to reflect the $30,000 stock sale to Bobbye Miller.

b. Prepare a balance sheet for Offshore Public Relations, Inc., as of January 3, 2003, to reflect both the $30,000 stock sale to Bobbye Miller and the sale of the bonds, assuming the bonds sold at their par value.

c. Calculate the amount of interest Offshore Public Relations, Inc., must pay each July 2 and January 2.

d. How much would Offshore Public Relations, Inc., have received from the sale of the bonds on January 3, 2003, if the bonds had sold at 99 (a discount)?

e. How much would Offshore Public Relations, Inc., have received from the sale of the bonds on January 3, 2003, if they had sold at 105 (a premium)?

LO 2: CORPORATE BALANCE SHEET PREPARATION

3–29. The following information is taken from accounting records of Seth Industries, Inc., as of December 31, 2003:

Cash	$ 33,000
Land	120,000
Building	580,000
Office equipment	15,000
Notes payable	650,000
Common stock (no par)	98,000

Required:

    a. Classify each item as follows:

        A = Asset
        L = Liability
        EQ = Equity

    b. Prepare a balance sheet for the company as of December 31, 2003.

LO 2: CORPORATE BALANCE SHEET PREPARATION

3–30. The following information is taken from accounting records of Zhang Corporation as of December 31, 2003:

Cash	$ 28,000
Inventory	92,000
Store equipment	5,000
Notes payable	35,000
Common stock (no par)	90,000

Required:

    a. Classify each item as follows:

        A = Asset
        L = Liability
        EQ = Equity

    b. Prepare a balance sheet for the company as of December 31, 2003.

LO 2: CORPORATE BALANCE SHEET PREPARATION

3–31. The following information is taken from accounting records of Amanda's Cooking Supplies as of December 31, 2003:

Cash	$ 53,000
Notes payable	118,000
Land	100,000
Building	120,000
Equipment	18,000
Common stock, $1 par	10,000
Additional paid-in capital	163,000

Required: Prepare a balance sheet for the company as of December 31, 2003.

LO 2: CORPORATE BALANCE SHEET PREPARATION

3–32. The following information is taken from accounting records of Bill Hudik's Photo Shop as of December 31, 2003:

Cash	$ 18,000
Inventory	81,000
Supplies inventory	3,000
Delivery truck	18,000
Notes payable	24,000
Bonds payable	51,000
Common stock, $2 par	1,500
Additional paid-in capital	43,500

Required:

    a. Classify each item as follows:

        A = Asset
        L = Liability
        EQ = Equity

    b. Prepare a balance sheet as of December 31, 2003.

LO 2: CORPORATE BALANCE SHEET PREPARATION

3–33. The following information is taken from accounting records of Levine Company as of December 31, 2003:

Cash	$ 89,000
Merchandise inventory	320,000
Store supplies inventory	4,000
Delivery truck	21,000
Notes payable	20,000
Bonds payable	125,000
Common stock, $3 par	15,000
Additional paid-in capital	274,000

Required: Prepare a balance sheet as of December 31, 2003.

LO 2: CORPORATE BALANCE SHEET PREPARATION

3–34. The following information is taken from accounting records of Stacy's Giftware, Inc., as of December 31, 2003:

Cash	$ 13,000
Supplies inventory	3,000
Land	242,000
Building	378,000
Delivery truck	15,000
Notes payable	24,000
Bonds payable	30,000
Common stock, $5 par	55,000
Additional paid-in capital—common	439,000
Preferred stock, $100 par	100,000
Additional paid-in capital—preferred	3,000

Required: Prepare a balance sheet for the company as of December 31, 2003.

LO 2: CORPORATE BALANCE SHEET PREPARATION

3–35. The following information is taken from accounting records of Sherry's Frame Shop as of December 31, 2003:

Preferred stock, $50 par	$ 75,000
Additional paid-in capital—preferred	2,000
Common stock, $1 par	62,000
Additional paid-in capital—common	188,000
Cash	55,000
Land	380,000
Buildings	698,000
Equipment	35,000
Notes payable	41,000
Bonds payable	800,000

Required: Prepare a balance sheet as of December 31, 2003.

LO 2: CORPORATE BALANCE SHEET PREPARATION

3–36. The following information is taken from accounting records of Sexton Sales Corporation as of December 31, 2003:

Common stock (no par)	$ 76,000
Preferred stock, $75 par	90,000
Additional paid-in capital—preferred	4,000
Inventory	40,000
Cash	11,000
Supplies inventory	1,000
Land	35,000
Building	87,000
Store equipment	23,000
Notes payable	27,000

Required: Prepare a balance sheet for the company as of December 31, 2003.

LO 2: CORPORATE BALANCE SHEET PREPARATION

3–37. The following information is taken from accounting records of Maupin Promotion Company as of December 31, 2003:

Cash	$ 11,000
Office equipment	65,000
Notes payable	8,000
Common stock, $1 par	500
Additional paid-in capital—common	14,500
Preferred stock, $50 par	50,000
Additional paid-in capital—preferred	3,000

Required: Prepare a balance sheet as of December 31, 2003.

LO 2: CORRECTION AND PREPARATION OF SIMPLE CORPORATE BALANCE SHEET

3–38. Examine the following balance sheet:

Karen Bean Enterprises
Balance Sheet
December 31, 2003

Assets:			Liabilities and owner's equity:	
Land	$100,000		Cash	$ 20,000
Less: Notes payable	20,000		Common stock, $10 par value	40,000
			Additional paid-in capital	50,000
			Retained earnings	10,000
Total assets	$120,000		Total liabilities and owner's equity	$120,000

Required:

    a. List the errors in the balance sheet.
    b. Prepare a corrected balance sheet.

LO 2: CORRECTION AND PREPARATION OF SIMPLE CORPORATE BALANCE SHEET

3–39. Examine the following balance sheet:

L. Stallworth, Inc.
Balance Sheet
December 31, 2003

Assets:			Liabilities and owner's equity:	
Cash	$50,000		Notes payable	$10,000
Retained earnings	10,000		Stallworth, capital, $10 par value	40,000
			Equipment	10,000
Total assets	$60,000		Total liabilities and owner's equity	$60,000

Required:

    a. List the errors in the balance sheet.
    b. Prepare a corrected balance sheet.

LO 2: CORRECTION AND PREPARATION OF SIMPLE CORPORATE BALANCE SHEET

3–40. Examine the following balance sheet:

Sweet Corporation
Balance Sheet
For the Year Ended December 31, 2003

Assets:			Liabilities and owner's equity:	
Cash	$120,000		Notes payable	$30,000
			Common stock, $1 par value	20,000
Additional paid-in capital	40,000		Retained earnings	30,000
Total assets	$160,000		Total liabilities and owner's equity	$80,000

Required:

    a. List the errors in the balance sheet.

    b. Prepare a corrected balance sheet.

LO 2 & 3: BALANCE SHEET PREPARATION—PROPRIETORSHIP, PARTNERSHIP, AND CORPORATION

3–41. On January 2, 2003, Randy Peoples started an appliance repair business.

Required:

    a. Prepare a balance sheet as of January 2, 2003, assuming Randy's company is a proprietorship named Randy Peoples Enterprises and that he invested $5,000 cash in the operation.

    b. Now assume that the business organized on January 2, 2003, was a partnership started by Randy and his brother Sandy, which they have named R&S Enterprises. Randy invested $2,000 and Sandy invested $3,000. Prepare a balance sheet as of January 2, 2003, for the partnership to reflect the partners' investment.

    c. Now assume that the business organized on January 2, 2003, was a corporation started by Randy and his brother Sandy, which they have named R&S Enterprises, Inc. Randy invested $2,000 and received 200 shares of common stock. Sandy invested $3,000 and received 300 shares of common stock. The common stock has a par value of $2 per share. Prepare a balance sheet as of January 2, 2003, for the company to reflect the stockholders' investment.

    d. Assume the same facts as in requirement c, except that the common stock is no-par stock. Prepare a balance sheet as of January 2, 2003, for the company to reflect the stockholders' investment.

LO 2 & 3: BALANCE SHEET PREPARATION—PROPRIETORSHIP, PARTNERSHIP, AND CORPORATION

3–42. On June 2, 2003, Arthur Johnson started a manufacturing business.

Required:

    a. Prepare a balance sheet as of June 2, 2003, assuming Arthur's company is a proprietorship named Arthur Johnson Enterprises and that he invested $50,000 cash in the operation.

    b. Now assume that the business organized on June 2, 2003, was a partnership started by Arthur and his friend Charles Smith, which they have named A&C Enterprises. Arthur invested $50,000 and Charles invested $30,000. Prepare a balance sheet as of June 2, 2003, for the partnership to reflect the partners' investment.

    c. Now assume that the business organized on June 2, 2003, was a corporation started by Arthur and his friend Charles, which they have named A&C Enterprises, Inc. Arthur invested $50,000 and received 5,000 shares of common stock. Charles invested $30,000 and received 3,000 shares of common stock. The common stock has a par value of $1 per share. Prepare a balance sheet as of June 2, 2003, for the company to reflect the stockholders' investment.

    d. Assume the same facts as in requirement c, except that the common stock is no-par stock. Prepare a balance sheet as of June 2, 2003, for the company to reflect the stockholders' investment.

LO 2 & 3: BALANCE SHEET PREPARATION—PROPRIETORSHIP, PARTNERSHIP, AND CORPORATION

3–43. On July 1, 2003, Fred Berfel started a retail business.

Required:

    a. Prepare a balance sheet as of July 1, 2003, assuming Fred's company is a proprietorship named Fred Berfel Enterprises and that he invested $90,000 cash in the operation.

    b. Now assume that the business organized on July 1, 2003, was a partnership started by Fred and his father Dan, which they have named F&D Enterprises. Fred invested $40,000 and Dan invested $50,000. Prepare a balance sheet as of July 1, 2003, for the partnership to reflect the partners' investment.

c. Now assume that the business organized on July 1, 2003, was a corporation started by Fred and his father Dan, which they have named F&D Enterprises, Inc. Fred invested $40,000 and received 4,000 shares of common stock. Dan invested $50,000 and received 5,000 shares of common stock. The common stock has a par value of $2 per share. Prepare a balance sheet as of July 1, 2003, for the company to reflect the stockholders' investment.

d. Assume the same facts as in requirement c, except that the common stock is no-par stock. Prepare a balance sheet as of July 1, 2003, for the company to reflect the stockholders' investment.

LO 2 & 3: BALANCE SHEET PREPARATION—PROPRIETORSHIP, PARTNERSHIP, AND CORPORATION

3–44. On March 1, 2003, Sandy Sanders started a business.

Required:

a. Prepare a balance sheet as of March 1, 2003, assuming Sandy's company is a sole proprietorship named Sandy Sanders Enterprises and that he invested $40,000 cash in the operation and a piece of land valued at $5,000.

b. Now assume that the business organized on March 1, 2003, was a partnership started by Sandy and his brother Darryl, which they have named S&D Enterprises. Sandy invested $40,000 cash and a piece of land valued at $10,000, and Darryl invested $30,000 cash. Prepare a balance sheet as of March 1, 2003, for the partnership to reflect the partners' investment.

c. Now assume that the business organized on March 1, 2003, was a corporation started by Sandy and his brother Darryl, which they have named S&D Enterprises, Inc. Sandy invested $40,000 cash and the piece of land valued at $10,000 and received 5,000 shares of common stock. Darryl invested $30,000 cash and received 3,000 shares of common stock. The common stock has a par value of $1 per share. Prepare a balance sheet as of March 1, 2003, for the company to reflect the stockholders' investment.

d. Assume the same facts as in requirement c, except that the common stock is no-par stock. Prepare a balance sheet as of March 1, 2003, for the company to reflect the stockholders' investment.

LO 2: COMPARE, CONTRAST BALANCE SHEETS OF THREE TYPES OF BUSINESS ORGANIZATIONS

3–45. The chapter discusses the balance sheet presentations for each of the three forms of business organization. Discuss the similarities and differences in the balance sheets of proprietorships, partnerships, and corporations.

LO 2 & 3: INTERPRETING STOCKHOLDERS' EQUITY

3–46. The balance sheet of Ramona Rahill, Inc., contains the following information in its equity section:

Stockholders' equity:	
Common stock, $5 par value, 1,000,000 shares authorized,	
800,000 shares issued and outstanding	$ 4,000,000
Additional paid-in capital	4,800,000
Retained earnings	2,000,000
Total stockholders' equity	$10,800,000

Required:

a. What is the maximum number of shares of stock that Rahill could issue if the board of directors desired to do so?

b. When the corporation sold its stock, what was the average selling price per share?

c. If the board of directors declared a $1.25 per share dividend, how much cash would be required to pay the dividend?

d. If Rahill has distributed $3,500,000 to shareholders since its formation, how much profit has the corporation earned since its formation?

LO 3: INTERPRETING STOCKHOLDERS' EQUITY

3–47. The balance sheet of Juliette Richard Corporation contains the following information in its equity section:

Stockholders' equity:
Common stock, $10 par value, 1,000,000 shares authorized,

800,000 shares issued and outstanding	$ 8,000,000
Additional paid-in capital	8,000,000
Retained earnings	9,500,000
Total stockholders' equity	$25,500,000

Required:

a. What is the maximum number of shares of stock that Richard Corporation could sell if the board of directors desired to do so?

b. When the corporation sold its stock, what was the average selling price per share?

c. If the board of directors declared a $2 per share dividend, how much cash would be required to issue the dividend?

d. If Richard has distributed $5,500,000 to shareholders since its formation, how much profit has the corporation earned since its formation?

e. If the board of directors wished to raise $5,000,000, how much would the average price per share need to be if all available shares were sold?

LO 2 & 3: INTERPRETING STOCKHOLDERS' EQUITY

3–48. The balance sheet of David Luza Corporation contains the following information in its equity section:

Stockholders' equity:
Common stock, $10 par value, 1,000,000 shares

authorized and issued and outstanding	$10,000,000
Additional paid-in capital	8,000,000
Retained earnings	9,500,000
Total stockholders' equity	$27,500,000

Required:

a. What is the maximum number of shares of stock that the corporation could sell if the board of directors desired to do so?

b. When the corporation sold its stock, what was the average selling price per share?

c. If the board of directors declared a $1.50 per share dividend, how much cash would be required to issue the dividend?

d. If Luza has earned $9,500,000 since its formation, how much profit has the corporation distributed to stockholders in the form of dividends since its formation?

e. If the current market price of the stock is $60 per share, how much cash could the board of directors raise if it sold all available shares?

LO 4 & 6: NOTES VS. BONDS

3–49. Miller Company needs to borrow funds to modernize its plant. Miller decided to issue $50 million worth of 30-year bonds in the bond market. Explain why Miller Company might issue bonds rather than borrowing from a bank.

LO 4: CALCULATING BOND PROCEEDS, BOND INTEREST, AND TOTAL BOND PAYMENTS

3–50. Assume that Zhang Company sells 6,500 of its five-year, $1,000 bonds paying 8 percent interest at 96.

Required:

a. How much cash will the company receive from the bond sale?

b. How much cash will the company pay to all the bondholders each year as interest?

c. Determine the total cash payments the company must make for each $1,000 bond to pay the bondholders their return on investment (interest) and the return of their investment.

d. Is the effective (market) interest rate less than, equal to, or greater than 8 percent? How can you determine this?

LO 4: CALCULATING BOND PROCEEDS, BOND INTEREST, AND TOTAL BOND PAYMENTS

3–51. Assume Sherry Company sells 2,500 of its five-year, $1,000 bonds paying 12 percent interest at 103.

Required:

    a. How much cash will the company receive from the bond sale?

    b. How much cash will the company pay to all the bondholders each year as interest?

    c. Determine the total cash payments the company must make for each $1,000 bond to pay the bondholders their return on investment (interest) and the return of their investment.

    d. Is the effective (market) interest rate less than, equal to, or greater than 12 percent? How can you determine this?

LO 4: BOND INTEREST AND PAYMENT CALCULATIONS

3–52. Assume that Phil Handley pays $950 for a five-year, $1,000, 9 percent bond.

Required:

    a. How much cash will Handley receive each year as interest?

    b. Calculate the amount of cash the bondholder will receive for his return on investment and the return of his investment for the $1,000 bond.

    c. Is the effective (market) interest rate less than, equal to, or greater than 9 percent? How can you determine this?

LO 4 & 5: BOND INTEREST AND PAYMENT CALCULATIONS

3–53. Assume Suzanne Weiser pays $1,040 for a five-year, $1,000 bond paying 8 percent interest.

Required:

    a. How much cash will Suzanne receive each year as interest?

    b. Calculate the amount of cash the bondholder will receive for her return on investment and the return of her investment for the $1,000 bond.

    c. Is the effective (market) interest rate less than, equal to, or greater than 8 percent? How can you determine this?

LO 5: COMPUTATION OF INTEREST

3–54. July 1, 2003, Alto, Inc., borrowed $10,000 from National Bank. Alto signed a 10 percent promissory note due on December 31, 2003.

Required:

    a. Determine the total amount Alto will have to pay (principal and interest) on December 31, 2003.

    b. How much interest will National Bank earn on this note?

    c. How would your answer to part b differ if the company borrowed the money on October 1, 2003?

LO 5: COMPUTATION OF INTEREST AND PRINCIPAL

3–55. The Leverett Company borrowed $20,000 to finance its business operation. The loan is due on December 31, 2004.

Required: Calculate the interest and principal Leverett Company would have to pay the bank on December 31, 2004, under each of the following assumptions:

    a. The loan is at 12 percent, borrowed on January 2, 2004.

    b. The loan is at 10 percent, borrowed on January 2, 2004.

    c. The loan is at 12 percent, borrowed on April 1, 2004.

    d. The loan is at 9 percent, borrowed on September 1, 2004.

LO 5: COMPUTATION OF INTEREST AND PRINCIPAL

3–56. The Habiger Company borrowed $100,000 due on December 31, 2004.

Required: Calculate the interest Habiger would have pay to the bank on December 31, 2004, under each of the following assumptions:

    a. The loan is at 6 percent interest, borrowed on January 2, 2004.
    b. The loan is at 8 percent interest, borrowed on January 2, 2004.
    c. The loan is at 6 percent interest, borrowed on May 1, 2004.
    d. The loan is at 8 percent interest, borrowed on August 1, 2004.

LO 4: EFFECT OF MARKET INTEREST ON BOND SELLING PRICES

3–57. Assume a company is selling 6 percent bonds. Explain how an increase in the market rate of interest will impact the selling price of the company's 6 percent bonds.

LO 4: EFFECT OF MARKET INTEREST ON BOND SELLING PRICES

3–58. Assume a company is selling 6 percent bonds. Explain how a decrease in the market rate of interest will impact the selling price of the 6 percent bonds.

LO 4: EFFECT OF MARKET INTEREST ON BOND SELLING PRICES

3–59. King Corporation is prepared to issue 5,000 of its 6 percent, $1,000 par value bonds. If the market rate of interest for such bonds is currently 6½ percent, would you expect the bonds to sell at par value, at a premium, or at a discount? Explain your answer.

LO 4: EFFECT OF MARKET INTEREST ON BOND SELLING PRICES

3–60. Tamara Corporation has decided to issue 9,000 of the company's 7 percent bonds, each with a par value of $1,000. If the market rate of interest for such securities is currently 6¾ percent, would you expect the bonds to sell at par value, at a premium, or at a discount? Explain your answer.

LO 4: EFFECT OF MARKET INTEREST ON BOND SELLING PRICES

3–61. Stacy Corporation has decided to sell 7,000 of its 5 percent bonds, each with a par value of $1,000. If the market rate of interest is currently 5¼ percent, would you expect the bonds to sell at par value, at a premium, or at a discount? Explain your answer.

LO 5: STOCK ISSUANCES

3–62. Klauss Corporation began operations in 1972 by issuing 20,000 shares of its no-par common stock for $5 per share. The following details provide information about the company's stock in the years since that time.

    1. In 1992, the company issued an additional 50,000 shares of common stock for $15 per share.
    2. Klauss Corporation stock is traded on the ***New York Stock Exchange (NYSE).*** During an average year, about 25,000 shares of its common stock are sold by one set of investors to another.
    3. On December 31, 2002, Klauss Corporation common stock was quoted on the ***NYSE*** at $38 per share.
    4. On December 31, 2003, Klauss Corporation common stock was quoted on the ***NYSE*** at $55 per share.

Required:

    a. How much money has Klauss Corporation received in total from the sales of its common stock since it was incorporated in 1972?
    b. When Klauss Corporation prepares its balance sheet as of December 31, 2003, what dollar amount will it show in the owners' equity section for common stock?
    c. What, if anything, can you infer about Klauss Corporation's performance during 2003 from the price of its common stock on December 31, 2002, and December 31, 2003?

LO 5: STOCK ISSUANCES

3–63. Shiner Corporation began operations in 1988 by issuing 35,000 shares of its $2 par value common stock for $10 per share. The following details provide information about the company's stock in the years since that time.

1. In 1998, the company issued an additional 80,000 shares of common stock for $15 per share.
2. Shiner Corporation stock is traded on the *American Stock Exchange (AMEX).* During an average year, about 40,000 shares of its common stock are sold by one set of investors to another.
3. On December 31, 2002, Shiner Corporation common stock was quoted on the *AMEX* at $79 per share.
4. On December 31, 2003, Shiner Corporation common stock was quoted on the *AMEX* at $45 per share.

Required:

a. How much money has Shiner Corporation received in total from the sales of its common stock since it was incorporated in 1988?
b. When Shiner Corporation prepares its balance sheet as of December 31, 2003, what dollar amount will it show in the owners' equity section for common stock?
c. What, if anything, can you infer about Shiner Corporation's performance during 2003 from the price of its common stock on December 31, 2002, and December 31, 2003?

LO 5: STOCK ISSUANCES

3–64. La Forge Corporation began operations in January, 1992, by issuing 90,000 shares of its no-par common stock for $25 per share and 10,000 shares of its $100 par value, 6 percent preferred stock for $100 per share. The following details provide information about the company's stock in the years since that time.

1. In January 1999, the company issued an additional 50,000 shares of common stock for $35 per share and 5,000 shares of preferred stock for $150 per share.
2. La Forge Corporation stock is traded on the *New York Stock Exchange (NYSE).* During an average year, about 100,000 shares of its common stock and 6,000 shares of preferred stock are sold by one set of investors to another.
3. On December 31, 2002, La Forge Corporation common stock was quoted on the *NYSE* at $55 per share. The preferred stock was quoted at $135 per share.
4. On December 31, 2003, La Forge Corporation common stock was quoted on the *NYSE* at $65 per share. The preferred stock was quoted at $150 per share.

Required:

a. How much money has La Forge Corporation received in total from the sales of its stock since it was incorporated in 1992?
b. When La Forge Corporation prepares its balance sheet as of December 31, 2003, what dollar amount will it show in the owners' equity section for common stock and for preferred stock?
c. What is the market value of La Forge's stock on December 31, 2002, and December 31, 2003?

LO 5: STOCK ISSUANCES

3–65. Bennett Corporation began operations in 1979 by issuing 40,000 shares of its no-par common stock for $10 per share. The following details provide information about the company's stock in the years since that time.

1. In 1998, the company issued an additional 70,000 shares of common stock for $15 per share.
2. Bennett Corporation stock is traded on the *New York Stock Exchange (NYSE).* During an average year, about 50,000 shares of its common stock are sold by one set of investors to another.
3. On December 31, 2002, Bennett Corporation common stock was quoted on the *NYSE* at $56 per share.
4. On December 31, 2003, Bennett Corporation common stock was quoted on the *NYSE* at $35 per share.

Required:

a. How much money has Bennett Corporation received in total from the sales of its common stock since it was incorporated in 1979?

    b. When Bennett Corporation prepares its balance sheet as of December 31, 2003, what dollar amount will it show in the owners' equity section for common stock?

    c. What, if anything, can you infer about Bennett Corporation's performance during 2003 from the price of its common stock on December 31, 2002, and December 31, 2003?

LO 6: EQUITY VS. DEBT

3–66. This chapter discussed two very different forms of financing available to corporations: debt and equity.

Required:

    a. Explain why a corporation might prefer to issue bonds rather than shares of common stock.

    b. Explain why an investor might prefer to purchase shares of a company's common stock rather than a company's corporate bonds.

LO 6: EQUITY VS. DEBT

3–67. Define *nominal interest rate* and *market interest rate* relative to bonds, and briefly explain how these rates affect a bond's selling price.

LO 6: DEBT VS. EQUITY INVESTMENTS

3–68. Ed Furgol has $20,000 to invest. His options are as follows:

    Option 1: Big Company's five-year, $1,000 par value, 8 percent bonds, which are selling for 98 on the bond market. (Exactly three years remaining to maturity.)

    Option 2: Little Company's initial offering of no-par common stock, which is selling for $20 per share. Although there is no formal requirement to pay dividends, it is anticipated that Little Company will pay an annual dividend of $0.80 per share on its common stock.

Required:

    a. How many of the Big Company bonds can Ed buy with the $20,000 he has to invest?

    b. How much cash will Ed receive from Big Company each year if he buys the bonds?

    c. What will Ed's return on investment and return of investment be for the bonds if he holds them until maturity?

    d. How many shares of Little Company's common stock can Ed purchase with the $20,000 he has to invest?

    e. Assuming Little Company does pay the anticipated annual dividend on its common stock, how much will Ed receive each year if he invests his $20,000 in the stock?

LO 6: EQUITY VS. DEBT

3–69. Joshua Pak has $50,000 to invest. His options are as follows:

    Option 1: Grand Oil Company's five-year, $1,000 par value, 12 percent bonds, which are selling for 103 on the bond market. (Exactly five years remaining to maturity.)

    Option 2: Little Giant Oil Company's initial offering of no-par common stock, which is selling for $75 per share. Although there is no formal requirement to pay dividends, it is anticipated that Little Giant will pay an annual dividend of $2 per share on its common stock.

Required:

    a. How many of the Grand Oil bonds can Joshua buy with the $50,000 he has to invest?

    b. How much cash will Joshua receive from Grand Oil each year if he buys the bonds?

    c. What will Joshua's return on investment and return of investment be for the bonds if he holds them until maturity?

    d. How many shares of Little Giant's common stock can Joshua purchase with the $50,000 he has to invest?

    e. Assuming Little Giant does pay the anticipated annual dividend on its common stock, how much will Joshua receive each year if he invests his $50,000 in the stock?

LO 7: STATEMENT OF CASH FLOWS PREPARATION—SIMPLE INVESTING AND FINANCING ACTIVITIES ONLY

3–70. The following information is from the records of the Elsea Corporation for the year ended December 31, 2003.

1. Sold Elsea Corporation common stock for cash of $95,500
2. Purchased equipment for cash $28,000
3. Borrowed $7,000 from Miami National Bank
4. Cash balance at December 31, 2003, was $30,000

Required: Prepare a statement of cash flows for Elsea Corporation for the year ended December 31, 2003.

LO 7: STATEMENT OF CASH FLOWS PREPARATION—SIMPLE INVESTING AND FINANCING ACTIVITIES ONLY

3–71. The following information is from the records of the Steinmann Industries for the year ended December 31, 2003.

1. Sold Steinmann Industries common stock for cash of $30,000
2. Borrowed $120,000 by selling bonds
3. Purchased land for $40,000 cash
4. Purchased a building for $60,000 cash
5. Cash balance at December 31, 2002, was $20,000

Required: Prepare a statement of cash flows for Steinmann Industries for the year ended December 31, 2003.

LO 7: STATEMENT OF CASH FLOWS PREPARATION—SIMPLE INVESTING AND FINANCING ACTIVITIES ONLY

3–72. The following information is from the records of the Shandra Industries for the year ended December 31, 2003.

1. Sold Shandra Industries common stock for cash of $73,000
2. Sold Shandra bonds for $200,000 cash
3. Borrowed $70,000 from XYZ Bank
4. Purchased equipment for cash $240,000
5. Purchased land for $35,000 cash
6. Cash balance at December 31, 2002, was $20,000

Required: Prepare a statement of cash flows for Shandra Industries for the year ended December 31, 2003.

LO 7: STATEMENT OF CASH FLOWS PREPARATION—SIMPLE INVESTING AND FINANCING ACTIVITIES ONLY

3–73. The following information is from the records of the Jessie Lynne Company for the year ended December 31, 2003.

1. Sold Jessie Lynne Company common stock for cash of $55,000
2. Sold Jessie Lynne Company preferred stock for cash of $25,000
3. Borrowed $100,000 from XYZ Bank
4. Sold Jessie Lynne bonds for $120,000 cash
5. Purchased equipment for cash $60,000
6. Sold equipment for cash $1,500
7. Cash balance at December 31, 2002, was $20,000

Required: Prepare a statement of cash flows for Jessie Lynne Company for the year ended December 31, 2003.

LO 7: STATEMENT OF CASH FLOWS PREPARATION—SIMPLE INVESTING AND FINANCING ACTIVITIES ONLY

3–74. The following information is from the records of the Alto Corporation for the year ended December 31, 2003.

1. Sold Alto Corporation common stock for cash of $65,000
2. Sold Alto Corporation preferred stock for cash of $50,000
3. Purchased equipment for cash $60,000
4. Sold Alto bonds for $300,000 cash
5. Sold equipment for cash $12,000
6. Paid $500 cash dividend
7. Borrowed $70,000 from Miami National Bank
8. Purchased IBM stock $15,000
9. Purchased land for $120,000 cash
10. Purchased building for $150,000 cash
11. Cash balance at December 31, 2002, was $30,000

Required: Prepare a statement of cash flows for Alto Corporation for the year ended December 31, 2003.

LO 7: STATEMENT OF CASH FLOWS PREPARATION—SIMPLE INVESTING AND FINANCING ACTIVITIES ONLY

3–75. The following information is from the records of the Foxmore Company for the year ended December 31, 2003.

1. Sold Foxmore Company common stock for cash of $195,000
2. Sold Foxmore Company preferred stock for cash of $75,000
3. Purchased equipment for cash $9,000
4. Sold equipment for cash $3,000
5. Borrowed $170,000 from **Bank of America,** signing a promissory note
6. Sold Foxmore bonds for $250,000 cash
7. Purchased land for $30,000 cash
8. Purchased building for $50,000 cash
9. Purchased machinery to use in the business for 180,000 cash
10. Paid cash dividend of $2,000
11. Cash balance at December 31, 2002, was $30,000

Required: Prepare a statement of cash flows for Foxmore Company for the year ended December 31, 2003.

LO 7: STATEMENT OF CASH FLOWS PREPARATION—SIMPLE INVESTING AND FINANCING ACTIVITIES ONLY

3–76. During the year ended December 31, 2003, Dale's Computer Center sold some of its common stock for cash of $90,000. In addition, the company purchased equipment for cash of $68,000 and borrowed $25,000 from **Bank of America.** The company's cash balance at December 31, 2002, was $22,000.

Required: Prepare a statement of cash flows for the company for the year ended December 31, 2003.

LO 7: STATEMENT OF CASH FLOWS PREPARATION—SIMPLE INVESTING AND FINANCING ACTIVITIES ONLY

3–77. During the year ended December 31, 2003, Ace Corporation sold some of its common stock for cash of $86,000. In addition, the company purchased land for cash of $33,000 and sold Ace bonds for $55,000 cash. The company's cash balance at December 31, 2002, was $12,000.

Required: Prepare a statement of cash flows for the company for the year ended December 31, 2003.

LO 7: STATEMENT OF CASH FLOWS PREPARATION—SIMPLE INVESTING AND FINANCING ACTIVITIES ONLY

3–78. During the year ended December 31, 2003, Ventura Corporation sold some of its common stock for cash of $180,000. In addition, the company borrowed $120,000 by selling bonds and $50,000 by signing a promissory note to the Bank of Key Largo. The company purchased land for $40,000 and a building for $60,000 cash. The company's cash balance at December 31, 2002, was $22,000.

Required: Prepare a statement of cash flows for the company for the year ended December 31, 2003.

LO 7: STATEMENT OF CASH FLOWS PREPARATION—SIMPLE INVESTING AND FINANCING ACTIVITIES ONLY

3–79. During the year ended December 31, 2003, Mini-Me Corporation sold some of its common stock for cash of $400,000. In addition, the company borrowed $150,000 by selling bonds and $150,000 by signing a promissory note to the Bank of Brevard. The company purchased land for $210,000 and a building for $360,000 cash. The company's cash balance at December 31, 2002, was $88,000.

Required: Prepare a statement of cash flows for the company for the year ended December 31, 2003.

LO 8: FINANCIAL RATIO CALCULATIONS—PROPRIETORSHIP

3–80. The following balance sheet of Gerner Enterprises was compiled shortly after Edward Gerner started his business:

Gerner Enterprises
Balance Sheet
October 1, 2003

Assets		Liabilities and owner's equity:	
Cash	$100,000	Notes payable—Union Bank	$ 50,000
Land	50,000	Graham Gerner, capital	100,000
Total assets	$150,000	Total liabilities and owner's equity	$150,000

Required:

a. Based on the information provided in Gerner's balance sheet, write a brief paragraph that describes what Edward Gerner did financially to start his business.
b. What type of business organization is Gerner Enterprises?
c. Calculate the debt ratio for the company.
d. Calculate the debt-to-equity ratio for the company.
e. What do the ratios in parts c and d tell you about the company?

LO 8: FINANCIAL RATIO CALCULATIONS—PARTNERSHIP

3–81. The following balance sheet of Susan Drake and Associates was compiled at the end of its first year of operations:

Susan Drake and Associates
Balance Sheet
December 31, 2003

Assets:		Liabilities and owners' equity:	
Cash	$40,000	Notes payable—Central Bank	$10,000
Land	20,000	Susan Drake, capital	25,000
		Julie Pham, capital	25,000
Total assets	$60,000	Total liabilities and owners' equity	$60,000

Required:

a. Write a paragraph that describes what this balance sheet tells you about the financial position of the company.
b. What type of business organization is Susan Drake and Associates?
c. Calculate the debt ratio for the company.
d. Calculate the debt-to-equity ratio for the company.
e. What do the ratios in parts c and d tell you about the company?

LO 8: FINANCIAL RATIO CALCULATIONS—CORPORATION

3–82. The following balance sheet was compiled for Quynh Vu Enterprises at the end of its first year of operations:

Quynh Vu Enterprises
Balance Sheet
December 31, 2003

Assets:		Liabilities and stockholders' equity:	
Cash	$120,000	Notes payable—Sooner Bank	$ 20,000
		Common stock, $10 par value	40,000
		Additional paid-in capital	50,000
		Retained earnings	10,000
		Total liabilities and stockholders'	
Total assets	$120,000	equity	$120,000

Required:

a. Write a paragraph that describes what this balance sheet tells you about the financial position of the company.
b. Assuming the company did not distribute any of its earnings to its owners, from the information provided, can you determine how much profit the company made in its first year?
c. Can you tell how many stockholders Quynh Vu Enterprises has? Explain your answer.
d. How many shares of stock did Quynh Vu Enterprises sell and what was the stock's average selling price per share?
e. Calculate the debt ratio for the company.
f. Calculate the debt-to-equity ratio for the company.
g. What do the ratios in parts e and f tell you about the company?

LO 8: FINANCIAL RATIO CALCULATIONS—CORPORATION

3–83. The balance sheet below was compiled for Lauren Elsea Tour Enterprises, Inc.

Lauren Elsea Tour Enterprises, Inc.
Balance Sheet
December 31, 2003

Assets:		Liabilities:	
Cash	$15,000	Notes payable	$144,000
Land	120,000	Bonds payable	441,000
Building	215,000	Total liabilities	585,000
Office equipment	28,000	Stockholders' equity:	
Tour trolleys	149,000	Common stock	$ 57,000
Charter boat	205,000	Additional paid-in capital—common	90,000
		Total stockholders' equity	147,000
		Total liabilities and stockholders'	
Total assets	$732,000	equity	$732,000

Required:

a. Calculate the debt ratio for the company.
b. Calculate the debt-to-equity ratio for the company.
c. What do the ratios in parts a and b tell you about the company?

LO 8: FINANCIAL RATIO CALCULATIONS—CORPORATION

3–84. The balance sheet below was compiled for South Beach Dive Center, Inc.

South Beach Dive Center, Inc.
Balance Sheet
November 30, 2003

Assets:		Liabilities:	
Cash	$11,000	Accounts payable	$ 62,000
Merchandise inventory	96,000	Notes payable	77,000
Computer system	6,000	Total liabilities	139,000
Office equipment	8,000	Stockholders' equity:	
Dive boat	188,000	Common stock	$68,000
		Additional paid-in capital—common	102,000
		Total stockholders' equity	170,000
		Total liabilities and stockholders'	
Total assets	$309,000	equity	$309,000

Required:

    a. Calculate the debt ratio for the company.
    b. Calculate the debt-to-equity ratio for the company.
    c. What do the ratios in parts a and b tell you about the company?

LO 6: FINANCIAL RATIO CALCULATIONS—CORPORATION

3–85. The balance sheet below was compiled for Panama City Charters, Inc.

Panama City Charters, Inc.
Balance Sheet
June 30, 2003

Assets:		Liabilities:	
Cash	$ 7,000	Accounts payable	$ 12,000
Office furniture inventory	15,000	Notes payable	52,000
Office equipment	8,000	Total liabilities	64,000
Computer equipment	18,000	Stockholders' equity:	
Tour buses	377,000	Common stock	$ 92,000
		Additional paid-in capital—common	269,000
		Total stockholders' equity	361,000
		Total liabilities and stockholders'	
Total assets	$425,000	equity	$425,000

Required:

    a. Calculate the debt ratio for the company.
    b. Calculate the debt-to-equity ratio for the company.
    c. What do the ratios in parts a and b tell you about the company?

LO 8: FINANCIAL RATIO CALCULATIONS—CORPORATION

3–86. Refer to the balance sheets presented in problems 3–83, 3–84, and 3–85.

Required:

    a. What industry would you say each of the three companies is in?
    b. Do they seem to be in the same industry?
    c. Calculate the debt ratios for each company.
    d. Calculate the debt-to-equity ratios for each company.
    e. Create a well-organized table that shows each of the company's names and their debt and debt-to-equity ratios.
    f. Assume each company has applied for a loan and you are the loan office evaluating their applications. Rank the companies according to their loan risk based on the information in the table you prepared for requirement e. Explain your ranking.

Financial Reporting Exercises   •

LO 1, 2, & 6: GATHERING EQUITY INFORMATION FROM PUBLISHED ANNUAL REPORT

3–87. Refer to *Pier 1 Imports* annual report on page F–503 to answer the following questions.

Required:

    a. What types of stock are reported on the company's balance sheet?
    b. For each type of stock listed, identify the number of shares authorized, the number issued, and the number outstanding for each year presented on the balance sheet.
    c. Why might *Pier 1* issue preferred stock?
    d. Present the accounting equation with dollar amounts for *Pier 1* for each of its balance sheets presented in the company's annual report.

LO 1, 2, & 6: GATHERING EQUITY INFORMATION FROM PUBLISHED ANNUAL REPORT

3–88. Go to the PHLIP Web site for this book to find the link to *Barnes & Noble Inc.* Refer to the information listed under February 2, 2002, and answer the following questions.

Required:

    a. What types of stock are reported on the balance sheet?

    b. If there is common and/or preferred stock, identify the number of shares authorized, the number issued, and the number outstanding. If there is treasury stock, list the number of shares.

    c. What is the total cost of the shares held in the treasury? What was the cost of these per share to the company?

    d. Write the accounting equation for **Barnes & Noble Inc.,** as of February 2, 2002.

LO 1, 2, 4, & 6: VARIOUS. GATHERING DEBT AND EQUITY INFORMATION FROM PUBLISHED ANNUAL REPORT

3–89. Go to the PHLIP Web site for this book to find the link to **Emerson Radio Corporation.** Refer to the information listed under January 31, 2002, and answer the following questions.

Required:

    a. What types of stock are reported on the balance sheet?

    b. If there is common and/or preferred stock, identify the number of shares authorized, the number issued, and the number outstanding. If there is treasury stock, list the number of shares.

    c. What is the total cost of the shares held in the treasury? What was the original cost per share to the company?

    d. Write the accounting equation for **Emerson Radio Corp.,** as of January 31, 2002.

LO — VARIOUS. INTERPRETING DEBT INFORMATION FROM PUBLISHED ANNUAL REPORT

3–90. In its 2002 10-K Report, **Dell Computer Corporation** reported total long-term liabilities of $520,000,000. Of that amount, $300,000,000 represented 4.87% debentures due in 2028.

Required:

    a. What is a debenture?

    b. Why might there be a difference in the current value of the bonds and the amount the company has listed?

    c. What percentage of the company's long-term liabilities are bonds?

    d. Assuming the bonds were issued in 2002, how much total interest will **Dell Computer Corporation** pay on them? Is this number dependent on the market?

LO — VARIOUS. INTERPRETING DEBT INFORMATION FROM PUBLISHED ANNUAL REPORT

3–91. **Procter & Gamble Co.,** multinational producer and marketer of such products as *Tide* laundry detergent, *Charmin* toilet paper, and *Pampers* diapers, included the following in its 2001 10-K Notes to Consolidated Financial Statements:

    Long-term debt maturities during the next five years are as follows: 2002—$622,000,000; 2003—$1,117,000,000; 2004—$1,040,000,000; 2005—$1,912,000,000 and 2006—$32,000,000.

Required:

    a. Why would **Procter & Gamble Co.** include this information in the annual report?

    b. What information does this provide the annual report readers?

    c. If you were making a loan to **Procter & Gamble Co.,** in which one of the five years would you prefer to schedule the company's loan repayment to you?

LO 1, 2, 6, & 8: VARIOUS. INTERPRETING DEBT AND EQUITY INFORMATION, CALCULATING FINANCIAL RATIOS

3–92. Go to the PHLIP Web site for the link to look up the total liabilities and total stockholders' equity for **Blockbuster, Inc.,** from the 10-K Report's balance sheet under the listing for December 31, 2001.

Required:

    a. How much are the company's total assets?

    b. Calculate the debt ratio for the company.

c. Calculate the debt-to-equity ratio for the company.

d. What do these ratios tell you about ***Blockbuster, Inc?*** Do they tell you anything relative to the risk of investing in the company?

 3–93. Go to the PHLIP Web site for the link to look up the total liabilities and total stockholders' equity for ***Elizabeth Arden, Inc.,*** from the 10-K Report's balance sheet under the listing for January 31, 2002.

Required:

a. How much are the company's total assets?

b. Calculate the debt ratio for the company.

c. Calculate the debt-to-equity ratio for the company.

d. What do these ratios tell you about ***Elizabeth Arden, Inc?*** Do they tell you anything relative to the risk of investing in the company?

ANNUAL REPORT PROJECT

3–94. Section 3—Basic Balance Sheet Information

In this assignment, you will prepare a report based on your company's balance sheet and other information.

Required: Prepare a report that includes the following information:

a. Describe your company's balance sheet presentation and the important information it includes. For example, how many years of balance sheet information does your company present? Does your company use the report form or the account form for its balance sheet presentation? Does it matter to you which format your company uses? Explain your reasoning.

b. Discuss the important items and amounts that appear on the balance sheet. What is the company's most significant asset? Which is the least significant? Is there any reason for this?

c. If your company has long-term debt, summarize the pertinent facts relating to the debt. Information for this requirement can be found in the notes to the financial statements.

d. Go to the notes to the financial statements and find the note regarding contingencies. Does your company have any contingent liabilities? If it does, provide a brief description of each. Describe why this information is important.

e. Does the balance sheet include categories called something similar to "other assets"? If it does, use information from the notes to the financial statement to describe the items in this category.

f. Does the balance sheet include categories called something similar to "other liabilities"? If it does, use information from the notes to the financial statement to describe the items in this category.

g. Prepare a schedule for your company that presents the following financial ratios:

- Debt ratio for two years
- Debt-to-equity ratio for two years

h. Comment in your report on the information that each ratio provides. Include comments regarding the changes in the amounts of ratios over time. Is the proportion of debt financing increasing or decreasing? Comment on your company's external financing including the relative proportions of liabilities and equity.

i. Your report should conclude with a summary of what you think of the company in light of what you discovered as you completed this assignment.

4

Income Statement and Statement of Owners' Equity

Imagine for a moment that you are a fairly new commercial loan officer at **Bank of America** and you are evaluating the risk of lending $150,000 to a particular corporate customer. (Management considers you a rising star, so they have entrusted you with this evaluation even though you have never done one before.) Your job as a loan officer is to lend as much money as possible, but only to those corporations that will pay it back. It's quite a responsibility and you are naturally a bit nervous. If you fail to lend to a credit-worthy customer, the bank could lose interest revenue. Worse, the bank could lose the entire $150,000 if you approve a loan to a company that cannot repay it. The company applying for the loan has provided you with a set of financial statements—a balance sheet, an income statement, a statement of owners' equity, and a statement of cash flows.

As you sit in your office gazing at all these numbers, you remember a phrase from your accounting text in college: Sometimes trying to sift through all this information is like trying to empty the ocean with a teaspoon to get to the treasure on the sea floor. Well, the amount of material in these financial statements certainly seems to reflect that situation.

Unsure of exactly how to proceed, you seek the advice of Barney Barnes, an experienced loan officer who has been acting as a mentor to you. When you ask him what financial information is really important in helping you make sound lending decisions, he responds with a long list of things to consider, such as gross profit on sales (percentage and dollars), net profit margin (percentage and dollars), the amount of debt compared to equity, retained earnings, capital structure, the ability to generate cash through operations, dividends paid in the past, and, of course, how the financial statements articulate.

Your head is swimming as you return to your office. Some of these items you know come from the balance sheet, others from the income statement, and still others from the statement of owners' equity and the statement of cash flows. It's obvious to you that you need a solid understanding of all the financial statements and the information they provide as you assess whether to make the loan. You already know about the balance sheet and the information it provides. Certainly, this information is helpful, but it is not sufficient. Even though the balance sheet shows the present financial position of a company, it is only one of the pieces of information you should assemble before you make a final decision. For example, you also need to assess whether the company's business activities result in profits that are adequate enough for the company to remain viable.

In this chapter, you will learn how the income statement depicts this type of information. The income statement provides information about a company's economic performance over a specific period of time.

This chapter will also introduce you to the statement of owners' equity. This financial statement provides a bridge between the information the income statement provides and the information the balance sheet provides. It does this by tracing the changes in owners' equity (of which net income from the income statement is a part) from the beginning to the end of the accounting period.

The activity reflected by the income statement has a profound impact on cash flow, specifically cash flow from operating activities. Because so many decision makers look toward cash as their ultimate reward in business, information about cash and how it increases or decreases over time is critically important to them. In this chapter, we will show how the statement of cash flows reflects the sources and uses of cash from operating activities.

Financial statements provide so much information that it can become difficult to ascertain the relationships of the various financial statement amounts. As we learned in prior chapters, financial statement analysis is the process of evaluating financial statements and the relationships among the amounts they contain. In this chapter, we will discuss financial statement analysis associated with the income statement.

By the time you've finished this chapter, you will have explored four financial statements—the balance sheet, the income statement, the statement of owners' equity, and the statement of cash flows. Bear in mind that these are financial information tools for economic decision makers. Their importance lies in their usefulness and their contribution to the decision making process.

Learning Objectives

After completing your work on this chapter, you should be able to do the following:

1. Prepare a basic income statement and describe the information it provides.
2. Distinguish between single-step and multiple-step income statements.
3. Explain the impact of net income or net loss on owners' equity.
4. Prepare a basic statement of owners' equity for a proprietorship, a partnership, and a corporation and describe the information the statement provides.
5. Define drawings and dividends and discuss the circumstances under which they are paid.
6. Describe the articulation of income statements, statements of owners' equity, and balance sheets.
7. Explain the content and purpose of the operating activities section of the statement of cash flows.
8. Use financial ratios to evaluate business profits.

◆ INTRODUCTION TO THE INCOME STATEMENT

income statement A financial statement providing information about an entity's past performance. Its purpose is to measure the results of the entity's operations for some specific time period.

The **income statement** is a financial tool that provides information about a company's past performance. Recall that in our presentation of the balance sheet in Chapter 3 we discussed assets, liabilities, and owners' equity (including investments by owners)—four of the accounting elements described by the Financial Accounting Standards Board (FASB) in the *Conceptual Framework of Accounting*. The income statement also includes accounting elements (see Exhibit 4–1). The italicized definitions in the following discussion are provided by the FASB. A less formal definition of each element follows the words of the FASB.

revenue An accounting element representing the inflows of assets as a result of an entity's ongoing major or central operations. These are the rewards of doing business.

expense An accounting element representing the outflow of assets resulting from an entity's ongoing major or central operations. These are the sacrifices required to attain the rewards (revenues) of doing business.

- **Revenues**—*Inflows or other enhancements of assets to an entity . . . from delivering or producing goods, rendering services, or other activities that constitute the entity's ongoing major or central operations* (Statement of Financial Accounting Concepts No. 6, paragraph 78). Revenue represents what a company charges its customers for the goods and services it provides. If a company deposits money in a bank, the interest the company earns on that money is also revenue. Revenues are the reward of doing business.
- **Expenses**—*Outflows or other using up of assets . . . from delivering or producing goods, rendering services, or carrying out other activities that constitute the entity's major or central operations* (Statement of Financial Accounting Concepts No. 6, paragraph 80). Expenses are the sacrifices required to generate revenues. Unlike assets, which have future value, expenses are the costs of doing business that no longer have future value.

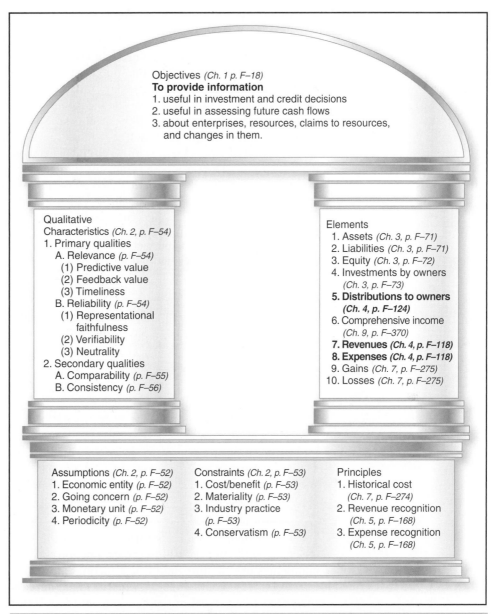

Objectives *(Ch. 1 p. F–18)*
To provide information
1. useful in investment and credit decisions
2. useful in assessing future cash flows
3. about enterprises, resources, claims to resources, and changes in them.

Qualitative
Characteristics *(Ch. 2, p. F–54)*
1. Primary qualities
   A. Relevance *(p. F–54)*
     (1) Predictive value
     (2) Feedback value
     (3) Timeliness
   B. Reliability *(p. F–54)*
     (1) Representational
       faithfulness
     (2) Verifiability
     (3) Neutrality
2. Secondary qualities
   A. Comparability *(p. F–55)*
   B. Consistency *(p. F–56)*

Elements
1. Assets *(Ch. 3, p. F–71)*
2. Liabilities *(Ch. 3, p. F–71)*
3. Equity *(Ch. 3, p. F–72)*
4. Investments by owners
   (Ch. 3, p. F–73)
5. **Distributions to owners**
   (Ch. 4, p. F–124)
6. Comprehensive income
   (Ch. 9, p. F–370)
7. **Revenues *(Ch. 4, p. F–118)***
8. **Expenses *(Ch. 4, p. F–118)***
9. Gains *(Ch. 7, p. F–275)*
10. Losses *(Ch. 7, p. F–275)*

Assumptions *(Ch. 2, p. F–52)*
1. Economic entity *(p. F–52)*
2. Going concern *(p. F–52)*
3. Monetary unit *(p. F–52)*
4. Periodicity *(p. F–52)*

Constraints *(Ch. 2, p. F–53)*
1. Cost/benefit *(p. F–53)*
2. Materiality *(p. F–53)*
3. Industry practice
   (p. F–53)
4. Conservatism *(p. F–53)*

Principles
1. Historical cost
   (Ch. 7, p. F–274)
2. Revenue recognition
   (Ch. 5, p. F–168)
3. Expense recognition
   (Ch. 5, p. F–168)

EXHIBIT 4–1   Accounting Elements

net income   The amount of profit that remains after all costs have been considered. The net reward of doing business for a specific time period.

net loss   The difference between revenues and expenses of a period in which expenses are greater than revenues.

    The excess of the rewards (revenues) over the sacrifices (expenses) for a given time period is the net reward of doing business, which we call **net income.** Accountants also call net income *earnings, net earnings,* or *net profit.* If the expenses for the period are greater than the revenues for the period, the result is a **net loss.** The relationship between revenues, expenses, and either net income or net loss can be represented by the following equation:

$$\text{Revenues} - \text{Expenses} = \text{Net Income (or Net Loss)}$$

This income statement equation forms the basis for the income statement itself. As we study the income statement, we will deal with the equation again and again, so fix its meaning in your mind!

Discussion Questions

4–1. Of the transactions in your personal finances during the last month, which would you describe as revenues? Which would you describe as expenses?

4–2. Use the income statement equation and your responses to Discussion Question 4–1 to determine whether you had a net income or a net loss for the month.

BUILDING THE INCOME STATEMENT

As an example of the basic format, the income statement of ***Tiffany & Co.*** is shown in Exhibit 4–2. Note that the heading includes the name of the business, the name of the statement, and the time period the statement depicts. As you recall, the heading for the balance sheet includes the precise date for which the information is being presented. While the balance sheet is a "snapshot" of a business at a particular point in time, the income statement is something like a "home video" of a company for a period of time (usually a month, quarter, or year). For this reason, the income statement heading identifies a period of time—not just a single date. The income statement indicates that during this specific time period, the company earned so much revenue, incurred so much expense, and produced either a net income or a net loss. Companies prepare income statements for external users annually and quarterly. Additionally, for internal decision makers, accountants prepare income statements monthly, or for any other time interval that would provide information managers need.

EXHIBIT 4–2 *Tiffany & Co.* Income Statement

Tiffany & Co.
Income Statement
For the Year Ended January 31, 2001
(In thousands)

Net Sales	$1,668,056
Cost of sales	719,642
Gross profit	948,414
Selling, general and administrative expense	621,018
Earnings from operations	327,396
Interest expense and financing cost	(16,207)
Other income, net	6,452
Earnings before income taxes	317,641
Provision for income taxes	127,057
Net earnings	$ 190,584

The income statement's formal name is the *statement of results of operations*, which is a far better description of its function than *income statement*. However, most companies use the informal title, "Income Statement." The authors of *Accounting Trends and Techniques*[1] report that of 600 companies surveyed in 2001, 284 used *income* as a key word in the headings of their 2000 financial statements, 198 used *operations*, and 108 used *earnings*.

A company may have more than one type of revenue. Revenues comprise earned inflows of the company arising from both primary operations and secondary company activities. A service firm's primary operation is providing service, and merchandising and manufacturing firms obtain and sell tangible products. In addition to revenues from its primary operations, a company may generate revenues through other activities. For example, a company may earn rent revenue by renting out extra space in its office building or it may earn interest revenue from investing some of its cash in certificates of deposit.

Discussion Question ●

4–3. For each of the following, determine whether the company's primary revenue comes from obtaining and selling products or providing services.

  a. ***General Motors***
  b. ***ExxonMobil***
  c. ***Starbucks***
  d. ***Prudential Insurance***
  e. ***B. Dalton Bookstores***
  f. ***AOL***

---

[1]*Accounting Trends and Techniques* (AICPA, 2001), 289.

Income statements show various expenses. Expenses take many different forms, such as salaries and wages expense for employees, rent expense for land and buildings occupied by the business, electricity expense for the electricity used by the company, fuel expense, and maintenance expense for vehicles the business owns. These are just a few examples of the numerous expenses a company may have.

The cost of the products that merchandisers and manufacturers sell make up an expense called the **cost of goods sold,** sometimes called *cost of sales*, or *cost of products sold*. For many companies, cost of goods sold comprises the major expense of doing business. For example, in its **2001** income statement, **_Best Buy_** reported total expenses (in thousands) of $14,722,244. Of this total, $12,267,459, or 83 percent, was cost of goods sold.

In the United States, companies must pay **income tax,** which is a tax based on the amount of income a company has earned. The specifics for calculating the amount of income tax a company should pay or the amount it should report as income tax expense is beyond the scope of this course. But basically, the way it works is that the amount of taxable income is multiplied by the company's tax rate.

$$\text{Taxable Income} \times \text{Tax Rate} = \text{Income Tax Expense}$$

If you were to compare the tax rates of various companies, you would notice that each one has a somewhat different tax rate from the next. This is because of several factors including the fact that tax rates increase as income increases. The more income a company generates, the more income tax expense it will have.

INCOME STATEMENT FORMATS

There are two commonly used income statement formats: the single-step and the multiple-step formats. Of the 600 companies surveyed in 2001, the authors of *Accounting Trends and Techniques* reported that 134 companies used the single-step format and 466 used the multiple-step format for their 2000 income statements.

Although the presentation of the information differs between the single-step and the multiple-step income statements, the bottom line, or net income, would be the same regardless of the format used. However, there are some subtle but important differences between the two formats, so let's take a look at them.

SINGLE-STEP FORMAT OF THE INCOME STATEMENT

In the **single-step income statement** format, all revenues are grouped together and then totaled. Similarly, all expenses are grouped together and totaled. This format is called the single-step income statement because in one step, total expenses are subtracted from total revenues to determine net income or net loss. In actual practice, one exception to grouping *all* expenses together when the single-step format is used stands out. Of the 134 companies that used the single-step format in 2000, *Accounting Trends and Techniques* reported that every one of them showed income tax as a separate item and listed it just above net income. Accordingly, this is the format we will use for our presentations for the single-step format.

To illustrate the single-step format of the income statement, let's return to Jessica's Beauty Supply, Inc., the company we used in Chapter 3 to introduce the balance sheet. Assume that the company had $3,230 in sales revenue during January 2003 from selling hair care supplies to beauty shops. Additionally, the business earned $990 in rent revenue by renting some spare space in the back of its building during January. Also assume that expenses during the period were $955 for cost of goods sold, $675 for wages, $310 for utilities, and $120 for interest payments. Exhibit 4–3 on page F–122 shows a single-step income statement for Jessica's Beauty Supply, Inc., for the month ended January 31, 2003.

Income statements for proprietorships, partnerships, and corporations are quite similar to one another. The main difference between them is that corporations pay income tax, while proprietorships and partnerships do not. Therefore, if we were to prepare an income statement for our example company assuming it was organized as

cost of goods sold The cost of the product sold as the primary business activity of a company.

income tax A tax based on the amount of income a company has earned.

single-step income statement A format of the income statement that gathers all revenues into "total revenues" and all expenses into "total expenses." Net income is calculated as a subtraction of total expenses from total revenues.

Jessica's Beauty Supply, Inc.
Income Statement
For the Month Ended January 31, 2003

Revenues:		
Sales	$3,230	
Rent revenue	990	
Total revenues		$4,220
Expenses:		
Cost of goods sold	955	
Wages expense	675	
Utilities expense	310	
Interest expense	120	
Total expenses		(2,060)
Income before income tax		2,160
Income tax expense		540
Net income		$1,620

EXHIBIT 4–3   Single-Step Income Statement Format

either a proprietorship or a partnership, the only differences would be the company names and the absence of income tax. Accordingly, if Jessica's business was organized under the proprietorship form or the partnership form, the company's net income in either case would be the $2,160 instead of the after-tax amount of $1,620.

MULTIPLE-STEP FORMAT OF THE INCOME STATEMENT

The **multiple-step income statement** provides two items of information not presented in a single-step income statement: (1) **gross margin** or *gross profit* and (2) **operating income** or *income from operations*. The single-step income statement format simply sums all revenues and all expenses. No special consideration is given to any specific revenue or expense. In contrast, the multiple-step format arranges revenue and expense items to highlight their relationship to one another. Exhibit 4–4 shows a multiple-step income statement for Jessica's Beauty Supply, Inc., for the month ended January 31, 2003. As you can see, the net income using the multiple-step format is the same as that shown on the single-step income statement in Exhibit 4–3. Notice, though, that the multiple-step format makes two important stops before arriving at the bottom line: gross margin and operating income (thus the term *multiple-step*).

Gross margin is an important piece of information shown on a multiple-step income statement. This item highlights the relationship between sales revenue and cost of goods sold. Recall that **sales revenue,** sometimes simply called *sales*, is the revenue generated from the sale of tangible products. Cost of goods sold is the cost of the products that have been sold. Sales revenue minus cost of goods sold equals gross margin, or gross profit as it is sometimes called. For example, *Nike* sells running shoes and other products to generate sales revenue. *Nike*'s cost of goods sold is the cost of all the products it actually sells during a particular period. The difference between these amounts represents *Nike*'s gross margin. For 2001, *Nike* reported sales of $9.49 billion and cost of goods sold totaling $5.78 billion. The company's 2001 gross margin, therefore, was $3.71 billion.

multiple-step income statement An income statement format that highlights gross margin and operating income.

gross margin An item shown on a multiple-step income statement, calculated as: Sales – Cost of goods sold.

operating income Income produced by the major business activity of the company. An item shown on the multiple-step income statement.

sales revenue The revenue generated from the sale of a tangible product as a major business activity.

Discussion Question ●

4–4. Identify two manufacturing or merchandising companies and describe their source of sales revenue and the components of their cost of goods sold.

A merchandiser or manufacturer cannot be profitable unless it sells its products for more than it pays for them. Gross margin represents how much more a company

Jessica's Beauty Supply, Inc.
Income Statement
For the Month Ended January 31, 2003

Sales		$3,230
Less: Cost of goods sold		955
Gross margin		2,275
Operating expenses:		
Wages expense	$675	
Utilities expense	310	
Total operating expenses		(985)
Operating income		1,290
Other revenues:		
Rent revenue		990
Other expenses:		
Interest expense		(120)
Income before income tax		2,160
Income tax expense		(540)
Net income		$1,620

EXHIBIT 4–4 Multiple-Step Income Statement Format

received from the sale of its products than what the products cost the company. It also represents the amount available from sales to cover all other expenses the company incurs. For example, assume Kay Carnes Merchandising Company sells its product for $30 per unit. Assume further that each unit costs Carnes $24. If the company sold 5,000 units of product in January, it would have a gross margin of $30,000, calculated as follows:

Sales (5,000 × $30)	$150,000
LESS: Cost of goods sold (5,000 × $24)	120,000
Gross margin	$ 30,000

This $30,000 represents the amount Carnes has to cover all the company's other expenses for January. Assuming the company had no revenues other than sales, if those other expenses were less than $30,000, the company would have a net income for the month; if the other expenses were greater than $30,000, the company would experience a net loss.

Economic decision makers use gross margin as one measure to evaluate the performance of a manufacturing or merchandising company. Examining gross margin allows financial statement readers to quickly see the relationship among revenue produced by selling a product, the cost of the product, and all the other expenses the company incurs.

Discussion Question

4–5. Consider the following simplified multiple-step income statement:

Kanaly Company
Income Statement
For the Year Ended December 31, 2003

Sales (1,000 units)	$375,000
LESS: Cost of goods sold	380,000
Gross margin	$ (5,000)
LESS: Operating expenses	(32,000)
Net income (loss)	$ (37,000)

a. What can you learn about Kanaly Company from its gross margin?
b. If the selling price per unit remains constant, how many units must the company sell to earn a net income of $2,000?
c. If the company sells 1,000 units, at what selling price per unit would Kanaly earn a $5,000 net income?

In addition to highlighting the relationship between sales and cost of goods sold, the multiple-step income statement separates income generated by a firm's ongoing major business activity from revenues and expenses generated by secondary or incidental sources. Operating income or income from operations denotes the results associated with a company's primary business activity. For example, for a merchandiser, operating income would include all revenue and expenses related to the sale of products but would exclude revenues and expenses associated with incidental activities such as interest revenue, rent revenue, and interest expense. A quick look back at Exhibit 4–4 demonstrates this for Jessica's Beauty Supply, Inc. By separating the revenue and expenses in this way, a financial statement user learns not only the amount of the company's net income, but also the sources of that net income. When economic decision makers are attempting to use the past performance of a company as presented on the income statement to predict the future, operating income may be more useful than net income as an indicator of future performance. Therefore, multiple-step income statements may prove more useful than single-step statements.

NET INCOME AS AN INCREASE IN OWNERS' EQUITY

Net income increases the owners' equity in the business. Recall from our discussion of the elements found in a balance sheet, one of the two sources of owners' equity is earned equity. In this context, when we talk about a company's "earnings," we are really talking about its net income. Each revenue increases earned equity and each expense decreases earned equity. A net income, therefore, increases earned equity, while a net loss decreases earned equity.

A company's equity will change by the amount of its net income or loss. This means that the amounts reflected on the income statement have a direct effect on the amounts that appear on the balance sheet. A company that has income on its income statement will have a greater amount of retained earnings. This link is very logical when you realize that the past performance of a company is at least partially responsible for its present condition.

◆ DISTRIBUTIONS TO OWNERS

distributions to owners
Decreases in equity resulting from transferring assets to the owners of an enterprise.

In time, if the operations of a company are profitable, owners' equity will increase. Eventually, the owners will expect the company to distribute at least some of the earned equity to them. **Distributions to owners** is another accounting element shown in Exhibit 4–1. The FASB's *Conceptual Framework* defines distributions to owners as *decreases in equity of a particular business enterprise resulting from transferring assets, rendering services, or incurring liabilities by the enterprise to owners. Distributions to owners decrease ownership interest (or equity) in an enterprise* (Statement of Financial Accounting Concepts No. 6, paragraph 67). Just as net income increases owners' equity, distributions to owners decrease owners' equity.

Don't think of these distributions as salaries or wages paid to the owners. Distributions to owners are a distribution of income, *not* part of the expenses deducted from revenue to calculate income. Thus, they are not shown on the income statement. Distributions to owners represent a return on the investment they made. Regardless of the organizational form of the company, distributions to owners reduce total owners' equity.

PROPRIETORSHIPS AND PARTNERSHIPS—DRAWINGS

In the case of a proprietorship or partnership, little beyond common sense restricts the owners from taking money out of the company. If the cash is available and is not

drawings Distributions to the owners of proprietorships and partnerships. Also called withdrawals.

needed by the business, the owner or owners may take it for their personal use. The distributions to the owners of proprietorships and partnerships are called **drawings** or *withdrawals*.

Partnership agreements may state explicitly when and in what amounts partners may take withdrawals, or they may leave it to the discretion of the partners. Clearly, the partnership must have sufficient cash to support the actions of its owners. When thinking of making a withdrawal of cash from the company, a partner must consider the impact of this action on his or her capital in the partnership. Partners may take withdrawals that are disproportionate to the profit-sharing arrangement. Frequently, partners agree to allow one partner to take larger withdrawals because of an unusual personal need. Another partner may decide to not take normal withdrawals but to leave the capital in the business. The timing and amount of partners' withdrawals are a common source of partnership conflict and, in severe cases, can lead to the dissolution of a partnership.

CORPORATIONS—DIVIDENDS

dividends A distribution of earnings from a corporation to its owners. Dividends are most commonly distributed in the form of cash.

Owners of corporations (stockholders) may have much less control over when and in what amount they receive a distribution than do owners of proprietorships or partnerships. This is particularly true in large corporations. As we have already mentioned, distributions to owners of a corporation are called **dividends.** By law, unless there are contractual arrangements to the contrary, dividend distributions to shareholders must be proportionate to the number of shares they own. Although not legally required to do so, virtually all corporations pay dividends at some point in their existence.

Why do corporations pay dividends if they are not legally required to do so? In the long run, corporate investors demand this distribution. A number of factors cause a company's stock to either increase or decrease in value, but probably the most important factor is whether or not the company is profitable. Profitability is vital because investors know that profits lead to future dividends. A profitable corporation is more likely to pay dividends, and more profit ultimately means more dividends. On the other hand, if a corporation sustains losses or lacks the free cash to pay dividends, investors react and the demand for the company's stock declines. This decline in demand will result in falling stock prices. When this situation occurs, the corporation may find it difficult to obtain funds necessary to support its operations. Opportunities for both major types of external funding—issuing stock and borrowing funds—may disappear. Eventually, if enough people lose faith in the company, it will run out of cash and cease to exist. This explains why corporate executives are so interested in investor perception.

Some successful companies resist the pressure to pay dividends in order to reinvest profits to build the company for a better future, and they clearly communicate this strategy to the stockholders. *Microsoft* is one such company. Investors have accepted *Microsoft*'s reinvestment policy as a wise business strategy, and the company's stock price has not suffered.

The board of directors makes all decisions associated with the corporation's dividend policy. The policy includes whether or not to pay a dividend, the type of dividend to be paid, and when the dividend will be paid. The board of directors can also choose to distribute additional shares of the firm's stock as a dividend, called a stock dividend. It is, however, much more common for companies to distribute cash dividends. Of the 600 companies surveyed in 2001 by *Accounting Trends and Techniques*, 403 paid a cash dividend in 2000.[2]

CASH DIVIDENDS ON COMMON STOCK

A cash payment is what comes to mind when we hear the word *dividend*. To be able to pay a cash dividend, a corporation must have two things: sufficient retained earnings and sufficient cash.

---

[2]*Accounting Trends and Techniques* (AICPA, 2001), 433.

1. *Sufficient Retained Earnings.* Dividends are distributions of earnings; however, corporations are not restricted to the current year's earnings to cover the distribution. Although it may be desirable for a company to declare dividends from the current year's earnings, dividends are actually declared from retained earnings. Remember, net income is only this period's addition to retained earnings; thus, it is not necessary that current net income be greater than the dividend amount. The legal requirement is that the retained earnings balance exceeds the amount of the dividend. Exhibit 4–5 shows how retained earnings increase over time and how net income, net losses, and dividends affect them.

EXHIBIT 4–5	Effect of Net Income, Net Losses, and Dividends on Retained Earnings				
Year	2001	2002	2003	2004	2005
Beginning retained Earnings balance	$ -0-	$ 800	$1,300	$ 700	$1,150
Net income (loss)	800	1,000	(100)	950	400
	800	1,800	1,200	1,650	1,550
Dividends	-0-	(500)	(500)	(500)	(500)
Ending retained Earnings balance	$ 800	$1,300	$ 700	$1,150	$1,050

Note two things as you look at Exhibit 4–5. First, the ending balance of one period (in this case, a year) becomes the beginning balance of the next period. This is something you should know and understand because, in addition to its applicability to retained earnings, it is a very common phenomenon in accounting in general. Second, the payment of dividends is not directly related to the profits of a given period. In 2003, for example, this company paid dividends even though it experienced a net loss for the year, and in 2005, it paid out more in dividends than it earned for the year. This company appears to have adopted a policy of paying $500 per year in total dividends, regardless of its net income or loss for a particular year. This policy is perfectly acceptable, as long as the company has both sufficient retained earnings and sufficient cash each year to cover the dividend amount.

2. *Sufficient Cash.* Bear in mind that retained earnings is not cash. The only item on the balance sheet that represents cash is the cash amount. Basically, retained earnings is the sum of all profits earned by the corporation since its inception minus all dividends. Except by extraordinary coincidence, the amount of retained earnings and the amount of cash on hand will differ. (In Chapter 5, we explore the reasons for the difference between cash and retained earnings.) A corporation must make certain it has, or can get, sufficient cash to pay the dividend. A company may feel so compelled to pay its regular cash dividend that it will borrow the cash it needs if the company's cash balance is insufficient.

Dividend Dates

The shares of stock of most large corporations are owned by thousands of investors and these shares change hands constantly. It is impossible for these publicly traded corporations to know exactly who owns their stock at a given moment because the stock is bought and sold every day and it takes time for the corporations to obtain and record the stock transaction information. For this reason, corporations do not declare and pay a dividend on the same day.

Three important dates are associated with the payment of a cash dividend:

1. **Date of Declaration.** As stated earlier, the board of directors decides whether and when to pay a cash dividend. The day the board votes to pay a dividend is the date of declaration. The date of declaration marks the creation of the corporation's legal liability to pay the dividend.

date of declaration The date upon which a corporation announces plans to distribute a dividend. At this point, the corporation becomes legally obligated to make the distribution: A liability is created.

date of record Owners of the shares of stock on this day are the ones who will receive the dividend announced on the date of declaration.

date of payment The date a corporate dividend is actually paid. The payment date is generally announced on the date of declaration.

2. **Date of Record.** Whoever owns shares of stock on the date of record will receive the dividend. Every time a company's stock changes hands, the company is notified, although that notification may take several days or even weeks, especially in large corporations. Accordingly, the date of record may follow the date of declaration by several weeks.

3. **Date of Payment.** The date the dividend is actually paid is the date of payment. The corporation pays the dividend to whoever owned shares of stock on the date of record, even though some of those people may have sold their shares of stock between the date of record and the date of payment. The payment of the cash dividend satisfies the company's liability for the dividend.

Generally, on the date the board of directors declares a dividend, the date of record and the date of payment are publicly announced as shown in Exhibit 4–6.

EXHIBIT 4–6	Examples of Dividends Reported in 2002				
Company	*Per.*	*Amount*	*Declaration Date*	*Record Date*	*Payment Date*
IBM	Q	$.15	Apr. 30, 2002	May 10, 2002	June 10, 2002
Boeing	Q	.17	June 24, 2002	Aug. 16, 2002	Sept. 6, 2002
Southwest Airlines	Q	.045	July 18, 2002	Sept. 4, 2002	Sept. 25, 2002
ExxonMobil	Q	.23	Aug. 9, 2002	Aug. 13, 2002	Sept. 10, 2002
Wendy's Intl. Inc.	Q	.06	July 25, 2002	Aug. 5, 2002	Aug. 19, 2002

Discussion Questions

Let's say today is August 15, 2002. Use the information in Exhibit 4–6 to answer Discussion Questions 4–6 through 4–9.

4–6. You own 100 shares of ***ExxonMobil*** stock. How much is the next dividend you expect to receive and when do you expect to receive it?

4–7. How would the information in Exhibit 4–6 affect you if you were going to sell your shares of ***Southwest Airlines*** stock in the next few days?

4–8. You own 200 shares of ***Wendy's International.*** About how much would you expect to receive in dividends during the next year?

4–9. Which of the stocks listed has a dividend rate per share nearest to that of ***Boeing?***

4–10. An outspoken investor advocate, Ms. Nadera Ralphino, has just criticized Mega-Millions because the company paid only a $.60 per share dividend even though it has retained earnings of $6 billion. Why might Ms. Ralphino's criticism be unjustified?

CASH DIVIDENDS ON PREFERRED STOCK

The procedures associated with the payment of dividends on preferred stock are exactly the same as those for common stock. As with dividends on common stock, the board of directors declares preferred dividends and the dividends are paid in accordance with the three dividend dates outlined previously. The distinctions between common and preferred dividends are based on the preference features of preferred stocks. If a corporation has preferred stock and it elects to pay dividends, the preferred stockholders receive their dividend before the common stockholders can be paid.

◆ **INTRODUCTION TO THE STATEMENT OF OWNERS' EQUITY**

The **statement of owners' equity** is a bridge between the income statement and the balance sheet. The statement of owners' equity shows the changes to owners' equity from the beginning of the income statement period to the end of that period. The ending bal-

statement of owners' equity   The financial statement that reports activity in the capital accounts of proprietorships and partnerships and in the stockholders' equity accounts of corporations. The statement of owners' equity serves as a bridge between the income statement and the balance sheet.

ance shown on the statement of owners' equity is equal to the amount shown for owners' equity on the balance sheet.

Owners' equity has three basic components: *contributions by owners, earned equity*, and *distributions to owners*. The earned equity, of course, is a culmination of all the revenues and expenses, netted to arrive at net income or net loss. For the remainder of our discussion here, we will use net income or net loss in place of earnings or revenues and expenses. The basic idea of the statement of owners' equity is expressed in the following equation:

$$
\begin{aligned}
&\text{Beginning Owners' Equity}\\
+\ &\text{Contributions by Owners}\\
+\ &\text{Net Income}\\
-\ &\underline{\text{Distributions to Owners}}\\
=\ &\text{Ending Owners' Equity}
\end{aligned}
$$

Although the specifics of the statement vary according to the organizational form of the company, all statements include a beginning equity balance, the changes in equity caused by the three components of equity, and an ending balance.

PROPRIETORSHIPS—STATEMENT OF CAPITAL

statement of capital   A statement of owner's equity for a proprietorship.

Earned equity goes by various names, depending on the form of the business. Proprietorships and partnerships usually make no distinction between the equity from owner investments and earned equity. Because both forms of business are legally considered mere extensions of their owner or owners, the contributed equity and earned equity are combined and shown as one amount under the title "owners' equity" or "owners' capital." The statement of owner's equity for a sole proprietorship is generally called the **statement of capital.** In this context, the word *capital* refers to owner's equity. Exhibit 4–7 shows the format of a proprietorship's statement of capital using Jessica's Beauty Supply as an example. Note that the statement shows the changes in capital arising from the three components of equity and that the heading indicates the particular time period the statement reflects. This time period is usually the same one used in preparation of the income statement. Remember that, generally speaking, the ending balance of one period becomes the beginning balance for the next. Since this is Jessica's first month of operation, there was no beginning balance. The $10,000 contribution by owner is the investment Jessica made to start her business, as we discussed in Chapter 3. Remember, because a proprietorship pays no income tax, the company's net income would be $2,160, as we mentioned earlier in this chapter. We can also see that Jessica took a draw of $500, shown as a reduction of capital on the statement. The ending balance is calculated by combining the beginning balance of owner's capital, the contribution by owner, and the net income for the month. Then the distribution to Jessica is deducted to arrive at the ending balance of capital. It is important to note that this ending balance appears not only on the statement of capital but also in the owner's equity section of the balance sheet. Earlier, we said that the statement of owners' equity acts as a bridge between the income statement and the balance sheet. Now you

---

EXHIBIT 4–7   Statement of Capital for a Proprietorship

Jessica's Beauty Supply
Statement of Capital
For the Month Ended January 31, 2003

Jessica, capital, January 1, 2003	$ 0
ADD: Contributions by owner	10,000
Net income	2,160
	12,160
DEDUCT: Drawings (distributions to owner)	(500)
Jessica, capital, January 31, 2003	$11,660

can see that it bridges the statements by using the net income figure from the income statement to help calculate the ending owners' equity that appears on the balance sheet.

PARTNERSHIPS—STATEMENT OF CAPITAL

statement of partners' capital A statement of owners' equity for a partnership.

A statement of capital for a partnership would follow the same general outline as that for a proprietorship but might be designated a **statement of partners' capital.** As we mentioned earlier in this chapter, because a partnership pays no income tax, the company's net income would be $2,160. Of course, there would be a capital balance for each partner, and the partners would share the net income of $2,160 according to their partnership agreement. Using Jessica and Stephanie's partnership as an example, Exhibit 4–8 shows a statement of capital for this type of business form assuming Jessica's drawings were $400 and Stephanie's drawings were $100.

Exhibit 4–8 assumes that the partners, Jessica and Stephanie, have agreed to share the net income in the same proportion as their initial investments. Thus, Jessica is entitled to a capital increase of 60 percent of the total net income for the period, and Stephanie is entitled to an increase of 40 percent of the net income.

EXHIBIT 4–8 Statement of Partners' Capital for a Partnership

Jessica and Stephanie's Beauty Supply
Statement of Partners' Capital
For the Month Ended January 31, 2003

Jessica, capital, January 1, 2003	$ 0	
ADD: Jessica's contribution	6,000	
Net income	1,296	
LESS: Drawings (distributions to owners)	(400)	
Jessica, capital, January 31, 2003		$ 6,896
Stephanie, capital, January 1, 2003	0	
ADD: Stephanie's contribution	4,000	
Net income	864	
LESS: Drawings (distributions to owners)	(100)	
Stephanie, capital, January 31, 2003		4,764
Total partners' capital, January 31, 2003		$11,660

As you can see from the exhibit, this statement of capital shows the impact of a withdrawal made by the partners. Jessica has taken a withdrawal of $400 while Stephanie took a withdrawal of only $100. This action reduces the amount of their capital accounts and the total amount of partners' equity.

CORPORATIONS—STATEMENT OF STOCKHOLDERS' EQUITY

statement of stockholders' equity The financial statement that shows the changes in owners' equity for a corporation for a given time period.

The statement that shows the changes in owners' equity for a corporation is called the **statement of stockholders' equity.** Corporations are legally required to keep the equity from owners' investment and the earned equity separate. In corporations, you will recall, the investment by owners is called *contributed capital* and earned equity is called *retained earnings*.

The format of the statement of stockholders' equity varies somewhat from company to company, but the main idea is to trace the balances in stock, additional paid-in capital, and retained earnings from the beginning of the period to the end. The statement of stockholders' equity for Jessica's Beauty Supply, Inc., in Exhibit 4–9 on page F–130 traces common and preferred stock, additional paid-in capital, and retained earnings from their balances on January 1 to their balances on January 31, 2003.

The beginning balances on the statement of stockholders' equity are the previous period's ending balances. All the beginning balances are zero in this statement because

Jessica's Beauty Supply, Inc.
Statement of Stockholders' Equity
For the Month Ended January 31, 2003

	Preferred Stock	Additional Paid-in Capital Preferred	Common Stock	Additional Paid-in Capital Common	Retained Earnings	Total Stockholders' Equity
Balance, January 1, 2003	$ 0	$ 0	$ 0	$ 0	$ 0	$ 0
Common stock issued			4,000	36,000		40,000
Preferred stock issued	20,000	1,000				21,000
Net income					1,620	1,620
Preferred dividends					(100)	(100)
Common dividends					(400)	(400)
Balance, January 31	$20,000	$1,000	$4,000	$36,000	$1,120	$62,120

EXHIBIT 4–9 Statement of Stockholders' Equity for Jessica's Beauty Supply, Inc.

this is the company's first month of operation. Notice that the statement of stockholders' equity reflects activity in both types of owners' equity—contributed capital and earned equity. Common and preferred stock and additional paid-in capital are components of contributed capital, and retained earnings represents the earned equity portion of stockholders' equity. The amount of retained earnings is increased by net income each period or decreased by net loss and decreased by dividend distributions to stockholders. The net income figure comes directly from the income statement. The dividend of $500 is comprised of $400 for common stock (4,000 × $.10 per share) and $100 for preferred stock (200 × $.50 per share), and it reduces retained earnings. Notice that the income and dividends affect only the retained earnings section. Both net income and dividends change the balance in retained earnings, but neither affects any part of contributed capital. We use the totals at the bottom of the statement of stockholders' equity to prepare the stockholders' equity section of the balance sheet.

Exhibit 4–10 outlines the differences among owners' equity for the three business forms we examined for Jessica's beauty supply company.

EXHIBIT 4–10 Owners' Equity by Business Organizational Form

	Proprietorship	*Partnership*	*Corporation*
Name of Statement	Statement of capital	Statement of partners' capital	• Statement of stockholders' equity
Statement Sections	Capital	Partner's capital	• Contributed capital • Retained earnings
Equity Account Titles	Jessica, capital	Jessica, capital Stephanie, capital	• Common stock • Preferred stock • Additional paid-in capital • Retained earnings

Discussion Question

4–11. How would it be possible for Jessica's Beauty Supply, Inc., to have a zero balance in retained earnings on January 1, 2003, even if January 2003 was not the company's first month of business? Is there any other financial statement information that might confirm that this was the first month of operations?

statement of retained earnings A corporate financial statement that shows the changes in retained earnings during a particular period.

STATEMENT OF RETAINED EARNINGS

If a corporation has not issued stock or engaged in any other activity that would affect contributed capital, it may issue a **statement of retained earnings** instead of the more comprehensive statement of stockholders' equity. A statement of retained earnings is similar in form to the statement of capital for proprietorships and partnerships. Exhibit 4–11 presents a statement of retained earnings for Jessica's Beauty Supply, Inc.

EXHIBIT 4–11   Statement of Retained Earnings for Jessica's Beauty Supply, Inc.

Jessica's Beauty Supply, Inc.
Statement of Retained Earnings
For the Month Ended January 31, 2003

Retained earnings, January 1, 2003		$ 0
ADD: Net income		1,620
		$1,620
DEDUCT: Preferred dividends	(100)	
Common dividends	(400)	(500)
Retained earnings, January 31, 2003		$1,120

This simpler statement is an acceptable substitute for the statement of stockholders' equity only if no changes have been made in a corporation's contributed capital. However, because most corporations are frequently involved in activities affecting their stock or other parts of their contributed capital, corporations use the statement of stockholders' equity more often than the statement of retained earnings. Of the 600 companies surveyed in 2001 by *Accounting Trends and Techniques*, 577 used the statement of stockholders' equity in 2000.[3] Only seven of the corporations presented a statement of retained earnings. The remaining group did not present either form of this "bridge statement," but rather placed a schedule in the notes to their financial statements.

◆ **ARTICULATION**

articulation The links among the financial statements.

Earlier in this chapter, we referred to the link between income and owners' equity. We call this link the **articulation** (or connection) of the financial statements. When preparing financial statements, accountants prepare the income statement first, the statement of owners' equity second, and the balance sheet last. This is because the net income amount must be taken from the income statement and placed on the statement of owners' equity. Further, the ending balances from the statement of owners' equity are used to prepare the balance sheet. Amounts from one statement are needed to complete the next statement. While we will demonstrate articulation using only the corporate form, the concept is the same for proprietorships and partnerships. The blue lines on the financial statements in Exhibit 4–12 on page F–132 depict the articulation among the statements for Jessica's Beauty Supply, Inc.

As Exhibit 4–12 demonstrates, we prepare the income statement first to calculate net income. Then, we use net income from the income statement to prepare the statement of stockholders' equity. Finally, we use the ending balances shown on the statement of stockholders' equity to prepare the balance sheet. And after all this, the accounting equation shows that this important relationship still holds true.

$$\text{Assets} = \text{Liabilities} + \text{Owners' Equity}$$
$$\$312,120 = \$250,000 + \$62,120$$

Discussion Question •

4–12. If a clerk in Jessica's Beauty Supply, Inc., decided to slip the cash from a sale into his pocket and not record the sale, how would each of the statements in Exhibit 4–12 be affected?

---

[3]*Accounting Trends and Techniques* (AICPA, 2001), 43.

Jessica's Beauty Supply, Inc.
Income Statement
For the Month Ended January 31, 2003

Sales		$3,230
Less cost of goods sold		955
Gross margin		2,275
Operating expenses:		
Wages expense	$675	
Utilities expense	310	
Total operating expenses		(985)
Operating income		1,290
Other revenues:		
Rent revenue		990
Other expenses:		
Interest expense		(120)
Income before income tax		2,160
Income tax expense		(540)
Net income		$1,620

Statement of Stockholders' Equity
For the Month Ended January 31, 2003

	Preferred Stock	Additional Paid-in Capital Preferred	Common Stock	Additional Paid-in Capital Common	Retained Earnings	Total Stockholders' Equity
Balance, January 1, 2003	$ 0	$ 0	$ 0	$ 0	$ 0	$ 0
Common stock issued			4,000	36,000		40,000
Preferred stock issued	20,000	1,000				21,000
Net income					1,620	1,620
Preferred dividends					(100)	(100)
Common dividends					(400)	(400)
Balance, January 31	$20,000	$1,000	$4,000	$36,000	$1,120	$62,120

Balance Sheet
January 31, 2003

Assets:		Liabilities:	
Cash	$ 82,120	Notes payable	$ 50,000
Land	50,000	Bonds payable	200,000
Building	120,000	Total liabilites	250,000
Computer equipment	35,000	Stockholders' equity:	
Truck	25,000	Preferred stock	$ 20,000
		Additional paid-in capital—preferred	1,000
		Common stock	4,000
		Additional paid-in capital—common	36,000
		Total contributed capital	61,000
		Retained earnings	1,120
		Total stockholders' equity	62,120
Total Assets	$312,120	Total liabilities and stockholders' equity	$312,120

EXHIBIT 4–12   Articulation Among Financial Statements for Jessica's Beauty Supply, Inc.

◆ STATEMENT OF CASH FLOWS

operating activities
Activities that result in cash inflows and outflows generated from the normal course of business.

As we mentioned in Chapter 3, the **operating activities** section of the statement of cash flows includes cash inflows and outflows for revenues and expenses associated with a company's ongoing business operations. Basically, these activities are related to the items found on the income statement. To simplify our introduction to the operating activities section of the statement of cash flows, we will assume that all of Jessica's Beauty Supply, Inc.'s revenues and expenses are received and paid in cash. Exhibit 4–13 shows the statement of cash flows for Jessica's Beauty Supply, Inc., for the month ended January 31, 2003.

Except for adding the $500 cash paid for dividends, we used the cash flow from investing and financing activities prepared in Chapter 3 for Jessica's Beauty Supply, Inc. As you can see, the statement of cash flows provides a wealth of important information. Not only does the statement show the ending cash balance, but it also tells us about the sources and uses of cash.

Discussion Questions •••••••••••••••••••••••••••••••••

4–13. Where did Jessica's Beauty Supply, Inc., get most of its cash?
4–14. Where did Jessica's Beauty Supply, Inc., use the most cash?
4–15. The cash balance for Jessica's Beauty Supply, Inc., grew to $82,120 during its first month of business. Based on the statement of cash flows in Exhibit 4–13, do you think there are any problems with the company's cash situation?

EXHIBIT 4–13   Statement of Cash Flows for Jessica's Beauty Supply, Inc.

Jessica's Beauty Supply, Inc.
Statement of Cash Flows
For the Month Ended January 31, 2003

Cash flows from operating activities:		
Cash collections from customers	$ 3,230	
Cash received for rent	990	
Cash paid for merchandise	(955)	
Cash paid for wages	(675)	
Cash paid for utilities	(310)	
Cash paid for interest	(120)	
Cash paid for income tax	(540)	
Net cash flows from operating activities		$ 1,620
Cash flows from investing activities:		
Purchase of land	(50,000)	
Purchase of building	(120,000)	
Purchase of computer equipment	(35,000)	
Purchase of truck	(25,000)	
Net cash flows from investing activities		(230,000)
Cash flows from financing activities:		
Sale of common stock	40,000	
Sale of preferred stock	21,000	
Borrowing on notes payable	50,000	
Sale of bonds	200,000	
Cash paid for preferred dividends	(100)	
Cash paid for common dividends	(400)	
Net cash flows from financing activities		310,500
Increase in cash		82,120
Cash at the beginning of the period		0
Cash at the end of the period		$ 82,120

Now that we have a complete set of financial statements for Jessica's Beauty Supply, Inc., the question is, how is the company doing? Would it be a good investment? Would it be a good credit risk?

At the beginning of the chapter, we posed the hypothetical situation in which you were a loan officer evaluating the credit risk of a particular customer. Let's assume that Jessica's Beauty Supply, Inc., is that customer. Should you lend the $150,000 to Jessica's Beauty Supply, Inc.? It may be difficult to tell without additional information and without analyzing Jessica's financial statements.

PROFITABILITY RATIOS

In this chapter, we will present seven ratios used to evaluate profitability: gross profit margin ratio, net profit margin ratio, rate of return on assets ratio, rate of return on common equity ratio, dividend payout ratio, earnings per share, and the price-to-earnings ratio.

Gross Profit Margin Ratio

gross profit margin ratio
A financial ratio that expresses a company's gross profit (often called gross margin on the financial statements) as a percentage of sales revenue.

The **gross profit margin ratio** expresses a company's gross profit (often called gross margin on the financial statements) as a percentage of sales revenue. The formula for this ratio is:

$$\text{Gross Profit Margin Ratio} = \frac{\text{Gross Profit}}{\text{Net Sales}}$$

Using the information from the financial statements for Jessica's Beauty Supply, Inc., in Exhibit 4–12, the calculation is as follows:

$$\frac{\$2,275}{\$3,230} = .704 \text{ or } 70.4\%$$

The gross profit margin ratio for Jessica's company indicates that gross profit is 70.4 percent of sales.

This ratio calculation tells us that after covering the cost of products sold during the month, Jessica had 70.4 percent of each sales dollar remaining to cover all the company's operating expenses, interest cost, and income taxes. You can also look at it this way: For every one dollar of sales, the company had about 70.4 cents remaining after it paid for the merchandise it sold. This 70.4 cents is what Jessica's Beauty Supply, Inc., has left to pay all its other costs. Gross profit margin ratios vary from industry to industry, but clearly, the higher the gross profit margin percentage, the better.

Net Profit Margin Ratio

net profit margin ratio
A financial ratio that expresses a company's net profit (almost always called either net income or net earnings on the financial statements) as a percentage of sales revenue. It indicates the amount of net income generated by a dollar of sales.

The **net profit margin ratio** expresses a company's net profit (almost always called either net income or net earnings on the financial statements) as a percentage of sales revenue. It indicates the amount of net income generated by a dollar of sales. The formula for this ratio is:

$$\text{Net Profit Margin Ratio} = \frac{\text{Net Profit}}{\text{Net Sales}}$$

Using the information from the financial statements for Jessica's Beauty Supply, Inc., in Exhibit 4–12, the calculation is as follows:

$$\frac{\$1,620}{\$3,230} = .502 \text{ or } 50.2\%$$

This ratio tells us that during the month, Jessica's Beauty Supply, Inc., had 50.2 percent of each sales dollar remaining as profit after covering the cost of products sold, all operating expenses, interest cost, and income taxes. In other words, it reveals the percentage of each sales dollar remaining after *all* the costs of running the business for the year. So for every one dollar of sales, Jessica's had about 50.2 cents (of each sales dollar) remaining after it paid its costs for the year. Net profit margin ratios vary from industry to industry, but clearly, the higher the net profit margin percentage, the better.

Rate of Return on Assets Ratio

rate of return on assets ratio A financial ratio that shows the amount of profit (net income) produced for a given level of assets.

The **rate of return on assets ratio** shows the amount of profit (net income) produced for a given level of assets. This is an important ratio because it indicates how effectively the company uses its total assets to generate net income. The formula for this ratio is:

$$\text{Rate of Return on Assets Ratio} = \frac{\text{Net Income}}{\text{Average Total Assets}}$$

The net income amount we use in the numerator of this ratio comes directly from the income statement. The amount we use as the denominator requires a bit of explanation. Since the net income in the numerator was earned throughout the month of January 2003 (some in the first week, some in the second, etc.), we want to know the amount of assets employed throughout the month. We determine this by calculating the average of the total assets. This is done by adding the beginning balance of total assets to the ending balance of total assets and then dividing that number by two. Since January 2003 is the first month of operation for Jessica's Beauty Supply, Inc., the beginning balance of total assets is $0. The ending balance comes from the January 31, 2003, balance sheet ($312,120). The average total assets for the month of January is $156,060 ($0 + $312,120 = $312,120/2 = $156,060). We calculate Jessica's rate of return on assets for January 2003 as:

$$\frac{\$1,620}{\$156,060} = .0104 \text{ or } 1.04\%$$

The return on assets for Jessica's Beauty Supply, Inc., indicates the company earned a return of only 1 percent on average total assets during January 2003. Even though the return on assets will vary depending on the industry and company, this return seems particularly low. What do you think?

Rate of Return on Common Equity Ratio

rate of return on common equity ratio A financial ratio that shows the amount of profit (net income) in relation to the amount of investment by the company's owners.

The **rate of return on common equity ratio** shows the amount of profit (net income) in relation to the amount of investment by the company's owners. The purpose of this ratio is similar to that of the rate of return on assets ratio except that it focuses on the owners' investment (represented by the equity), rather than total assets. The formula for this ratio is:

$$\text{Rate of Return on Common Equity Ratio} = \frac{\text{Net Income} - \text{Total Preferred Dividends}}{\text{Average Common Stockholders' Equity}}$$

The net income used in the numerator of this ratio comes from the income statement, but it must be adjusted for any preferred stock dividend requirement, because that amount is not available to common stockholders. As Jessica's Beauty Supply, Inc.'s statement of stockholders' equity shows, the company paid a preferred dividend totaling $100 to Stephanie ($0.50 × 200 shares).

We use an average amount for the denominator in this calculation for the same reason we did in the rate of return on assets ratio. Since the net income in the numerator was earned throughout the month of January, we want to know the amount of common equity throughout the month. We determine this by calculating the average of the common stockholders' equity. This is done by adding the beginning balance of common stockholders' equity to the ending balance of common stockholders' equity and then dividing that number by two. Since January 2003 is the first month of operation for Jessica's Beauty Supply, Inc., the beginning balance of common stockholders' equity is $0. The ending balance comes from the January 31, 2003, balance sheet ($62,120 − $21,000 preferred stock = $41,120). The average common stockholders' equity for the month of January is $20,560 ($0 + $41,120 = $41,120/2 = $20,560). We calculate Jessica's rate of return on common equity for January 2003 as:

$$\frac{\$1,620 - \$100}{\$20,560} = .074 \text{ or } 7.4\%$$

This ratio tells us that during January 2003, Jessica's Beauty Supply, Inc.'s earned a 7.4 percent return on the owners' holdings in the company. Do not confuse this with what the owners themselves earned on their investment. The owners' return is a combination of the dividends they receive and appreciation of the stock's price in the marketplace. The company's rate of return on common equity does, however, greatly influence the market price of the company's stock and, therefore, the stockholders' return on their investment.

Dividend Payout Ratio

The **dividend payout ratio** shows what portion of a company's net income for a given year was paid to its owners as cash dividends during that year. The formula for this ratio is:

$$\text{Dividend Payout Ratio} = \frac{\text{Total Cash Dividends}}{\text{Net Income}}$$

We can determine the amount of cash dividends to use in the numerator by examining the statement of stockholders' equity in Exhibit 4–12. The denominator is simply net income from the income statement. We calculate Jessica's Beauty Supply, Inc.'s dividend payout ratio for January 2003 as:

$$\frac{\$500}{\$1,620} = .309 \text{ or } 30.9\%$$

This ratio tells us that during January 2003, Jessica's paid out 30.9 percent of its net income to its stockholders as dividends. On the surface, it might seem that a high-dividend payout ratio is better than a low one, and for some investors this is true (those who count on dividends as a significant portion of their yearly income). Many investors and analysts, however, believe a low-dividend payout ratio is superior to a high one. The reason is actually pretty simple. Remember that a company can do only two things with the profits it earns: It can either distribute them to the stockholders as dividends, or it can reinvest them in the business in the form of property, plant, and equipment or new products and processes. A high-dividend payout ratio may indicate that a company is not investing sufficiently for the future.

Earnings per Share

Earnings per share expresses the net income of a company as a per share amount on common stock. The formula for this ratio is:

$$\text{Earnings per Share} = \frac{\text{Net Income} - \text{Total Preferred Dividend}}{\text{Average Common Shares Outstanding}}$$

As you can see, preferred stock dividends have been deducted from net income in the numerator of this ratio. This is because the part of net income distributed to the preferred shareholders is not available to the common shareholders. The denominator of the ratio uses an average amount for the same reason earlier ratios did. Since the profit was earned throughout the period, we want to know the average number of shares outstanding for the period covered by the calculation of earnings per share. In this case, we use 4,000 common shares because the number of shares has been constant throughout the company's entire existence. Most companies must calculate a weighted average number of common shares because the number of shares outstanding changes. Earnings per share calculations, including the calculations for the number of weighted average common shares outstanding, is covered in more detail in Chapter 9.

Earnings per share is never calculated for preferred stock, so the number of preferred shares is never used in the calculation. The calculations for earnings per share for large publicly traded companies is quite complicated due to the ever-changing number of common shares outstanding and other factors that may be present that could dilute (lessen) the earnings per share amount. Using the information from the financial statements for Jessica's Beauty Supply, Inc., in Exhibit 4–12, we present the calculation for earnings per share in its most basic form as follows:

$$\frac{\$1,620 - \$100}{4,000 \text{ Shares}} = \$.38 \text{ per Share}$$

The earnings per share for Jessica's Beauty Supply, Inc., indicates the company earned 38 cents per share. Notice that the preferred dividends were deducted from net income before it was divided by common shares. Earnings per share is not an indication of how much the common stockholders received from the company. It reflects the amount earned, of which only a part is typically distributed to shareholders. In this case, the common shareholder, Jessica, only received $400 of the $1,620 available to common shareholders so she did not get 38 cents per share in dividends. Generally, the greater the earnings per share, the better. In fact, earnings per share has a huge impact on the value of publicly traded stocks.

Price-to-Earnings Ratio

price-to-earnings ratio
A financial ratio that is often called simply the PE ratio that expresses the relationship between a company's earnings per share and the market value of the company's stock.

The **price-to-earnings ratio** (often referred to as simply the PE ratio) expresses the relationship between a company's earnings per share and the market value of the company's stock. Financial analysts use this measure to decide whether a company's stock is *under*valued or *over*valued. This ratio is considered so valuable that it is published daily in stock market reports along with a stock's high and low prices and the volume of shares traded. The formula for this ratio is:

$$\text{Price-to-Earnings Ratio} = \frac{\text{Average Market Price per Share of Stock}}{\text{Earnings per Share}}$$

The numerator for this ratio is not found in any of a company's financial statements. Rather, it is the average price of the stock in the stock market. This is a subject we will discuss in much greater detail in Chapter 11. For now, let's assume that Jessica's Beauty Supply, Inc., has an average market price of $6.00 per share. The denominator is earnings per share from the income statement. We calculate Jessica's price to earnings ratio for January 2003 as:

$$\frac{\$6.00}{\$.38} = 15.79 \text{ times}$$

This ratio calculation tells us that Jessica's stock was selling for 15.79 times its earnings per share in January 2003. This is a difficult ratio to interpret because it means different things to different analysts. A high PE ratio may indicate that the stock is overvalued (and may be an unwise investment), whereas a low PE ratio may indicate that it is undervalued (and may be a wise investment). Since the market value of a stock is not directly related to earnings per share, smart analysts evaluate this ratio in conjunction with many other factors.

ANALYSIS OF THE STATEMENT OF CASH FLOWS

The statement of cash flows itself presents the results of an analysis of cash flows. Company accountants have done most of the analytical calculations so financial statement users are able to do more interpreting with less calculating. You already know that the statement of cash flows presents sources and uses of cash for operating, investing, and financing activities. As a financial statement user, you should evaluate not only the appropriateness of the uses of cash, but also the appropriateness of the sources of cash as well.

Cash Flow from Operating Activities

Net cash inflow from operating activities is a healthy sign. This is because a net cash inflow from operating activities constitutes cash that the company has generated internally instead of from additional investments by owners, borrowing, or selling off investments. In the long run, businesses must generate cash from operating activities to pay for investments and to pay a return to its owners and to pay its creditors. In evaluating a business's cash flow, you should examine the proportion of cash that comes from operating activities versus the amount that comes from investing and financing activities. Also compare net cash inflow from operations with net income to evaluate how much of the net income is actually being realized in cash.

Cash Flow from Investing Activities

Net cash *inflow* from investing activities may be an indication that the company is not investing in the land, buildings, equipment, and other assets it will need for the future, and in fact, it is selling off assets. You can just about count on a net cash *outflow* from investing activities in such companies as **Starbucks, Wal-Mart, McDonalds,** and other successful companies because they are constantly expanding by investing in new stores. Generally speaking, investments pay off in the future. If the company does not invest, there will be no payoff. Substantial, sustained cash outflows for investing in securities may indicate that the company is retaining cash that it really doesn't need for business operations. In such a case, perhaps some of the excess funds would be better used to pay down debt or to pay dividends to stockholders.

Cash Flow from Financing Activities

Unless the business is just beginning or expanding, net cash inflow from financing activities is not necessarily a positive indication. Any business can have a sizable stream of cash inflows from borrowing, at least for a while. But when a substantial portion of a company's cash routinely comes from borrowing, this ultimately spells trouble. Increased borrowing entails higher interest cost, and the loan must be repaid at some point. Within reason, it is generally better to see net cash outflow in the financing section of the statement of cash flows unless the company is in the start-up or expansion mode.

By now you should have a basic understanding of financial statements and how they relate to one another. The more you know about financial statements, the better you can utilize them for economic decisions. In the next chapter, we will introduce two bases of economic measurement: the cash basis and the accrual basis.

Summary

The income statement is a financial tool that provides information about a company's past performance. Like the balance sheet, the income statement is made up of accounting elements. The two elements included in the income statement are revenues and expenses, and the statement can be expressed by the following equation:

$$\text{Revenues} - \text{Expenses} = \text{Net Income (or Net Loss)}$$

The income statement equation forms the basis for the income statement itself. The income statement indicates that during this specific time period, the company earned so much revenue, incurred so much expense, and produced either a net income or a net loss. Publicly traded companies are required to prepare income statements for external users annually and quarterly. The income statement's formal name is the statement of results of operations.

There are two commonly used income statement formats: the single-step and the multiple-step formats. In the single-step income statement format, all revenues are grouped together and then totaled. This format is called the single-step income statement because in one step, total expenses are subtracted from total revenues to determine net income or net loss. The multiple-step income statement provides two items of information not presented in a single-step income statement: (1) gross margin (gross profit) and (2) operating income (income from operations).

A company's equity changes by the amount of its net income or loss. Net income increases the owners' equity in the business. Each revenue increases earned equity and each expense decreases earned equity. A net income, therefore, increases earned equity, while a net loss decreases earned equity.

Just as net income increases owners' equity, distributions to owners—another accounting element—decrease owners' equity. In the case of proprietorships and partnerships, distributions to owners are called drawings or withdrawals. Distributions to owners of a corporation are called dividends. To be able to pay a cash dividend, a corporation must have two things: sufficient retained earnings and sufficient cash.

The statement of owners' equity is a bridge between the income statement and the balance sheet. This statement shows the changes to owners' equity from the beginning of the income statement period to the end of that period. The ending balance shown on the statement of owners' equity is equal to the amount shown for owners' equity on the balance sheet. The statement of owners' equity for a sole proprietorship is generally called the statement of capital, and for a partnership, it is usually called the statement of partners' capital. Corporations generally call this statement the statement of stockholders' equity, although if there have been no changes in contributed capital during the period, the company may prepare a statement of retained earnings, which is similar in form to the statement of capital for proprietorships and partnerships.

The income statement, the statement of owners' equity, and the balance sheet have a special relationship of interdependence to one another called articulation. Articulation means that the net income shown on the income statement causes an increase in equity on the statement of owners' equity. Then, the ending balances from the statement of owners' equity are included in the equity section of the balance sheet. The ending balance of cash on the statement of cash flows should be the same as the balance of cash on the balance sheet. The operating activities section of the statement of cash flows includes cash inflows and outflows for revenues and expenses associated with a company's ongoing business operations.

Over time, financial analysts have developed several ratios to evaluate a company's profitability performance. In this chapter, we presented seven of them: the gross profit margin ratio, the net profit margin ratio, the rate of return on assets ratio, the rate of return on common equity ratio, the dividend payout ratio, earnings per share, and the price-to-earnings ratio.

Key Terms

- articulation, F–131
- cost of goods sold, F–121
- cost of products sold. *See* cost of goods sold
- cost of sales. *See* cost of goods sold
- date of declaration, F–126
- date of payment, F–127
- date of record, F–127
- distributions to owners, F–124
- dividend payout ratio, F–136
- dividends, F–125
- drawings, F–125
- earnings per share, F–136
- expense, F–118
- gross margin, F–122

- gross profit. *See* gross margin
- gross profit margin ratio, F–134
- income from operations. *See* operating income
- income statement, F–118
- income tax, F–121
- multiple-step income statement, F–122
- net earnings. *See* net income
- net income, F–119
- net loss, F–119
- net profit. *See* net income
- net profit margin ratio, F–134
- operating activities, F–133
- operating income, F–122
- price-to-earnings ratio, F–137

- rate of return on assets ratio, F–135
- rate of return on common equity ratio, F–135
- revenue, F–118
- sales revenue, F–122
- single-step income statement, F–121
- statement of capital, F–128
- statement of owners' equity, F–128
- statement of partners' capital, F–129
- statement of results of operations. *See* income statement
- statement of retained earnings, F–130
- statement of stockholders' equity, F–129
- withdrawals. *See* drawings

Review the Facts

A. Name and define in your own words the accounting elements used to determine net income.

B. What is the major expense of merchandisers and manufacturers?

C. Name the two formats of the income statement, and describe the differences between them.

D. What item is responsible for the primary increase in the capital account?

E. What is the difference between a statement of stockholders' equity and a statement of retained earnings?

F. What is the effect of owners' drawings and on what financial statement is this information reported?

G. Under what circumstances is a corporation unable to pay a dividend?

H. How is a corporation's financial position affected by the payment of a dividend?

I. Explain the following terms: *date of declaration, date of record*, and *date of payment*.

J. Describe the meaning of articulation as it is used in accounting.

K. Describe the operating activities sections of the statement of cash flows.

L. List and describe each of the seven profitability ratios.

M. Describe what you would prefer to see in a company's net cash inflows/outflows for each section of the statement of cash flows.

Apply What You Have Learned • • • • • • • • • • • • • • • • • •

LO 1: TERMINOLOGY

4–16. Below is a list of items relating to the concepts discussed in this chapter, followed by definitions and examples of those items in scrambled order:

a. Assets   d. Revenues
b. Liabilities   e. Expenses
c. Equity

1. _____ Debts of the company
2. _____ Sales
3. _____ Probable future economic benefits
4. _____ Inflows of assets from delivering or producing goods, rendering services, or other activities
5. _____ "Things" of value a company has
6. _____ The residual interest in the assets of an entity that remains after deducting its liabilities
7. _____ Probable future sacrifices of economic benefits
8. _____ Outflows or other using up of assets from delivering or producing goods, rendering services, or carrying out other activities
9. _____ Costs that have no future value
10. _____ What the company owes
11. _____ What the company has less what it owes
12. _____ The owner's interest in the company

Required: Match the letter next to each item on the list with the appropriate definition. Letters may be used more than once.

LO 1: INCOME STATEMENT TERMINOLOGY

4–17. Define the following terms in your own words:

a. Revenue   d. Net loss
b. Expense   e. Profit
c. Net income   f. Earnings

LO 1, 5, & 6: TERMINOLOGY

4–18. Below is a list of items relating to the concepts discussed in this chapter, followed by definitions of those items in scrambled order:

a. Revenues   f. Drawings
b. Expenses   g. Date of declaration
c. Income statement   h. Date of record
d. Statement of owners' equity   i. Date of payment
e. Dividends   j. Articulation

1. _____ The date distributions of earnings to owners of a corporation are actually paid
2. _____ Inflows of assets from delivering or producing goods, rendering services, or other activities
3. _____ Distribution of earnings to the owners of a corporation
4. _____ The link between the income statement and the balance sheet
5. _____ A bridge statement showing how the income statement and balance sheet are related
6. _____ Distribution of earnings to the owners of proprietorships and partnerships
7. _____ Outflows or other using up of assets from delivering or producing goods, rendering services, or carrying out other activities
8. _____ The date a corporation announces it will make a distribution of earnings to its owners
9. _____ A financial tool providing information about an entity's past performance
10. _____ Whoever owns shares of stock on this date will receive the distribution of earnings previously declared

Required: Match the letter next to each item on the list with the appropriate definition. Use each letter only once.

LO 1 & 2: SIMPLE INCOME STATEMENT PREPARATION—NO INCOME TAXES

4–19. Phil Brock and Company had $75,985 in sales revenue during 2004. In addition to the regular sales revenue, Brock rented out a small building it owned and received $4,800 for the year. Cost of goods sold for the year totaled $31,812. Other expenses for the year were as follows:

Rent	$10,500
Utilities	2,195
Advertising	4,265
Wages	12,619
Interest	996

Required:

    a. Prepare a 2004 income statement for Phil Brock and Company using a single-step format.

    b. Prepare a 2004 income statement for Phil Brock and Company using a multiple-step format.

LO 1 & 2: SIMPLE INCOME STATEMENT PREPARATION—NO INCOME TAXES

4–20. Sam Sosa and Company had $245,000 in sales revenue during 2004. In addition, Sosa had interest revenue of $7,600 for the year. Cost of goods sold for the year totaled $102,000. Other expenses for the year were:

Rent	$24,000
Wages	13,500
Advertising	2,200
Utilities	2,900

Required:

    a. Prepare a 2004 income statement for Sam Sosa and Company using a single-step format.

    b. Prepare a 2004 income statement for Sam Sosa and Company using a multiple-step format.

LO 1 & 2: SIMPLE INCOME STATEMENT PREPARATION—CORPORATE

4–21. Pipkin's Camera and Video, Inc., had sales revenue of $770,000 during 2003. Expenses for the year were:

Wages	$ 72,000
Rent	64,000
Advertising	16,400
Cost of goods sold	550,000
Utilities	13,600
Income tax expense	16,200

Required:

    a. Prepare a 2003 income statement for Pipkin's Camera and Video, Inc., using a single-step format.

    b. Prepare a 2003 income statement for Pipkin's Camera and Video, Inc., using a multiple-step format.

LO 1 & 2: INCOME STATEMENT PREPARATION—CORPORATE

4–22. The following information is taken from the accounting records of Alex's Baseball Card Shop, Inc., for 2004:

Sales	$650,000
Wages	120,000
Store rent	39,000
Interest expense	42,000
Advertising	28,200

Electricity	6,800
Telephone	1,400
Cost of goods sold	420,000
Rent revenue	18,000
Income tax expense	2,120

Required:

  a. Prepare a 2004 income statement for Alex's Baseball Card Shop, Inc., using a single-step format.
  b. Prepare a 2004 income statement for Alex's Baseball Card Shop, Inc., using a multiple-step format.
  c. If you were the owner of the company, which format of income statement would you prefer to use? Why?

LO 1 & 2: CORPORATE INCOME STATEMENT PREPARATION

4–23. The following information is taken from accounting records of Nancy's Chocolate Factory for the year ended December 31, 2003:

Sales	$356,000
Cost of goods sold	275,000
Wages and salaries	30,000
Rent	20,000
Electricity	9,000
Telephone	7,000
Advertising	5,000
Maintenance	1,000
Interest expense	4,000
Income tax	2,000

Required:

  a. Prepare a 2003 income statement for the company using the single-step format.
  b. Prepare a 2003 income statement for the company using a multiple-step format.

LO 1 & 2: CORPORATE INCOME STATEMENT PREPARATION

4–24. The following information is taken from accounting records of Al's Boating Supplies, Inc., for the year ended December 31, 2003:

Sales	$1,343,000
Cost of goods sold	1,100,000
Wages and salaries	80,000
Rent	70,000
Electricity	25,000
Telephone	23,000
Advertising	14,000
Maintenance	4,000
Interest revenue	9,000
Interest expense	12,000
Income tax	6,000

Required:

  a. Prepare a 2003 income statement for the company using the single-step format.
  b. Prepare a 2003 income statement for the company using a multiple-step format.

LO 1, 2, 4, & 6: CORPORATE INCOME STATEMENT AND RETAINED EARNINGS STATEMENT PREPARATION

4–25. The following information is taken from accounting records of Gina's Nail Salon for the year ended December 31, 2003:

Sales	$123,000
Cost of goods sold	75,000
Operating expenses	40,280
Interest revenue	1,200

Interest expense	6,240
Income tax	536
Beginning retained earnings balance	10,650
Dividends	500

Required:

a. Prepare a 2003 income statement for the company using the single-step format.
b. Prepare a 2003 income statement for the company using a multiple-step format.
c. Prepare a 2003 retained earnings statement for the company.

LO 1, 2, 4, & 6: CORPORATE INCOME STATEMENT AND RETAINED EARNINGS STATEMENT PREPARATION

4–26. The following information is taken from accounting records of Michelle's Catering Co. for the year ended December 31, 2003:

Sales	$350,000
Cost of goods sold	265,400
Operating expenses	56,300
Rent revenue	2,400
Interest expense	9,850
Income tax	4,170
Beginning retained earnings balance	45,800
Dividends	1,500

Required:

a. Prepare a 2003 income statement for the company using the single-step format.
b. Prepare a 2003 income statement for the company using a multiple-step format.
c. Prepare a 2003 retained earnings statement for the company.

LO 1, 2, 4, & 6: CORPORATE INCOME STATEMENT AND RETAINED EARNINGS STATEMENT PREPARATION

4–27. The following information is taken from accounting records of Jerry's Hunting & Fishing Supplies for the year ended December 31, 2003:

Sales	$538,400
Cost of goods sold	318,520
Operating expenses	198,560
Rent revenue	4,260
Interest expense	12,500
Income tax	3,270
Beginning retained earnings balance	36,800
Dividends	1,000

Required:

a. Prepare a 2003 income statement for the company using the single-step format.
b. Prepare a 2003 income statement for the company using a multiple-step format.
c. Prepare a 2003 retained earnings statement for the company.

LO 1, 2, 4, & 6: CORPORATE INCOME STATEMENT AND RETAINED EARNINGS STATEMENT PREPARATION

4–28. The following information is taken from accounting records of Martha's Books for Kids for the year ended December 31, 2003:

Sales	$126,500
Cost of goods sold	80,520
Wages and salaries	22,000
Rent	12,000
Electricity	2,400
Telephone	1,200
Interest revenue	600
Interest expense	2,000

Income tax	1,745
Beginning retained earnings balance	21,000
Dividends	500

Required:

   a. Prepare a 2003 income statement for the company using the single-step format.
   b. Prepare a 2003 income statement for the company using a multiple-step format.
   c. Prepare a 2003 retained earnings statement for the company.

LO 1 & 2: INCOME STATEMENT PREPARATION–INCOME TAX DISREGARDED

4–29. The following information is taken from the accounting records of Bea's Pet Shop, Inc., for 2003:

Sales	$830,000
Cost of goods sold	440,000
Wages	280,000
Utilities	34,000
Rent	28,000
Advertising	22,000
Interest revenue	5,000

Required:

   a. Prepare a 2003 income statement for Bea's Pet Shop, Inc., using a single-step format.
   b. Prepare a 2003 income statement for Bea's Pet Shop, Inc., using a multiple-step format.

LO 3 & 4: IMPACT OF NET INCOME ON OWNERS' EQUITY

4–30. Refer to Bea's Pet Shop, Inc., in 4–29.

Required:

   a. Prepare the statement of capital for Bea's Pet Shop, Inc., for 2003 assuming that it operates as the sole proprietorship of Beatrice Wilson who had a beginning capital balance of $10,000 and withdrew $20,000 during 2003.
   b. Now assuming the company is a corporation, prepare the statement of retained earnings for Bea's Pet Shop, Inc., for 2003 assuming that Bea is the sole stockholder, the beginning retained earnings balance is $21,000, and Bea paid a dividend of $12,000.

LO 2 & 3: IMPACT OF NET INCOME ON OWNERS' EQUITY—PROPRIETORSHIP

4–31. The Alvin Smith Company reported the following information in the records for 2003:

Sales	$250,000
Cost of goods sold	120,000
Salaries	70,000
Utilities	4,000
Rent	3,000
Advertising	1,000
Interest expense	2,000

Required:

   a. Prepare the income statement for the Alvin Smith Company for the year of 2003 using the multiple-step format.
   b. Explain how the result determined in part a will affect the owner's equity for the year assuming that the company is a sole proprietorship.

LO 3 & 4: IMPACT OF NET INCOME ON OWNERS' EQUITY— PROPRIETORSHIP, PARTNERSHIP

4–32. Refer to the Alvin Smith Company in 4–31.

Required:

   a. Prepare the statement of capital for Alvin Smith Company assuming it operates as the sole proprietorship of Alvin Smith, Sr., who had a beginning capital balance of $50,000.

b. Prepare the statement of partners' capital for Alvin Smith Company assuming it operates as a partnership between Alvin Smith, Sr., and Alvin Smith, Jr.

	Smith, Sr.	Smith, Jr.
Partners' share of profits	60%	40%
Beginning capital balance	$50,000	$ 5,000
Withdrawals	$20,000	$20,000

LO 2 & 3: IMPACT OF NET INCOME ON OWNERS' EQUITY—PROPRIETORSHIP, CORPORATION, TAX DISREGARDED

4–33. The Ben Jones Company, Inc., reported the following information in the records for 2003:

Sales	$530,000
Cost of goods sold	220,000
Wages	160,000
Utilities	74,000
Rent	8,000
Advertising	11,000
Interest revenue	3,000

Required:

a. Prepare the income statement for the Ben Jones Company, Inc., for the year 2003 using the single-step format.
b. Explain how the result determined in part a will affect the owner's equity for the year assuming that the company is a sole proprietorship.
c. Explain how the result determined in part a will affect the equity of the corporation.

LO 3 & 4: IMPACT OF NET INCOME ON OWNERS' EQUITY—PROPRIETORSHIP, PARTNERSHIP, AND CORPORATION

4–34. Refer to the Ben Jones Company, Inc., in 4–33.

Required:

a. Prepare the statement of capital for Ben Jones Company, Inc., assuming it operates as the sole proprietorship of Ben Jones who had a beginning capital balance of $50,000.
b. Prepare the statement of partners' capital for Ben Jones Company, Inc., assuming it operates as a partnership between Ben Jones and Kathy Jones.

	Ben Jones	Kathy Jones
Partners' share of profits	35%	65%
Beginning capital balance	$15,000	$45,000
Withdrawals	$12,000	$25,000
Additional capital contributions	$ 5,000	$ 0

LO 3 & 4: IMPACT OF NET INCOME ON RETAINED EARNINGS

4–35. The Carl Smythe Company reported the following information in its records for the year ended December 31, 2004:

Sales	$85,000
Beginning balance—retained earnings	26,000
Cost of sales	55,000
Expenses	35,000
Dividends	2,000

Required:

a. Prepare a single-step income statement for 2004.
b. Prepare the statement of retained earnings for 2004.
c. What is the balance of retained earnings at the end of 2004?

LO 4, 5, & 6: PREPARATION OF A STATEMENT OF EQUITY—PROPRIETORSHIP, PARTNERSHIP, AND CORPORATION

4–36. Pfister Company was organized on January 3, 2003, and had modest net income of $9,500 in its first year.

Required:

    a. Prepare a statement of capital for Pfister Company for the year ended December 31, 2003, assuming Ken Pfister began the company as a sole proprietorship by investing $20,000 of his own money. Also assume Ken took no drawings from the company.

    b. Prepare a statement of partners' capital for Pfister Company for the year ended December 31, 2003, assuming Ken Pfister, Stephanie Winters, and Harriet Higgins began the company as a partnership. Assume the three partners have taken no drawings from the company and have agreed to share any income or loss in the same proportion as their initial investments, which were as follows:

Name	Investment
Pfister	$ 6,000
Winters	4,000
Higgins	2,000
Total	$12,000

    c. Prepare a statement of stockholders' equity for Pfister Company for the year ended December 31, 2003. Assume Ken Pfister, Stephanie Winters, and Harriet Higgins organized the company as a corporation and that the company did not pay a dividend in 2003. The corporate charter authorized 50,000 shares of $2 par value common stock. The following shares were issued on January 3, 2003 (all at $10 per share):

500 shares to Pfister	$ 5,000
300 shares to Winters	3,000
200 shares to Higgins	2,000
Total	$10,000

LO 4, 5, & 6: PREPARATION OF STATEMENT OF EQUITY—SECOND YEAR, PROPRIETORSHIP, PARTNERSHIP, AND CORPORATION

4–37. This problem is a continuation of problem 4–36 for Pfister Company. Now assume it is the end of the company's second year, that is, December 31, 2004, and it is time to prepare the statement of owners' equity for Pfister Company. Net income for the year ended December 31, 2004, was $18,000, and there were no additional owners' investments during the year.

Required:

    a. Prepare a statement of capital for Pfister Company for the year ended December 31, 2004, assuming the business was a proprietorship and that Pfister took drawings totaling $8,000 during 2004.

    b. Prepare a statement of partners' capital for Pfister Company for the year ended December 31, 2004, assuming the partnership form. Recall from the previous problem that the partners share income in the same proportion as their initial investment. Drawings by the three partners during 2004 were as follows:

Name	Drawings
Pfister	$4,000
Winters	2,500
Higgins	1,500
Total	$8,000

    c. Prepare a statement of stockholders' equity for Pfister Company for the year ended December 31, 2004, assuming the corporate form. Recall from the previous problem that 1,000 shares of common stock were issued at the time of incorporation. Dividends paid during the year were $6 per share.

    d. Prepare a statement of retained earnings for Pfister Company assuming the same information given in part c.

LO 4, 5, & 6: PREPARATION OF A STATEMENT OF EQUITY—PROPRIETORSHIP, PARTNERSHIP, AND CORPORATION

4–38. Modell Company was organized on January 3, 2003, and the company experienced a modest net loss of $4,500 in 2003.

Required:

    a. Prepare a statement of capital for Modell Company for the year ended December 31, 2003, assuming Art Modell began the company as a sole proprietorship by investing $50,000 of his own money. During 2003, Modell took no drawings.

    b. Prepare a statement of partners' capital for Modell Company for the year ended December 31, 2003, assuming Art Modell, Sally Weber, and Hillary Hager began the company as a partnership. During 2003, the partners took no drawings. The three partners have agreed to share any income or loss in the same proportion as their initial investments, which were as follows:

Name	Investment
Modell	$ 5,000
Weber	4,000
Hager	1,000
Total	$10,000

    c. Prepare a statement of stockholders' equity for Modell Company for the year ended December 31, 2003, assuming Modell, Weber, and Hager organized the company as a corporation. The corporate charter authorized 100,000 shares of $5 par value common stock. During 2003, the company paid no dividends. The following shares were issued on January 3, 2003 (all at $10 per share):

500 shares to Modell	$ 5,000
400 shares to Weber	4,000
100 shares to Hager	1,000
Total	$10,000

LO 4, 5, & 6: PREPARATION OF A STATEMENT OF EQUITY—SECOND YEAR, PROPRIETORSHIP, PARTNERSHIP, AND CORPORATION

4–39. This problem is a continuation of problem 4–38 for Modell Company. Now assume it is the end of the company's second year of business, December 31, 2004. Net income for the year ended December 31, 2004, was $54,000 and there were no additional owners' investments during the year.

Required:

    a. Prepare a statement of capital for Modell Company for the year ended December 31, 2004, assuming the business was a proprietorship and that Modell took drawings totaling $18,000 during 2004.

    b. Prepare a statement of partners' capital for Modell Company for the year ended December 31, 2004, assuming the partnership form. Recall from the previous problem that the partners share income in the same proportion as their initial investment. Drawings by the three partners during 2004 were as follows:

Name	Drawings
Modell	$ 8,000
Weber	5,000
Hager	5,000
Total	$18,000

    c. Prepare a statement of stockholders' equity for Modell Company for the year ended December 31, 2004, assuming Modell Company took the corporate form. Recall from the previous problem that 1,000 shares of common stock were issued at the time of incorporation. Dividends paid during the year were $3 per share.

    d. Prepare a statement of retained earnings for Modell Company assuming the same information given in part c.

LO 4, 5, & 6: PREPARE STATEMENT OF STOCKHOLDERS' EQUITY AND STATEMENT OF RETAINED EARNINGS

4–40. The Wynn Corporation had the following information available for 2004:

Common stock ($1 par value, 100,000 shares issued and outstanding)	$100,000
Net income for 2004	10,000
Dividends for 2004	5,000
Retained earnings at January 1, 2004	250,000
Additional paid-in capital	50,000

Required:

    a. Prepare a statement of stockholders' equity for 2004 for the Wynn Corporation. No stock transactions occurred during 2004.

    b. Prepare a statement of retained earnings for 2004 for the Wynn Corporation.

    c. Explain the difference between the two statements.

LO 4, 5, & 6: PREPARE STATEMENT OF STOCKHOLDERS' EQUITY AND STATEMENT OF RETAINED EARNINGS

4–41. The Bishop Corporation had the following information available at the end of 2004:

Common stock, January 1, 2004 ($5 par value, 50,000 shares authorized, 25,000 issued and outstanding)	$125,000
Net income for 2004	20,000
Dividends for 2004	10,000
Retained earnings at January 1, 2004	70,000
Additional paid-in capital, January 1, 2004	150,000
Sale of additional 5,000 shares of stock	75,000

Required:

    a. Prepare a statement of stockholders' equity for 2004 for the Bishop Corporation.

    b. Prepare a statement of retained earnings for 2004 for the Bishop Corporation.

    c. Explain the difference between the two statements. Considering the transactions that occurred this year, which statement would be most informative to the user?

LO 4, 5, & 6: PREPARE STATEMENT OF STOCKHOLDERS' EQUITY AND STATEMENT OF RETAINED EARNINGS

4–42. The Rook Corporation had the following information available for 2003:

Common stock, January 1, 2003 (no par value, 50,000 shares authorized, 25,000 shares issued and outstanding)	$175,000
Net loss for 2003	35,000
Dividends for 2003	10,000
Retained earnings at January 1, 2003	197,000
Sale of 10,000 shares of no-par stock during 2003	100,000

Required:

    a. Prepare a statement of stockholders' equity for 2003 for the Rook Corporation.

    b. Prepare a statement of retained earnings for 2003 for the Rook Corporation.

    c. Explain the difference between the two statements. Considering the transactions that occurred this year, which statement would be most informative to the user?

LO 4, 5, & 6: SHAREHOLDERS' EQUITY VS. RETAINED EARNINGS STATEMENTS—WITH TREASURY STOCK

4–43. The Einstein Corporation had the following information available for 2004:

Common stock, January 1, 2004 ($10 par value, 150,000 shares authorized, 25,000 shares issued and outstanding)	$250,000
Net income for 2004	55,000
Dividends for 2004	25,000
Retained earnings at January 1, 2004	160,000
Additional paid-in capital, January 1, 2004	75,000
Sale of 10,000 shares on March 10	150,000

Required: Prepare a statement of stockholders' equity for 2004 for the Einstein Corporation.

LO 5: DIVIDEND TERMINOLOGY

4–44. The Simpson Company decided to pay a cash dividend to its stockholders. This dividend is the first that has ever been paid and the board of directors questions the proper procedure.

Required: With respect to corporate dividend payments, there are three important dates to consider. Explain what happens on each of these important dates and how they help facilitate the payment of dividends.

LO 5: DIVIDENDS

4–45. The board of directors of McCormick Corporation is trying to decide whether or not to declare a cash dividend for the current year.

Required: Identify and discuss the various business and legal issues that the board of directors must consider as they contemplate whether or not to pay a dividend.

LO 1, 2, 4, 5, & 6: CORPORATE INCOME STATEMENT, RETAINED EARNINGS STATEMENT, AND BALANCE SHEET PREPARATION

4–46. The following information is taken from accounting records of Christie's Cheerleading Supplies for the year ended December 31, 2003:

Sales	$100,000
Cost of goods sold	60,000
Operating expenses	30,000
Income tax	2,500
Beginning retained earnings balance	12,000
Dividends	1,000
Cash	3,500
Inventory	12,000
Equipment	9,000
Notes payable	2,000
Common stock	500
Additional paid-in capital—common	3,500

Required:

a. Classify each item as follows:

   Asset = A
   Liability = L
   Equity = EQ
   Revenue = R
   Expense = EX

b. Prepare a 2003 income statement for the company using the single-step format.
c. Prepare a 2003 income statement for the company using a multiple-step format.
d. Prepare a 2003 retained earnings statement for the company.
e. Prepare a balance sheet for the company as of the end of the accounting period.

LO 1, 2, 4, 5, & 6: CORPORATE INCOME STATEMENT, RETAINED EARNINGS STATEMENT, AND BALANCE SHEET PREPARATION

4–47. The following information is taken from accounting records of Salon of Dadeland for the year ended December 31, 2003:

Sales	$129,850
Operating expenses	86,540
Rent revenue	2,000
Interest expense	280
Income tax	13,509
Beginning retained earnings balance	27,680
Dividends	20,000
Cash	12,680
Supplies	860

Equipment	27,500
Office equipment	1,685
Computer system	3,480
Notes payable	2,400
Common stock	1,200
Additional paid-in capital—common	3,404

Required:

a. Classify each item as follows:

> Asset = A
> Liability = L
> Equity = EQ
> Revenue = R
> Expense = EX

b. Prepare a 2003 income statement for the company using the single-step format.
c. Prepare a 2003 income statement for the company using a multiple-step format.
d. Prepare a 2003 retained earnings statement for the company.
e. Prepare a balance sheet for the company as of the end of the accounting period.

LO 1, 2, 4, 5, & 6: CORPORATE INCOME STATEMENT, RETAINED EARNINGS STATEMENT, AND BALANCE SHEET PREPARATION

4–48. The following information is taken from accounting records of Manny's Auto Parts for the year ended December 31, 2003:

Sales	$34,620
Cost of goods sold	22,860
Operating expenses	7,680
Interest expense	600
Income tax	870
Beginning retained earnings balance	10,840
Dividends	250
Cash	1,980
Inventory	8,540
Equipment	13,850
Notes payable	7,000
Common stock	1,350
Additional paid-in capital—common	2,820

Required:

a. Prepare a 2003 income statement for the company using the single-step format.
b. Prepare a 2003 income statement for the company using a multiple-step format.
c. Prepare a 2003 retained earnings statement for the company.
d. Prepare a balance sheet for the company as of the end of the accounting period.

LO 1, 2, 4, 5, & 6: CORPORATE INCOME STATEMENT, RETAINED EARNINGS STATEMENT, AND BALANCE SHEET PREPARATION

4–49. The following information is taken from accounting records of the Hurricane Restaurant for the year ended December 31, 2003:

Sales	$864,200
Operating expenses	743,860
Interest expense	42,640
Income tax	24,864
Beginning retained earnings balance	254,630
Dividends	30,000
Cash	4,268
Land	120,680
Building	587,960

Equipment	128,520
Accounts payable	3,840
Notes payable	278,640
Bonds payable	200,000
Common stock	17,000
Additional paid-in capital—Common	64,482

Required:

a. Classify each item as follows:

   Asset = A
   Liability = L
   Equity = EQ
   Revenue = R
   Expense = EX

b. Prepare a 2003 income statement for the company using the single-step format.
c. Prepare a 2003 income statement for the company using a multiple-step format.
d. Prepare a 2003 retained earnings statement for the company.
e. Prepare a balance sheet for the company as of the end of the accounting period.

LO 1, 2, 4, 5, & 6: CORPORATE INCOME STATEMENT, RETAINED EARNINGS STATEMENT, AND BALANCE SHEET PREPARATION

4–50. The following information is taken from accounting records of Roger's Bike Sales for the year ended December 31, 2003:

Sales	$260,500
Cost of goods sold	182,530
Operating expenses	53,000
Rent revenue	2,100
Interest expense	4,570
Income tax	5,625
Beginning retained earnings balance	64,580
Dividends	2,900
Cash	5,800
Accounts receivable	12,300
Inventory	26,800
Supplies	575
Land	40,650
Building	68,450
Equipment	3,850
Computer system	1,550
Delivery truck	26,960
Accounts payable	6,860
Notes payable	5,000
Common stock	1,000
Additional paid-in capital—common	95,520

Required:

a. Classify each item as follows:

   Asset = A
   Liability = L
   Equity = EQ
   Revenue = R
   Expense = EX

b. Prepare a 2003 income statement for the company using the single-step format.
c. Prepare a 2003 income statement for the company using a multiple-step format.
d. Prepare a 2003 retained earnings statement for the company.
e. Prepare a balance sheet for the company as of the end of the accounting period.

LO 1, 2, 4, 5, & 6: CORPORATE INCOME STATEMENT, RETAINED EARNINGS STATEMENT, AND BALANCE SHEET PREPARATION

4–51. The following information is taken from accounting records of Tressa's Treasures for the year ended December 31, 2003:

Sales	$120,000
Cost of goods sold	80,000
Operating expenses	22,000
Interest revenue	2,000
Interest expense	5,000
Income tax	6,000
Beginning retained earnings balance	42,670
Dividends	3,000
Cash	11,000
Accounts receivable	22,000
Inventory	37,000
Land	35,800
Building	59,750
Equipment	13,000
Accounts payable	18,000
Notes payable	16,000
Common stock	7,000
Additional paid-in capital—common	88,880

Required:

a. Prepare a 2003 income statement for the company using the single-step format.
b. Prepare a 2003 income statement for the company using a multiple-step format.
c. Prepare a 2003 retained earnings statement for the company.
d. Prepare a balance sheet for the company as of the end of the accounting period.

LO 1, 2, 4, 5, & 6: CORPORATE INCOME STATEMENT, RETAINED EARNINGS STATEMENT, AND BALANCE SHEET PREPARATION

4–52. The following information is taken from accounting records of Home Pet Supplies, Inc., for the year ended December 31, 2003:

Sales	$56,250
Cost of goods sold	24,630
Wages and salaries	22,800
Rent	2,400
Electricity	1,260
Telephone	625
Interest expense	900
Income tax	727
Beginning retained earnings balance	12,850
Dividends	500
Cash	2,680
Inventory	8,880
Equipment	9,640
Computer system	3,750
Delivery truck	12,600
Accounts payable	5,480
Notes payable	4,500
Common stock	2,000
Additional paid-in capital—common	10,312

Required:

a. Prepare a 2003 income statement for the company using the single-step format.
b. Prepare a 2003 income statement for the company using a multiple-step format.
c. Prepare a 2003 retained earnings statement for the company.
d. Prepare a balance sheet for the company as of the end of the accounting period.

LO 1, 2, 4, 5, & 6: CORPORATE INCOME STATEMENT, RETAINED EARNINGS STATEMENT, AND BALANCE SHEET PREPARATION

4–53. The following information is taken from accounting records of Mendelsohn Electronics for the year ended December 31, 2003:

Sales	$12,856,850
Cost of goods sold	9,458,560
Operating expenses	3,128,950
Rent revenue	36,000
Interest expense	13,340
Income tax	99,280
Beginning retained earnings balance	2,460,350
Dividends	25,000
Cash	1,920,650
Accounts receivable	263,520
Inventory	2,462,250
Supplies	1,200
Land	750,520
Building	1,385,520
Equipment	265,220
Accounts payable	1,985,640
Notes payable	736,580
Bonds payable	500,000
Preferred stock	200,000
Common stock	998,590

Required:

a. Classify each item as follows:

    Asset = A
    Liability = L
    Equity = EQ
    Revenue = R
    Expense = EX

b. Prepare a 2003 income statement for the company using the single-step format.
c. Prepare a 2003 income statement for the company using a multiple-step format.
d. Prepare a 2003 retained earnings statement for the company.
e. Prepare a balance sheet for the company as of the end of the accounting period.

LO 1, 2, 4, 5, & 6: CORPORATE INCOME STATEMENT, RETAINED EARNINGS STATEMENT, AND BALANCE SHEET PREPARATION

4–54. The following information is taken from accounting records of Louie's Landscaping Co. for the year ended December 31, 2003:

Sales	$2,650,500
Cost of goods sold	1,825,000
Wages and salaries	420,000
Rent	108,000
Electricity	10,200
Telephone	4,200
Interest revenue	1,600
Interest expense	36,000
Income tax	79,584
Beginning retained earnings balance	43,116
Dividends	20,000
Cash	34,500
Accounts receivable	152,500
Inventory	231,232
Supplies	2,500
Delivery truck	20,300
Accounts payable	155,300

Notes payable	5,000
Bonds payable	31,000
Common stock	2,500
Additional paid-in capital—common	55,000

Required:

a. Classify each item as follows:

Asset = A
Liability = L
Equity = EQ
Revenue = R
Expense = EX

b. Prepare a 2003 income statement for the company using the single-step format.
c. Prepare a 2003 income statement for the company using a multiple-step format.
d. Prepare a 2003 retained earnings statement for the company.
e. Prepare a balance sheet for the company as of the end of the accounting period.

LO 1, 2, 4, 5, & 6: CORPORATE INCOME STATEMENT, RETAINED EARNINGS STATEMENT, AND BALANCE SHEET PREPARATION

4–55. The following information is taken from accounting records of Cupcake's Specialty Bakery for the year ended December 31, 2003:

Sales	$1,265,300
Cost of goods sold	862,150
Operating expenses	345,890
Interest revenue	1,280
Interest expense	3,690
Income tax	16,455
Beginning retained earnings balance	225,950
Cash	37,560
Inventory	195,850
Supplies	2,000
Land	105,750
Building	225,500
Office equipment	26,800
Computer equipment	4,850
Delivery truck	23,800
Accounts payable	51,280
Notes payable	9,500
Bonds payable	27,000
Preferred stock	80,000
Additional paid-in capital—preferred	2,000
Common stock	32,000
Additional paid-in capital—common	155,985

Required:

a. Prepare a 2003 income statement for the company using the single-step format.
b. Prepare a 2003 income statement for the company using a multiple-step format.
c. Prepare a 2003 retained earnings statement for the company.
d. Prepare a balance sheet for the company as of the end of the accounting period.

LO 1, 2, 4, 5, & 6: CORPORATE SERVICE BUSINESS INCOME STATEMENT, RETAINED EARNINGS STATEMENT, AND BALANCE SHEET PREPARATION

4–56. The following information is taken from accounting records of Medical Service, Inc., for the year ended December 31, 2003:

Sales	$1,162,530
Operating expenses	485,600
Wages and salaries	485,600
Rent	36,000
Electricity	4,800

Telephone	1,250
Advertising	19,860
Maintenance	2,200
Rent revenue	2,400
Interest expense	6,200
Income tax	37,026
Beginning retained earnings balance	182,600
Dividends	40,000
Cash	125,800
Accounts receivable	98,560
Supplies	22,000
Equipment	295,000
Office equipment	3,600
Computer system	2,600
Computer equipment	2,560
Accounts payable	12,350
Notes payable	65,740
Preferred stock	28,000
Additional paid-in capital—preferred	400
Common stock	54,000
Additional paid-in capital—common	160,636

Required:

a. Prepare a 2003 income statement for the company using the single-step format.
b. Prepare a 2003 income statement for the company using a multiple-step format.
c. Prepare a 2003 retained earnings statement for the company.
d. Prepare a balance sheet for the company as of the end of the accounting period.

LO 1, 2, 4, 5, & 6: CORPORATE INCOME STATEMENT, RETAINED EARNINGS STATEMENT, AND BALANCE SHEET PREPARATION

4–57. The following information is taken from accounting records of Oxy's Toy Store for the year ended December 31, 2003:

Sales	$985,570
Cost of goods sold	654,340
Wages and salaries	195,820
Rent	24,000
Electricity	6,200
Telephone	2,460
Advertising	3,640
Maintenance	690
Interest revenue	520
Rent revenue	600
Interest expense	1,840
Income tax	31,264
Beginning retained earnings balance	235,860
Dividends	5,400
Cash	56,250
Accounts receivable	96,230
Inventory	275,860
Supplies	1,330
Equipment	13,590
Office equipment	35,980
Computer system	26,850
Delivery truck	28,460
Accounts payable	135,870
Notes payable	9,450
Bonds payable	10,000
Preferred stock	20,000
Additional paid-in capital—preferred	100
Common stock	3,200
Additional paid-in capital—common	59,034

Required:

a. Prepare a 2003 income statement for the company using the single-step format.
b. Prepare a 2003 income statement for the company using a multiple-step format.
c. Prepare a 2003 retained earnings statement for the company.
d. Prepare a balance sheet for the company as of the end of the accounting period.

LO 7: PREPARE A SIMPLE STATEMENT OF CASH FLOWS

4–58. The following information is from the records of the Super 211 Company for the year ended December 31, 2003.

1. Cash sales to customers, $50,000
2. Sold Super 211 Company stock for cash, $3,000
3. Paid cash for merchandise, $24,000
4. Paid cash dividend, $200
5. Purchased ***IBM*** stock, $1,000
6. Received cash dividend from ***IBM,*** $100
7. Loaned $500 to ABC Company
8. Paid cash for operating expenses, $4,000
9. Paid income tax, $5,500
10. Cash balance at December 31, 2002, was $20,000

Required: Prepare a statement of cash flows for Super 211 Company for the year ended December 31, 2003.

LO 7: PREPARE A SIMPLE STATEMENT OF CASH FLOWS

4–59. The following information is from the records of the Fox Company for the year ended December 31, 2003.

1. Sold Fox Company stock for cash, $5,500
2. Purchased equipment for cash, $8,000
3. Cash sales to customers, $60,000
4. Paid cash for merchandise, $25,000
5. Paid $500 cash dividend
6. Borrowed $7,000 from Miami National Bank
7. Purchased ***Dow Chemical*** stock, $3,000
8. Paid cash for operating expenses, $4,000
9. Paid income tax, $7,500
10. Cash balance at December 31, 2002, was $30,000

Required: Prepare a statement of cash flows for Fox Company for the year ended December 31, 2003.

LO 7: PREPARE A SIMPLE STATEMENT OF CASH FLOWS

4–60. The following information is from the records of the McCarthy Company for the year ended December 31, 2003.

1. Cash sales to customers, $50,000
2. Borrowed $7,000 from XYZ Bank
3. Purchased equipment for cash, $10,000
4. Sold equipment for cash, $1,500
5. Sold McCarthy Company stock for cash, $3,000
6. Made a loan payment to XYZ Bank for $1,090, which included $90 interest
7. Paid cash for merchandise, $24,000
8. Paid cash dividend, $200
9. Purchased ***IBM*** stock, $1,000
10. Received cash dividend from ***IBM,*** $100
11. Paid cash to employees for wages, $6,000
12. Loaned $500 to ABC Company
13. Paid cash for other expenses, $4,000
14. Paid income tax, $4,000
15. Cash balance at December 31, 2002, was $20,000

Required: Prepare a statement of cash flows for McCarthy Company for the year ended December 31, 2003.

LO 7: PREPARE A SIMPLE STATEMENT OF CASH FLOWS

4–61. The following information is from the records of the Jaspers Computer, Inc., for the year ended December 31, 2003.

1. Cash sales to customers, $75,000
2. Borrowed from XYZ Bank, $9,000
3. Purchased equipment for cash, $12,000
4. Sold equipment for cash, $3,000
5. Sold Jaspers Computer, Inc., stock for cash of $3,000
6. Made a loan payment to XYZ Bank for $1,200, which included $150 interest
7. Paid cash for merchandise, $38,000
8. Paid $300 cash dividend
9. Purchased *IBM* stock, $1,300
10. Received cash dividend from *IBM,* $120
11. Paid cash to employees for wages, $8,000
12. Loaned $500 to ABC Company
13. Paid cash for other expenses, $10,000
14. Paid income tax, $2,500
15. Cash balance at December 31, 2002, was $25,000

Required: Prepare a statement of cash flows for Jaspers Computer, Inc., for the year ended December 31, 2003.

LO 7: PREPARE A SIMPLE STATEMENT OF CASH FLOWS

4–62. The following information is from the records of the Thomas Wholesale Company for the year ended December 31, 2003.

1. Loaned $1,500 to Smith Company
2. Sold Thomas Wholesale Company stock for cash, $6,000
3. Purchased equipment for cash, $11,000
4. Cash sales to customers totaled $70,000
5. Sold equipment for cash, $2,000
6. Paid cash to employees for wages, $5,000
7. Paid cash for merchandise, $35,000
8. Paid $500 cash dividend
9. Borrowed $5,000 from Miami National Bank
10. Purchased *Dow Chemical* stock, $3,000
11. Received cash dividend from *Dow Chemical,* $100
12. Paid cash for other expenses, $6,000
13. Paid income tax, $3,000
14. Made a loan payment to Miami National Bank for $1,100, which included $100 interest
15. Cash balance at December 31, 2002, was $40,000

Required: Prepare a statement of cash flows for Thomas Wholesale Company for the year ended December 31, 2003.

LO 7: PREPARE A SIMPLE STATEMENT OF CASH FLOWS

4–63. The following information is from the records of the Smith & Daughters Company for the year ended December 31, 2003.

1. Loaned $2,000 to Lynne Company
2. Sold Smith & Daughters Company stock for cash, $8,500
3. Purchased equipment for cash, $35,000
4. Cash sales to customers, $90,000
5. Sold equipment for cash, $2,000
6. Paid cash to employees for wages, $12,000
7. Paid cash for merchandise, $50,000
8. Paid $200 cash dividend
9. Borrowed $20,000 from Miami National Bank
10. Purchased *Dow Chemical* stock, $5,000
11. Received cash dividend from *Dow Chemical,* $500
12. Paid cash for other expenses, $14,000
13. Made a loan payment to Miami National Bank for $2,300, which included $300 interest.

14. Paid income tax, $6,000
15. Cash balance at December 31, 2002, was $9,000

Required: Prepare a statement of cash flows for Smith & Daughters Company for the year ended December 31, 2003.

LO 8: PROFITABILITY RATIO CALCULATIONS

4–64. The following information is available for the Matheis Company for the year ended December 31, 2003:

- Net sales were $13,552,000.
- Gross profit for 2003 was $3,132,200.
- Net income for the year was $709,500.
- Interest expense for the year totaled $103,400.
- The company's assets totaled $5,067,800 at December 31, 2002, and $5,520,200 at December 31, 2003.
- The company paid preferred dividends for the year totaling $26,000.
- The company paid common dividends for the year totaling $64,000.
- Common stockholders' equity totaled $3,156,800 at December 31, 2002, and $3,776,300 at December 31, 2003.
- Average number of common shares outstanding during the year was 825,000 shares.
- The company's common stock had an average market price of $16.50 per share.

Required:

a. Calculate the following profitability ratios for the company:

1. The gross profit margin ratio
2. The net profit margin ratio
3. The rate of return on assets ratio
4. The rate of return on common equity ratio
5. The dividend payout ratio
6. The company's earnings per share
7. The price-to-earnings ratio

b. Explain what the ratios tell you about the company

LO 8: PROFITABILITY RATIO CALCULATIONS

4–65. The following information is available for Rex International, Inc., for the year ended December 31, 2003:

- Net sales were $544,000.
- Gross profit for 2003 was $106,080.
- Net income for the year was $40,800.
- Interest expense for the year totaled $10,400.
- The company's assets totaled $1,300,000 at December 31, 2002, and $1,360,000 at December 31, 2003.
- The company paid preferred dividends for the year totaling $2,000.
- The company paid common dividends for the year totaling $4,000.
- Common stockholders' equity totaled $1,120,000 at December 31, 2002, and $1,154,800 at December 31, 2003.
- Average number of common shares outstanding during the year was 76,500 shares.
- The company's common stock had an average market price of $2.85 per share.

Required:

a. Calculate the following profitability ratios for the company:

1. The gross profit margin ratio
2. The net profit margin ratio
3. The rate of return on assets ratio
4. The rate of return on common equity ratio
5. The dividend payout ratio
6. The company's earnings per share
7. The price-to-earnings ratio

b. Explain what the ratios tell you about the company.

LO 8: PROFITABILITY RATIO CALCULATIONS

4–66. The following information is available for SOBE Entertainment, Inc., for the year ended December 31, 2003:

- Net sales were $846,000.
- Gross profit for 2003 was $448,500.
- Net income for the year was $80,900.
- Interest expense for the year totaled $20,500.
- The company's assets totaled $725,600 at December 31, 2002, and $795,400 at December 31, 2003.
- The company paid preferred dividends for the year totaling $12,000.
- The company paid common dividends for the year totaling $6,900.
- Common stockholders' equity totaled $345,000 at December 31, 2002, and $407,000 at December 31, 2003.
- Average number of common shares outstanding during the year was 110,250 shares.
- The company's common stock had an average market price of $12.59 per share.

Required:

a. Calculate the following profitability ratios for the company:

1. The gross profit margin ratio
2. The net profit margin ratio
3. The rate of return on assets ratio
4. The rate of return on common equity ratio
5. The dividend payout ratio
6. The company's earnings per share
7. The price-to-earnings ratio

b. Explain what the ratios tell you about the company.

LO 8: PROFITABILITY RATIO CALCULATIONS

4–67. The following information is available for Tom Robinson Industries, Inc.

Tom Robinson Industries, Inc.
Income Statement
For the Year Ended December 31, 2004
(In thousands)

Sales	$88,230
Less cost of goods sold	36,120
Gross margin	52,110
Operating expenses	(43,930)
Operating income	8,180
Other revenues:	
Rent revenue	80
Other expenses:	
Interest expense	(110)
Income before income tax	8,150
Income tax expense	2,771
Net income	$ 5,379

Statement of Stockholders' Equity
For the Year Ended December 31, 2004
(In thousands)

	Preferred Stock	Additional Paid-in Capital Preferred	Common Stock	Additional Paid-in Capital Common	Retained Earnings	Total Stockholders' Equity
Balance, January 1, 2004	$5,500	$ 250	$3,581	$22,872	$18,676	$50,879
Common stock issued						
Preferred stock issued						
Net income					5,379	5,379
Preferred dividend					(385)	(385)
Common dividends					(550)	(550)
Balance, December 31, 2004	$5,500	$ 250	$3,581	$22,872	$23,120	$55,323

Balance Sheet
December 31, 2004
(In thousands)

Assets:		Liabilities:	
Cash	$ 8,820	Current payable	$ 7,860
Land	27,548	Bonds payable	10,390
Building	33,750	Total liabilities	18,250
Other assets	3,455	Stockholders' equity:	
		Preferred stock, $50 par, 110 shares	
		issued and outstanding	$ 5,500
		Additional paid-in capital—preferred	250
		Common stock, $1 par, 3,581 shares	
		issued and outstanding	3,581
		Additional paid-in capital—common	22,872
		Total contributed capital	32,203
		Retained earnings	23,120
		Total stockholders' equity	55,323
Total assets	$73,573	Total liabilities and stockholders' equity	$73,573

Required: Assume the company's assets totaled $68,450 at December 31, 2003. Assume the company's common stock had an average market price of $12.90 per share as of December 31, 2004. Calculate the following profitability ratios for the company:

a. The gross profit margin ratio
b. The net profit margin ratio
c. The rate of return on assets ratio
d. The rate of return on common equity ratio
e. The dividend payout ratio
f. The company's earnings per share
g. The price-to-earnings ratio

LO 8: PROFITABILITY RATIO CALCULATIONS

4–68. The president of Wayne Industries, Inc., cannot understand why his company is having trouble obtaining additional external financing. "After all," he says, "the company earned a net income of over $1.7 million in 2004." The following information is also available:

Wayne Industries, Inc.
Income Statement
For the Year Ended December 31, 2004
(In thousands)

Sales	$144,230
Less cost of goods sold	110,090
Gross margin	34,140
Operating expenses	(30,710)
Operating income	3,430
Other revenues—rent revenue	30
Other expenses—interest expense	(990)
Income before income tax	2,470
Income tax expense	741
Net income	$ 1,729

Statement of Stockholders' Equity
For the Year Ended December 31, 2004
(In thousands)

	Preferred Stock	Additional Paid-in Capital Preferred	Common Stock	Additional Paid-in Capital Common	Retained Earnings	Total Stockholders' Equity
Balance, January 1, 2004	$5,000	$ 50	$9,320	$122,442	$11,801	$148,613
Common stock issued						
Preferred stock issued						
Net income					1,729	1,729
Preferred dividend					(400)	(400)
Common dividends					0	0
Balance, December 31, 2004	$5,000	$ 250	$9,320	$122,442	$13,130	$149,942

Balance Sheet
December 31, 2004
(In thousands)

Assets:		Liabilities:	
Cash	$ 1,820	Current payable	$ 44,560
Land	100,448	Bonds payable	12,375
Building	83,750	Total liabilities	56,935
Other assets	20,859	Stockholders' equity:	
		Preferred stock, $100 par, 50 shares issued and outstanding	$ 5,000
		Additional paid-in capital—preferred	50
		Common stock, $.25 par, 37,280 shares issued and outstanding	9,320
		Additional paid-in capital—common	122,442
		Total contributed capital	136,812
		Retained earnings	13,130
		Total stockholders' equity	149,942
Total assets	$206,877	Total liabilities and stockholders' equity	$206,877

Required:

a. Assume the company's assets totaled $201,443 at December 31, 2003. Note that the company had no common stock transactions during 2004, so the amount for common stock and additional paid-in capital for common did not change during the year. The average market price for the company's stock is $0.27 per share. Calculate the following profitability ratios for the company:

1. The gross profit margin ratio
2. The net profit margin ratio
3. The rate of return on assets ratio
4. The rate of return on common equity ratio
5. The dividend payout ratio
6. The company's earnings per share
7. The price-to-earnings ratio

b. Based on the ratios you calculated, discuss the reasons that the company may be having difficulty securing additional external financing.

LO 8: PROFITABILITY RATIO CALCULATIONS

4–69. The president of Stacy Sexton Industries, Inc., is expanding and would like to obtain additional external financing. The following information is also available:

Stacy Sexton Industries, Inc.
Income Statement
For the Year Ended December 31, 2004

Sales	$12,188,720
Less cost of goods sold	7,910,050
Gross margin	4,278,670
Operating expenses	(2,158,080)
Operating income	2,120,590
Other expenses—interest expense	(32,690)
Income before income tax	2,087,900
Income tax expense	751,644
Net income	$ 1,336,256

Balance Sheet
December 31, 2004

Total assets	$ 9,518,822
Total liabilities	408,625
Stockholders' equity:	
Preferred stock, no par, 8,000 shares	
issued and outstanding	800,000
Common stock, no par, 750,000 shares	
issued and outstanding	2,150,327
Retained earnings	6,159,870
Total stockholders' equity	9,110,197
Total liabilities and stockholders' equity	$ 9,518,822

Required: Assume the following:

- The company's common stock had an average market price of $34.29 per share.
- The company paid preferred dividends for the year totaling $56,000.
- The company paid common dividends for the year totaling $130,000.
- The company's assets totaled $8,947,877 at December 31, 2003.
- Retained earnings totaled $5,009,614 at December 31, 2003.
- No common stock transactions occurred during the year.

a. Calculate the following profitability ratios for the company:

1. The gross profit margin ratio
2. The net profit margin ratio
3. The rate of return on assets ratio
4. The rate of return on common equity ratio
5. The dividend payout ratio
6. The company's earnings per share
7. The price-to-earnings ratio

b. Based on the ratios you calculated, do you feel the company will have difficulty securing additional external financing? Explain your answer.

LO: COMPREHENSIVE

4–70. The Cronin Corporation has been a profitable company for many years and has paid a quarterly dividend for each of the past 45 quarters. The company's board of directors is meeting and will discuss the quarterly dividend declaration. The current quarter incurred a $150,000 net loss, which is not unusual for a second quarter of the year. Unfortunately, Cronin does not have enough cash to pay the dividend and to support its operation during the next 45 days.

Required:

a. Assuming the company could get the cash somehow, would the current quarter's loss preclude the company from paying a cash dividend? Explain your answer.
b. The problem indicates the company does not have enough cash to pay the dividend. What could the company do to get the cash it needs to pay the dividend?
c. Are there any reasons the company's board of directors would want to pay the cur-

rent quarterly dividend even though the company suffered a second-quarter loss and is temporarily short of cash?

   d. What do you think the board of directors should do?

LO 1, 2, & 4: INCOME STATEMENT, CAPITAL STATEMENT—PROPRIETORSHIP

4–71. The Michelle Miller Company began on January 15, 2003, when Ms. Miller contributed $10,000 to a business account. During 2003, she contributed another $10,000 on June 1 and $15,000 on September 30. Ms. Miller withdrew $5,000 on December 20. The following is a summary of the remaining receipts and expenditures for the year of 2003:

Receipts:	
Sales	$235,000
Inventory loan from bank	50,000
Expenditures:	
Inventory purchased and sold	140,000
Repayment of loan	40,000
Interest expense	2,000
Operating expenses:	
Selling expenses	37,000
Administrative expenses	39,000

Required:

   a. Prepare a multiple-step income statement for 2003 for Michelle Miller Company.

   b. Prepare a statement of capital for Michelle Miller Company for the year of 2003.

LO 1 & 4: STATEMENT OF STOCKHOLDERS' EQUITY—CORPORATION

4–72. Pezant, Inc., began operations during 2004. During that year, the corporation issued 30,000 shares of $10 par value stock on the following dates for the indicated amounts:

Date	Number of Shares	Price per Share
March 19	10,000	$15
May 16	15,000	$16
November 6	5,000	$20

The corporation earned a net income of $5,600 during 2004 and declared a modest $0.10 per share dividend on December 1 to shareholders of record on December 15, and paid the dividend on December 30.

Required: Prepare a statement of stockholders' equity for 2004.

Financial Reporting Exercises •

LO 8: PROFITABILITY RATIOS

4–73. Using the *SEC*'s *EDGAR* system, obtain a copy of the *Office Depot, Inc.,* income statement, balance sheet, and statement of retained earnings from the company's Form 10K from 2001.

Required: Calculate the following profitability ratios for the company for 2001:

   1. The gross profit margin ratio

   2. The net profit margin ratio

   3. The rate of return on assets ratio

   4. The rate of return on common equity ratio

   5. Why does this company not have a dividend payout ratio? What is their reasoning for this?

   6. The company's earnings per share

   7. The price-to-earnings ratio given that the average market price per share is $29.83

LO 8: PROFITABILITY RATIOS

4–74. Using the *SEC*'s *EDGAR* system, obtain a copy of the *OfficeMax, Inc.,* income statement, balance sheet, and statement of retained earnings from the company's 2001 Form 10K.

Required:

    a. Calculate the following profitability ratios for the company for each year presented:

        1. The gross profit margin ratio
        2. The net profit margin ratio
        3. The rate of return on assets ratio
        4. The rate of return on common equity ratio
        5. Why does this company not have a dividend payout ratio? What is their reasoning for this?
        6. The company's earnings per share
        7. Why doesn't this company have a price-to-earnings ratio?

    b. Look at the ratios for ***OfficeMax, Inc.,*** compared to ***Office Depot, Inc.*** For each ratio, circle which company has a more favorable ratio and why you think it is better. In which company would you rather invest? Why?

LO 8: PROFITABILITY RATIOS

4–75. Using the ***SEC***'s ***EDGAR*** system, obtain a copy of ***Staples, Inc.,*** income statement, balance sheet, and statement of retained earnings from the company's 2001 Form 10K.

Required:

    a. Calculate the following solvency ratios for the company for 2001:

        1. The debt ratio
        2. The debt-to-equity ratio

    b. Calculate the following profitability ratios for the company for 2001:

        1. The gross profit margin ratio
        2. The net profit margin ratio
        3. The rate of return on assets ratio
        4. The rate of return on common equity ratio
        5. Why does this company not have a dividend payout ratio? What is their reasoning for this?
        6. The company's earnings per share
        7. The price-to-earnings ratio given that the average market price per share of common stock is $16.32

    c. List for each ratio which of the three companies (***Office Depot, OfficeMax,*** or ***Staples***) is the most favorable.
    d. Which of the three companies would you be most likely to invest in and why?

LO 8: PROFITABILITY RATIOS

4–76. Select a publicly traded company that has positive earnings, preferred stock, pays dividends, and any other guidelines established by your instructor. Using the ***SEC***'s ***EDGAR*** system, obtain a copy of the company's income statement, its balance sheet, and its statement of retained earnings from the company's latest Form 10K.

Required:

    a. Calculate the following solvency ratios for the company for the most recent year:

        1. The debt ratio
        2. The debt-to-equity ratio

    b. Calculate the following profitability ratios for the company for the most recent year:

        1. The gross profit margin ratio
        2. The net profit margin ratio
        3. The rate of return on assets ratio
        4. The rate of return on common equity ratio
        5. The dividend payout ratio
        6. The company's earnings per share
        7. The price-to-earnings ratio

    c. What do the ratios tell you about the company? Would you rather invest in this company or a company from one of the previous three problems? Why?

ANNUAL REPORT PROJECT

4–77. Section 4—Basic Income Statement and Statement of Stockholders' Equity

In this assignment, you will prepare a report based on your company's income statement, its balance sheet, and other information.

Required: Prepare a report for your company that includes the following:

a. Companies are required to provide information on the various segments of their businesses. Describe your company's business segments. Describe the types of information your company's annual report includes for its various business segments. Indicate which segment you think contributes the most toward the success of your company. Explain your reasoning. Indicate which segment you think contributes the least. Explain your reasoning. Does the business segment information hint that the company should consider changing its business strategy or focus? Explain your reasoning.

b. Describe your company's income statement presentation and the important information it includes. For example, how many years of income statement information does your company present? Does your company use the single-step or multiple-step income statement format? Do you think there is any reason your company might use one format rather than the other? Which format would you prefer your company to use? Explain your reasoning. Discuss the important items and amounts that appear on the income statement. Is there a category on the income statement called something similar to "other income"? If so, use information from the notes to the financial statement to describe the items this category includes.

c. Describe your company's statement of stockholders' equity presentation. For example, how many years does your company present? Did your company issue stock during the year? Provide an explanation. What item seems to cause the most significant changes in stockholders equity? Your report should mention the number of common shares of stock authorized and the number outstanding, the number of preferred shares of stock authorized (if any) and the number outstanding. If your company has treasury stock, list the number of treasury shares presented and describe why you think the company reacquired its own stock. *Hint*: Check the managements' discussion and analysis and look in the note to the financial statements for this information.

d. Prepare a schedule that presents the following financial ratios:

- Gross profit margin ratios for three years
- Net profit margin ratios for three years
- Return on assets ratio for the latest year
- Return on common equity ratio for the latest year
- Dividend payout ratio for three years
- Earnings per share for three years
- Price-to-earnings ratio for the latest year

e. Comment in your report on the information that each one of the ratios provides. Where applicable, comment on the changes in the amounts of ratios over time.

f. Your report should conclude with a summary of your impressions of the company in light of what you discovered as you completed this assignment.

Keeping Score: Bases of Economic Measurement

At the end of your sophomore year, you decide to start a small business to help with your college expenses. You spot an advertisement in the campus newspaper—"Used Delivery Truck for Sale." After some investigation into the potential services you could provide with it, you decide to buy the truck for $12,000 cash and begin to offer delivery services of furniture and mattresses around town. During your first month of business, you receive cash in the amount of $1,300 from Mattress City and bill Furniture Giant $2,100 for the delivery services you provided for them. In addition, you charge $225 for gasoline on your *Citibank VISA* card.

Your best friend is intrigued by your venture and asks what your company's income was for its first month of business. How do you respond? Do you say that the company earned $1,300 because you received that much cash and you really didn't pay out any cash for expenses? Or, since you paid cash for the truck, do you deduct the $12,000 from the $1,300 and say your business lost $10,700 in its first month? What about the $2,100 invoice to Furniture Giant that you won't collect on until next month? And how do you account for the gasoline you charged on the *VISA* card? Even though no cash changed hands, should you include those amounts in your income calculation?

What *was* your company's profit for its first month? Which amount is correct? Well, depending how you base your measurement, they are all correct, but the real question is this: Which figure best represents what actually happened in your business?

In the preceding two chapters, we explored the development of three financial tools—the balance sheet, the income statement, and the statement of owners' equity. We also showed how items on the balance sheet and income statement affect the statement of cash flows. Each of these statements measures economic activity. However, before decision makers can use these measurements with confidence, they must know the answer to one basic question: *From what perspective have the measurements been made?* Unless decision makers know what basis of economic measurement was used to prepare the financial statements, the information provided will be of little value to them.

There are two general bases of economic measurement—the cash basis and the accrual basis. In this chapter, we will consider these two approaches to measuring revenue and expense for a particular time period and explore in detail the distinctions between them.

Learning Objectives

After completing your work on this chapter, you should be able to do the following:

1. Explain the difference between reality and the measurement of reality.
2. Apply the criteria for revenue and expense recognition under the cash basis of accounting to determine periodic net income.
3. Apply the criteria for revenue and expense recognition under the accrual basis of accounting to determine periodic net income.

4. Explain the concept of matching and describe how it relates to depreciation.

5. Describe the difference between accruals and deferrals and identify examples of each.

6. Contrast the cash basis and accrual basis of economic measurement, describing the relative strengths and weaknesses of each.

◆ REALITY VERSUS THE MEASUREMENT OF REALITY

Every company performs a variety of functions. Some of the more common are purchasing inventory, selling goods, providing services, investing resources, and paying employees. These activities make up the actual events—the reality—of being in business and doing business. Every company must also measure these activities. As events occur, their effects are recorded in an attempt to measure the reality of the business. But remember this: *No matter how accurately the measurement of reality reflects reality, it is not reality.*

As an example of what we're talking about, assume a company purchased some office supplies and wrote a check for $480. In recording the check in the check register, the bookkeeper read the amount of the check incorrectly and entered $48. After deducting the $48, the check register indicated a balance of $1,127. The fact that the bookkeeper entered the wrong amount for the check in no way changes the reality of how much money the company spent and how much actually remains in the company's checking account.

Discussion Questions ●

5–1. Assuming there are no other errors in the check register, what is the actual cash balance in the company's checking account?

5–2. In what ways could this incorrect measurement of reality have an effect on reality? Explain.

THE PROBLEMS OF PERIODIC MEASUREMENT

Errors are one cause of differences between reality and the measurement of reality. However, there are also legitimate reasons for discrepancies between reality and its measure. An example is best demonstrated in the measurement of the revenues and expenses reported in a company's income statement for a particular period.

Most differences between reality and its measure occur when earnings activities are measured for a specific period of time. Regardless of the time period being measured (month, quarter, year, etc.), it is not always obvious which revenues and which expenses should be included in determining the earnings (net income) of that period.

Discussion Question ●

5–3. Checker Business Systems sells computer equipment to small businesses. During 2004, the sales activity was as follows:

February: Sold $6,000 of equipment to credit card or charge account customers (on account). The customers paid in full on March 15.

March: Sold $4,500 of equipment on account. Customers paid in full on April 15.

What activity would be included in each period if the business activity were measured

a. each month?
b. each quarter?
c. each year?

The only true measure of net income for a company is a comparison between revenues and expenses over the entire life of that company. In the fifteenth century, determining true net income was easier and more precise than it is today. In the era of Christopher Columbus, if an entrepreneur sailed to the New World and brought back goods to sell, the net income for that particular venture could be measured accurately. The entrepreneur began with a pile of money. With that, he bought a ship and supplies and hired men to help with the expedition. The group set sail, gathered up treasures and commodities from the New World, returned, and sold the goods. Then the workers were paid off, the ship was sold, and the entrepreneur ended up, once again, with a pile of money. If the pile of money he had at the end of his venture was greater than the pile of money he began with, the difference was a net income. If the amount of money he ended up with was smaller than the amount he started with, the entrepreneur suffered a net loss on the venture.

In today's world, it is unrealistic to expect companies to stop operations periodically and sell off all their assets so they can determine their "true" net income. So although lifetime net income is the only truly precise measurement of an operation's success or failure, users of accounting information demand current information every year, or quarter, or month. It is this need to artificially break the company's operations into time periods that requires us to make decisions about when revenues and expenses should be reported.

REVENUE AND EXPENSE RECOGNITION

In the base of the arch we have used to depict the Financial Accounting Standards Board's (FASB's) *Conceptual Framework of Accounting* (see Exhibit 5–1), certain accounting principles are listed. Revenue recognition and expense recognition are the two we will discuss in this chapter. As in previous chapters, the italicized definitions in the following discussion are provided by the FASB. A less formal discussion of certain items follows the words of the FASB.

In the *Conceptual Framework*, the FASB defined recognition in accounting as . . . *the process of formally recording or incorporating an item into the financial statements of an entity as an asset, liability, revenue, expense, or the like. Recognition includes depiction of an item in both words and numbers, with the amount included in the totals of the financial statements* (Statement of Financial Accounting Concepts No. 5, paragraph 6). **Recognition** in accounting, then, is the process of (1) recording in the books and (2) reporting on the financial statements.

recognition The process of recording an event in accounting records and reporting it in your financial statements.

The problem of when to recognize an item applies to all of the accounting elements we have discussed so far, as well as to the ones we have yet to discuss. The greatest difficulties, however, concern when to recognize revenues and expenses.

When should revenue be recognized? When should an expense be recognized? These are two very difficult questions, for which there are no clear-cut "right" answers. For financial statements of different companies to be comparable, there must be a consistently applied set of criteria to determine when accounting elements, particularly revenues and expenses, are recognized. Those of you who have taken another accounting class may have been taught a particular set of criteria for revenue and expense recognition and we are not asking you to forget what you learned. What we are asking you to do is slide those criteria to the back of your mind, because what you learned in the other accounting class is *a* set of criteria, not *the* set of criteria.

Discussion Questions

5–4. If revenue is defined as the reward of doing business, at what point do you think it should be recognized? Explain.

5–5. If an expense is defined as the sacrifice necessary to obtain a revenue, at what point do you think it should be recognized? Explain.

BASES OF ECONOMIC MEASUREMENT

There are two basic approaches to recording economic activity—the *cash basis* of economic measurement and the *accrual basis* of economic measurement. As they are discussed, you will see that each has certain advantages over the other. Neither of them is "correct" in the sense of being in accordance with some natural law of finance and accounting. They are simply different approaches to the measurement of revenues, expenses, assets, liabilities, and owners' equity.

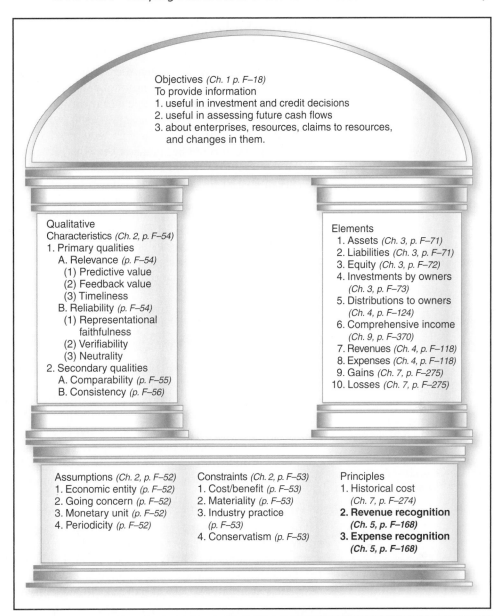

Objectives *(Ch. 1 p. F–18)*
To provide information
1. useful in investment and credit decisions
2. useful in assessing future cash flows
3. about enterprises, resources, claims to resources, and changes in them.

Qualitative
Characteristics *(Ch. 2, p. F–54)*
1. Primary qualities
   A. Relevance *(p. F–54)*
     (1) Predictive value
     (2) Feedback value
     (3) Timeliness
   B. Reliability *(p. F–54)*
     (1) Representational
        faithfulness
     (2) Verifiability
     (3) Neutrality
2. Secondary qualities
   A. Comparability *(p. F–55)*
   B. Consistency *(p. F–56)*

Elements
1. Assets *(Ch. 3, p. F–71)*
2. Liabilities *(Ch. 3, p. F–71)*
3. Equity *(Ch. 3, p. F–72)*
4. Investments by owners
   (Ch. 3, p. F–73)
5. Distributions to owners
   (Ch. 4, p. F–124)
6. Comprehensive income
   (Ch. 9, p. F–370)
7. Revenues *(Ch. 4, p. F–118)*
8. Expenses *(Ch. 4, p. F–118)*
9. Gains *(Ch. 7, p. F–275)*
10. Losses *(Ch. 7, p. F–275)*

Assumptions *(Ch. 2, p. F–52)*
1. Economic entity *(p. F–52)*
2. Going concern *(p. F–52)*
3. Monetary unit *(p. F–52)*
4. Periodicity *(p. F–52)*

Constraints *(Ch. 2, p. F–53)*
1. Cost/benefit *(p. F–53)*
2. Materiality *(p. F–53)*
3. Industry practice
   (p. F–53)
4. Conservatism *(p. F–53)*

Principles
1. Historical cost
   (Ch. 7, p. F–274)
2. Revenue recognition
   (Ch. 5, p. F–168)
3. Expense recognition
   (Ch. 5, p. F–168)

EXHIBIT 5–1 The Conceptual Framework of Accounting

We will use a single set of data to illustrate the two bases of measurement. Consider the following information concerning Corkel Incorporated, a dealer of sophisticated exercise equipment with a target market of movie stars and eccentric millionaires:

1. Max Corkel started the company on January 2, 2003, by incorporating and immediately purchasing 2,000 shares of the company's no-par common stock for $200,000.
2. Corkel Incorporated borrowed $100,000 from ***Citibank*** on January 2, by signing a one-year, 12 percent note payable. Although the $100,000 does not have to be repaid until January 2, 2004, the interest charge must be paid each month, beginning on February 2, 2003.
3. The company purchased a vehicle on January 2 for $14,000 cash. Max's best guess is that the vehicle will fill the company's needs for four years, after which he estimates the vehicle can be sold for $2,000.

4. The company paid cash for $75,000 of merchandise inventory on January 8.
5. On January 15, the company sold $42,000 of the merchandise inventory for a total selling price of $78,000 and collected cash the same day.
6. On January 22, the company sold $15,000 of the merchandise inventory for a total selling price of $32,000 on account (a credit sale). The terms of the sale were 30 days, meaning Corkel can expect to receive payment by February 22.
7. Cash payments for operating expenses in January totaled $22,500.
8. At the end of the month, the company owed $2,000 to employees of the company for work performed in January. They will be paid on February 3.
9. The company owed $700 at the end of the month for a utility bill that was received on January 26 and will be paid on February 15.

The above information is the reality of what happened in Corkel Incorporated during the month of January 2003. The measurement of that reality will be different, depending on whether you use the cash basis of accounting or the accrual basis of accounting. Remember, both treatments are based on exactly the same reality. They are simply different methods of measuring reality.

◆ CASH BASIS OF ECONOMIC MEASUREMENT

cash basis accounting
A basis of accounting in which cash is the major criterion used in measuring revenue and expense for a given income statement period. Revenue is recognized when the associated cash is received, and expense is recognized when the associated cash is paid.

The first approach we'll look at to measure economic activity is **cash basis accounting.** It is the simpler of the two bases, because everyone understands what cash is and can therefore readily grasp the measurement criterion of this method. Its greatest strength lies in the fact that it keeps the user's eye on the ball. As its name implies, the cash basis has only one measurement criterion: *CASH!*

As you recall, one of the three objectives of accounting information outlined by the FASB in the *Conceptual Framework* dealt specifically with cash. That objective says that to be useful, the information should help users assess a company's ability to generate sufficient cash to meet its obligations, support its operations, and to pay dividends. To do this, the FASB states that ... *financial reporting should provide information to help investors, creditors, and others assess the amounts, timing, and uncertainty of prospective net cash inflows to the related enterprise* (Statement of Financial Accounting Concepts No. 1, paragraph 37). The underlying theoretical justification for the cash basis of accounting is that it keeps the users focused on cash flow. Under cash basis accounting, we recognize economic activity only when we receive or pay cash.

CASH BASIS REVENUE RECOGNITION

There are two things to keep in mind when considering cash basis revenue recognition. First, a company recognizes revenue only when it receives the associated cash. Second, cash basis accounting considers only cash received as a result of the earnings process to be revenue. For example, the cash a business receives from its owners is an investment by those owners rather than revenue. Also, the business considers the cash it receives when it borrows as a liability rather than revenue. Transactions such as these, which involve cash but are not considered revenues, are reported on the statement of owners' equity and/or on the balance sheet, but not on the income statement.

CASH BASIS EXPENSE RECOGNITION

A company recognizes an expense only when it pays the associated cash. As with revenues, under cash basis accounting, not all cash a company pays out is an expense. If a company pays a dividend to its owners, for example, the cash paid out is not an expense to the company. Such a payment is a distribution of profits or a return on the owners' original investment. Transactions such as these, which involve cash but are not considered expenses, are reported on the statement of owners' equity and/or on the balance sheet, but not on the income statement.

CASH BASIS FINANCIAL STATEMENTS

There are two keys, then, to revenue and expense recognition under the cash basis. First, cash must be involved in the transaction. Second, the receipt or disbursement must relate to delivering or producing goods, rendering services, or other profit-related activities. If a transaction meets both of these requirements, it is a revenue or expense transaction (depending on whether the cash is received or paid) and will be reported on the income statement.

In preparing the income statement, the statement of owners' equity, and the balance sheet using the cash basis, you must first isolate the events and transactions involving cash. For our example of Corkel Incorporated, of the nine transactions and events we listed earlier, only the following events and transactions involve cash:

1. Max Corkel started the company on January 2, 2003, by incorporating and immediately purchasing 2,000 shares of the company's no-par common stock for $200,000.
2. Corkel Incorporated borrowed $100,000 from **Citibank** on January 2, by signing a one-year, 12 percent note payable. Although the $100,000 does not have to be repaid until January 2, 2004, the interest charge must be paid each month, beginning on February 2, 2003.
3. The company purchased a vehicle on January 2 for $14,000 cash. Max's best guess is that the vehicle will fill the company's needs for four years, after which he estimates the vehicle can be sold for $2,000.
4. The company paid cash for $75,000 of merchandise inventory on January 8.
5. On January 15, the company sold $42,000 of the merchandise inventory for a total selling price of $78,000 and collected cash the same day.
7. Cash payments for operating expenses in January totaled $22,500.

Corkel records these transactions in its books and reports the results on one or more of the financial statements: the income statement, the statement of owners' equity, or the balance sheet.

In order to determine which of the transactions should be reported on the income statement, we must determine which relate directly to Corkel's major or central operation, which is the buying and selling of sophisticated exercise equipment. Transactions 3, 4, 5, and 7 meet that criterion. Exhibit 5–2 shows a multiple-step income statement for the month of January 2003 using the cash basis of accounting.

- *Sales revenue.* Because the company received $78,000 in cash from sales in the month of January, that is the amount it shows as revenue.
- *Cost of goods sold.* Corkel paid $75,000 in cash for merchandise inventory during January. Thus, that is the amount recognized as cost of goods sold.
- *Expenses.* The cash expenses of $22,500 plus the entire $14,000 for the vehicle the company purchased were recognized as expenses in January. The company will recognize the remaining expenses as it pays the cash.

EXHIBIT 5–2   Cash Basis Income Statement

Corkel Incorporated
Income Statement
For the Month Ended January 31, 2003

Sales revenue		$ 78,000
Cost of goods sold		(75,000)
Gross margin		$ 3,000
Expenses:		
Cost of vehicle	$14,000	
Cash operating expenses	22,500	
Total operating expenses		(36,500)
Net loss		($ 33,500)

Transaction 1, Max Corkel's investment of $200,000, reflects an inflow of cash, so the cash basis of measurement requires that it be recognized. This investment by the owner increases the company's capital, while the net loss determined in Exhibit 5–2 decreases capital. Exhibit 5–3 shows the statement of owners' equity prepared using the cash basis of accounting.

EXHIBIT 5–3   Cash Basis Statement of Owners' Equity

Corkel Incorporated
Statement of Stockholders' Equity
For the Month Ended January 31, 2003

	Common Stock	Retained Earnings	Total
Balances as of January 1, 2003	$ 0	$ 0	$ 0
Sale of common stock	200,000		200,000
Net loss		(33,500)	(33,500)
Balances as of January 31, 2003	$200,000	($33,500)	$166,500

The remaining cash transaction of Corkel Incorporated during January 2003 is Transaction 2, the $100,000 bank loan. Borrowing money creates a liability that appears on the balance sheet. Exhibit 5–4 shows Corkel Incorporated's balance sheet at January 31, 2003, under cash basis accounting.

EXHIBIT 5–4   Cash Basis Balance Sheet

Corkel Incorporated
Balance Sheet
January 31, 2003

Assets:		Liabilities:	
Cash	$266,500	Note payable	$100,000
		Stockholders' equity:	
		Common stock	200,000
		Retained earnings	(33,500)
		Total stockholders' equity	166,500
Total assets	$266,500	Total liabilities and stockholders' equity	$266,500

Notice the articulation of the financial statements for Corkel Incorporated. The net loss from the income statement is shown on the statement of owners' equity, and the ending balances from the statement of owners' equity are used on the balance sheet. The cash amount showing on the balance sheet is simply the $200,000 the owner invested in the company plus the $100,000 borrowed from the bank less the $33,500 net loss for the month of January.

Discussion Questions •

5–6. Assume for a moment that you are Corkel's loan officer at the bank. How would you evaluate the income statement and balance sheet presented in Exhibits 5–2 and 5–4 in terms of the primary qualitative characteristic of relevance, including predictive value and feedback value? (*Hint*: See Chapter 2.)

5–7. If your response to Question 5–6 led you to the conclusion that there is a problem in terms of predictive value and feedback value, what item or items do you feel caused the problem? How do you think the company could account for the item or items to better relate costs to the revenues they generate?

STRENGTHS AND WEAKNESSES OF CASH BASIS ACCOUNTING

The greatest strength of cash basis accounting is that it keeps the focus on cash flow, and because of that, it is relatively simple to use. Further, it is relatively objective. Because cash is the only measurement criterion, the cash basis requires less subjective judgment than the accrual basis measurement, which we will discuss next. This is not to say that cash basis accounting is totally objective. For example, a company can manipulate the expenses it reports in a particular income statement period simply by delaying the payment of amounts owed. The greatest weakness of the cash basis is that it makes no attempt to recognize expenses in the same period as the revenues they helped generate. This makes the cash basis income statement very difficult to use either for predicting future profitability or for assessing past performance in cases in which cash is not immediately received when it is earned or paid when it is owed.

Discussion Question   •

5–8. The cash basis of accounting is very similar to maintaining a checking account balance. Provide two examples of situations in which your checkbook balance did not provide relevant information.

◆ ACCRUAL BASIS OF ECONOMIC MEASUREMENT

accrual basis accounting
A method of accounting in which revenues are recognized when they are earned, regardless of when the associated cash is collected. The expenses incurred in generating the revenue are recognized when the benefit is derived rather than when the associated cash is paid.

accrue   As used in accounting, to come into being as a legally enforceable claim.

The second basis of economic measurement we will discuss is **accrual basis accounting.** The key to understanding accrual basis accounting is to understand what the word **accrue** means, which is *to come into being as a legally enforceable claim.* This system does not rely on the receipt or payment of cash to determine when revenues and expenses should be recognized.

Essentially, in accrual basis accounting, a company recognizes sales, purchases, and all other business transactions whenever a legally enforceable claim to the associated cash is established. A legally enforceable claim to cash means that if somebody owes you money and they don't pay, you can legally force them to pay (or vice versa). The main focus of accrual accounting is determining when a legally enforceable claim to cash or other assets or services has been established between the parties involved in the transaction.

The legal considerations just discussed are all well and good, but more importantly from a practical standpoint, at least, is what accrual accounting and the resultant financial information is attempting to capture. Essentially, accrual accounting focuses on the earnings process rather than the cash flows resulting from that process. This is important because what it means is that accrual accounting takes the user's eye off the ball (cash). The FASB, in the *Conceptual Framework*, had this to say about accrual accounting:

> *Accrual accounting attempts to record the financial effects on an entity of transactions and other events and circumstances that have cash consequences for the entity in the periods in which those transactions, events, and circumstances occur rather than only in the periods in which cash is received or paid by the entity. Accrual accounting is concerned with an entity's acquiring of goods and services and using them to produce and distribute other goods or services. It is concerned with the process by which cash expended on resources and activities is returned as more (or perhaps less) cash to the entity, not just with the beginning and end of that process. It recognizes that the buying, producing, selling, distributing, and other operations of an entity during a period, as well as other events that affect entity performance, often do not coincide with the cash receipts and payments of the period* (Statement of Financial Accounting Concepts No. 6, paragraph 139).

Included in the concept of accrual accounting are the revenue and expense recognition principles the FASB discussed in the *Conceptual Framework*. Following the FASB's italicized words, we will explain how the principles are applied.

ACCRUAL BASIS REVENUE RECOGNITION

The FASB said this about accrual basis revenue recognition:

> *Revenues and gains of an enterprise during a period are generally measured by the exchange values of assets (goods or services) or liabilities involved, and recognition involves consideration of two factors (A) being realized or realizable and (B) being earned, with sometimes one and sometimes the other being the more important consideration* (Statement of Financial Accounting Concepts No. 5, paragraph 83).

First, let's address the FASB's reference to *revenues* and *gains*. While revenues and gains are similar, revenues result from a company's primary or central operations and gains result from what we call incidental or peripheral transactions. *Gains* are one of the 10 accounting elements listed on the arch, and we will discuss this topic in Chapter 7. For now we will focus on revenues that result from a company's primary operations.

If we are using accrual accounting then, we recognize revenue when it is *realized* or *realizable* or when we consider it *earned*. Revenues are realized when a company exchanges goods or services for cash or claims to cash. They are realizable when a company receives assets other than cash or claims to cash, when those assets can be exchanged for known amounts of cash or claims to cash. If you think this all sounds pretty confusing, you're not alone. Even practicing accountants with years of experience sometimes disagree about precisely what the concept of realized or realizable means and how it applies to day-to-day business transactions and events. For this reason, our focus will be on recognizing revenue when we consider it earned.

Under accrual accounting, we recognize revenue when it is deemed to be earned—that is, a company recognizes revenue when it has a legally enforceable claim to the cash associated with that revenue. Since in many instances the cash is collected some time other than when the revenue is earned, under accrual accounting, revenue recognition is completely unrelated to when the cash is received.

There are three possible relationships between when a company receives cash and when it recognizes revenue:

1. Cash is received at the time the revenue is earned. An example of this is when you buy a pair of jeans at *Gap* and pay cash. *Gap* receives cash at the same time as the store recognizes revenue from the sale.
2. Cash is received after the revenue has been earned. An example of this is a sale of merchandise on account (a credit sale). ***NAPA Auto Parts*** records revenue for sales made to its credit card customers in January but does not collect the cash until February.
3. Cash is received before the revenue has been earned. An example of this is when ***Time*** magazine receives the payment in advance from a customer for a year's subscription.

Remember that under accrual accounting, the trigger mechanism for determining when revenue should be recognized is the earning process, not when the cash is received. In Examples 1 and 2, the revenue is recorded in the books and shown on the financial statements at the time the sale is made. The fact that in Example 2 the company did not receive cash at that time does not affect recognition of the revenue. In Example 3, the receipt of cash does not cause revenue to be recognized because, under accrual accounting, the revenue is not recognized until it is earned (when the magazines have been sent to the customer).

Identifying the point in time when revenue is earned is not always a simple matter. There are three questions accountants try to answer to determine when revenue has been earned and should therefore be recognized:

title Legal ownership of something.

1. Has **title** (legal ownership) to whatever was sold been transferred to the customer? If the answer to this question is yes, the seller should definitely recognize the revenue.
2. Has an exchange taken place? In other words, has the customer received whatever he or she purchased? If the answer to this question is yes, the seller will likely recognize the revenue.

3. Is the earnings process virtually complete? This is the toughest of the three questions to answer. Let's say, for example, that you have contracted with Joe Dokes to remodel your kitchen. It's a two-week job, and midway through the second week, Joe decides that he doesn't want to be a remodeler anymore. Are you obligated to pay him for removing your old cabinets, stripping the wallpaper, and making a hole in the wall for the new window? Probably not. He cannot recognize revenue until the job is "virtually" complete.

The answer to all three questions need not be "yes" for a business to recognize revenue. In most cases, a positive answer to any one question is persuasive evidence that revenue has been earned and should be recognized.

Discussion Questions

5–9. On Saturday morning, you decide to buy a computer at Carl's Computer Mart. The salesperson has agreed to have all the software you need installed and have the machine delivered to you by Tuesday afternoon. Because you purchased your last computer at Carl's, the store has agreed to extend credit to you as an established customer. You have 30 days to pay for your new computer. As of Monday,

    a. has title passed?
    b. has an exchange taken place?
    c. is the earnings process complete?

5–10. When should Carl's Computer Mart recognize revenue:

    a. under the cash basis?
    b. under the accrual basis?

ACCRUAL BASIS EXPENSE RECOGNITION

The FASB said this about accrual basis expense recognition:

> *Expenses and losses are generally recognized when an entity's economic benefits are used up in delivering or producing goods, rendering services, or other activities that constitute its ongoing major or central operations or when previously recognized assets are expected to provide reduced or no further benefits* (Statement of Financial Accounting Concepts No. 5, paragraph 85).

First, let's address the FASB's reference to *expenses* and *losses*. Expenses and losses are similar, and in the reference just cited, the FASB states that both expenses and losses result from a company's ongoing or central operations. While it is true that some losses do result from a company's day-to-day operations, you should think of expenses as resulting from a company's primary or central operations, and consider losses as resulting from incidental or peripheral transactions. *Losses* are one of the 10 accounting elements in the arch, and we will discuss them in Chapter 7. For now, we will focus on expenses that result from a company's day-to-day operations.

According to the FASB, then, an entity should recognize expenses when its *economic benefits* are used up in delivering or producing goods or rendering services. Economic benefits, as you recall from Chapter 3, are assets. So expenses are assets used up in delivering or producing goods or rendering services. As with revenue recognition, expense recognition under accrual accounting is completely unrelated to the movement of cash.

Again, there are three possible relationships between when a company pays cash and when it recognizes an expense:

1. Cash is paid at the time the expense is incurred. An example of this is a check the manager of a **Gap** store writes to the catering company for food served at the store Christmas party held that same day.

2. Cash is paid after the expense has been incurred. An example of this is **NAPA Auto Parts'** payment of a utility bill in February that was for electricity used in January.

3. Cash is paid before the expense has been incurred. An example of this is insurance. *Time* magazine buys insurance coverage for a full year and pays the entire premium when the policy is purchased.

The key to expense recognition under accrual accounting is revenue recognition. That's right—*revenue recognition.* Remember that to be useful in predicting future profitability and cash flow, an income statement should measure revenues for a specific period of time *and* the expenses required to obtain those revenues. Thus, accrual accounting attempts to establish a relationship between revenues and expenses. This relationship is referred to as **matching.**

THE CONCEPT OF MATCHING

In the *Conceptual Framework*, the FASB stated:

> *Accrual accounting uses accrual, deferral, and allocation procedures whose goal is to relate revenues, expenses, gains, and losses to periods to reflect an entity's performance during a period instead of merely listing its cash receipts and outlays. Thus, recognition of revenues, expenses, gains, and losses and the related increments and decrements in assets and liabilities—including matching of costs and revenues, allocation, and amortization—is the essence of using accrual accounting to measure performance of entities* (Statement of Financial Accounting Concepts No. 6, paragraph 145).

The first step in the accrual matching process is to determine in which income statement period a company should recognize a particular revenue. The second step is to determine which expenses helped to generate that revenue. The company then recognizes those expenses in that same financial statement period. This approach makes the income statement for that time period more reflective of true earnings results and, therefore, more relevant for predicting future potential. It is important to note that it can be very difficult to determine which expenses generated which revenue, so a significant amount of judgment is required in recognizing expenses under the accrual basis of accounting. There are two possible relationships between revenues and expenses, and these determine when expenses are recognized: (1) direct cause and effect and (2) no direct cause and effect.

1. *Direct cause and effect.* This situation, in which a direct link can be found between an expense and the revenue it helped generate, is the more desirable of the two relationships. An example is sales commissions. If **Prudential Insurance Company** pays a 10 percent sales commission to its salespersons, and a sales representative makes a sale of $1,000, the company incurs a $100 expense. Once the company determines in which income statement period it should recognize the $1,000 revenue, it recognizes the $100 expense in that same period. Unfortunately, relatively few expenses can be linked directly to the revenues they help generate.

2. *No direct cause and effect.* This is the more common relationship. In this case, there are two possible treatments: (a) allocation to the periods benefited and (b) immediate recognition.

   a. *Allocation to the periods benefited.* If a purchased item has discernible benefit to future income statement periods and the periods can be reasonably estimated, a company records the item as an asset when purchased. The cost of that item is then systematically converted to expense in the periods benefited. An example of this is insurance. If a company pays a premium for two years of insurance coverage, there is no question that a benefit to future periods exists. Further, the estimate of those periods is clear—benefits will be derived for two years. As time passes during the two years, the company converts the cost of the insurance coverage to expense. This allows each of the two years covered by the insurance to show an equal amount of expense.

   b. *Immediate recognition.* There are two situations in which recording the expense immediately is the most appropriate action. First, if a purchased item has no dis-

---

matching Accounting principle that relates the expenses to the revenues of a particular income statement period. Once it is determined in which period a revenue should be recognized, the expenses that helped to generate the revenue are matched to that same period.

cernible future benefit, or the periods benefited cannot be reasonably estimated, a company should recognize the cost of the item as an expense immediately. A good example of an expense requiring immediate recognition is ***Ford Motor Company***'s television advertising to promote the sale of its cars and trucks. The future benefit of this type of advertising is not discernible. Television ads purchased and presented to the public in one period almost certainly benefit future periods, but how many periods and how much in each of those periods cannot be reasonably estimated. Thus, companies usually recognize the cost of television advertising as an expense in the periods when the ads are purchased.

The second situation requiring the immediate recognition of an expense is when allocation of the cost of a purchased item provides no additional useful information. An example of this situation is the purchase of a $10 item such as a stapler. Even if the stapler will be used in the office for five years, allocation of the $10 cost over the five-year period serves no useful purpose. Remember, the purpose of accounting is to provide information useful to decision makers. Will allocating this minor cost over a five-year period provide useful accounting information? Since most decision makers would be unaffected by the treatment of a $10 item, the answer is no. The record-keeping cost of recording the stapler as an asset on the balance sheet and then converting a portion of that cost per year as an expense on each of the next five year's income statements far outweighs the benefit of doing so. Recognizing the $10 cost as an immediate expense makes more sense. This is a perfect example of the materiality and cost/benefit constraints we discussed in Chapter 2.

The concept of "allocation to the periods benefited" has a more widely used application than the one just described. When assets that will benefit the company for several periods (often many years) are acquired, the cost is recorded as an asset on the balance sheet. As time passes, the cost is transferred to expense on the income statement. This form of "allocation to the periods benefited" is a process known as depreciation. Depreciation is applied to a variety of long-lived assets such as machinery, buildings, and equipment. One asset that has a long life, but is not depreciated, is land.

DEPRECIATION—WHAT IT IS *AND* WHAT IT IS NOT

depreciation   The systematic and rational conversion of a long-lived asset's cost from asset to expense in the income statement periods benefited.

Depreciation is a systematic (methodical) and rational (reasoned) allocation of the cost of a long-lived item from asset to expense. You should recall that under cash basis accounting, Corkel Incorporated recognized the purchase of a $14,000 vehicle as a $14,000 expense because that amount of cash was spent. The real question is whether this asset has been "used up" (has the company received the total benefit from the vehicle?) or does the asset still have a future benefit? The answer is clearly that the asset (vehicle) has not been used up; the company has not received all the benefit from it. The accrual basis of measurement takes the position that the company should not recognize this cash payment of $14,000 as an expense at the time the cash is paid. Rather than recognize the cost of the vehicle as an expense immediately, under the accrual basis, it is recorded as an asset because it has probable future benefit. Over time, the cost of the vehicle will be converted from asset to expense as the benefit is derived from the use of the vehicle. The resulting expense is called depreciation expense.

There is probably nothing in all of accounting as misunderstood as the concept of depreciation. The confusion is caused by the difference between the meaning of *depreciation* in accounting and in ordinary speech. In virtually every context except accounting, depreciation means the lowering of value. In accounting, it simply means the allocation of cost to the periods benefited. This allocation requires two highly subjective estimates: (1) the useful life of the asset and (2) the residual value of the asset.

The useful life of an asset is the length of time that the asset will be of use to the company, not the length of time the asset will exist. Notice that in the case of Corkel Incorporated, Max Corkel feels that the vehicle will fill the company's needs for four years. This is not the same thing as saying the vehicle will last four years. This is an important distinction.

If the estimated useful life of an asset is less than the physical life of that asset, it follows that the asset will probably be sold at the end of its useful life. The estimated amount for which the asset can be sold at the end of its useful life is known as its residual value (sometimes called *salvage value* or *scrap value*).

In calculating depreciation, we subtract any estimated residual value from the cost of an asset to arrive at what is called the *depreciable base* or *depreciable amount*. In the case of Corkel Incorporated, the cost of the vehicle was $14,000, and the company estimated that at the end of its useful life, the vehicle could be sold for $2,000. The depreciable amount, therefore, is $12,000 ($14,000 − $2,000). In one sense, then, the true cost of the vehicle to Corkel is $12,000, because the company expects to recoup $2,000 of the purchase price when the vehicle is sold.

Once we have estimated the useful life and residual value of the asset, we must select a method of depreciation. Several have been developed over the years. The simplest method is straight-line depreciation, and we will use it to demonstrate how depreciation expense is calculated.

The straight-line approach allocates an equal amount of depreciation expense to each period of the asset's estimated useful life. The amount of expense is calculated by dividing the estimated useful life of the asset into the depreciable amount of the asset. In the case of Corkel's vehicle, which cost $14,000 and has a four-year estimated useful life and a $2,000 residual value, the amount of expense works out to $3,000 per year calculated as follows:

$$\frac{\text{Cost} - \text{Residual Value}}{\text{Useful Life}} = \frac{\$14,000 - \$2,000}{4} = \frac{\$12,000}{4} = \$3,000$$

Each year of the four-year estimated useful life, Corkel will transfer $3,000 of the asset "vehicle" on the balance sheet into the expense "depreciation" on the income statement. At the end of the four years, the company will have recognized the entire cost of the vehicle (except the $2,000 residual value) as expense.

Depreciation is an important process that is based on accrual accounting's attempt to recognize expenses in the periods in which they help to generate revenue. Even though all of the $14,000 in cash was spent during January 2003 for Corkel Incorporated's vehicle, the entire benefit expected from the asset has not been received at that time. Because the company expects the asset to help generate revenues in future periods, it will allocate part of the cost to depreciation expense in each of those periods. The depreciation process is just one result of accrual accounting's attempt to match expenses and revenues. We'll explore others next.

Discussion Question ●

5–11. Recall the scenario, introduced in Discussion Question 5–9, involving your purchase of a computer from Carl's Computer Mart. If the computer is to be used in the business you operate from your home, how should the purchase be treated:

  a. under the cash basis?
  b. under the accrual basis?

ACCRUALS AND DEFERRALS

adjustments Changes made in recorded amounts of revenues and expenses in order to follow the guidelines of accrual accounting.

Because accrual accounting attempts to recognize revenues in the income statement period they are earned, and attempts to match the expenses that generated that revenue to the same income statement period, **adjustments** must be made each period to ensure that these guidelines have been followed. The adjustment process takes place at the end of the financial statement period before the financial statements are prepared. This process involves reviewing the financial records to be sure that all items that should be recognized in the current period have been recorded. In addition, during the adjustment process, it is ascertained that no items that should be recognized in future periods appear in the current period's records. The two basic types of adjustments that are necessary are accruals and deferrals.

accruals Adjustments made to record items that should be included on the income statement but have not yet been recorded.

accrued revenues Revenues appropriately recognized under accrual accounting in one income statement period although the associated cash will be received in a later income statement period.

accrued expenses Expenses appropriately recognized under accrual accounting in one income statement period although the associated cash will be paid in a later income statement period.

deferrals Situations in which cash is either received or paid, but the income statement effect is delayed until some later period. Deferred revenues are recorded as liabilities, and deferred expenses are recorded as assets.

deferred revenues Revenues created when cash is received before the revenue is earned. Because the cash received has not yet been earned, an obligation is created and a liability is recorded. Later, when the cash is deemed to have been earned, it will be recognized as a revenue.

deferred expenses Expenses created when cash is paid before any benefit is received. Because the benefit to be derived is in the future, the item is recorded as an asset. Later, when the benefit is received from the item, it will be recognized as an expense.

1. **Accruals.** These adjustments are made to recognize items that should be included in the income statement period but have not yet been recorded. Accrual adjustments recognize revenue or expense *before* the associated cash is received or paid. In other words, this type of adjustment comes before the cash flow takes place. There are two types of accruals:

   a. **Accrued revenues.** These are revenues considered earned during the financial statement period because they met the criteria (answers to questions 1, 2, and 3 on pages F–174–F–175 were "yes"), but which have not yet been recognized. Consider Warner Management Consulting Services, Inc. For the clients that use its services on an ongoing basis, the company sends bills on the 2nd of each month for work done during the previous month. Warner has a legal claim at the end of December to what was earned in that month. Revenues recognized (recorded) should reflect the amount earned in December, even though the clients will not be billed until January 2 of the next year.

   b. **Accrued expenses.** These are expenses deemed to have been incurred during the financial statement period, but which have not yet been recognized. An example of this is accrued wages for employees. Assume Pellum Company pays its employees every two weeks for work performed in the previous two weeks. If part of the two-week pay period is in 2004 and part is in 2005, Pellum must make an adjustment at the end of 2004 to recognize the portion of wages expense incurred during that period. Even though the company will not spend any money until payday in January of 2005, part of that pay period's wages are 2004 expenses.

2. **Deferrals.** These are postponements of the recognition of revenue or expense even though the cash has been received or paid. Deferrals are the adjustment of revenues for which the cash has been collected but not yet earned, and of expenses for which cash has been paid but no benefit has yet been received. In other words, this type of adjustment comes after the cash flow has already taken place. There are two types of deferrals: (a) deferred revenues and (b) deferred expenses.

   a. **Deferred revenues.** These are created when cash is received before it is earned. For example, Larry's Lawn Service provides lawn care to many wealthy Miami families. On June 1, the Weatherby family sends Larry's Lawn Service $450 for the cost of lawn service for June, July, and August. As of June 1, Larry's Lawn Service has not earned any revenue, even though it has received cash. In fact, at that point, a liability has been created. The company owes the Weatherby family either three months of lawn service or their money back. The key here is who has legal claim to the cash. Because Larry's Lawn Service has no legal claim to the cash, it cannot rightly account for it as earned. By the time financial statements are prepared at the end of June, however, one month's worth of lawn service was performed, and $150 should be recognized as revenue. The remaining $300, representing two months of service, is deferred revenue. This amount represents a liability for Larry's Lawn Service and will remain so until the company either performs the services required to attain a legal claim to the cash or returns the cash to the Weatherby family.

   b. **Deferred expenses.** These are created when cash is paid before an expense has been incurred. On January 2, 2004, Crockett Cookie Company purchased a three-year insurance policy for $2,175. By December 31, 2004, one third of the insurance coverage has expired (one third of the benefit has been received). Financial statements prepared for 2004 should reflect the fact that one third of the cost of the policy ($725) is an expense for that year. The remaining portion of the policy, two years' worth of coverage, is an asset providing future benefits to the company. Even though the entire $2,175 was spent in 2004, two thirds of the cost is a deferred expense, an asset that will be recognized as an expense in future periods.

Accruals and deferrals are adjustments made to be sure that the financial statements reflect the guidelines of accrual accounting. Accruals occur in situations where the cash flow has not yet taken place, but the revenue or expense should be recognized.

Deferrals are necessary in cases when the cash flow has already taken place, but the associated revenue or expense should not be recognized yet. Understand, too, that the original transaction (the receipt or payment of cash) is not an adjustment, but rather creates a situation where an adjustment will be necessary later.

Whether they reflect expenses or revenues, accruals and deferrals will always possess the following three characteristics:

1. *A revenue item or an expense item will always be affected.* This is logical because the whole purpose of the adjustment process is to make certain that revenues and expenses associated with a given financial statement period are recognized in that period. Clearly, adjustments will always affect the income statement.
2. *An asset item or a liability item will always be affected.* This means the balance sheet will also be affected by the adjustment process.
3. *Cash is never affected by accruals or deferrals.* Remember, adjustments are made to properly recognize accounting elements. It is assumed that inflows and outflows of cash were properly recorded at the time they occurred.

ACCRUAL BASIS FINANCIAL STATEMENTS

Let us once again turn to the transactions of Corkel Incorporated for the month of January 2003. Again, here are the descriptions of the company's transactions:

1. Max Corkel started Corkel Incorporated on January 2, 2003, by incorporating and immediately purchasing 2,000 shares of the company's no-par common stock for $200,000.
2. Corkel Incorporated borrowed $100,000 from **Citibank** on January 2, by signing a one-year, 12 percent note payable. Although the $100,000 does not have to be repaid until January 2, 2004, the interest charge must be paid each month, beginning on February 2, 2003.
3. The company purchased a vehicle on January 2 for $14,000 cash. Max's best guess is that the vehicle will fill the company's needs for four years, after which he estimates the vehicle can be sold for $2,000.
4. The company paid cash for $75,000 of merchandise inventory on January 8.
5. On January 15, the company sold $42,000 of the merchandise inventory for a total selling price of $78,000 and collected cash the same day.
6. On January 22, the company sold $15,000 of the merchandise inventory for a total selling price of $32,000 on account (a credit sale). The terms of the sale were 30 days, meaning Corkel can expect to receive payment by February 22.
7. Cash payments for operating expenses in January totaled $22,500.
8. At the end of the month, the company owed $2,000 to employees of the company for work performed in January. They will be paid on February 3.
9. The company owed $700 at the end of the month for a utility bill that was received on January 26 and will be paid on February 15.

All nine transactions will affect the income statement and/or the balance sheet and the statement of owners' equity under the accrual basis of accounting. The income statement for January 2003 is presented in Exhibit 5–5.

Most of the items on this income statement differ from those on the income statement prepared under the cash basis (Exhibit 5–2). Let's discuss each item:

- *Sales revenue.* Under the accrual basis, a company recognizes revenue when it is earned, regardless of when the associated cash is received. Transaction 6 says the company made a $32,000 sale on January 22. The fact that the cash is not expected to be received until February 22 is irrelevant. Therefore, total sales revenue for the month using accrual accounting is $110,000 ($78,000 cash sale + $32,000 credit sale).
- *Cost of goods sold.* Under accrual accounting, we attempt to match all expenses to the same income statement period as the revenues they help generate. In the case of merchandise inventory, it is relatively easy to establish a direct cause and effect

Corkel Incorporated
Income Statement
For the Month Ended January 31, 2003

Sales revenue		$110,000
Cost of goods sold		57,000
Gross margin		$ 53,000
Expenses:		
Cash operating expenses	$22,500	
Wages expense	2,000	
Utilities expense	700	
Depreciation expense	250	
Total operating expenses		(25,450)
Operating income		27,550
Other expenses—interest		(1,000)
Net income		$ 26,550

EXHIBIT 5–5 Accrual Basis Income Statement

between the revenue (sale of the inventory) and the expense (cost of the inventory sold). Transaction 5 says $42,000 of merchandise inventory was sold on January 15, and transaction 6 says $15,000 of merchandise inventory was sold on January 22. The total cost of this merchandise is $57,000, so this is the amount shown on the accrual basis income statement as cost of goods sold. This means, of course, that there is $18,000 of merchandise inventory not yet accounted for ($75,000 purchased − $57,000 sold). We will discuss this remaining inventory when we talk about the balance sheet.

- *Cash operating expenses.* This is the clearest and most understandable expense figure on Corkel Incorporated's income statement. Under both cash basis and accrual basis measurement, expenses paid in cash this period to support operations during this period are considered to be expenses for this period.
- *Wages expense of $2,000.* Because these wages were earned by employees during January, Corkel has a legal liability at January 31 for this amount. Further, since the benefit derived from the employees' work was in January, the expense should be recognized in January regardless of when the employees will actually be paid.
- *Utilities expense of $700.* Since the bill was received in January, let us assume that it was for utilities purchased and used during January. In that case, the expense should be recognized in January.
- *Depreciation expense of $250.* Under cash accounting, the cost of the vehicle was considered an expense the day it was paid for. But as explained earlier, under accrual accounting, only a portion of the cost is recognized as expense each period. Using straight-line depreciation, the amount of depreciation is calculated as ($14,000 − $2,000)/4 = $3,000. This $3,000 represents the amount of depreciation expense that should be recognized during each year of the asset's useful life. Because the financial statements we are using in the Corkel Incorporated example are for only the month of January 2003, the amount of depreciation expense would be only $250 ($3,000/12) for the month.
- *Interest expense of $1,000.* The cost of the $100,000 loan is the interest Corkel must pay. Because the company had the $100,000 throughout the month of January, the interest cost for the month should be recognized as an expense even though it will not be paid until February 2. The amount is calculated using the formula explained in Chapter 3:

$$\text{Principal} \times \text{Rate} \times \text{Time} = \text{Interest Expense}$$
$$\$100,000 \times 12\% \times 1/12 = \$1,000 \text{ Interest Expense for January}$$

Discussion Questions

5-12. Reexamine each item on Corkel Incorporated's accrual basis income statement and identify the items that are a result of the adjustment process.

5-13. Consider the following statement as it relates to the accrual basis of economic measurement: "Net income is an opinion; cash is a fact." What do you think this means?

Now that we have discussed the effect of accrual accounting on the income statement, we can look at what effects this system has on the statement of owners' equity. The owner's investment of $200,000 is treated just as it was under the cash basis. However, the results presented on the income statement under accrual accounting will be different, so the statement of owners' equity (Exhibit 5–6) will also be different under the accrual basis of measurement.

EXHIBIT 5-6   Accrual Basis Statement of Owners' (Stockholders') Equity

Corkel Incorporated
Statement of Stockholders' Equity
For the Month Ended January 31, 2003

	Common Stock	Retained Earnings	Total
Balances as of January 1, 2003	$ 0	$ 0	$ 0
Sale of common stock	200,000		200,000
Net income		26,550	26,550
Balances as of January 31, 2003	$200,000	$26,550	$226,550

The balance sheet for Corkel Incorporated at January 31, 2003, using the accrual basis of accounting is presented in Exhibit 5–7. Note that the items we discussed for the income statement have had an effect on the balance sheet as well.

EXHIBIT 5-7   Accrual Basis Balance Sheet

Corkel Incorporated
Balance Sheet
January 31, 2003

Assets:		Liabilities:	
Cash	$266,500	Accounts payable	$ 700
Accounts receivable	32,000	Wages payable	2,000
Inventory	18,000	Interest payable	1,000
Vehicle	14,000	Note payable	100,000
Less accumulated depreciation	(250)	Total liabilities	103,700
Vehicle, net	13,750	Stockholders' equity:	
		Common stock	200,000
		Retained earnings	26,550
		Total stockholders' equity	226,550
Total assets	$330,250	Total liabilities and stockholders' equity	$330,250

Again, many items on this balance sheet differ from those on the balance sheet prepared under the cash basis (Exhibit 5–4). Each item on the statement will be discussed in turn.

- *Cash of $266,500.* The amount of cash is counted and reported. Regardless of the basis of economic measurement, the amount of cash on hand cannot be changed. Note, however, that under the accrual basis, several items not directly related to cash affect net income. Therefore, net income is not equal to the increase in cash.
- *Accounts receivable of $32,000.* Transaction 6 created this asset. Corkel recognized the sale because an exchange had taken place and title to the merchandise inventory had passed to the customer. When that transaction occurred, Corkel had a legal claim to the $32,000. This is certainly an item that has probable future benefit to the business; it is therefore shown as an asset. It will remain classified as an asset until such time as the customer pays Corkel the cash.
- *Inventory of $18,000.* This is the remaining amount of merchandise inventory not recognized as cost of goods sold on the income statement. It is classified on the balance sheet as an asset because Corkel has not yet sacrificed it to generate revenue (it has probable future benefit). It will remain classified as an asset until such time as it is sold.
- *Vehicle of $14,000.* The original cost of the vehicle still shows on the balance sheet.
- *Accumulated depreciation of $250.* To show that a portion of the original cost of the vehicle has been converted to expense, an amount called accumulated depreciation has been deducted to arrive at what is called the net amount of the asset. This amount, $13,750, is also called the *book value* of the vehicle. In future periods, as more depreciation expense is recorded, the total amount recorded since the asset was acquired is shown as **accumulated depreciation.** Therefore, as time passes, accumulated depreciation increases and the book value of the asset decreases. This method of presentation tells decision makers the original cost of the asset and the amount not yet converted to expense (depreciated).
- *Accounts payable of $700.* This is for the utilities; the liability was created when Corkel recorded receiving the bill. Corkel has recognized the utilities expense, but the bill has not yet been paid. It is properly classified as a liability because it is an amount owed by the company and will require the sacrifice of assets (in this case, cash) in the future. It will remain classified as a liability until such time as Corkel pays the bill.
- *Wages payable of $2,000.* This is the amount Corkel owes its employees at the balance sheet date; the liability was created in the adjustment process.
- *Interest payable of $1,000.* This is the amount of interest Corkel owes the bank at the balance sheet date. Again, this liability was created in the adjustment process.
- *Note payable of $100,000.* This is a liability representing the amount Corkel Incorporated owes to **Citibank.**
- *Equity of $226,550.* This is the ending balance shown on the accrual basis statement of stockholders' equity. This amount is different from the equity balance shown on the cash basis balance sheet because of the difference in net income.

accumulated depreciation The total amount of cost that has been systematically converted to expense since a long-lived asset was first purchased.

STRENGTHS AND WEAKNESSES OF ACCRUAL BASIS ACCOUNTING

The strength of the accrual basis is that it establishes a relationship between revenues and the expenses incurred to generate the revenue. This is helpful to economic decision makers as they assess the past performance of a company and as they attempt to predict a company's future profitability.

Accrual accounting's most glaring weakness is that it takes the user's eye off cash. Accrual basis income statements do not provide information about inflows or outflows of cash. Because revenue and expense recognition under the accrual basis are totally unrelated to the receipt or payment of cash, net income does not represent an increase in cash for the period covered by the income statement. Neither does a net loss represent a decrease in cash.

Discussion Question ●

5–14. What complications can you see if revenue is recognized in December 2004, but the cash is not collected until January 2005?

◆ COMPARING THE TWO BASES OF ECONOMIC MEASUREMENT

Exhibits 5–8 and 5–9 depict two sets of financial statements for Corkel Incorporated. The first set is cash basis statements and the second set is accrual basis statements.

Each set illustrates the articulation of financial statements. The net loss presented on the cash basis income statement results in a reduction of owners' equity presented on the statement of stockholders' equity. The accrual basis income statement shows a net income of $26,550, which acts to increase owners' equity presented on the statement of stockholders' equity. In both sets of statements, the ending balance shown on the statement of owners' equity is used on the balance sheet.

Remember that both sets of statements are based on exactly the same transactions and events. The measurement criteria for the cash basis of accounting versus the measurement criteria for the accrual basis of accounting caused the differences, not the reality of what happened in Corkel Incorporated during the month.

Discussion Questions

5–15. Which of the two sets of financial statements do you think more closely relates the measurement of reality to reality? In other words, which set do you think is

EXHIBIT 5–8 Set of Cash Basis Financial Statements

Corkel Incorporated
Income Statement
For the Month Ended January 31, 2003

Sales revenue		$78,000
Cost of goods sold		75,000
Gross margin		$ 3,000
Expenses:		
Cost of vehicle	$14,000	
Cash operating expenses	22,500	
Total operating expenses		(36,500)
Net loss		($33,500)

Corkel Incorporated
Statement of Stockholders' Equity
For the Month Ended January 31, 2003

	Common Stock	Retained Earnings	Total
Balance as of January 1, 2003	$ 0	$ 0	$ 0
Sale of common stock	200,000		200,000
Net loss		(33,500)	(33,500)
Balance as of January 1, 2003	$200,000	($33,500)	$166,500

Corkel Incorporated
Balance Sheet
January 31, 2003

Assets:		Liabilites:	
Cash	$266,500	Notes payable	$100,000
		Stockholders' equity:	
		Common stock	200,000
		Retained earnings	(33,500)
		Total stockholders' equity	166,500
Total assets	$266,500	Total liabilities and stockholders' equity	$266,500

the better presentation of what actually happened during January 2003? Explain.

5–16. Which of the two sets of financial statements do you think better reflects Corkel Incorporated's future profit potential? Explain.

5–17. Are you coming to the conclusion that accounting lacks the exactness you once thought it possessed? Explain.

So, which of the bases is better? Well, that's not an easy question to answer. Each has strengths and weaknesses in relation to the other, and each is appropriate for certain entities in certain situations. However, having two valid bases of economic measurement does present a problem to economic decision makers, who often evaluate

---

EXHIBIT 5–9   Set of Accrual Basis Financial Statements

Corkel Incorporated
Income Statement
For the Month Ended January 31, 2003

Sales revenue		$110,000
Cost of goods sold		57,000
Gross margin		$ 53,000
Expenses:		
Cash operating expenses	$22,500	
Wages expense	2,000	
Utilities expense	700	
Depreciation expense	250	
Total operating expenses		(25,450)
Operating income		27,550
Other expenses—interest		1,000
Net income		$ 26,550

Corkel Incorporated
Statement of Stockholders' Equity
For the Month Ended January 31, 2003

	Common Stock	Retained Earnings	Total
Balance as of January 1, 2003	$ 0	$ 0	$ 0
Sale of common stock	200,000		200,000
Net income		26,550	26,550
Balance as of January 31, 2003	$200,000	$26,550	$226,550

Corkel Incorporated
Balance Sheet
January 31, 2003

Assets:		Liabilities:	
Cash	$266,500	Accounts payable	$ 700
Accounts receivable	32,000	Wages payable	2,000
Inventory	18,000	Interest payable	1,000
Vehicle	14,000	Note payable	100,000
Less accumulated depreciation	(250)	Total liabilites	103,700
Vehicle, net	13,750	Stockholders' equity:	
		Common stock	200,000
		Retained earnings	26,550
		Total stockholders' equity	226,550
Total assets	$330,250	Total liabilities and stockholders' equity	$330,250

choices among various companies. If one company uses cash basis accounting and another uses accrual accounting, what are decision makers to do? We have seen the different outcomes when we use the two different measurement bases to measure the same reality. Imagine how difficult it would be to evaluate two sets of financial statements with different measurement bases and different business activities!

Because the accounting profession has deemed that accrual accounting provides more useful information to economic decision makers than does cash accounting, accrual accounting has been adopted as the method used by those companies required to follow generally accepted accounting principles (GAAP). According to the FASB in the *Conceptual Framework*:

> *The information measured by accrual accounting generally provides a better indication of an organization's performance than does information about cash receipts and payments. Accrual accounting attempts to record the financial effects of transactions, events, and circumstances that have cash consequences for an organization in the periods in which those transactions, events, and circumstances occur rather than in only the periods in which cash is received or paid by the organization. Accrual accounting is concerned with the process by which cash is obtained and used, not with just the beginning and end of that process. It recognizes that the acquisition of resources needed to provide services and the rendering of services by an organization during a period often do not coincide with the cash receipts and payments of the period* (Statement of Financial Accounting Concepts No. 4, paragraph 50).

With that said, using accrual accounting does not, in and of itself, provide comparability. Even if the companies we are comparing both use the accrual basis of measurement, a number of factors could complicate the comparison. Chapters 7 and 8 explore areas in accounting that permit flexibility in the recognition of revenues and expenses. These variations reduce comparability of financial statement information between companies. In order to make the best use of accounting information, be aware of the variations. There is also the problem that accrual accounting takes the focus off cash flow. This problem has been addressed by the development of the statement of cash flows, which we have discussed briefly in previous chapters, and which we will discuss in much greater detail in Chapter 10.

Summary •

There are two things going on in business. First, there is the reality of business transactions and events. Second, there is the attempt to measure that reality in the accounting records and reports. For a number of reasons, the measurement of reality may not precisely reflect reality. Some of the differences between reality and the measurement of reality are a result of the basis selected to recognize revenues and expenses in a particular time period. This chapter presented two distinct bases: the cash basis and the accrual basis.

Under cash basis accounting, economic activity is recognized only when cash is paid or received. Under this basis, a company recognizes revenue only when it receives the associated cash. Remember, however, that cash basis accounting considers revenue only the cash that is received as a result of the earnings process.

Under cash basis accounting, a company recognizes an expense only when it pays the associated cash. However, under cash basis accounting, not all cash a company pays out is an expense. If a company pays a dividend to its owners, or pays the principal on a debt, the cash paid out is not an expense to the company. Because cash is the only measurement criterion, cash basis accounting requires less subjective judgment than the accrual basis measurement, but it has a weakness in that it makes no attempt to recognize expenses in the same period as the revenues they helped generate.

Under accrual basis accounting, a company recognizes sales, purchases, and all other business transactions whenever a legally enforceable claim to the associated cash is established. Essentially, accrual accounting focuses on the earnings process rather than the cash flows resulting from that process.

Under accrual accounting, revenue is recognized when it is deemed to be earned—that is, a company recognizes revenue when it has a legally enforceable claim to the cash associated with that revenue. Since in many instances the cash is collected some time other than when the revenue is earned, under accrual accounting, revenue recognition is completely unrelated to when the cash is received.

There are three possible relationships between when a company receives cash and when it recognizes a revenue: Cash is received at the time the revenue is earned, cash is received after the revenue has been earned, or cash is received before the revenue has been earned.

Under accrual accounting, we recognize expenses when their benefit is received (i.e., they produce revenues), regardless of when the associated cash is paid. As with revenue recognition, expense recognition under accrual accounting is completely unrelated to the movement of cash.

Accrual accounting attempts to establish a relationship between revenues and expenses. The first step in the accrual matching process is to determine in which income statement period a company should recognize a particular revenue. The company then recognizes those expenses in that same financial statement period.

Accrual accounting's most glaring weakness is that it takes the user's eye off cash. Accrual basis income statements do not provide information about inflows or outflows of cash. Because revenue and expense recognition under the accrual basis are totally unrelated to the receipt or payment of cash, net income does not represent an increase in cash for the period covered by the income statement.

If one company uses cash basis accounting and another uses accrual accounting, what are decision makers to do? Because the accounting profession has deemed that accrual accounting provides more useful information to economic decision makers than does cash accounting, accrual accounting has been adopted as the method used by those companies required to follow generally accepted accounting principles.

Key Terms

- accrual basis accounting, F–173
- accruals, F–179
- accrue, F–173
- accrued expenses, F–179
- accrued revenues, F–179

- accumulated depreciation, F–183
- adjustments, F–178
- cash basis accounting, F–170
- deferrals, F–179
- deferred expenses, F–179

- deferred revenues, F–179
- depreciation, F–177
- matching, F–176
- recognition, F–168
- title, F–174

Review the Facts

A. Explain the difference between reality and the measurement of reality, and provide an example of each.
B. In accounting, what does it mean for an item to be "recognized"?
C. Under the cash basis of measurement, when does revenue recognition occur?
D. Under the cash basis, when are expenses recognized?
E. What is the greatest strength of the cash basis?
F. What is the greatest weakness of the cash basis?
G. Under the accrual basis of measurement, when does revenue recognition occur?
H. Under the accrual basis, when are expenses recognized?
I. Explain the concept of matching.
J. What is depreciation and why is it necessary in accrual accounting?
K. What are accruals?
L. What are deferrals?
M. What is the greatest strength of the accrual basis?
N. What is the greatest weakness of the accrual basis?

Apply What You Have Learned ●

LO 1, 2, 3, & 4: TERMINOLOGY

5–18. Below is a list of items relating to the concepts discussed in this chapter, followed by definitions of those items in scrambled order:

a. Cash basis revenues
b. Accrual basis expenses
c. Immediate recognition
d. Matching principle
e. Title passes to customer

f. Depreciation
g. No direct cause and effect between costs and revenues
h. Cash basis expenses
i. Accrual basis revenues

1. _____ Recognized when cash associated with a sale is received
2. _____ The situation that causes costs to be either recognized immediately as an expense or allocated to the income statement periods supposed benefited
3. _____ One of three evidences that revenue has been earned under accrual accounting
4. _____ Recognized when the cash associated with a cost is paid
5. _____ Recognized when there is a legal claim to the cash associated with a sale
6. _____ An attempt to recognize expenses in the same income statement period as the revenues they generate
7. _____ Recognized when the benefit is received rather than when the cash is paid
8. _____ The process of converting the cost of a long-lived item from asset to expense
9. _____ The treatment for costs when no future benefit can be determined or allocation to future periods serves no useful purpose

Required: Match the letter next to each item on the list with the appropriate definition. Use each letter only once.

LO 1 & 2: CASH BASIS MEASUREMENT

5–19. Linda VanHook Company began operation on January 2, 2004. During its first month of operation, the company had the following transactions:

- Purchased $35,000 of merchandise inventory on January 2. The amount due is payable on February 2.
- Paid January office rent of $3,000 on January 3.
- Purchased $10,000 of merchandise inventory on January 5. Paid cash at the time of purchase.
- Sold inventory that cost $18,000 for $30,000 to a customer on January 10 and received the cash on that date.
- Sold inventory that cost $5,000 for $9,000 to a customer on January 20. The sale was on account and the customer has until February 20 to pay.
- Paid cash expenses during January of $7,500.
- Received bills for utilities, advertising, and phone service totaling $1,500. All these bills were for services received in January. They will all be paid the first week in February.

Required:

a. Prepare a January 2004 multiple-step income statement for Linda VanHook Company using the cash basis of accounting.
b. Do you think the income statement you prepared for the previous requirement provides a good measure of the reality of the company's performance during January? Explain your reasoning.

LO 3: ACCRUAL BASIS MEASUREMENT

5–20. Linda VanHook Company began operation on January 2, 2004. During its first month of operation, the company had the same seven transactions as noted in problem 5–19.

Required:

a. Prepare a January 2004 multiple-step income statement for Linda VanHook Company using the accrual basis of accounting.
b. Do you think the income statement you prepared for the previous requirement provides a good measure of the reality of the company's performance during January? Explain your reasoning.

LO 1 & 2: CASH BASIS MEASUREMENT

5–21. Snow and Ice Company began operation on June 1, 2004. During its first month of operation, the company had the following transactions:

- Purchased $40,000 of merchandise inventory on June 1. The amount due is payable on August 1.
- Paid June office rent of $2,000 on June 3.
- Purchased $20,000 of merchandise inventory on June 4. Paid cash at the time of purchase.
- Sold inventory that cost $30,000 for $42,000 to a customer on June 10 and received the cash on that date.
- Sold inventory that cost $10,000 for $14,000 to a customer on June 20. The sale was on account and the customer has until July 20 to pay.
- Paid cash expenses during June of $9,500.
- Received bills for utilities, advertising, and phone service totaling $3,500. All these bills were for services received in June. They will all be paid the first week in July.

Required:

  a. Prepare a June 2004 multiple-step income statement for Snow and Ice Company using the cash basis of accounting.
  b. Do you think the income statement you prepared for the previous requirement provides a good measure of the reality of the company's performance during June? Explain your reasoning.

LO 3: ACCRUAL BASIS MEASUREMENT

5–22. Snow and Ice Company began operation on June 1, 2004. During its first month of operation, the company had the same seven transactions as noted in problem 5–21.

Required:

  a. Prepare a June 2004 multiple-step income statement for Snow and Ice Company using the accrual basis of accounting.
  b. Do you think the income statement you prepared for the previous requirement provides a good measure of the reality of the company's performance during June? Explain your reasoning.

LO 2 & 3: CASH VS. ACCRUAL

5–23. Bob Franks and Company began operation on January 2, 2004. During its first month of operation, the company had the following transactions:

- Paid January office rent of $2,000 on January 2.
- Purchased $25,000 of merchandise inventory on January 5. The amount due is payable on February 5.
- Purchased $15,000 of merchandise inventory on January 8. Paid cash at the time of purchase.
- Sold merchandise that cost $12,000 for $18,000 to a customer on January 16 and received the cash on that date.
- Sold merchandise that cost $9,000 for $13,500 to a customer on January 26. The sale was on account and the customer has until February 26 to pay.
- Paid February office rent of $2,000 on January 31.

Required:

  a. Prepare a January 2004 multiple-step income statement for Bob Franks and Company using the cash basis of accounting.
  b. Prepare a January 2004 multiple-step income statement for Bob Franks and Company using the accrual basis of accounting.
  c. Explain what caused the differences between the income statement prepared under the cash basis and the one prepared under the accrual basis.
  d. Which of the two income statement presentations do you think:

  1. Provides better information as to cash flow for the month of January?
  2. Provides better information as to what Franks earned during the month of January?
  3. Better reflects Franks' ability to generate future earnings and cash flow?

LO 2, 3, & 4: CONTINUATION CASH VS. ACCRUAL—SECOND MONTH

5–24. This is a continuation of the Bob Franks and Company problem begun in 5–23. During its second month of business, that's February 2004, the company had the following transactions:

- Sold the entire merchandise inventory it had on hand at the beginning of February for $28,500 cash on February 2.
- On February 5, the company paid the $25,000 it owed for the merchandise inventory it purchased on January 5.
- Purchased $20,000 of merchandise inventory on February 11. Paid cash at the time of purchase.
- Sold the merchandise that cost $20,000 it had purchased on February 11 for $30,000 to a customer on February 21 and received the cash on that date.
- On February 26, Franks collected the $13,500 from the sale of January 26.

Required:

a. Prepare a February 2004 multiple-step income statement for Bob Franks and Company using the cash basis of accounting.
b. Prepare a February 2004 multiple-step income statement for Bob Franks and Company using the accrual basis of accounting.
c. Explain what caused the differences between the income statement prepared under the cash basis and the one prepared under the accrual basis.
d. Which of the two income statement presentations do you think:

   1. Provides better information as to cash flow for the month of February?
   2. Provides better information as to what Franks earned during the month of February?
   3. Better reflects Franks' ability to generate future earnings and cash flow?

e. What is the total net income for January and February combined using the cash basis?
f. What is the total net income for January and February combined using the accrual basis?
g. What does the results of requirements e and f tell you?

LO 2, 3, & 4: CASH VS. ACCRUAL

5–25. Tom Dunn and Company began operation on August 2, 2004. During its first month of operation, the company had the following transactions:

- Paid August office rent of $3,000 on August 2.
- Purchased $35,000 of merchandise inventory on August 5. The amount due is payable on September 5.
- Purchased $25,000 of merchandise inventory on August 8. Paid cash at the time of purchase.
- Sold merchandise that cost $22,000 for $33,000 to a customer on August 16 and received the cash on that date.
- Sold merchandise that cost $10,000 for $15,000 to a customer on August 26. The sale was on account and the customer has until September 26 to pay.
- Paid September office rent of $3,000 on August 31.

Required:

a. Prepare an August 2004 multiple-step income statement for Tom Dunn and Company using the cash basis of accounting.
b. Prepare an August 2004 multiple-step income statement for Tom Dunn and Company using the accrual basis of accounting.
c. Explain in your own words what caused the differences between the income statement prepared under the cash basis and the one prepared under the accrual basis.
d. Which of the two income statement presentations do you think:

   1. Provides better information as to cash flow for the month of August?
   2. Provides better information as to what Tom Dunn earned during the month of August?
   3. Better reflects Tom Dunn's ability to generate future earnings and cash flow?

LO 2, 3, & 4: CONTINUATION CASH VS. ACCRUAL—SECOND MONTH

5–26. This is a continuation of the Tom Dunn and Company problem begun in 5–25. During the company's second month of business, September 2004, the company had the following transactions:

- Sold all merchandise inventory it had on hand at the beginning of September for $42,000 cash on September 2.
- On September 5, the company paid the $35,000 it owed for the merchandise inventory it purchased on August 5.
- Purchased $30,000 of merchandise inventory on September 11. Paid cash at the time of purchase.
- Sold merchandise that cost $30,000 it had purchased on September 11 for $45,000 to a customer on September 21 and received the cash on that date.
- On September 26, Tom Dunn and Company collected the $15,000 from the sale of August 26.

Required:

a. Prepare a September 2004 multiple-step income statement for Tom Dunn and Company using the cash basis of accounting.

b. Prepare a September 2004 multiple-step income statement for Tom Dunn and Company using the accrual basis of accounting.

c. Explain in your own words what caused the differences between the income statement prepared under the cash basis and the one prepared under the accrual basis.

d. Which of the two income statement presentations do you think:

1. Provides better information as to cash flow for the month of September?
2. Provides better information as to what Tom Dunn and Company earned during the month of September?
3. Better reflects Tom Dunn and Company's ability to generate future earnings and cash flow?

e. What is the total net income for August and September combined using the cash basis?

f. What is the total net income for August and September combined using the accrual basis?

g. What do the results of requirements e and f tell you?

LO 4: THE MATCHING PRINCIPLE

5–27. Maria Giudici, Inc., purchased $65,000 worth of inventory for cash in December 2003. The company sold $25,000 worth of the inventory in December and the remaining inventory of $40,000 in January 2004.

Required:

a. Calculate how much of the $65,000 of merchandise would appear in Cost of Goods Sold on the December 2003 income statement and how much would appear in Cost of Goods Sold on the January 2004 income statement if Giudici uses the cash basis of accounting.

b. Calculate how much of the $65,000 of merchandise would appear in Cost of Goods Sold on the December 2003 income statement and how much would appear in Cost of Goods Sold on the January 2004 income statement if Giudici uses the accrual basis of accounting.

LO 4: THE MATCHING PRINCIPLE

5–28. Alberto Pons Inc., purchased $100,000 of merchandise inventory on December 15, 2004, on a 30-day account. It sold merchandise that cost $35,000 in December and the remainder in January 2005.

Required:

a. On what date should Pons pay for the merchandise?

b. Calculate how much of the $100,000 of merchandise appears in Cost of Goods Sold on the December 2004 income statement and how much appears on the balance sheet in Merchandise Inventory on December 31, 2004, if Pons uses the cash basis of accounting.

c. Calculate how much of the $100,000 of merchandise appears in Cost of Goods Sold on the December 2004 income statement and how much appears on the balance sheet in Merchandise Inventory on December 31, 2004, if Pons uses the accrual basis of accounting.

LO 4: THE MATCHING PRINCIPLE

5–29. On December 5, 2004, Phil Handley, Inc., purchased $150,000 of merchandise inventory on account. The $150,000 is due in 90 days. It sold merchandise that cost $55,000 in December and $70,000 in January 2005.

Required:

 a. On what date should Handley pay for the merchandise?
 b. Calculate how much of the $150,000 of merchandise appears in Cost of Goods Sold on the December 2004 income statement and how much appears on the balance sheet in Merchandise Inventory on December 31, 2004, if Handley uses the cash basis of accounting.
 c. Calculate how much of the $150,000 of merchandise appears in Cost of Goods Sold on the January 2005 income statement and how much appears on the balance sheet in Merchandise Inventory on January 31, 2005, if Handley uses the cash basis of accounting.
 d. Calculate how much of the $150,000 of merchandise appears in Cost of Goods Sold on the December 2004 income statement and how much appears on the balance sheet in Merchandise Inventory on December 31, 2004, if Handley uses the accrual basis of accounting.
 e. Calculate how much of the $150,000 of merchandise appears in Cost of Goods Sold on the January 2005 income statement and how much appears on the balance sheet in Merchandise Inventory on January 31, 2005, if Handley uses the accrual basis of accounting.

LO 4: THE MATCHING PRINCIPLE

5–30. Davenport Corporation purchased a two-year insurance policy on May 1, 2004, by paying $4,800 on that date.

Required:

 a. Indicate how Davenport will list information concerning this policy on its 2004 income statement and its December 31, 2004, balance sheet under the cash basis.
 b. Indicate how Davenport will list information concerning this policy on its 2004 income statement and its December 31, 2004, balance sheet under the accrual basis.
 c. Indicate how Davenport will list information concerning this policy on its 2005 income statement and its December 31, 2005, balance sheet under the cash basis.
 d. Indicate how Davenport will list information concerning this policy on its 2005 income statement and its December 31, 2005, balance sheet under the accrual basis.

LO 4: THE MATCHING PRINCIPLE

5–31. Belski & Miglio paid their landlord $10,000 for five months' rent paid in advance on November 1, 2004. The partnership has a calendar year end.

Required:

 a. Indicate how Belski & Miglio will list information concerning this rental on its 2004 income statement and its December 31, 2004, balance sheet under the cash basis.
 b. Indicate how Belski & Miglio will list information concerning this rental on its 2004 income statement and its December 31, 2004, balance sheet under the accrual basis.
 c. Indicate how Belski & Miglio will list information concerning this rental on its 2005 income statement and its December 31, 2005, balance sheet under the cash basis.
 d. Indicate how Belski & Miglio will list information concerning this rental on its 2005 income statement and its December 31, 2005, balance sheet under the accrual basis.

LO 4: THE MATCHING PRINCIPLE

5–32. Avonia's Clothes paid its landlord $1,600 for the first and last months' rent on March 1, 2004, when Avonia opened her business. The lease on her shop is for one year.

Required:

 a. Indicate how Avonia's Clothes will list information concerning this rental on its March 2004 income statement and its March 31, 2004, balance sheet under the cash basis.
 b. Indicate how Avonia's Clothes will list information concerning this rental on its March 2004 income statement and its March 31, 2004, balance sheet under the accrual basis.

LO 4: THE MATCHING PRINCIPLE

5–33. Flemming Real Estate Company collected $10,000 from Phillips & Arguello for five months' rent paid in advance on November 1, 2004. Flemming operates on a February 28 year end.

Required:

  a. How much rental revenue will Flemming recognize in its income statement for the year ended February 28, 2005, under the cash basis? How will this affect the February 28, 2005, balance sheet?
  b. How much rental revenue will Flemming recognize in its income statement for the year ended February 28, 2005, under the accrual basis? How will this affect the February 28, 2005, balance sheet?
  c. How much rental revenue will Flemming recognize in its income statement for the year ended February 28, 2006, under the cash basis? How will this affect the February 28, 2006, balance sheet?
  d. How much rental revenue will Flemming recognize in its income statement for the year ended February 28, 2006, under the accrual basis? How will this affect the February 28, 2006, balance sheet?

LO 4: THE MATCHING PRINCIPLE

5–34. On December 1, 2004, Jeanette Park paid her accountant, Diane Clifford, $675 for three months' services. The services are to be performed evenly over December, January, and February. By the end of December, Clifford had completed the December services.

Required:

  a. How much should Clifford report as revenue for the year ended December 31, 2004, under the cash basis? How will this affect Clifford's December 31, 2004, balance sheet?
  b. How much should Clifford report as revenue for the year ended December 31, 2004, under the accrual basis? How will this affect Clifford's December 31, 2004, balance sheet?
  c. How should Park report this payment on her income statement and balance sheet for December 31, 2004, under the cash basis?
  d. How should Park report this payment on her income statement and balance sheet for December 31, 2004, under the accrual basis?

LO 4: THE MATCHING PRINCIPLE

5–35. Mike Fisher borrowed $15,000 for his business, Fisher Inc., at 9 percent interest from the Nations Bank on June 1, 2004; principal and interest are due on May 31, 2005.

Required:

  a. How much interest will Fisher owe the bank when he pays the note on May 31, 2005?
  b. How will Fisher report the interest on his income statement and balance sheet for calendar year 2004 if he uses the cash basis of accounting?
  c. How will Fisher report the interest on his income statement and balance sheet for calendar year 2004 if he uses the accrual basis of accounting?

LO 4: THE MATCHING PRINCIPLE AND DEPRECIATION

5–36. Todd's Toppers bought a commercial stitching machine on July 1, 2004, for $25,000. Todd estimates this machine will be useful for five years and will have no residual value because there is little market for used stitching machines.

Required:

  a. Assuming Todd uses the cash basis of accounting, how much will he recognize as expense for the stitching machine on his income statements for each of 2004, 2005, and 2006?
  b. Assuming Todd uses the accrual basis of accounting, how much will he recognize as expense for the stitching machine on his income statements for each of 2004, 2005, and 2006?
  c. Assuming Todd uses the cash basis of accounting, how will he report this on his ending balance sheets for 2004, 2005, and 2006?
  d. Assuming Todd uses the accrual basis of accounting, how will he report this on his ending balance sheets for 2004, 2005, and 2006?

LO 4: THE MATCHING PRINCIPLE AND DEPRECIATION

5–37. Carole's Delivery Service purchased a van on October 1, 2003, to deliver parcels for local merchants. Carole estimates that the van will last four years and can be sold for $2,000 at the end of the fourth year.

Required:

    a. For accrual basis accounting, how much will Carole recognize as depreciation expense for each of the calendar years 2003, 2005, and 2007 if the cost of the van was

        1. $26,000?
        2. $34,000?

    b. What will be the balance of Accumulated Depreciation on December 31, 2003, 2005, and 2007, if the cost of the van was

        1. $26,000?
        2. $34,000?

LO 5: ACCRUALS AND DEFERRALS

5–38. Explain the difference between a deferred expense and an accrued expense and include at least one example of each in your answer.

LO 5: ACCRUALS AND DEFERRALS

5–39. Explain why accruals and deferrals are necessary under accrual basis accounting but not under cash basis accounting. In your answer, include an explanation of accruals and deferrals as they apply to both revenues and expenses.

LO 5: ACCRUALS AND DEFERRALS

5–40. The Fowks Company reported sales of $200,000 for the year ended December 31, 2005. Sales were reported on the accrual basis. The accounts receivable at December 31, 2004, were $25,000, and at December 31, 2005, the receivables were $12,000.

Required: Calculate the amount Fowks collected from customers for 2005.

LO 6: IMPACT OF THEFT ON FINANCIAL STATEMENTS

5–41. Reynolds, Inc., sold some merchandise inventory for cash during the current month. Unfortunately, the company's accounting clerk simply slipped the cash from the sale into his pocket and did not record the sale. Reynolds uses accrual accounting.

Required:

    a. Explain how each of the following financial statements would be affected by the accounting clerk's behavior. Avoid using one-word responses such as understated and overstated. You should approach this requirement as if you were explaining the effects to someone with no knowledge of accounting or financial statements.

        1. Income statement
        2. Statement of stockholders' equity
        3. Balance sheet

    b. Briefly explain how your answer would differ if Reynolds used the cash basis of accounting.

LO 6: IMPACT OF ACCOUNTING ERROR ON FINANCIAL STATEMENTS

5–42. The bookkeeper for Sunny Corporation mistakenly recorded a disbursement for equipment as if the payment had been for repairs and maintenance expense.

Required:

    a. Explain how each of the following financial statements would be affected by the bookkeeper's error. Avoid using one-word responses such as understated and overstated. You should approach this requirement as if you were explaining the effects to someone with no knowledge of accounting or financial statements.

1. Income statement
2. Statement of stockholders' equity
3. Balance sheet

b. Briefly explain how your answer would differ if Sunny used the cash basis of accounting.

LO 6: IMPACT OF ACCOUNTING ERROR ON FINANCIAL STATEMENTS

5–43. The bookkeeper for Joan Rodgers Corporation mistakenly recorded a disbursement for advertising expense as if the payment had been for office furniture.

Required:

a. Explain how each of the following financial statements would be affected by the bookkeeper's error. Avoid using one-word responses such as understated and overstated. You should approach this requirement as if you were explaining the effects to someone with no knowledge of accounting or financial statements.

1. Income statement
2. Statement of stockholders' equity
3. Balance sheet

b. Briefly explain how your answer would differ if Rodgers used the cash basis of accounting.

LO 6: IMPACT OF ACCOUNTING ERROR ON FINANCIAL STATEMENTS

5–44. The bookkeeper for Heart Corporation mistakenly recorded a disbursement for rent expense as if the payment had been for an insurance expense.

Required:

a. Explain how each of the following financial statements would be affected by the bookkeeper's error. Avoid using one-word responses such as understated and overstated. You should approach this requirement as if you were explaining the effects to someone with no knowledge of accounting or financial statements.

1. Income statement
2. Statement of stockholders' equity
3. Balance sheet

b. Briefly explain how your answer would differ if Heart used the cash basis of accounting.

LO 6: CASH VS. ACCRUAL REVENUE RECOGNITION

5–45. Simon Corporation uses the accrual basis of accounting. Simon recognizes revenue at the time it delivers product or provides a service. The entity engages in the following activities during August:

1. Collects $5,000 from customers for the sale of merchandise in the month of August.
2. Collects $10,000 from customers for the sale of merchandise in the month of July.
3. Collects $4,000 from customers for merchandise to be delivered in September.

Required:

a. Calculate the amount of revenue Simon should recognize in August.
b. Calculate the amount of revenue Simon should recognize in August if the company were on a cash basis.

LO 6: CASH VS. ACCRUAL REVENUE RECOGNITION

5–46. Knowles Corporation uses the accrual basis of accounting. Knowles recognizes revenue at the time it delivers product or provides a service. The entity engages in the following activities during November:

1. Collects $10,000 from customers for the sale of merchandise in the month of October.
2. Collects $18,000 from customers for the sale of merchandise in the month of November.
3. Collects $12,000 from customers for merchandise to be delivered in December and January.

Required:

    a. Calculate the amount of revenue Knowles should recognize in November.

    b. Calculate the amount of revenue Knowles should recognize in November if the company were on a cash basis.

LO 4 & 6: CASH VS. ACCRUAL EXPENSE RECOGNITION

5–47. Green Corporation uses the accrual basis of accounting. Green recognizes expenses in accordance with the matching principle. The entity engaged in the following activities during July:

    1. Paid $20,000 to suppliers for office supplies used in the month of July.

    2. Paid $22,000 for radio and television advertising that aired in June.

    3. Paid $6,000 for insurance that covers the months of July, August, and September.

Required:

    a. Calculate the amount of expense Green should recognize in the month of July.

    b. Calculate the amount of expense Green should recognize in July if the company were on a cash basis.

LO 4 & 6: CASH VS. ACCRUAL EXPENSE RECOGNITION

5–48. Glenna Corporation uses the accrual basis of accounting. Glenna recognizes expenses in accordance with the matching principle. The entity engaged in the following activities during December:

    1. Paid $8,000 in December for December's office equipment rental.

    2. Paid $32,000 in December for radio and television advertising that aired in November.

    3. Paid $8,000 in December for insurance expense that covers the months of December through March.

Required:

    a. Calculate the amount of expense Glenna should recognize in December.

    b. Calculate the amount of expense Glenna should recognize in December if the company were on a cash basis.

LO 6: CASH VS. ACCRUAL DETERMINATION OF NET INCOME

5–49. The following list pertains to the Searcy Company for the month of January 2004:

    1. Purchased $10,000 of merchandise for resale paying cash.

    2. Paid $2,000 for office rent for January and February.

    3. Ordered $15,000 worth of merchandise to sell.

    4. Paid $3,000 for a piece of office furniture that will last five years with no residual value.

    5. Received and paid for merchandise ordered in transaction 3.

    6. Sold merchandise that cost $2,000 for $6,000 cash.

    7. Paid one month's salary of $3,500.

    8. Sold merchandise on credit for $20,000 that cost $7,000. Payment was received in February.

    9. Purchased advertising for January on credit for $2,000 agreeing to pay for it in February.

Required:

    a. Determine the net income or net loss for the month of January on a cash basis.

    b. Determine the net income or net loss for the month of January on the accrual basis.

LO 6: CASH VS. ACCRUAL DETERMINATION OF NET INCOME

5–50. The Friedman Corporation entered into the following transactions during February 2004:

    1. Purchased $56,000 of merchandise for cash.

    2. Paid $3,600 for office rent for January and February.

    3. Ordered $45,000 worth of merchandise to sell.

    4. Paid $5,400 for a computer for the accounting department. The computer should last three years with no residual value.

5. Received the merchandise ordered in transaction 3. Payment is due to the vendor on March 10.
6. Sold merchandise that cost $24,000 for $38,000 cash.
7. Paid weekly salaries of $4,500 for the first three weeks. The last week's salary will be paid March 1.
8. Sold merchandise on credit for $80,000 that cost $45,000. Payment was received in February.
9. Paid for advertising for January of $12,000. February's ads were $8,000 and will be paid by March 15.

Required:

   a. Determine February's net income or net loss on a cash basis.
   b. Determine February's net income or net loss on the accrual basis.

LO 6: CASH VS. ACCRUAL DETERMINATION OF NET INCOME

5–51. Nancy Jackson Enterprises completed the following transactions in November 2004:

1. Paid cash for purchase of $100,000 worth of merchandise for resale.
2. Paid $12,000 for office rent. The $12,000 covers rent for 12 months.
3. Ordered $85,000 worth of merchandise for resale.
4. Purchased a delivery van for $25,000 that should last five years.
5. Received the merchandise ordered in transaction 3. Payment is due in 30 days.
6. Sold merchandise that cost $72,000 for $106,000 cash.
7. Paid one month's salaries of $13,500.
8. Sold merchandise on credit for $72,000 that cost $54,000. Payment was received in December.
9. Purchased advertising for November on credit for $9,000 agreeing to pay for it in December.

Required:

   a. Determine the net income or net loss for the month of November on a cash basis.
   b. Determine the net income or net loss for the month of November on the accrual basis.

Financial Reporting Exercises

LO 3: ACCRUAL BASIS IN FINANCIAL REPORTS

5–52. Obtain **Carnival Cruise Lines**' balance sheet by using the Securities and Exchange Commission's (SEC's) Electronic Data Gathering, Analysis, and Retrieval (EDGAR) system. On the SEC site, locate **Carnival Cruise Lines** and select their 2001 Form 10-K. The Form 10K will include the company's balance sheet.

   Once you have **Carnival**'s balance sheet, find the liability **Carnival** calls *Customer Deposits*. This item represents payments **Carnival** has received from customers for future travel.

Required:

   a. How much does **Carnival** report for Customer Deposits? How significant is the amount relative to the various other liabilities the company lists?
   b. Like all companies that conform to GAAP, **Carnival** uses the accrual basis of accounting. If, however, **Carnival** used the cash basis instead of the accrual basis, how would the company report these deposits received from customers for future travel?

LO 3: ACCRUAL BASIS IN FINANCIAL REPORTS

5–53. Obtain the 10-K of **Readers Digest Association, Inc.,** through the SEC's EDGAR system. Use the balance sheet to classify the following.

Required:

   a. Does the company have deferred expenses? If so, what are they and what is the amount?
   b. Does the company have deferred revenues? If so, what are they and what is the amount?

c. Does the company have accrued expenses? If so, what are they and what is the amount?

d. Does the company have accrued revenues? If so, what are they and what is the amount?

e. Comparing the amounts above, do any of them seem significant? Are any substantially larger or smaller than the others? If so, can you think of a reason why?

f. For the one above that doesn't apply to ***Readers Digest Association, Inc.,*** why do you think that it doesn't? Name three companies that would and why.

LO: COMPREHENSIVE

5–54. Visit the ***Walt Disney Corporation*** Web site by finding the link on the PHLIP Web site for this book at *www.prenhall.com/werner*. Look up the current annual report and go to the footnotes section. Footnote 1 should describe the business and summarize the significant accounting policies.

Required: Does Disney use the cash or accrual basis of accounting? Write a one-page summary of the important issues discussed in the first footnote.

ANNUAL REPORT PROJECT

5–55. Section 5—Strengths, Weaknesses, Opportunities, and Threats (SWOT)

This section of the annual report project involves SWOT analysis for your selected company. The acronym SWOT stands for strengths, weaknesses, opportunities, and threats. This part of your project should be very interesting and informative. It should improve your ability to come to an overall conclusion about your company at the end of the project.

The strengths and weaknesses of the company should be viewed from an internal perspective, and the opportunities and threats are viewed from an external perspective.

Press releases and articles published about your company and its industry will be helpful in finding the necessary information you will need to complete this assignment. Another major source of information for this part of the project is the management's discussion and analysis section of your company's annual report.

Let's focus on the strengths and weaknesses first.

Required:

a. Prepare a schedule that specifies your company's strengths and weaknesses in the following areas:

A. Corporate Structure

1. Does the company seem to have a strong corporate structure?
2. Does the structure seem to fit the current business environment?

B. Corporate Culture

1. Can you readily determine the company's overall goals, beliefs, and values?
2. Is the corporate mission clear to employees, customers, and the community?
3. Is the corporate mission consistent with the corporate beliefs and values?
4. Is the mission carried out well?

C. Corporate Resources—How strong or weak are the following resources?

1. Human resources
2. Financial resources
3. Management information system
4. Manufacturing
5. Research and development
6. Marketing
7. Distinctive competencies (something this company is known for doing very well)

b. Prepare a summary of your thoughts regarding the strengths and weaknesses of your company's internal environment.

Next, let's focus on the opportunities and threats facing your company. The opportunities and threats are viewed from an external perspective.

c. Prepare a schedule that specifies your company's opportunities and threats in the following areas:

  A. Industry Environment—What specific problems or opportunities exist for your company with the following groups?

    1. Customers
    2. Suppliers
    3. Competitors
    4. Substitute products or services

  B. Macro-environment—What specific problems or opportunities exist for your company in the following areas?

    1. Economic
    2. Social (changes in societal trends and attitudes)
    3. Political/Legal
    4. Technology
    5. Globalization
    6. Demographics

d. Prepare a summary of your thoughts regarding the opportunities and threats for your company's external environment.
e. Prepare a summary that summarizes your overall feelings regarding the SWOT analysis for your company.

CHAPTER 6

The Accounting System

Let's assume for a moment that you are a division manager for a major software corporation. You are trying to determine why the amount you owe your vendors and suppliers (accounts payable) is so high, so you call your company's general accounting department. You complain that your accounts payable balance has *increased* by $150,000 even after they had told you that it would be *credited* for this amount. After listening to your inquiry, an accounting clerk explains to you that a credit to accounts payable actually increases the account, it does not decrease it.

Hmm. Without at least a basic understanding of how accounting works, you'd have difficulty comprehending the logic of what the accounting clerk has told you. In a very real way, you'd be at the mercy of the accounting clerk—you'd need to rely on her to explain the situation to you in terms that you could understand. This is why everyone in business, not just accountants, needs to have at least a rudimentary understanding of how accountants transform economic facts and figures into useful information.

Although financial statement users are not generally concerned with the mechanics of how accounting gathers data and converts them to useful information, the better a user understands the accounting process, the better he or she can appreciate how business events and transactions will affect financial statements. Knowledgeable users do not blindly accept the information accountants provide. Instead, they understand where it comes from and how it finds its way into financial statements and other accounting reports and schedules.

This chapter is divided into two sections, Part I and Part II. Part I introduces the accounting system. It describes the accounting cycle and the documents accountants use to help them convert facts and figures into useful accounting information. Part II covers the application of accounting procedures. This section includes the application of debit and credit entries, adjusting entries, closing entries, as well as the use of T-accounts, journals, ledgers, the trial balance, and the worksheet.

Part I: Introduction to the Accounting System

Every business has hundreds if not thousands of transactions and economic events each year. In Part I of this chapter, we describe the procedures accountants use to analyze, classify, and record these economic events and transactions. We will explore how an accounting system transforms basic facts and figures into the valuable economic information that decision makers need.

Learning Objectives

After you complete your work on Part I of this chapter, you should be able to do the following:

1. Describe the basic classification structure accounting uses.
2. Describe the nine steps of the accounting cycle.

3. Describe and use journals and ledgers.
4. Explain the purpose of preparing a trial balance.
5. Explain why accountants make adjusting entries and what these entries accomplish.
6. Explain the closing process and the reason for it.

◆ ACCOUNTING'S BASIC CLASSIFICATION STRUCTURE

To convert raw data into useful information, an accounting system needs some means of classifying economic events and transactions. As we have seen in previous chapters, accounting elements such as assets, liabilities, and equity are some basic classifications, but they are too broad to render the level of detail that is needed for the resulting information to be useful to decision makers. Therefore, accountants use subclassifications of these accounting elements. For example, some subclassifications that may be found under assets are accounts receivable, office supplies, and property, plant, and equipment. Under expenses, we may find wages, rent, and advertising.

accounts Subclassifications used to classify and record economic events and transactions. For example, some accounts that may be found under assets are accounts receivable, office supplies, and property, plant, and equipment. Under expenses, we may find wages, rent, and advertising.

These subclassifications are called **accounts** or **general ledger accounts.** The reason accounts are sometimes called *general ledger accounts* is that historically they were kept in a ledger book. Today, although most accounting systems are computerized, all the accounts together are called the **general ledger.** The term *account* used in this context may be confusing. Just remember this: Generally, in accounting and certainly in this chapter, when we use the word *account*, we mean a general ledger account unless we state otherwise.

general ledger accounts The same thing as accounts.

general ledger A book of final entry that contains a page for each account listed in the chart of accounts.

Each account in the general ledger is assigned a title. These account titles are not dictated by generally accepted accounting principles (GAAP) or by any other accounting rules. Rather, companies choose their own account titles based on the needs and desires of the firm. The only real requirement is that account titles adequately describe the items they represent.

Accounts are almost always also assigned account numbers. Again, accounting rules do not establish the numbering scheme; businesses are free to choose their own numbering system. Companies generally develop a numbering system that groups similar types of accounts together. For example, assets might be assigned account numbers in a particular numerical range, say 1000 to 1999, and liabilities might be assigned account numbers in the next range, say 2000 to 2999, and so forth.

The number of accounts a company uses depends on the diversity of its business activity and the level of detail the company needs. Some companies have hundreds of accounts, others have only a few.

chart of accounts A list of all the accounts used by a business entity. The list usually contains the name of the account and the account number.

A reference document that lists all of the company's accounts and their account numbers is called a **chart of accounts.** Companies can add accounts to their chart of accounts as needed to record new and different transactions. Each business entity tailors its chart of accounts to its business activities. Exhibit 6–1 on page F–202 shows the chart of accounts for Collins Container Corporation, a wholesaler that sells boxes, barrels, and ash urns to crematoriums.

The chart of accounts normally lists accounts by account number. Most companies design their numbering system so that the accounts are listed in the order they will appear on the balance sheet and then the income statement. Now that you are familiar with the basic accounting classifications, we can turn our attention to the accounting cycle.

◆ THE ACCOUNTING CYCLE

In the previous chapters, we were able to prepare financial statements without a formal accounting system because there were so few transactions, and we were easily able to keep track of how they affected the financial statements. But when a business has thousands of transactions, such a simplistic approach just doesn't work. In such cases, we need a formal accounting system to gather, record, and classify transactions data. In a

---

Collins Container Corporation
Chart of Accounts

Assets:
101 Cash
110 Accounts receivable
120 Merchandise inventory
130 Office supplies
140 Prepaid insurance
150 Delivery truck
155 Accumulated depreciation on delivery truck

Liabilities:
200 Accounts payable
210 Wages payable
220 Interest payable
240 Accrued expenses
245 Unearned revenue
250 Notes payable

Stockholders' Equity:
300 Common stock
310 Additional paid-in capital
320 Retained earnings
325 Dividends

Revenues:
400 Sales
410 Delivery service revenue
420 Interest revenue

Expenses:
500 Cost of goods sold
620 Wages expense
630 Rent expense
640 Electricity expense
645 Supplies expense
650 Gasoline expense
655 Insurance expense
660 Depreciation expense
670 Bank service charge expense
680 Interest expense

EXHIBIT 6–1   Chart of Accounts for Collins Container Corporation

formal accounting system, some events occur daily, some monthly, and some occur annually. As one year ends and another begins, the process begins anew. That is why the steps that accountants take to transform data into meaningful information are called the accounting cycle. The steps in the accounting cycle are as follows:

Step 1: Analyze economic events and transactions
Step 2: Journalize transactions
Step 3: Post transactions to the general ledger
Step 4: Prepare a trial balance
Step 5: Prepare, journalize, and post adjusting entries
Step 6: Prepare an adjusted trial balance
Step 7: Prepare financial statements
Step 8: Prepare, journalize, and post closing entries
Step 9: Prepare the post-closing trial balance

Before we delve into the specifics of accounting entries and procedures, let's look at the accounting cycle by presenting a general overview of each of its nine steps.

STEP 1: ANALYZING ECONOMIC EVENTS AND TRANSACTIONS

Analyzing transactions, the most important step in the accounting cycle, consists of two parts. The first part is determining if and when an economic event or transaction should be recorded in the accounting system. We record an economic event or transaction when it affects one or more accounting elements or accounts. For example, if a company buys merchandise on account, inventory increases as does accounts payable. In such a case, both assets and liabilities are affected. But what if the company had merely ordered the merchandise for delivery at a later time instead of purchasing it? Should we record this event in the company's accounting system? No, because the event has not affected assets, liabilities, equity, or any other accounting element. We do not record the event until title to the merchandise passes from the vendor to the buyer and the seller has the cash or a legally enforceable claim to cash. At that moment, the company has a new asset and a new liability.

The second part of analyzing transactions is identifying the nature of the transaction in terms of how the company's accounts are affected. All economic events and transactions that are recorded by accountants affect at least two areas and therefore at least two general ledger accounts. In a way, this makes sense because if every accounting entry affects the accounting equation, a change in one element of the equation would require a change in another to keep the equation in balance. This concept is the origin of the term *double-entry bookkeeping*. For example, if you use your credit card to buy a new television for $500, the transaction affects two things. First, you now have a new asset, a $500 television. Second, you now have a new $500 liability. When you pay the credit card company for the television, two things are affected as well. First, an asset (cash) decreases by $500, and second, liabilities decrease by $500.

When analyzing transactions, you should take a common sense look at the situation to figure out what has happened. Then, you can select and use accounts that will appropriately reflect the reality of the situation.

Discussion Question ●

6–1. Why do you think it takes common sense and not just an accounting background to analyze economic events and transactions?

STEP 2. JOURNALIZING TRANSACTIONS

Journalizing transactions is the act of recording accounting transactions in a journal. Many people keep a daily personal journal—a chronological record of the things that happen in their life. Each day's entry includes the date and all the pertinent facts associated with the events they enter. An accounting **journal** is quite similar. It is a chronological record of the economic events and transactions that affect the accounting elements (the accounts) of a company. Each entry is dated, it indicates the accounts that were increased or decreased and the dollar amount of the change, and it may also include a description of the entry to provide additional detail. The first place an economic event or transaction is recorded is in a journal. For this reason, journals are sometimes called **books of original entry.**

In a **manual accounting system,** the accountants and bookkeepers write all of the entries by hand in pen and ink. In this case, the journals are nothing more than books with pages and pages of journal entries. In a **computerized accounting system,** the accountants and bookkeepers make entries in a computer system, and the journals are more likely to consist of a listing of transactions on a computer printout or a file in the computer's memory.

Regardless of its form, a journal lists transactions in the order of occurrence. Employees, managers, and auditors frequently use the journal's chronological listing of transactions to trace events and answer inquiries. For this reason, we record transactions formally into journals daily, weekly, or sometimes monthly for small businesses. Large companies use online, real-time processing techniques that make the journal entries as the transactions occur. Sophisticated cash register systems often create journal entries as the cashier scans the items sold.

journal A book of original entry used to record the economic events and transactions that affect the accounts of a company.

book of original entry The same thing as a journal.

manual accounting system An accounting system in which the accountants and bookkeepers write all of the entries by hand in pen and ink.

computerized accounting system An accounting system in which the accountants and bookkeepers make entries in a computer system where the journals and ledgers consist of listings of transactions on computer printouts or in files in the computer's memory.

Typically, a business will use not one, but several journals. Each journal is designed to record a particular type of transaction. For example, a cash receipts journal is used to record all cash collections, a cash payments journal is used to record all cash payments, and a sales journal is used to record all sales on account. A journal that is created to record a particular type of transaction is called a **special journal.** Special journals help to streamline the accounting process and greatly enhance accounting efficiency. In addition to special journals, every company has a **general journal** to record any transactions for which there is no special journal. If a company has no special journals, all transactions are recorded in the general journal. If a company has a full complement of special journals, very few transactions are recorded in the general journal.

STEP 3. POSTING TRANSACTIONS TO THE GENERAL LEDGER

Journals provide a wealth of valuable information about each transaction, but, when hundreds of transactions are involved, journals do not work well to provide information account by account. For example, if we wanted to know how much cash the company had received, how much it had paid out, and how much it had left, a journal would not be very much help. Even if the company's journal is 50 pages long and there were hundreds of transactions that affected cash, the only way to determine the balance in the cash account would be to page through the journal and find all the entries that impacted cash. Then, you would have to add them up to gain insight into what happened to cash. For this reason, a ledger page is prepared for each account. As we mentioned earlier, all these ledger pages are kept in a book called the general ledger. This is why accounts are sometimes called general ledger accounts. In computerized accounting systems, the general ledger consists of computer files and printouts.

The entries made in the journal are transcribed to the ledger in a process called **posting.** Posting is a fairly simple process of copying information from the journal to the appropriate ledger. What this means is that all the journal entries that affect cash are posted to the cash account, all the entries that affect supplies are posted to the supplies account, and so forth. See Exhibit 6–2 for an illustration of posting. Generally, the

special journal   A book of original entry designed to record a specific type of transaction.

general journal   A book of original entry in which is recorded all transactions not otherwise recorded in special journals.

posting   The process of transcribing information from journals to the ledger.

EXHIBIT 6–2   Posting from the Journals to the General Ledger

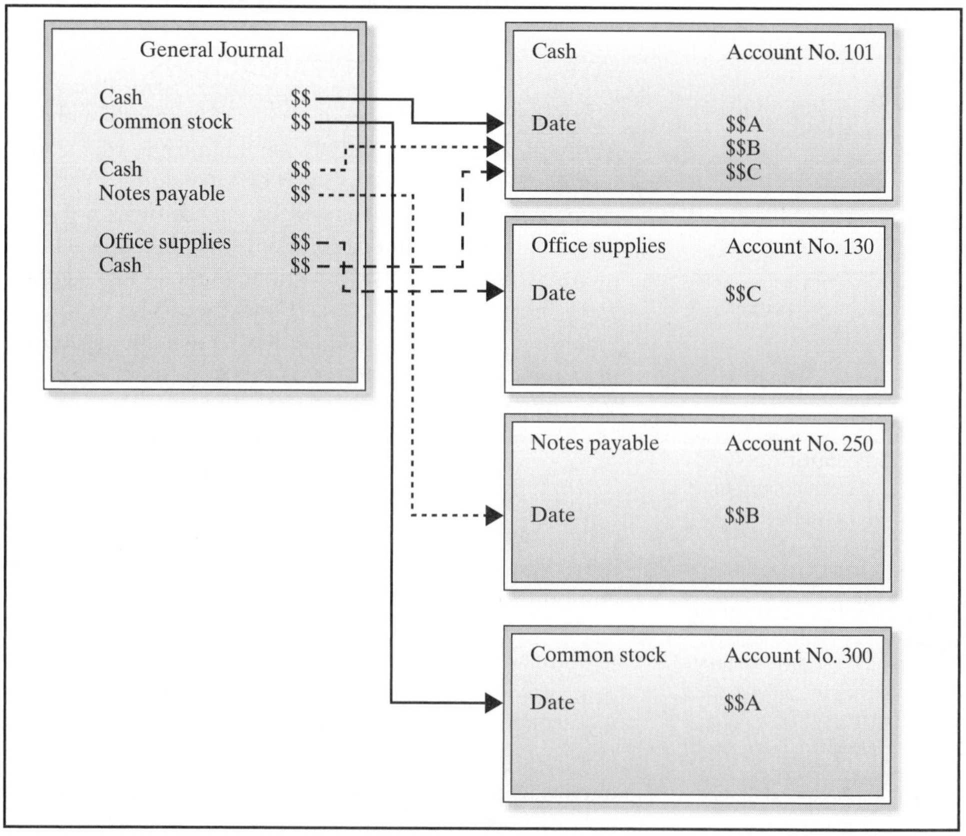

journal entries are posted to the general ledger at least monthly. Computers can perform this function in seconds.

Once all the journal entries have been posted to the general ledger, we add all increases and subtract all decreases to the previous balance of the account to arrive at a new account balance. We use the general ledger account balances to prepare financial statements after two additional steps in the accounting cycle.

Discussion Question ·

6–2. Why would a company need journals and a general ledger? Why wouldn't just one or the other be good enough?

STEP 4. PREPARING A TRIAL BALANCE

trial balance The listing of the general ledger account balances, which proves that the general ledger and therefore the accounting equation is in balance.

From time to time, we need to know the balances in the general ledger accounts to make sure that the accounting equation is in balance, or to review the general ledger balances as we prepare to make financial statements. To get these balances, instead of looking at each page of the general ledger, we prepare a trial balance. A **trial balance** is simply a listing of all the general ledger accounts and their balances. In manual accounting systems, preparing a trial balance is just a matter of accounting personnel paging through the general ledger and listing the account names and their balances. In a computerized system, accounting personnel select the appropriate menu option and the accounting software package creates the trial balance automatically. See Exhibit 6–3 for an illustration of a trial balance.

STEP 5. ADJUSTING THE GENERAL LEDGER ACCOUNTS

You might think that accountants are able to keep general ledger account balances up to date moment by moment. Unfortunately, this is not the case. Even when every member of the accounting staff has done his or her job perfectly, there are differences between what accounting records show and the reality of the situation. Why does this

EXHIBIT 6–3   Preparing the Trial Balance

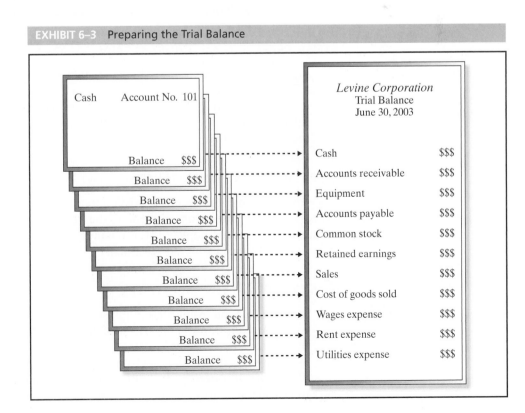

happen? Well, there are a number of reasons, but often it's simply a matter of timing. For example, there is almost always a difference between when economic events actually occur and when the accounting staff records the events. Sometimes, the events are recorded too soon (so what is recorded is not totally accurate), but more often, they are not recorded soon enough (so the accounting system doesn't provide timely information). Also, business situations can change over time. In those cases, the account balances that resulted when the accounting staff originally recorded the transaction fail to capture the essence of the new situation. So, accountants must review and update account balances before they prepare financial statements. Making entries to bring account balances up to date in order to prepare the most up-to-the-minute financial statements is part of the adjusting process.

Prior to preparing financial statements, accountants review each general ledger account to determine whether the account balances reflect the company's situation as of the end of the accounting period. Then, they make **adjusting entries** as necessary so that all revenue earned is reported, but no more; that all expenses incurred are reported, but no more; and that asset, liability, and equity accounts are properly stated as of the balance sheet date. The adjustment process may involve entries to defer or accrue revenues or expenses, as we discussed in Chapter 5. During the adjusting process, accountants follow a step-by-step procedure. First, they examine each account in light of the situation that existed at the very end of the accounting period to determine whether the ending balances are appropriate. Second, when they find accounts that have inappropriate balances, they must determine the amount by which they need to increase or decrease those accounts. Finally, they make an adjusting entry in the general journal to change the ending account balances to the appropriate amount.

As part of the adjusting process, accountants frequently use a **worksheet** to help them prepare financial statements. We will examine the details of the worksheet later in this chapter.

Once the accounting staff has made all the necessary adjusting entries, the account balances are ready to prepare the adjusted trial balance.

adjusting entries The entries to modify account balances so that all revenue earned and all expenses incurred are recorded and all asset, liability, and equity accounts are properly stated as of the balance sheet date.

worksheet A tool used by the accountant to accumulate the necessary information used to prepare the financial statements.

Discussion Question

6–3. List and discuss two situations that would result in the need to adjust accounting records even though all the company's accounting had been done properly.

STEP 6. PREPARING AN ADJUSTED TRIAL BALANCE

adjusted trial balance A trial balance that is prepared after all of the adjusting entries have been made.

The **adjusted trial balance** is a trial balance that is prepared after all of the adjusting entries have been made. It is like any other trial balance except that it reflects account balances that are up to the minute and as accurate as reasonably possible. The adjusted trial balance provides the accounting staff with the account balances they need to prepare the company's financial statements.

STEP 7. PREPARING FINANCIAL STATEMENTS

Once the company accountant is satisfied that the account balances are correct as of the balance sheet date, he or she prepares the financial statements. The accountant uses the amounts from the adjusted trial balance to prepare the income statement, the statement of owners' equity, and the balance sheet.

Discussion Questions

6–4. Imagine that you own a large retail stereo and electronics business. With respect to your need for information, how often do you think your company should prepare financial statements?

6–5. Assume your stereo and electronics business has borrowed a substantial sum from **Bank of America.** How often do you think the bank will want your business to provide them with financial statements?

STEP 8. PREPARING AND POSTING CLOSING ENTRIES

The closing process involves closing out one year of business and getting ready for the next. To understand the closing process, we must first understand a little bit about how accounts are used to provide information. Revenue and expense accounts are what we might call "accumulator accounts." This is because they accumulate, or keep a running total of the revenues and expenses a company has had during the year. Similarly, distributions to owners accounts, such as dividends, keep a running total of the amounts distributed to owners throughout the year. Once a fiscal (business) year comes to a close, it is time to prepare the company's books so that new running totals can be maintained for the next year. What this means is that revenues, expenses, and dividends should begin the new year with a blank slate—that is, zero balances. To accomplish this, accountants make a series of **closing entries** to reset revenues, expenses, and dividends to zero. The entries ultimately move the balances in revenue, expense, and dividend accounts into retained earnings.

Accounts that are closed during the closing process—generally, revenues, expenses, and dividends—are called **temporary** (or **nominal**) **accounts.** The closing entries zero out temporary account balances much like a trip-switch zeros out the mileage on an automobile trip odometer. We do not close all general ledger accounts, however. Unlike income statement accounts (temporary accounts) that keep running totals of business activity, balance sheet accounts represent what a company has (its assets), what it owes (its liabilities), and the owners' interest in the company (its equity) as of a moment in time. Balance sheet accounts present a picture of "what is." Balance sheet accounts are called **permanent** (or **real**) **accounts** because they are not closed during the closing process. Permanent accounts include asset, liability, and equity accounts, except for distributions to owners such as the dividend account.

The closing process consists of four steps and uses a temporary account called *income summary*. As you can see by the following list of closing steps for a corporation, the income summary account is created and then closed during the closing process.

1. Close the revenue accounts to income summary.
2. Close the expense accounts to income summary.
3. Close income summary to retained earnings.
4. Close the dividends account to retained earnings.

Although it might not seem so, the closing process is really quite interesting. In prior chapters, we said that net income increases owners' equity and distributions to owners' decreases it. If you examine the four steps of the closing process, you will see just how owners' equity, through retained earnings, is increased by net income (revenues less expenses) and decreased by distributions to owners (dividends.) An understanding of this concept will be critically important as you are learning how and why debits and credits affect revenues, expenses, and dividends.

Discussion Question

6–6. We have said that income increases owners' equity in a business. Why are the owners entitled to the income instead of the employees who worked to earn the income in the first place?

STEP 9. PREPARING THE POST-CLOSING TRIAL BALANCE

After we prepare the closing entries and post them to the general ledger, only the permanent accounts (the balance sheet accounts) will have balances remaining. Revenues, expenses, and any owner withdrawal or dividend accounts should have zero balances. As part of a final check of the closing process, we prepare a **post-closing trial balance** after posting closing entries to confirm that the closing entries have zeroed the temporary accounts. In a computerized system, this step is crucial to verify the integrity of the closing process and to ensure that the accounting equation remains in balance.

closing entries A series of entries to reset revenues, expenses, and dividends to zero in preparation for a new accounting year.

temporary (nominal) accounts The general ledger accounts that are closed to a zero balance at the end of the fiscal year as the net income or net loss is transferred to the appropriate equity account. Temporary accounts include revenues, expenses, gains, losses, owner withdrawal, and dividend accounts.

permanent (real) accounts The general ledger accounts that are never closed. The permanent accounts include assets, liabilities, and equity accounts except for owner withdrawals.

post-closing trial balance A trial balance prepared after all closing entries have been posted, which proves that the only accounts remaining in the general ledger are the permanent accounts and that the accounting equation remains in balance.

Before we look at the specifics of how the accounting cycle works, let's see how accountants use debits and credits to increase and decrease account balances.

Part II: Application of Accounting Procedures

Now that you are familiar with the accounting cycle's nine steps, we are ready to explore the details of how accountants transform transaction data into useful accounting information.

Learning Objectives

After completing your work on Part II of this chapter, you should be able to do the following:

1. Understand the effects of debits and credits and use them to make accounting entries.
2. Make accounting entries using T-accounts and the general journal.
3. Post journal entries to the general ledger.
4. Prepare a trial balance.
5. Prepare adjusting journal entries and reconcile a bank account.
6. Prepare a worksheet and an adjusted trial balance.
7. Prepare financial statements from a worksheet or an adjusted trial balance.
8. Prepare closing journal entries and a post-closing trial balance.

◆ DEBITS AND CREDITS

Accountants do not use pluses (+) and minuses (−) to increase and decrease dollar amounts in accounting records; instead they use a system of *debits* and *credits*. This is because the debit and credit system enables accountants to keep the accounting system in balance more readily than would the use of pluses and minuses. At any given point in the accounting process, whether we examine a single accounting entry or the balances in an entire accounting system, the total dollar amount of the debits should equal the total dollar amount of the credits.

Making debit and credit entries is not really difficult, but to be successful, it requires you to bring three important areas of understanding together. These areas are:

1. You must understand the accounting elements and accounts. As we mentioned earlier, the accounting elements basically comprise a system for classifying economic events and transactions. The accounting elements are further broken down into subclassifications called accounts or general ledger accounts.
2. You must understand how to analyze economic events and transactions to determine their impact, if any, on the accounting elements and specific general ledger accounts.
3. You must understand how debits and credits increase and decrease account balances.

Knowing any one or two of the areas is not enough; you must understand all three. By now, you should have a firm grasp of the accounting elements we covered in the first five chapters of this book. If not, review them before proceeding further. You are probably less familiar with how accountants analyze transactions, so we provide several step-by-step examples in the remainder of this chapter. If you are like most people who take a beginning accounting course, you probably don't know much about debits and credits at all, so our coverage of this topic will be extensive.

◆ THE IMPACT OF DEBITS AND CREDITS ON ASSETS, LIABILITIES, AND EQUITY

Accounting and accounting entries are based on the accounting equation we first presented in Chapter 1 (Assets = Liabilities + Equity). As we know from mathematics, a change in one side of the equation requires a change in the other side to keep the equation in balance. This concept is the basis of the double-entry bookkeeping.

The double-entry system we use today is based on the writings of Luca Pacioli of Venice, Italy. In his book, *Summa de Arithmetica, Geometria, Proportioni et Proportionalita* (Everything About Arithmetic, Geometry and Proportion), published in 1494, Pacioli described the double-entry system of bookkeeping being used by merchants in Venice at that time. The ledger he described was very similar to the ones we use in modern accounting today. It included notations for the date and a description of the event, with debits on the left side (*deve dare*) and credits on the right (*deve avere*). Even today, debits are always on the left and credits are always on the right.

When we apply this debits on the left, credits on the right logic to the accounting equation, assets (the accounting element on the left side of the equation) are on the debit (left) side of the equation, while liabilities and equity (the elements on the right side of the equation) are on the credit (right) side of the equation. When an accounting system is in balance, the debits equal the credits; left equals right.

$$\text{Assets} = \text{Liabilities} + \text{Equity}$$
$$\text{Left Side of the Equation} = \text{Right Side of the Equation}$$
$$\text{Debit Side} = \text{Credit Side}$$

Because of their position in the accounting equation, assets normally have debit balances and liabilities and equity accounts normally have credit balances. The debit or credit balance an account typically has is called the account's **normal balance.**

normal balance The balance of the account derived from the type of entry (debit or credit) that increases the account.

$$\text{Assets} = \text{Liabilities} + \text{Equity}$$
Normal Balances: $\quad$ Debit Balance = Credit Balance* + Credit Balance*

An account's normal balance dictates the type of entry that increases the account; debits increase debit balance accounts and credits increase credit balance accounts. Accounts that are increased by debits are decreased by credits and accounts that are increased by credits are decreased by debits. Exhibit 6–4 shows a summary of normal account balances and the effects of debits and credits on assets, liabilities, and equity.

EXHIBIT 6–4 Effects of Debits and Credits on Assets, Liabilities, and Equity

	Assets	*Liabilities*	*Equity*
Normal Balance	Debit	Credit	Credit
Increased by:	Debits	Credits	Credits
Decreased by:	Credits	Debits	Debits

Understanding how debits and credits affect account balances is essential. Through logic or memorization, you must comprehend how debits and credits work to increase and decrease account balances. With this knowledge and a familiarity with the accounting elements and accounts, and an ability to analyze transactions, you can make debit and credit entries in asset, liability, and equity accounts. But first, you will need to know an acceptable format for your debit/credit entries. The format we will use initially is the T-account.

THE T-ACCOUNT

The T-account gets its name because it is nothing more than a big "T" drawn under an account name with space for debits on the left and credits on the right. T-accounts for cash and supplies are presented below:

Cash

Debit side	Credit side

Supplies

Debit side	Credit side

*The two credit balances must equal the debit balance.

To debit a T-account, all we have to do is to place the dollar amount of the debit on the left side of the T-account account. To credit a T-account, we place the dollar amount on the right side. Dollar signs ($) are not necessary for T-account entries. For example, assume **Holiday Isle Resorts** buys $300 dollars worth of supplies for cash and they wish to make a T-account entry for this transaction. The company is receiving supplies in exchange for cash so we should increase the supplies account and decrease the cash account. Both supplies and cash are asset accounts, and, as we already know, assets are increased by debits and decreased by credits, so the T-account entry would appear as follows:

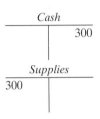

As we have already mentioned, whenever you make an accounting entry, in whatever format, debits will always be on the left while credits will always be on the right. In addition, the total dollar amount of the debits should always equal the total dollar amount of the credits.

When we said debit cash for $300 to increase it, the entry may have seemed entirely backwards to you. The reason debits and credits seem to work backwards to a lot of us is that the account records we generally see are not our own, but rather those of banks or credit card companies. So, the debits and credits you have seen in the past on your bank statement are from the *bank's* perspective, *not yours*. What you probably do not realize is that when you look at your bank statement, you are not really looking at a *cash* account at all, but rather the bank's *liability* account to you. The bank has a liability to you because the bank has your money and, at some point, must pay it back. To increase a liability, the bank credits the liability account. So the reason debits and credits may seem backwards to you is that, probably for the first time, you are viewing the situation from the perspective of making entries in your own accounting records (or those of the company for which you are doing the accounting) rather than from the perspective of a bank or credit card company.

THE IMPACT OF DEBITS AND CREDITS ON REVENUES, EXPENSES, AND DIVIDENDS

By now you should be familiar with how debits and credits affect assets, liabilities, and equity. But what about making debit and credit entries to revenue and expense accounts? To understand how debits and credits affect revenues and expenses, we need to bear in mind that revenues and expenses are really part of equity. In a corporate setting, revenues and expenses are a part of retained earnings. The more revenue a company has, the more its retained earnings will increase. The more expenses a company has, the more retained earnings will decrease. So, revenues increase retained earnings while expenses decrease it. We should also mention that dividends also decrease retained earnings.

Remember, equity normally carries a credit balance, and because it is part of equity, so does retained earnings. What this means is that credits increase retained earnings while debits decrease it. Revenues are the source of credits that increase retained earnings and expenses and dividends are the sources of debits that decrease retained earnings. So, revenues normally have credit balances while expenses and dividends normally have debit balances. Exhibit 6–5 shows the accounting equation and how the debits and credits from revenues, expenses, and dividends affect equity.

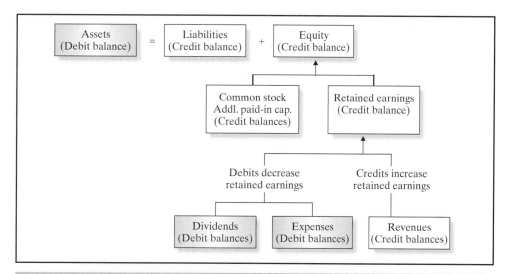

EXHIBIT 6–5   The Accounting Equation and the Effects of Debits and Credits to Revenues, Expenses, and Dividends on Equity

Exhibit 6–5 shows the logic of how debits and credits affect revenues, expenses, and dividends. To put this knowledge to use, we will make T-account entries to record the following three transactions for A. R. Oddo Leasing Corporation.

a. On July 31, 2004, Oddo Leasing collected $500 for July rent.
b. On July 31, the company paid $200 for July's property taxes.
c. On July 31, the company paid dividends of $120 to its owners.

Cash

(a.) 500 | 200 (b.)
| 120 (c.)

Rent Revenue

| 500 (a.)

Property Tax Expense

(b.) 200 |

Dividends

(c.) 120 |

Although a basic understanding of how debits and credits increase and decrease account balances is essential, don't be concerned if you have yet to fully understand how debits and credits work. You will have plenty of opportunities to enhance your understanding as we proceed through each step of the accounting cycle.

Exhibit 6–6 summarizes the effects of debits and credits on assets, liabilities, equity, revenues, expenses, and dividends.

EXHIBIT 6–6   Effects of Debits and Credits on Account Balances

	Assets	*Liabilities*	*Equity*	*Revenues*	*Expenses*	*Dividends*
Normal Balance	Debit	Credit	Credit	Credit	Debit	Debit
Increased by:	Debits	Credits	Credits	Credits	Debits	Debits
Decreased by:	Credits	Debits	Debits	Debits	Credits	Credits

◆ THE GENERAL JOURNAL

Although T-accounts worked well to introduce debits and credits, in accounting, their use is generally limited to informal illustrations of accounting entries and procedures; they are not a formal part of an accounting system. Instead of using T-accounts, businesses initially record transactions in a journal. As we indicated earlier in this chapter, there are several types of journals. For simplicity, in this chapter, we will use only the general journal, because the general journal can be used to record virtually any accounting entry. Before you begin to make accounting entries, you must first understand the correct format for entries in the general journal. Exhibit 6–7 illustrates a general journal and shows the entry to record the 2004 transactions for A. R. Oddo Leasing Corporation that we previously showed in T-account form.

EXHIBIT 6–7 Sample General Journal Entry

	General Journal			Page xx
Date 2004	Description	**Post. Ref.**	**Debit**	**Credit**
Jul 31	Cash		500	
	Rent revenue			500
	To record rent collected for July.			
31	Property tax expense		200	
	Cash			200
	To record July property taxes.			
31	Dividends		120	
	Cash			120
	To record cash dividends paid to owners.			

The date column of the general journal provides information about the effective date of the entry. It is not necessarily the date that the accounting staff made the entry; rather it is the date the accounting staff wants the entry to take effect. As a practical matter, accounting entries are often made after an economic event has occurred. When dating a journal entry, the year is placed at the top of the date column, followed by an abbreviation for the month, and finally the day. Once the month has been indicated on the journal, it need not be entered again until it changes.

The description column of the general journal provides space for the account names and for an optional description of the entry. Accounting custom dictates that the debits for an entry are made first, followed by the credits. Then an optional description may be presented to provide additional detail about the transaction. Note that the title of the credited account has been indented. This indenting is one of the indications that the account was credited. Making the debit part of the general journal entry first and indenting the credited account title are two important accounting customs.

The posting reference column of the general journal is not used when the entry is originally recorded in the journal; rather it is used when the entry is posted to the general ledger. As part of the posting process, accountants record the account number that corresponds to the account to which the transaction was posted.

The general journal's debit column is used to record the dollar amount of the debit entries and the credit column is used to record the dollar amount of the credits. Note that it is not necessary to use dollar signs ($) when making entries in a journal.

◆ **ANALYZING AND JOURNALIZING TRANSACTIONS**

As part of the process of making the accounting entries, we must analyze each of the company's economic events and transactions. As we said earlier in this chapter, analyzing a transaction entails a common sense look at the situation to determine if a transaction has occurred and, if one has, the transaction's impact on the general ledger accounts. To help you analyze transactions and make general journal entries, we suggest the following four steps:

1. Determine if and when a transaction occurred, what accounts were affected, which account balances should increase, which should decrease, and by how much.
2. Determine which accounts should be debited and which should be credited.
3. Make the journal entry.
4. Review the entry to ensure it is in proper form and that the debits equal the credits.

We will follow these four steps as we examine a series of transactions for the Collins Container Corporation. As we proceed, try to develop the skills necessary to analyze transactions and make the entries on your own. Keep in mind that the entries we show are a small sample of the thousands that are possible. Accordingly, try to develop a technique for analyzing events and transactions and then making appropriate entries, rather than trying to memorize the entries we make for our example transactions. We will begin with the transactions listed in Exhibit 6–8. These initial transactions affect only assets, liabilities, and equity.

EXHIBIT 6–8 Transactions a. Through h. for the Collins Container Corporation

a. On January 1, 2004, Collins Container Corporation began by issuing 1,000 shares of its $1 par common stock in exchange for $10,000 in cash.

b. On January 1, the company borrowed cash of $20,000 on a 9%, one-year promissory note from *Bank of America.*

c. On January 1, the company purchased a one-year insurance policy for $2,400 cash.

d. On January 1, the company purchased a $15,000 delivery truck for cash.

e. On January 4, the company ordered $4,200 worth of shipping supplies. The shipping supplies are to be delivered in early February.

f. On January 7, the company purchased office supplies for $2,000 on account (on a charge account).

g. On January 8, the company purchased merchandise inventory costing $16,000 on account.

h. On January 12, the company paid $750 on account toward the office supplies purchased on January 7, 2004, in item f.

a. **On January 1, 2004, Collins Container Corporation began by issuing 1,000 shares of its $1 par common stock in exchange for $10,000 in cash.**

1. This transaction took place on January 1, 2004, and affects cash, common stock, and additional paid-in capital. The balances of each of the accounts should be increased: cash by $10,000, common stock by $1,000, and additional paid-in capital by $9,000.

2. Because cash is an asset account, it is on the left side of the accounting equation and is increased with a debit. Common stock and additional paid-in capital are both equity accounts and are on the right side of the accounting equation, so they are increased by credits.

3. The general journal entry:

2004
Jan 1   Cash   10,000
*   Common stock   1,000*
*   Additional paid-in capital   9,000*

4. A final check of the entry reveals that we dated the entry, we made the debit part of the entry first, we indented the credit account titles, we did not use dollar signs, and the dollar amount of the debits equals that of the credits.

b. **On January 1, 2004, the company borrowed cash of $20,000 on a 9 percent, one-year promissory note from *Bank of America*.**

   1. This transaction took place on January 1, 2004, and affects cash and notes payable. The balances of both accounts should be increased by $20,000. (*Note*: Because Collins has just borrowed the money, no time has passed for interest to accrue, so we need not include interest in the entry we are making at this time.)

   2. Because cash is an asset account, it is on the left side of the accounting equation and is increased with a debit. Notes payable, a liability account, is on the right side of the accounting equation, so it is increased by a credit.

   3. The general journal entry:

Jan 1   Cash   20,000
*   Notes payable   20,000*

   4. A final check of the entry reveals that the entry is in good form and the dollar amount of the debits equals that of the credits.

c. **On January 1, 2004, the company purchased a one-year insurance policy for $2,400 cash.**

   1. This transaction took place on January 1, 2004. With this $2,400 payment, the company now owns an insurance policy that will benefit the company for the next 12 months. Therefore, the payment for this insurance has future value to the company and we should consider it an asset. Expenses paid in advance are called *prepaid expenses*, so in this case, prepaid insurance and cash are affected by the transaction. The balance of the prepaid insurance account should be increased by $2,400 and the balance of the cash account should be decreased by $2,400.

   2. Because prepaid insurance is an asset account, it is on the left side of the accounting equation and is increased by a debit. Cash is also an asset account, and, because assets are on the left side of the accounting equation, they are decreased by credits. In this case, we want to decrease the account, so the cash account is credited.

   3. The general journal entry:

Jan 1   Prepaid insurance   2,400
*   Cash   2,400*

   4. A final check of the entry reveals that the dollar amount of the debits equals that of the credits.

Discussion Question •

6–7. When accountants review an entry to make sure it balances, they check to see that debits equal credits. Why couldn't they do the same thing with pluses and minuses?

d. On January 1, 2004, the company purchased a $15,000 delivery truck for cash.

1. This transaction took place on January 1, 2004. Based on this transaction, Collins Container Corporation owns a new asset, a delivery truck. In addition, cash was used to pay for the truck, so cash should be decreased. The delivery truck account should be increased by the $15,000 cost of the truck and the cash account should be decreased by the $15,000 paid for the truck.

2. Because the delivery truck account is an asset account, it is on the left side of the accounting equation and is increased by a debit. Cash is also an asset account, and, because assets are on the left side of the accounting equation, they are decreased by credits. In this case, we want to decrease the account, so the cash account is credited.

3. The general journal entry:

Jan 1	Delivery truck	15,000	
	Cash		15,000

4. A final check of the entry reveals that the entry is in good form and the dollar amount of the debits equals that of the credits.

e. On January 4, the company ordered $4,200 worth of shipping supplies. The shipping supplies are to be purchased for cash in early February.

1. Actually, a transaction has not yet occurred with respect to item e. Merely ordering material such as supplies does not impact an accounting element or account. The transaction will occur when Collins Container Corporation purchases the supplies in February. No accounting entry is necessary at this time. This item does not change the balance in any account. We have not purchased the supplies and do not own them yet, so we should *not* increase the shipping supplies account balance. In addition, we have not yet paid any cash for the supplies, so we should *not* decrease the cash account. Again, no entry should be made for this item at this time, so our analysis can end here.

f. On January 7, 2004, the company purchased office supplies for $2,000 on account (on a charge account).

1. This transaction took place on January 7, 2004. In this transaction, the company purchased office supplies that it can use in the future. The company has not paid for the office supplies however; rather, it purchased them "on account," so a liability (accounts payable) has been created. The balance of the office supplies account should be increased by the $2,000 cost of the supplies acquired. The accounts payable account should be increased by the $2,000 the company now owes on account.

2. Because office supplies is an asset account, it is on the left side of the accounting equation and is increased by a debit. Accounts payable is a liability account and on the right side of the accounting equation, so it is increased by a credit.

3. The general journal entry:

Jan 7	Office supplies	2,000	
	Accounts payable		2,000

4. A final check of the entry reveals that the dollar amount of the debits equals that of the credits.

g. On January 8, the company purchased merchandise inventory costing $16,000 on account.

1. This transaction took place on January 8, 2004. In this transaction, the company purchased merchandise that it will sell to customers in the future. Merchandise inventory, an asset, should be increased, and, because the company has not yet paid for the merchandise, accounts payable should be increased for the purchase. The balance of the merchandise inventory account should be increased by the

$16,000 cost of the merchandise purchased. The accounts payable account should be increased by the $16,000 the company now owes on account for this purchase.

2. Because merchandise inventory is an asset account, it is on the left side of the accounting equation and is increased by a debit. Accounts payable is a liability account, so it is on the right side of the accounting equation and is increased by a credit.

3. The general journal entry:

    Jan 8   Merchandise inventory   16,000
                Accounts payable   16,000

4. A final check of the entry reveals that the dollar amount of the debits equals that of the credits.

h. On January 12, 2004, the company paid $750 on account toward the office supplies purchased on January 7, 2004, in item f.

1. This transaction took place on January 12, 2004. In this transaction, the company is paying part of its $2,000 accounts payable liability. The company is paying with cash, so cash should be reduced. Also, the amount the company owes will be reduced by the payment, so accounts payable should also be reduced. Both the cash account and accounts payable account should be reduced by the $750 paid. Note that the company is *not* acquiring more office supplies, it is simply paying the liability incurred for the office supplies it purchased previously. Accordingly, the office supplies account is not affected by this entry.

2. Accounts payable is a liability account, so it is on the right side of the accounting equation and is decreased by a debit. Because cash is an asset account, it is on the left side of the accounting equation and is decreased by a credit.

3. The general journal entry:

    Jan 12   Accounts payable   750
                 Cash   750

4. A final check of the entry reveals that the dollar amount of the debits equals that of the credits.

Now we continue our Collins Container Corporation example with some additional items that impact not only assets, liabilities, and equities, but also revenues and expenses as well. See Exhibit 6–9.

EXHIBIT 6–9   Transactions i. Through p. for the Collins Container Corporation

i. On January 22, Collins Container Corporation received cash of $8,000 for merchandise it sold and delivered to customers that day. The merchandise originally cost Collins $5,000.

j. Collins Container Corporation billed customers $12,600 for merchandise delivered to customers on January 26. This merchandise originally cost Collins $7,400.

k. Collins Corporation provides delivery services to some neighboring businesses to help utilize its delivery truck. On January 26, Collins Corporation billed one of these businesses $300 and collected cash of $150 from another business for delivery services. Thus, the total for delivery services for neighboring businesses was $450.

l. On January 27, the company paid $90 for gasoline used in the company's delivery truck during the month of January.

m. On January 27, the company paid wages to employees of $1,500.

n. On January 28, the company received a $2,700 order from a customer for goods to be delivered in February.

o. On January 31, the company paid $500 for January's rent.

p. On January 31, the company paid a dividend to its shareholders of $300.

i. On January 22, Collins Container Corporation received cash of $8,000 for merchandise it sold and delivered to customers that day. The merchandise originally cost Collins $5,000.

1. This transaction took place on January 22, 2004. Generally speaking, sales transactions have two distinct parts we must deal with. First, the company has sold merchandise for cash, so we should increase both sales and cash. Second, the company has delivered merchandise to the customer from its inventory, so we should decrease merchandise inventory and increase cost of goods sold. The amount of the sale and the cash received is $8,000, so we should increase the sales account and the cash account by this amount. The company's cost of the inventory it sold is $5,000, so we should decrease the merchandise inventory account and increase the cost of goods sold account by this amount.

2. As you know, because cash is an asset account, we increase it with a debit. Sales is a revenue account and revenue increases equity. Equity accounts are increased with a credit, so we should credit the sales revenue account. Cost of goods sold is an expense account and expenses decrease equity. Therefore, we increase expense accounts such as cost of goods sold with a debit. Merchandise inventory is an asset account, so we decrease it with a credit. This item actually requires two separate entries, or an entry that includes multiple parts. Entries that include multiple parts are called **compound entries.**

compound entries
Entries recorded in the general journal that contain more than two accounts.

3. The two separate entries are:

Jan 22	Cash	8,000	
	Sales		8,000
22	Cost of goods sold	5,000	
	Merchandise inventory		5,000

Or, to accomplish the same changes to the account balances, we can make the following compound entry:

Jan 22	Cash	8,000	
	Cost of goods sold	5,000	
	Sales		8,000
	Merchandise inventory		5,000

4. A final check of both sets of entries reveals that the dollar amount of the debits equals that of the credits. You can make either two separate entries or a compound entry for an item such as this. The choice is yours.

j. Collins Container Corporation billed customers $12,600 for merchandise delivered to customers on January 26. This merchandise originally cost Collins $7,400.

1. This transaction took place on January 26, 2004. As we said before, sales transactions generally have two distinct parts. In this case, the company has sold merchandise on account, so we should increase sales and accounts receivable. Also, the company has delivered merchandise to the customer from its inventory, so we should decrease merchandise inventory and increase cost of goods sold. The amount of the sale and the amount that the customer owes Collins is $12,600, so we should increase the sales account and the accounts receivable account by this amount. The company's cost of the inventory it sold is $7,400, so we should decrease the merchandise inventory account and increase the cost of goods sold account by this amount.

2. Accounts receivable is an asset account, so we increase it with a debit. We increase sales, a revenue account, with a credit. Cost of goods sold is an expense account, so we increase it with a debit. Merchandise inventory is an asset account, so we decrease it with a credit.

3. Like **item *i,*** this item requires two separate entries or a compound entry. The entries are:

Jan 26	Accounts receivable	12,600	
	Sales		12,600
26	Cost of goods sold	7,400	
	Merchandise inventory		7,400

Or, to accomplish the same changes to the account balances, we can make the following compound entry:

Jan 26	Accounts receivable	12,600	
	Cost of goods sold	7,400	
	Sales		12,600
	Merchandise inventory		7,400

4. A final check of both sets of entries reveals that the dollar amount of the debits equals that of the credits. Just as was the case for **item h,** you can make either two separate entries or a compound entry for an item such as this.

Discussion Question

6–8. You may have noticed that when we make an entry to record a sale and its associated cost of goods sold, we do not subtract the cost from the sale amount to determine the income on the sale. When *would* we subtract cost of goods sold from sales to determine gross profit on sales?

k. Collins Corporation provides delivery services to some neighboring businesses to help utilize its delivery truck. On January 26, Collins Corporation billed one of these businesses $300 and collected cash of $150 from another business for delivery services. Thus, the total for delivery services for neighboring businesses totaled $450.

1. This transaction took place on January 26, 2004. In this transaction, Collins received some cash, so cash should be increased. The company has also billed customers, so accounts receivable should be increased. The company has earned revenue from providing delivery services, so delivery service revenue should be increased. The amount of cash received was $150, billings to customers on account were $300, and the total delivery service revenue earned was $450.

2. We increase the cash account and accounts receivable with debits, while the delivery service revenue account is increased with a credit.

3. The journal entry:

Jan 26	Cash	150	
	Accounts receivable	300	
	Delivery service revenue		450

Or, to accomplish the same changes to the account balances, we can make the following two entries:

Jan 26	Cash	150	
	Delivery service revenue		150
	Accounts receivable	300	
	Delivery service revenue		300

4. A final check of both sets of entries reveals that the dollar amount of the debits equals that of the credits. Again, you can make either a compound entry or two separate entries for an item such as this.

l. On January 27, the company paid $90 for gasoline used in the company's delivery truck during the month of January.

1. This transaction took place on January 27, 2004. The company paid cash for the fuel, so cash should be decreased. The company purchased and used the fuel, so gasoline expense should be increased. The cash account should be decreased by the $90 paid for the gasoline. The gasoline expense account should be increased by the $90 cost of the gasoline purchased and used.

2. We increase the gasoline expense account with a debit and we decrease the cash account with a credit.

3. The general journal entry:

Jan 27 Gasoline expense   90
        Cash   90

4. A final check of the entry reveals that the dollar amounts of the debits and credits are equal.

m. On January 27, the company paid wages to employees of $1,500.

1. This transaction took place on January 27, 2004. The company paid cash for wages, so cash should be decreased and wages expense should be increased. The cash account should be decreased by $1,500 and the wages expense account increased by the $1,500 paid for the wages.

2. We increase the wages expense account with a debit and decrease the cash account with a credit.

3. The general journal entry:

Jan 27 Wages expense   1,500
        Cash   1,500

4. A final check of the entry reveals that the dollar amounts of the debits and credits are equal.

n. On January 28, the company received a $2,700 order from a customer for goods to be delivered in February.

1. This item does not affect any accounts or accounting elements. Although an entry will be required in February when the sale actually takes place, no entry should be made at this time.

o. January 31, the company paid $500 for January's rent.

1. This transaction took place on January 31, 2004. Collins paid cash for rent, so we should increase the rent expense account and decrease the cash account by the amount of the $500 rent payment.

2. We increase the rent expense account with a debit and decrease the cash account with a credit.

3. The general journal entry:

Jan 31 Rent expense   500
        Cash   500

4. A final check of the entry reveals that the dollar amounts of the debits and credits are equal.

Discussion Question

6–9. If Collins Corporation paid $1,500 on January 31 for rent for February, March, and April, should it debit rent expense? If not, what type of account should it debit? Why?

p. On January 31, the company paid a dividend to its shareholders of $300.

1. This transaction took place on January 31, 2004. Collins is making a cash dividend distribution to its owners, so we should decrease cash and increase dividends. We should increase the dividends account and decrease the cash account by the $300 amount of the dividend.

contra-account An account that carries a normal balance that decreases the accounting element in which it is classified.

2. Although the dividends account is an equity account, its normal balance actually works to decrease equity. An account that carries a normal balance that decreases the accounting element in which it is classified is called a **contra account.** Dividends, a contra equity account, decreases equity, so we increase the dividend account with a debit. We decrease the cash account, of course, with a credit.

3. The general journal entry:

    Jan 31   Dividends   300
                Cash   300

4. A final check of the entry reveals that the dollar amounts of the debits and credits are equal.

Exhibit 6–10 shows the general journal for Collins Container Corporation with all the journal entries we have made so far.

EXHIBIT 6–10 General Journal for Collins Container Corporation

Date 2004	Description	Post. Ref.	Debit	Credit
	General Journal			Page 1
Jan 1	Cash		10,000	
	Common stock			1,000
	Additional paid-in capital			9,000
	To record the sale of 1,000 shares of			
	$1 par common stock for $10,000 cash.			
1	Cash		20,000	
	Notes payable			20,000
	To record $20,000, 9%, one-year promissory			
	note to Bank of America.			
1	Prepaid insurance		2,400	
	Cash			2,400
	To record the purchase of a one-year			
	insurance policy effective January 1.			
1	Delivery truck		15,000	
	Cash			15,000
	To record purchase of a delivery truck for			
	cash.			
7	Office supplies		2,000	
	Accounts payable			2,000
	To record the purchase of office supplies on			
	account.			
8	Merchandise inventory		16,000	
	Accounts payable			16,000
	To record the purchase of merchandise on			
	account.			
12	Accounts payable		750	
	Cash			750
	To record $750 payment on account.			

General Journal				Page 2
Date 2004	Description	Post. Ref.	Debit	Credit
Jan 22	Cash		8,000	
	Sales			8,000
	Cost of goods sold		5,000	
	Merchandise inventory			5,000
	To record $8,000 sale for cash of goods that cost			
	$5,000.			
26	Accounts receivable		12,600	
	Sales			12,600
	Cost of goods sold		7,400	
	Merchandise inventory			7,400
	To record $12,600 sale on account of goods that			
	cost $7400.			
26	Cash		150	
	Accounts receivable		300	
	Delivery service revenue			450
	To record revenue for miscellaneous deliveries.			
27	Gasoline expense		90	
	Cash			90
	To record the purchase of gasoline for cash.			
27	Wages expense		1,500	
	Cash			1,500
	To record the payment of wages to employees.			
31	Rent expense		500	
	Cash			500
	To record the payment of January's rent.			
31	Dividends		300	
	Cash			300
	To record payment of dividends to common			
	stockholders.			

EXHIBIT 6–10   *Continued*

Now that the transactions have been journalized, we can post them to the general ledger.

STEP 3. POSTING THE TRANSACTIONS TO THE GENERAL LEDGER

Posting transactions to the general ledger is a simple process of transcribing entries from company journals to the general ledger. Although it is tedious and time consuming, the posting process presents no serious challenge. Posting requires attention to detail, and the accounting staff generally follows procedures similar to the following:

1. Locate the account in the general ledger.
2. Record the transaction date on the account's general ledger page. When posting from the general journal, we use the date of the journal entry.

3. The description column of the general ledger is often left blank. However, you can enter a notation about the transaction in this column if you feel that such information will be valuable in the future.

4. The posting reference column is very important. The notation in this column is the key to tracing an entry in the general ledger back to the original entry in the journal. Identifying the journal and the page number of original entry in the general ledger's posting reference column does this. For example, if the entry was originally journalized on page 212 of the general journal, GJ 212 is entered in the posting reference column on the general ledger.

5. Next, you record the amount of the entry in the appropriate debit or credit column. It is not necessary to use dollar signs ($) when posting amounts to the general ledger.

6. The last step in the posting process is a bit unusual but critically important. It is unusual because, instead of making this final notation in the *general ledger*, you make the entry back in the *journal*. In this step, we record the general ledger account number in the journal's posting reference column. Like the ledger's posting reference notations, the journal's posting references are critical in tracing journal entries forward to the appropriate general ledger account.

EXHIBIT 6–11 Posting to the General Ledger

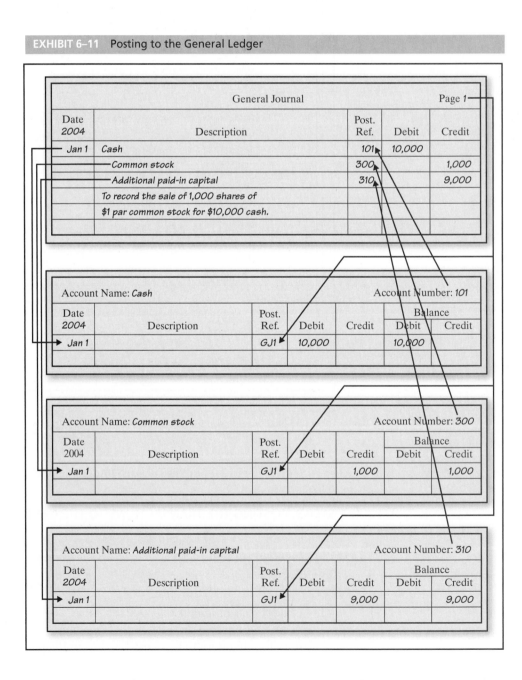

Exhibit 6–11 shows the posting of Collins Container Corporation's first journal entry. Then, Exhibit 6–12 presents the general ledger for the Collins Container Corporation once we have posted all the entries from the general journal. Once all the entries are posted, we can prepare a trial balance.

EXHIBIT 6–12   General Ledger for Collins Container Corporation

Account Name: *Cash* — Account Number: *101*

Date 2004	Description	Post. Ref.	Debit	Credit	Balance Debit	Balance Credit
Jan 1		GJ1	10,000			
1		GJ1	20,000			
1	Ck. #101	GJ1		2,400		
1	Ck. #102	GJ1		15,000		
12	Ck. #103	GJ1		750		
22		GJ2	8,000			
26		GJ2	150			
27	Ck. #104	GJ2		90		
27	Ck. #105	GJ2		1,500		
31	Ck. #106	GJ2		500		
31	Ck. #107	GJ2		300	17,610	

Account Name: *Accounts receivable* — Account Number: *110*

Date 2004	Description	Post. Ref.	Debit	Credit	Balance Debit	Balance Credit
Jan 26		GJ2	12,600			
26		GJ2	300		12,900	

Account Name: *Merchandise inventory* — Account Number: *120*

Date 2004	Description	Post. Ref.	Debit	Credit	Balance Debit	Balance Credit
Jan 8		GJ1	16,000			
22		GJ2		5,000		
26		GJ2		7,400	3,600	

Account Name: *Office supplies* — Account Number: *130*

Date 2004	Description	Post. Ref.	Debit	Credit	Balance Debit	Balance Credit
Jan 7		GJ1	2,000		2,000	

Account Name: *Prepaid insurance* — Account Number: *140*

Date 2004	Description	Post. Ref.	Debit	Credit	Balance Debit	Balance Credit
Jan 1		GJ1	2,400		2,400	

continued

Account Name: *Delivery truck*   **Account Number:** *150*

Date 2004	Description	Post. Ref.	Debit	Credit	Balance Debit	Balance Credit
Jan 1		GJ1	15,000		15,000	

Account Name: *Accounts payable*   **Account Number:** *200*

Date 2004	Description	Post. Ref.	Debit	Credit	Balance Debit	Balance Credit
Jan 7		GJ1		2,000		
8		GJ1		16,000		
12		GJ1	750			17,250

Account Name: *Notes payable*   **Account Number:** *250*

Date 2004	Description	Post. Ref.	Debit	Credit	Balance Debit	Balance Credit
Jan 1		GJ1		20,000		20,000

Account Name: *Common stock*   **Account Number:** *300*

Date 2004	Description	Post. Ref.	Debit	Credit	Balance Debit	Balance Credit
Jan 1		GJ1		1,000		1,000

Account Name: *Additional paid-in capital*   **Account Number:** *310*

Date 2004	Description	Post. Ref.	Debit	Credit	Balance Debit	Balance Credit
Jan 1		GJ1		9,000		9,000

Account Name: *Dividends*   **Account Number:** *325*

Date 2004	Description	Post. Ref.	Debit	Credit	Balance Debit	Balance Credit
Jan 31		GJ2	300		300	

EXHIBIT 6–12   *Continued*

Account Name: *Sales* — **Account Number:** *400*

Date 2004	Description	Post. Ref.	Debit	Credit	Balance Debit	Balance Credit
Jan 22		GJ2		8,000		
26		GJ2		12,600		20,600

Account Name: *Delivery service revenue* — **Account Number:** *410*

Date 2004	Description	Post. Ref.	Debit	Credit	Balance Debit	Balance Credit
Jan 26		GJ2		450		450

Account Name: *Cost of goods sold* — **Account Number:** *500*

Date 2004	Description	Post. Ref.	Debit	Credit	Balance Debit	Balance Credit
Jan 22		GJ2	5,000			
26		GJ2	7,400		12,400	

Account Name: *Wages expense* — **Account Number:** *620*

Date 2004	Description	Post. Ref.	Debit	Credit	Balance Debit	Balance Credit
Jan 27		GJ2	1,500		1,500	

Account Name: *Rent expense* — **Account Number:** *630*

Date 2004	Description	Post. Ref.	Debit	Credit	Balance Debit	Balance Credit
Jan 27		GJ2	500		500	

Account Name: *Gasoline expense* — **Account Number:** *650*

Date 2004	Description	Post. Ref.	Debit	Credit	Balance Debit	Balance Credit
Jan 27		GJ2	90		90	

EXHIBIT 6–12 *Continued*

STEP 4. PREPARING A TRIAL BALANCE

To prepare the trial balance, we simply list the general ledger accounts and their balances, include an appropriate heading, and provide totals for the debit and credit columns. You may have noticed that we are not yet using some accounts shown on Collins Container Corporation's chart of accounts. When we prepare a trial balance, we only list the accounts that we are currently using and that have balances. The trial balance for Collins Container Corporation appears in Exhibit 6–13. The fact that the debit and credit columns equal is an indication that our general ledger is in balance.

EXHIBIT 6–13 Trial Balance for the Collins Container Corporation

Collins Container Corporation
Trial Balance
January 31, 2004

Account	Debit	Credit
101 Cash	$17,610	
110 Accounts receivable	12,900	
120 Merchandise inventory	3,600	
130 Office supplies	2,000	
140 Prepaid insurance	2,400	
150 Delivery truck	15,000	
200 Accounts payable		$17,250
250 Notes payable		20,000
300 Common stock		1,000
310 Additional paid-in capital		9,000
325 Dividends	300	
400 Sales		20,600
410 Delivery service revenue		450
500 Cost of goods sold	12,400	
620 Wages expense	1,500	
630 Rent expense	500	
650 Gasoline expense	90	
Total	$68,300	$68,300

Discussion Questions

6–10. If the debits equal the credits on the trial balance, does this mean that everything in the general ledger is correct? Explain your answer.

6–11. If the debits do not equal the credits, what might have caused the imbalance?

STEP 5. ADJUSTING THE GENERAL LEDGER ACCOUNT BALANCES

We examine each account to see whether the balance is reasonable and to determine whether any accrual, deferral, or some other adjusting entry is needed. As we mentioned earlier in this chapter, the adjusting process basically consists of three steps:

1. **Examine each account and determine the appropriate ending account balances.** Examine each account in light of the situation as it exists on the last day of the accounting period to determine whether the ending account balances are appropriate. If an account's ending balance is not appropriate for the situation that exists at the end of the accounting period, determine the appropriate ending account balance.

2. **Determine the required increase or decrease.** Determine the amount by which the account should be increased or decreased so the account reflects the appropriate balance.
3. **Make an adjusting entry.** Make the adjusting journal entries to change the ending account balances to the appropriate amounts.

Accountants develop various techniques and procedures to ensure that they have made all of the adjusting entries needed. An accountant might begin by reviewing last year's adjusting entries, and then he or she might examine the trial balance and the general ledger. Accountants also collect additional information by talking to managers and employees throughout the company to determine the present state of business affairs and whether the general ledger account balances reflect these affairs.

For Collins Container Corporation, we will methodically examine each account listed on Collins Container Corporation's chart of accounts, beginning with cash. The idea is to use the chart of accounts to direct our attention to each business area so we can determine the adjusting entries required.

Cash   The best way to determine whether the cash account's balance is appropriate is to reconcile it to the bank statement. Conceptually, the bank reconciliation is simple. We compare the amounts on the bank statement to those on our books to determine the differences that exist. For each of those differences, we need to indicate whether the bank's balance or our general ledger cash balance should be adjusted, and by how much.

Each month, banks send statements to each of their customers. These statements trace bank account balances from the beginning of the month to the end of the month and show each and every addition and deduction that affected each customer's account. Although there are some miscellaneous items, the additions consist primarily of deposits and the deductions consist primarily of checks the bank has paid from the accounts.

When you review your bank statement, the debits and credits may seem to be the exact opposite of what you have learned so far in this chapter. This may surprise you, but you are not looking at a cash account, but rather at the bank's liability account to you. That's right, the statement you receive from your bank reflects its liability to you, not a cash account. With this in mind, the debits and credits on the statement make perfect sense.

There are many acceptable formats that you could use to reconcile a bank account. As Exhibit 6–14 on page F–228 shows, we will use one that reflects the bank's cash balance and our own general ledger cash balance, followed by the changes required to adjust each of these balances to the correct cash amount.

Before we get started, we should make sure we have all the documents and information we need to do the reconciliation. To do the bank reconciliation, you need:

1. The prior month's bank reconciliation
2. The bank statement
3. The company's cash records. Generally, this would include the company's general ledger cash account and its journals if the ledger does not provide enough detail.

For our example, we will need to collect the appropriate documents for Collins Container Corporation. Although the bank statement and general ledger are available for the company, Collins is a new company and just opened its bank account in January, so we will not have a prior month's bank reconciliation.

Reconciling a bank statement uses the following process:

1. Record the ending general ledger cash account balance on the appropriate space on the bank reconciliation form.
2. Match and check off each item on the prior month's bank reconciliation to the bank statement and the company's records to determine whether the items have been resolved and the appropriate entries made.

Company Name
Bank Reconciliation
For the Month of _____

Balance per bank statement $ _____
Add:
   Deposits in transit:

   _____ $ _____

   _____   _____

   _____   _____   _____

   Other reconciling items:

   _____   _____   _____

Deduct:
   Outstanding checks:

   _____   _____

   _____   _____

   _____   _____

   _____   _____

   Other reconciling items:

   _____   _____

Correct cash balance $ _____

Balance per bank statement $ _____
Add:

   _____ $ _____

   _____   _____

   _____   _____   _____

Deduct:
   Bank service charge   _____
   Other reconciling items:

   _____   _____

   _____   _____

   _____   _____   _____

Correct cash balance $ _____

EXHIBIT 6–14   Sample Bank Reconciliation Form

3. Match and check off each item on the bank statement to the company's cash records (the general ledger or, if necessary, the journals) to determine which items appear on the statement, but not on the company's books, or vice versa.

4. Examine the prior month's bank reconciliation, the bank statement, and the company's cash records (the general ledger cash account, or, if necessary, the journals) in search of any cash items that you could not check off in steps 2 and 3. This is a very important step because we are actively seeking items that are causing the difference between the bank's balance and our own. We will list these items, called **reconciling items,** in the appropriate places on our bank reconciliation form.

5. Any item on the prior month's bank reconciliation that you did not check off was probably not recorded by the bank or the company. Place such items on the current bank reconciliation in the same position they occupied on the prior month's reconciliation.

6. If the bank statement appropriately reflects an item but the company's cash account does not, you should add or subtract the item as appropriate on the company's part of the reconciliation.

7. If the company's cash account appropriately reflects an item but the bank statement does not, you should add or subtract the item on the bank's part of the reconciliation.

8. Once you have entered all the reconciling items on the bank reconciliation, you are ready to determine the correct cash balance. To do this, adjust the bank's bal-

reconciling items   Items that are causing the difference between a bank's cash balance and the balance shown on a company's records. These items are listed in the appropriate places on the company's bank reconciliation form.

ance and the general ledger cash balance shown on the reconciliation as appropriate by the reconciling items. When you are done, both parts of the reconciliation should arrive at the same amount as the correct cash balance.

If your bank reconciliation does not balance, you will have to recheck your work. You should look for the following types of problems:

a. *Not checking an item.* Look for items that you should have checked off but did not.

b. *Checking an item by mistake.* Look for items that you should not have checked off but you did.

c. *Forgetting to put an item on the bank reconciliation.* Look for items that you did not check off that you failed to place on the bank reconciliation.

d. *Putting an item in the wrong place on the bank reconciliation.* Look for items that you put in the wrong place on the bank reconciliation form. Remember, if the item is on the bank statement but not on our books, we need to include it in our books (to our side of the bank reconciliation), and if an item is on our books but not on the bank statement, we need to include it on the bank's side of the reconciliation.

e. *Mathematical errors.* Review the bank reconciliation to ensure you have added items that should have been added and subtracted the items that should have been subtracted, and that your math is correct. Also, look for transposed numbers—a distinct possibility if the unreconciled difference is divisible by 9.

Exhibit 6–15 on page F–230 shows Collins Container Corporation's bank statement and general ledger cash account for January with the appropriate items checked off.

Once the bank reconciliation is complete, the next step is to make the appropriate entries in the general journal to adjust the cash account to the correct amount. The bank reconciliation for Collins Container Corporation in Exhibit 6–16 on page F–231 indicates that we need to make two entries to our cash account: one to increase cash and increase interest revenue and the other to decrease cash and increase bank service charge expense. Therefore, we should make the following adjusting entries.

a.	Jan 31	Cash	28	
		Interest revenue		28
	31	Bank service charge	32	
		Cash		32

Often, the items that appear on the bank's part of the bank reconciliation are due to timing differences. Timing differences are those that resolve themselves in due course as the bank finally pays our checks and records our deposits. Sometimes, however, in addition to the adjustments we make in our books, we may also need to call the bank to tell them about mistakes they have made or adjustments they need to make.

Now that we have made the adjusting entries to the company's cash account, we will continue down the trial balance and review each of the other general accounts.

Accounts Receivable   Try to verify the correctness of the accounts receivable balance by actively seeking any transactions where "sales" on account were recorded but the sale was not actually made and where sales were actually made but, for one reason or another, were not recorded. In addition, we should verify that all collections on account are properly recorded. In the case of Collins Container Corporation, the accounts receivable balance appears to include all the appropriate entries, and therefore, no adjusting entry seems to be needed.

Merchandise Inventory   As we will explore in Chapter 8, companies generally compare the balance of the inventory account to a physical count of the inventory. Accountants then make adjusting entries as needed for the differences. In addition, accountants must ensure that the inventory account includes all of the inventory the company owns, and no more. In the case of Collins Container Corporation, the ending inventory account balance seems appropriate, so no adjusting entry is required.

Bank of America

555 Any Street   Anytown, TX

Collins Container Corporation
1234 Any Road
Anytown, TX

Account Number: 123 456789

Your Account Balance at a Glance

Beginning Balance on 01-01-04	$	0
Deposits and Other Additions +	+	38,028
Checks Posted	–	19,650
Other Subtractions	–	32
Ending Balance on 01-31-04	$	18,346

Account Additions and Subtractions

Date	Amount ($)	Resulting Balance	Transaction
01-02	✓20,000+	20,000	Deposit
01-02	✓10,000+	30,000	Deposit
01-03	✓15,000–	15,000	Check 102
01-06	✓2,400–	12,600	Check 101
01-15	✓750–	11,850	Check 103
01-23	✓8,000–	19,850	Deposit
01-29	✓1,500–	18,350	Check 105
01-31	32–	18,318	Service Charge
01-31	28+	18,346	Interest

Account Name: *Cash*   Account Number: *101*

Date 2004	Description	Post. Ref.	Debit	Credit	Balance Debit	Balance Credit
Jan 1		GJ1	✓10,000			
1		GJ1	✓20,000			
1	Ck. #101	GJ1		✓2,400		
1	Ck. #102	GJ1		✓15,000		
12	Ck. #103	GJ1		✓750		
22		GJ2	✓8,000			
26		GJ2	150			
27	Ck. #104	GJ2		90		
27	Ck. #105	GJ2		✓1,500		
31	Ck. #106	GJ2		500		
31	Ck. #107	GJ2		300	17,610	

EXHIBIT 6–15   Collins Container Corporation's Bank Statement and General Ledger Cash Account

Office Supplies   On January 31, employees at Collins Container Corporation counted the office supplies that remained in the storage cabinet. They found that office supplies costing $1,650 were unused and still on hand at January 31, 2004. If the company originally purchased $2,000 worth of supplies and $1,650 are left, they must have used $350 worth of supplies. We should make an adjusting entry for these office supplies used during the month. As the following calculations show, the adjusting entry should

Collins Container Corporation
Bank Reconciliation
For the Month of January, 2004

Balance per bank statement			$ 18,346
Add:			
Deposits in transit:			
January 26		$ 150	
_____		_____	150
Other reconciling items:			
_____			
Deduct:			
Outstanding checks:			
104 _____	90		
106 _____	500		
107 _____	300		
_____			890
Other reconciling items:			
_____			
Correct cash balance			$ 17,606
Balance per books (per general ledger cash account)			$ 17,610
Add:			
January interest		$ 28	
_____			
_____			28
Deduct:			
Bank service charge		32	
Other reconciling items:			
_____			
_____			
_____			32
Correct cash balance			$ 17,606

EXHIBIT 6–16 Bank Reconciliation for Collins Container Corporation

decrease office supplies to the amount on hand at January 31 and increase office supplies expense for the $350 worth of supplies used.

Office Supplies:
Unadjusted Account Balance	$2,000	Debit
Adjusted Account Balance	1,650	Debit
Required Adjusting Entry	$ 350	Credit

Office Expense:
Unadjusted Account Balance	$ 0	
Adjusted Account Balance	350	Debit
Required Adjusting Entry	$ 350	Debit

Adjusting entry to accrue wages:

b. Jan 31   *Office supplies expense*   *350*
             Office supplies   *350*

Prepaid Insurance The company's $2,400 insurance policy covers a 12-month time period. Since January has passed, only 11 of those months remain. Therefore, the prepaid insurance account's balance should only include the 11 months' worth of insurance. As the following calculations show, the adjusting entry to record the expiration of insurance during January should decrease prepaid insurance and increase insurance expense by $200.

Prepaid Insurance:

Unadjusted Account Balance (12 months)	$2,400	Debit
Adjusted Account Balance (11 months)	2,200	Debit
Required Adjusting Entry (1 month)	$ 200	Credit

Insurance Expense:

Unadjusted Account Balance	$ 0	
Adjusted Account Balance	200	Debit
Required Adjusting Entry	$ 200	Debit

Adjusting entry to accrue wages:

c.	Jan 31	Insurance expense	200
		Prepaid insurance	200

Delivery Truck   The delivery truck account correctly reflects the fact that the company owns a delivery truck, so the account balance seems correct and no adjusting entry is necessary.

Accumulated Depreciation on Delivery Truck   Since the company used the truck to earn revenue for a month, we should make an adjusting entry to record one month's depreciation. As we learned in Chapter 5, one way we can compute the depreciation is to subtract the truck's residual value from its cost and divide the result by the estimated useful life of the truck. In this case, the truck cost $15,000, its estimated useful life is five years or 60 months, and its estimated residual value is $1,500. Therefore, the truck's depreciation expense equals $225 for January calculated as follows:

$$\text{Depreciation Expense} = \frac{\text{Asset's Cost} - \text{Estimated Residual Value}}{\text{Estimated Useful Life of the Asset}}$$

$$\frac{\$15,000 - \$1,500}{60 \text{ Months}} = \$225$$

As the following calculations show, the adjusting entry to record depreciation expense should increase both accumulated depreciation and depreciation expense. Keep in mind that accumulated depreciation is a *contra asset* account because, although it is part of the asset classification, it works to reduce the total asset balance. Unlike regular asset accounts that are increased with debits, contra asset accounts work to decrease total assets, so they are increased with credits. Depreciation expense, like any other expense, should be increased with a debit.

Accumulated Depreciation on Delivery Truck:

Unadjusted Account Balance	$ 0	
Adjusted Account Balance	225	Credit
Required Adjusting Entry	$225	Credit

Depreciation Expense:

Unadjusted Account Balance	$ 0	
Adjusted Account Balance	225	Debit
Required Adjusting Entry	$225	Debit

Adjusting entry for delivery truck depreciation:

d.	Jan 31	Depreciation expense	225
		Accumulated depreciation on delivery truck	225

Accounts Payable   After reviewing its suppliers' accounts, Collins determines that this account includes everything it should, and no more, so its balance seems appropriate. No adjusting entry is needed.

Wages Payable   Collins Container Corporation hired its employees on Tuesday, January 21, 2004, and pays them $300 per day based on a five-day workweek. The company paid its employees on Tuesday, January 28, for their work up to Monday, January 27. The company did not pay its employees until February 4 for their work on January 28, 29, 30, and 31. Therefore, we should accrue wages of $1,200 for the four days at $300 per day. As the following calculations show, the adjusting entry to record the $1,200 wage accrual should increase both wages payable and wages expense.

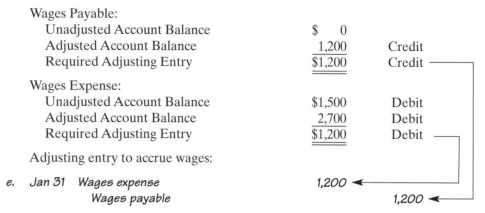

Wages Payable:
Unadjusted Account Balance	$ 0	
Adjusted Account Balance	1,200	Credit
Required Adjusting Entry	$1,200	Credit

Wages Expense:
Unadjusted Account Balance	$1,500	Debit
Adjusted Account Balance	2,700	Debit
Required Adjusting Entry	$1,200	Debit

Adjusting entry to accrue wages:

e. Jan 31   Wages expense   1,200
                    Wages payable   1,200

Interest Payable   On January 1, 2004, Collins Container Corporation signed a one-year, 9 percent promissory note to ***Bank of America*** for $20,000. Because the company used the loan to fund its business operations during January, we should accrue interest for the month. We compute January's loan interest as follows:

$$\text{Interest} = \text{Principal } \$20,000 \times \text{Rate } 9\% \times \text{Time } 1/12 = \$150$$

Interest Payable:
Unadjusted Account Balance	$ 0	
Adjusted Account Balance	150	Credit
Required Adjusting Entry	$150	Credit

Interest Expense:
Unadjusted Account Balance	$150	
Adjusted Account Balance	0	Debit
Required Adjusting Entry	$150	Debit

Adjusting entry to accrue interest expense:

f. Jan 31   Interest expense   150
                    Interest payable   150

Accrued Expenses   Let's assume that on February 3, the company received an electric bill for $120 dated January 31, 2004. The bill is for electricity the company used during the month of January, so it should be included in electricity expense for January. When bills and invoices are recorded as part of the adjusting process, instead of including their liability in accounts payable, a liability account called **accrued expenses** is used. Make a special effort to remember that *accrued expenses* is a liability account, not an expense account, because this is a common point of confusion. As the following calculations show, the adjusting entry to record the accrual of the $120 electric bill should increase both the accrued expenses liability account and electricity expense.

accrued expenses
Expenses appropriately recognized under accrual accounting in one income statement period although the associated cash will be paid in a later income statement period.

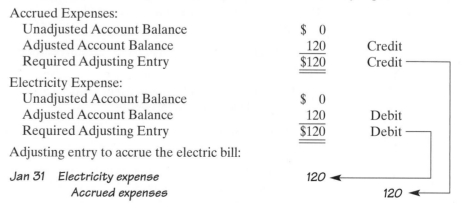

Accrued Expenses:
Unadjusted Account Balance	$ 0	
Adjusted Account Balance	120	Credit
Required Adjusting Entry	$120	Credit

Electricity Expense:
Unadjusted Account Balance	$ 0	
Adjusted Account Balance	120	Debit
Required Adjusting Entry	$120	Debit

Adjusting entry to accrue the electric bill:

g. Jan 31   Electricity expense   120
                    Accrued expenses   120

Unearned Revenue   Unearned revenue is a liability account used to defer (put off) the recognition of revenue. We use it when customers pay in advance for products or

unearned revenue A liability account used to record a company's liability to provide goods or services, which customers have paid for but have not yet received.

services yet to be delivered. In such cases, the seller has the cash but has not yet earned the revenue—the revenue is *unearned.* As was the case with accrued expenses, avoid making a common error by noting that **unearned revenue** is a liability account, not a revenue account. To determine if any revenue has been recorded but not earned, company accountants must seek out any situations in which customers have paid and revenue has been recorded, but the company has yet to perform. In the case of Collins Container Corporation, let's assume we have discovered that of the $450 of delivery service revenue, only $375 has been earned because $75 of the delivery service revenue recorded in January is actually for a delivery the company will make in February. As the following calculations show, the adjusting entry to defer the recognition of the unearned $75 delivery service revenue should increase unearned revenue and decrease delivery service revenue.

Unearned Revenue:
    Unadjusted Account Balance $ 0
    Adjusted Account Balance   75   Credit
    Required Adjusting Entry $ 75   Credit

Delivery Service Revenue:
    Unadjusted Account Balance $ 450   Credit
    Adjusted Account Balance   375   Credit
    Required Adjusting Entry $ 75   Debit

Adjusting entry to accrue the electric bill:

h. Jan 31 *Delivery service revenue*   75
                Unearned revenue   75

Notes Payable   This account includes everything it should include, and no more, so its balance seems appropriate.

Common Stock   This account includes everything it should include, and no more, so its balance seems appropriate.

Additional Paid-in Capital   This account includes everything it should include, and no more, so its balance seems appropriate.

Retained Earnings   We will determine the appropriate balance for retained earnings when we do the statement of stockholders' equity for Collins Container Corporation. Generally, aside from closing entries, we seldom change or adjust the retained earnings account.

Dividends   We have already recorded all the dividends paid, so this account includes everything it should, and no more. No adjustment is needed.

Sales   This account includes everything it should include, and no more, so its balance seems appropriate.

Delivery Service Revenue   We made the adjusting entry to this account when we reviewed unearned revenue.

Interest Revenue   We made the adjusting entry to interest revenue when we reviewed cash.

Cost of Goods Sold   This account includes everything it should include, and no more, so its balance seems appropriate.

Wages Expense   We made the adjusting entry to wages expense when we reviewed wages payable.

Rent Expense   This account includes everything it should include, and no more, so its balance seems appropriate.

Electricity Expense   We made the adjusting entry to electricity expense when we reviewed accrued expenses.

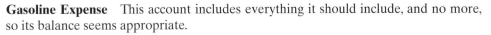

Gasoline Expense This account includes everything it should include, and no more, so its balance seems appropriate.

Depreciation Expense We made the adjusting entry to depreciation expense when we reviewed accumulated depreciation.

Bank Service Charge Expense We made the adjusting entry to bank service charge expense when we reviewed cash.

Interest Expense We made the adjusting entry to interest expense when we reviewed interest payable.

Next, we will enter the adjusting entries on the worksheet. As we mentioned earlier, the worksheet is an optional step in the accounting cycle. It is an informal procedure that accountants often perform before they formally journalize and post each of the adjusting entries. Exhibit 6–17 on page F–236 shows the worksheet for Collins Container Corporation including all of January's adjusting entries.

To prepare the worksheet:

1. We begin with an appropriate heading.
2. Then we list all the accounts included on the company's chart of accounts. Alternatively, we could copy the trial balance onto the worksheet, but then we would have to leave space to add accounts as they are needed.
3. Next, we enter the account balances from the trial balance and total them to assure that they are in balance.
4. We then enter the adjusting entries in the appropriate columns next to the accounts we are adjusting. We then total the adjusting entries columns to make sure our adjusting entries balance.
5. Once we enter all the adjusting entries on the worksheet, we add across each line to determine the amounts for the adjusted trial balance columns. We then total the adjusted trial balance columns to assure that our worksheet still balances.
6. Once we determine that the adjusted account balances, we place the adjusted balance for each account in the income statement and balance sheet columns as appropriate. Of course, income statement accounts go in the income statement columns and balance sheet accounts go in the balance sheet columns.
7. In the final steps of preparing the worksheet, we total the income statement and balance sheet columns but, at this point, they do *not* balance. For these columns to balance, we must enter the net income figure as shown on the worksheet and then calculate our final totals.

Do not make the mistake of believing that the trial balance totals or any other worksheet totals provide significant information aside from an indication that debits and credits equal. They do not. Except for assuring us that our debits equal our credits and that our worksheet is in balance, none of the worksheet totals really mean much.

In summary, the work sheet begins with the unadjusted trial balance and includes columns for the adjusting entries. Then the adjusting entries are incorporated into the account balances to arrive at the adjusted trial balance. Finally, the adjusted trial balances are moved over to the appropriate income statement or balance sheet columns and each column on the worksheet is totaled to ensure that debits equal credits.

STEP 6. JOURNALIZING AND POSTING THE ADJUSTING ENTRIES AND PREPARING THE ADJUSTED TRIAL BALANCE

Whether or not we use a worksheet, we must formally journalize all of the adjusting entries and post them to the general ledger. Then we prepare a trial balance called the adjusted trial balance. The adjusted trial balance is prepared after all the adjusting entries are journalized and posted to the general ledger. Exhibit 6–18 on page 237 shows the adjusted trial balance for Collins Container Corporation.

EXHIBIT 6-17 Worksheet for Collins Container Corporation

Collins Container Corporation
Worksheet
For the Month Ended January 31, 2004

Account	Trial Balance Debit	Trial Balance Credit	Adjusting Entries Debit	Adjusting Entries Credit	Adjusted Trial Balance Debit	Adjusted Trial Balance Credit	Income Statement Debit	Income Statement Credit	Balance Sheet Debit	Balance Sheet Credit
101 Cash	17,610		28	32	17,606				17,606	
110 Accounts receivable	12,900				12,900				12,900	
120 Merchandise inventory	3,600				3,600				3,600	
130 Office supplies	2,000			350	1,650				1,650	
140 Prepaid insurance	2,400			200	2,200				2,200	
150 Delivery truck	15,000				15,000				15,000	
155 Accumulated depreciation				225		225				225
200 Accounts payable		17,250				17,250				17,250
210 Wages payable				1,200		1,200				1,200
220 Interest payable				150		150				150
240 Accrued expenses				120		120				120
245 Unearned revenue				75		75				75
250 Notes payable		20,000				20,000				20,000
300 Common stock		1,000				1,000				1,000
310 Additional paid-in capital		9,000				9,000				9,000
320 Retained earnings										
325 Dividends	300				300				300	
400 Sales		20,600				20,600		20,600		
410 Delivery service revenue		450	75			375		375		
420 Interest revenue				28		28		28		
500 Cost of goods sold	12,400				12,400		12,400			
620 Wages expense	1,500		1,200		2,700		2,700			
630 Rent expense	500				500		500			
640 Electricity expense			120		120		120			
645 Office supplies expense			350		350		350			
650 Gasoline expense	90				90		90			
655 Insurance expense			200		200		200			
660 Depreciation expense			225		225		225			
670 Bank service charge expense			32		32		32			
680 Interest expense			150		150		150			
Total	68,300	68,300	2,380	2,380	70,023	70,023	16,767	21,003	53,256	49,020
Net income							4,236			4,236
Total							21,003	21,003	53,256	53,256

Collins Container Corporation
Adjusted Trial Balance
January 31, 2004

Account	Debit	Credit
101 Cash	$17,606	
110 Accounts receivable	12,900	
120 Merchandise inventory	3,600	
130 Office supplies	1,650	
140 Prepaid insurance	2,200	
150 Delivery truck	15,000	
155 Accumulated depreciation on delivery truck		$ 225
200 Accounts payable		17,250
210 Wages payable		1,200
220 Interest payable		150
240 Accrued expenses		120
245 Unearned revenue		75
250 Notes payable		20,000
300 Common stock		1,000
310 Additional paid-in capital		9,000
320 Retained earnings		
325 Dividends	300	
400 Sales		20,600
410 Delivery service revenue		375
420 Interest revenue		28
500 Cost of goods sold	12,400	
620 Wages expense	2,700	
630 Rent expense	500	
640 Electricity expense	120	
645 Office supplies expense	350	
650 Gasoline expense	90	
655 Insurance expense	200	
660 Depreciation expense	225	
670 Bank service charge expense	32	
680 Interest expense	150	
Total	$70,023	$70,023

EXHIBIT 6–18   Adjusted Trial Balance for Collins Container Corporation

STEP 7. PREPARING FINANCIAL STATEMENTS

The trial balance, or the worksheet if we have prepared one, includes all the information we need to prepare formal financial statements. Exhibit 6–19 on page F–238 shows the income statement, the statement of owners' equity, and the balance sheet for Collins Container Corporation using information from the adjusted trial balance as of January 31, 2004.

STEP 8. PREPARING AND POSTING CLOSING ENTRIES

As we mentioned earlier, companies close their books at the end of each business year to prepare them for the next business year. The four steps of the closing process for a corporation are:

1. Close all revenue and gain accounts to income summary.
2. Close all expense and loss accounts to income summary.

Collins Container Corporation
Income Statement
For the Month Ended January 31, 2004

Sales		$20,600
Less: Cost of goods sold		12,400
Gross margin		8,200
Operating expenses:		
Wages expense	$2,700	
Rent expense	500	
Electricity expense	120	
Office supplies expense	350	
Gasoline expense	90	
Insurance expense	200	
Depreciation expense	225	
Total operating expense		(4,185)
Operating income		4,015
Other revenues:		
Delivery service revenue	375	
Internet revenue	28	403
Other expenses:		
Bank service charge expense	32	
Internet expense	150	(182)
Net income		$ 4,236

Collins Container Corporation
Statement of Stockholders' Equity
For the Month Ended January 31, 2004

	Common Stock	Additional Paid-in Capital	Retained Earnings	Total Stockholders' Equity
Balance, January 1, 2004	$ 0	$ 0	$ 0	$ 0
Stock issued	1,000	9,000		10,000
Net income			4,236	4,236
Dividends (distributions to owners)			(300)	(300)
Balance, January 31, 2004	$1,000	$9,000	$3,936	$13,936

Collins Container Corporation
Balance Sheet
January 31, 2004

Assets:			Liabilities:		
Cash		$17,606	Accounts payable	$17,250	
Accounts receivable		12,900	Wages payable	1,200	
Merchandise inventory		3,600	Interest payable	150	
Office supplies		1,650	Accrued expenses	120	
Prepaid insurance		2,200	Unearned revenue	75	
Delivery truck	15,000		Notes payable	20,000	
Less accumulated depreciation	(225)		Total liabilities:		$38,795
Delivery truck, net		14,775	Stockholders' equity:		
			Common stock	1,000	
			Additional paid-in capital	9,000	
			Total contributed capital	10,000	
			Retained earnings	3,936	
			Total stockholders' equity		13,936
Total assets		$52,731	Total liabilities and stockholders' equity		$52,731

EXHIBIT 6–19 Financial Statements for Collins Container Corporation

3. Close the income summary account to retained earnings.
4. Close the dividends account to the retained earnings.

Although it is unrealistic for a business to end its business year one month after the company was established, for demonstration purposes, we will assume that Collins Container Corporation ends its business year on January 31. The adjusted trial balance in Exhibit 6–18 on page F–237 provides us with all the information we need to make the closing entries. The closing entries for Collins Container Corporation are as follows:

Step 1. Close all revenue and gain accounts to income summary.

Jan 31	Sales	20,600	
	Delivery service revenue	375	
	Interest revenue	28	
	Income summary		21,003

Step 2. Close all expense and loss accounts to income summary.

Jan 31	Income summary	16,767	
	Cost of goods sold		12,400
	Wages expense		2,700
	Rent expense		500
	Electricity expense		120
	Office supplies expense		350
	Gasoline expense		90
	Insurance expense		200
	Depreciation expense		225
	Bank service charge expense		32
	Interest expense		150

Step 3. Close the income summary account to retained earnings.

| Jan 31 | Income summary | 4,236 | |
| | Retained earnings | | 4,236 |

Step 4. Close the dividends account to the retained earnings.

| Jan 31 | Retained earnings | 300 | |
| | Dividends | | 300 |

The closing process is quite interesting in that we finally see how income actually becomes part of equity as the balances of revenues and expenses are transferred into retained earnings. Once we have made the closing entries, it is a good idea to prepare a post-closing trial balance to ensure that all temporary accounts are closed and all permanent accounts still remain.

STEP 9. PREPARING THE POST-CLOSING TRIAL BALANCE

We have reached the final step in the process. We prepare a post-closing trial balance to verify that each temporary account is closed, that all the permanent accounts remain, and that the general ledger remains in balance. The account balances on the post-closing trial balance become the opening balances for the new fiscal year. Exhibit 6–20 on page F–240 shows the January 31, 2004, post-closing trial balance for Collins Container Corporation.

Discussion Question ●

6–12. In addition to closing temporary accounts, why don't we also close permanent accounts? Wouldn't it be better to begin the new year with a blank slate for all accounts? Discuss your answers.

Collins Container Corporation
Post-Closing Trial Balance
January 31, 2004

Account	Debit	Credit
101 Cash	$17,606	
110 Accounts receivable	12,900	
120 Merchandise inventory	3,600	
130 Office supplies	1,650	
140 Prepaid insurance	2,200	
150 Delivery truck	15,000	
155 Accumulated depreciation on delivery truck		$ 225
200 Accounts payable		17,250
210 Wages payable		1,200
220 Interest payable		150
240 Accrued expenses		120
245 Unearned revenue		75
250 Notes payable		20,000
300 Common stock		1,000
310 Additional paid-in capital		9,000
320 Retained earnings		3,936
Total	$52,956	$52,956

EXHIBIT 6–20 Post-Closing Trial Balance for Collins Container Corporation

In this chapter, we have examined how accountants and their staff analyze, classify, and record transactions. In addition, we have reviewed the entire accounting cycle from its beginnings, through the preparation of financial statements, to closing entries.

Summary

Every business has hundreds if not thousands of transactions and economic events each year. To record these transactions and events and to convert these raw data into useful information, company accountants utilize an accounting system—a mechanism used to subclassify the accounting elements (assets, liabilities, etc.) that are affected by these various transactions. These subclassifications are called accounts or general ledger accounts.

Each account in the general ledger is assigned a title. These account titles are not dictated by generally accepted accounting principles or by any other accounting rules. Accounts are not only given descriptive names (cash, sales, rent expense, etc.), they are usually assigned account numbers as well. Companies generally develop a numbering system that groups similar types of accounts together. A reference document that lists all of the company's accounts and their account numbers is called a chart of accounts.

We journalize an economic event or transaction when it affects one or more accounting elements or accounts. Journalizing transactions means recording accounting transactions in a journal. A journal is a chronological record of the economic events and transactions that affect the accounting elements (the accounts) of a company. Special journals help to streamline the accounting process and greatly enhance accounting efficiency. If a company has no special journals, all transactions are recorded in the general journal. Periodically, the transactions recorded in a company's journals are transferred (posted) to the general ledger.

Accountants use a system of debits and credits to record transactions and events in journals and post to the general ledger. The accounting system records transactions as either debits or credits. Debit means left side and credit means right side, referring to the sides of the accounting equation. Debits must always equal credits in each transaction, each journal, and the general ledger to keep the equation in balance. Debits increase assets, expenses, and dividends and decrease liabilities, equity, and revenue. Credits increase liabilities, equity, and revenues and decrease assets and expenses.

Companies have some transactions and economic events that occur daily, some monthly, and some annually. As one year ends and the next begins, the process begins anew. The recording and reporting of these various transactions is called the accounting cycle. The steps in the accounting cycle are as follows:

Step 1: Analyze economic events and transactions
Step 2: Journalize transactions
Step 3: Post transactions to the general ledger
Step 4: Prepare a trial balance
Step 5: Prepare, journalize, and post adjusting entries
Step 6: Prepare an adjusted trial balance
Step 7: Prepare financial statements
Step 8: Prepare, journalize, and post closing entries
Step 9: Prepare the post-closing trial balance

These steps, when followed consistently, allow a company's accounting system to keep track of all the transactions and economic events the company experiences, and to produce accounting reports economic decision makers can use to make informed decisions.

Key Terms

- accounts, F–201
- accrued expenses, F–233
- adjusted trial balance, F–206
- adjusting entries, F–206
- book of original entry, F–203
- chart of accounts, F–201
- closing entries, F–207
- compound entries, F–217
- computerized accounting system, F–203
- contra account, F–220
- general journal, F–204
- general ledger, F–201
- general ledger accounts, F–201
- journal, F–203
- manual accounting system, F–203
- normal balance, F–209
- permanent (real) accounts, F–207
- post-closing trial balance, F–207
- posting, F–204
- reconciling items, F–228
- special journal, F–204
- temporary (nominal) accounts, F–207
- trial balance, F–205
- unearned revenue, F–234
- worksheet, F–206

Review the Facts—Part I

A. What is a general ledger account?
B. What information does a chart of accounts provide?
C. List the nine steps in the accounting cycle.
D. Describe the differences between a journal and a ledger.
E. Explain the purposes of special journals.
F. List the important elements of a general journal entry.
G. What is posting?
H. What information is shown on a trial balance?
I. Why do accountants make adjusting entries?
J. What is the difference between an unadjusted trial balance and an adjusted trial balance?
K. What is the difference between temporary and permanent accounts?
L. What is the purpose of the closing entries?
M. Describe the contents of the post-closing trial balance and explain its purpose.

Review the Facts—Part II ●

N. Distinguish between debits and credits and explain how they relate to the accounting equation.
O. Explain how a T-account is used.
P. What are the four steps for making general journal entries?
Q. What is the purpose of the general ledger?
R. How are posting references helpful?
S. With respect to bank reconciliations, what are deposits in transit? What are outstanding checks?
T. What type of account is accrued expenses? What is it used for?
U. Describe the information contained on the worksheet.
V. What are the four steps of the closing process?

Apply What You Have Learned—Part I ● ● ● ● ● ● ● ● ● ● ● ● ● ● ● ● ●

LO PART I, 1: ACCOUNT CLASSIFICATION

6–13. **Required:** Indicate the classification of each of the accounts as follows. Each letter may be used more than once.

  a. Asset   d. Revenue
  b. Liability   e. Expense
  c. Equity

  1. _____ Prepaid taxes
  2. _____ Notes payable
  3. _____ Advertising expense
  4. _____ Retained earnings
  5. _____ Bonds payable
  6. _____ Depreciation expense
  7. _____ Rent revenue
  8. _____ Land
  9. _____ Automotive equipment
  10. _____ Additional paid-in capital
  11. _____ Sales
  12. _____ Truck expense
  13. _____ Accounts payable
  14. _____ Gasoline expense
  15. _____ Common stock

LO PART I, 1: ACCOUNT CLASSIFICATION

6–14. **Required:** Indicate the classification of each of the accounts as follows. Each letter may be used more than once.

  a. Asset   d. Revenue
  b. Liability   e. Expense
  c. Equity

  1. _____ Accounts receivable
  2. _____ Sales
  3. _____ Notes payable
  4. _____ Prepaid rent
  5. _____ Supplies inventory
  6. _____ Delivery service revenue
  7. _____ Insurance expense
  8. _____ Income tax expense
  9. _____ Wages payable
  10. _____ Additional paid-in capital

LO PART I, 2: THE ACCOUNTING CYCLE

6–15. Identify and list in order of occurrence the steps of the accounting cycle.

LO PART I, 1, 3, 4, 5, & 6: TERMINOLOGY

6–16. Define the following terms:

  a. Journal
  b. Ledger
  c. Posting
  d. Trial balance
  e. Adjusting entries
  f. Closing entries

LO PART I, 1, 2, 3, & 4: TERMINOLOGY

6–17. Below is a list of items relating to the concepts discussed in this chapter, followed by definitions of those items in scrambled order:

  a. Accounting cycle   e. Journalizing
  b. General journal   f. Account
  c. General ledger   g. Chart of accounts
  d. Trial balance   h. Posting

  1. _____ A subclassification of the broad accounting elements such as asset, liabilities, and equity
  2. _____ The series of steps repeated each accounting period to enable a business entity to record, classify, and summarize financial information
  3. _____ A book of original entry
  4. _____ A device used to sort accounting data into similar groupings
  5. _____ The process of recording into the general ledger from a journal
  6. _____ The process of recording transactions into the book of original entry
  7. _____ A listing to prove the equality of debits and credits
  8. _____ The complete list of the account titles used by an entity

Required: Match the letter next to each item on the list with the appropriate definition. Use each letter only once.

LO PART I, 6: PERMANENT OR TEMPORARY ACCOUNTS

6–18. Examine the following accounts:

  1. _____ Cash
  2. _____ Accounts payable
  3. _____ Additional paid-in capital
  4. _____ Sales revenue
  5. _____ Prepaid insurance
  6. _____ Merchandise inventory
  7. _____ Dividends
  8. _____ Rent expense
  9. _____ Income tax expense
  10. _____ Income taxes payable
  11. _____ Common stock

Required: In the space provided, indicate whether the type of account is permanent (P) or temporary (T).

LO PART I, 6: PERMANENT OR TEMPORARY ACCOUNTS

6–19. Examine the following accounts:

  1. _____ Accounts receivable
  2. _____ Notes payable
  3. _____ Dividends
  4. _____ Sales
  5. _____ Service revenue
  6. _____ Prepaid rent
  7. _____ Supplies inventory
  8. _____ Insurance expense
  9. _____ Income tax expense

10. _____Wages payable
11. _____Retained earnings

Required: In the space provided, indicate whether the type of account is permanent (P) or temporary (T).

Apply What You Have Learned—Part II • • • • • • • • • • • • • • • • • •

LO PART I, 1 AND LO PART II, 1 & 5: ACCOUNT CLASSIFICATION

6–20. **Required:** Indicate the classification of each of the accounts as follows. Each letter may be used more than once.

a. Asset   e. Contra equity
b. Contra asset   f. Revenue
c. Liability   g. Expense
d. Equity

1. _____ Cash
2. _____ Accounts payable
3. _____ Accumulated depreciation
4. _____ Additional paid-in capital
5. _____ Revenues
6. _____ Prepaid insurance
7. _____ Unearned revenue
8. _____ Dividends
9. _____ Merchandise inventory
10. _____ Rent expense
11. _____ Income tax expense
12. _____ Income taxes payable
13. _____ Preferred stock

LO PART II, 1: NORMAL ACCOUNT BALANCES

6–21. Examine the following accounts:

1. _____ Accounts receivable
2. _____ Notes payable
3. _____ Dividends
4. _____ Sales
5. _____ Prepaid rent
6. _____ Supplies inventory
7. _____ Insurance expense
8. _____ Income tax expense
9. _____ Wages payable
10. _____ Retained earnings

Required: In the space provided, indicate whether the normal balance of each account is a debit (DR) or credit (CR).

LO PART II, 1: NORMAL ACCOUNT BALANCES

6–22. Examine the following accounts:

1. _____ Cash
2. _____ Accounts payable
3. _____ Additional paid-in capital
4. _____ Revenues
5. _____ Prepaid insurance
6. _____ Merchandise inventory
7. _____ Rent expense
8. _____ Income tax expense
9. _____ Income taxes payable
10. _____ Common stock

Required: In the space provided, indicate whether the normal balance of each account is a debit (DR) or credit (CR).

LO PART II, 1: NORMAL ACCOUNT BALANCES

6–23. Examine the following accounts:

1. _____ Prepaid taxes
2. _____ Advertising expense
3. _____ Retained earnings
4. _____ Depreciation expense
5. _____ Rent revenue
6. _____ Automotive equipment
7. _____ Allowance for doubtful accounts
8. _____ Truck expense
9. _____ Gasoline expense
10. _____ Common stock

Required: In the space provided, indicate whether the normal balance of each account is a debit (DR) or credit (CR).

LO PART II, 2: SIMPLE T-ACCOUNT ENTRIES—BALANCE SHEET ACCOUNTS ONLY

6–24. **Required:** Prepare T-account entries for the following transactions:

Jan 1 Borrowed $10,000 from the bank for two years at 8 percent.
1 Purchased merchandise inventory for $2,800 on account.
2 Purchased equipment for $2,000 cash.
3 Purchased supplies for $1,000 cash.
10 Paid for the merchandise purchased on January 1.

LO PART II, 2: SIMPLE GENERAL JOURNAL ENTRIES—BALANCE SHEET ACCOUNTS ONLY

6–25. **Required:** Prepare general journal entries for the following transactions:

Feb 1 Sold 1,000 shares of the company's no-par common stock for $5,000 cash.
5 Purchased a delivery truck for $18,000 by signing a promissory note for the entire $18,000.
6 Purchased supplies for $200 on account.
9 Paid $2,400 cash for a one-year insurance policy.
16 Paid for the supplies purchased on February 6.

LO PART II, 2: SIMPLE GENERAL JOURNAL ENTRIES—BALANCE SHEET ACCOUNTS ONLY

6–26. **Required:** Prepare general journal entries for the following transactions:

Mar 1 Sold 1,000 shares of the company's no-par preferred stock for $9,000 cash.
1 Borrowed $10,000, signing a promissory note.
7 Purchased production equipment for $11,000 cash.
8 Purchased inventory for $1,400 on account.
9 Purchased office furniture for $3,000 cash.
18 Paid for the inventory supplies purchased on March 8.

LO PART II, 2: SERVICE COMPANY SIMPLE T-ACCOUNT ENTRIES—BALANCE SHEET AND INCOME STATEMENT ACCOUNTS

6–27. **Required:** Prepare T-account entries for the following transactions:

Apr 1 Borrowed $8,000, signing a promissory note.
7 Purchased lawn equipment for $2,000 cash.
8 Billed a customer $300 for lawn services performed.
9 Received $150 from cash customers for lawn services performed.
9 Paid wages to helpers of $120.

LO PART II, 2: SERVICE COMPANY SIMPLE GENERAL JOURNAL ENTRIES—BALANCE SHEET AND INCOME STATEMENT ACCOUNTS

6–28. **Required:** Prepare general journal entries for the following transactions:

May 1 Sold 500 shares of $1 par common stock for $7,000 cash.
   2 Purchased computer equipment for $3,500 on account.
  18 Collected $600 cash for word processing services performed.
  29 Billed a customer $400 for word processing services performed.
  30 Paid $90 for electricity used in May.

LO PART II, 2: SERVICE COMPANY SIMPLE GENERAL JOURNAL ENTRIES—BALANCE SHEET AND INCOME STATEMENT ACCOUNTS

6–29. **Required:** Prepare general journal entries for the following transactions:

Jun 1 Sold 1,000 shares of $2 par common stock for $8,000 cash.
   2 Purchased equipment for $3,500 on account.
   2 Purchased garage supplies for $300 cash.
  15 Billed Smith for $1,900 for repair services performed.
  27 Received $1,200 cash from Jones for repair services performed.
  30 Paid $120 for electricity used in June.

LO PART II, 2: MERCHANDISING COMPANY SIMPLE T-ACCOUNT ENTRIES—BALANCE SHEET AND INCOME STATEMENT ACCOUNTS

6–30. **Required:** Prepare T-account entries for the following transactions:

Jul 1 Borrowed $12,000 on a promissory note.
   2 Purchased merchandise inventory for $8,500 on account.
   2 Purchased store supplies for $800 cash.
  15 Sold merchandise that cost $2,000 for $4,500 cash.
  27 Sold merchandise that cost $1,500 on account for $3,250.
  30 Paid wages of $300.

LO PART II, 2: MERCHANDISING COMPANY SIMPLE GENERAL JOURNAL ENTRIES—BALANCE SHEET AND INCOME STATEMENT ACCOUNTS

6–31. **Required:** Prepare general journal entries for the following transactions:

Aug 1 Sold 2,000 shares of no-par common stock for cash of $11,000.
   3 Purchased store equipment for $2,800 cash.
   3 Purchased merchandise inventory on account for $9,000.
  10 Sold merchandise that cost $3,000 for cash of $5,000.
  30 Sold merchandise that cost $2,000 on account for $4,000.
  30 Paid sales salaries of $300.

LO PART II, 2: MERCHANDISING COMPANY SIMPLE GENERAL JOURNAL ENTRIES—BALANCE SHEET AND INCOME STATEMENT ACCOUNTS

6–32. **Required:** Prepare general journal entries for the following transactions:

Sept 1 Sold 200 shares of $100 par preferred stock for cash of $20,300.
   2 Paid $3,600 for a one-year insurance policy.
   3 Purchased merchandise inventory on account for $18,000.
  15 Sold merchandise that cost $9,000 for cash of $15,000.
  29 Sold merchandise that cost $5,000 on account for $8,000.
  30 Paid sales salaries of $1,500.
  30 Paid $450 for electricity used in September.

LO PART II, 2: TRANSACTION ANALYSIS AND JOURNAL ENTRIES

6–33. On May 1, Bill Simon Computer Repair was begun when the company sold 1,000 shares of its no-par common stock for $7,000 cash. Also on May 1, the company paid two months' rent in advance totaling $400. On May 3, the company purchased computer repair supplies for $700 cash and three computers at a total cost of $4,500 on account. On May 3, the company hired a student helper, agreeing to pay the helper $1,000 per month. On May 12, the company billed a customer $700 for repair services rendered. The company paid the helper $500 on May 15. On May 25, the company paid $200 for a newspaper advertisement, which appeared in the paper a week earlier to announce the opening of the business. On May 31, the company paid another $500 to the helper. On May 31, the company received cash of $2,800 for repair services rendered to another customer.

Required: Prepare journal entries to record these transactions.

LO PART II, 2: TRANSACTION ANALYSIS AND JOURNAL ENTRIES

6–34. On July 1, Mead Travel Agency, Inc., was established when it sold 3,000 shares of no-par common stock for $10,000 cash. On July 2, the company paid $500 for one month's rent. On July 5, the company purchased office supplies for $700 on account and three desks at a total cost of $1,500 cash. On July 6, the company hired a travel consultant, agreeing to pay her $20 per hour. The consultant worked 100 hours in July, which the company will pay on August 1. The company paid $100 on July 29 for a newspaper advertisement that had appeared in the paper the week before to announce the opening of its business. On July 22, the company received $800 from East Coast Cruise Lines for commission revenue in connection with bookings Mead Travel made in July. On July 31, the company borrowed $12,000 from the ***Bank of America*** for two years at 7 percent.

Required: Prepare journal entries to record these transactions.

LO PART II, 2: TRANSACTION ANALYSIS AND JOURNAL ENTRIES

6–35. On December 1, 2004, Wayne Cox Enterprises, Inc., was established when the company sold 500 shares of no-par common stock for cash of $5,000. Also on December 1, the company paid office rent for December 2004 and January and February 2005 totaling $900. On December 2, the company purchased office furniture for cash of $1,500 and bought $250 worth of office supplies on account. The company also purchased computer equipment by signing a three-year, 6 percent promissory note for $1,500.

Required: Prepare journal entries to record these transactions.

LO PART II, 2: T-ACCOUNT AND JOURNAL ENTRIES

6–36. The transactions for September 2004 for Frank Collins Two Mile High Flight School are as follows:

Sept 1 Sold 25,000 shares of its $1 par common stock for $125,000 cash.
    1 Purchased an airplane for cash of $80,000.
    2 Paid $260 for a newspaper advertisement.
    2 Paid $3,000 for six months rent on an airplane hangar.
    5 Collected $900 for lessons given to students.
    5 Borrowed $10,000 from the bank for two years at 8 percent.
    6 Purchased office supplies for $250 cash.
    8 Collected $1,100 for lessons given to students.
    12 Paid a dividend of $850.
    20 Ordered $320 of repair parts for the airplane.
    23 Received the parts ordered on the 20th, paying cash.
    29 Paid cash of $400 for the fuel the airplane used in September.
    29 Paid September's electric bill for $150.

Required:

    a. Prepare T-account entries for the above transactions.
    b. Prepare general journal entries for the above transactions.

LO PART II, 3 & 4: CONTINUATION OF 6–36—CHART OF ACCOUNTS, POSTING TRANSACTIONS, TRIAL BALANCE

6–37. Refer to problem 6–36 for Frank Collins Two Mile High Flight School.

Required:

    a. Prepare a chart of accounts for the company based on the accounts you used for the journal entries.
    b. Post the transactions in the general ledger.
    c. Prepare a trial balance after completion of the posting process.

LO PART II, 2: RECORDING TRANSACTIONS—COMMON AND PREFERRED STOCK

6–38. Transactions for XXX Pest Control for October 2005 are as follows:

Oct 1 XXX Pest Control was formed when the company sold 3,500 shares of its $1 par stock for cash of $35,000.
1 The company sold 100 shares of its $100 par preferred stock for $10,500 cash.
1 Purchased a truck for $18,000 cash.
1 Borrowed $8,000 from the bank using the truck as collateral. Interest of 9 percent will be paid monthly on the first day of each month.
2 Purchased spraying equipment for the truck costing $3,500 cash including $400 of chemicals ($3,100 for the equipment and $400 for the chemicals).
2 Paid $600 for a newspaper advertisement to run each week in October.
2 Paid rent on an office for six months in advance totaling $6,000.
5 Collected $75 upon completion of spraying a new residence.
5 Billed a customer $150 upon completion of spraying the lawn.
6 Purchased office supplies for $200 cash.
8 Collected $100 for a termite inspection.
9 Collected the $150 from the customer on the 5th.
12 Paid a $500 dividend.
20 Ordered $1,000 of chemicals.
23 Received the chemicals ordered on the 20th with payment due in 10 days.
28 Collected $2,300 for completed termite inspections done for a loan company and billed an apartment complex $1,200 upon completion of spraying 40 units.
29 Paid the power company $135 for electricity used in October.

Required: Prepare general journal entries for the above transactions.

LO PART II, 3 & 4: CONTINUATION OF 6–38—CHART OF ACCOUNTS, POSTING TRANSACTIONS, TRIAL BALANCE

6–39. Refer to problem 6–38 for XXX Pest Control.

Required:

a. Prepare a chart of accounts for the company based on the accounts you used for the journal entries.
b. Post the transactions in the general ledger.
c. Prepare a trial balance after completion of the posting process.

LO PART II, 2: RECORDING TRANSACTIONS

6–40. The transactions for December 2004 for Brad Sanders Auto Repair Shop are as follows:

Dec 1 Sold 5,000 shares of $5 par common stock for $45,000 cash.
1 Purchased a wrecker for $30,000 cash.
1 Borrowed $25,000 on a one-year, 8 percent note from the bank. Interest is payable monthly on the first day of the month.
2 Purchased shop equipment for cash of $12,500.
2 Paid $360 for a newspaper advertisement to announce the opening of his business.
2 Paid rent on garage and office for six months in advance totaling $8,100.
5 Signed a contract to perform maintenance service on all auto equipment for a car rental agency.
5 Billed a customer $250 upon completion of auto repairs.
6 Purchased office supplies for $250 cash.
8 Billed the rental agency $2,500 upon completion of work performed.
10 Collected the $250 from the customer billed on the 5th.
12 Paid a cash dividend of $500.
15 Paid the December's telephone bill of $300.
21 Paid the local parts distributor $600 for parts already used on repair jobs (parts expense).
21 Ordered $1,300 of parts for parts inventory.
25 Received the parts ordered on the 21st and paid cash on delivery.
29 Paid $320 to the power company for electricity used in December.
31 Billed the rental agency $3,600 upon completion of repair services. Used $680 worth of the parts inventory for these repairs.

Required: Prepare general journal entries for the preceding transactions.

LO PART II, 3 & 4: CONTINUATION OF 6–40—CHART OF ACCOUNTS, POSTING TRANSACTIONS, TRIAL BALANCE

6–41. Refer to problem 6–40.

Required:

  a. Prepare a chart of accounts for the company based on the accounts you used for the journal entries.
  b. Post the transactions in the general ledger.
  c. Prepare a trial balance after completion of the posting process.

LO PART II, 5: SIMPLE ACCRUAL ADJUSTING ENTRIES

6–42. The Carlos Garcia Company had the following accrual information available at the end of the year 2004:

  a. Wages earned but unrecorded and unpaid as of December 31, 2004, were $2,500.
  b. Unpaid and unrecorded interest to date on a bank loan was $1,000.
  c. On January 12, 2005, the company received a $280 electric bill for December's electricity. The amount is unrecorded and unpaid.
  d. A customer owed one year's interest on a note to Garcia for $400 as of December 31. No entry has been made to record this transaction.
  e. As of December 31, 2004, Garcia has completed $2,300 of repair service in connection with a service contract. The amount will not be billed until January when the rest of the work is completely done.

Required: Prepare the appropriate general journal entries with explanations to record the above adjustments as of December 31, 2004.

LO PART II, 5: ADJUSTING ENTRIES

6–43. The Ray Placid Corporation had the following information available for the year ended December 31, 2004:

  a. The accountant completed the 2004 depreciation schedule, which showed the total depreciation expense of $10,520 for the year. The depreciation expense account has a balance of $8,500.
  b. Commissions for December of $22,000 will be paid to Placid's sales staff on January 5. The commissions payable account has a zero balance.
  c. The company loaned $20,000 to a customer on July 1 for one year at 8 percent interest. The customer will pay the principal and interest on the loan on June 30, 2005. No interest in connection with this loan has been recorded.
  d. On July 1, Placid paid an entire year's rent of $14,000 for a warehouse. In July, the bookkeeper recorded this payment as rent expense.

Required: Prepare the appropriate general journal entries with explanations to record the above adjustments as of December 31, 2004.

LO PART II, 5: ADJUSTING ENTRIES

6–44. The Butler Company has the following information available for the year ended December 31, 2004:

  a. Wages earned by employees but not paid at year end is $4,000.
  b. A one-year insurance policy was paid for on October 1 for $2,520. The insurance expense account's current balance is $2,520.
  c. Service revenue earned but not collected at year end is $14,000. Accounts receivable has a zero balance.
  d. Real estate taxes unrecorded and unpaid at year end are $3,900.
  e. Interest owed to the bank but not recorded or paid at year end is $2,200.

Required: Prepare the appropriate general journal entries with explanations to record the above adjustments as of December 31, 2004.

LO PART II, 5: DEFERRAL ADJUSTING ENTRIES

6–45. The Cohen Company's trial balance at June 30, 2004, has the following balances before adjustments:

Unearned rental revenue	$7,200
Prepaid rent expense	3,600
Prepaid insurance	4,800
Supplies inventory	1,200

   a. On May 1, the company paid the rent for one year in the amount of $3,600.

   b. On April 1, the company collected rental revenue in advance for the following 24 months in the amount of $7,200.

   c. On June 1, the company paid for its one-year business insurance policy in the amount of $4,800.

   d. At June 30, 2004, the physical count of the supplies inventory indicated that $295 of supplies were on hand.

Required: Prepare the appropriate adjusting entries with explanations to record the above information as of June 30, 2004.

LO PART II, 5: DEFERRAL ADJUSTING ENTRIES

6–46. As of June 30, 2004, the Jones Company has the following account balances before adjustments:

Unearned rental revenue	$4,800
Prepaid rent	3,600
Insurance expense	2,400
Prepaid insurance	0
Supplies inventory	700

   a. On January 1, the company paid the rent expense of $3,600 for one year's rent in advance.

   b. On March 1, the company collected 24 months' rent in advance totaling $4,800.

   c. On May 1, the company paid $2,400 for a one-year catastrophe insurance policy. This was the only policy in force.

   d. On June 30, the physical count of the supplies inventory on hand was $400.

Required: The company's year end is June 30. Prepare the appropriate adjusting entries as of June 30, 2004, with explanations to record the above adjustments.

LO PART II, 5: COMPLEX DEFERRAL ADJUSTING ENTRIES

6–47. In the first few days of January 2004, *Hearty Cooking* magazine sold 1,000 annual subscriptions to its monthly magazine for $16 each. It also sold 500 two-year subscriptions for $25 each and 250 three-year subscriptions for $32 each.

Required:

   a. Prepare the appropriate adjusting entries with explanations to record the adjustments necessary at December 31, 2004, and at December 31, 2005. Assume the subscriptions were all sold at the beginning of January 2004 and were originally recorded as income in the subscriptions revenue account.

   b. Prepare the appropriate adjusting entries with explanations to record the adjustments necessary at December 31, 2004, and at December 31, 2005. Assume the subscriptions were all sold at the beginning of January 2004 and were originally recorded as a liability in the unearned subscriptions revenue account.

LO PART II, 5: SIMPLE DEPRECIATION ADJUSTING ENTRIES

6–48. On January 1, 2004, the Stevens Company purchased a copy machine for $2,000. The firm believed the machine would have an estimated useful life of six years and a residual value of $200. The firm also purchased a delivery van costing $28,000 with an estimated useful life of four years and a residual value of $4,000. The company uses straight-line depreciation for all of its assets.

Required: Prepare the appropriate entries with explanations to record the depreciation expense for the first year for the copy machine and delivery van.

LO PART II, 5: SIMPLE DEPRECIATION ADJUSTING ENTRIES

6–49. On January 1, 2004, the Bishop Company purchased equipment for $3,000. The firm believed the equipment would have an estimated useful life of four years and a residual value of $200. The firm also purchased a tractor costing $56,000 with an estimated useful life of six years and a residual value of $2,000. The company uses straight-line depreciation for all of its assets.

Required: Prepare the appropriate adjusting entries with explanations to record the depreciation adjustment for December 31, 2004, for the equipment and the tractor.

LO PART II, 5: SIMPLE DEPRECIATION ADJUSTING ENTRIES

6–50. At the start of the year 2004, the Mitchell Corporation purchased a piece of equipment for $36,000. The firm believed the machine would have an estimated useful life of five years and a residual value of $6,000. The firm also purchased a building costing $200,000 with an estimated useful life of 40 years and no residual value. The company uses straight-line depreciation for all of its assets.

Required: Prepare the appropriate adjusting entries with explanations to record the depreciation adjustment at the end of the first year for the equipment and the building.

LO PART II, 4 & 5: ADJUSTING ENTRIES USING TRIAL BALANCE AND SUPPLEMENTAL INFORMATION

6–51. The following is a partial trial balance for the Weiss Company as of December 31, 2004:

The Weiss Company
Partial Trial Balance
December 31, 2004

	Debit	Credit
Prepaid insurance	$18,000	
Prepaid rent expense	12,000	
Interest receivable	0	
Wages payable		$10,000
Unearned service revenue		36,000
Interest revenue		0

Additional information includes the following:

a. As of December 31, 2004, seven months remain on the 12-month insurance policy that originally cost $18,000.
b. Weiss has a note receivable with $2,500 of interest due and payable on January 1, 2005.
c. The books show that two thirds of the fees paid in advance by a customer on June 30 have now been earned. Only one customer has paid Weiss Company in advance during 2004.
d. The company prepaid its rent of $12,000 for nine months on July 1.
e. The wages payable on December 31, 2004, were $7,000. The amount in the wages payable account is from December 31, 2003.

Required: Record the adjusting entries required based on the above information as of December 31, 2004.

LO PART II, 5: ADJUSTING ENTRIES USING TRIAL BALANCE AND SUPPLEMENTAL INFORMATION

6–52. The following is a partial trial balance for the Brown Company as of December 31, 2005:

The Brown Company
Partial Trial Balance
December 31, 2005

	Debit	Credit
Prepaid insurance	$ 7,200	
Prepaid rent expense	10,000	
Interest payable		$ 0
Subscription revenue		72,000
Wages expense	25,000	
Interest expense	0	

Additional information includes the following:

a. The company paid a $7,200 premium on a one-year business insurance policy on July 1, 2005.
b. Brown borrowed $200,000 on January 2, 2005, and must pay 12 percent interest on January 2, 2006, for the entire year of 2005.
c. Of the $72,000 of subscription revenue, $60,000 was earned as of December 31, 2005, and the balance will be earned in 2006.
d. The company prepaid 10 months' rent in advance on November 1, 2005, to take advantage of a special discount that reduced the rent to $1,000 per month.
e. Wages for work done by employees on December 31, 2005, of $3,000 will be paid to the employees on January 6, 2006.

Required: Record the adjusting entries required based on the above information as of December 31, 2005.

LO PART II, 5: ADJUSTING ENTRIES USING TRIAL BALANCE AND SUPPLEMENTAL INFORMATION

6–53. The following is a partial trial balance for the Mendoza Company as of December 31, 2004:

The Mendoza Company
Partial Trial Balance
December 31, 2004

	Debit	Credit
Office supply inventory	$ 1,400	
Wages payable		$0
Office supply expense	36,000	
Wage expense	45,500	

Additional information includes the following:

a. Office supplies on hand at year end were $1,230.
b. The total payroll cost for the year 2004 was $50,000. At December 31, 2004, the company owed employees $4,500 for wages earned in 2004.

Required: Record the adjusting entries required at December 31, 2004, based on the above information.

LO PART II, 5: SIMPLE BANK RECONCILIATION

6–54. The Clarke Company showed a balance for cash on their books of $2,517 on November 30, 2004. The company received the bank statement dated November 30, 2004, that showed a balance of $2,750. The differences between the company's book balance of cash and the bank statement balance are:

- A deposit of $500 that was made on November 30 was not included in the bank statement.
- Outstanding checks on November 30 were $1,280.
- Regular bank service charges imposed by the bank were $35.
- Bank service charge for credit card collections was $512.

Required:

a. Prepare the bank reconciliation for the Clarke Company for November 30, 2004.
b. Prepare any necessary adjusting journal entries at November 30, 2004.

LO PART II, 5: SIMPLE BANK RECONCILIATION

6–55. The Clifford Company received the bank statement for October 2004. The following information is available as of October 31, 2004:

Cash balance per general ledger	$7,500
Cash balance per bank statement	8,023
Interest earned shown on the bank statement but unrecorded by Clifford	18
Outstanding checks total	2,365

| Deposits in transit | 1,800 |
| Bank charges | 60 |

Required:

    a. Prepare the bank reconciliation for the Clifford Company for October 31, 2004.

    b. Prepare any necessary adjusting journal entries at October 31, 2004.

LO PART II, 5: SIMPLE BANK RECONCILIATION

6–56. The Patten Company showed a cash balance of $1,838 on its books as of December 31, 2004, but the December 31, 2004, bank statement showed a balance of $2,116. The differences between the company's book balance for cash and the bank statement's balance include:

    1. A deposit of $300 that was made on December 31 was not included in the bank statement.

    2. Outstanding checks on December 31 were $1,280.

    3. Bank service charges imposed by the bank were $28.

    4. The bank included a debit memo for bank charges for credit card handling fees totaling $690.

    5. The bank statement reflected interest revenue of $16.

Required:

    a. Prepare the bank reconciliation for the Patten Company for December 31, 2004.

    b. Prepare any adjusting journal entries at December 31, 2004.

LO PART II, 5: BANK RECONCILIATION

6–57. The following bank statement and cash journal are for the Whitaker Company's first month of business during 2004:

Any Bank

555 Any Street   Narberth, PA

Page 1 of 1
Statement Period:
11-01-04 through 11-30-04

Whitaker Company
1234 Any Road
Anytown, PA

Account Number: 123 456789

Your Account Balance at a Glance

Beginning Balance on 11-01-04	$	0
Deposits and Other Additions +	+	10,773
Checks Posted	–	1,603
Other Subtractions	–	45
Ending Balance on 11-30-04	$	9,125

Account Additions and Subtractions

Date	Amount ($)	Resulting Balance	Transaction
11-02	1,500+	1,500	Deposit
11-02	128–	1,372	Check 1001
11-03	1,254+	2,626	Deposit
11-06	425–	2,201	Check 1002
11-15	550–	1,651	Check 1004
11-23	8,000+	9,651	Deposit
11-29	500–	9,151	Check 1005
11-30	45–	9,106	Service Charge
11-30	19+	9,125	Interest

Account Name: *Cash*					Account Number: *111*	
Date 2004	Description	Post. Ref.	Debit	Credit	Balance Debit	Balance Credit
Nov 1	Deposit	GJ1	1,500			
1	Deposit	GJ1	1,254			
1	Ck. #1001	GJ1		128		
1	Ck. #1002	GJ1		425		
12	Ck. #1003	GJ1		785		
22	Deposit	GJ2	8,000			
26	Deposit	GJ2	150			
27	Ck. #1004	GJ2		550		
27	Ck. #1005	GJ2		500		
30	Ck. #1006	GJ2		95		
30	Ck. #1007	GJ2		130	8,291	

Required:

a. Prepare the bank reconciliation for the Whitaker Company for November 30, 2004.
b. Prepare any necessary adjusting journal entries at November 30, 2004.

LO PART II, 5: BANK RECONCILIATION

6–58. The following bank statement and cash journal are for the Levine Company's first month of business:

University Bank

555 Dixie Highway   Coral Gables, FL

Page 1 of 1
Statement Period:
11-01-04 through 11-30-04

Levine Company
317 Jenkins Drive
Coral Gables, FL

Account Number: 123 456789

Your Account Balance at a Glance

Beginning Balance on 11-01-04	$	0
Deposits and Other Additions +	+	6,362
Checks Posted	–	5,441
Other Subtractions	–	36
Ending Balance on 11-30-04	$	885

Account Additions and Subtractions

Date	Amount ($)	Resulting Balance	Transaction
11-02	2,750+	2,750	Deposit
11-02	3,000+	5,750	Deposit
11-03	2,250–	3,500	Check 2001
11-06	1,125–	2,375	Check 2002
11-15	55–	2,320	Check 2004
11-22	1,965–	355	Check 2003
11-23	600+	955	Deposit
11-29	46–	909	Check 2006
11-30	12+	921	Interest
11-30	36–	885	Service Charge

Account Name: *Cash*					Account Number: *111*	
Date		Post.			Balance	
2004	Description	Ref.	Debit	Credit	Debit	Credit
Nov 1	*Deposit*	GJ1	2,750			
1	*Deposit*	GJ1	3,000			
1	*Ck. #2001*	GJ1		2,250		
1	*Ck. #2002*	GJ1		1,125		
12	*Ck. #2003*	GJ1		1,965		
22	*Deposit*	GJ2	600			
27	*Deposit*	GJ2	1,150			
27	*Ck. #2004*	GJ2		55		
28	*Ck. #2005*	GJ2		79		
30	*Ck. #2006*	GJ2		46		
30	*Ck. #2007*	GJ2		122		
30	*Ck. #2008*	GJ2		139		
30	*Deposit*	GJ2	750		2,469	

Required:

    a. Prepare the bank reconciliation for the Levine Company for November 30, 2004.

    b. Prepare any necessary adjusting journal entries at November 30, 2004.

LO PART II, 5: ADJUSTING ENTRIES USING TRIAL BALANCE
AND SUPPLEMENTAL INFORMATION, FINANCIAL STATEMENT IMPACT

6–59. The Thompson Company has the following account balances for the year ended December 31, 2004 (all have normal balances):

Prepaid insurance	$ 6,000
Insurance expense	0
Rental revenue	44,800
Unearned revenue	0
Wages expense	7,660
Wages payable	0
Interest revenue	2,325
Interest receivable	0

The company also has the following information available at the end of the year:

    1. $4,000 of the prepaid insurance has now expired.

    2. Of the $44,800 of rental revenue, $2,200 has not yet been earned.

    3. The company must accrue an additional $1,500 of wages expense.

    4. The company has earned an additional $500 of interest revenue.

Required:

    a. Prepare the adjusting journal entries necessary based on the above information.

    b. Use T-accounts to compute the account balances of the income statement and balance sheet accounts.

LO PART II, 5: ADJUSTING ENTRIES USING TRIAL BALANCE
AND SUPPLEMENTAL INFORMATION, FINANCIAL STATEMENT IMPACT

6–60. The Carol Levine Company has the following account balances for the year ended December 31, 2004 (all have normal balances):

Insurance expense	$4,000
Prepaid insurance	0
Unearned rental revenue	3,800
Rental revenue	135,200

Wages payable	0
Wages expense	53,800
Property tax expense	4,398
Property tax payable	0
Depreciation expense	0
Accumulated depreciation	17,486

The company also has the following information available at the end of the year:

1. $1,000 of the insurance policy has not yet expired.
2. $1,600 of the unearned rental revenue has now been earned.
3. As of the end of the year, the company owes employees $1,200 of wages.
4. The company owes an additional $4,900 in real estate taxes.
5. Depreciation expense for the year totals $8,743.

Required:

a. Prepare any necessary adjusting journal entries based on the above information at December 31, 2004.
b. Use T-accounts to compute the account balances of the income statement and balance sheet accounts at December 31, 2004.

LO PART II, 5: ADJUSTING ENTRIES USING TRIAL BALANCE AND SUPPLEMENTAL INFORMATION, FINANCIAL STATEMENT IMPACT

6–61. The Alvarez Company has the following account balances for the year ended December 31, 2004 (all have normal balances):

Insurance expense	$ 5,400
Prepaid insurance	0
Unearned service revenue	3,525
Service revenue	235,750
Wages payable	0
Wage expense	64,820
Advertising expense	9,500
Prepaid advertising	0
Depreciation expense	0
Accumulated depreciation	24,000

The company also has the following information available at the end of the year:

1. $3,200 of the company's insurance has not yet expired.
2. $1,200 of the unearned service revenue was earned in the last month of the year.
3. The company must accrue an additional $1,800 of wages expense.
4. The company paid $6,000 for advertisements that will run for the next six months beginning next month. The $6,000 is included in the advertising expense account balance.
5. Depreciation expense for the year is a total of $8,000.

Required:

a. Prepare any necessary adjusting journal entries based on the above information at December 31, 2004.
b. Use T-accounts to compute the account balances of the income statement and balance sheet accounts.

LO PART II, 5: ADJUSTING ENTRIES USING TRIAL BALANCE AND SUPPLEMENTAL INFORMATION, FINANCIAL STATEMENT IMPACT

6–62. The Holmes Company has the following account balances for the year ended December 31, 2005 (all have normal balances):

Supplies expense	$2,000
Supplies	730
Unearned subscription revenue	3,758
Prepaid rent expense	4,950
Depreciation expense	0
Accumulated depreciation	24,652

The company also has the following information available at the end of the year:

1. Only $500 of the supplies are still on hand.
2. $1,785 of the unearned subscription revenue has now been earned.
3. With respect to prepaid rent, there are two months' rent remaining at $850 per month.
4. Depreciation expense for the year totals $12,326.

Required:

a. Prepare any necessary adjusting journal entries based on the above information at December 31, 2005.
b. Use T-accounts to compute the account balances of the income statement and balance sheet accounts.

LO PART II, 8: CLOSING ENTRIES

6–63. **Required:** Prepare closing entries based on the following information available for the year ended December 31, 2004:

	Debit	Credit
Cash	$20,180	
Supplies	4,340	
Prepaid expenses	1,685	
Notes payable		$ 2,400
Common stock		1,200
Additional paid-in capital—common		3,404
Retained earnings		7,680
Dividends	20,000	
Sales		129,850
Salaries expense	68,458	
Rent expense	18,082	
Rent revenue		2,000
Interest expense	280	
Income tax expense	13,509	

LO PART II, 8: CLOSING ENTRIES

6–64. **Required:** Prepare closing entries based on the following information available for the year ended June 30, 2005:

	Debit	Credit
Cash	$3,500	
Inventory	12,000	
Equipment	9,000	
Notes payable		$ 2,000
Common stock		500
Additional paid-in capital—common		3,500
Retained earnings		12,000
Dividends	1,000	
Sales		100,000
Cost of goods sold	60,000	
Wages expense	15,000	
Rent expense	9,000	
Electricity expense	4,000	
Telephone expense	2,000	
Income tax	2,500	

LO PART II, 8: CLOSING ENTRIES

6–65. **Required:** Prepare closing entries based on the following information available for the year ended December 31, 2005:

	Debit	Credit
Cash	$ 1,980	
Inventory	8,540	
Equipment	13,850	
Notes payable		$ 7,000

Common stock		1,350
Additional paid-in capital—common		2,820
Retained earnings		10,840
Dividends	250	
Sales		34,620
Cost of goods sold	22,860	
Wages expense	6,500	
Rent expense	1,180	
Interest expense	600	
Income tax expense	870	

LO PART II, 8: CLOSING ENTRIES

6–66. **Required:** Prepare closing entries based on the following information available for the year ended December 31, 2004 (all have normal balances):

Cash	$ 5,800
Accounts receivable	12,300
Inventory	26,800
Supplies	575
Land	40,650
Building	88,450
Accumulated depreciation—building	20,000
Equipment	4,950
Accumulated depreciation—equipment	1,100
Computer system	1,850
Accumulated depreciation—computer system	300
Delivery truck	29,960
Accumulated depreciation—delivery truck	3,000
Accounts payable	6,860
Notes payable	5,000
Common stock	1,000
Additional paid-in capital—common	95,520
Retained earnings	64,580
Dividends	2,900
Sales	260,500
Cost of goods sold	182,530
Wages expense	33,000
Depreciation expense	15,000
Electricity expense	3,500
Telephone expense	1,500
Rent revenue	2,100
Interest expense	4,570
Income tax	5,625

LO PART II, 8: CLOSING ENTRIES

6–67. **Required:** Prepare closing entries based on the following information available for the year ended June 30, 2005 (all have normal balances):

Cash	$ 2,680
Inventory	8,880
Equipment	12,640
Accumulated depreciation—equipment	3,000
Computer system	4,850
Accumulated depreciation—computer system	1,100
Delivery truck	18,600
Accumulated depreciation—delivery truck	6,000
Accounts payable	5,480
Notes payable	4,500
Common stock	2,000
Additional paid-in capital—common	10,312
Retained earnings	12,850
Dividends	500
Sales	56,250

Cost of goods sold	24,630
Salaries expense	18,400
Depreciation expense	4,400
Rent expense	2,400
Electricity expense	1,260
Telephone expense	625
Interest expense	900
Income tax expense	727

LO PART II, 8: CLOSING ENTRIES

6–68. **Required:** Prepare closing entries based on the following information available for the year ended December 31, 2004 (all have normal balances):

Cash	$ 1,920,650
Accounts receivable	263,520
Inventory	2,462,250
Supplies	1,200
Land	750,520
Building	1,685,520
Accumulated depreciation—building	300,000
Equipment	385,220
Accumulated depreciation—equipment	120,000
Accounts payable	1,985,640
Notes payable	736,580
Bonds payable	500,000
Preferred stock	200,000
Common stock	998,590
Retained earnings	2,460,350
Dividends	25,000
Sales	12,856,850
Cost of goods sold	9,458,560
Salaries expense	2,771,518
Depreciation expense	190,000
Rent expense	105,642
Electricity expense	24,995
Telephone expense	36,795
Rent revenue	36,000
Interest expense	13,340
Income tax expense	99,280

Mini Practice Sets ●

LO PART II, 1, 2, 3, 4, 5, & 7: JOURNALIZE AND POST TRANSACTIONS, AND TRIAL BALANCE AND FINANCIAL STATEMENT PREPARATION

6–69. The Best Home Improvement Center began operations on November 1, 2004. Transactions for the month of November are as follows:

Nov 1 Best Home Improvement Center sold 1,500 shares of $1 par Best common stock for cash of $45,000.

    1 Borrowed $5,000 from ***First National Bank,*** signing a 9 percent, 90-day note with interest payable on the first day of each month.

    1 Purchased a forklift to move merchandise for $5,000 cash.

    5 Best signed a lease on a store and paid six months' rent in advance beginning November 1, $9,450.

    6 Purchased $500 of office supplies from Helen's Office Supply on account.

    8 Purchased merchandise for $25,000 from Associated Supply on account.

   11 Paid $175 for a radio ad to run in November to announce the store's opening.

   14 Sold merchandise for cash of $4,000 that cost $2,400.

   15 Sold merchandise that cost $1,750 for $2,500 on a 30-day account to J. Park.

   17 Sold merchandise that cost $1,950 for $3,000 on a 30-day account to H. Clark.

   19 Purchased $10,000 merchandise from the Sun Company on account.

   20 Sold merchandise that cost $13,200 for $20,000 cash.

   21 Paid Helen's Office Supply for purchase on November 6th.

23 Paid Associated Supply for the purchase on the 8th.
24 Collected payment in full from H. Clark.
25 Paid Sun Company for the purchase on the 19th.
25 Received payment in full from J. Park.
28 Paid $800 to the power company for electricity used in the month of November.
29 Paid all the wages for the month of $4,000.
30 Paid a cash dividend of $1,000.

Required:

a. Journalize the transactions for the month of November in the general journal.
b. Open the general ledger accounts and post the November transactions to the appropriate accounts in the general ledger.
c. Prepare an unadjusted trial balance at November 30, 2004.
d. Prepare adjusting general journal entries and post them to the ledger accounts. The following additional information is available:

1. Best depreciated the forklift for the month of November, using straight-line depreciation with a $200 residual value and an eight-year (96-month) estimated life.
2. Best accrued the interest on the bank loan for November. The interest will be paid on December 1.
3. On December 8, Best received the phone bill for November phone service for $190.

e. Prepare an income statement, a statement of stockholders' equity, and a balance sheet for the month of November.

LO PART II, 1, 2, 3, 4, 5, 6, & 7: JOURNALIZE AND POST TRANSACTIONS, AND TRIAL BALANCE, WORKSHEET, AND FINANCIAL STATEMENT PREPARATION

6–70. Robertson Distributing, Inc., began operations on December 1, 2004. Transactions for the month of December are as follows:

Dec 1 Robertson Distributing, Inc., sold 7,500 shares of its $2 par value common stock for $75,000 cash.
1 Borrowed $10,000 from *First National Bank,* signing a 10 percent, 180-day note.
1 Robertson signed a lease on a warehouse and paid $6,000 for six months' rent in advance.
1 Purchased a truck to deliver merchandise for $14,000 cash.
5 Purchased $1,500 of office supplies from Market Office Supply on account.
7 Purchased merchandise for $15,000 from Acme Supply on account.
11 Paid the *Time Express* newspaper $350 for an ad to announce the grand opening of the distribution center. The ad ran in December.
13 Sold merchandise that cost $6,300 for $8,200 cash.
14 Sold merchandise that cost $3,725 for $5,000 to M. Real on account.
16 Sold merchandise that cost $3,050 for $4,000 to E. Johnson on account.
17 Purchased merchandise for $20,000 from the Davis Company on account.
19 Sold merchandise that cost $7,950 for $10,000 cash.
21 Paid Market Office Supply for the purchase on the 5th.
22 Paid Acme Supply for the purchase on the 7th.
24 Collected payment in full from M. Real.
26 Paid Davis Company for the purchase on the 17th.
27 Received payment in full from E. Johnson.
30 Paid the power company $1,800 for electricity used in December.
31 Paid wages for the month of $7,000.
31 Paid a cash dividend of $1,800.

Required:

a. Journalize the transactions for the month of December in the general journal.
b. Open the necessary accounts in the general ledger and post the December transactions to the appropriate accounts in the general ledger.
c. Prepare an unadjusted trial balance at December 31, 2004.

d. Prepare a worksheet and adjusting general journal entries and post them to the ledger accounts. In addition to information from the entries you made previously, the following additional information is available:

   1. Robertson depreciated the truck for the entire month of December, using straight-line depreciation with a $1,400 residual value and a 5-year (60-month) estimated life.
   2. Robertson accrued the interest on the bank loan for the month of December.
   3. As of December 31, Robertson owes wages of $1,900 for the month of December.

e. Prepare an income statement and a statement of stockholders' equity for the month ended December 31, 2004, and prepare a balance sheet as of December 31, 2004.

LO PART II, 1, 2, 3, 4, 5, & 7: PROPRIETORSHIP JOURNAL ENTRIES, POSTING, TRIAL BALANCE, ADJUSTING ENTRIES, AND FINANCIAL STATEMENTS

6–71. John Fox began his retail clothing business, Fineries, on November 1, 2004, as a sole proprietorship. The post-closing trial balance at November 30, 2004, appeared as follows:

Fineries
Post-Closing Trial Balance
November 30, 2004

	Debits	Credits
Cash	$38,500	
Prepaid rent	200	
Merchandise inventory	24,000	
Equipment	6,000	
Accumulated depreciation		$ 1,000
Common stock (no par)		67,700
Totals	$68,700	$68,700

The following transactions occurred in the month of December, 2004:

Dec 1 Fineries sold an additional 5,000 shares of stock for $100,000 cash.
   1 Bought equipment on account from the Acme Company for $13,600.
   1 Paid six months' rent in advance, $12,000.
   5 Purchased $28,000 of merchandise on account from Rose Company.
   7 Paid for a 12-month contents policy for fire damage at a cost of $1,440.
   8 Purchased merchandise for resale for $25,000 cash.
   10 Sold merchandise costing $6,300 to M. Powers on account for $12,600.
   12 Paid the balance due to Rose Company.
   15 Cash sales for the first half of the month totaled $27,500 for merchandise costing $13,750.
   16 Sold merchandise costing $5,000 to Alan Foster on account for $10,000.
   16 Paid wages for the first half of the month totaling $5,500.
   18 Purchased merchandise on account from King Company for $9,500.
   20 Purchased office supplies totaling $250 cash.
   22 Received a check from M. Powers for her invoice.
   25 Received a check from Alan Foster for payment of invoice.
   28 Sold merchandise costing $4,300 to Paul Munter for $8,600 on account.
   28 Paid cash of $300 for electricity used in December.
   28 Received but did not pay a $100 telephone bill for December's phone service.
   28 Paid King Company for the invoice of December 18.
   31 Recorded cash sales for the second half of December totaling $44,900 for merchandise costing $22,450.
   31 Paid wages for the second half of December, $4,500.
   31 Received a bill for delivery expense for December, $250.

Required:

a. Journalize the transactions for the month of December in the general journal.
b. Open the necessary accounts in the general ledger and post the December transactions to the appropriate accounts.
c. Prepare an unadjusted trial balance at December 31, 2004.

d. Prepare adjusting general journal entries and post them to the ledger accounts. In addition to the entries you have previously made, the following information is also available:

1. The company owes wages of $900 for work done in the last three days of the month.
2. Depreciation expense to be recorded for the month of December is $250.

e. Prepare an adjusted trial balance for the company.
f. Prepare a balance sheet as of December 31, 2004, and an income statement and a statement of owners' equity for the month ended December 31, 2004.

LO PART II, 1, 2 ,3, 4, 5, 7, & 8: JOURNAL ENTRIES, POSTING, TRIAL BALANCE, ADJUSTING ENTRIES, FINANCIAL STATEMENTS INCLUDING STATEMENT OF CASH FLOWS, CLOSING ENTRIES

6–72. Michael Sharpe started a retail hardware store, Sharpe's Home Haven, Inc., on December 1, 2005. The following transactions occurred in the month of December:

Dec 1 Sharpe's Home Haven, Inc., sold Michael 100,000 shares of its common stock for cash of $200,000. The stock has a par value of $1 per share, and there were 200,000 shares authorized.
1 Bought store equipment on account from the Ace Company for $22,000.
1 Paid three months' rent in advance, $9,000.
5 Purchased merchandise on account from Taylor Company for $50,000.
7 Paid $1,200 for a 12-month insurance policy.
8 Purchased merchandise for resale for $30,000 cash.
10 Sold merchandise costing $12,000 to Hill on account, $24,000.
12 Paid the balance due to Taylor Company.
15 Cash sales for the first half of the month totaled $30,000 for merchandise costing $15,000.
16 Sold merchandise costing $2,500 to Scott Dunn Company on account, $5,000.
16 Paid wages for the first half of the month totaling $7,000.
18 Purchased merchandise on account from M. Lynne Company for $18,000.
20 Purchased office supplies for cash of $400.
22 Received a check from Hill for payment of the December 10 invoice.
25 Received a check from Scott Dunn for payment of invoice.
28 Sold merchandise that cost $6,300 for $12,600 to David Brown Supply on account.
28 Paid cash of $600 for electricity used in December.
28 Received but did not pay the telephone bill for $200 for the month of December. It is due on January 12.
28 Paid M. Lynne Company for the invoice of December 18.
31 Recorded cash sales for the second half of December totaling $35,200 for merchandise that cost $17,600.
31 Paid wages for the second half of December, $7,500.
31 Received a bill for delivery expense for December for $400 due January 10.
31 Paid a $.10 per share cash dividend.

Required:

a. Journalize the transactions for the month of December in the general journal.
b. Open the necessary accounts in the general ledger and post the December transactions to the appropriate accounts.
c. Prepare an unadjusted trial balance at December 31, 2005.
d. Prepare adjusting general journal entries and post them to the ledger accounts. In addition to the entries you have previously made, the following information is also available:

1. As of December 31, Sharpe owes wages of $900 for the last two days of December.
2. Equipment is depreciated using the straight-line method over five years with $2,200 residual value.

e. Prepare an adjusted trial balance for the company.
f. Using the information from the adjusted trial balance, prepare an income statement and a statement of retained earnings for the month of December 2005 and a balance sheet as of December 31, 2005.

g. Using information from the cash entries on the general journal, prepare a statement of cash flows for the company.

h. Prepare and post the closing entries as of December 31, 2005, to close the year.

i. Prepare a post-closing trial balance at December 31, 2005.

LO PART II, 1, 2 ,3, 4, 5, 7, & 8: JOURNAL ENTRIES, POSTING, TRIAL BALANCE, ADJUSTING ENTRIES, FINANCIAL STATEMENTS INCLUDING STATEMENT OF CASH FLOWS, CLOSING ENTRIES

6–73. James and William Blues began a management consulting business on October 1, 2005, called Blues Brothers Consulting, Inc. The following transactions occurred in the month of October 2005:

Oct 1   Blues Brothers Consulting, Inc., sold 1,000 shares of its $1 par common stock for $10,000 cash.

     1   Purchased office equipment for $5,000, paying $1,000 cash and signing a 10 percent, one-year promissory note for the balance. The equipment has an expected life of five years with a $500 residual value.

     1   Paid three months' rent in advance totaling $3,000.

     5   Purchased office supplies on account from Spring Company for $700.

     6   Paid $600 for a one-year insurance policy.

   10   Performed consulting services and billed Sam Hall Company $14,000 on account.

   11   Provided consulting services for Betty Collins Corporation receiving cash of $4,000.

   15   Paid for the office supplies purchased from Spring Company on the 5th.

   15   Provided consulting services to Lynne Munter Interior Design, Inc., receiving cash of $2,000.

   15   Billed Gary Sumter Enterprises $5,000 for consulting fees earned.

   16   Paid secretary wages for the first half of the month totaling $1,000.

   19   Purchased computer supplies on account from Dale Company, $400.

   20   Purchased office supplies for cash totaling $400.

   20   Received payment from Sam Hall for payment of his October 10 invoice.

   25   Received a check from Gary Sumter Enterprises for payment of invoice.

   28   Provided services on account to Dan Lee for $1,600.

   28   Paid $300 for electricity used during October.

   28   Received telephone bill for $250 for telephone service for the month of October.

   28   Paid Dale Company for the invoice of October 19.

   31   Paid wages for the second half of October, $1,500.

   31   Received a bill from ***Kinko's*** for October's copy services for $100.

   31   Paid cash dividends of $2,700.

Required:

a. Journalize the transactions for the month of October in the general journal.

b. Open the necessary accounts in the general ledger and post the October transactions to the appropriate accounts.

c. Prepare an unadjusted trial balance at October 31, 2005.

d. Prepare adjusting general journal entries and post them to the ledger accounts. In addition to the entries you have previously made, the following information is also available:

   1. Office supplies of $100 were on hand at October 31.

   2. There were no computer supplies left at year end.

e. Prepare an adjusted trial balance.

f. Using the information from the adjusted trial balance, prepare an income statement and statement of stockholders' equity for the month of October 2005 and a balance sheet as of October 31, 2005.

g. Using information from the cash entries on the general journal, prepare a statement of cash flows for the company.

h. Assume that Blues Brothers Consulting, Inc., selected October 31 as the year end. Prepare and post the closing entries to close the year.

i. Prepare a post-closing trial balance at October 31, 2005.

ANNUAL REPORT PROJECT

6–74. Section 6—Finding Peer Companies and Peer Company Comparisons

By now you have learned a lot about the company you selected for your annual report project. For this assignment, you will select another company in the same industry, a peer company. Peer companies are companies that are similar to one another, usually in the same industry and of similar size, which analysts use for financial comparisons.

Required:

a. Select a peer company. Sometimes peer companies are obvious. For example, if you were analyzing a large airline like ***American,*** it is fairly obvious that you would select another large airline like ***United.*** If you are having trouble selecting a peer company, one way you can find one is to use the Securities and Exchange Commission's (SEC's) Electronic Data Gathering, Analysis, and Retrieval (EDGAR) system. In case you need it, we have listed the step-by-step instructions to help you find a peer company using the SEC's EDGAR system.

Step-by-step instructions to find peer companies using the SEC's Web site:

1. Go to the SEC's home page at *www.sec.gov.*
2. Click on *Search for Company Filings* (listed under *"Filings and Forms (EDGAR)"*).
3. Click on *Search Companies and Filings.*
4. Enter your company's name (the name of the company you selected for your project) in the appropriate place and click *Find Companies.*
5. The company's Standard Industrial Classification (SIC) code and a description of the company's industry will appear just under the company's name in the upper left area of the page. For example, for ***Pier 1 Imports, Inc.,*** the following information appears on the Web page just under the SEC's logo and seal:

```
PIER 1 IMPORTS INC
SIC: 5700 - Retail - Home Furniture, Furnishings & Equipment Stores
```

6. Click on your company's SIC code. In ***Pier 1***'s case, you would click on 5700.
7. A list of companies classified under that SIC code will appear.
8. Click on several of the companies and examine their Form 10-K to find a company that is a good fit. Try to find a company of similar size (based on sales revenues or total assets) in a business that appears to closely match that of the company you selected for your annual report project.

b. Once you have selected a peer company, locate its latest Form 10-K in the EDGAR system. You will need to print out the peer company's Form 10-K to obtain the information necessary to calculate financial ratios for this and later sections of this annual report project.

c. Prepare a report that compares the following ratios for your company with those of the peer company you selected. Keep in mind that you have already calculated each of the ratios for your company in earlier sections of this project.

- Debt ratio for two years
- Debt-to-equity ratio for two years
- Gross profit margin ratios for three years
- Net profit margin ratios for three years
- Rate of return on assets ratio for the latest year
- Rate of return on common equity ratio for the latest year
- Dividend payout ratio for three years
- Earnings per share for three years
- Price-to-earnings ratio for the latest year

d. Comment in your report on the information that the comparison of each one of the ratios provides. How does your company compare to its peer? And where applicable, comment on how your company has performed over time relative to the peer company you selected.

e. Your report should conclude with comments regarding what you think of your company and how you think your company compares to its peer in light of the work you did in connection with this assignment.

CHAPTER 7

Long-Lived Depreciable Assets— A Closer Look

Let's say you are about to invest in one of two moving and storage companies. Both companies appear interesting, but you would like to review some of the companies' financial information before you make a decision. At your request, the companies, Straight-Line Movers and Accelerated Movers, provide you with 2002 financial statements, the data from which appear in Exhibit 7–1 on page F–266.

After reviewing the two companies' financial statements, you conclude that Straight-Line Movers definitely appears to be the stronger of the two. Not only does Straight-Line have greater net income, but its assets and its equity are greater as well. The investment decision seems easy. But is it really that simple? Is Straight-Line Movers really a more solid company than Accelerated? Upon closer examination, you notice that depreciation expense plays a major role in the differences between the two companies. You need to have a good understanding of depreciation before you can tell for sure which company is stronger. This chapter will provide you with a basic understanding of the most popular depreciation methods and will help you understand depreciation's influence on the amounts that appear on financial statements.

In virtually every context except accounting, the word depreciation is associated with the declining value of assets over time. One might say that his or her car depreciates by $2,000 a year, meaning that the car's value declines each year by $2,000. In accounting, however, the word depreciation has an entirely different meaning. As you recall from Chapter 5, in an accounting context, **depreciation** is defined as a systematic and rational allocation of the cost of a long-lived asset. You must know about the accounting implications of depreciation because it is a component of the financial reports of ***Target, Eastman Kodak, Sprint,*** and every other company in the United States.

In this chapter, we will extend our coverage of depreciation by considering several issues that further complicate the depreciation process. In Chapter 5, we mentioned that management must estimate an asset's useful life and its residual value in order to calculate annual depreciation expense. In this chapter, we will explore how these estimates affect depreciation expense, net income, and the book value of assets. In addition, we will explore the two most popular methods of depreciation, which are the straight-line method and the double-declining-balance method. Finally, we will look at the gains and losses that occur when a company sells a depreciable asset and how management's estimates and their choice of depreciation method greatly impact the gains or losses the company will recognize.

depreciation The systematic and rational conversion of a long-lived asset's cost from asset to expense in the income statement periods benefited.

Learning Objectives

After completing your work on this chapter, you should be able to do the following:

1. Explain the process of depreciating long-lived assets.

2. Determine depreciation expense using the straight-line and the double-declining-balance depreciation methods.

3. Describe how the use of different depreciation methods affects the income statement and the balance sheet.

Income Statements
For the Year Ended December 31, 2002

	Straight-Line Movers	Accelerated Movers
Sales	$ 769,000	$ 769,000
LESS: Cost of goods sold	295,500	295,500
Gross margin	$ 473,500	$ 473,500
Wages expense	$ 67,500	$ 67,500
Utilities expense	31,000	31,000
Depreciation expense	34,000	114,000
Total operating expenses	(132,500)	(212,500)
Operating income	$ 341,000	$ 261,000
Other revenues and expenses:		
Interest expense	(120,000)	(120,000)
Net income	$ 221,000	$ 141,000

Balance Sheets
December 31, 2002

	Straight-Line Movers	Accelerated Movers
Assets:		
Cash	$226,000	$ 226,000
Accounts receivable	198,000	198,000
Inventory	223,000	223,000
Trucks	$228,000	$228,000
Accumulated depreciation	(34,000)	(114,000)
Trucks, net	194,000	114,000
Total assets	$841,000	$ 761,000
Liabilities:		
Accounts payable	$ 22,000	$ 22,000
Notes payable	61,000	61,000
Total liabilities	$ 83,000	$ 83,000
Owners' equity:		
Common stock	$200,000	$ 200,000
Additional paid-in capital	194,000	194,000
Contributed capital	$394,000	$ 394,000
Retained earnings	364,000	284,000
Total shareholders' equity	758,000	678,000
Total liabilities and owners' equity	$841,000	$ 761,000

EXHIBIT 7–1   2002 Financial Statements of Straight-Line Movers and Accelerated Movers

4. Compare and contrast gains and losses with revenues and expenses.

5. Calculate gains and losses on the disposal of depreciable assets.

6. Describe the true meaning of gains and losses on the disposal of depreciable assets.

7. Prepare journal entries associated with long-lived depreciable assets. (Appendix)

◆ DEPRECIATION

As we've said, *depreciation* is a systematic and rational allocation of the cost of a long-lived asset to the accounting periods benefited. Companies initially record the cost of long-lived property, plant, and equipment as assets. This is appropriate because, like all assets, the property, plant, and equipment have future value. Firms can use these long-lived assets for years to come, usually to help earn revenue. As a company benefits from the use of property, plant, and equipment, accountants use depreciation as a means of transferring their cost from assets to expense. In this way, a company recognizes expense in the period benefited by the use of the asset. As a result, depreciation helps match the expense of using long-lived assets with the revenues the assets helped to produce. What this means is that when **Southwest Airlines** depreciates one of its airplanes, it is trying to match the cost of the aircraft to the revenue that aircraft helped to produce.

When a company determines that it will use an item for more than one income statement period, the company should not recognize the item's entire cost as an expense immediately. Instead, the company should record the item as an asset. Then, in each year of the asset's *useful life*, the company should recognize a portion of the item's cost as an expense. Just how much the company should recognize as expense in a given year depends on several factors, including the company's estimates for the asset's useful life, its residual value (what the company estimates it will be able to sell the asset for at the end of its useful life), and the company's choice of depreciation method.

THE EFFECT OF ESTIMATES

A company's estimates of the length of the asset's useful life and the amount of its residual value directly affect the amount of depreciation expense the company will recognize each year. For example, assume a division of **3Com** purchases a new copy machine for $20,000. If management estimates that the copier has a residual value of $4,000, the asset has a depreciable base of $16,000. An asset's **depreciable base** is the asset's cost less its estimated residual value (also commonly referred to as *salvage value* or *scrap value*). The depreciation expense a company recognizes will differ if it estimates a $3,000 residual value rather than $4,000. By the same token, the amount of depreciation expense a company recognizes each year will differ if the company estimates a useful life of four years rather than five. Exhibit 7–2 shows examples of how residual value and useful life estimates can impact depreciation expense.

depreciable base The total amount of depreciation expense that is allowed to be claimed for an asset during its useful life. The depreciable base is the cost of the asset less its residual value.

EXHIBIT 7–2 Effects of Estimates on Depreciation

Options	Depreciable Base	Annual Expense
Residual value: $4,000, useful life: 4 years	$16,000	$4,000
Residual value: $4,000, useful life: 5 years	$16,000	$3,200
Residual value: $3,000, useful life: 4 years	$17,000	$4,250
Residual value: $3,000, useful life: 5 years	$17,000	$3,400

Discussion Questions

7–1. What factors do you think a company should consider when it determines the estimated useful life of a long-lived asset? How do you think a company determines the asset's estimated residual value?

7–2. Assume that you are the manager of the **3Com** division that has just purchased the $20,000 copy machine. How would the depreciation estimates you make affect how your division's performance appears on the company's financial reports? Would you have any control over this?

7–3. Consider a long-lived asset that costs $30,000. How would net income be affected by using an estimated useful life of four years and an estimated residual value of $5,000 rather than a five-year estimated useful life and a residual value of $5,000? Explain.

As you review financial information, be aware that the estimates companies use for calculating depreciation vary. For example, **UAL Corporation (United Air Lines)** typically depreciates its aircraft over four to 30 years while *Delta* depreciates its flight equipment over 15 to 25 years.

THE EFFECTS OF DIFFERENT DEPRECIATION METHODS

Within generally accepted accounting principles (GAAP), there is some latitude permitted so companies can select accounting procedures that are best suited to fit their needs. Companies may use any of several acceptable methods of depreciation. However, GAAP require companies to provide information about their depreciation estimates and the depreciation methods they choose to use. This information is not generally on the face of the financial statements; it is usually found in the financial statement notes. For example, you won't find the words "depreciation expense" on *General Mills*' income statement, but on page 6, note B, of its 2001 annual report, the company reports it depreciates buildings over 40 to 50 years and equipment over three to 15 years, primarily using the straight-line method. The note goes on to say that depreciation charges for 2001 were $194 million. Although *General Mills* does not specifically show the depreciation expense of $194 million on its income statement, the company includes the amount as part of cost of goods sold, selling, general and administrative expense, and perhaps as other expense classifications as well.

Most companies have more than one depreciable asset, and they are free to choose one method of depreciation for one asset and a totally different method for another. Although many companies use the same depreciation method for all their depreciable assets, some do choose to use more than one depreciation method.

As users of the financial accounting information, it is important that you understand the impact of depreciation method choice on financial statements. To illustrate these effects, we will explore in detail the two most commonly used depreciation methods. The first method we will examine is **straight-line depreciation,** which records an equal amount of depreciation expense in each year of an asset's life. Not only is this the simplest method of depreciation, it is also the one most widely used by companies in the United States. Of the 600 companies surveyed by the authors of *Accounting Trends and Techniques* in 2001, 96 percent used the straight-line method to calculate depreciation expense reported in their financial statements for the year 2000 for at least some of their assets.

The second depreciation method we will study records a larger amount of depreciation expense in the early years of an asset's life and less in the later years. There are several depreciation methods that work this way, and collectively, they are known as **accelerated depreciation methods.** During 2000, about 14 percent of the companies surveyed by the authors of *Accounting Trends and Techniques* used some type of accelerated depreciation for some of their assets. Remember, some companies use more than one type of method. For example, *Chevron Corporation* generally uses an accelerated method to depreciate its plant and equipment in the United States and the straight-line method to depreciate international plant and equipment.

How do companies choose between using straight-line depreciation and an accelerated depreciation method? Recall that a basic premise of accrual accounting is that we should match expenses to the revenues they help produce. Theoretically, then, companies should use straight-line depreciation for assets that produce the same amount of revenue in each period of their useful lives. Conversely, companies should use accelerated depreciation methods for assets that produce more revenue in the early years and a lesser amount as time goes by. However, companies are more likely to choose one depreciation method over another based on the anticipated effect on the financial statements during the asset's useful life. Exhibit 7–3 contrasts straight-line depreciation expense to the amount recorded if an accelerated method is used.

As we explore different depreciation methods, you will see the significant impact a company's choice of depreciation method can have on the accounting information offered to economic decision makers. To illustrate this impact on financial statements, we will contrast straight-line depreciation with the most popular accelerated depreciation method—the double-declining-balance method. We will explore the application of these methods so you can learn the mechanics of how to use them and, more importantly, to demonstrate their impact on reported net income.

---

straight-line depreciation A method of calculating periodic depreciation. The depreciable base of an asset is divided by its estimated useful life. The result is the amount of depreciation expense to be recognized in each year of the item's useful life: (Cost − Residual Value)/N = Annual Depreciation Expense.

accelerated depreciation methods Those methods that record more depreciation expense in the early years of an asset's life and less in the later years.

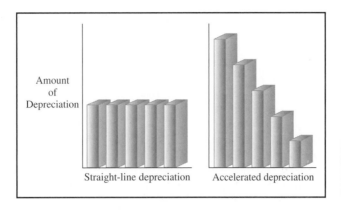

EXHIBIT 7–3   Straight-Line versus Accelerated Depreciation

STRAIGHT-LINE DEPRECIATION

In Chapter 5, we introduced the concept of depreciation with an example of the straight-line method. To review how straight-line depreciation is calculated, assume Barlow Paving Corporation purchased an asphalt paving machine on January 2, 2002, for a total cost of $300,000.

In accounting, when we calculate the cost of a depreciable asset, we include all the costs to bring an asset to a usable state. This includes the invoice price, applicable sales tax, installation costs, cost of insurance while in transit, shipping costs, and cost of training personnel to use the machine. It does not include repairs and maintenance or insurance once the asset becomes productive.

Barlow's management estimates the useful life of this machine to be five years, at the end of which the machine will be sold for an estimated $25,000. For simplicity, we will assume that this machine is the only long-lived asset Barlow owns.

Using the straight-line method, Barlow's yearly depreciation expense is $55,000. To calculate this amount, we determine the depreciable base of $275,000 ($300,000 cost less the $25,000 estimated residual value) and then divide that base by the five-year estimated useful life ($275,000/5 years = $55,000 per year).

What this means is that for each of the five years, $55,000 is removed from the asset total on the balance sheet and is shown as depreciation expense on the income statement. While accountants could accomplish the transfer by decreasing the asset amount itself, they don't. Instead, they use a separate account called *accumulated depreciation* to record the reduction. This way, a company can determine the asset's original cost at any time by simply examining the asset account, in this case, the machine account. Additionally, the company can determine the asset's depreciation to date by examining the accumulated depreciation account, in this case, the accumulated depreciation—machine account. So, the total depreciation expense recognized since the asset was put in service is called **accumulated depreciation.** In other words, accumulated depreciation keeps a running total of all the depreciation that has ever been taken on an asset. When we examine the financial statements for Barlow Paving Corporation, we will see depreciation expense on the income statements of $55,000 for each year and a yearly increase in the balance of accumulated depreciation for the same amount. To illustrate this point, we present Barlow Paving Corporation's income statements and balance sheets for the years 2002 through 2006 using straight-line depreciation in Exhibit 7–4 on page F–270. For ease of interpretation, we have kept the financial statement items not affected by depreciation constant.

Regardless of what else happened in Barlow's operations for the years 2002 through 2006, the depreciation expense remained the same amount each year. Constant depreciation expense is one of the main characteristics of straight-line depreciation. Also note that there is a direct relationship between the yearly depreciation expense on the income statement and the machine's book value on the balance sheets. You will recall from Chapter 5 that **book value** is the cost of a long-lived asset less all the depreciation expense recognized since the asset was placed in service. Therefore,

Cost − Accumulated Depreciation = Book Value

accumulated depreciation   The total amount of cost that has been systematically converted to expense since a long-lived asset was first purchased.

book value   The original cost of a long-lived asset less its accumulated depreciation. This item is often shown on the balance sheet.

Income Statements					
	2002	2003	2004	2005	2006
Sales	$755,000	$755,000	$755,000	$755,000	$755,000
Cost of goods sold	422,000	422,000	422,000	422,000	422,000
Gross margin	$333,000	$333,000	$333,000	$333,000	$333,000
Operating expenses other than depreciation	(236,000)	(236,000)	(236,000)	(236,000)	(236,000)
Depreciation expense	(55,000)	(55,000)	(55,000)	(55,000)	(55,000)
Net income	$ 42,000	$ 42,000	$ 42,000	$ 42,000	$ 42,000

Balance Sheets					
	2002	2003	2004	2005	2006
Assets:					
Cash	$ 50,000	$ 96,000	$157,000	$213,000	$289,000
Accounts receivable	206,000	257,000	293,000	334,000	355,000
Inventory	77,000	77,000	77,000	77,000	77,000
Machine	300,000	300,000	300,000	300,000	300,000
LESS: Accumulated depreciation	(55,000)	(110,000)	(165,000)	(220,000)	(275,000)
Total assets	$578,000	$620,000	$662,000	$704,000	$746,000
Liabilities and stockholders' equity:					
Accounts payable	$206,000	$206,000	$206,000	$206,000	$206,000
Notes payable	170,000	170,000	170,000	170,000	170,000
Common stock	100,000	100,000	100,000	100,000	100,000
Additional paid-in capital	10,000	10,000	10,000	10,000	10,000
Retained earnings	92,000	134,000	176,000	218,000	260,000
Total liabilities and stockholders' equity	$578,000	$620,000	$662,000	$704,000	$746,000

EXHIBIT 7–4 Barlow Paving Corporation's Financial Statements Using Straight-Line Depreciation

Each year, as the company recognizes $55,000 in depreciation expense, the balance of accumulated depreciation increases by that amount. The net effect is a reduction in the asset's book value by that same $55,000. This example illustrates that straight-line depreciation causes the book value of assets to decrease by the same amount each year. Barlow recorded a total of $275,000 in depreciation expense. The book value at the end of 2006 is $25,000 ($300,000 cost − $275,000 accumulated depreciation). An asset's depreciable base is equal to the total amount of depreciation expense allowed throughout the asset's life. Once all of the allowable depreciation expense has been recognized for an assets entire useful life, the asset is **fully depreciated.** So you see, it is no coincidence that the book value of a fully depreciated asset is equal to the asset's estimated residual value.

fully depreciated   When all of the allowable depreciation expense has been recognized for an asset's entire useful life.

Discussion Question

7–4. Refer to Exhibit 7–2, which illustrates *3Com*'s four estimate options for its new copy machine. For each option, determine what the book value would be after three years of straight-line depreciation.

Obviously, a different estimated useful life or a different estimated residual value would cause the amount of yearly depreciation expense to be different. So, too, would the selection of a different method of calculating yearly depreciation expense. To demonstrate the effect of selecting one depreciation method over another, we will now explore the most widely used accelerated depreciation method.

DOUBLE-DECLINING-BALANCE DEPRECIATION

double-declining-balance method   An accelerated depreciation method in which depreciation expense is twice the straight-line percentage multiplied by the book value of the asset.

The **double-declining-balance method** got its name because it calculates depreciation expense at twice the straight-line depreciation rate. Note that we said twice the straight-line *rate*, not twice the straight-line *amount*. The difference is subtle, but very important. If you don't pick up on that difference (which we'll demonstrate shortly), you will fall into the trap of thinking that double-declining-balance depreciation records twice as much depreciation expense each year as the amount recorded using straight-line depreciation.

Rather than using the depreciable base to calculate yearly depreciation expense as the straight-line method does, double-declining-balance calculates depreciation expense for a given year by applying a percentage depreciation rate to the current book value of the asset. As a result, the double-declining-balance method ignores the estimated residual value in the depreciation calculation—though, as we will see, companies using this method must be careful not to depreciate an asset beyond its residual value.

There are three steps to calculating depreciation using the double-declining-balance method:

1. Determine the straight-line rate of depreciation as a percentage. (100% / N, where N = number of years in the asset's useful life.)
2. Double the straight-line percentage.
3. Apply that percentage to the current book value of the asset. Book value declines with the deduction of each year's depreciation so that even though the percentage applied is constant, the amount of depreciation expense decreases each year.

As an example, let's use the double-declining-balance method to determine the depreciation expense for Barlow's paving machine.

1. 100% / 5 = 20% (per year)
2. 20% × 2 = 40% (per year)
3. $300,000 × 40% = $120,000 (for the first year)

For 2002, Barlow Paving Corporation would record $120,000 depreciation expense using the double-declining-balance method.

Note that in the first year of the asset's useful life, before any depreciation has been recorded, the book value of the asset we use in Step 3 equals the cost of the asset. In later years, however, the book value of the asset equals the asset's cost minus its accumulated depreciation.

Exhibit 7–5 shows how yearly depreciation expense would be calculated on Barlow's $300,000 machine using double-declining-balance depreciation, a $25,000 residual value, and a five-year estimated useful life.

EXHIBIT 7–5   Book Value and Double-Declining-Balance Depreciation Calculations

	Book Value Calculation			Depreciation Calculation		
Year	Cost	Accumulated Depreciation	Book Value	Book Value	Rate	Depreciation Expense
2002	$300,000 −	$ 0 =	$300,000	$300,000 ×	40% =	$120,000
2003	$300,000 −	$120,000 =	$180,000	$180,000 ×	40% =	$ 72,000
2004	$300,000 −	$192,000 =	$108,000	$108,000 ×	40% =	$ 43,200
2005	$300,000 −	$235,200 =	$ 64,800	$ 64,800 ×	40% =	$ 25,920
2006	$300,000 −	$261,120 =	$ 38,880			$ 13,880
2007	$300,000 −	$275,000 =	$ 25,000			$ 0
				Total depreciation expense		$275,000

As you examine the calculations in the exhibit, note several points. First, the book value of the machine declines each year by the amount of depreciation expense of the prior year. For example, the book value at the beginning of 2002 is the full $300,000 cost of the machine. At the beginning of 2003, the book value drops to $180,000 (the $300,000 cost − $120,000 depreciation for 2002). The book value of the machine continues to drop until, at the beginning of 2006, it is $38,880.

The second thing to note in Exhibit 7–5 is that depreciation expense for 2006 ($13,880) is not 40 percent of the book value at the beginning of the year. The amount of depreciation expense in 2006 is limited to $13,880 because companies are not allowed to depreciate assets beyond the point at which the book value of the asset is equal to its estimated residual value. In other words, the book value of an asset may never be lower than its residual value. As Exhibit 7–5 shows, total depreciation over the five-year life of the asset is $275,000, and it is not by chance that this amount is the asset's depreciable base. Even when double-declining-balance depreciation is used, total depreciation expense over the life of the asset cannot exceed the asset's depreciable base (cost − residual value). As the book value declines toward the residual value of the asset and the accumulated depreciation rises toward the maximum depreciation allowed, we must be careful not to exceed the limits. When the double-declining-balance depreciation method is used, the last year's depreciation expense is not equal to the asset's book value times the double-declining-balance rate; rather, it is the amount required to reduce the book value of the asset to its estimated residual value. This is the maximum depreciation expense allowed in that period. At that point, the asset is fully depreciated.

The third point to note about the double-declining-balance calculations is that during an asset's useful life, yearly depreciation expense starts out high but quickly decreases. This decrease is characteristic of all accelerated depreciation methods and has a profound effect on the financial statements of companies using accelerated depreciation. Exhibit 7–6 illustrates this with Barlow Paving Corporation's income statements and balance sheets for 2002 through 2006, this time using the double-declining-balance depreciation method. As with our straight-line depreciation presentation, we have kept the items not affected by the company's choice of depreciation method constant from year to year.

Discussion Questions •••

7–5. Based on Barlow Paving Corporation's financial statements in Exhibit 7–6, and assuming no dividends were declared during 2002, what was the balance in retained earnings at the beginning of 2002?

7–6. Prepare the 2002 statement of retained earnings assuming Barlow Paving Corporation had not recorded *any* depreciation on its paving machine.

UNDERSTANDING THE IMPACT OF DEPRECIATION METHOD CHOICE

When you compare Barlow Paving Corporation's financial statements using straight-line depreciation (Exhibit 7–4) with Barlow's financial statements for the same period using double-declining-balance depreciation (Exhibit 7–6), notice several differences and several similarities:

- There is a significant difference in Barlow's depreciation expense in each of the five years.
- There is a significant difference in Barlow's net income in each of the five years.
- *Total* depreciation expense and *total* net income over the entire five-year period are exactly the same regardless of which depreciation method Barlow uses. The differences occur in the individual years but balance out by the time the asset is fully depreciated.
- There is a significant difference in the amounts of accumulated depreciation on the balance sheets for each of the years from 2002 through 2005. The 2006 balance

Income Statements

	2002	2003	2004	2005	2006
Sales	$755,000	$755,000	$755,000	$755,000	$755,000
Cost of goods sold	422,000	422,000	422,000	422,000	422,000
Gross margin	$333,000	$333,000	$333,000	$333,000	$333,000
Operating expenses other than depreciation	(236,000)	(236,000)	(236,000)	(236,000)	(236,000)
Depreciation expense	(120,000)	(72,000)	(43,200)	(25,920)	(13,880)
Net income	$(23,000)	$ 25,000	$ 53,800	$ 71,080	$ 83,120

Balance Sheets

	2002	2003	2004	2005	2006
Assets:					
Cash	$ 50,000	$ 96,000	$157,000	$213,000	$289,000
Accounts receivable	206,000	257,000	293,000	334,000	355,000
Inventory	77,000	77,000	77,000	77,000	77,000
Machine	300,000	300,000	300,000	300,000	300,000
LESS: Accumulated depreciation	(120,000)	(192,000)	(235,200)	(261,120)	(275,000)
Total assets	$513,000	$538,000	$591,800	$662,880	$746,000
Liabilities and stockholders' equity:					
Accounts payable	$206,000	$206,000	$206,000	$206,000	$206,000
Notes payable	170,000	170,000	170,000	170,000	170,000
Common stock	100,000	100,000	100,000	100,000	100,000
Additional paid-in capital	10,000	10,000	10,000	10,000	10,000
Retained earnings	27,000	52,000	105,800	176,880	260,000
Total liabilities and stockholders' equity	$513,000	$538,000	$591,800	$662,880	$746,000

EXHIBIT 7–6   Barlow Paving Corporation's Financial Statements Using Double-Declining-Balance Depreciation

sheet, however, shows exactly the same amount of accumulated depreciation in both presentations. In fact, the 2006 balance sheets in the two presentations are identical.

We are not saying that one method of depreciation is better than the other. But our presentation does point out that, if we look at a company's financial statements from one year to the next, the company's choice of one depreciation method over another will affect its reported net income and certain amounts that appear on its balance sheets.

Discussion Questions

7–7. Examine Exhibits 7–4 and 7–6 and explain why the 2006 balance sheets on the exhibits are identical even though they reflect different depreciation methods. Also explain why all five income statements and the first four years' balance sheets are different.

7–8. Examine Exhibits 7–4 and 7–6. How does the amount of cash Barlow shows using straight-line depreciation each year compare to what the company shows when we assume it uses double-declining-balance depreciation? Explain your findings.

We have now seen how Barlow's machine would be depreciated using either the straight-line method or the double-declining-balance method. Exhibit 7–7 summarizes the results by presenting a comparison of the depreciation expense, net income, and book value of the machine using the two different methods.

EXHIBIT 7–7   Straight-Line vs. Double-Declining-Balance Depreciation—A Comparison of Depreciation Expense, Net Income, and Book Value

	Straight-Line			*Double-Declining-Balance*		
Year	*Depreciation Expense*	*Net Income*	*Book Value of Machine*	*Depreciation Expense*	*Net Income*	*Book Value of Machine*
2002	$ 55,000	$ 42,000	$245,000	$120,000	($ 23,000)	$180,000
2003	$ 55,000	$ 42,000	$190,000	$ 72,000	$ 25,000	$108,000
2004	$ 55,000	$ 42,000	$135,000	$ 43,200	$ 53,800	$ 64,800
2005	$ 55,000	$ 42,000	$ 80,000	$ 25,920	$ 71,080	$ 38,880
2006	$ 55,000	$ 42,000	$ 25,000	$ 13,880	$ 83,120	$ 25,000
Total	$275,000	$210,000		$275,000	$210,000	

We used double-declining-balance depreciation to demonstrate the impact of accelerated depreciation on financial statements. Other accelerated methods include the 150 percent-declining-balance method and the sum-of-the-year's-digits method. **Boeing,** for example, uses the 150 percent-declining-balance method for buildings and land improvements and the sum-of-the-year's-digits method for machinery and equipment. Although we will not delve into the calculations for these methods, if you see them in financial reports, you should know that although they are not as aggressive as the double-declining-balance method, they are accelerated depreciation methods all the same.

Discussion Question

7–9. Assume that Exhibit 7–7 depicts information from two different companies, one using straight-line and the other double-declining-balance. If you were making an investment decision based solely on information available up to 2002, which company would *appear* to be the most attractive investment? Explain why this appearance could be deceptive.

◆ DISPOSAL OF DEPRECIABLE ASSETS

historical cost principal
The accounting principal that requires balance sheet amounts generally to be shown at acquisition price rather than fair value.

In a perfect world, a company would use a depreciable asset for exactly the time it had originally estimated, and then it would sell the asset for an amount equal to the asset's original estimated residual value. In reality, this almost never happens. The actual useful life of an asset may differ greatly from its estimated useful life. In fact, a company may dispose of (sell or scrap) an asset at any time, even long before the asset reaches the end of its estimated useful life. No laws prohibit a company from selling an asset before the end of its depreciable life, nor must a company stop using or dispose of an asset when it is fully depreciated. For example, the fact that **UPS** estimates the useful life of its delivery vans to be five years does not mean that the company cannot use the vans for a longer period of time. From a business perspective, **UPS** should continue to use a delivery van as long as the van is economically serviceable regardless of the van's estimated useful life.

According to the conceptual framework's **historical cost principal,** amounts are generally shown on the balance sheet at acquisition price, not at fair value. Therefore it is unlikely that an asset will be sold for the amount shown on the balance sheet. Additionally, there is no guarantee that a company will receive an amount equal to the asset's estimated residual value when it finally sells the asset. When companies sell their used equipment, machinery, trucks, and other depreciable assets, they may sell them for more or less than their estimated residual value. Companies try to sell these assets for as much as they reasonably can, but they do not limit their selling price by the estimated residual value, nor do they insist on receiving an amount equal to the asset's residual value when the asset is just not worth that much. They sell the assets for what they can get. Generally, estimated useful lives and estimated residual values used for depreciation calculation are not significant considerations in decisions regarding whether or not a company should dispose of an asset or the amount for which depreciable assets should be sold.

Disposing of depreciable assets is usually not associated with a company's ongoing major or central activity. Rather, this type of transaction is most often incidental or peripheral to the day-to-day operation of the business. For this reason, we do not normally classify any increase in equity from the disposal of depreciable assets as revenue, or any decrease in equity associated with this type of transaction as expense. Instead, accountants classify net inflows from the disposal of depreciable assets as gains and net outflows from the disposal of depreciable assets as losses.

GAINS AND LOSSES

Gains and losses are two of the accounting elements discussed by the Financial Accounting Standards Board (FASB) in its *Conceptual Framework of Accounting* (see Exhibit 7–8 on page F–276). As we discuss these two elements, we will provide the actual FASB definitions in italics, followed by a brief explanation of each.

gains Net inflows resulting from peripheral activities of a company. An example is the sale of an asset for more than its book value.

- **Gains**—*Increases in equity from peripheral or incidental transactions of an entity and from all other transactions and other events and circumstances affecting the entity except those that result from revenues or investments by owners* (Statement of Financial Accounting Concepts No. 6, paragraph 82). As you may recall from our discussion of revenue recognition in Chapter 5, gains are very similar to revenues because both are inflows of assets. The source of the inflows is what distinguishes these two elements from one another. Revenues are generated by the company's major business activities while gains result from peripheral or incidental business activities. As we will soon learn, another distinction between revenues and gains is that revenues generally represent only inflows of assets, but gains often represent the netting of inflows and outflows associated with a particular transaction or type of transaction.

losses Net outflows resulting from peripheral activities of a company. An example is the sale of an asset for less than its book value.

- **Losses**—*Decreases in equity from peripheral or incidental transactions of an entity and from all other transactions and other events and circumstances affecting the entity except those that result from expenses or distributions to owners* (Statement of Financial Accounting Concepts No. 6, paragraph 83). Recall from our discussion of expense recognition in Chapter 5 that losses are very similar to expenses because both are outflows of assets. As was the case with gains and revenues, losses and expenses differ by source. Expenses are the results of the company's major business activity, whereas losses generally result from other activities. Unlike gains, which are always associated with peripheral or incidental transactions, losses are sometimes associated with a company's major business activity. Losses of this type generally reflect the decline in value of operating assets, such as inventory. Another distinction between expenses and losses is that expenses generally represent only outflows of assets, but losses often represent the netting of the inflows and outflows associated with a particular transaction or type of transaction.

Keep in mind that an income statement provides information about the past performance of a company. This type of information can help decision makers better predict a company's future performance. Because all gains and many losses are incidental to a company's central operations, they may be less significant to decision makers than the revenues and expenses from the company's central operations. To allow decision makers to evaluate the inflows from a company's major or central operations (revenues) separately from the inflows from incidental activities (gains), the two are reported separately on the income statement. For example, *AMC Entertainment, Inc.,* reported a $664,000 gain on the disposal of assets in 2002 separately from theater admissions and concession revenue. The same treatment applies to expenses and

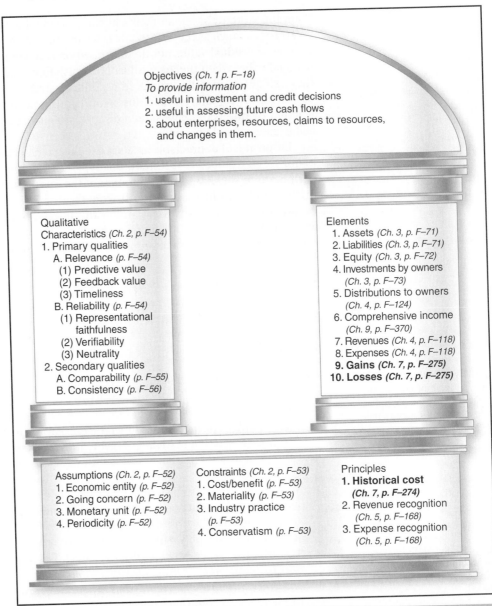

Objectives *(Ch. 1 p. F–18)*
To provide information
1. useful in investment and credit decisions
2. useful in assessing future cash flows
3. about enterprises, resources, claims to resources, and changes in them.

Qualitative
Characteristics *(Ch. 2, p. F–54)*
1. Primary qualities
  A. Relevance *(p. F–54)*
    (1) Predictive value
    (2) Feedback value
    (3) Timeliness
  B. Reliability *(p. F–54)*
    (1) Representational
       faithfulness
    (2) Verifiability
    (3) Neutrality
2. Secondary qualities
  A. Comparability *(p. F–55)*
  B. Consistency *(p. F–56)*

Elements
1. Assets *(Ch. 3, p. F–71)*
2. Liabilities *(Ch. 3, p. F–71)*
3. Equity *(Ch. 3, p. F–72)*
4. Investments by owners
   (Ch. 3, p. F–73)
5. Distributions to owners
   (Ch. 4, p. F–124)
6. Comprehensive income
   (Ch. 9, p. F–370)
7. Revenues *(Ch. 4, p. F–118)*
8. Expenses *(Ch. 4, p. F–118)*
9. Gains *(Ch. 7, p. F–275)*
10. Losses *(Ch. 7, p. F–275)*

Assumptions *(Ch. 2, p. F–52)*
1. Economic entity *(p. F–52)*
2. Going concern *(p. F–52)*
3. Monetary unit *(p. F–52)*
4. Periodicity *(p. F–52)*

Constraints *(Ch. 2, p. F–53)*
1. Cost/benefit *(p. F–53)*
2. Materiality *(p. F–53)*
3. Industry practice
  (p. F–53)
4. Conservatism *(p. F–53)*

Principles
1. Historical cost
   (Ch. 7, p. F–274)
2. Revenue recognition
   (Ch. 5, p. F–168)
3. Expense recognition
   (Ch. 5, p. F–168)

EXHIBIT 7–8   Conceptual Framework of Accounting—Gains and Losses Highlighted

losses. The income statement reports the outflows from major or central business operations (expenses) separately from outflows from incidental activities (losses).

Although the income statement reports revenues separate from gains, and expenses separate from losses, gains affect net income in exactly the same way that revenues do, and the effect of losses is exactly the same as that of expenses. With the addition of gains and losses, we can expand the income statement equation introduced in Chapter 4 as follows:

$$\text{Revenues} + \text{Gains} - \text{Expenses} - \text{Losses} = \text{Net Income}$$

CALCULATING GAINS AND LOSSES

Calculating gains and losses that result from the disposal of depreciable assets is straightforward. When a company sells a depreciable asset, the difference between the amount the company receives (most often cash) and the book value of the asset sold is the amount of gain or loss on the sale. Let's return once again to the Barlow Paving Corporation and its $300,000 paving machine. Assume Barlow depreciated this machine using the straight-line method over a five-year estimated useful life, with an estimated residual value of $25,000 (Exhibit 7–4). Assume further that it is now January 2, 2007, and Barlow is selling the machine. As of the end of 2006, the machine has a $25,000 book value ($300,000 cost − $275,000 accumulated depreciation). For how much should Barlow sell the machine? If your answer is $25,000, you should reconsider — $25,000 is the book value of the machine, not its market value. Barlow will sell the machine for as much as it can get. The book value is based on an estimate made way back in 2002. In truth, potential buyers will neither know nor care about the book value as reflected in Barlow's records. A buyer will pay what she or he thinks the item is worth. This amount will depend on a number of factors, such as the condition of the machine, the state of technology, and the selling prices of comparable used machines. It's highly unlikely that Barlow will receive exactly $25,000, but we do not have enough information to determine whether Barlow will receive more or less.

Gain on Disposal

Assume Barlow is able to sell the machine for a cash price of $32,000. Because Barlow has received more than the book value of the machine, there is a gain, which we calculated as $7,000 ($32,000 cash received − $25,000 book value). Barlow will report the $7,000 as a gain on its income statement for the year 2007. Exhibit 7–9 shows Barlow's income statements and balance sheets for 2006 and 2007 reflecting a $7,000 gain on the disposal of its machine.

EXHIBIT 7–9   Barlow Paving Corporation's Financial Statements Reflecting a Gain on the Sale of Machine

Barlow Paving Corporation
Income Statements

	2006	2007
Sales	$755,000	$941,000
Cost of goods sold	422,000	525,000
Gross margin	$333,000	$416,000
Operating expenses other than depreciation	(236,000)	(319,000)
Depreciation expense	(55,000)	0
Operating income	$ 42,000	$ 97,000
Gain on sale of machine	0	7,000
Net income	$ 42,000	$104,000

Balance Sheets

	2006	2007
Assets:		
Cash	$289,000	$225,000
Accounts receivable	355,000	313,000
Inventory	77,000	172,000
Machine	300,000	0
LESS: Accumulated depreciation	(275,000)	0
Total assets	$746,000	$710,000
Liabilities and stockholders' equity:		
Accounts payable	$206,000	$216,000
Notes payable	170,000	20,000
Common stock	100,000	100,000
Additional paid-in capital	10,000	10,000
Retained earnings	260,000	364,000
Total liabilities and stockholders' equity	$746,000	$710,000

As you examine the financial statements in Exhibit 7–9, there are several things to note:

- Barlow's 2007 income statement shows the $7,000 gain in a different place than it shows the revenues from its ongoing major operations.
- The $7,000 gain has exactly the same effect on net income as revenues from Barlow's ongoing major operations.
- Because Barlow no longer owns the machine, it has removed both the cost of the machine ($300,000) and the machine's accumulated depreciation ($275,000) from its balance sheet as of the end of 2007.

Discussion Question

7–10. Note that Barlow Paving Corporation's income statements are presented in a multiple-step format in Exhibit 7–9. What specific items on the income statements are unique to this format and would not appear on a single-step statement?

Loss on Disposal

Now assume Barlow is able to sell the machine for a cash price of only $19,000. Because the company received less than the book value of the machine, there is a loss, which we calculate as $6,000 ($19,000 cash received − $25,000 book value). Barlow will report the $6,000 as a loss on its income statement for the year 2007. Exhibit 7–10 shows Barlow's income statements and balance sheets for 2006 and 2007 reflecting the $6,000 loss on the disposal of its machine.

EXHIBIT 7–10 Barlow Paving Corporation's Financial Statements Reflecting a Loss on the Sale of Machine

Barlow Paving Corporation
Income Statements

	2006	2007
Sales	$755,000	$941,000
Cost of goods sold	422,000	525,000
Gross margin	$333,000	$416,000
Operating expenses other than depreciation	(236,000)	(319,000)
Depreciation expense	(55,000)	0
Operating income	$ 42,000	$ 97,000
Loss on sale of machine	0	(6,000)
Net income	$ 42,000	$ 91,000

Balance Sheets

	2006	2007
Assets:		
Cash	$289,000	$212,000
Accounts receivable	355,000	313,000
Inventory	77,000	172,000
Machine	300,000	0
LESS: Accumulated depreciation	(275,000)	0
Total assets	$746,000	$697,000
Liabilities and stockholders' equity:		
Accounts payable	$206,000	$216,000
Notes payable	170,000	20,000
Common stock	100,000	100,000
Additional paid-in capital	10,000	10,000
Retained earnings	260,000	351,000
Total liabilities and stockholders' equity	$746,000	$697,000

As you examine the financial statements in Exhibit 7–10, there are several things to note:

- Barlow's 2007 income statement shows the $6,000 loss in a different place than it shows the expenses required for its ongoing major operations.
- The $6,000 loss has exactly the same effect on net income as expenses required for Barlow's ongoing major operations.
- Because Barlow no longer owns the machine, it has removed both the cost of the machine ($300,000) and the accumulated depreciation ($275,000) from its balance sheet as of the end of 2007.

In our examples of both a gain and a loss, we have assumed that Barlow was able to sell its machine for some amount of cash. However, there are times when an asset has no market value, so the company must simply scrap it. If this were the case with Barlow's machine, it would result in a loss of $25,000 ($0 cash received − $25,000 book value).

Discussion Question

7–11. Refer to Barlow Paving Corporation's income statements and balance sheets in Exhibit 7–10. What items on the financial statements for the year 2007 would be different (and by how much) if Barlow had scrapped the machine?

Disposal with No Gain or Loss

Now let's assume Barlow is able to sell the machine for a cash price of $25,000. Because the company received exactly the book value of the machine, there is neither a gain nor a loss ($25,000 cash received −$25,000 book value = $0 gain or loss). As Exhibit 7–11 shows, under these circumstances, the sale of the machine will not directly affect the income statement for the year 2007, but it will affect the balance sheet.

EXHIBIT 7–11   Barlow Paving Corporation's Financial Statements Reflecting the Sale of Its Machine for Book Value

Barlow Paving Corporation
Income Statements

	2006	2007
Sales	$755,000	$941,000
Cost of goods sold	422,000	525,000
Gross margin	$333,000	$416,000
Operating expenses other than depreciation	(236,000)	(319,000)
Depreciation expense	(55,000)	0
Operating income	$ 42,000	$ 97,000
Gain (loss) on sale of machine	0	0
Net income	$ 42,000	$ 97,000

Balance Sheets

	2006	2007
Assets:		
Cash	$289,000	$218,000
Accounts receivable	355,000	313,000
Inventory	77,000	172,000
Machine	300,000	0
LESS: Accumulated depreciation	(275,000)	0
Total assets	$746,000	$703,000
Liabilities and stockholders' equity:		
Accounts payable	$206,000	$216,000
Notes payable	170,000	20,000
Common stock	100,000	100,000
Additional paid-in capital	10,000	10,000
Retained earnings	260,000	357,000
Total liabilities and stockholders' equity	$746,000	$703,000

As you examine the financial statements in Exhibit 7–11, there are two things to note:

- There is no gain or loss from the disposal of the machine on the income statement for the year 2007.
- Because Barlow no longer owns the machine, it has removed both the cost of the machine ($300,000) and the accumulated depreciation ($275,000) from its balance sheet as of the end of 2007.

Thus far, we have examined how to calculate gains and losses, as well as how these elements affect a company's financial statements. Next, we will explore how to interpret gains and losses from the sale of depreciable assets in light of the effects of depreciation estimates and the selection of one depreciation method over another.

◆ UNDERSTANDING THE TRUE MEANING OF GAINS AND LOSSES

To demonstrate the true meaning of gains and losses, let's assume there are two companies—Straight-Line Movers and Accelerated Movers—whose business activities are identical in almost every respect. The companies have the exact same sales for the year, and all their operating expenses (except depreciation) are the same.

Each company purchased a fleet of trucks for $228,000 on January 2, 2002. In addition, both companies estimated a useful life of four years and a residual value of $92,000 for the trucks. Because Straight-Line Movers uses—you guessed it—straight-line depreciation and Accelerated Movers uses the double-declining-balance (accelerated) method, we would expect to see differences in their financial statements. The 2002 income statement and balance sheet for each company appear in Exhibit 7–12.

Discussion Questions ●

Refer to Exhibit 7–12 to answer the following questions:

7–12. The income statements show the amount of depreciation expense for each company. Provide computations that show how each company determined its depreciation expense.

7–13. Between companies, four items on the income statements differ and six items on the balance sheets differ. Identify each item and explain the cause of the difference.

The impact of the choice of depreciation method becomes even more evident over time. Exhibit 7–13 on page F–282 shows the income statements and balance sheets of Straight-Line Movers and Accelerated Movers at the end of 2003. Again, we have held constant the items that are not affected by using different depreciation methods.

Discussion Question ●

7–14. Provide computations and an explanation to show how Accelerated Movers determined the depreciation expense of $22,000 shown in Exhibit 7–13.

As we have seen, the use of different depreciation methods causes a profound effect on depreciation expense and other financial statement amounts. An even more striking impact occurs when we examine the effect of the use of different depreciation methods on the gains and losses companies recognize when they sell depreciable assets. For example, suppose that Straight-Line Movers and Accelerated Movers both decide to sell their trucks on December 31, 2003. The assets the companies are selling are identical in age, condition, and market value. Each company receives $150,000 cash in exchange for its trucks, the market value of the trucks on the day of the sale. Even though the companies are selling their trucks, they still have to record depreciation for 2003 because they used the trucks all year. Therefore, the companies would still show depreciation expense on their financial statements for 2003, just as we showed in the previous exhibits.

Income Statements
For the Year Ended December 31, 2002

	Straight-Line Movers	Accelerated Movers
Sales	$769,000	$769,000
LESS: Cost of goods sold	295,500	295,500
Gross margin	$473,500	$473,500
Wages expense	$ 67,500	$ 67,500
Utilities expense	31,000	31,000
Depreciation expense	34,000	114,000
Total operating expenses	(132,500)	(212,500)
Operating income	$341,000	$261,000
Other revenues and expenses:		
Interest expense	(120,000)	(120,000)
Net income	$221,000	$141,000

Balance Sheets
December 31, 2002

	Straight-Line Movers	Accelerated Movers
Assets:		
Cash	$226,000	$226,000
Accounts receivable	198,000	198,000
Inventory	223,000	223,000
Trucks	$228,000	$228,000
Accumulated depreciation	(34,000)	(114,000)
Trucks, net	194,000	114,000
Total assets	$841,000	$761,000
Liabilities:		
Accounts payable	$ 22,000	$ 22,000
Notes payable	61,000	61,000
Total liabilities	$ 83,000	$ 83,000
Owners' equity:		
Common stock	$200,000	$200,000
Additional paid-in capital	194,000	194,000
Contributed capital	$394,000	$394,000
Retained earnings	364,000	284,000
Total shareholders' equity	758,000	678,000
Total liabilities and owners' equity	$841,000	$761,000

EXHIBIT 7–12 2002 Financial Statements of Straight-Line Movers and Accelerated Movers

Discussion Question ●

7–15. Were the companies wise to sell the assets? Did they get "a good deal"? Did one company make a better deal than the other? What information might you want before deciding whether each company made a smart move?

Even though Straight-Line Movers and Accelerated Movers' business activity is identical, the financial statement presentation of the results of the sale of their trucks would be quite different, as Exhibit 7–14 on page F–283 shows.

The most obvious financial statement impact of the different depreciation methods is the resulting gain or loss on the sale of the trucks. Note that Straight-Line Movers recorded a $10,000 loss, but the exact same activity resulted in a $58,000 gain for Accelerated Movers. The moral of the story is that smart financial statement users are not overly impressed by gains or overly alarmed by losses associated with the dis-

Income Statements
For the Year Ended December 31, 2003

	Straight-Line Movers	Accelerated Movers
Sales	$769,000	$769,000
LESS: Cost of goods sold	295,500	295,500
Gross margin	$473,500	$473,500
Wages expense	$ 67,500	$ 67,500
Utilities expense	31,000	31,000
Depreciation expense	34,000	22,000
Total operating expenses	(132,500)	(120,500)
Operating income	$341,000	$353,000
Other revenues and expenses:		
Interest expense	(120,000)	(120,000)
Net income	$221,000	$233,000

Balance Sheets
December 31, 2003

	Straight-Line Movers	Accelerated Movers
Assets:		
Cash	$ 426,000	$426,000
Accounts receivable	253,000	253,000
Inventory	223,000	223,000
Trucks	$ 228,000	$228,000
Accumulated depreciation	(68,000)	(136,000)
Trucks, net	160,000	92,000
Total assets	$1,062,000	$994,000
Liabilities:		
Accounts payable	$ 22,000	$ 22,000
Notes payable	61,000	61,000
Total liabilities	$ 83,000	$ 83,000
Owners' equity:		
Common stock	$ 200,000	$200,000
Additional paid-in capital	194,000	194,000
Contributed capital	$ 394,000	$394,000
Retained earnings	585,000	517,000
Total shareholders' equity	979,000	911,000
Total liabilities and owners' equity	$1,062,000	$994,000

EXHIBIT 7–13   2003 Financial Statements of Straight-Line Movers and Accelerated Movers

posal of depreciable assets. Such gains and losses are merely a result of the difference between the book value and the market value of assets sold. We cannot always assume that a gain from the sale of depreciable assets reflects something that was "good" for business. Likewise, we cannot assume that a loss means that management made a bad move. In our example, there is not enough information available to determine whether the sale of the trucks for $150,000 was a wise business decision or a poor one. Clearly, though, the sale was no wiser for one company than for the other.

Also note that the retained earnings balances for Straight-Line Movers and Accelerated Movers in Exhibit 7–14 are exactly the same—$575,000. As you know, the depreciation process transfers the cost of property, plant, and equipment from assets on the balance sheet to expense on the income statement. By claiming a larger amount of depreciation in the early years of an asset's life—as happens when a company uses accelerated depreciation—a company's net income will be less in those early years. In this way, the company also lowers the asset's book value, which then may be much

Income Statements
For the Year Ended December 31, 2003

	Straight-Line Movers	Accelerated Movers
Sales	$769,000	$769,000
LESS: Cost of goods sold	295,500	295,500
Gross margin	$473,500	$473,500
Wages expense	$ 67,500	$ 67,500
Utilities expense	31,000	31,000
Depreciation expense	34,000	22,000
Total operating expenses	(132,500)	(120,500)
Operating income	$341,000	$353,000
Other revenues and expenses:		
Gain on sale of truck		58,000
Loss on sale of truck	(10,000)	
Interest expense	(120,000)	(120,000)
Net income	$211,000	$291,000

Balance Sheets
December 31, 2003

	Straight-Line Movers	Accelerated Movers
Assets:		
Cash	$ 576,000	$ 576,000
Accounts receivable	253,000	253,000
Inventory	223,000	223,000
Trucks	0	0
Accumulated depreciation	0	0
Trucks, net	0	0
Total assets	$1,052,000	$1,052,000
Liabilities:		
Accounts payable	$ 22,000	$ 22,000
Notes payable	61,000	61,000
Total liabilities	$ 83,000	$ 83,000
Owners' equity:		
Common stock	$ 200,000	$ 200,000
Additional paid-in capital	194,000	194,000
Contributed capital	$ 394,000	$ 394,000
Retained earnings	575,000	575,000
Total shareholders' equity	969,000	969,000
Total liabilities and owners' equity	$1,052,000	$1,052,000

EXHIBIT 7–14   Impact of the Sale of Trucks at the End of 2003 on the Financial Statements of Straight-Line Movers and Accelerated Movers

lower than the asset's market value. In our example, the book value of Accelerated Movers' trucks was so low that the company registered quite a large gain on their sale. Conversely, if a company claims a smaller amount of depreciation in the early years—as happens when using the straight-line method—the asset's book value will be higher. In our example, the book value of Straight-Line Movers' trucks was so high at the time of sale that the company incurred a loss.

Exhibit 7–15 on page F–284 illustrates the effect of the method of depreciation on net income in our example. Note that there are differences between the amounts shown for the two companies in individual years, but over the entire period of ownership, the differences balance out, so the company's choice of depreciation method ultimately has no effect on net income.

	Straight-Line	*Accelerated*
2002 Depreciation expense	$(34,000)	$(114,000)
2003 Depreciation expense	(34,000)	(22,000)
2003 Gain or (loss) resulting from sale of asset	(10,000)	58,000
Total Impact of Asset Ownership	**$(78,000)**	**$ (78,000)**

EXHIBIT 7–15   Long-Term Impact of Depreciation Method on Net Income

Exhibit 7–15 illustrates why it isn't wise for decision makers to focus too much on the impact of gains and losses from the sale of assets without considering the bigger picture. Clearly, gains and losses that result from the sale of assets are only part of the overall financial impact of asset ownership.

◆ OTHER DEPRECIATION METHODS

Thus far, we have examined the two most popular depreciation methods. Although straight-line and double-declining-balance depreciation are the most widely used, there are other methods of depreciation that are worth looking at. These methods include the units-of-production depreciation method and the Modified Accelerated Cost Recovery System (MACRS), the depreciation method that income tax regulations permit.

UNITS-OF-PRODUCTION DEPRECIATION METHOD

units-of-production depreciation method
A straight-line depreciation method that uses production activity as the basis of allocating depreciation expense. Instead of using an amount of depreciation per year, an amount of depreciation per unit produced is used.

Instead of using the estimated useful life in years as the basis for their straight-line depreciation calculations, some companies use the estimated number of units of production. The **units-of-production depreciation method,** or *units-of-activity method* as it is sometimes called, is a straight-line depreciation method that uses production activity as the basis of allocating depreciation expense. Instead of calculating an amount of depreciation per year, when a company uses the units-of-production method, it calculates an amount of depreciation per unit produced. Here, we are using the word *production* to mean whatever the asset normally produces. For example, we would probably define the "production" of a delivery truck as the number of miles traveled and the production of a milling machine as the number of units of product manufactured. *Freeport-McMoran Copper & Gold, Inc.,* uses units-of-production depreciation for its copper mining equipment based on the estimated copper the machines will recover.

To demonstrate the calculations for the units-of-production depreciation method, assume that on January 2, 2003, Rodriguez Trucking purchased a long-haul delivery truck for $125,000. Rodriguez Trucking estimates that it will use the truck for 400,000 miles. At the end of the truck's useful life, Rodriguez estimates that it can sell the truck for $25,000. Using the units-of-production depreciation method, Rodriguez's depreciation expense is $.25 per mile. To calculate this amount, we determine the depreciable base of $100,000 ($125,000 cost less the $25,000 estimated residual value) and then divide that base by the estimated number of miles ($100,000/400,000 miles = $0.25 per mile). If Rodriguez Trucking drives the truck 94,000 miles in 2003, the depreciation expense would be $23,500 (94,000 × $.25). We would calculate depreciation in subsequent years in the same fashion as Exhibit 7–16 shows.

Exhibit 7–16 shows that we used 58,000 miles to calculate the depreciation expense for 2007. However, this does not necessarily mean Rodriguez drove the truck only 58,000 miles that year. Although the company may have used the truck for many more than the 58,000 miles we used to calculate the depreciation expense for 2007, once the company has recorded depreciation on a total of 400,000 miles, the truck is fully depreciated and it should not be depreciated further.

Year	Actual Miles Driven		Depreciation per Mile		Depreciation Expense
2003	94,000	×	$.25	=	$ 23,500
2004	88,000	×	.25	=	22,000
2005	84,000	×	.25	=	21,000
2006	76,000	×	.25	=	19,000
2007	58,000	×	.25	=	14,500
Total	400,000				$100,000

EXHIBIT 7–16   Units-of-Production Depreciation Method

DEPRECIATION AND FEDERAL INCOME TAXES

Federal income tax regulations permit companies to deduct depreciation expense as part of their taxable income calculation. However, the ***Internal Revenue Service (IRS)*** requires that businesses use either of two prescribed depreciation methods for income tax purposes. The first is an accelerated depreciation method originally called the Accelerated Cost Recovery System (ACRS) when it was adopted by the federal government in 1981. ACRS was modified somewhat in 1986 and became known as the **Modified Accelerated Cost Recovery System (MACRS).** The other depreciation method allowed under IRS regulations is a form of the straight-line method.

Modified Accelerated Cost Recovery System (MACRS) Depreciation method taxpayers use to calculate depreciation expense for tax purposes.

Under MACRS, companies must use ***IRS***-mandated service lives regardless of how long the company feels its assets will last. Additionally, the residual value assigned to assets is zero under MACRS. Bear in mind that the purpose of tax regulations, and MACRS for that matter, is to provide a conduit for collecting taxes. MACRS is a departure from generally accepted accounting principles (GAAP) because it does not allow companies to estimate appropriate useful lives or residual values for their assets, and it is not designed to enhance the information provided to economic decision makers. Accordingly, the use of MACRS is not generally used for financial accounting purposes.

◆ DEPRECIATION'S IMPACT ON CASH

Depreciation expense has an important characteristic that distinguishes it from most other expenses. Depreciation does *not* require the outflow of cash. That is, depreciation is a *noncash* expense. Think about it. Expenses like wages expense, electricity expense, and rent expense all require the outflow of cash. But no company has to pay cash to anyone for depreciation expense. Depreciation is an allocation process that transfers the cost of an asset from assets to expense. No cash changes hands in that allocation process.

The fact that depreciation expense does not require an outflow of cash has tremendous implications to economic decision makers. They must think of depreciation expense differently than they do other expenses as they attempt to predict a company's future cash flows. In fact, banks and other lending institutions typically eliminate depreciation expense from the income statement and treat it as though it is not an expense at all. This is accomplished by *adding back* depreciation expense to net income. Exhibit 7–17 on page F–286 shows 2006 and 2007 income statements for Barlow Paving Corporation with depreciation added back for 2006. You will recall that in the Barlow examples we held everything constant from one year to the next except the items affected by depreciation. There was no depreciation in 2007, so once the depreciation is added back for 2006, the adjusted income for 2006 equals the new income for 2007.

In this chapter, we demonstrated that depreciation and the disposal of depreciable assets can have a significant impact on a company's net income and other financial

	2006	2007
Barlow Paving Corporation Income Statements		
Sales	$755,000	$941,000
Cost of goods sold	422,000	525,000
Gross margin	$333,000	$416,000
Operating expenses other than depreciation	(236,000)	(319,000)
Depreciation expense	(55,000)	0
Operating income	$ 42,000	$ 97,000
Gain (loss) on sale of machine	0	0
Net income	$ 42,000	$ 97,000
Add back depreciation expense	55,000	0
Adjusted net income	$ 97,000	$ 97,000

EXHIBIT 7–17 Barlow Paving Corporation's Net Income—Depreciation Expense Added Back

information. Economic decision makers must understand depreciation if they are to use financial statements for predicting a company's future or assessing its past performance.

Depreciation is but one of the complex areas that affect accrual basis financial statements. We will continue our discussion of these complications in Chapter 8, where we consider issues associated with sale of merchandise inventory.

Summary

Depreciation is the process of allocating the cost of long-lived assets to the periods in which the assets help to earn revenues. When a company purchases property, plant, and equipment, it records it as an asset and shows it on its balance sheet. As time passes, the cost is transferred from an asset on the balance sheet to an expense on the income statement. Recording depreciation expense accomplishes this transfer. The amount of an asset's accumulated depreciation represents the total of all of the asset's depreciation expense recognized thus far. Accumulated depreciation is reported on the balance sheet as a reduction of the asset cost.

GAAP rules allow several depreciation methods. The straight-line method allocates cost evenly over the life of the asset being depreciated. Accelerated depreciation methods, such as the double-declining-balance method, recognize a greater amount of depreciation expense in the early years of an asset's life and a smaller amount in later years.

The choice of depreciation methods affects companies' financial statements. In total, over the useful life of an asset, straight-line and double-declining-balance depreciation methods record the same amount of depreciation expense. However, in any particular period, different depreciation methods usually result in different amounts of depreciation expense, and this causes a difference in reported net income. Because the amount of depreciation expense affects accumulated depreciation, the balance sheets of companies using different depreciation methods will also be different during most of the life of the assets.

From time to time, companies sell some of their depreciable assets, and these transactions often result in gains or losses. Gains and losses affect net income in a manner similar to that of revenues and expenses, but they are shown as separate items on the income statement. Gains and losses result from activities peripheral to the major activity of the company; revenues and expenses are direct results of the company's primary business activity.

An asset's book value is its cost less the amount of its accumulated depreciation. If an asset is sold for more than its book value, the transaction results in a gain. Conversely, selling an asset for less than its book value results in a loss.

If the disposal of an asset results in a gain or loss, that outcome is reported on the income statement. If, however, an asset is sold for exactly its book value, the transaction results in no gain or loss. In any case, when a company disposes of an asset, both the asset and its corresponding accumulated depreciation account are removed from the balance sheet.

If the sale of an asset results in a gain, it cannot be assumed that this was a "wise move" or that management received a good price for the asset. A gain simply indicates that the asset was sold for more than its book value. Conversely, disposing of an asset at a loss is not necessarily an indication of poor management. Losses result when less than the book value is received for the asset. Depreciation method choice and estimates of the useful life and residual value of the asset affect book values of assets. Selling price is determined by what the buyer is willing to pay for the asset. Gains and losses are merely an indication of the relationship between book value and selling price. They should not be interpreted as anything more than that.

Recording Long-Lived Assets and Depreciation

After completing your work on this chapter appendix, you should be able to prepare the journal entries associated with long-lived depreciable assets.

DEPRECIABLE ASSET ENTRIES

The recording process for depreciable assets involves three basic types of transactions:

Transaction 1—The purchase or other acquisitions of long-lived depreciable assets.
Transaction 2—The depreciation of long-lived assets.
Transaction 3—The sale or other disposals of depreciable assets.

To record these transactions, accountants generally use the following general ledger accounts:

1. *Long-lived asset accounts.* In our example, the account we will use is "Machine."
2. *An accumulated depreciation account for each asset account.* In our example, we will use "Accumulated depreciation—machine."
3. *Depreciation expense*
4. *Gain on disposal of assets*
5. *Loss on disposal of assets*

Recall that debits increase assets, expenses, and losses, and credits increase liabilities, equity, revenues, and gains. Also recall that debits and credits must equal for each journal entry. We will now examine the journal entries that the Barlow Paving Corporation would make to record the transactions for its asphalt paving machine. The first set of transactions illustrates Barlow's purchase of the machine, its use of straight-line depreciation, and its sale of the machine for $32,000. Where it is appropriate and nonrepetitive, we will analyze each transaction using the four steps we introduced in Chapter 6.

1. Determine if and when a transaction occurred, what accounts were affected, which account balances should increase, which should decrease, and by how much.
2. Determine which accounts should be debited and which should be credited.
3. Make the journal entry.
4. Review the entry to ensure it is in proper form and that the debits equal the credits.

DEPRECIABLE ASSET ENTRIES—ASSUMING STRAIGHT-LINE DEPRECIATION

Transaction 1: On January 2, 2002, Barlow Paving Corporation purchased an asphalt paving machine for cash of $300,000.

1. This transaction took place on January 2, 2002. The transaction affects the machine account and cash. The balance of the machine account should be increased by $300,000 and the balance in cash should be decreased by the same amount.
2. Because the machine account is an asset account, it is on the left side of the accounting equation and increased with a debit. Cash is also an asset account and should be decreased with a credit.
3. The general journal entry:

```
2002
Jan 2   Machine                              300,000
             Cash                                        300,000
```

4. A final check of the entry reveals that we dated it correctly, made the debit part of the entry first, indented the credit account title, and the dollar amount of the debits equals that of the credits. The entry is fine.

Transaction 2: On December 31, 2002, Barlow Paving Corporation records straight-line depreciation for its paving machine in the amount of $55,000.

1. This "transaction" took place a little at a time, each day of the year. Companies can record depreciation on a routine basis, say monthly, or they can wait until the end of the year and use the balance sheet date for depreciation entries, even though they are recording depreciation for an entire accounting period. In this case, we will assume

Barlow records its depreciation at the end of the year, so we will use December 31, 2002. Depreciation transfers the cost of an asset from assets to expense. Although we could accomplish the transfer by decreasing the asset account itself, in accounting, we use a separate account called accumulated depreciation to record the reduction. In this case, the account would be accumulated depreciation—machine. This way, we can determine the asset's original cost at any time by simply examining the asset account, in this case, the machine account. Additionally, we can determine the asset's depreciation to date by examining the accumulated depreciation account. So, the transaction affects depreciation expense and the contra-asset account, accumulated depreciation—machine. We should increase the depreciation expense account by $55,000. What about accumulated depreciation? To determine the machine's book value, we subtract its accumulated depreciation from the machine account. Therefore, to reduce the machines book value, accumulated depreciation—machine should be increased by $55,000.

2. To increase depreciation expense, we debit it, and to increase accumulated depreciation—machine, a contra-asset account, we credit it.

3. The general journal entry:

2002
Dec 31   *Depreciation expense*   *55,000*
                Accumulated depreciation—machine   *55,000*

4. A final check of the entry reveals that the entry is fine.

We are not going to prepare entries for each year's depreciation because, except for the date, the depreciation entries for 2003, 2004, 2005, and 2006 would be identical to the one we made for December 31, 2002.

Recording a Gain on Disposal of Assets

Before we record the disposal of an asset, we must record depreciation up to the moment the asset is taken out of service. Because Barlow's paving machine was fully depreciated at the time of its sale, no additional depreciation entry is needed.

The entry we make to record the disposal of the paving machine removes the asset and the accumulated depreciation associated with the asset from Barlow's books. Removing the asset and its accumulated depreciation from Barlow's books is reasonable because, once the machine is sold, Barlow no longer owns it. The entry also records the gain or loss on the sale of the asset.

Transaction 3: Barlow sold its paving machine on January 2, 2007, for cash of $32,000 resulting in a $7,000 gain.

1. This transaction took place on January 2, 2007. Since Barlow is selling the paving machine, we should remove it and its accumulated depreciation from Barlow's books. We should also record the cash Barlow receives and the resulting gain or loss on the disposal. Accordingly, we should decrease the machine account and accumulated depreciation—machine and increase cash. In this particular disposal transaction, we should increase gain on disposal of assets because the proceeds from the sale of the asset exceed its book value. We should increase cash by the $32,000 Barlow received. We should decrease the machine account and accumulated depreciation—machine by $300,000 and $275,000, respectively, to reduce their balance to zero. We should increase gain on disposal of assets by the amount that the proceeds from the sale exceed the book value of the asset, in this case, $7,000.

2. We increase cash with a debit, decrease accumulated depreciation—machine with a debit, decrease machine with a credit, and increase gain on disposal of assets with a credit.

3. The general journal entry:

2007
Jan 2   *Cash*   *32,000*
              Accumulated depreciation—machine   *275,000*
                    Machine   *300,000*
                    Gain on disposal of assets   *7,000*

4. A final check of the entry reveals that the entry is fine.

Exhibit 7A–1 on page F–290 shows T-account entries for the Barlow machine assuming the company used straight-line depreciation. Keep in mind that for this presentation, we show all of the depreciation entries in the depreciation expense account even though the company would actually close the depreciation expense account to zero at the end of each year as part of the closing process.

Machine					Cash	
1-2-02 300,000						300,000 *1-2-02*
	300,000 *1-2-07*			1-2-07 32,000		
0						

Accumulated Depreciation				Depreciation Expense	
	55,000 *12-31-02*		12-31-02 55,000		
	55,000 *12-31-03*		12-31-03 55,000		
	55,000 *12-31-04*		12-31-04 55,000		
	55,000 *12-31-05*		12-31-05 55,000		
	55,000 *12-31-06*		12-31-06 55,000		
T3 1-2-07 275,000					
	0				

Gain on Disposal of Assets	
	7,000 *1-2-07*

EXHIBIT 7A–1   T-Account Entries for Barlow's Paving Machine Assuming Straight-Line Depreciation

Recording a Loss on Disposal of Assets

To demonstrate recording a loss on disposal of assets, let's assume that instead of receiving $32,000 for its paving machine, Barlow only received $19,000 (transaction 3). This change would not affect the acquisition entry or the depreciation entries, but, as we show below, the entry to record the disposal of the paving machine is different under this assumption.

Transaction 3: Assume Barlow sold its paving machine on January 2, 2007, for cash of $19,000 resulting in a $6,000 loss.

1. This transaction took place on January 2, 2007. As before, since we are selling the paving machine, we should remove it and its accumulated depreciation. We should also record the cash received and the resulting gain or loss on the disposal. In this particular disposal transaction, *loss* on disposal of assets should be increased because the proceeds from the sale of the asset are less than its book value. We should increase cash by the $19,000 Barlow received. We should decrease the machine account and accumulated depreciation—machine by $300,000 and $275,000, respectively, to reduce their balance to zero. We should increase loss on disposal of assets by the amount that the book value of the asset sold exceeds the proceeds from the sale, in this case, $6,000.
2. We increase cash with a debit, decrease accumulated depreciation—machine with a debit, and increase loss on disposal of assets with a debit. We decrease machine with a credit.
3. The general journal entry:

```
2007
Jan 2   Cash                                     19,000
          Accumulated depreciation—machine       275,000
          Loss on disposal of assets              6,000
             Machine                                        300,000
```

4. The entry seems fine.

Next we will record the disposal of Barlow's paving machine assuming the company sold it for $25,000.

Sale of an Asset for Book Value

When the selling price of an asset is exactly equal to the asset's book value, there is no gain or loss. The following entry shows a journal entry to record the sale of Barlow's paving machine for an amount exactly equal to its book value. This is an unlikely event indeed.

Transaction 3: Assume Barlow sold its paving machine on January 2, 2007, for cash of $25,000, an amount equal to the machine's book value.

1. This transaction took place on January 2, 2007. The increases and decreases for this version of Transaction 3 are the same as they were for the first two versions except that there is no gain or loss to record. We should increase cash by the $25,000 Barlow received. Again, we should decrease the machine account and accumulated depreciation—machine by $300,000 and $275,000, respectively. There is no gain or loss to record on this version of the transaction because we assume that Barlow sold the asset for an amount equal to its book value.

2. We increase cash with a debit, decrease accumulated depreciation—machine with a debit, and decrease machine with a credit.

3. The general journal entry:

2007			
Jan 2	Cash	25,000	
	Accumulated depreciation—machine	275,000	
	Machine		300,000

4. The entry seems fine.

Depreciable Asset Entries—Assuming Double-Declining-Balance Depreciation

The entries associated with depreciable assets are basically the same regardless of the depreciation method the company uses. So, whether a company uses the double-declining-balance depreciation method or straight-line, its depreciable asset entries will be pretty much the same except for the dollar amounts. The entries follow the same format and use the same accounts. The only differences are associated with the amount of annual depreciation expense. Because the double-declining-balance entries are so similar to straight-line entries, to avoid repetition, we will not present them.

Appendix Summary

When recording transactions for long-lived assets, the accounts companies use include a long-lived asset account, accumulated depreciation, depreciation expense, and a gain or loss account for disposal of assets. Companies record the original purchase of an asset as a debit to the asset account. Recording annual depreciation results in a debit to depreciation expense and a credit to accumulated depreciation, a contra-asset account. When a company sells an asset, it must record depreciation up to the moment the asset is taken out of service, then the company debits the asset received (usually cash), debits accumulated depreciation, credits the asset sold, and credits a gain on the sale or debits a loss on the sale to balance the journal entry.

Key Terms

- accelerated depreciation methods, F–268
- accumulated depreciation, F–269
- book value, F–269
- depreciable base, F–267
- depreciation, F–265
- double-declining-balance method, F–271
- fully depreciated, F–270
- gains, F–275
- historical cost principle, F–274
- losses, F–275
- Modified Accelerated Cost Recovery System (MACRS), F–285
- straight-line depreciation, F–268
- units-of-production depreciation method, F–284

Review the Facts

A. Provide three examples of long-lived depreciable assets.
B. In an accounting context, how is depreciation defined?
C. What two estimates made by management will affect the amount of depreciation recorded each period?
D. What is the depreciable base of an asset?
E. Explain what is meant by an accelerated depreciation method.
F. Theoretically, in what situation is an accelerated depreciation method the appropriate choice?
G. Explain how the amount of depreciation expense is calculated using straight-line depreciation.

H. What is meant by an asset's book value?
I. What does the amount of accumulated depreciation represent?
J. Describe the process of determining depreciation expense using the double-declining-balance method.
K. Compared to straight-line depreciation, what is the effect of an accelerated depreciation method on the balance sheet? On the income statement?
L. Regardless of what depreciation method is used, at what point is an asset considered "fully depreciated"?
M. On what financial statement do gains and losses appear?
N. What is the difference between a revenue and a gain? A loss and an expense?
O. How is a gain or loss calculated for the sale of an asset?
P. Describe the units-of-production method of depreciation.
Q. How do MACRS depreciation and depreciation under GAAP differ?

Apply What You Have Learned ●

LO 1, 2, 3, & 4: TERMINOLOGY

7–16. Presented below is a list of items relating to the concepts discussed in this chapter, followed by definitions of those items in scrambled order:

a. Accelerated depreciation
b. Book value
c. Gain on sale of asset
d. Losses
e. Estimated useful life
f. Straight-line depreciation
g. Gains
h. Loss on sale of asset
i. Depreciable base
j. Production method

1. _____ A factor determining how much of an asset's cost will be allocated to the periods supposedly benefited.
2. _____ A depreciation method that uses activity instead of time as the basis of allocation.
3. _____ More of the cost of a long-lived asset is converted to expense in the early years of its life than in later years.
4. _____ The cost of a long-lived asset less the estimated residual value.
5. _____ Results when a depreciable asset is sold for more than its book value.
6. _____ An equal amount of a long-lived asset's cost is converted to expense in each year of its useful life.
7. _____ Net inflows resulting from peripheral activities.
8. _____ The cost of a long-lived depreciable asset less its accumulated depreciation.
9. _____ Results when a depreciable asset is sold for less than its book value.
10. _____ Net outflows resulting from peripheral activities.

Required: Match the letter next to each item on the list with the appropriate definition. Use each letter only once.

LO 1: DEPRECIATION PROCESS

7–17. Evaluate the following statement and write a brief response: "The depreciation process is an accounting process designed to value fixed assets on the balance sheet."

LO 2: COMPUTE DEPRECIATION EXPENSE—STRAIGHT-LINE METHOD

7–18. **Required:** Compute annual straight-line depreciation expense for the following situation:

Equipment cost	$74,840
Estimated residual value	$12,000
Estimated useful life	5 Years

LO 2: COMPUTE DEPRECIATION EXPENSE—STRAIGHT-LINE METHOD

7–19. **Required:** Compute annual straight-line depreciation expense for the following situation:

Machinery cost	$643,778
Estimated residual value	$50,000
Estimated useful life	7 Years

LO 2: COMPUTE DEPRECIATION EXPENSE—STRAIGHT-LINE METHOD

7–20. **Required:** Compute annual straight-line depreciation expense for the following situation:

Production equipment cost	$207,888
Estimated residual value	$20,000
Estimated useful life	8 Years

LO 2: COMPUTE DEPRECIATION EXPENSE—STRAIGHT-LINE METHOD

7–21. Jerry Proctor and Company purchased a lathe for use in its manufacturing operation. The machine cost $150,000, has a five-year estimated useful life, and will be depreciated using the straight-line method. The only thing remaining to be determined before yearly depreciation expense can be calculated is the lathe's estimated residual value.

The alternatives are

1. $10,000 estimated residual value
2. $20,000 estimated residual value
3. $30,000 estimated residual value

Required:

   a. Calculate the yearly depreciation expense for the new lathe under each of the alternatives given.
   b. Which of the three alternatives will result in the highest net income?
   c. How long will the new lathe be useful as an asset to Proctor and Company? What factors could change this time period?

LO 2: COMPUTE DEPRECIATION EXPENSE—STRAIGHT-LINE METHOD

7–22. Betty Hart Company, Inc., has just purchased a computer for use in its manufacturing operation. The machine cost $75,000, has a four-year estimated useful life, and will be depreciated using the straight-line method. The only thing remaining to be determined before yearly depreciation expense can be calculated is the estimated residual value.

The alternatives are

1. $7,500 estimated residual value
2. $12,500 estimated residual value
3. $17,500 estimated residual value

Required:

   a. Calculate the yearly depreciation expense for the new computer under each of the alternatives given.
   b. Which of the three alternatives will result in the highest net income? Which of the three alternatives will result in the lowest net income?
   c. How long will the new computer be useful as an asset to Hart? What factors could change this time period?

LO 2: COMPUTE DEPRECIATION EXPENSE—STRAIGHT-LINE METHOD

7–23. Carl Young Publishing Company purchased a new printing press for a total installed cost of $700,000. The printing press will be depreciated using the straight-line method. Michael Hoff, the corporate controller, is trying to decide on an estimated useful life and an estimated residual value for the asset.

The alternatives are

1. A six-year estimated useful life with a $40,000 estimated residual value
2. A five-year estimated useful life with a $100,000 estimated residual value
3. A four-year estimated useful life with a $140,000 estimated residual value

Required:

   a. Calculate the yearly depreciation expense for the new printing press under each of the alternatives given.
   b. Which of the three alternatives will result in the lowest yearly net income? Which of the three alternatives will result in the highest yearly net income?
   c. What should be the deciding factor in selecting among the three alternatives?

LO 2: COMPUTE DEPRECIATION EXPENSE—STRAIGHT-LINE METHOD

7–24. The Pizzeria Restaurant Company purchased a new walk-in freezer for a total installed cost of $250,000. The walk-in freezer will be depreciated using the straight-line method. Richard Porter, the corporate controller, is trying to determine an estimated useful life and residual value for the asset.

His alternatives are

1. A five-year estimated useful life with a $10,000 estimated residual value
2. A four-year estimated useful life with a $25,000 estimated residual value
3. A three-year estimated useful life with a $50,000 estimated residual value

Required:

a. Calculate the yearly depreciation expense for the new freezer under each of the alternatives given.
b. Which of the three alternatives will result in the lowest yearly net income? Which of the three alternatives will result in the highest yearly net income?
c. What should be the deciding factor in selecting among the three alternatives?

LO 2: COMPUTE DEPRECIATION EXPENSE—DOUBLE-DECLINING-BALANCE METHOD

7–25. **Required:** Based on the following information, prepare a table that shows the depreciation expense for each year using the double-declining-balance method:

Computer equipment cost	$36,000
Estimated residual value	$6000
Estimated useful life	5 Years

LO 2: COMPUTE DEPRECIATION EXPENSE—DOUBLE-DECLINING-BALANCE METHOD

7–26. **Required:** Based on the following information, prepare a table that shows the depreciation expense for each year using the double-declining-balance method:

Machinery cost	$76,000
Estimated residual value	$5,000
Estimated useful life	4 Years

LO 2: COMPUTE DEPRECIATION EXPENSE—DOUBLE-DECLINING-BALANCE METHOD

7–27. **Required:** Based on the following information, prepare a table that shows the depreciation expense for each year using the double-declining-balance method:

Production machinery cost	$16,000
Estimated residual value	$2,000
Estimated useful life	5 Years

LO 2: COMPUTE DEPRECIATION EXPENSE—STRAIGHT-LINE AND DOUBLE-DECLINING-BALANCE METHODS

7–28. The following information is available:

Machinery cost	$203,475
Estimated residual value	$25,000
Estimated useful life	5 Years

Required:

a. Compute annual straight-line depreciation expense.
b. Prepare a table that shows the depreciation expense for each year using the double-declining-balance method.

LO 2: COMPUTE DEPRECIATION EXPENSE—STRAIGHT-LINE AND DOUBLE-DECLINING-BALANCE METHODS

7–29. The following information is available for Oxy's of Pinecrest, Inc.:

Equipment cost	$5,932
Estimated residual value	$900
Estimated useful life	4 Years

Required:

  a. Compute annual straight-line depreciation expense.
  b. Prepare a table that shows the depreciation expense for each year using the double-declining-balance method.

LO 2: COMPUTE DEPRECIATION EXPENSE—STRAIGHT-LINE AND DOUBLE-DECLINING-BALANCE METHODS

7–30. The following information is available:

Truck cost	$46,390
Estimated residual value	$7,000
Estimated useful life	5 Years

Required:

  a. Compute annual straight-line depreciation expense.
  b. Prepare a table that shows the depreciation expense for each year using the double-declining-balance method.

LO 2: COMPUTE DEPRECIATION EXPENSE AND BOOK VALUE— DOUBLE-DECLINING-BALANCE METHOD

7–31. Cramer Company purchased a high-tech assembler on January 2, 2004, for a total cost of $600,000. The assembler has an estimated useful life to the company of five years. Cramer thinks it can sell the used assembler for $60,000 after five years. The company chose to depreciate the new assembler using the double-declining-balance method.

Required:

  a. Prepare a schedule showing the amount of depreciation expense for each of the five years of the estimated useful life.
  b. What will be the book value of the assembler at the end of the five-year estimated useful life?
  c. What does book value represent?

LO 2: COMPUTE DEPRECIATION EXPENSE AND BOOK VALUE— DOUBLE-DECLINING-BALANCE METHOD

7–32. Winch Company purchased an earthmoving machine on January 2, 2003, for a total cost of $900,000. The earthmover has an estimated useful life to the company of four years. Winch believes it can sell the used earthmover for $80,000 after four years. The company selected the double-declining-balance method of depreciation.

Required:

  a. Prepare a schedule showing the amount of depreciation expense for each of the four years of the estimated useful life.
  b. What will be the book value of the earthmover at the end of the four-year estimated useful life?
  c. What does book value represent?

LO 2: COMPUTE DEPRECIATION EXPENSE—STRAIGHT-LINE AND DOUBLE-DECLINING-BALANCE METHODS

7–33. Danielle Company purchased a sophisticated stamping machine on January 2, 2004, for $480,000. The estimated useful life of the stamping machine is six years. Danielle estimates the machine's residual value is $54,000.

Required:

    a. Calculate the yearly depreciation expense for the stamping machine assuming the company uses the straight-line depreciation method.

    b. Prepare a schedule showing the amount of depreciation expense for each of the six years of the estimated useful life assuming the company uses the double-declining-balance depreciation method.

LO 2: COMPUTE DEPRECIATION EXPENSE—STRAIGHT-LINE AND DOUBLE-DECLINING-BALANCE METHODS

7–34. Hal Clark, Inc., purchased a pasteurizing machine on January 2, 2004, for $375,000. The estimated useful life of the machine is four years with a residual value of $45,000.

Required:

    a. Calculate the yearly depreciation expense for the machine assuming the company uses the straight-line depreciation method.

    b. Prepare a schedule showing the amount of depreciation expense for each of the four years of the estimated useful life assuming the company uses the double-declining-balance depreciation method.

LO 1, 2, & 3: COMPUTE DEPRECIATION EXPENSE—STRAIGHT-LINE AND DOUBLE-DECLINING-BALANCE METHODS

7–35. David Brown, Inc., purchased a fleet of delivery trucks on January 2, 2004, for $700,000. The estimated useful life of the fleet is four years, after which Brown estimates it can sell the entire fleet for $50,000.

Required:

    a. Calculate the yearly depreciation expense for the fleet of vehicles assuming the company uses the straight-line depreciation method.

    b. Prepare a schedule showing the amount of depreciation expense for each of the four years of the estimated useful life assuming the company uses the double-declining-balance depreciation method.

    c. Address the following questions:

        1. Double-declining-balance calculates depreciation at twice the straight-line rate. Why is the amount of depreciation expense in 2004 under double-declining-balance not exactly twice the amount under straight-line for 2004?

        2. Over the four-year estimated useful life of the vehicles, how much depreciation expense will be charged against income using the straight-line method? How much will be charged against income using the double-declining-balance method?

        3. Discuss the impact on the net income of each method of depreciation in the first two years of the life of the asset.

LO 1, 2, & 3: COMPUTE DEPRECIATION EXPENSE—STRAIGHT-LINE AND DOUBLE-DECLINING-BALANCE METHODS

7–36. Mandy and Jessie, Inc., purchased equipment on January 2, 2004, for $600,000. The corporation estimates the useful life of the equipment is three years, after which it can sell the equipment for $51,000.

Required:

    a. Calculate the yearly depreciation expense for the equipment assuming the company uses the straight-line depreciation method.

    b. Prepare a schedule showing the amount of depreciation expense for each of the three years of the estimated useful life assuming the company uses the double-declining-balance depreciation method.

    c. Address the following questions:

        1. Double-declining-balance calculates depreciation at twice the straight-line rate. Why is the amount of depreciation expense in 2004 under double-declining-balance not exactly twice the amount under straight-line for 2004?

2. Over the three-year estimated useful life of the equipment, how much depreciation expense will be charged against income using the straight-line method? How much will be charged against income using the double-declining-balance method?
3. Discuss the impact on the net income of each method of depreciation in the first two years of partial year life of the asset.

LO 2 & 5: COMPUTE PARTIAL YEAR DEPRECIATION EXPENSE AND GAIN OR LOSS—STRAIGHT-LINE METHOD

7–37. Roberts Company purchased a machine in January 2003 for $200,000. When originally purchased, the machine had an estimated useful life of five years and an estimated residual value of $30,000. The company uses straight-line depreciation. It is now June 30, 2006, and the company has decided to dispose of the machine.

Required:

a. Calculate the book value of the machine as of June 30, 2006.
b. Calculate the gain or loss on the sale of the machine assuming Roberts sells it for $102,000.
c. Calculate the gain or loss on the sale of the machine assuming Roberts sells it for $25,000.

LO 2 & 5: COMPUTE PARTIAL YEAR DEPRECIATION EXPENSE AND GAIN OR LOSS—STRAIGHT-LINE METHOD

7–38. Cohen Company purchased a machine in January 2004 and paid $150,000 for it. When originally purchased, the machine had an estimated useful life of four years and an estimated residual value of $10,000. The company uses straight-line depreciation. It is now September 30, 2006, and the company has decided to dispose of the machine.

Required:

a. Calculate the book value of the machine as of September 30, 2006.
b. Calculate the gain or loss on the sale of the machine assuming Cohen sells it for $172,000.
c. Calculate the gain or loss on the sale of the machine assuming Cohen sells it for $25,000.

LO 2 & 5: COMPUTE DEPRECIATION EXPENSE AND GAIN OR LOSS—STRAIGHT-LINE METHOD

7–39. Colton Company purchased a machine in January 2003 for $450,000. When originally purchased, the machine had an estimated useful life of 10 years and an estimated residual value of $60,000. The company uses straight-line depreciation. It is now January 2, 2009, and the company has decided to dispose of the machine.

Required:

a. Calculate the book value of the machine as of December 31, 2008.
b. Calculate the gain or loss on the sale of the machine assuming Colton sells it for $130,000.
c. Calculate the gain or loss on the sale of the machine assuming Colton sells it for $30,000.

LO 1, 2, 3, 4, 5, & 6: IMPACT OF DEPRECIATION METHOD ON GAINS AND LOSSES

7–40. Pam and Cam are twins. Each of them has her own company. Three years ago, on the same day, they each purchased copiers for use by their companies. The machines were identical in every way and cost exactly the same amount ($28,000). The machines had the same estimated useful life (five years) and the same estimated residual value ($3,000). The only difference was the depreciation method chosen. Nails by Pam chose to depreciate its copier using the straight-line method, while Cam's Sportswear chose an accelerated depreciation method.

Due to technological developments in copy machines, at the end of two years, Pam decided to sell her old machine and buy a new one. Cam decided to do the same thing. In fact, they each received exactly the same amount when they sold their machines ($16,500). Later, while they were having lunch together, Cam mentioned that when she sold her copier, she had a gain of $6,420 on the sale. Pam kept quiet but was confused because she knew she had sold her copier for exactly the same amount as Cam, yet the sale of her copier had resulted in a loss of $1,500.

Required: Explain how Pam could have had a loss of $1,500 on the sale of her copier, while Cam had a sizable gain.

LO 2, 3, 5, & 6: IMPACT OF DEPRECIATION METHOD ON GAINS AND LOSSES

7–41. Leroy Bowden and Bill Hudik each ran their own automotive repair shop. On January 2, 2004, each of them bought a new hydraulic vehicle lift costing $10,000. Each of the lifts was expected to have an eight-year life and a $2,000 residual value. Bowden Auto Repair used straight-line depreciation, and Hudik Automotive Service used the double-declining-balance method. At the end of three years, each of them sold their lifts for $5,500.

Required:

    a. Compute the depreciation for both Bowden and Hudik through the third year.
    b. Compute the gain or loss that each would recognize on the sale of their machine.
    c. If the gain or loss is different for each of them, explain why.

LO 2, 3, 5, & 6: IMPACT OF DEPRECIATION METHOD ON GAINS AND LOSSES

7–42. Penny and Linda each ran their own cooking school. Each bought a new piece of equipment costing $20,000 on January 2, 2004. The equipment was expected to have a five-year useful life and a $2,000 residual value. Cooking with Penny used straight-line depreciation and Linda's Kitchen used double-declining-balance depreciation. At the end of three years, each of them sold their equipment for $11,000.

Required:

    a. Compute the depreciation for both Penny and Linda through the third year.
    b. Compute the gain or loss that each would recognize on the sale of the equipment.
    c. If the gain or loss is different for each of them, explain why.

LO 2, 3, 5, & 6: IMPACT OF DEPRECIATION METHOD ON GAINS AND LOSSES

7–43. Jerry and Pete each ran their own construction business. Each bought a new piece of equipment costing $40,000 on January 2, 2004. The equipment was expected to have a five-year useful life and $4,000 residual value. Jerry's Home Repairs used straight-line depreciation and Pete's Custom Kitchens used double-declining-balance depreciation. At the end of three years, each of them sold their machines for $22,000.

Required:

    a. Compute the depreciation for both Jerry and Pete through the third year.
    b. Compute the gain or loss that each would recognize on the sale of the machine.
    c. If the gain or loss is different for each of them, explain why.

LO 4: MEANING OF GAINS AND LOSSES

7–44. Explain in your own words what a gain or loss on the sale of long-lived depreciable assets means and how the gain or loss relates to depreciation expense.

LO 2: COMPUTE DEPRECIATION EXPENSE—UNITS-OF-PRODUCTION METHOD

7–45. Strickland, Inc., purchased a delivery truck on January 2, 2003, for $70,000. Strickland estimates the useful life of the vehicle is 200,000 miles and the residual value at $10,000. The truck is driven 40,000 miles in 2003; 45,000 miles in 2004; 60,000 miles in 2005; and 65,000 miles in 2006.

Required: Calculate the yearly depreciation expense for the vehicle assuming the company uses the units-of-production depreciation method.

LO 2: COMPUTE DEPRECIATION EXPENSE—UNITS-OF-PRODUCTION METHOD

7–46. McLeod, Inc., purchased a printing press on January 2, 2003, for $95,000. McLeod estimates the useful life of the press is 2,000,000 pages or five years, after which he can sell the press for $5,000. The press produces 500,000 pages in 2003; 400,000 pages in 2004; 430,000 pages in 2005; 600,000 pages in 2006; and 350,000 pages in 2007.

Required: Calculate the yearly depreciation expense for the press assuming the company uses the units-of-production depreciation method.

LO 2: COMPUTE DEPRECIATION EXPENSE—UNITS-OF-PRODUCTION METHOD

7–47. Patten, Inc., purchased a lathe on January 2, 2003, for $200,000. Patten estimates its useful life as 10,000 hours or four years and its residual value at $4,000. He uses the lathe for 2,000 hours in 2003; 2,800 hours in 2004; 3,200 hours in 2005; and 2,600 hours in 2006.

Required: Calculate the yearly depreciation expense for the machine assuming the company uses the units-of-production depreciation method.

LO 2 & 7: APPENDIX—RECORDING ASSETS AND STRAIGHT-LINE DEPRECIATION

7–48. On January 2, 2004, Cunningham Corporation purchased a new piece of equipment for $60,000 cash. Cunningham uses straight-line depreciation and estimates the useful life of the equipment at five years with a residual value of $10,000.

Required:
    a. Prepare the journal entry to record the purchase of the asset.
    b. Prepare the journal entries to record the depreciation for the first year of life of the asset.

LO 2 & 7: APPENDIX—RECORDING ASSETS AND STRAIGHT-LINE DEPRECIATION

7–49. On January 2, 2004, Holzmann, Inc., purchased a new piece of equipment for $560,000. The company paid $125,000 in cash and signed a promissory note to finance the balance. Holzmann uses straight-line depreciation and estimates the useful life of the equipment at six years with a residual value of $50,000.

Required:
    a. Prepare the journal entry to record the purchase of the asset.
    b. Prepare the journal entry to record the depreciation for the first year of life of the asset.

LO 2 & 7: APPENDIX—RECORDING ASSETS AND STRAIGHT-LINE DEPRECIATION

7–50. On January 2, 2004, Miceli Corporation purchased a new piece of equipment for $75,000 cash. Miceli uses straight-line depreciation and estimates the useful life of the equipment at seven years with a residual value of $5,000.

Required:
    a. Prepare the journal entry to record the purchase of the asset.
    b. Prepare the journal entry to record the depreciation for the first year of life of the asset.

LO 2 & 7: APPENDIX—RECORDING ASSETS AND STRAIGHT-LINE DEPRECIATION

7–51. On January 2, 2004, Chris Scott Corporation purchased a new piece of equipment for $85,000. The company paid $8,000 in cash and signed a promissory note for the balance. Scott uses straight-line depreciation and estimates the useful life of the equipment at seven years with a residual value of $11,500.

Required:

    a. Prepare the journal entry to record the purchase of the asset.

    b. Prepare the journal entry to record the depreciation for the first year of the life of the asset.

LO 2, 5, & 7: APPENDIX—COMPUTE GAIN OR LOSS, STRAIGHT-LINE DEPRECIATION, RECORD SALE OF ASSET

7–52. On January 2, 2005, Esposito, Inc., purchased a new piece of equipment for $650,000. The company paid $130,000 in cash and borrowed the remainder from the bank. Esposito uses straight-line depreciation and estimates the useful life of the equipment at six years with a residual value of $75,000.

Required:

    a. Compute the gain or loss if the company uses straight-line depreciation and sells the equipment for $86,000 at the end of the fourth year.

    b. Prepare the journal entry to record the sale of the equipment.

LO 2, 5, & 7: APPENDIX—COMPUTE DOUBLE-DECLINING-BALANCE DEPRECIATION, COMPUTE GAIN OR LOSS, RECORD SALE OF ASSET

7–53. On January 2, 2004, Allen Corporation purchased a new piece of equipment for $75,000. The company paid $5,000 in cash and borrowed the remainder from the bank. Allen estimates the useful life of the equipment at seven years with a residual value of $12,000.

Required:

    a. Compute the gain or loss if the company uses double-declining-balance depreciation and sells the equipment for $8,000 at the end of the fourth year.

    b. Prepare the journal entry to record the sale of the equipment.

LO 2, 5, & 7: APPENDIX—COMPUTE AND RECORD STRAIGHT-LINE DEPRECIATION, COMPUTE GAIN OR LOSS, RECORD SALE OF ASSET

7–54. J. T. Company purchased a stamping machine on January 2, 2004, for $480,000. The estimated useful life of the stamping machine is five years. The machine has an estimated residual value of $40,000.

Required:

    a. Calculate the yearly depreciation expense for the stamping machine assuming the company uses the straight-line depreciation method.

    b. Record the journal entries for the depreciation that would be required each year.

    c. Prepare the required journal entries to record the sale of the machine at the end of two years for $350,000.

LO 2, 5, 6, & 7: APPENDIX—COMPUTE AND RECORD DOUBLE-DECLINING-BALANCE DEPRECIATION, COMPUTE GAIN OR LOSS, RECORD SALE OF ASSET

7–55. Cooke Company purchased a pasteurizing machine on January 2, 2004, for $375,000. The estimated useful life of the machine is five years. The machine has an estimated residual value of $40,000.

Required:

    a. Calculate the yearly depreciation expense for the machine assuming the company uses the double-declining-balance depreciation method and prepare the journal entries to record depreciation each year.

    b. Assuming the machine is sold at the end of December 2006 for $50,000, prepare the required entry to record the sale.

    c. Assuming the machine is sold at the end of April 2006 for $50,000, prepare the required entry to record the sale.

    d. Is it better to sell the machine in April or December? Explain your answer.

LO 2, 5, 6, & 7: APPENDIX—COMPUTE AND RECORD STRAIGHT-LINE DEPRECIATION, COMPUTE GAIN OR LOSS, RECORD SALE OF ASSET

7–56. Suzanne, Inc., purchased a delivery truck on January 2, 2004, for $70,000. The estimated useful life of the vehicle is four years, after which Suzanne thinks it will be able to sell it for $5,000.

Required:

a. Calculate the yearly depreciation expense for the vehicle assuming the company uses the straight-line depreciation method and prepare the journal entries to record the depreciation.
b. Assume the truck is sold at the end of December of the fourth year for $7,000. Prepare the journal entry to record the transaction.
c. Assume the truck is sold on March 31, 2007, for $3,000. Prepare the journal entry to record the transaction.
d. Is it better to sell the truck at the end of December of the fourth year or on March 31, 2007? Explain your answer.

LO 2, 3, 5, & 7: APPENDIX—COMPUTE AND RECORD STRAIGHT-LINE AND DOUBLE-DECLINING-BALANCE DEPRECIATION, COMPUTE GAIN OR LOSS, RECORD SALE OF ASSET

7–57. Jerry and Pete each run their own construction business. Each bought a new piece of equipment costing $40,000 on January 2, 2004. The equipment is expected to have a five-year useful life and a $4,000 residual value. Jerry's Home Repairs uses straight-line depreciation and Pete's Custom Kitchens uses double-declining-balance depreciation. On June 30, 2007, each of them sold their machines for $22,000.

Required:

a. Compute the depreciation for both Jerry and Pete through the date of sale.
b. Compute the gain or loss that each would recognize on the sale of the equipment.
c. Prepare the journal entries necessary to record the purchase, annual depreciation, and sale of Jerry's and Pete's equipment.

Financial Reporting Exercises ●

7–58. Go to *Pier 1*'s annual report on page F–503. Look in the notes to consolidated financial statements section under the subheading Properties, Maintenance, and Repairs to answer the following.

Required:

a. For which of the items listed does *Pier 1 Imports, Inc.,* use depreciation?
b. How long are the average useful lives for the items listed?
c. For which of the items listed does *Pier 1 Imports, Inc.,* not use depreciation? Why?
d. What type of depreciation calculations do they use?
e. What were their total depreciation costs in 2000–2002?
f. What do they do when they sell/dispose of an asset that has been partially or fully depreciated?

7–59. Go to the *Securities and Exchange Commission's (SEC's) Electronic Data Gathering, Analysis, and Retrieval (EDGAR)* system and find the 2001 Form 10-K for *Williams Sonoma, Inc.* Use the information in note A of the notes to consolidated financial statements and the statement of cash flows to answer the following.

Required:

a. What type of depreciation method does *Williams Sonoma, Inc.,* employ?
b. What are the useful lives assigned to the different types of assets by *Williams Sonoma, Inc.?*
c. What was its total depreciation cost in 2000–2002?

7–60. Go to the SEC's EDGAR system and find the 2001 Form 10-K for *Bed Bath & Beyond, Inc.* Use the information in the notes to consolidated financial statements to answer the following.

Required:

    a. Determine the type of depreciation methods used for different types of long-lived assets.

    b. What are the useful lives assigned to the different types of assets by ***Bed Bath & Beyond, Inc.?***

    c. What was its total depreciation cost in 2000–2002?

7–61. Continuation of problems 7–58, 7–59, and 7–60.

Required:

    a. Prepare a list that compares the depreciation methods and amounts of depreciation of ***Pier 1 Imports, Inc., Williams Sonoma, Inc.,*** and ***Bed Bath & Beyond, Inc.***

    b. What are the similarities or significant differences that you see? What do you think they mean?

ANNUAL REPORT PROJECT

7–62. Section 7—Long-Lived Assets

This section of the annual report project focuses on your company's property, plant, and equipment and its depreciation.

Required: Prepare a report that includes the following information:

    a. A schedule that presents and compares the property, plant, and equipment of your company and the peer company you selected for the assignment for Section 6. For example, include a presentation of each company's property, plant, and equipment for the two years listed in the financial reports. Also, present the total of accumulated depreciation associated with property, plant, and equipment for each company for each year. You can find information about property, plant, and equipment and depreciation in the balance sheet and the notes to the financial statements.

    b. Identify the method or methods of depreciation used by the two companies. In addition, comment on the significance of any similarities or differences between the depreciation methods used by the two companies.

    c. Comment on the estimates used by the two companies for depreciation calculations. For example, what are the estimates used by each company? Comment on the significance of any similarities or differences between the estimates used by the two companies.

    d. A schedule that presents and compares the intangible assets of your company and the peer company you selected. Comment on the intangible assets of each company. For example, which is most significant? Has either company recognized any sizable losses due to the impaired value of intangible assets? If so, read the notes to the financial statements and fully explain the circumstances relating to the loss. For example, did the loss relate to a new accounting pronouncement? Does the company comment on whether it is likely that such a loss will occur again in the future?

    e. Your report should conclude with comments regarding what you think of your company and how you think your company compares to its peer in light of the work you did in connection with this assignment.

CHAPTER 8

Accounting for Inventory

Palmer Nursery has been in business for over 20 years. It sells the same products—plants, shrubs, trees, and garden supplies—year in and year out. But the owners feel that because the company's business practices might be out of step with the times, their sales may be suffering. They hire you, a business consultant, to suggest ways they can improve performance.

One of the first things you do is review Palmer's financial statements. You notice that the dollar amount of inventory shown on their balance sheet seems quite low. Surely, you reason, such a low dollar value can't represent much in the way of salable product. You are alarmed by this, so you check other companies in the industry and confirm that there must be a problem. These other companies (which are of comparable size to Palmer) all show much higher dollar amounts of inventory on their balance sheets. You wonder if Palmer's low inventory might be resulting in lost sales. When you make your first site visit, you are surprised to see that Palmer has plenty of saleable merchandise on hand. In fact, they may have *too much*! There are trees, shrubs, shovels, and hoses everywhere. How, you ask yourself, can there be so much physical inventory on hand when the balance sheet shows such a low inventory dollar amount? So you approach the company's bookkeeper and ask her to explain it. She looks at you and says one word: LIFO.

You decide—wisely—that you had better go back to your office and learn more about accounting for inventory before you say much more to the folks at Palmer.

In Chapter 7, we explored the impact that the latitude generally accepted accounting principles (GAAP) permit in accounting for long-lived depreciable assets has on financial statements. Similarly, GAAP permit a considerable degree of latitude in accounting cost of products companies sell, and this latitude also can have a significant effect on financial statements.

Accrual accounting generally requires companies to recognize revenue when it is earned and when it is realized or realizable. Therefore, accrual accounting requires companies to match expenses—in this case, the cost of the product sold—with the revenues the expenses helped generate. GAAP permit companies to select from a variety of acceptable accounting methods to match sales revenue with the cost of the goods sold. In this chapter, we will look at three of them. Like depreciation, this is an example of how the financial statements of companies may vary under accrual accounting. In fact, the way companies account for the flow of merchandise inventory costs can have a direct and significant impact on their reported net income and on the dollar amounts they show for inventory on their balance sheets.

Learning Objectives

After completing your work on this chapter, you should be able to do the following:

1. Describe goods available for sale and name its components.

2. Explain the relationship between ending inventory and cost of goods sold.

3. Differentiate between the physical flow of merchandise and the cost flow of merchandise.

4. Explain the differences between periodic and perpetual inventory systems.

5. List three different inventory cost flow assumptions and contrast how they affect net income.

6. Calculate cost of goods sold and the cost of ending inventory using FIFO, LIFO, and average cost inventory cost flow assumptions.

7. Calculate and interpret the inventory turnover ratio.

8. Describe the impact of payment terms and freight terms. (Appendix A)

9. Prepare journal entries associated with the purchase and sale of merchandise inventory. (Appendix B)

◆ TRACKING INVENTORY COSTS

merchandise inventory
The physical units (goods) a company buys to resell as part of its business operation. Also called inventory.

inventory The stockpile of tangible product that a company has on hand to sell.

In Chapter 1, we introduced the three major types of businesses—manufacturing firms, merchandising firms, and service firms. Recall that manufacturers make the products they sell, merchandisers buy the products they sell, and service companies sell services rather than tangible products. The stockpile of tangible products that a merchandiser has on hand to sell is called **merchandise inventory,** or simply **inventory.** For example, *Wal-Mart Corporation*'s inventory includes toys, lawnmowers, clothing, and thousands of other products. *Bassett Furniture Company*'s inventory includes beds, dressers, tables, desks, and chairs. *General Motors* owns desks and chairs also, but these items are not inventory because they are things *General Motors* uses, not things it sells. Inventory is the stock of items a company holds for resale. The inventory of *General Motors* includes cars, trucks, vans, and a variety of automotive parts and accessories.

The terms *merchandise inventory* and *inventory* are often used to describe the *cost* of the items as well as the items themselves. Therefore, when you see the term *merchandise inventory*, you will have to determine whether it is describing the actual physical units of inventory or the cost of that inventory.

We should mention that a company's inventory cost generally includes the cost of the product itself, plus any additional costs for freight to bring the product in, plus any other costs associated with getting the product ready to sell. For example, if Carolina's Shoe Store pays $10,000 for shoes, $200 for freight to have the shoes delivered to the store, and another $300 to put the shoes into custom shoe boxes to get them ready to sell, the company's total cost for the inventory is $10,500. Only costs that are directly related to obtaining the product or getting the product ready to sell should be treated as part of inventory cost. Accordingly, the cost of inventory generally should not include operating expenses such as store rent, sales salaries, and electricity expense.

beginning inventory
The amount of merchandise inventory (units or dollars) on hand at the beginning of the income statement period.

purchases The amount of merchandise inventory bought during the income statement period.

goods available for sale
The total amount of merchandise inventory a company has available to sell in a given income statement period.

Beginning inventory is the amount of salable merchandise a company has on hand at the first moment of a particular accounting period. **Purchases** is the amount of salable merchandise a company buys during that particular period. Again, both of these terms may refer to the cost of products or to the products themselves. **Goods available for sale** is the amount of merchandise a company starts with (beginning inventory) plus the amount it buys (purchases) during the accounting period. Goods available for sale represents the total amount of merchandise inventory a company could sell in a given income statement period. Once again, the term *goods available for sale* describes both the physical amount of merchandise inventory and the cost of that inventory. Whether we are referring to the physical amount of inventory or its cost, the following relationship among beginning inventory, purchases, and goods available for sale holds true:

Beginning Inventory + Purchases = Goods Available for Sale

Companies report the inventory they have on hand as an asset because it has probable future benefit (it should generate future sales revenues). **Cost of goods sold**

cost of goods sold The cost of the product sold as the primary business activity of a company.

cost of sales Another name for cost of goods sold.

(sometimes called **cost of sales**) is the cost of all of the merchandise (products) a company has transferred (sold) to its customers during a particular income statement period. When a company sells some of its inventory, we should transfer the cost of the merchandise sold from inventory, an asset on the balance sheet, to cost of goods sold, an expense on the income statement. We can determine cost of goods sold by subtracting the amount of inventory on hand at the end of the period, called ending inventory, from goods available for sale. In other words, the total amount that we could have sold (goods available for sale) minus the amount we still had at the end of the period (ending inventory) equals the amount we must have sold (cost of goods sold):

Goods Available for Sale − Ending Inventory = Cost of Goods Sold

Conversely, if we know a company's goods available for sale and its cost of goods sold, we can determine a company's ending merchandise inventory:

Goods Available for Sale − Cost of Goods Sold = Ending Inventory

Again, these relationships are true whether we are considering the amount of physical units of inventory or the cost of the inventory. Exhibit 8–1 shows an example of these relationships in terms of both units and dollar amounts.

EXHIBIT 8–1 Relationships Among Goods Available for Sale, Ending Inventory, and Cost of Goods Sold in Both Units and Dollars

	Units	Cost
Beginning Inventory	20	$200
+ Purchases	70	700
= Goods Available for Sale	90	900
− Less: Ending Inventory	(15)	(150)
= Cost of Goods Sold	75	$750

OR

	Units	Cost
Beginning Inventory	20	$200
+ Purchases	70	700
= Goods Available for Sale	90	900
− Less: Cost of Goods Sold	(75)	(750)
= Ending Inventory	15	$150

In the first calculation, we subtract ending inventory to arrive at units sold and cost of goods sold. In the second calculation, we subtract units sold and cost of goods sold to determine ending inventory. It is important to learn from these two calculations that *the total of ending inventory and cost of goods sold always equals goods available for sale.*

To illustrate, consider the ***Virgin Record Store.*** All the CDs and tapes in the store on January 1 (beginning inventory) plus any new CDs and tapes the store buys during January (purchases) equals the total of all the CDs and tapes the store has available to sell (goods available for sale). By the end of January, the products that constituted goods available for sale are either gone or still in the store. If items are gone, we presume the store sold them and consider them part of cost of goods sold. (*Note:* Some of the items could have been broken or stolen, but generally companies consider this cost as part of cost of goods sold.) The CDs and tapes that are still in the store at the end of January are the store's ending inventory. What this means is that *all goods available for sale become either cost of goods sold or ending inventory.*

Exhibit 8–2 on page F–306 shows the movement of inventory through a merchandising operation. Notice that beginning inventory and purchases comprise goods avail-

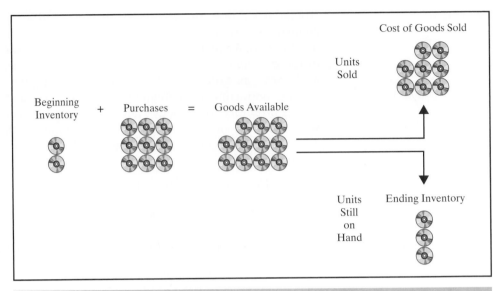

EXHIBIT 8–2 The Flow of Inventory and Its Cost

able for sale. By the end of the period, goods available for sale becomes either cost of goods sold or ending inventory.

Discussion Question

8–1. Assume that you decide to throw a party and begin to plan for it by checking out what's in the house. You find you have some hot dogs, rolls, and pretzels. That's a good start, but you go to the store to buy soda, chips, dip, peanuts, and ice cream. The party is a great hit. Your guests devour all the food and drinks, except for the ice cream — it was never touched! In terms of the party items we have mentioned, what was your:

    a. beginning inventory?
    b. purchases?
    c. goods available?
    d. ending inventory?
    e. "cost" of the party?

Now, let's look closer at the process of tracking a company's inventory and its cost as items are bought and sold.

◆ PHYSICAL FLOW OF INVENTORY (REALITY)

Assume that Computer Exchange, Inc., purchased a computer on January 17, 2003, for $800 and placed it in its warehouse. Also assume the company sold the computer to a customer on February 6, 2003, for $1,500.

Because Computer Exchange purchased the computer for the purpose of reselling it, the company should consider the computer merchandise inventory. Had the company bought the computer for its own use, the company would have considered it a long-lived depreciable asset instead of inventory. Exhibit 8–3 illustrates the physical

EXHIBIT 8–3 Physical Movement of a Computer Purchased by Computer Exchange

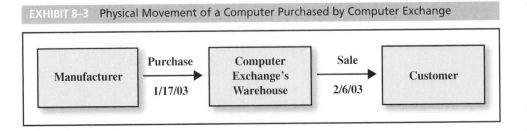

movement of the computer from the time Computer Exchange purchased it until the company sold it and delivered it to the customer.

For many companies, it is important to "rotate their stock"—to sell old merchandise before they sell newer merchandise. This is particularly true of companies selling perishable products such as produce and dairy products. We could describe this physical flow as first-in, first out (FIFO).

Discussion Question ●

8–2. For what other products would it be important for the first units of merchandise purchased to be the first ones sold? Explain.

For some products, it is unimportant or impractical to sell the first units purchased first. For example, it is both unimportant and impractical for a nursery to sell its oldest sand before it sells sand purchased later. When a truckload of sand arrives, the driver dumps the new sand right on top of the remnants of the old sand pile. It would be silly to dig down into the pile and attempt to sell the oldest sand first. In such cases, goods may be sold in random order, or perhaps the merchandise is sold from the top of the pile so that the last units in are the first units taken out of inventory and sold. We could describe this physical flow as last-in, first out (LIFO).

Sometimes it is impossible to tell which units were sold first because the product becomes so intermixed. This is the case with liquid or gas products such as gasoline and propane. For example, it would be impossible for Chevron to tell which gasoline it was selling first from one of its huge storage tanks, and impossible for Chevron's retailers to tell which gasoline it is selling first from its underground tanks. When the retailer receives the load of gasoline, the new product simply blends together with the old. The gasoline she or he sells will consist of a blend of the old and new. We could describe this physical flow as an average of old product and new product.

Discussion Questions ●

8–3. Once again, assume you are Palmer Nursery's consultant. With respect to the physical units themselves, would you advise Palmer to use LIFO for its potting soil? Do you think LIFO is acceptable for all of the nursery's products or should it use FIFO or average for some of them? Explain your answers.

8–4. If you owned a retail camera shop, what possible reasons would you have for insisting that your employees sell the first Nikon cameras received before the ones that arrived at the store later?

You might suppose that accounting rules require that the flow of inventory costs through a company's accounting records reflect the reality of how the physical units flow through the company's warehouse. For example, if a company sells bread, it will sell older loaves before newer ones to ensure product freshness. It seems logical to expect that the company would be required to recognize the cost of the older product as expense before it recognizes the cost of the newer product. However, accounting rules *do not* require that the cost flow for inventory mirror the physical flow of inventory. There are several acceptable cost flow methods allowed by GAAP, and we will discuss four of them a little later in this chapter. For now, we will introduce you to the inventory cost flow in a very general way.

◆ INVENTORY COST FLOW (MEASUREMENT OF REALITY)

Let's return to our Computer Exchange example. Under accrual accounting, Computer Exchange must attempt to match expenses to the same income statement period as the revenues they help generate. For this reason, the company would not recognize the cost of the $800 computer as an expense when it was purchased. Instead, the company would consider the computer and its $800 cost as an asset.

As of January 31, 2003, the company had not sold the computer—it was in the company's warehouse. Therefore, the company should show the computer's cost on the balance sheet prepared at the end of January as merchandise inventory. The company would not report anything related to the computer on its January income statement. The calculations below show the cost of goods sold and ending inventory for Computer Exchange, Inc., assuming the company purchased the computer but has not sold it yet.

	Units	Cost
Beginning Inventory, January 1	0	$ 0
+ Purchases	1	800
= Goods Available for Sale	1	800
− Cost of Goods Sold	0	0
= Ending Inventory, January 31	1	$800

Exhibit 8–4 shows Computer Exchange's income statement for the month of January 2003 and its balance sheet at January 31, 2003, assuming the company had no business transactions during January except those related to the computer and warehouse rent.

Discussion Question

8–5. Can you tell how long Computer Exchange, Inc., has been in business by looking at the income statement and balance sheet in Exhibit 8–4? Explain.

EXHIBIT 8–4 Computer Exchange's Financial Statements—Before Sale of Computer

Computer Exchange, Inc.
Income Statement
For the Month Ended January 31, 2003

Sales	$ 0
LESS: Cost of goods sold	0
Gross margin	$ 0
Operating expenses:	
Warehouse rent	$ (200)
Net income (loss)	$ (200)

Computer Exchange, Inc.
Statement of Retained Earnings
For the Month Ended January 31, 2003

Beginning retained earnings	$ 0
Net income (loss)	(200)
	$ (200)
Less dividends	$ 0
Ending retained earnings	$ (200)

Computer Exchange, Inc.
Balance Sheet
January 31, 2003

Assets:	
Cash	$22,000
Merchandise inventory	800
Total assets	$22,800
Liabilities and stockholders' equity:	
Common stock	$15,000
Additional paid-in capital	8,000
Retained earnings	(200)
Total liabilities and stockholders' equity	$22,800

Recall that Computer Exchange sold the computer for $1,500 on February 6, 2003, and delivered it to the customer on that day. The calculations below show the cost of goods sold and ending inventory for Computer Exchange at the end of February.

	Units	*Cost*
Beginning Inventory, January 1	0	$ 0
+ Purchases	1	800
= Goods Available for Sale	1	800
− Cost of Goods Sold	1	800
= Ending Inventory, February 28	0	$ 0

Exhibit 8–5 shows Computer Exchange's income statement for the month of February 2003 and its balance sheets at January 31, 2003, and February 28, 2003, assuming the company had no business transactions during February except those related to the computer and the warehouse rent.

We have included the presale (January 31) balance sheet as well as the postsale (February 28) balance sheet in Exhibit 8–5 to demonstrate how the $800 cost of the computer flowed through the financial statements. Computer Exchange reported the $800 as an asset (merchandise inventory) on the January 31 balance sheet. Because the company sold the computer during February and has no other merchandise to sell, there is no merchandise inventory on the February 28 balance sheet. Instead, Computer Exchange shows the computer's $800 cost as an expense and reports it on

EXHIBIT 8–5   Computer Exchange's Financial Statements Showing Effects of Sale of Computer

Computer Exchange, Inc.
Income Statement
For the Month Ended February 28, 2003

Sales	$ 1,500
LESS: Cost of goods sold	800
Gross margin	$ 700
Operating expenses:	
Warehouse rent	$ (200)
Net income (loss)	$ 500

Computer Exchange, Inc.
Statement of Retained Earnings
For the Month Ended January 31, 2003

Beginning retained earnings	$ (200)
Net income (loss)	500
	$ 300
Less dividends	$ 0
Ending retained earnings	$ 300

Computer Exchange, Inc.
Balance Sheets
January 31, 2003, and February 28, 2003

Assets:	January 31	February 28
Cash	$22,000	$21,800
Accounts receivable	-0-	1,500
Merchandise inventory	800	0
Total assets	$22,800	$23,300
Liabilities and stockholders' equity:		
Common stock	$15,000	$15,000
Additional paid-in capital	8,000	8,000
Retained earnings	(200)	300
Total liabilities and stockholders' equity	$22,800	$23,300

the February income statement as cost of goods sold. As you can see, cost of goods sold affects the gross margin, and thus the net income as well. The February 28 balance sheet reflects the $500 net income as an increase in both the total assets and total liabilities and stockholders' equity. The company's total assets increased by $500 because, while the company sacrificed $1,000 of assets during February ($800 cost of goods sold and $200 rent on the warehouse), those sacrifices generated a $1,500 asset (accounts receivable). As the arrow in Exhibit 8–5 shows, stockholders' equity increases by $500 as a result of combining the net income figure for February with the previous retained earnings balance (which in this case was negative) to arrive at the updated retained earnings balance of $300.

Discussion Question

8–6. Can you tell by looking at the income statement and balance sheets in Exhibit 8–5 whether the customer who purchased the computer from Computer Exchange has paid for it by the end of February 2003? Explain.

Exhibit 8–3 on page F–306 illustrates the physical movement of the computer from the time Computer Exchange purchased it to the time it was sold to the customer. Exhibit 8–6 shows both the physical flow of the computer and the flow of the cost associated with the computer.

Computer Exchange purchased a computer and put it in the company's warehouse. This is reality. Then, Computer Exchange sold the computer, took it out of the warehouse, and delivered it to its customer. This, too, is reality. The company initially reported the computer's $800 cost on its balance sheet as an asset. When it sold the computer, the company transferred the $800 cost to an expense, cost of goods sold, on the income statement. This is the measurement of reality. As Exhibit 8–6 shows, in this simple example involving only one unit of inventory, the physical flow of the merchandise inventory and the flow of the cost associated with the merchandise inventory coincide. As we will see later in this chapter, however, when a company has many units of inventory, the physical flow of merchandise (reality) and the cost flow of that merchandise (measurement of reality) do not necessarily coincide. This situation is another source of variation among companies' accounting information. To some degree, a company's financial information is influenced by its choice of one inventory costing method over another.

EXHIBIT 8–6 The Physical Movement of the Computer from the Time Computer Exchange Purchased It to the Time It Was Sold to the Customer

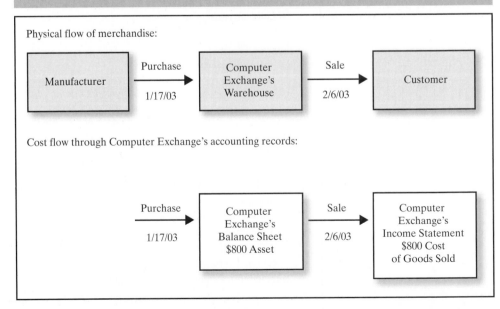

◆   **INVENTORY SYSTEMS**

In our previous example, Computer Exchange, Inc., transferred the $800 cost of the computer from an asset to an expense when the item was sold on February 6, 2003. Over time, two major inventory systems have been developed to account for this transfer. As we will see, each has advantages and disadvantages in comparison to the other.

PERIODIC INVENTORY SYSTEM

periodic inventory system   An inventory system in which all inventory and cost of goods sold calculations are done at the end of the income statement period.

Under a **periodic inventory system,** companies do their inventory and cost of goods sold calculations at the end of the income statement period. When a company uses a periodic inventory system, it does not update the detailed inventory records during the period. Further, the accounting records of a company using this system do not provide up-to-date information about which products have been sold during the period and which remain in inventory. Under this system, only at the end of the accounting period, when a company prepares its financial statements, does it calculate the cost of its ending inventory and its cost of the goods sold. It is only then that the company adjusts its accounting records to reflect the cost of ending inventory to show on its balance sheet and the cost of goods sold to show on its income statement.

The strength of the periodic inventory system is that it involves relatively little record keeping. Its greatest weakness is that it does not provide the company with any day-to-day information about the status of its inventory or its cost of goods sold.

Prior to the computer age, virtually all companies used the periodic inventory system because keeping detailed inventory records manually was too time consuming. Now, however, the availability of powerful and affordable computer technology makes the task of keeping daily inventory records an efficient process. For this reason, most companies now use the perpetual inventory system. Because of its overwhelming popularity, all our remaining examples are based on the perpetual inventory system.

PERPETUAL INVENTORY SYSTEM

perpetual inventory system   An inventory system in which both the physical count of inventory units and the cost classification (asset or expense) are updated when a transaction involves inventory.

Under a **perpetual inventory system,** companies update their inventory records continually to keep track of both the physical count of inventory units and the cost of those units. The inventory records are updated whenever there is a transaction involving inventory. What this means is that when a company uses the perpetual system, it updates its accounting records to provide up-to-date information about which products it has sold and which products still remain in inventory. To illustrate, let's return to our example of Computer Exchange. Under a perpetual system, Computer Exchange would have an inventory report similar to the one shown in Exhibit 8–7.

EXHIBIT 8–7   Inventory Control Report Under Perpetual Inventory System Merchandise

		Purchases			Cost of Goods Sold			Inventory Balance		
Date	*Explanation*	*Units*	*Unit Cost*	*Total Cost*	*Units*	*Unit Cost*	*Total Cost*	*Units*	*Unit Cost*	*Total Cost*
1/17	Purchase	1	$800	$800				1	$800	$800
2/06	Sale				1	$800	$800	0		$0

Since the report keeps a running balance of merchandise inventory (the far right side of the report), the company can tell the number of physical units it has on hand at any time. The report also shows the dollar amount that the company has transferred from assets (merchandise inventory) on the balance sheet to expense (cost of goods sold) on the income statement.

Computer Exchange uses a computerized accounting system to generate its inventory reports automatically. Purchases and sales of inventory are registered either by keyboard entries or by a bar-code scanning device. Retailers use scanners to read bar codes—formally known as universal product codes, or UPCs—printed on their inventory. Companies program their computers to assign a given cost to each inventory item and to perform the necessary functions to update their inventory records. Chances are, when you purchased this book, the clerk at the bookstore's checkout counter scanned the UPC on the book's back cover. In addition to ringing up the sale of the book, the bookstore's computer probably also updated the bookstore's inventory records. The bookstore's computer made entries to update the number of physical units on hand and to transfer the book's cost from merchandise inventory to cost of goods sold. By utilizing this technology, the bookstore's computer can provide employees with valuable information about the number of books sold and the number of books remaining on the shelf. If everything in the system works correctly, the bookstore's management can tell how many books are on the shelf without having to physically count them.

Discussion Question ●

8–7. Assume the inventory report at the bookstore for this textbook shows 25 books remaining on the shelf. Just to make sure, the bookstore manager goes over to the shelf, counts the remaining books, and finds there are only 22. What might explain the discrepancy?

◆ THE NECESSITY OF A PHYSICAL INVENTORY COUNT

book inventory The amount of ending inventory (units and dollars) resulting from transactions recorded by a perpetual inventory system.

The inventory amounts in units and dollars that a company's perpetual inventory system shows is called **book inventory.** Book inventory may or may not coincide with the merchandise inventory actually on hand at the end of the period. Errors in recording inventory transactions and theft of inventory are two potential causes of differences between book inventory and actual inventory. Others are damaged and discarded inventory and, in the case of perishable inventory, spoilage. Because discrepancies between book inventory and the actual physical inventory on hand are bound to occur, companies must physically count their inventory. Accounting rules dictate that every company governed by GAAP must take a physical count of its inventory at least annually.

Results of a physical inventory count take precedence over the book inventory the inventory system generates. Companies must adjust their book inventory to match the actual physical inventory on hand. To accomplish such an adjustment, the book inventory is adjusted and offset by a corresponding adjustment of cost of goods sold. To illustrate, Exhibit 8–8 shows the calculation of cost of goods sold and ending inventory generated by a perpetual inventory system.

EXHIBIT 8–8 Record of Ending Inventory Based on Book Inventory

	Units	Cost
Beginning Inventory, January 1	20	$200
+ Purchases	70	700
= Goods Available for Sale	90	900
− Cost of Goods Sold	75	750
= Ending Inventory, February 28	15	$150

The figures in this exhibit came from the company's records. The ending inventory of 15 units and $150 is the company's book inventory. However, a physical count reveals that there are only 13 units on hand. In this case, the company must adjust its records to reflect reality. The amount the balance sheet shows as ending inventory must be the amount the company actually had on hand. Since we know that cost of goods available for sale ($900 in this example) will end up as either cost of goods sold or ending inventory, a change in the ending inventory amount will cause a change in the amount of cost of goods sold. After the necessary adjustments, the company's records would look like Exhibit 8–9.

	Units	Cost
Beginning Inventory, January 1	20	$200
+ Purchases	70	700
= Goods Available for Sale	90	900
− Cost of Goods Sold	77	770
= Ending Inventory, February 28	13	$130

EXHIBIT 8–9   Adjusted Record of Ending Inventory After Physical Count

The cost of goods sold the company reports as an expense on its income statement for the period would be $770. The merchandise inventory the company reports as an asset on its balance sheet would be $130, which reflects the reality of the number of units actually on hand at the end of the period. With this adjustment, the company's financial statement will more accurately reflect reality.

Some accountants argue that because the book inventory under a perpetual inventory system is adjusted to the physical count periodically, all companies really end up using a form of the periodic inventory method.

Discussion Question ●

8–8. If careless employees break inventory items and discard them, or dishonest employees steal inventory items, how is a company's income statement affected?

◆ INVENTORY COST FLOW METHODS

Now that we have introduced you to the two inventory systems and have discussed the flow of inventory costs through a company's accounting records in a general way, we will now present four different inventory costing methods companies use, depending on their circumstances. The first of these methods is the specific identification method.

SPECIFIC IDENTIFICATION COST FLOW METHOD

specific identification method The method of inventory cost flow that identifies each item sold by a company.

Under the **specific identification method,** company accountants move the actual cost of individual units of inventory through the company's accounting records to exactly match the physical flow of units through the company's inventory. In other words, when a company uses the specific inventory method, its cost of goods sold is the actual cost of specific units of inventory the company sold, and the cost the company assigns to its ending inventory is the actual cost of specific units still on hand. Generally, this method is used only by companies that sell expensive, unique items such as airplanes, antiques, and boats. As an example, assume that Dobbs Motor Company sells antique automobiles and appropriately uses the specific identification method. Exhibit 8–10 shows the details of the automobiles in inventory at the beginning of March, those Dobbs purchased in March, and those Dobbs sold during the month.

EXHIBIT 8–10   Dobbs Motor Company's Detailed Inventory Information

Date Purchased	Description	Cost	Date Sold	Selling Price
Beginning Inventory				
10-15-2002	1926 Bentley	$35,000	03-05-2003	$45,000
12-20-2002	1960 Mercedes	15,000		
01-25-2003	1955 Thunderbird	25,000	03-09-2003	38,000
02-10-2003	1929 Model A Ford	24,000	03-18-2003	36,000
Purchases				
03-10-2003	1955 Cadillac	20,000		
03-25-2003	1964 Corvette	31,000		
Cost of Goods Available		**$150,000**		

When a company uses the specific identification inventory method, it keeps track of the cost of the actual units of inventory it sold. Let's assume that Dobbs sold the Bentley, the Thunderbird, and the Model A Ford during March. Exhibit 8–11 shows a summary of the sales and the cost of the automobiles sold.

EXHIBIT 8–11   Specific Identification Sales and Cost of Goods Sold

	Date Sold	Selling Price	Cost
1926 Bentley	03-05-2003	$ 45,000	$35,000
1955 Thunderbird	03-09-2003	38,000	25,000
1929 Model A Ford	03-18-2003	36,000	24,000
Total		**$119,000**	**$84,000**

The dollar amount assigned to the ending inventory under specific identification consists of the cost of the actual units of inventory still on hand at the end of the accounting period. In Dobbs's case, the ending inventory consists of the Mercedes, the Cadillac, and the Corvette. Exhibit 8–12 shows the cost that Dobbs would assign to its ending inventory.

EXHIBIT 8–12   Specific Identification Ending Inventory

Date Purchased	Description	Cost	Date Sold	Selling Price
12-20-2002	1960 Mercedes	$15,000		
3-10-2003	1955 Cadillac	20,000		
3-25-2003	1964 Corvette	31,000		
Ending Inventory Cost		$66,000		

Exhibit 8–13 presents a summary of the inventory cost flow for Dobbs Motor Company under the specific identification inventory method.

EXHIBIT 8–13   Dobbs Motor Company's Inventory Amounts Using Specific Identification

Beginning Inventory	$ 99,000
+ Purchases	51,000
= Goods Available for Sale	150,000
− Cost of Goods Sold	84,000
= Ending Inventory	$ 66,000

The specific identification method is both logical and intuitive. It is logical because it adheres to a rational set of procedures, and it is intuitive because the flow of costs through the accounting records is exactly the same as the physical flow of inventory. In many instances, however, it is impractical, unnecessary, or even impossible for the cost flow to exactly correspond to the physical flow of units through the inventory. GAAP do not require the flow of costs through a company's accounting records to reflect the reality of how the physical units flow through the company's inventory, as was the case with the antique car example we just used. Rather, these accounting rules allow companies to cost their products based on some *assumption* of how units of product physically flow through the company.

COST FLOW ASSUMPTIONS

Over time, the accounting profession has developed several cost flow assumptions to account for the movement of product cost through a company's accounting system. The three we will discuss in this chapter are the first-in, first-out (FIFO) method, the last-in, first-out (LIFO) method, and the average cost method. These cost flow assumptions are logical because they adhere to rational procedures. They are not, however, as intuitive as the specific identification method, because the flow of costs is not in any way related to how the physical inventory moves through a company. For example, ***Holsum Bakery*** makes certain it sells its oldest bread first. If it sold its freshest bread first, the older bread would go stale, leaving ***Holsum*** with merchandise it couldn't sell. For product costing purposes, however, ***Holsum*** can use any cost flow assumption it wishes without regard to how its inventory physically flows through the bakery. That is, accounting rules do not require the flow of inventory costs through accounting records to mirror the flow of physical units. Accounting rules permit companies to use any cost flow assumption—FIFO, LIFO, or average cost—regardless of the physical flow of inventory through their warehouses. This is yet another example of how reality and the measurement of reality may differ, and this difference can result in a difference between reality and the measurement of reality in accrual accounting. As financial statement users, you need to understand how companies track their inventory costs and how they arrive at the amounts they present on their financial statements. We will now explore three acceptable cost flow assumptions and the impact they have on inventory, cost of goods sold; and net income.

Generally, product costs change over time. For some products, prices rise regularly; wholesalers often warn the retailers to whom they sell goods of price increases months in advance. Products based on technology often fall in price as more and more companies offer the products and competition drives prices down. Prices may rise or fall over time, or they may fluctuate in unexpected patterns, but rarely will they remain constant for long periods.

When prices are changing, the cost flow assumption a company chooses will have a dramatic impact on its cost of goods sold and ending inventory. To illustrate, we will examine the effect of three cost flow assumptions on a product sold by Montoya Emergency Equipment Corporation. As the company's name implies, Montoya sells various kinds of emergency equipment to hospitals, ambulance services, and governments at the local and state level. The product we will focus on is the model EG241 emergency generator, which provides electric power whenever regular electricity service is unavailable. Montoya purchases these generators directly from the manufacturer and then sells them to its customers. For purposes of this example, we will assume that Montoya's cost for the generators is increasing, but due to competition, Montoya is unable to increase its retail selling price.

Montoya began March 2003 with only one model EG241 generator in stock. The company's cost for this generator was $800. During March, the company purchased five more generators. As Exhibit 8–14 shows, Montoya's cost for the generators is increasing even though the five generators purchased in March are identical to the one the company had on hand at the beginning of the month.

EXHIBIT 8–14   Montoya's March Beginning Inventory and March Purchases

Date		Quantity	Cost per Unit
March 1	Beginning Inventory	1	$ 800
March 3	Purchase	2	1,000
March 17	Purchase	1	1,200
March 26	Purchase	1	1,300
March 29	Purchase	1	1,400

Montoya Emergency Equipment sold one generator on March 22 and another on March 30 for $1,500 each. Remember, though, that because of competition, Montoya is unable to raise its $1,500 selling price per generator. Exhibit 8–15 on page F–316 shows Montoya's beginning inventory, its purchases, and the two sales.

Considering what you know about when Montoya purchased the generators and the dates of the two sales, which one do you think Montoya Emergency Equipment Corporation sold on March 22 and which do you think it sold on March 30? Different

Date		Quantity	Cost per Unit
March 1	Beginning Inventory	1	$ 800
March 3	Purchase	2	1,000
March 17	Purchase	1	1,200
March 22	Sale	(1)	
March 26	Purchase	1	1,300
March 29	Purchase	1	1,400
March 30	Sale	(1)	
March 31	Ending Inventory	4	

EXHIBIT 8–15 Montoya's March Beginning Inventory, March Purchases, and March Sales

answers are possible, but the generators the company actually sold were probably the ones most conveniently located in the warehouse (i.e., those closest to the door). In this case, the generators are identical, so it doesn't really matter which ones are sold first. About the only thing you can determine for sure is that the generator Montoya sold on March 22 was either the $800 one, one of the $1,000 ones, or the $1,200 one; and that the one Montoya sold on March 30 was one of the five still in the warehouse on that day.

Discussion Question

8–9. Why must the generator sold on March 22 have been one costing $800, $1,000, or $1,200?

Because Montoya's cost of the generators varied, it is impossible for us to determine the cost of the actual physical goods sold if we don't know exactly which generators the company sold. What we need is a method to calculate cost of goods sold that will work regardless of which specific products were sold.

In the sections that follow, we discuss three acceptable inventory cost flow assumptions. Before we do so, however, we must make three important points:

1. None of the three methods we discuss attempts to reflect the physical movement of the actual units of merchandise inventory.
2. Our discussions of the three methods are not intended to be exhaustive. Our aim is to give you a basic understanding of these methods so that you will understand how a particular inventory cost flow assumption can significantly affect a company's financial statements.
3. Our illustrations of cost flow methods assume that a perpetual inventory system is in place. Accordingly, we will keep a running inventory balance and we will calculate cost of goods sold each time a generator is sold.

The number of generators Montoya Emergency Equipment Corporation purchased, the date they were purchased, and their cost to Montoya are all facts. Likewise, the quantity of generators Montoya sold and when it sold them are also facts. The cost flow assumption Montoya uses cannot change these facts. What we *can* change is our *assumption* of which particular generator Montoya sold for product costing purposes. The cost flow assumptions we make will affect the amount Montoya records as cost of goods sold and also the amount Montoya shows as the cost of its ending inventory.

As we mentioned earlier in this chapter, cost of goods available for sale is the total cost of the inventory on hand at the beginning of the period plus the cost of inventory purchased during the period. Exhibit 8–16 shows the calculation of Montoya Emergency Equipment Corporation's cost of goods available for sale for March 2003.

The various cost flow assumptions we will apply to this situation will separate the $6,700 into two portions: (1) the cost that we will assign to the two generators Montoya sold (cost of goods sold), and (2) the cost we will assign to the four generators Montoya still has on hand at the end of March (ending inventory). Each cost flow assumption will take a different approach to determining which items we assume were sold on March 22 and March 30 and, thus, to determining the cost of goods sold for the month.

Date		Quantity	Cost per Unit	Total Cost
March 1	Beginning Inventory	1	$ 800	$ 800
March 3	Purchase	2	1,000	2,000
March 17	Purchase	1	1,200	1,200
March 26	Purchase	1	1,300	1,300
March 29	Purchase	1	1,400	1,400
	Total Goods Available for Sale			$6,700

EXHIBIT 8–16 Montoya Emergency Equipment Corporation's Cost of Goods Available for Sale

Because we will use the perpetual inventory system, we will determine the cost of goods sold at the time of each sale. The portion of the cost of goods available for sale not included in cost of goods sold, then, must be the cost of ending inventory.

FIRST-IN, FIRST-OUT (FIFO) METHOD

The **first-in, first-out (FIFO)** inventory cost flow method is so named because it *assumes* that the first units placed in inventory are the first units sold. Let's apply the FIFO inventory method to our example.

The first sale took place on March 22. One generator was sold, but which one? What inventory items were available on the sale date? Exhibit 8–17 answers that question. Then, applying FIFO logic, we assume that the generator sold on March 22 must have been the oldest one, the one from beginning inventory. That is, the first generator in was the first one out. Therefore, cost of goods sold for the March 22 sale was $800.

EXHIBIT 8–17 Inventory Items Available for Sale on March 22

Date		Quantity	Cost per Unit	Total Cost
March 1	Beginning Inventory	1	$ 800	$ 800
March 3	Purchase	2	1,000	2,000
March 17	Purchase	1	1,200	1,200

The next sale took place on March 30. What inventory items were on hand at the time of the sale? Exhibit 8–18 answers that question. Under FIFO, which of the generators should we assume was sold on March 30? At this point in time, the first generator into inventory was one of those Montoya purchased on March 3, so we assume one of those was sold. Therefore, cost of goods sold for the March 30 sale is $1,000.

EXHIBIT 8–18 Inventory Items Available for Sale on March 30 Under FIFO Assumption

Date		Quantity	Cost per Unit	Total Cost
March 3	Purchase	2	$1,000	$2,000
March 17	Purchase	1	1,200	1,200
March 26	Purchase	1	1,300	1,300
March 29	Purchase	1	1,400	1,400

We can now calculate the cost of goods sold that Montoya Emergency Equipment Corporation should report on its March income statement. Since cost of goods sold for the month is the total of the cost of goods sold for each sale, Montoya should report cost of goods sold of $1,800 ($800 + $1,000). Exhibit 8–19 on page F–318 summarizes Montoya's inventory cost flow under the FIFO inventory method.

At the time of each sale, cost of goods sold is determined using the assumption that the first items into inventory are the first ones to be sold. As Exhibit 8–19 shows, we assume that the generator from beginning inventory was the one Montoya sold on March 22 and one of the generators Montoya purchased on March 3 was sold on March 30. Montoya's ending inventory consists of the cost of the four unsold generators: one of the generators it purchased on March 3 and the ones it purchased on

first-in, first-out (FIFO)
The inventory flow concept based on the assumption that the first units of inventory purchased are the first ones sold.

Goods Available

Date		Quantity	Cost per Unit	Total Cost
March 1	Beginning Inventory	1	$ 800	$ 800
March 3	Purchase	2	1,000	2,000
March 17	Purchase	1	1,200	1,200
March 26	Purchase	1	1,300	1,300
March 29	Purchase	1	1,400	1,400
	Total Cost of Goods Available for Sale			$6,700

Cost of Goods Sold

Date	Quantity	Cost per Unit	Total Cost
March 22 Sale	1	$ 800	$ 800
March 30 Sale	1	$1,000	1,000
Total Cost of Goods Sold	2		$1,800

Ending Inventory

Date		Quantity	Cost per Unit	Total Cost
March 3	Purchase	1	$1,000	$1,000
March 17	Purchase	1	1,200	1,200
March 26	Purchase	1	1,300	1,300
March 29	Purchase	1	1,400	1,400
March 31	Ending Inventory	4		$4,900

EXHIBIT 8–19   Cost of Goods Sold and Ending Inventory Cost Under FIFO

March 17, 26, and 29. By totaling the costs of these four generators, we determine that the cost of Montoya's ending inventory for March is $4,900.

Discussion Question ●

8–10. If Montoya Emergency Equipment Corporation sells two more generators before purchasing any more, which two would we assume the company sold under FIFO?

Even if we didn't identify and cost the items we assumed were remaining in ending inventory as we did in Exhibit 8–19, we could determine the ending inventory cost. Since we know the cost of goods available for sale is $6,700 and the cost of goods sold is $1,800, we can determine the cost of the company's ending inventory for March 2003 by subtracting cost of goods sold from the cost of goods available:

$$\text{Cost of Goods Available} - \text{Cost of Goods Sold} = \text{Ending Inventory}$$
$$\$6,700 \qquad - \qquad \$1,800 \qquad = \qquad \$4,900$$

Note that we separated cost of goods available for sale ($6,700) into cost of goods sold ($1,800) and cost of ending inventory ($4,900). Cost of goods sold is shown as an expense on the income statement, and ending inventory is shown as an asset on the balance sheet.

Exhibit 8–20 shows Montoya's financial statements assuming it used the FIFO inventory method and had no business transactions during March except those related to the generators and its rent payment.

We included both the February 28 and the March 31 balance sheets in Exhibit 8–20 to demonstrate how the cost of inventory flows through the financial statements. Montoya had only $800 in merchandise inventory on February 28, as its balance sheet reflects. This was the beginning inventory for March. During March, the company purchased five generators for a total of $5,900. Some of the $6,700 cost of goods available for sale becomes part of the merchandise inventory on the March

Montoya Emergency Equipment Corporation
Income Statement
For the Month Ended March 31, 2003

Sales	$ 3,000
LESS: Cost of goods sold	1,800
Gross margin	$1,200
Operating expenses:	
Warehouse rent	$ (200)
Net income (loss)	$ 1,000

Montoya Emergency Equipment Corporation
Balance Sheets
February 28, 2003, and March 31, 2003

	February 28	March 31
Assets:		
Cash	$21,000	$22,300
Accounts receivable	1,500	3,000
Merchandise inventory	800	4,900
Total assets	$23,300	$30,200
Liabilities and stockholders' equity:		
Accounts payable	$ 0	$ 5,900
Common stock	15,000	15,000
Additional paid-in capital	8,000	8,000
Retained earnings	300	1,300
Total liabilities and stockholders' equity	$23,300	$30,200

EXHIBIT 8–20   Montoya Emergency Equipment Corporation's Financial Statements—FIFO Inventory Method

balance sheet ($4,900) while the rest becomes cost of goods sold on the March income statement ($1,800). The $4,900 merchandise inventory on the March 31 balance sheet represents the unsold generators, while the $1,800 cost of goods sold represents the two generators Montoya sold in March. The cost of goods sold affects the gross margin and thus the net income as well. We combine the $1,000 net income with the previous retained earnings balance of $300 to arrive at the March 31 retained earnings balance of $1,300.

Discussion Question

8–11. Can you tell by looking at Montoya's financial statements in Exhibit 8–20 whether, as of March 31, the company had paid for the five generators purchased during March 2003? Explain.

As you can see, even though it may not be intuitive, FIFO is logical because it adheres to a rational set of procedures. Next, we will explore the LIFO method, which is no less logical than FIFO but results in different amounts for cost of goods sold and ending inventory.

LAST-IN, FIRST-OUT (LIFO) METHOD

last-in, first-out (LIFO)
The inventory flow concept based on the assumption that the last units of inventory purchased are the first ones sold.

The **last-in, first-out (LIFO)** method is so named because it *assumes* that the last units placed in inventory are the first units sold. In other words, regardless of the physical flow of merchandise through the warehouse, under LIFO, the cost of the goods most recently purchased is the first cost recognized as cost of goods sold. Exhibit 8–21 shows Montoya Emergency Equipment Corporation's goods available for sale when the company makes its first sale of the month on March 22.

Date		Quantity	Cost per Unit	Total Cost
March 1	Beginning Inventory	1	$ 800	$ 800
March 3	Purchase	2	1,000	2,000
March 17	Purchase	1	1,200	1,200

EXHIBIT 8–21 Inventory Items Available for Sale on March 22

Applying LIFO logic, we assume that the generator sold on March 22 was the one Montoya purchased on March 17. That is, the last one in was the first one out. Therefore, cost of goods sold for the March 22 sale was $1,200.

The next sale took place on March 30. Exhibit 8–22 shows what inventory items were on hand at the time of the sale.

EXHIBIT 8–22 Inventory Items Available for Sale on March 30 Under LIFO Assumption

Date		Quantity	Cost per Unit	Total Cost
March 1	Purchase	1	$ 800	$ 800
March 3	Purchase	2	1,000	2,000
March 26	Purchase	1	1,300	1,300
March 29	Purchase	1	1,400	1,400

Under LIFO, we assume that the generator sold on March 30 was the last one into inventory—that is, the generator Montoya purchased on March 29. Therefore, cost of goods sold for the March 30 sale is $1,400.

We can now calculate the cost of goods sold that Montoya Emergency Equipment Corporation should report on its March income statement: $2,600 ($1,200 + $1,400). Montoya's ending inventory cost consists of the cost of the four unsold generators. Exhibit 8–23 summarizes Montoya's inventory cost flow under the LIFO inventory method.

EXHIBIT 8–23 Cost of Goods Sold and Ending Inventory Cost Under LIFO

Goods Available

Date		Quantity	Cost per Unit	Total Cost
March 1	Beginning Inventory	1	$ 800	$ 800
March 3	Purchase	2	1,000	2,000
March 17	Purchase	1	1,200	1,200
March 26	Purchase	1	1,300	1,300
March 29	Purchase	1	1,400	1,400
	Total Cost of Goods Available for Sale			$6,700

Cost of Goods Sold

Date	Quantity	Cost per Unit	Total Cost
March 22 Sale	1	$1,200	$1,200
March 30 Sale	1	1,400	1,400
Total Cost of Goods Sold	2		$2,600

Ending Inventory

Date		Quantity	Cost per Unit	Total Cost
March 1	Beginning Inventory	1	$ 800	$ 800
March 3	Purchase	2	1,000	2,000
March 26	Purchase	1	1,300	1,300
March 31	Ending Inventory	4		$4,100

As Exhibit 8–23 indicates, we assume that the generator purchased on March 17 was sold on March 22 and the generator purchased on March 29 was sold on March 30. The generators remaining in ending inventory are the one from beginning inventory, the two Montoya purchased on March 3, and the one it purchased on March 26. By adding up the costs of these four generators, we determine that the cost of Montoya's ending inventory is $4,100.

Discussion Question

8–12. If Montoya sells two more generators before purchasing any more, under LIFO, which two would we assume the company sold next?

Even if we didn't identify and cost the items we assumed were remaining in ending inventory as we did in Exhibit 8–23, we could determine Montoya's ending inventory cost. Since we know the cost of goods available for sale is $6,700 and the cost of goods sold is $2,600, we can determine the cost of the company's ending inventory for March 2003 by subtracting cost of goods sold from the cost of goods available:

Cost of Goods Available − Cost of Goods Sold = Ending Inventory
$6,700   − $2,600   = $4,100

Exhibit 8–24 shows Montoya's financial statements assuming the company used the LIFO inventory method and had no business transactions during March except those related to the generators and its rent payment.

EXHIBIT 8–24 Montoya Emergency Equipment Corporation's Financial Statements—LIFO Inventory Method

Montoya Emergency Equipment Corporation
Income Statement
For the Month Ended March 31, 2003

Sales	$ 3,000
LESS: Cost of goods sold	2,600
Gross margin	$ 400
Operating expenses:	
Warehouse rent	(200)
Net income (loss)	$ 200

Montoya Emergency Equipment Corporation
Balance Sheets
February 28, 2003, and March 31, 2003

	February 28	March 31
Assets:		
Cash	$21,000	$22,300
Accounts receivable	1,500	3,000
Merchandise inventory	800	4,100
Total assets	$23,300	$29,400
Liabilities and stockholders' equity:		
Accounts payable	$ 0	$ 5,900
Common stock	15,000	15,000
Additional paid-in capital	8,000	8,000
Retained earnings	300	500
Total liabilities and stockholders' equity	$23,300	$29,400

As with the FIFO presentation, we included both the February 28 and March 31 balance sheets in Exhibit 8–24 to demonstrate how the cost of inventory items flows through the financial statements. The $800 in merchandise inventory Montoya had on February 28 becomes the company's beginning inventory for March. During March, Montoya purchased $5,900 of generators. Some of the $6,700 cost of goods available for sale becomes part of the merchandise inventory on the March balance sheet ($4,100), while the rest becomes cost of goods sold on the March income statement

($2,600). The $4,100 merchandise inventory on the March 31 balance sheet represents the unsold generators, while the $2,600 cost of goods sold represents the two generators Montoya sold in March. We combine the $200 net income with the previous retained earnings balance of $300 to arrive at the March 31 retained earnings balance of $500. Now let's compare the financial statements prepared for Montoya Emergency Equipment Corporation using FIFO (Exhibit 8–20) with those prepared using LIFO (Exhibit 8–24). Remember, the two sets of financial statements are based on exactly the same facts. Yet, applying the FIFO inventory method, the company reports net income of $1,000, whereas under the LIFO inventory method, the company reports net income of $200. Moreover, using FIFO, we see results in total assets on the March 31 balance sheet of $30,200, while using LIFO results in total assets on the March 31 balance sheet of $29,400. This demonstrates that when prices are increasing, using FIFO results in both higher reported net income and a higher reported inventory amount. When prices are decreasing, however, LIFO would result in higher reported net income and a higher reported inventory amount. Keep in mind that companies may use either LIFO or FIFO, regardless of their inventory's physical flow.

Discussion Questions

8–13. The FIFO financial statements in Exhibit 8–20 show Montoya Emergency Equipment Corporation to be more profitable than do the LIFO financial statements in Exhibit 8–24. Is the company really more profitable if it uses the FIFO method rather than the LIFO method? Explain.

8–14. How would you explain the differences between these two sets of financial statements to someone who did not know the facts behind them?

8–15. In a time of rising prices, which inventory method would you choose for your company if you were trying to impress a banker with your company's success?

The third cost flow assumption we will discuss is the average cost method. It is as logical as both FIFO and LIFO, and many people also think it is more intuitive.

AVERAGE COST METHOD

average cost method
The inventory cost flow method that assigns an average cost to the units of inventory on hand at the time of each sale.

The **average cost method** is so named because it uses an average cost per unit to determine the cost of goods sold and the cost of goods in ending inventory. Under this method, the average cost per unit for a product changes each time more of that product is purchased and added to inventory. As a practical matter, companies generally calculate a new average cost per unit at the time of each sale or when they otherwise need to know the cost per unit. As Exhibit 8–25 shows, we calculate the average cost per unit by dividing the cost of goods available for sale by the total number of units available for sale.

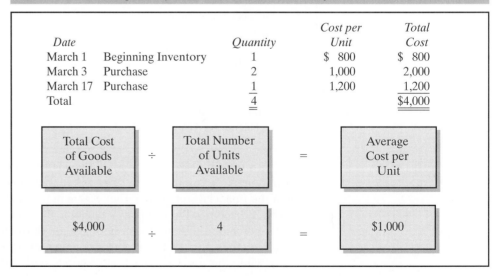

EXHIBIT 8–25 Average Cost per Unit Calculation for Montoya's March 22 Sale

Montoya sold one generator on March 22, and we assigned each of the four generators on hand at that time an average cost of $1,000. Therefore, cost of goods sold for the generator sold on March 22 was $1,000. After the March 22 sale, there are three generators in inventory at an average cost of $1,000 each.

The next sale of a generator took place on March 30. But before that, Montoya purchased two more generators—one on March 26 and one on March 29. We must consider these purchases when we calculate the new average cost per unit for the March 30 sale. So, on March 30, in total, there were five generators in inventory at a total cost of $5,700 resulting in an average cost per unit of $1,140. So, the cost of goods sold for the generator sold on March 30 is $1,140.

Exhibit 8–26 shows the calculation for the new average cost per unit at the time of the March 30 sale. We can now calculate the cost of goods sold that should be reported on Montoya's March income statement. Cost of goods sold for the month is the total of the cost of goods sold for each sale. Therefore, cost of goods sold is:

$$\$1{,}000 + \$1{,}140 = \$2{,}140$$

We can also now calculate the cost of ending inventory. After the March 30 sale, the four generators that were left constitute ending inventory. Therefore, the cost of the company's ending inventory for March is:

$$4 \text{ Units} \times \$1{,}140 = \$4{,}560$$

There is an alternative to this ending inventory calculation. As we indicated for both the FIFO and LIFO methods, by knowing the amount of cost of goods available for sale ($6,700) and the cost of goods sold ($2,140), we can determine the cost of the company's ending inventory for March 2003:

Cost of Goods Available − Cost of Goods Sold = Ending Inventory
$6,700   − $2,140   = $4,560

EXHIBIT 8–26   Average Cost per Unit Calculation for Montoya's March 30 Sale

Date		Quantity	Cost per Unit	Total Cost
March 22	Inventory	3	$1,000	$3,000
March 26	Purchase	1	1,300	1,300
March 29	Purchase	1	1,400	1,400
Total		5		$5,700

Total Cost of Goods Available	÷	Total Number of Untits Available	=	Available Cost per Unit
$5,700	÷	5	=	$1,140

Discussion Question

8–16. If Montoya Emergency Equipment Corporation sells two more generators before purchasing any more, which two would we assume the company sold under the average cost method?

Exhibit 8–27 shows Montoya's financial statement assuming it used the average cost method and had no business transactions during March except those related to the generators and its rent payment.

As with the FIFO and LIFO presentations, we have included both the February 28 and the March 31 balance sheets in Exhibit 8–27 to demonstrate how the cost of inventory items flows through the financial statements. The $800 in merchandise inventory

Montoya Emergency Equipment Corporation
Income Statement
For the Month Ended March 31, 2003

Sales	$ 3,000
LESS: Cost of goods sold	2,140
Gross margin	$ 860
Operating expenses:	
Warehouse rent	$ (200)
Net income (loss)	$ 660

Montoya Emergency Equipment Corporation
Balance Sheets
February 28, 2003, and March 31, 2003

Assets:	February 28	March 31
Cash	$21,000	$22,300
Accounts receivable	1,500	3,000
Merchandise inventory	800	4,560
Total assets	$23,300	$29,860
Liabilities and stockholders' equity:		
Accounts payable	$ 0	$ 5,900
Common stock	15,000	15,000
Additional paid-in capital	8,000	8,000
Retained earnings	300	960
Total liabilities and stockholders' equity	$23,300	$29,860

EXHIBIT 8–27   Montoya Emergency Equipment Corporation's Financial Statements—
Average Cost Method

Montoya had on February 28 becomes the beginning inventory for March. During
March, the company purchased $5,900 of generators. Some of the $6,700 cost of goods
available for sale becomes part of the merchandise inventory on the March balance
sheet ($4,560), while the rest becomes cost of goods sold on the March income state-
ment ($2,140). The $4,560 of merchandise inventory on Montoya's March 31 balance
sheet represents the unsold generators, while the $2,140 cost of goods sold represents
the two generators Montoya sold in March. We combine the $660 net income with the
previous retained earnings balance of $300 to arrive at the March 31 retained earnings
balance of $960.

Discussion Question ●

8–17. Using Montoya Emergency Equipment Corporation's financial statements in
Exhibit 8–27, explain the increase in cash from $21,000 to $22,300.

We have explored four popular inventory approaches and have seen how they
result in different cost of goods sold and ending inventory amounts. Now we will further explore how the inventory cost flow method a company selects affects its financial
statements.

◆ THE EFFECTS OF INVENTORY COST FLOW METHOD CHOICE

The financial statements we prepared for Montoya Emergency Equipment Corporation using the average cost method (Exhibit 8–27) are based on exactly the same set of
facts as the ones we prepared using FIFO (Exhibit 8–20) and LIFO (Exhibit 8–24).
That is, the reality is the same. What differs is the measurement of that reality. Exhibit
8–28 summarizes the differences that result from using the three different cost flow
assumptions.

	FIFO	LIFO	Average Cost
Goods Available for Sale	$6,700	$6,700	$6,700
Income Statement:			
Cost of Goods Sold	$1,800	$2,600	$2,140
Net Income	$1,000	$200	$660
Balance Sheet:			
Ending Inventory	$4,900	$4,100	$4,560
Retained Earnings	$1,300	$ 500	$ 960

EXHIBIT 8–28 Effect of Inventory Cost Flow Assumptions

It appears that Montoya Emergency Equipment Corporation is most profitable if it employs the FIFO method and least profitable if it uses the LIFO method. The average cost method results in profits somewhere between FIFO and LIFO. In reality, a company is no "better off" when it selects one cost flow method over another. Let's take a closer look at the two opposite ends of the inventory spectrum, FIFO and LIFO.

EFFECTS OF FIFO

As you have seen, FIFO matches the oldest product cost with current sales revenue. What this means is that, when inventory prices are changing, it is probable that sales revenue will be matched with costs that are different (older) than the current replacement costs of the products sold. This is because FIFO assumes that the earliest goods were sold first and that the most current costs are associated with goods left in ending merchandise inventory. Financial statement users should be aware of this when they are trying to determine the future earnings potential of a company that uses FIFO.

FIFO provides good information to decision makers trying to determine the present condition of a company because it values inventory with costs that are the most recent and up to date. When a company uses FIFO, it assigns the most current product cost to ending inventory. Therefore, the ending inventory cost shown on a company's balance sheet would closely approximate the current value of the inventory.

EFFECTS OF LIFO

As you have seen, LIFO matches the most recent product cost with sales revenue. LIFO probably provides the best information available for financial decision makers trying to determine the future earnings potential of a company. However, over time, LIFO may distort the dollar amount companies assign to inventory on their balance sheets because the costs used to value LIFO ending inventories may be so old they are severely outdated. For example, if a company has had a product in inventory continually for 20 years, at least part of the cost assigned to that product will be cost from 20 years ago. If prices are increasing, the dollar amount the balance sheet shows for inventory will be unrealistically low. This is what happened at Palmer Nursery, the example we used in the opening vignette for this chapter. Remember that you were concerned when you looked at the company's balance sheet because the dollar amount of inventory was so low. And yet, when you made your site visit, you found a huge amount of physical inventory. To demonstrate how this happened at Palmer (and could happen in any company), we will look at just one item from Palmer's operation, an aloe vera plant.

Let's say that Palmer purchased 1,000 aloe vera plants at the beginning of 1983 for $1.00 each. Since 1983, the company has purchased and sold countless aloe vera plants but always keeps a minimum of 1,000 plants in inventory. So, at the end of 2003, Palmer has 1,000 aloe vera plants on hand. Now, you know that these are not the same 1,000 plants Palmer purchased in 1983. Those were sold long ago, as were the ones Palmer bought in 1984, 1985, and so on. Remember, that is physical flow and we're talking here about cost flow. Now let's assume that the cost of nursery plants has increased by about 3 percent each year. Exhibit 8–29 shows how Palmer's cost per aloe vera plant has increased since 1983.

Year	Cost at Beginning of Year	Percent Increase	Cost at End of Year
1983	$1.00	103%	$1.03
1984	1.03	103%	1.06
1985	1.06	103%	1.09
1986	1.09	103%	1.13
1987	1.13	103%	1.16
1988	1.16	103%	1.19
1989	1.19	103%	1.23
1990	1.23	103%	1.27
1991	1.27	103%	1.30
1992	1.30	103%	1.34
1993	1.34	103%	1.38
1994	1.38	103%	1.43
1995	1.43	103%	1.47
1996	1.47	103%	1.51
1997	1.51	103%	1.56
1998	1.56	103%	1.60
1999	1.60	103%	1.65
2000	1.65	103%	1.70
2001	1.70	103%	1.75
2002	1.75	103%	1.81
2003	1.81	103%	1.86

EXHIBIT 8–29 Cost Increase of Aloe Vera Plants Since 1983

Even though Palmer's 2003 replacement cost for the 1,000 aloe vera plants is $1,860 (1,000 × $1.86), under LIFO, Palmer would value the plants on hand at the end of 2003 at $1,000 (1,000 × $1.00) for its December 31, 2003, inventory. This is because Palmer uses the cost of the most recently purchased products for its cost of goods sold (last-in, first-out), and it uses the cost of the inventory it purchased earliest to value its ending inventory. A plant that costs Palmer $1.86 today cost the company only $1.00 in 1983. Because the physical inventory of plants has never fallen below 1,000 units, the 1,000 aloe vera plants on hand at the end of 2003 each carry a 1983 cost ($1.00). If this were the case for all of the products in Palmer's inventory, the total dollar amount of inventory reported on the company's balance sheet would be dramatically lower than the replacement cost of the inventory. This is why LIFO does not provide the best information for decision makers trying to determine the present condition of a company because LIFO values inventory with costs that can be years out of date.

When the authors of *Accounting Trends and Techniques* surveyed 600 companies to determine which inventory cost flow method they used for the year 2000, this was the response:

FIFO	386
LIFO	283
Average Cost	180
Other	38
Total	887

The total of 887 far exceeds the number of companies surveyed because many companies have more than one type of inventory and use more than one method. Montoya, for example, might use the average cost method on its generators, but FIFO on the emergency food supplies it sells.

As was the case with accounting for depreciation of long-lived assets, accounting for the cost of merchandise inventory affects the net income a company reports for a given period. The amount of inventory a company reports is also affected. Remember that the total cost of goods available for sale will be shown as either cost of goods sold (expense on the income statement) or as the cost of ending inventory (asset on the balance sheet). If more of that total cost is shown as expense on the income statement (as would be the case with LIFO in a time of rising prices), then less of that total cost will be shown as the asset inventory on the balance sheet. Informed users of financial statements must have an understanding of the effect of the various inventory cost flow methods if they hope to use accounting information to its fullest potential.

◆ STATEMENT OF CASH FLOWS

As we mentioned in previous chapters, the operating activities section of the statement of cash flows includes cash flows for the revenues and expenses that are associated with a company's ongoing business operations. With respect to the sale of merchandise inventory, operating activities include cash received from customers for sales and cash payments to suppliers for merchandise. In the case of Montoya Emergency Equipment Corporation, cash flow from operating activities for March 2003 does not equal the company's income from operations because of two important factors. First, Montoya's March sales were credit sales rather than cash sales. Second, Montoya purchased the generators in March on account instead of paying cash for them. Rather than confusing you at this point by presenting the statement of cash flows with these complicating factors, we will cover the handling of such complications (and others) in Chapter 10, when we take a closer look at the statement of cash flows.

◆ USING FINANCIAL INFORMATION

Next, we will present a measure that economic decision makers use to evaluate inventory levels—the inventory turnover ratio. As an example, we will use the financial statements for Palmer Nursery we show in Exhibit 8–30.

EXHIBIT 8–30 Palmer Nursery, Inc.'s Financial Statements—LIFO Inventory Method

Palmer Nursery, Inc.
Income Statement
For the Year Ended December 31, 2003

Sales	$1,850,000
LESS: Cost of goods sold	1,125,000
Gross margin	$ 725,000
Operating expenses	(577,000)
Net income (loss)	$ 148,000

Palmer Nursery, Inc.
Balance Sheets
As of December 31, 2003 and 2002

Assets:	2003	2002
Cash	$175,000	$116,000
Merchandise inventory	100,000	106,000
Other assets	415,000	315,000
Total assets	$690,000	$537,000
Liabilities:		
Accounts payable	$ 75,000	$ 70,000
Stockholders' equity:		
Common stock	$ 25,000	$ 25,000
Additional paid-in capital	10,000	10,000
Retained earnings	580,000	432,000
Total stockholders' equity	$615,000	$467,000
Total liabilities and stockholders' equity	$690,000	$537,000

INVENTORY TURNOVER RATIO

inventory turnover ratio
A liquidity ratio that indicates how long a company holds its inventory.

The **inventory turnover ratio** expresses the theoretical number of times the complete inventory was sold during the year. For example, if cost of goods sold is $400,000 and average inventory is $100,000, the inventory turned over or was sold four times ($400,000/$100,000). The formula for this ratio is:

$$\text{Inventory turnover ratio} = \frac{\text{Cost of goods sold}}{\text{Average inventory}}$$

The cost of goods sold figure in the numerator comes from the income statement. The denominator is normally based on the inventory shown on the balance sheet. However, if we are analyzing a company that uses the LIFO inventory method (as Palmer does), it is a common practice to use the company's FIFO inventory value when computing the inventory turnover ratio. By doing so, the inventory turnover calculation is based on the most current costs for both cost of goods sold and inventories. We use an average amount for this ratio for the same reason we used an average amount in earlier ratios. Since the cost of goods sold in the numerator occurred throughout 2003, we should use the amount of inventory throughout the year. We will assume that Palmer has disclosed in its notes to the financial statements that the FIFO value of its 2002 and 2003 inventories were $191,860 and $186,000, respectively, so we determine the average inventory of $188,930 ($191,860 + $186,000 = $377,860/2 = $188,930). We calculate Palmer's inventory turnover ratio for 2003 as:

$$\frac{\$1,125,000}{\$188,930} = 5.95 \text{ times}$$

The inventory turnover ratio for Palmer indicates that its inventory turns over 5.95 times per year. That is, in theory, the company sells its entire inventory the equivalent of nearly six times each year. Inventory turnover varies greatly from industry to industry and company to company, but generally, the higher the inventory turnover without sacrificing customer satisfaction, the better.

You might note that because Palmer's LIFO inventory value is so low, the company's inventory turnover would have been 10.92 times per year had we used its LIFO inventory values. Now, if you think back to the opening vignette of this chapter, you can see how Palmer's inventory value as shown on the balance sheet might have appeared to be too low when in fact the company had plenty of product (maybe even too much).

Palmer's inventory turnover of 5.95 times per year becomes easier to comprehend if we extend the calculation to determine average length of time product is held in inventory before it is sold. To calculate the **average inventory holding period,** we divide the inventory turnover ratio into 365 (the number of days in a year). Palmer's average inventory holding period is:

average inventory holding period The average length of time product is held in inventory.

$$\text{Average inventory holding period in days} = \frac{365}{\text{Inventory turnover ratio}}$$

$$\frac{365}{5.95} = 61.34 \text{ days}$$

This calculation indicates that Palmer's inventory turns over every 61.34 days. That is, in theory, the company sells the equivalent of its entire inventory every 61.34 days. In general, the fewer days sales in inventory, the better, as long as the company has enough inventory to maintain the desired level of customer satisfaction.

Now that you have an understanding of some of the issues and situations that impact financial statements, in Chapter 9, we will explore the balance sheet and income statement in more detail.

Summary •

The term *merchandise inventory* (or *inventory*) refers to the physical units of goods that a company plans to sell. Inventory on hand at the beginning of a given income statement period (beginning inventory) and the inventory bought during the period (purchases) constitute the total amount of goods the company could sell (goods available for sale). Goods available for sale will either be on hand at the end of the period or be assumed sold.

Under accrual accounting, when inventory is purchased, its cost is considered an asset to the company and is listed as such on the balance sheet. As inventory is sold, its cost is converted from an asset to an expense, which is listed on the income statement as cost of goods sold. It follows, then, that the total cost of goods available for sale will end up either as ending inventory (an asset on the balance sheet) or as cost of goods sold (an expense on the income statement).

Two types of systems have been developed to track the cost of inventory. The periodic system counts inventory and traces costs only at the end of each income statement period, while the perpetual system updates inventory counts and costs each time a sale or purchase is made. Perpetual inventory systems usually make use of computer technology and scanners that read UPCs. Even though inventory records are updated often when a perpetual system is in place, physical inventory counts are still necessary. Determining the actual amount of inventory on hand may uncover theft, damage, or spoilage of inventory.

The physical flow of inventory can be quite different from the flow of inventory costs. Several methods have been developed to trace inventory costs as they move from the balance sheet to the income statement. Of the four methods we presented in this chapter, only under the specific identification method is the physical flow and the cost flow the same. The other three methods are cost flow assumptions that prescribe which inventory items are assumed to be the ones sold. The first-in, first-out (FIFO) method assumes that the first units of inventory purchased are the first ones sold. Conversely, the last-in, first-out (LIFO) method assumes that the last units of inventory purchased are the first sold. The average cost method assigns an average cost to the units of inventory on hand at the time of each sale. Companies may choose to use any of these cost flow methods. If the price they pay for inventory items varies during the period, the choice will impact several amounts reported on the company's financial statements.

Inventory Purchasing Issues

This appendix covers two important issues that companies must contend with when they purchase merchandise inventory—payment terms and freight terms.

PAYMENT TERMS AND CASH DISCOUNTS

Suppliers frequently encourage their customer to pay invoices more quickly by offering a relatively small discount, say 2 percent, in exchange for the customer's prompt payment. Sellers spell out such discounts in their *payment terms*. Payment terms are also called *terms of sale, sales terms*, or simply *terms*. Sellers devise payment terms that best suit their needs and appeal to their customers. Sometimes payment terms are spelled out and easy to understand. For example, the terms might say: *A 2% discount is allowed if paid within 10 days, net invoice amount is due if paid within 30 days*. Or the same terms may be presented in a popular, yet more cryptic, fashion as follows: *2/10, N/30*. In either case, the terms specify that a 2 percent discount is allowed if paid within 10 days from the invoice date; otherwise, full payment is due 30 days after the invoice date. Terms of *1/10, EOM, net 60 days EOM* means that a 1 percent discount is allowed if paid within 10 days after the end of the month (EOM) of the sale; otherwise, full payment is due 60 days from the end of the month of the sale.

To demonstrate, let's return to the Montoya Emergency Equipment Corporation example we used in the chapter to present the cost flow assumptions. Recall that Montoya purchased two generators on March 3 for $1,000 each. If that purchase had terms of 2/10, net 30, Montoya must pay the invoice by March 13 to receive a 2 percent discount. Otherwise, Montoya could wait until April 3 but would have to pay the full invoice amount.

To take advantage of the prompt payment discount, more commonly called the *cash discount*, Montoya would pay 98 percent of $2,000, or $1,960 ($2,000 × .98), by March 13. In this case, the discount amounts to $40 (2% × $2,000). Cash discounts are considered part of inventory acquisition cost and therefore reduce the cost of inventory purchases.

Although cash discounts seem relatively small—commonly 1, 2, or 3 percent for example—on an annualized basis, the amounts are substantial. Let's consider cash terms of 2 percent 10 days, net 30 days. In this situation, the seller is offering a 2 percent discount if the buyer will pay within 10 days. If the buyer does not take advantage of the discount, the buyer must pay the invoice in 30 days, or 20 days after the prompt payment date has passed. Therefore, the 2 percent is offered in return for paying the invoice 20 days earlier. This means that the buyer gets 2 percent for a short 20-day investment. There are 18.25 20-day periods in a year (365/20) and if the buyer could get 2 percent for each of these periods, the buyer would earn a 36.5 percent (18.25 × 2%) return on an annualized basis.

FREIGHT TERMS

Freight terms define the point at which title passes from the seller to the buyer. FOB (free on board) shipping point indicates that the title passes when the merchandise leaves the seller's shipping dock. FOB destination indicates that the title passes when the merchandise arrives at the purchaser's unloading dock.

Freight cost may be paid by either the buyer or seller. If the shipment is made *freight collect*, the buyer must pay the freight costs. On the other hand, if the shipment is made *freight prepaid*, the seller pays the freight costs. Freight costs that the buyer pays are considered part of inventory acquisition cost and therefore increase the cost of inventory purchases.

In some cases, the point at which title transfers to the buyer is used as an indication of which party is responsible for the shipping cost. In such a case, if the terms are FOB shipping point, title passes at the sellers shipping dock and the buyer bears the freight expense. If the terms are FOB destination, the seller owns the goods until delivery and bears the freight expense. Keep in mind that this is not always the case, however. For example, when **Eastman Kodak Company** ships merchandise from its warehouse in Rochester to **Pitman Photo Supply** in Miami, **Kodak** ships it FOB shipping point, freight prepaid. In this case, title passes to **Pitman** as soon as the trucking company picks up the merchandise, but **Kodak** pays the freight bill.

If Montoya Emergency Equipment Corporation bought two generators from Taylor Equipment, Inc., on March 3 with terms of FOB shipping point, freight collect, Montoya will pay the shipping costs directly to the freight company (sometimes called the *common carrier* or simply the *carrier*). This is freight paid to ship merchandise *in* to Montoya—in this case, Montoya is the buyer—and therefore the company should increase its cost of the generators accordingly.

We should not confuse freight paid to ship merchandise *in* with freight paid to ship merchandise *out* to customers. Freight paid to ship merchandise out to customers—when Montoya is selling merchandise—would be considered part of selling expense.

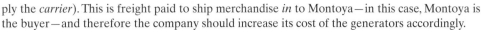

◆◆◆ Appendix B

Recording Inventory Transactions

The accounting procedures in Part II of Chapter 6 and those in this chapter (including Appendix A) have prepared you to understand the following entries regarding the purchase and sale of merchandise inventory. After completing your work on this appendix, you should be able to prepare the journal entries associated with purchase and sale of merchandise inventory.

The recording process for merchandise inventory involves seven basic types of transactions:

Transaction 1: Purchasing inventory
Transaction 2: Paying freight charges on purchases
Transaction 3: Paying the vendor for merchandise
Transaction 4: Returning merchandise
Transaction 5: Selling merchandise to customers
Transaction 6: Receiving cash from customer
Transaction 7: Adjusting inventory records to the physical count

To record these transactions, accountants use the following general ledger accounts:

- Asset accounts:

  Inventory or *Merchandise inventory*

- Expense accounts:

  Cost of goods sold
  Purchase discounts (a contra-account to *Cost of goods sold*)
  Freight-out (a selling expense)

- Revenue accounts:

  Sales or *Sales revenue*
  Sales returns and allowances
  Sales discounts

Recall that debits increase assets, expenses, and losses, and credits increase liabilities, equity, revenues, and gains. You should also recall that debits and credits must equal for each journal entry. We will now examine the journal entries that the Montoya Emergency Equipment Corporation would make to record the transactions for its purchase and sale of merchandise inventory. The entries in this appendix demonstrate the perpetual inventory system, which is far and away the system most commonly used today. Where it is appropriate and nonrepetitive, we will analyze each transaction using the four steps we introduced in Chapter 6.

1. Determine if and when a transaction occurred, which accounts were affected, which account balances should increase and which should decrease, and by how much.
2. Determine which accounts should be debited and which should be credited.
3. Make the journal entry.
4. Review the entry to ensure it is in proper form and that the debits equal the credits.

Transaction 1: On March 3, Montoya Emergency Equipment Corporation purchased two generators on account for $2,000, 2/10, net 30, FOB destination, freight collect.

1. This transaction took place on March 3, 2003. The transaction affects merchandise inventory and accounts payable. We should increase the balances of both merchandise inventory and accounts payable by $2,000.
2. We increase merchandise inventory, an asset account, with a debit, and we increase accounts payable, a liability account, with a credit.
3. The general journal entry:

	2003			
	Mar 3	Merchandise inventory	2,000	
		Accounts payable		2,000

4. A final check of the entry reveals that we dated it correctly, we made the debit part of the entry first, and the entry is in balance. The entry is fine.

Transaction 2: On March 4, Montoya paid the freight bill of $125 from UPS to deliver the generators purchased on March 3 to Montoya's warehouse.

1. This transaction took place on March 4, 2003. Because the freight is for shipping the generators to Montoya's warehouse, it is treated as part of the cost of the merchandise. Therefore, we should increase merchandise inventory. Also, Montoya paid UPS, so it should decrease cash. We should increase the balance of merchandise inventory and decrease cash by $125.
2. We increase merchandise inventory with a debit and decrease cash with a credit.
3. The general journal entry:

	2003			
	Mar 4	Merchandise inventory	125	
		Cash		125

4. A final check of the entry reveals that it is fine.

Transaction 3: First Assumption: Assume that on March 12, 2003, Montoya paid for the generators it purchased on March 3. Note that Montoya paid the invoice within the discount period.

1. This transaction took place on March 12, 2003. Montoya took the 2 percent cash discount of $40 ($2,000 × .02) and paid only the remaining 98 percent of the invoice, which amounts to $1,960 ($2,000 × .98). The transaction affects accounts payable, cash, and, because the discount is considered a reduction in the inventory's acquisition cost, merchandise inventory. Instead of affecting the merchandise inventory account, some companies use an account called *purchase discounts*. We should decrease the balance of accounts payable by the amount of the liability satisfied by the payment. In this case, even though Montoya is paying less than the full invoice amount, the payment satisfies the entire liability. Therefore, we should decrease accounts payable by $2,000, decrease cash by the $1,960 paid, and decrease merchandise inventory by the $40 cash discount.
2. We decrease accounts payable with a debit, and we decrease both cash and inventory with credits.
3. The general journal entry:

	2003			
	Mar 12	Accounts payable	2,000	
		Cash		1,960
		Merchandise inventory (or purchase discounts)		40

4. A final check of the entry reveals that it is fine.

Transaction 3: Second Assumption: Now assume that Montoya didn't pay for the generators it purchased on March 3 until April 2, 2003. Note that under this assumption, Montoya did not pay for the generators in time to earn the cash discount.

1. Under this assumption, this transaction took place on April 2, 2003. Because Montoya did not pay for the generators within the discount period, it paid the full invoice amount and took no discount. Therefore, the transaction affects accounts payable and cash. We should decrease the balances of both accounts payable and cash by the $2,000 Montoya paid.
2. We decrease accounts payable with a debit, and we decrease cash with a credit.
3 The general journal entry:

	2003			
	Apr 2	Accounts payable	2,000	
		Cash		2,000

4. A final check of the entry reveals that it is fine.

Transaction 4: Now let's assume that instead of paying for the generators, Montoya returned them to the manufacturer on March 8, 2003.

1. This transaction took place on March 8, 2003. When a company uses a perpetual inventory system, the entry to record a return of merchandise is simply a reversal of the entry made to record the purchase. Therefore, the entry affects accounts payable and merchandise inventory. We should decrease the balances of both accounts payable and merchandise inventory by the $2,000 cost of the merchandise Montoya returned.
2. We decrease accounts payable with a debit, and we decrease merchandise inventory with a credit.
3. The general journal entry:

```
2003
Mar 8   Accounts payable                    2,000
             Merchandise inventory                    2,000
```

4. A final check of the entry reveals that it is fine.

Transaction 5: On March 17, Montoya sold a generator to Earheart Industries for $1,500 on account with terms of 2/10, net/30.

1. This transaction took place on March 17, 2003. Montoya sold the generator to Earheart on account, so the transaction affects sales and accounts receivable. Also, under the perpetual method, we must make an entry to move the cost of the sold generator from merchandise inventory to cost of goods sold. We should increase both sales and accounts receivable by the $1,500 selling price. In addition, assuming Montoya Emergency Equipment Corporation uses FIFO, we should increase cost of goods sold and decrease merchandise inventory by the generator's $800 cost.
2. We increase accounts receivable with a debit and increase sales with a credit. Also, we increase cost of goods sold, an expense, with a debit, and we decrease merchandise inventory with a credit.
3. The general journal entry:

```
2003
Mar 17   Accounts receivable                 1,500
              Sales                                    1,500
     17   Cost of goods sold                    800
              Merchandise inventory                    800
```

4. A final check of the entry reveals that it is fine.

Transaction 6: First Assumption: Assume that on March 26 Earheart Industries paid Montoya for the generator it purchased on March 17, 2003. Note that under this assumption, Earheart paid Montoya for the generator within the discount period.

1. This transaction took place on March 26, 2003. The customer deducted the 2 percent cash discount of $30 ($1,500 3 .02) from its payment, so Montoya will receive a payment of $1,470, which is 98 percent of the sale amount ($1,500 3 .98). This transaction affects cash and accounts receivable, and, when a customer takes a discount for prompt payment, the sales discounts account is used. We should increase cash by the $1,470 received and increase sales discounts by the $30 discount. We should decrease the balance of accounts receivable by the amount of the receivable satisfied by the customer's payment. In this case, even though the customer paid less than the full invoice amount, the payment satisfies the entire liability. Therefore, we should decrease accounts receivable by $1,500.
2. We increase cash with a debit, and we also increase sales discounts, a contra-revenue account, with a debit. We decrease accounts receivable with a credit.
3. The general journal entry:

```
2003
Mar 26   Cash                                1,470
              Sales discounts                       30
              Accounts receivable                    1,500
```

4. A final check of the entry reveals that it is fine.

Transaction 6: **Second Assumption: Now we will assume that Earheart Industries did not pay for the generator it purchased from Montoya until April 16, 2003. Note that under this assumption, Earheart paid Montoya too late to take the prompt payment discount.**

1. This transaction took place on April 16, 2003. The customer paid too late to take advantage of the cash discount, so it paid Montoya the full $1,500. Therefore, this transaction affects only cash and accounts receivable. We should increase cash and decrease accounts receivable by the $1,500 Montoya received.
2. We increase cash with a debit, and we decrease accounts receivable with a credit.
3. The general journal entry:

```
2003
Apr 16   Cash                              1,500
              Accounts receivable                    1,500
```

4. A final check of the entry reveals that it is fine.

Transaction 7: **Assume that on December 31, 2003, Montoya's accounting records reflected a perpetual inventory balance of nine generators at $1,400 each. Assume further that the company took a physical count of its inventory and discovered only eight generators in stock. Montoya Emergency Equipment Corporation must adjust its perpetual inventory records to reflect the reality of having only eight generators in inventory.**

1. It would be difficult, if not impossible, to determine when the missing generator disappeared. The discrepancy was detected when the physical inventory was taken on December 31. Therefore, we use December 31, 2003, as the date for the entry to adjust the perpetual inventory records to match the physical count. Generally, we adjust cost of goods sold and merchandise inventory as necessary to bring the accounting records in balance with the physical inventory count. In this case, since there is an inventory shortage, we decrease merchandise inventory and increase cost of goods sold by $1,400.
2. We increase cost of goods sold with a debit, and we decrease merchandise inventory with a credit.
3. The general journal entry:

```
2003
Dec 31   Cost of goods sold                1,400
              Merchandise inventory                  1,400
```

4. A final check of the entry reveals that it is fine.

In Transaction 7, we assumed that the perpetual inventory records reflected a lower amount of inventory than Montoya actually had in stock. If, on the other hand, Montoya's December 31 physical inventory count had revealed that the actual inventory was *more* than the amount the perpetual inventory reflected, the adjustment would have been a debit to merchandise inventory, and cost of goods sold would have been credited.

Key Terms •

- average cost method, F–322
- average inventory holding period, F–328
- beginning inventory, F–304
- book inventory, F–312
- cost of goods sold, F–305

- cost of sales, F–305
- first-in, first-out (FIFO), F–317
- goods available for sale, F–304
- inventory, F–304
- inventory turnover ratio, F–328
- last-in, first-out (LIFO), F–319

- merchandise inventory, F–304
- periodic inventory system, F–311
- perpetual inventory system, F–311
- purchases, F–304
- specific identification method, F–313

Review the Facts

A. Define the terms *inventory* and *merchandise inventory*.
B. What two amounts are added to determine goods available for sale?
C. Goods available for sale is allocated to two places in financial statements. Name them.
D. Under accrual accounting, the cost of inventory still on hand at the end of the period is shown on which financial statement?
E. Under accrual accounting, the cost of inventory no longer on hand at the end of the period is shown on which financial statement?
F. Explain the difference between the physical flow of merchandise and the cost flow of merchandise.
G. What are the two types of inventory systems? Explain the differences between them.
H. List three causes of differences between book inventory and the results of a physical inventory count.
I. Why are FIFO, LIFO, and average cost referred to as "assumptions"?
J. Describe in your own words the differences among the FIFO, LIFO, and average cost methods.
K. Name the financial ratio used to evaluate inventory. What does it tell you?
L. Describe what is meant by sales terms of 2/10, n/30. (Appendix A)
M. What is the difference between FOB shipping point and FOB destination? (Appendix A)
N. Describe the entry that would be necessary if a company's perpetual inventory records indicated a greater amount of inventory than what physically exists. (Appendix B)

Apply What You Have Learned

LO 1: TERMINOLOGY

8–18. Below is a list of items relating to the concepts presented in this chapter, followed by definitions of those items in scrambled order:

a. Periodic inventory system
b. Perpetual inventory system
c. Goods available for sale
d. Cost of goods sold

e. Merchandise inventory
f. First-in, first-out method
g. Last-in, first-out method
h. Average cost method

1. _____ The total amount of merchandise inventory a company can sell during a particular income statement period.
2. _____ All inventory and cost of goods sold calculations are done at the end of the period.
3. _____ Cost of goods sold is determined based on the assumption that the first units acquired are the first ones sold.
4. _____ Updates both the physical count of inventory units and the cost classification of those units when a transaction involves inventory.
5. _____ The physical units of product a company buys and then resells as part of its business operation.
6. _____ Cost of goods sold is based on the assumption that the last units acquired are the first ones sold.
7. _____ Cost of goods sold is determined based on the total cost of inventory units divided by the number of units.
8. _____ The cost of merchandise inventory that has been converted from an asset on the balance sheet to an expense on the income statement.

Required: Match the letter next to each item on the list with the appropriate definition. Each letter will be used only once.

LO 1: ELEMENTS OF GOODS AVAILABLE FOR SALE

8–19. Identify the various components of goods available for sale and define each component.

LO 1: ELEMENTS OF COST OF GOODS SOLD

8–20. Ned Flanders Company began the month of March 2004 with 304 units of product on hand at a total cost of $9,120. During the month, the company purchased an additional 818 units at $30 per unit. Sales for March were 732 units at a total cost of $21,960.

Required: From the information provided, complete the following schedule:

	Units	Cost
+ Beginning Inventory	_____	$_____
+ Purchases	_____	_____
= Goods Available for Sale	_____	_____
− Cost of Goods Sold	_____	_____
= Ending Inventory	_____	$_____

LO 7: CALCULATE INVENTORY TURNOVER RATIOS

8–21. This problem is a continuation of problem 8–20.

Required:

    a. Compute the inventory turnover ratio for the company.
    b. Compute the average inventory holding period for the company.

LO 1: ELEMENTS OF COST OF GOODS SOLD

8–22. Andrew D. Company began the month of June 2004 with 150 units of product on hand at a total cost of $3,000. During the month, the company purchased an additional 460 units at $20 per unit. Sales for June were 510 units at a total cost of $10,200.

Required: From the information provided, complete the following schedule:

	Units	Cost
+ Beginning Inventory	_____	$_____
+ Purchases	_____	_____
= Goods Available for Sale	_____	_____
− Ending Inventory	_____	_____
= Cost of Goods Sold	_____	$_____

LO 7: CALCULATE INVENTORY TURNOVER RATIOS

8–23. This problem is a continuation of problem 8–22.

Required:

    a. Compute the inventory turnover ratio for the company.
    b. Compute the average inventory holding period for the company.

LO 1: ELEMENTS OF COST OF GOODS SOLD

8–24. Bill Carter Company began the month of April 2005 with 452 units of product on hand at a cost of $54 per unit. During the month, the company purchased an additional 1,500 units at a total cost of $81,000. At the end of April, 616 units were still on hand at a cost of $33,264.

Required: From the information provided, complete the following schedule:

	Units	Cost
+ Beginning Inventory	_____	$_____
+ Purchases	_____	_____
= Goods Available for Sale	_____	_____
− Ending Inventory	_____	_____
= Cost of Goods Sold	_____	$_____

LO 1: ELEMENTS OF COST OF GOODS SOLD

8–25. Jones and Mosley Company began the month of July 2004 with 412 units of product on hand at a cost of $34 per unit. During the month, the company purchased an additional 1,300 units at a total cost of $44,200. At the end of July, 712 units were still on hand at a cost of $24,208.

Required: From the information provided, complete the following schedule:

	Units	Cost
+ Beginning Inventory	_____	$_____
+ Purchases	_____	_____
= Goods Available for Sale	_____	_____
− Ending Inventory	_____	_____
= Cost of Goods Sold	_____	$_____

LO 1: ELEMENTS OF COST OF GOODS SOLD

8–26. Nancy Keegan and Company began the month of February 2004 with 650 units of product on hand at a total cost of $11,050. During the month, the company purchased an additional 1,884 units at $17 per unit. Sales for February were 1,734 units at $64 per unit. The total cost of the units sold was $29,478, and operating expenses totaled $18,900.

Required:

a. From the information provided, complete the following schedule:

	Units	Cost
+ Beginning Inventory	_____	$_____
+ Purchases	_____	_____
= Goods Available for Sale	_____	_____
− Ending Inventory	_____	_____
= Cost of Goods Sold	_____	$_____

b. Prepare Nancy Keegan and Company's income statement for the month ended February 28, 2004.

LO 1: ELEMENTS OF COST OF GOODS SOLD

8–27. Bill Matheis and Company began the month of October 2005 with 470 units of product on hand at a total cost of $15,980. During the month, the company purchased an additional 1,244 units at $34 per unit. Sales for October were 1,280 units at $60 per unit. The total cost of the units sold was $43,520, and operating expenses totaled $11,300.

Required:

a. From the information provided, complete the following schedule:

	Units	Cost
+ Beginning Inventory	_____	$_____
+ Purchases	_____	_____
= Goods Available for Sale	_____	_____
− Ending Inventory	_____	_____
= Cost of Goods Sold	_____	$_____

b. Prepare Bill Matheis and Company's income statement for the month ended October 31, 2005.

LO 3 & 4: COST FLOW VERSUS PHYSICAL FLOW OF GOODS

8–28. Mary Reed TV Sales and Service began the month of March with two identical TV sets in inventory. During the month, six additional TV sets (identical to the two in beginning inventory) were purchased as follows:

2 on March 9
1 on March 13
3 on March 24

The company sold two of the TV sets on March 12, another one on March 17, and two more on March 28.

Required:

    a. Assume the company uses a perpetual inventory system and the first-in, first-out cost flow method, from a cost flow perspective:

        1. Which two TV sets were sold on March 12?
        2. Which one was sold on March 17?
        3. Which two TV sets were sold on March 28?
        4. The cost of which three TV sets will be included in Reed's inventory at the end of March?

    b. If the company uses a perpetual inventory system and the last-in, first-out cost flow method, the cost of which three TV sets will be included in Reed's inventory at the end of March?

LO 3 & 4: COST FLOW VERSUS PHYSICAL FLOW OF GOODS

8–29. Pfeiffer's Piano Sales & Service began the month of February with two identical pianos in inventory. During the month, six additional pianos (identical to the two in beginning inventory) were purchased as follows:

2 on February 10
1 on February 20
3 on February 26

The company sold two of the pianos on February 12, another one on February 17, and two more on February 28.

Required:

    a. Assume the company uses a perpetual inventory system and the first-in, first-out cost flow method, from a cost flow perspective:

        1. Which two pianos were sold on February 12?
        2. Which one was sold on February 17?
        3. Which two pianos were sold on February 28?
        4. The cost of which three pianos will be included in Pfeiffer's inventory at the end of February?

    b. If the company uses a perpetual inventory system and the last-in, first-out cost flow method, the cost of which three pianos will be included in Pfeiffer's inventory at the end of February?

LO 4: INVENTORY COST

8–30. The Tomlin Company purchased 500 drill presses from the Falcon Machinery Company. Each drill press cost $350. The presses are to be sold for $700 each. Tomlin paid $1,850 for freight to have them shipped in from Falcon and $260 for freight insurance while the presses were in transit. Tomlin Company hired two more salespeople for a cost of $4,000 per month.

Required: Calculate the cost of the inventory of drill presses to be recorded in the books and records.

LO 4: INVENTORY COST

8–31. The Baker Company acquired 4,000 hand saws from the Snaggletooth Saw Company. Each saw cost $10. The saws are to be sold for $25 each. Baker paid $750 for freight and $250 for insurance while the saws were in transit. Baker Company ran a special newspaper ad costing $800 to advertise the saws.

Required: Calculate the cost of the inventory of saws to be recorded in the books and records.

LO 4: INVENTORY COST

8–32. The Winter Company acquired 10,000 cases of wine from the Sonoma Wine Company. Each case of wine cost $130 and contains 12 bottles. The wine will sell for $20 per bottle.

Sonoma paid $1,200 for freight and $550 for freight insurance while the wine was in transit. Winter Company ran a special newspaper ad costing $1,800 to advertise the wine.

Required: Calculate the cost of the inventory of wine to be recorded in the books and records.

LO 4: INVENTORY COST

8–33. The Zeus Grocery Store began operations on July 1. The following transactions took place in the month of July.

  a. Cash purchases of merchandise during July were $500,000.
  b. Purchases of merchandise on account during July were $400,000.
  c. The cost of freight to bring the product in to Zeus was $25,000.
  d. Zeus returned $22,000 of merchandise purchased in part b to the supplier.
  e. The grocery store manager's salary is $3,000 for the month.

Required: Determine the amount that Zeus Grocery should use to calculate the cost of its merchandise inventory.

LO 4: INVENTORY COST

8–34. Chang's Gift Shop began operations on September 1. The following transactions took place in the month of September.

  a. Cash purchases of merchandise during September were $175,000.
  b. Purchases of merchandise on account during September were $225,000.
  c. The cost of freight to bring the merchandise in to Chang's was $5,000.
  d. Electricity cost totaled $800 for the month.
  e. Store rent was $2,400 for the month.
  f. Chang's returned $13,000 of merchandise purchased in part b to the supplier.
  g. The store manager's salary is $3,000 for the month.
  h. Advertising for the month of September totaled $4,000.

Required: Calculate the amount that Chang's should include in the valuation of its merchandise inventory.

LO 6: VERY SIMPLE FIFO, LIFO, AND AVERAGE INVENTORY CALCULATIONS— ONE SALE

8–35. The following information pertains to the inventory records of Gene's Pool Supply:

Date	Purchases (Units)	Cost per Unit	Total Cost
June 1	2,400	$100	$240,000
June 20	3,600	120	432,000
June 27	1,500	130	195,000
Total Goods Available for Sale	7,500		$867,000

The company's only sale occurred on June 30 when it sold 5,925 units. Inventory at the end of June was 1,575 units.

Required: Compute the cost of the inventory at June 30 and the cost of goods sold for the month of June under each of the following cost flow assumptions:

  a. FIFO
  b. LIFO
  c. Average cost method

LO 7: CALCULATE INVENTORY TURNOVER RATIOS

8–36. This problem is a continuation of problem 8–35.

Required:

    a. Compute the inventory turnover ratios for the company under FIFO, LIFO, and the average inventory cost methods.

    b. Compute the average inventory holding period for the company under FIFO, LIFO, and the average inventory cost methods.

    c. How does management's choice of inventory cost flow assumption impact the results of the inventory ratio calculations?

LO 6: VERY SIMPLE FIFO, LIFO, AND AVERAGE INVENTORY CALCULATIONS—ONE SALE

8–37. The following information pertains to one of the products sold by Casey's Computer Supply:

Date	Purchases (Units)	Cost per Unit	Total Cost
November 1	110	$28	$ 3,080
November 12	310	22	6,820
November 25	80	15	1,200
Total Goods Available for Sale	500		$11,100

The company's only sale occurred on November 30 when it sold 385 units. Inventory at the end of November was 115 units.

Required: Compute the cost of the inventory at November 30 and the cost of goods sold for the month of November under each of the following cost flow assumptions:

    a. FIFO
    b. LIFO
    c. Average cost method

LO 6: VERY SIMPLE FIFO, LIFO, AND AVERAGE INVENTORY CALCULATIONS—ONE SALE

8–38. The following information pertains to one of the products sold by William's Wholesale Supply:

Date	Purchases (Units)	Cost per Unit	Total Cost
December 1	800	$3.20	$2,560.00
December 17	750	3.55	2,662.50
December 29	950	3.95	3,752.50
Total Goods Available for Sale	2,500		$8,975.00

The company's only sale occurred on December 31 when it sold 1,580 units. Inventory at the end of December was 920 units.

Required: Compute the cost of the inventory at December 31 and the cost of goods sold for the month of December under each of the following cost flow assumptions:

    a. FIFO
    b. LIFO
    c. Average cost method

LO 6: SIMPLE FIFO, LIFO, AND AVERAGE INVENTORY CALCULATIONS—ONE SALE

8–39. Penny's Precious Metals Company purchases silver to sell by the ounce. During the month of August, its first month of operations, Penny's purchased the following silver:

Date	Purchases	Cost per Unit	Total Cost
August 1	50 ounces	$35.00	$1,750
August 8	25 ounces	39.00	975
August 19	30 ounces	42.00	1,260
August 22	15 ounces	43.00	645
August 29	20 ounces	45.00	900
Total Goods Available for Sale	140 ounces		$5,530

Penny's made only one sale during August. The sale occurred on August 30 and was for 108 ounces of silver. At the end of August, the company had 32 ounces of silver in inventory.

Required: Assuming the company uses a perpetual system, compute the cost of the inventory at August 31 and the cost of goods sold for the month of August under each of the following cost flow assumptions:

a. FIFO
b. LIFO
c. Average cost method

LO 7: CALCULATE INVENTORY TURNOVER RATIOS

8–40. This problem is a continuation of problem 8–39.

Required:

a. Compute the inventory turnover ratios for the company under the FIFO inventory cost flow assumption.
b. Compute the average inventory holding period for the company under the FIFO inventory cost flow assumption.
c. What do the results of these ratios tell you about the company?

LO 6: SIMPLE FIFO, LIFO, AND AVERAGE INVENTORY CALCULATIONS— ONE SALE

8–41. The Repo Rock Company purchases rock by the ton to sell to construction companies. During the month of June, its first month of operations, Repo purchased the following:

Date	Purchases (Tons)	Cost per Ton	Total Cost
June 1	700	$100	$ 70,000
June 6	250	120	30,000
June 17	300	125	37,500
June 24	150	130	19,500
June 29	200	145	29,000
Total Goods Available for Sale	1,600		$186,000

Repo Rock's only sale was on June 30. On June 30, the company sold 1,370 tons of rock. Inventory at the end of June was 230 tons.

Required: Assuming the company uses a perpetual system, compute the cost of the inventory at June 30 and the cost of goods sold for the month of June under each of the following cost flow assumptions:

a. FIFO
b. LIFO
c. Average cost method

LO 7: CALCULATE INVENTORY TURNOVER RATIOS

8–42. This problem is a continuation of problem 8–41.

Required:

a. Compute the inventory turnover ratios for the company under the FIFO inventory cost flow assumption.
b. Compute the average inventory holding period for the company under the FIFO inventory cost flow assumption.
c. What do the results of these ratios tell you about the company?

LO 2, 5, & 6: FIFO AND LIFO INVENTORY CALCULATIONS—MULTIPLE SALES

8–43. Majestic Commercial Supply reported the following information for the year 2004 for one of its products:

Date		Units	Unit Cost	Total Cost
Jan 2	Beginning Inventory	1,000	$10	$10,000
Jan 15	Purchased	1,500	11	16,500
Jan 20	Sold 1,400 Units			
Mar 23	Purchased	1,200	12	14,400
Apr 2	Sold 1,300 Units			
Jun 10	Purchased	1,000	13	13,000
Aug 18	Purchased	1,100	15	16,500
Sep 12	Sold 2,100 Units			
Dec 1	Purchased	1,400	16	22,400
Dec 20	Sold 600 Units			
Total Goods Available for Sale		7,200		$92,800

At the end of the year, a physical count is taken and there are 1,800 units left on December 31, 2004.

Required: Use the perpetual inventory system and determine the ending inventory and the cost of goods sold at December 31, 2004, using:

a. FIFO cost flow method
b. LIFO cost flow method

LO 2, 5, & 6: FIFO AND LIFO INVENTORY CALCULATIONS—MULTIPLE SALES

8–44. The Speace Electrical Supply Company reported the following information for the year 2005 for X-rite Switches:

Date		Units	Unit Cost	Total Cost
Jan 2	Beginning Inventory	500	$10	$ 5,000
Jan 23	Purchased	800	11	8,800
Mar 14	Purchased	600	12	7,200
Mar 18	Sold 1,000 Units			
Jul 5	Purchased	500	13	6,500
Aug 10	Purchased	1,100	14	15,400
Sep 2	Sold 1,300 Units			
Dec 15	Purchased	1,200	15	18,000
Dec 19	Sold 1,800 Units			
Total Goods Available for Sale		4,700		$60,900

A physical count taken on December 31, 2005, revealed that 600 units remained in inventory.

Required: Determine the ending inventory and the cost of goods sold at December 31, 2005, using:

a. FIFO cost flow method
b. LIFO cost flow method

LO 7: CALCULATE INVENTORY TURNOVER RATIOS

8–45. This problem is a continuation of problem 8–44.

Required:

a. Compute the inventory turnover ratios for the company under the FIFO inventory cost flow assumption.
b. Compute the average inventory holding period for the company under the FIFO inventory cost flow assumption.
c. What do the results of these ratios tell you about the company?

LO 2, 5, & 6: FIFO AND LIFO INVENTORY CALCULATIONS—MULTIPLE SALES

8–46. The Kundrat Widget Company reported the following information for the month of January, regarding widgets:

Date		Units	Unit Cost	Total Cost
Jan 1	Beginning Inventory	500	$71	$ 35,500
Jan 3	Purchased	800	73	58,400
Jan 6	Sold 1,020 Units			
Jan 10	Purchased	700	75	52,500
Jan 14	Sold 540 Units			
Jan 22	Purchased	600	80	48,000
Jan 25	Purchased	1,100	85	93,500
Jan 27	Sold 1,190 Units			
Jan 29	Purchased	1,200	87	104,400
Jan 30	Sold 1,315 Units			
Total Goods Available for Sale		4,900		$392,300

At the end of January, a physical count was taken revealing that there were 835 widgets left in inventory.

Required: Determine the January ending inventory and the cost of goods sold using:

a. FIFO cost flow method
b. LIFO cost flow method

LO 2, 5, & 6: FIFO, LIFO, AND AVERAGE COST INVENTORY CALCULATIONS— MULTIPLE SALES

8–47. The Spring Sales Company reported the following information for the year 2005, regarding their No. 123 spring:

Date		Units	Cost per Spring	Total Cost
Jan 2	Beginning Inventory	5,000	$15	$ 75,000
Purchases:				
Jan 23		8,000	14	112,000
Mar 14		7,000	13	91,000
Jul 5		6,000	11	66,000
Aug 10		11,000	9	99,000
Dec 15		12,000	8	96,000
Total Goods Available for Sale		49,000		$539,000

Sales of No. 123 springs occurred as follows:

Jan 28	Sold	6,000 springs
Feb 15	Sold	3,000 springs
Jul 6	Sold	15,000 springs
Aug 12	Sold	10,000 springs
Dec 24	Sold	6,600 springs

At the end of the year, a physical count is taken and there are 8,400 springs left on December 31, 2005.

Required: Use the perpetual inventory system and determine the December 31, 2005, ending inventory and the cost of goods sold using:

a. FIFO cost flow method
b. LIFO cost flow method
c. Average cost method

LO 2, 5, & 6: FIFO, LIFO, AND AVERAGE COST INVENTORY CALCULATIONS— MULTIPLE SALES

8–48. During the month of August, the first month of its operations, Maupin Mercantile Company had the following transactions:

		Units Purchased	Cost per Unit	Total Cost
Date				
August 1	Purchased	50	$35	$1,750
August 3	Sold 40 Units			
August 8	Purchased	25	40	1,000
August 11	Sold 20 Units			
August 19	Purchased	30	42	1,260
August 20	Sold 18 Units			
August 22	Purchased	10	43	430
August 29	Sold 30 Units			
August 30	Purchased	20	45	900
Total Goods Available for Sale		135		$5,340

Maupin's has 27 units left in inventory at the end of August.

Required: Assuming the company uses a perpetual system, compute the cost of the inventory at August 31 and the cost of goods sold for the month of August under each of the following cost flow assumptions:

a. FIFO cost flow method
b. LIFO cost flow method
c. Average cost method

LO 2, 5, & 6: FIFO, LIFO, AVERAGE COST INVENTORY CALCULATIONS—MULTIPLE SALES

8–49. During the month of June, its first month of operations, Walker Company had the following inventory transactions:

		Purchases (Units)	Cost per Unit	Total Cost
June 1	Purchased	700	$100	$ 70,000
June 3	Sold 400 units			
June 6	Purchased	250	105	26,250
June 17	Purchased	300	115	34,500
June 20	Sold 400 units			
June 24	Purchased	150	118	17,700
June 26	Sold 570 units			
June 30	Purchased	200	125	25,000
Total Goods Available for Sale		1,600		$173,450

Walker had 230 units left in inventory at the end of June. Assume a perpetual system of inventory.

Required: Compute the cost of the inventory at June 30 and the cost of goods sold for the month of June under each of the following cost flow assumptions:

a. FIFO cost flow assumption
b. LIFO cost flow assumption
c. Average cost method

LO 5 & 6: CALCULATION AND COMPARISON OF COST FLOW ASSUMPTIONS—INCREASING PRICES

8–50. Cox Company buys and then resells a product that is subject to rather severe cost increases. Following is information concerning Cox's inventory activity during the month of July 2005:

July 1: 431 units on hand, $3,017
July 2: Sold 220 units
July 9: Purchased 500 units @ $8.00 per unit
July 12: Purchased 200 units @ $8.50 per unit
July 16: Sold 300 units
July 21: Purchased 150 units @ $9.00 per unit

July 24: Purchased 50 units @ $9.75 per unit
July 29: Sold 500 units

Required:

   a. Assuming Cox employs a perpetual inventory system, calculate cost of goods sold for the month of July 2005 and ending inventory at July 31, 2005, using the following:

      1. FIFO cost flow assumption
      2. LIFO cost flow assumption
      3. Average cost method (round all unit cost calculations to the nearest penny)

   b. Which of the three methods resulted in the highest cost of goods sold for July?
   c. Which one would result in the highest net income for the company?
   d. Which one would provide the highest ending inventory value for Cox's balance sheet?
   e. In times of rising prices, which inventory cost flow assumption should Cox select if the company's intention is to favorably impress its banker?

LO 5 & 6: CALCULATION AND COMPARISON OF COST FLOW ASSUMPTIONS—DECREASING PRICES

8–51. The following information is available concerning Elsea Computer Component Company's inventory activity for the month of October 2005:

   October 1:   216 units on hand @ $14 per unit
   October 5:   Sold 80 units
   October 7:   Purchased 150 units @ $13 per unit
   October 11: Purchased 100 units @ $12 per unit
   October 15: Sold 200 units
   October 21: Purchased 300 units @ $10 per unit
   October 25: Purchased 50 units @ $8 per unit
   October 29: Sold 350 units

Required:

   a. Assuming Elsea employs a perpetual inventory system, calculate cost of goods sold (units and cost) for the month of October using the following:

      1. FIFO cost flow assumption
      2. LIFO cost flow assumption
      3. Average cost method (round all unit cost calculations to the nearest penny)

   b. Which of the three methods resulted in the highest cost of goods sold for October?
   c. Which one will provide the highest net income?
   d. Which one will provide the highest ending inventory value for Elsea's balance sheet?
   e. If the price of the products Elsea sells generally decreases over time, which inventory cost flow assumption should the company select if its intention is to favorably impress its banker?

LO 5 & 6: CALCULATION AND COMPARISON OF COST FLOW ASSUMPTIONS—INCREASING PRICES

8–52. Zingle's buys and then resells a single product as its primary business activity. Following is information concerning the Zingle's inventory activity for the product during August 2004:

   August 1:   210 units on hand @ $5.10 per unit
   August 5:   Sold 80 units
   August 7:   Purchased 160 units @ $5.25 per unit
   August 11: Purchased 110 units @ $5.30 per unit
   August 15: Sold 200 units
   August 21: Purchased 55 units @ $5.70 per unit
   August 25: Purchased 290 units @ $5.80 per unit
   August 29: Sold 350 units

Required:

a. Assuming Zingle's employs a perpetual inventory system, calculate cost of goods sold (units and cost) for the month of August using the following:

1. FIFO cost flow assumption
2. LIFO cost flow assumption
3. Average cost method (round all unit cost calculations to the nearest penny)

b. Which of the three methods resulted in the highest inventory amount for Zingle's August 31 balance sheet?
c. How would the differences among the three methods affect Zingle's income statement and balance sheet for the month?

LO 5 & 6: CALCULATION AND COMPARISON OF COST FLOW ASSUMPTIONS— DECREASING PRICES

8–53. David Harris Company buys and then resells a single product as its primary business activity. Following is information concerning the David Harris Company's inventory activity for the product during August 2005:

August 1: 200 units on hand @ $18 per unit
August 5: Sold 80 units
August 7: Purchased 170 units @ $17 per unit
August 11: Purchased 90 units @ $15 per unit
August 15: Sold 200 units
August 21: Purchased 275 units @ $14 per unit
August 25: Purchased 90 units @ $12 per unit
August 29: Sold 350 units

Required:

a. Assuming Harris employs a perpetual inventory system, calculate cost of goods sold (units and cost) for the month of August using the following:

1. FIFO cost flow assumption
2. LIFO cost flow assumption
3. Average cost method (round all unit cost calculations to the nearest penny)

b. Which of the three methods resulted in the highest inventory amount for Harris's August 31 balance sheet?
c. How would the differences among the three methods affect Harris's income statement and balance sheet for the month?

LO 5 & 6: CALCULATION AND COMPARISON OF COST FLOW ASSUMPTIONS— STABLE PRICES

8–54. Dennis Lee Company buys and then resells a single product as its primary business activity. Following is information concerning Lee's inventory activity for the product during the month of July 2004:

July 1: 220 units on hand @ $4 per unit
July 5: Sold 80 units
July 7: Purchased 140 units @ $4 per unit
July 11: Purchased 85 units @ $4 per unit
July 15: Sold 200 units
July 21: Purchased 320 units @ $4 per unit
July 25: Purchased 40 units @ $4 per unit
July 29: Sold 350 units

Required:

a. Assuming Lee employs a perpetual inventory system, calculate cost of goods sold (units and cost) for the month of July using the following:

1. First-in, first-out method
2. Last-in, first-out method
3. Average cost method (round all unit cost calculations to the nearest penny)

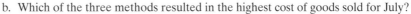

    b. Which of the three methods resulted in the highest cost of goods sold for July?

    c. Describe the differences among income statements and balance sheets prepared under the three cost flow assumptions.

LO 2 & 3: IMPACT OF DIFFERENCES BETWEEN PERPETUAL INVENTORY RECORDS AND PHYSICAL INVENTORY

8–55. The Corning Company's perpetual inventory records indicate that the ending inventory should be $160,000. In fact, when Corning Company's staff completed their annual physical inventory, they discovered that the inventory on hand was actually $156,000.

Required:

    a. With respect to the company's accounting records, what action should the Corning Company's accounting staff take regarding the difference between their perpetual inventory records and the inventory that is actually on hand?

    b. If no action is taken, how would this situation adversely impact the usefulness of the company's financial statements?

LO 2 & 3: IMPACT OF DIFFERENCES BETWEEN PERPETUAL INVENTORY RECORDS AND PHYSICAL INVENTORY

8–56. The Ace Company's perpetual inventory system reflected the following amounts for the year ended December 31, 2004:

Ending Inventory	$1,750,000
Cost of Goods Sold	$15,380,000

The staff completed a physical inventory and found that the inventory was actually $1,680,000.

Required:

    a. Name at least two possible reasons for the difference between the company's perpetual inventory records and the actual physical inventory on hand.

    b. With respect to security issues, name at least two actions the company could take to prevent such a thing from happening in the future.

    c. With regard to the company's accounting records, what action should the company take before it publishes its financial statements regarding the difference?

    d. If the company had already published its financial statements for 2004 when it discovered the difference, how would the situation adversely impact the usefulness of the financial statements? Be specific. Indicate which financial statement amounts would be in error and how much the error would be.

LO: COMPREHENSIVE

8–57. Benny Blades Company and Emeril Behar Company both began their operations on January 2, 2005. Both companies experienced exactly the same reality during 2005: They purchased exactly the same number of units of merchandise inventory during the year at exactly the same cost, and they sold exactly the same number of inventory units at exactly the same selling price during the year. They also purchased exactly the same type and amount of property, plant, and equipment and paid exactly the same amount for those purchases. At the end of 2005, the two companies prepared income statements for the year. Blades reported net income of $92,000 and Behar reported net income of $55,000.

Required: List and discuss all items you can think of that might have caused the reported net income for the two companies to be different. (*Note*: Do not restrict yourself only to items covered in Chapter 8.)

LO: COMPREHENSIVE

8–58. Pete Rush Merchandising Company uses a perpetual inventory system. Both the number of inventory units and the inventory costs are updated whenever an inventory transaction occurs. The company's perpetual inventory accounting records provide the following information for October 2005:

		Units	Cost
+	Beginning Inventory	200	$ 600
+	Purchases	1,700	5,100
=	Goods Available for Sale	1,900	5,700
−	Ending Inventory	400	1,200
=	Cost of Goods Sold	1,500	$4,500

On October 31, 2005, Rush conducted a physical count of its inventory and discovered there were only 375 units of inventory actually on hand.

Required:

a. Show Rush's schedule of cost of goods sold and ending inventory as it should be, to reflect the results of the physical inventory count on October 31.

b. Explain what the company should do regarding its accounting records in light of the physical count.

c. If Rush takes no action regarding its accounting records and the inventory difference, what financial statement amounts will be in error on its October 31 financial reports?

d. What are some possible causes of the difference between the inventory amounts in Rush's accounting records and the inventory amounts from the physical count?

LO 8: APPENDIX A—FREIGHT TERMS AND CASH DISCOUNTS

8–59. The Young Company made the following purchases from the Greene Company in August of the current year:

Aug 2   Purchased $5,000 of merchandise, terms 1/10, n/30, FOB shipping point. The goods were received on August 8.

Aug 5   Purchased $2,000 of merchandise, terms 2/10, n/45, FOB shipping point. The goods were received on August 15.

Aug 10 Purchased $4,000 of merchandise, terms 3/10, n/15, FOB destination. The goods were received on August 18.

Required: For each of the listed purchases, answer the following questions:

a. By what dates should the company pay each invoice in order to take advantage of the discount?

b. When is the payment of each invoice due if the company does not intend to take advantage of the discount?

c. What is the amount of the total cash discounts allowed?

d. Assuming the freight charges are $250 on each purchase and the seller pays freight on FOB destination orders and the buyer pays the freight on FOB shipping point orders and the company takes advantage of all the discounts, what is the total amount of inventory costs for the month of August?

LO 8: APPENDIX A—FREIGHT TERMS AND CASH DISCOUNTS

8–60. The Gruber Company made the following purchases from the Cope Company in May of the current year:

May 2   Purchased $3,000 of merchandise, terms 2/10, n/30, FOB destination. The goods were received on May 10.

May 10 Purchased $2,800 of merchandise, terms 2/10, n/60, FOB shipping point. The goods were received on May 19.

May 20 Purchased $6,000 of merchandise, terms 3/10, n/20, FOB destination. The goods were received on May 23.

Required: For each of the listed purchases, answer the following questions:

a. When is the payment for each invoice due assuming the company would like to take advantage of the discount?

b. When is the payment of each invoice due assuming the company does not intend to take advantage of the discount?

c. What is the total amount of the cash discounts allowed?

d. Assuming the freight charges are $400 on each purchase and the seller pays freight on FOB destination orders and the buyer pays the freight on FOB shipping point orders and the company takes advantage of all the discounts, what is the total amount of inventory costs for the month?

LO 8: APPENDIX A—FREIGHT TERMS AND CASH DISCOUNTS

8–61. The Payne Company made the following purchases from the Metz Company in July of the current year:

July 3   Purchased $7,000 of merchandise, terms 2/10, n/15, FOB shipping point. The goods were received on July 9.

July 7   Purchased $1,700 of merchandise, terms 1/10, n/60, FOB shipping point. The goods were received on July 17.

July 20   Purchased $9,000 of merchandise, terms 4/10, n/30, FOB destination. The goods were received on July 23.

Required: For each of the listed purchases, answer the following questions:

  a. When is the payment for each invoice due assuming the company would like to take advantage of the discount?
  b. When is the payment of each invoice due assuming the company does not intend to take advantage of the discount?
  c. What is the total amount of the cash discounts allowed?
  d. Assuming the freight charges are $100 on each purchase and the seller pays freight on FOB destination orders and the buyer pays the freight on FOB shipping point orders and the company takes advantage of all the discounts, what is the total amount of inventory costs for the month?

LO 8: APPENDIX B—SIMPLE JOURNAL ENTRIES—PURCHASES AND SALES OF INVENTORY

8–62. The Edwards Company had the following transactions during June:

June 1   Purchased 1,000 radios for cash of $20 each for a total of $20,000.
June 3   Purchased 2,500 clocks on account for $10 each for a total of $25,000.
June 5   Sold 250 of the radios that cost $20 each for cash of $8,000.
June 7   Sold, on account, 500 of the clocks that cost $10 each for a total of $7,000.
June 13   Paid for the clocks purchased on June 3.
June 19   Payment received for the June 7 sale.

Required: Prepare the general journal entries to record the June transactions using the perpetual inventory system.

LO 8: APPENDIX B—SIMPLE JOURNAL ENTRIES—PURCHASES AND SALES OF INVENTORY

8–63. The Scofield Wholesale Company had the following transactions during July:

July 7   Purchased 500 cookware sets on account for $56 each for a total of $28,000.
July 9   Purchased 750 cutting boards for cash of $8 each for a total of $6,000.
July 15   Sold 50 of the cookware sets that cost $56 each for cash of $4,150.
July 16   Sold, on account, 150 of the cutting boards that cost $8 each for a total of $1,800.
July 17   Paid for the cookware sets purchased on July 7.
July 27   Payment received for the July 16 sale.

Required: Prepare the general journal entries to record the July transactions using the perpetual inventory system.

LO 8: APPENDIX B—SIMPLE JOURNAL ENTRIES—PURCHASES AND SALES OF INVENTORY

8–64. Manny's Wholesale Sales had the following transactions during May:

May 4   Purchased, on account, inventory for $12,900.
May 5   Inventory purchased for cash of $3,800.
May 14   Sold, on account, merchandise that cost $880 for a total selling price of $1,390.
May 17   Merchandise sold that cost $750 for cash of $1,220.
May 24   Paid for the inventory purchased on May 4.
May 25   Payment received for the May 14 sale.

Required: Prepare the general journal entries to record the May transactions using the perpetual inventory system.

LO 8: APPENDIX B—JOURNAL ENTRIES—PURCHASES, PURCHASE RETURNS, FREIGHT, AND SALES

8–65. The Pierno Trading Company had the following transactions during May:

May 5   Purchased, on account, inventory for $11,900.
May 5   Paid cash in the amount of $120 for freight on inventory purchased.
May 6   Inventory purchased for cash of $1,800.
May 7   Returned and received credit for $900 of the inventory purchased on May 5.
May 11 Sold, on account, merchandise that cost $125 for a total selling price of $275.
May 16 Merchandise sold that cost $250 for cash of $430.
May 25 Paid for the inventory purchased on May 5.
May 27 Payment received for the May 11 sale.

Required: Prepare the general journal entries to record the May transactions using the perpetual inventory system.

LO 8: APPENDIX B—JOURNAL ENTRIES—PURCHASES, PURCHASE RETURNS, FREIGHT, AND SALES

8–66. Tatum Sales, Inc., had the following transactions during July:

July 2   Inventory purchased for cash of $880.
July 3   Sold, on account, merchandise that cost $220 for a total selling price of $330.
July 12 Inventory purchased on account for $950.
July 12 Paid cash of $40 for freight on inventory purchased.
July 16 Sold merchandise that cost $300 for cash of $450.
July 17 Returned and received credit for $130 of the inventory purchased on July 12.
July 25 Paid for the inventory purchased on July 12.
July 27 Payment received for the July 3 sale.

Required: Prepare the general journal entries to record the July transactions using the perpetual inventory system.

LO 8: APPENDIX B—JOURNAL ENTRIES—PURCHASES, PURCHASE RETURNS, FREIGHT, AND SALES

8–67. Florence Company had the following transactions during June:

June 5   Inventory purchased on account for $800.
June 5   Paid cash of $56 for freight on inventory purchased.
June 6   Inventory purchased for cash of $250.
June 7   Returned and received credit for $130 of the inventory purchased on June 5.
June 11 Sold, on account, merchandise that cost $260 for a total selling price of $520.
June 16 Sold merchandise that cost $420 for cash of $840.
June 25 Paid for the inventory purchased on June 5.
June 27 Payment received for the June 11 sale.

Required: Prepare the general journal entries to record the June transactions using the perpetual inventory system.

LO 8 & 9: APPENDIX B—RECORDING PURCHASE AND PURCHASE DISCOUNTS

8–68. Rodgers Company made the following purchases during August:

Aug 2   Purchased $1,000 of merchandise, terms 1% 10, net 30.
Aug 5   Purchased $3,000 of merchandise, terms 2% 10, net 45.
Aug 10   Purchased $7,000 of merchandise, terms 3% 10, net 50.

Required:

a. Prepare journal entries to record each of the purchase transactions.
b. Prepare the journal entries to record the payment of each of the transactions assuming the discount was taken.
c. Prepare the journal entries to record the payment of each of the transactions assuming the discount was not taken.

LO 8 & 9: APPENDIX B—RECORDING PURCHASE AND PURCHASE DISCOUNTS

8–69. Butterfield Wholesale Company made the following purchases during January:

Jan 1   Purchased $22,000 of merchandise, terms 2/10, n/30.
Jan 3   Purchased $33,500 of merchandise, terms 2/10, n/45.
Jan 5   Purchased $127,000 of merchandise, terms 3/10, n/60.

Required:

a. Prepare journal entries to record each of the purchase transactions.
b. Prepare the journal entries to record the payment of each of the transactions assuming the discount was taken.
c. Prepare the journal entries to record the payment of each of the transactions assuming the discount was not taken.

LO 8 & 9: APPENDIX B—RECORDING PURCHASE AND PURCHASE DISCOUNTS

8–70. Daisy Trading Company made the following purchases from the Alonso Company in November:

Nov 1 Purchased $22,000 of merchandise, terms 2/10, n/30.
Nov 3 Purchased $33,500 of merchandise, terms 1/10, n/45.
Nov 5 Purchased $127,000 of merchandise, terms 2/15, n/60.

Required:

a. Prepare journal entries to record each of the purchase transactions.
b. Prepare the journal entries to record the payment of each of the transactions assuming the discount was taken.
c. Prepare the journal entries to record the payment of each of the transactions assuming the discount was not taken.

LO 9: APPENDIX B—JOURNAL ENTRIES—PURCHASES, PURCHASE DISCOUNTS, FREIGHT, SALES, AND SALES DISCOUNTS

8–71. The Steve's Retailing Company had the following transactions:

May 1   Purchased inventory on account for $5,250, terms 2% 10, net 30.
May 1   Paid cash of $225 for freight on inventory purchased.
May 3   Purchased inventory on account for $8,300, terms 2% 20, net 45.
May 12   Sold merchandise that cost $1,600 for $2,200, terms 2% 10, net 30.
May 13   Paid for the inventory purchased on May 3. (Steve's took the discount.)
May 16   Sold merchandise that cost $1,900 for $3,800, terms 2% 10, net 30.
May 17   Returned and received credit for $250 of the inventory purchased on May 1.
May 22   Payment received for the May 12 sale. (Customer took the discount.)
May 22   Paid for inventory purchased on May 3. (Steve's took the discount.)
June 1   Paid for the balance of the inventory purchased on May 1. (Steve's did not take the discount.)
June 27 Received payment for the May 16 sale. (Customer did not take the discount.)

Required: Prepare the general journal entries to record the May and June transactions using the perpetual inventory system.

LO 9: APPENDIX B—JOURNAL ENTRIES—PURCHASES, PURCHASE DISCOUNTS, FREIGHT, SALES, AND SALES DISCOUNTS

8–72. Real Company had the following transactions:

June 5   Purchased inventory on account for $1,800, terms 2% 10, net 30.
June 6   Purchased inventory on account for $3,500, terms 2% 10, net 30.
June 6   Paid cash of $158 for freight on inventory purchased.
June 7   Returned and received credit for $800 of the inventory purchased on June 5.
June 11 Sold merchandise that cost $125 for $250, terms 2% 10, net 30.
June 16 Sold merchandise that cost $425 for $850, terms 2% 10, net 30.
June 14 Paid for the balance of the inventory purchased on June 5. (Real took the discount.)
June 21 Payment received for the June 11 sale. (Customer took the discount.)
July 6   Paid for the inventory purchased on June 6. (Real did not take the discount.)
July 29 Received payment for the June 16 sale. (Customer did not take the discount.)

Required: Prepare the general journal entries to record the June and July transactions using the perpetual inventory system.

LO 9: APPENDIX B—JOURNAL ENTRIES—PURCHASES, PURCHASE DISCOUNTS, FREIGHT, SALES, AND SALES DISCOUNTS

8–73. The Moon Merchandising Company had the following transactions:

May 5   Purchased inventory on account for $2,500, terms 2% 10, net 30.
May 6   Purchased inventory on account for $4,500, terms 2% 10, net 30.
May 6   Cash paid in the amount of $200 for freight on inventory purchased.
May 7   Returned and received credit for $250 of the inventory purchased on May 5.
May 11 Sold merchandise that cost $600 for $1,200, terms 2% 10, net 30.
May 16 Sold merchandise that cost $900 for $1,800, terms 2% 10, net 30.
May 14 Paid for the balance of the inventory purchased on May 5. (Moon took the discount.)
May 21 Payment received for the May 11 sale. (Customer took the discount.)
June 6 Paid for the inventory purchased on May 6. (Moon did not take the discount.)
June 29 Received payment for the May 16 sale. (Customer did not take the discount.)

Required: Prepare the general journal entries to record the May and June transactions using the perpetual inventory system.

LO 9: APPENDIX—ADJUSTING ENTRY FOR THE DIFFERENCE BETWEEN PERPETUAL INVENTORY RECORDS AND PHYSICAL INVENTORY COUNT

8–74. Dowers Company manufactures seats for the aircraft industry. At the end of the year, the company's perpetual inventory records showed the following balances:

Cost of Goods Sold	$996,000
Ending Inventory	$287,000

A physical count of the company's inventory revealed that the actual inventory in the warehouse at December 31, 2004, was $298,000.

Required: Prepare an appropriate adjusting journal entry in light of the discrepancy between the perpetual inventory records and the physical inventory on hand.

LO 9: APPENDIX—ADJUSTING ENTRY FOR THE DIFFERENCE BETWEEN PERPETUAL INVENTORY RECORDS AND PHYSICAL INVENTORY COUNT

8–75. Charles Company's perpetual inventory records indicate that the ending inventory should be $1,688,000. In fact, when Charles' staff completed their annual physical inventory, they discovered that the inventory on hand was actually $1,682,000.

Required:

   a. Prepare the adjusting entry for the difference between the perpetual inventory records and the inventory that is actually on hand.
   b. If no action is taken, how would this situation adversely impact the usefulness of the company's financial statements?

LO 9: APPENDIX—ADJUSTING ENTRY FOR THE DIFFERENCE BETWEEN PERPETUAL INVENTORY RECORDS AND PHYSICAL INVENTORY COUNT

8–76. The Alana Bradley Company's perpetual inventory system reflected the following amounts for the year ended December 31, 2004:

Ending Inventory	$1,680,000
Cost of Goods Sold	$15,900,000

The staff completed a physical inventory and found that the inventory was actually $1,676,000.

Required:

   a. Name at least two possible reasons for the difference between the company's perpetual inventory records and the actual physical inventory on hand.

b. With respect to security issues, name at least two actions the company could take to prevent such a thing from happening in the future.

c. Prepare a journal entry to address the difference between the perpetual inventory and the actual physical inventory on hand.

d. If the company fails to make the entry you propose in part c, how would the situation adversely impact the usefulness of the financial statements? Be specific. Indicate which financial statement amounts would be in error and how much the error would be.

Financial Reporting Exercises

8–77. Go to the Securities and Exchange Commission's (SEC's) Electronic Data Gathering, Analysis, and Retrieval (EDGAR) system and find the Inventories section under the Summary of Significant Accounting Policies in the 2001 Form 10-K for **Wal-Mart Stores, Inc.** Use that information to answer the following.

Required:

a. What kind of cost flow assumptions does **Wal-Mart Stores, Inc.,** use?

b. For each cost flow assumption used, list for what purpose it is used and why you think it is better for that specific purpose.

c. What potential problems do **Wal-Mart Stores, Inc.,** list that may affect future inventory? Come up with a situation that would lead to each of the problems listed for one product that they sell.

8–78. Go to the SEC's EDGAR system and find the financial statements and inventories section in the 2001 Form 10-K for **Home Depot, Inc.** Use that information to answer the following.

Required:

a. What cost flow assumption does **Home Depot, Inc.,** use?

b. What was their cost of goods sold for 2001?

c. What was their inventory at the end of 2001?

d. Using b and c, what was their goods available for sale for 2001?

8–79. Go to the SEC's EDGAR system and find the financial statements and inventories section in the 2001 Form 10-K for **General Electric Co.** Use that information to answer the following.

Required:

a. What cost flow assumption does the GE segment of the company mostly use? The GECS segment?

b. Using the inventory amounts listed for 2001 and 2000 on the financial statements, what is the inventory turnover for **General Electric Co.** assuming the LIFO adjustments have already been made?

c. Compute the inventory turnover ratio for the company.

d. Compute the average inventory holding period for the company.

e. Do the company's inventory ratios seem favorable? Why or why not?

ANNUAL REPORT PROJECT

8–80. Section 8—Inventory and Cost of Goods Sold

This section of the annual report project focuses on one of the most important costs for any merchandiser or manufacturer—the cost of inventory.

Required: Prepare a report that includes the following information:

a. A schedule that lists the various inventories for your firm and for those of the peer company you selected. List the inventory descriptions and dollar amounts for each year presented in the balance sheets.

b. Comment on the significance of the inventory. For example, relative to the other assets listed on the balance sheets, are inventories significant? How does your company's inventory compare to the peer company you are using? Over time, are the inventories increasing or decreasing? Are the products in your company's inventories perishable? If so, are they perishable because they are prone to spoilage like food, or because they are prone to technological obsolescence like computer processing chips?

c. Identify the inventory cost flow assumption or assumptions used by your company and those used by its peer. List the cost of goods sold and the gross profit for the two companies. Does the inventory cost flow assumption seem to have created any difference between your company and its peer company? Explain your reasoning. If one or both of the companies uses the LIFO inventory cost flow assumption, locate the financial statement note that relates to inventories and use the information it contains to prepare a schedule listing the LIFO inventory values, the inventory amounts had the inventories been valued under FIFO, and the difference between the LIFO and FIFO inventory values.

d. Calculate the inventory turnover ratio for your company and its peer for the current year. Comment on the information the ratio calculations provide.

e. Discuss which company seems to be using its investment in inventory more efficiently? Explain your reasoning.

f. Your report should conclude with comments regarding what you think of your company and how you think your company compares to its peer in light of the work you did in connection with this assignment.

CHAPTER 9

The Balance Sheet and Income Statement— A Closer Look

Your brother-in-law just sent you the annual report of a company that he believes will be the next *Microsoft.* He wants you to get in on the ground floor. You've looked at annual reports before, but none seemed this complex. The balance sheet includes a lot of "intangible" assets, but what are they? The income statement has numerous items after operating income. Should you really care about those figures? To top it off, the earnings per share has six different amounts! How can that be when you know earnings per share is the company's net income divided by the number of shares of common stock? Which one of them should you use to evaluate the stock's market price? The highest is only $0.45 a share, and your brother-in-law wants you to pay $12 per share for this stock. That is almost 27 times the annual income per share, if you are looking at the right one. Without an understanding of these financial statement complications, it is difficult to tell whether the investment your brother-in-law suggests is the right one for you.

Balance sheets and income statements are generally more complex than the ones we have explored so far, but they are organized in a manner that serves to clarify rather than complicate the information they provide to economic decision makers. An understanding of the organization of these two financial statements is crucial. In this chapter, we will explore the details and organization of the balance sheet and income statement.

Learning Objectives

After completing your work on this chapter, you should be able to do the following:

1. Describe how the balance sheet and income statement were developed as financial statements.

2. Explain the organization and purpose of the classified balance sheet.

3. Explain why recurring and nonrecurring items are presented separately on the income statement.

4. Interpret the net of tax disclosure of discontinued operations, extraordinary items, and accounting changes.

5. Calculate earnings per share and describe how it is presented on the income statement.

6. Describe the additional information provided by comparative financial statements.

7. Calculate several financial ratios based on income statement and balance sheet information.

◆ HISTORY AND DEVELOPMENT OF THE BALANCE SHEET AND INCOME STATEMENT

Human beings have kept track of their business affairs by accounting for economic events and transactions ever since they began living in organized societies. They recorded them first on stone or clay tablets, then on papyrus, then on paper, and now via computer technology.

Accounting records were originally kept to help business owners run their companies; accounting was not generally intended to provide information to outsiders. Amounts owed to suppliers, for example, were recorded primarily so a company could keep track of what had and had not been paid. As time went on, however, more and more companies turned to outsiders for financing and other needs. These outsiders were unwilling to become involved with a company blindly. They wanted to evaluate company financial information before they would put their funds at risk, so record keeping was expanded for the specific purpose of providing financial information to outsiders. Eventually, financial statements were developed to communicate this information. In *A History of Accounting Thought*, Michael Chatfield describes this transition as follows:

> *More than most accounting tools, financial statements are the result of cumulative historical influences. Before the Industrial Revolution they were usually prepared as arithmetic checks of ledger balances. Afterward the roles were reversed and it was account books which were reorganized to facilitate statement preparation. As statements became communication devices rather than simple bookkeeping summaries, the journal and ledger evolved from narratives to tabulations of figures from which balances could easily be taken.[1]*

Accounting has been with us since about 5000 B.C., but financial statements as we know them are a relatively recent phenomenon. The balance sheet's function as a financial statement only emerged during the Renaissance, around A.D. 1600. For the next several hundred years, the balance sheet was the primary output of the accounting process. Accountants developed the income statement in the late 1800s, but did not consider the information nearly as important as the balance sheet figures. In his landmark work, *Accounting Evolution to 1900*, A. C. Littleton makes the following observation:

> *. . . it seems that the primary motive for separate financial statements was to obtain information regarding capital; this was the center of the interest of partners, shareholders, lenders, and the basis of the calculation of early property taxes. Thus balance-sheet data were stressed and refined in various ways, while expense and income data were incidental—in fact, the latter in the seventeenth century were presented merely as a "proof of estate"—to demonstrate by another route the correctness of the balance sheet.[2]*

At the beginning of the 20th century, most U.S companies were financed by banks, so at this time, banks (i.e., creditors) were the primary users of financial statements. These creditors looked at balance sheets to help them evaluate a company's ability to repay its debts. During the first two decades of the 1900s, U.S. companies began to rely less on debt financing and more on equity financing. Companies began to borrow less from banks and issue more capital stock. When selling stock became an important source of external financing, stockholders became major users of financial statements. Stockholders were interested in the earnings of companies and the potential for earnings distributions (dividends), and the value of the company's stock. Stockholders focused on net income and considered the income statement more important than the balance sheet. Over time, creditors also realized that earning power was crucial to debt

---

[1]Michael Chatfield, *A History of Accounting Thought* (Huntington, NY: R. E. Kriger Publishing Co., 1974), 164.

[2]A. C. Littleton, *Accounting Evolution to 1900* (New York: Russell & Russell, 1966), 153.

repayment, so they also began to rely more on the income statement than on the balance sheet.

By the 1930s, it became apparent that neither the balance sheet nor the income statement is more important than the other; they are best used together. Each provides valuable information for economic decision makers. By learning more about the detailed structure of the balance sheet and income statement, you can make the best use of the information they provide.

In introducing the balance sheet in Chapter 3, we used this simple equation:

$$\text{Assets} = \text{Liabilities} + \text{Owners' equity}$$

The equation does not distinguish one asset from another or one liability from another. A balance sheet prepared for Eliason and Company, a chain of specialty furniture stores, at December 31, 2004, using the basic format would look like Exhibit 9–1.

EXHIBIT 9–1 Eliason and Company Balance Sheet

Eliason and Company Balance Sheet December 31, 2004	
Total assets	$1,566,800
Liabilities	$ 901,000
Stockholders' equity	665,800
Total liabilities and stockholders' equity	$1,566,800

Remember that economic decision makers are attempting to predict the amount and timing of future cash flows. The balance sheet in Exhibit 9–1 provides economic decision makers little useful information about the financial position of Eliason and Company at December 31, 2004. Even if the $1,566,800 of assets is all cash, we see no indication of how soon the $901,000 of liabilities must be paid or how much of the $665,800 of stockholders' equity represents contributed capital and how much represents retained earnings. In response to users' needs for additional information, accountants developed a more detailed balance sheet, called the classified balance sheet.

THE CLASSIFIED BALANCE SHEET

classified balance sheet A balance sheet that provides a breakdown of the composition of the items the balance sheet includes.

A **classified balance sheet** provides a breakdown of the composition of the items included. Rather than just presenting the totals of assets, liabilities, and owners' equity, this type of balance sheet provides much more detail about the nature of the assets, liabilities, and equities that make up the totals. Exhibit 9–2 on page F–358 shows a classified balance sheet prepared from the same accounting data as that used for the balance sheet in Exhibit 9–1. Notice that the assets still total $1,566,800; total liabilities are still $901,000; and stockholders' equity is still $665,800. The difference between the two balance sheet presentations is the amount of detail the balance sheets disclose.

We will refer to Eliason and Company's classified balance sheet presented in Exhibit 9–2 on page F–358 as we describe how the classified balance sheet is organized.

Discussion Question ·

9–1. Which of the two balance sheet presentations for Eliason and Company do you think would be more useful in predicting the future and timing of the company's cash flow? Provide three specific examples to support your position.

ASSETS

current assets Assets that are cash, will become cash, or will be consumed within the longer of one year or the current operating cycle.

Under GAAP, assets shown on the balance sheet at their historical cost and are grouped as either current assets or long-term assets. **Current assets** are defined as assets that either are cash already or are expected to become cash within one year or

Eliason and Company
Balance Sheet
December 31, 2004

ASSETS:

Current assets:

Cash			$ 100
Accounts receivable			251,000
Inventory			298,900
Prepaid expenses			50,000
Total current assets			$ 600,000
Long-term investments			34,000

Property, plant, and equipment:

Land		$125,000	
Plant and equipment	$1,075,000		
Less: Accumulated depreciation	(283,200)		
Plant and equipment, net		791,800	
Total property, plant, and equipment			916,800
Intangible asset—copyright			16,000
Total assets			$1,566,800

LIABILITIES:

Current liabilities:

Accounts payable			$ 501,000
Short-term notes payable			50,000
Total current liabilities			$ 551,000

Long-term liabilities:

Bonds payable			350,000
Total liabilities			$ 901,000

STOCKHOLDERS' EQUITY:

Contributed capital:

Common stock, $1 par value, 100,000 authorized, 10,000 shares issued and outstanding		$ 10,000	
Additional paid-in capital		390,000	
Total contributed capital		$400,000	
Retained earnings		265,800	
Total stockholders' equity			665,800
Total liabilities and stockholders' equity			$1,566,800

EXHIBIT 9–2   Classified Balance Sheet

one operating cycle, whichever is longer. An operating cycle is the length of time it takes for an entity to complete one revenue-producing cycle. For a manufacturer, a revenue cycle is the length of time from receiving raw materials to producing and selling the final product to collecting cash from its customers. For a merchandiser, the operating cycle is the time it takes from receiving merchandise to collecting the cash from its customers. Most businesses have several operating cycles within a year. Some businesses, such as wineries, timber operations, or long-term construction companies, have operating cycles that last five years or even longer. As you can see from Exhibit 9–2, cash, accounts receivable, inventory, and prepaid expenses are examples of current assets. Prepaid expenses that will be used within one year are included because, even though they will not become cash, they will benefit the company without requiring additional cash outflows. Although our example company does not have any, short-term investments would also be included in current assets. Short-term investments may be listed as trading securities, marketable securities, or short investments. It is also permissible for companies to show cash along with marketable securities that will be converted into cash within 90 days as a single balance sheet amount labeled *cash and cash equivalents.*

long-term assets Assets that are expected to benefit the company for longer than one year.

Long-term assets are defined as those assets that are expected to benefit the organization for more than one year, or that are not anticipated to become cash within one year. Although our example company does not use all of the classifications, there are several. The following long-term asset classifications are the ones most commonly used by businesses today.

long-term investments Sometimes called *investments.* Investments in securities such as stocks, bonds, and long-term notes receivable; investments in fixed assets that are not currently being used in operations; special funds established to set aside financial resources.

- **Long-term investments,** sometimes simply called *investments* include:
  - Investments in securities such as stocks, bonds, and long-term notes receivable
  - Investments in fixed assets such as land, buildings, and equipment that are not currently being used in operations
  - Special funds established to set aside financial resources (money) to pay for pension obligations, plant expansion, or to repay debt

property, plant, and equipment Physical long-lived assets used by the business including land, buildings, equipment, machinery, vehicles, and furniture.

- **Property, plant, and equipment** includes physical long-lived assets used by the business. Examples include land, buildings, equipment, machinery, vehicles, and furniture. As we learned in Chapter 7, except for land, accountants depreciate these durable assets to expense their cost in the periods they helped produce revenue.

intangible assets Things that have future value but lack physical presence such as patents, copyrights, trademarks, and purchased goodwill.

- **Intangible assets** include the company's cost of things that have future value but lack physical presence. Examples include patents, copyrights, trademarks, and purchased goodwill. We say *purchased* goodwill because goodwill can only be recorded in company accounting records when a business is purchased and the purchase price exceeds the fair value of the individual assets acquired. For example, assume that Gourmet Outlets, Inc., purchases Smith Produce, a very successful gourmet grocery store for $300,000. The fair value of Smith's assets is only $100,000, but Gourmet Outlets is willing to pay the $300,000 because Smith's business is so successful. In this situation, the $200,000 ($300,000 − $100,000) Gourmet Outlets pays in excess of the fair value of Smith's assets is goodwill.

  Like property, plant, and equipment, accountants systematically expense the cost of intangible assets in the accounting periods benefited by the use of the asset. As you know, for property, plant, and equipment, this systematic cost allocation is called depreciation. The systematic allocation of the cost of an intangible from assets to expense is called amortization. Not all intangible assets are amortized, however. According to the Financial Accounting Standards Board's (FASB's) Statement of Financial Accounting Standards (SFAS) Number 142 issued in June 2001, while intangible assets that have limited (finite) useful lives, such as patents, are amortized, intangible assets that have an indefinite useful life, such as goodwill, are not amortized.

  SFAS 142 also requires companies to review their intangible assets for impairment at least annually. In other words, every company must evaluate its intangible assets to assure that the amount the company reflects on its balance sheet does not exceed the value of the intangible assets. The impact of impairment tests can be significant. For example, in the first quarter of 2002, *AOL Time Warner* posted one of the largest losses in history because it was forced to record a write-down of goodwill amounting to approximately $54 billion.

other assets Long-term assets that do not fit into any other asset classification.

- **Other assets** are any long-term assets that do not fit into any other asset classification. Examples include property held for sale and long-term rent receivable.

Assets are listed on a classified balance sheet in order of decreasing liquidity. Liquidity means nearness to cash. Notice that we always list cash first on the balance sheet because by definition it is the most liquid asset. Generally, the farther down an item is found in the asset section of a classified balance sheet, the less likelihood there is that that item will be converted to cash in the near future. Because of the classified balance sheet's organization, users can tell in a glance just which assets (and their dollar amounts) the company thinks will be turned into cash within the next year (current assets) and which ones are not expected to be converted into cash (long-term assets).

In the case of Eliason and Company, current assets total $600,000 and property, plant, and equipment total $916,800. We would expect the $600,000 to be converted into cash before the $916,800.

Discussion Questions ●

9–2. Are there any items listed as current assets on Eliason's December 31, 2004, classified balance sheet (Exhibit 9–2) that you think will never be converted into cash? If there are, why do you think they are classified as current assets?

9–3. Property, plant, and equipment is not a current asset. Does this mean Eliason cannot sell one of its buildings in 2005? Explain your reasoning.

LIABILITIES

Generally, the balance sheet lists liabilities in order of how quickly they must be paid. Those liabilities that must be settled (paid or otherwise satisfied) first are listed first. Settlement often requires the payment of cash but may require other performance such as providing goods or services.

current liabilities
Liabilities that require settlement (payment) within one year or the current operating cycle, whichever is longer.

Current liabilities are those that require settlement within one year or the current operating cycle, whichever is longer. The operating cycle for the overwhelming majority of companies is less than one year, so the one-year criterion is the one most often used. Eliason and Company classifies the $501,000 it owes to suppliers (accounts payable) as a current liability because the suppliers expect Eliason to pay them within one year. Commercial suppliers usually require payment within 10 to 90 days, and the trend is to require payment sooner rather than later.

long-term liabilities
Liabilities that will not require settlement within one year or the current operating cycle.

Long-term liabilities are those that do not require settlement within one year or the current operating cycle. Eliason's bonds payable are not due within a year, so the company classifies the liability as long-term. If part of the bond liability was due within one year, the company would classify that part as current. In other words, current liabilities includes the current portion of any long-term debt.

Because of the way the balance sheet is organized, users can tell at a glance which liabilities are expected to be retired within the next year (current liabilities) and which ones are not (long-term liabilities). This enables them to assess future cash flows. Eliason's current liabilities total $551,000 and long-term liabilities total $350,000, so it must pay the $551,000 fairly soon, but the $350,000 is not due for at least a year. Exhibit 9–3 illustrates the current and long-term classifications of assets and liabilities.

EXHIBIT 9–3   Examples of Current and Long-Term Assets and Liabilities

Assets		Liabilities	
Current	*Long-Term*	*Current*	*Long-Term*
Cash	Long-term investments	Accounts payable	Notes payable
Marketable securities	Property, plant, and	Notes payable	Mortgages payable
Accounts receivable	equipment	Accrued expenses	Bonds payable
Inventory	Intangible assets	Unearned revenue	Others
Prepaid expenses	Other long-term assets	Payable for:	
		Wages	
		Taxes	
		Interest	
		Others	
		Current portion of long-term debt	

Discussion Questions ●

9–4. Provide two examples of current liabilities and two examples of long-term liabilities not shown on the Eliason and Company balance sheet in Exhibit 9–2.

9–5. Eliason shows $600,000 of current assets and $551,000 of current liabilities. Who might be interested in these amounts, and why?

OWNERS' EQUITY

contributed capital
Total amount invested in a corporation by its shareholders. Also called paid-in capital.

The stockholders' equity section of a classified balance sheet is also separated into two categories: contributed capital and retained earnings. **Contributed capital** (sometimes called *paid-in capital*) is the amount paid into the company by its owners in exchange for their ownership interest. In other words, contributed capital is the amount a company's stockholders paid for the stock they purchased. The contributed or paid-in capital section of equity generally begins with preferred stock. This is because preferred stockholders have first priority when it comes to dividends or distributions upon liquidation. Common stock is listed next, followed by the remaining contributed capital amounts. If the company has reacquired any of its capital stock (treasury stock), it is shown in the equity section of the balance sheet as a reduction in equity. In the case of Eliason and Company, we first list the $10,000 classified as common stock. The $10,000 is the amount associated with the stock's par value. The amount the company received in excess of a stock's par value ($390,000) is classified as additional paid-in capital. After listing all of the contributed capital items, we list retained earnings next.

retained earnings
Constitutes the earnings reinvested by the corporation and not distributed to owners in the form of dividends.

As we mentioned in Chapter 4, **retained earnings** constitutes the earnings reinvested by the corporation and not distributed to owners in the form of dividends. At December 31, 2004, Eliason and Company had a retained earnings balance of $265,800.

Discussion Questions ●

9–6. Explain the exact meaning of the $265,800 of retained earnings on Eliason and Company's balance sheet.

9–7. On average, how much did Eliason and Company receive for each share of stock sold?

9–8. Does Eliason's balance sheet provide an indication of the current market value of the company's stock? Explain your reasoning.

◆ ORGANIZATION OF THE INCOME STATEMENT

When we introduced the income statement in Chapter 4, we used the following simple equation:

$$\text{Revenues} - \text{Expenses} = \text{Net income}$$

An income statement prepared for Eliason and Company for the year ended December 31, 2004, using this simple format would look like the one in Exhibit 9–4.

EXHIBIT 9–4   Income Statement Prepared for Eliason and Company for the Year Ended December 31, 2004—Simple Format

Eliason and Company
Income Statement
For the Year Ended December 31, 2004

Revenue	$752,500
Less: Expenses	840,400
Net loss	$ (87,900)

Net income or net loss, of course, is the "bottom line" and discloses whether or not a company has been profitable for a given period. This is important, and we would never suggest otherwise. However, for Eliason and Company, there is more to the story than that told by the $87,900 loss.

The accounting profession follows established guidelines so income statements provide a fairly complete and relevant picture of what happens to businesses during an income statement period. Income statements that conform to these guidelines provide important information about the characteristics of the revenues and expenses they present. Exhibit 9–5 shows an income statement for Eliason and Company that conforms to the current income statement guidelines (except that the required earnings per share presentation is omitted).

EXHIBIT 9–5   Expanded Format Income Statement

Eliason and Company
Income Statement
For the Year Ended December 31, 2004

Sales revenue		$ 752,500
Less: Cost of goods sold		352,800
Gross profit on sales		$ 399,700
Less: Operating expenses:		
Selling	$60,250	
General and administrative	96,250	
Total operating expenses		(156,500)
Operating income		$ 243,200
Less other expenses:		
Interest expense		(30,650)
Income before taxes and extraordinary item		$ 212,550
Less: Income taxes		(64,660)
Income before extraordinary item		$ 147,890
Extraordinary loss (less: income taxes of $87,420)		(235,790)
Net loss		$ (87,900)

nonrecurring item
Results of activities that are not expected to occur again and, therefore, should not be used to predict future performance.

Although this income statement bears little resemblance to the one presented earlier in our discussion, revenues still total $752,500; total deductions from revenues still total $840,400; and the net loss is still $87,900. By now, this format should look familiar to you. In fact, only the last few lines are new.

Discussion Questions ●

9–9. Is Exhibit 9–5 a single-step or multiple-step income statement? How can you tell?

9–10. If you were considering some kind of economic involvement with Eliason and Company, which number on the expanded income statement would you consider most reliable in predicting the company's future profitability? Explain.

RECURRING AND NONRECURRING ITEMS

Besides presenting more detail concerning Eliason and Company's regular revenues and expenses for 2004, the income statement in Exhibit 9–5 shows an extraordinary loss of $235,790, which is separated from the company's regular, recurring revenues and expenses. An extraordinary gain or loss is one of the items the accounting profession has determined should be shown separately as a nonrecurring item on the income statement.

A **nonrecurring item** is any item (either positive or negative) that should not be considered a normal part of continuing operations because it is not expected to recur. Let's explore the logic of separating nonrecurring from recurring items on the income statement.

Suppose something—good or bad—happened to a company during the income statement period that was not expected to recur. The company must report it because it happened. In Eliason's case, the extraordinary loss reported on the 2004 income statement was caused by a flood that wiped out one of the company's retail outlets. This store was located in Phoenix, Arizona, where floods are *extremely* rare, so Eliason carried no flood insurance. If you were attempting to predict the company's ability to generate future profits and cash flows, and the company lumped this one-time "something" in with all its other revenues and expenses, you might be misled. Therefore, if nonrecurring items *do not* represent the ongoing results of a company's operations, it makes sense to report them separately from what *does* represent the company's ongoing business.

If the extraordinary (flood) loss is truly a nonrecurring item for Eliason, then the net loss of $87,900 for 2004 is not a good predictor of future profitability and cash flow. In fact, the best predictive number on Eliason's income statement is probably the $147,890 listed as income before extraordinary item.

Extraordinary items are but one type of nonrecurring item. Actually, there are three general types of nonrecurring items, listed in their order of presentation on the income statement:

1. Discontinued operations
2. Extraordinary items
3. Cumulative effect of changes in accounting principles

In the sections that follow, we will more fully explain the presentation and interpretation of these nonrecurring items and how they appear on a company's income statement. Throughout our discussion, we will use the income statement of Toy Box, Inc., a retailer specializing in top-of-the-line children's toys, as an example. The company's 2005 income statement is presented in Exhibit 9–6.

EXHIBIT 9–6   Income Statement for Toy Box, Inc., for the Year Ended December 31, 2005

Toy Box, Inc.
Income Statement
For the Year Ended December 31, 2005

Sales		$858,600
Less: Cost of goods sold		456,800
Gross profit on sales		$401,800
Less: Operating expenses:		
Selling expense	$94,450	
General and administrative expense	116,050	
Total operating expenses		(210,500)
Operating income		$191,300
Less: Interest expense		(30,650)
Income from continuing operations before taxes		$160,650
Less: Income taxes		(64,260)
Income from continuing operations		$ 96,390
Discontinued operations:		
Income from discontinued operations		
($118,800, less: income taxes of $47,520)	$71,280	
Loss on disposal of discontinued operation		
($90,000, less: income taxes of $36,000)	(54,000)	17,280
Income before extraordinary item and cumulative		
effect of a change in accounting principle		$113,670
Extraordinary gain ($220,000, less: income taxes of $88,000)		132,000
Income before cumulative effect of a change in accounting principle		245,670
Cumulative effect of a change in accounting principle		
($62,000, less: income taxes of $24,800)		(37,200)
Net income		$208,470

Income statements broadly separate the activities they report into those that are expected to recur and those that are not. The first half of Toy Box's income statement, up to income from continuing operations, reflects results of activities that will probably continue in the future.

The income tax of $64,260 is the tax on income from ongoing activities of the company. In practice, determining the amount of income tax associated with reported income is quite complex. First, company accountants must determine the revenue that is taxable according to the income tax regulations of the ***Internal Revenue Service (IRS).*** Next, the accountants must determine the costs the ***IRS*** allows to be deducted from taxable revenue to determine taxable income. Then, the accountants subtract the deductible costs from taxable revenue to determine taxable income. Finally, the amount of tax is calculated. The specifics for calculating the amount of income tax a company should pay or the amount it should report as income tax expense is beyond the scope of this course. But to get an approximation of income tax expense that is good enough for academic purposes, you can multiply income by an assumed income tax rate as we show below:

$$\text{Income} \times \text{Tax rate} = \text{Income tax expense}$$

We will use the above equation to calculate income tax whenever we need to determine a tax amount for something on Toy Box's income statement. The rough calculation to determine income tax expense for income from continuing operations is shown below:

$$\begin{array}{ccc} \text{Income from} & & \text{Income tax} \\ \text{continuing operations} \times \text{Tax rate} = & \text{on income from} \\ \text{before tax} & & \text{operations} \\ \\ \$160,650 \quad \times \quad 40\% \quad = \quad \$64,260 \end{array}$$

The $96,390 identified as *income from continuing operations* represents the net results of Toy Box's ongoing operations. We are probably safe to assume that this figure has a predictive value for future earnings. Information on the income statement below this point relates to nonrecurring items. The income from continuing operations is the dividing line between the recurring and nonrecurring activities. If a company does not have discontinued operations but does have extraordinary items, the company would use a title such as *income before extraordinary items*. If a company had no discontinued items and no extraordinary items but did have an accounting change to disclose, the company would use a title such as *income before cumulative effect of changes in accounting principle*. Regardless of the title, nonrecurring items always come after the income tax expense.

Proper classification of items as recurring or nonrecurring is critical to the usefulness of the accounting information. A company might be tempted to treat an item as nonrecurring because it reduces net income or to include an item with recurring revenues when it increases net income. To prevent companies from confusing the users of financial statements this way, the accounting profession restricts the items that may be considered nonrecurring. We will consider the criteria for each of these items after we discuss the income tax effects of these nonrecurring items.

INCOME TAX DISCLOSURE

We mentioned earlier that Toy Box's tax expense associated with the ongoing, recurring operation of the business income is $64,260. But how should the company disclose the income tax effect of the nonrecurring items shown on the income statement? The nonrecurring events cannot escape income tax consequences, and those consequences must be disclosed. Lumping together the income tax associated with nonrecurring items with that of income tax expense for continuing operations would distort the information. For example, the total of all income tax on Toy Box's income statement is $138,980 ($64,260 + $47,520 − $36,000 + $88,000 − $24,800). If Toy Box mistakenly presented the entire $138,980 as though all of it were associated with income from continuing operations, this part of the income statement would appear as follows:

Income from continuing operations before taxes		$160,650
Less:		
Income taxes on continuing operations	$64,260	
Income taxes on income from discontinued operations	47,520	
Income tax reduction from loss on disposal of discontinued operations	(36,000)	
Income taxes on extraordinary gain	88,000	
Income tax reduction from change in accounting principle	(24,800)	138,980
Income from continuing operations		$ 21,670

This presentation makes it appear that Toy Box is paying out about 86.5 percent ($138,980/$160,650) of its income from continuing operations for income taxes. That leaves a disproportionately small $21,670 for income from continuing operations after tax. The trouble with the preceding presentation is that it distorts the picture of continuing operations by including tax that is associated with nonrecurring items. To eliminate the distortion and confusion, the accounting profession decided that the only tax expense shown on the income statement as a separate line item will be the amount associated with continuing operations. Therefore, the three major types of nonrecurring items included on the income statement are shown "less income tax" or "net of tax."

net of tax The amount remaining for an item after income tax has been deducted.

Net of tax means the income tax has already been deducted from the amount shown for an item. For example, assume a company has an extraordinary gain of $100,000 and the income tax on the gain is $30,000. The extraordinary gain, net of tax would be $70,000 ($100,000 − $30,000). Next, we will calculate the income tax associated with the nonrecurring items for Toy Box, Inc.

Current accounting rules require that the tax effect of each of these nonrecurring items be disclosed either on the face of the income statement or in the related notes to the financial statements. Although it is not always the case, Toy Box's income statement shows the full amount of each nonrecurring item and its associated income tax. If the income statement does not show the full amount of a nonrecurring item, a financial statement user can calculate the amount by adding the item's net-of-tax amount to its associated income tax.

As we have already mentioned, we will calculate tax expense by simply multiplying the income by the effective tax rate. Before you can calculate the income tax for the nonrecurring items, you need to know each of their full amounts. As we show below, we can use the same basic calculation to determine the income tax expense for gains and the income tax savings associated with losses.

Income from operation of discontinued operations	$118,800 × 40% = $47,520
Disposal of discontinued operation	$ 90,000 × 40% = $36,000
Extraordinary gain	$220,000 × 40% = $88,000
Cumulative effect of accounting principle change	$ 62,000 × 40% = $24,800

When a business experiences a gain, the total income of the business increases and the **IRS** will require more taxes. The gain increases the amount of taxes owed, which in turn reduces the amount of the gain (see Exhibit 9–7 on page F–366). When a business experiences a loss, the total income of the business decreases and the **IRS** will require less taxes. The loss decreases the amount of taxes owed, which in turn reduces the amount of the loss. Therefore, we subtract income tax from the original amount of the nonrecurring item to get its net-of-tax amount.

Now look again at the income statement for Toy Box, Inc., in Exhibit 9–6. Notice that the statement includes examples of the three major types of nonrecurring items, and the statement presents each of them in the same general way: Each is shown below the *income from continuing operations*, and each is shown "net of tax." We now explore the criteria for, and specific presentation of, each type of nonrecurring item.

discontinued operations
The disposal of a business segment. One of the nonrecurring items shown net of tax on the income statement.

DISCONTINUED OPERATIONS

When a company eliminates a *major segment* of its business, that segment is called **discontinued operations.** When a company formally decides to dispose of a major seg-

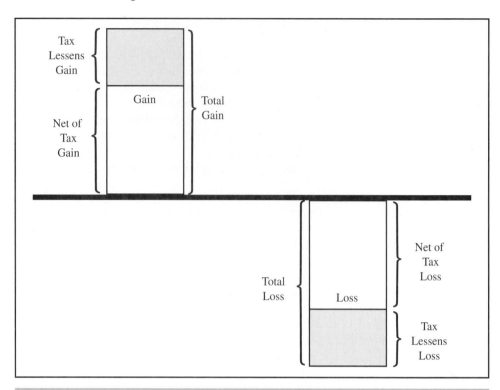

EXHIBIT 9–7   Effect of Tax on Gains and Losses

ment of its business, the income or loss on the operations of the segment that is to be eliminated and any gain or loss from the actual disposal of that business segment are reported as nonrecurring items on the income statement. A **business segment** may be a portion of an entity representing either a separate major line of business or a class of customer.

business segment   A portion of an entity representing either a separate major line of business or a class of customer.

> *The part of the business being eliminated is considered a business segment provided that its assets, results of operations, and activities can be clearly distinguished, physically and operationally and for financial reporting purposes, from the other assets, results of operations, and activities of the entity.*[3]

The following examples of situations meeting the criteria for disposal of a business segment will help you understand the application of these criteria.

1. *A sale by a diversified company of a major division, which represents the company's only activities in the electronics industry.*
2. *A sale by a meat packing company of a 25% interest in a professional football team.*
3. *A sale by a communications company of all its radio stations, which represent 30% of gross revenues. The company's remaining activities are three television stations and a publishing company.*
4. *A food distributor disposes of one of its two divisions. One division sells food wholesale primarily to supermarket chains and the other division sells food through its chain of fast food restaurants, some of which are franchised and some of which are company-owned.*[4]

Once a company determines that the disposal of a business segment should be considered a discontinued operation, generally accepted accounting principles (GAAP) require certain disclosures on the income statement. To illustrate, Toy Box, Inc., buys and resells toys. Many years ago, for reasons no one in the company's management even remembers, Toy Box purchased a company that manufactured hats. Although the hat manufacturing portion of the business has always been profitable,

---

[3]APB Opinion No. 30, paragraph 13.
[4]AICPA Accounting Interpretations, AIN-APB30, #1.

current management does not believe that the hat business fits into the corporation's strategic plans and sells it during 2005. Toy Box includes two items on its 2005 income statement to reflect the hat division's operation and disposal.

1. Toy Box reports income from discontinued operations of $71,280. In 2005, prior to being sold, the hat operation had revenues of $220,100 and expenses of $101,300. So its pretax income for the time Toy Box owned it during the year was $118,800 ($220,100 revenues − $101,300 expenses). Income taxes on the results of discontinued operations totaled $45,720, so the amount shown for income from discontinued operations on the income statement is $71,280 ($118,800 − $45,720).
2. Toy Box also reports a $54,000 loss on the disposal of discontinued operations. When the company sold the hat operation, it incurred a $90,000 pretax loss on the sale. Because this loss was deductible on the company's income tax return, it resulted in a reduction of $36,000 in income taxes for the year. The after-tax loss (the real loss to Toy Box) was $54,000 ($90,000 − $36,000).

After Toy Box reports the two components of the results of discontinued operations, it nets the two amounts. In other words, the company combines the $71,280 income from discontinued operations and the $54,000 loss on disposal of the discontinued operation, which results in a net gain of $17,280 under discontinued operations.

Discontinued operations occur more often than you might think. Of the 600 companies surveyed by the authors of *Accounting Trends and Techniques* in 2001, 60 companies reported discontinued operations in their 2000 income statements, including such companies as **American Home Products Corporation, Eaton Corporation,** and **International Multifoods Corporation.** It would be a mistake to think any time a company disposes of a major business segment, it is because that segment is unprofitable. **American Home Products,** for example, sold its crop protection and pest control products business in 2000 and reported after-tax profits from this discontinued operation of over $103 million in 2000. Sometimes, as was the case with Toy Box when it discontinued its hat manufacturing operation, the segment being disposed of just doesn't fit into the company's strategic plans.

EXTRAORDINARY ITEMS

extraordinary item
A gain or loss that is both unusual in nature and infrequent in occurrence. One of the nonrecurring items shown net of tax on the income statement.

In accounting, the word extraordinary has a very special meaning. Accounting rules define an **extraordinary item** as an event that is both *unusual* in nature and *infrequent* in occurrence. It can't be just one or the other, it must be both. When applying the criterion of "unusual in nature," accountants must consider the operating environment of the business entity.

The environment of an entity includes such factors as the characteristics of the industry or industries in which it is operating, the geographical location of its operations, and the nature and extent of government regulation. Thus, an event or transaction may be unusual in nature for one entity but not for another because of differences in their respective environments.[5]

So, a gain or loss that would be considered unusual for one company might be considered an ordinary event for another company.

Accountants must also consider the operating environment of the entity when applying the criterion of "infrequent in occurrence." To be considered infrequent, an event must be neither a recurrence of reasonably recent past events, nor should it be expected to recur in the foreseeable future. Earlier in this chapter, for example, we looked at Eliason and Company's income statement for 2004. Included in the statement was an extraordinary loss resulting from a flood in Phoenix, Arizona. Well, floods are both unusual and infrequent in Phoenix, so this loss can probably be considered extraordinary. However, if the store destroyed by a flood had been located in the flood plains of Iowa, where floods are quite common, the loss would not qualify as extraordinary.

---

[5]APB Opinion No. 30, paragraph 21.

According to *Accounting Trends and Techniques*, of the 600 companies surveyed in 2001, 55 companies reported extraordinary items in their 2000 income statements, including such companies as **Ingram Micro Inc., United Stationers,** and **ExxonMobil Corporation.**

What if an item is either unusual in nature *or* infrequent in occurrence, but not both? If the item is significant, the company should list it as a separate item, usually under other gains or other losses as appropriate. And, like the rest of the items included in other gains and other losses, the unusual *or* infrequent item should not be shown net of tax.

Although they are not necessarily unusual and infrequent, prior to May 2002, accounting rules required that any gain or loss that results from extinguishment of debt must be reported as extraordinary. Because companies do have gains and losses from extinguishment of debt from time to time, and because it is unlikely that any event would be both unusual in nature and infrequent in occurrence, in the past, the most popular extraordinary items companies reported were those associated with debt extinguishments. However, in April 2002, the FASB issued Statement No. 145, eliminating the requirement to treat all gains and losses related to extinguishments of debt as extraordinary. As a result, for financial statements issued on or after May 15, 2002, gains and losses from extinguishment of debt should be classified as extraordinary items only if they meet the criteria for treatment as an extraordinary item. That is, they must be unusual and infrequent. According to *Accounting Trends and Techniques*, of the 55 companies that reported extraordinary items in 2000, 48 were reporting extraordinary items associated with debt extinguishments. Although gains and losses related to extinguishments of debt have historically been the most common extraordinary items, you will seldom see them listed as extraordinary on income statements published after May 2002.

Extinguishment of debt means nothing more than paying off debt. Sometimes when a company pays off debt, especially if it pays it earlier than the due date, the company will pay either more or less than the actual loan amount. For example, assume that Smith, Inc., has a $1 million liability for some 12 percent corporate bonds that it would like to pay off. It would like to extinguish (pay off) these bonds even though they are not yet due because interest rates have fallen and the company can now borrow funds at an interest rate of 9 percent. But, will the bondholders readily agree to accept early payment of the debt when they are earning such a high rate of interest relative to current rates? Probably not. Smith will have to entice the bondholders by offering to pay them more than the face value of the bonds. Let's assume that the bondholders will accept no less than $1,115,000 as payment. If Smith pays the $1,115,000 to retire the debt, the difference between the $1 million liability on Smith's books and the amount Smith pays is a loss on extinguishment of debt.

Aside from gains and losses from the extinguishment of debt, which happened from time to time prior to May 2002, companies seldom report extraordinary items. Given the catastrophic events of September 11, 2001, you might expect that the number of companies reporting extraordinary items for 2001 would greatly increase from 2000. This, however, was not the case, at least as a result of the terrorist attacks of 9/11. In a landmark (and somewhat baffling) decision, the FASB, through its Emerging Issues Task Force (EITF), ruled that no losses as a result of 9/11 could be classified as extraordinary.

As you use financial statement information, a basic appreciation of how these criteria are applied will enhance your ability to interpret the impact of extraordinary items. The following events or transactions meet the criteria of both unusual and infrequent and should therefore be presented as extraordinary items on the income statement.

1. A hailstorm destroys a large portion of a tobacco manufacturer's crops in an area where hailstorms are rare.
2. A steel fabricating company sells the only land it owns. The company acquired the land 10 years ago for future expansion but shortly thereafter abandoned all plans for expansion and held the land for appreciation in value instead.

3. A company sells a block of common stock of a publicly traded company. The block of shares, which represents less than 10 percent of the publicly held company, is the only security investment the company has ever made.

4. An earthquake in Texas destroys one of the oil refineries owned by a large multinational oil company. (*Note*: Earthquakes generally do not occur in Texas.)

Discussion Question

9–11. The following examples do not qualify as extraordinary items. For each one, explain specifically what criterion/criteria have not been met.

 a. *A citrus grower's Florida crop is damaged by frost ...*
 b. *A company that operates a chain of warehouses sells excess land around one of its warehouses. Normally, when the company buys land for a new warehouse, it buys more land than it needs for the warehouse expecting that the land will appreciate in value ...*
 c. *A large diversified company sells from its portfolio a block of shares, which it has acquired for investment purposes. This is the first sale from its portfolio of securities ...*
 d. *A textile manufacturer with only one plant moves to another location. It has not relocated a plant in 20 years and has no plans to do so in the foreseeable future ...*[6]

The income statement for Toy Box, Inc. (Exhibit 9–6) reports an extraordinary gain of $132,000 ($220,000 less income taxes of $88,000). This gain resulted from the city government's purchase of Toy Box's land adjacent to the municipal airport. The government expropriated the land to complete an airport expansion, and Toy Box had no choice but to sell the property. Forced sales to government agencies will not create a taxable gain if the citizen or business entity replaces the property with property that costs as much as the proceeds of the sales. Because Toy Box decided not to replace the land, the transaction was taxable. This transaction is both unusual in nature and infrequent in occurrence for Toy Box. Therefore, the company appropriately reported it as an extraordinary item.

CHANGES IN ACCOUNTING PRINCIPLES

As we mentioned in Chapter 1, one of the secondary qualitative characteristics of useful accounting information is consistency. This means that companies should be consistent in their accounting and refrain from shifting from one accounting method to another. However, from time to time, business entities find it necessary to make changes. In fact, the FASB views changes in accounting principles or standards as part of accounting's natural progression. In its *Conceptual Framework*, the FASB stated:

> *Consistent use of accounting principles from one accounting period to another, if pushed too far, can inhibit accounting progress. No change to a preferred accounting method can be made without sacrificing consistency, yet there is no way that accounting can develop without change. Fortunately, it is possible to make the transition from a less preferred to a more preferred method of accounting and still retain the capacity to compare the periods before and after the change if the effects of the change of method are disclosed.*[7]

Disclosure of the effects of these changes results in the third major type of nonrecurring item that is shown on the income statement net of tax—cumulative effect of a change in accounting principle. This nonrecurring item can result from either of two

---

[6]AICPA Accounting Interpretations, AIN-APB30, #1.

[7]Statement of Accounting Concepts #2, paragraph 122.

scenarios. Bear in mind, however, that in both cases the company must be changing from one acceptable accounting treatment to another acceptable treatment.

The first scenario involves the adoption of a new accounting standard. When a company applies a new accounting method required by a new FASB standard, net income is often affected. Unless the FASB indicates otherwise, the change in net income is reported in the year the company implements the new accounting rule.

The second scenario springs from the fact that in many cases, companies can choose one of several acceptable methods of accounting, and from time to time, companies choose to change from one acceptable accounting method to another. For instance, in Chapter 7, we discussed two different methods for calculating periodic depreciation expense—straight-line and double-declining-balance. In Chapter 8, we presented four different methods of accounting for the cost of inventory—specific identification, FIFO, LIFO, and average cost. Changing from one accounting method to another can have a significant impact on reported net income. Therefore, companies should include the results of these changes on their income statements. We should also say that the decision to change accounting methods should be made after careful consideration. Investors, creditors, the Securities and Exchange Commission (SEC), and the IRS take a dim view of companies that change accounting methods without a good reason.

The required presentation for a cumulative effect of a change in accounting principle is the same whether the change was caused by a new accounting *rule* or was a discretionary *choice*. Often, a newly adopted accounting method impacts not only current income but past income as well. That is, if a company had used the newly adopted accounting procedures in prior years, the income in those past years would have been different. Except in a very few situations, accounting rules do not require or even permit companies to retroactively adjust the income reported in prior periods. Instead, the cumulative effect of the accounting change is presented on the current year's income statement. The **cumulative effect of an accounting change** is the total of the difference between the prior income a company actually reported and the income the company *would have* reported if the company had used the newly adopted accounting principle all along.

cumulative effect of an accounting change
Result of adopting a new accounting standard or changing from one acceptable method of accounting to another. One of the nonrecurring items shown net of tax on the income statement.

To illustrate, we return once again to Toy Box, Inc. Toy Box began operation in 1971, and from the beginning, it used the first-in, first-out (FIFO) method to account for its inventory transactions. Then, in 2005, Toy Box decided to change from FIFO to the average cost method. The effect of this change was a significant reduction in the company's cumulative net income. This arises because if we go back to 1971 and calculate the income as if the average cost method were used from 1971 to 2005, cost of goods sold would have been higher for the 30-year period, and therefore, net income would have been lower over that same time span.

Accounting rules require that the effect of Toy Box's change be reported in 2005. But to report the entire amount as an effect on cost of goods sold in 2005 would be misleading to those who use Toy Box's 2005 income statement to try to predict future results. Instead, the company rightly shows the cumulative effect of its change from FIFO to average cost as a nonrecurring item on its 2005 income statement (Exhibit 9–6).

Of the 600 companies surveyed by the authors of *Accounting Trends and Techniques* in 2001, 43 companies reported cumulative effect of accounting changes on their 2000 income statements, including such companies as **Dillard's, Inc., Greif Bros. Corporation,** and **Intergraph Corporation.**

◆ COMPREHENSIVE INCOME

So far, when we have mentioned the word *income*, we have been talking about income that appears on the income statement. But you may be surprised to learn that accounting rules do not permit all "gains" and "losses" to appear on the income statement. So, the FASB created comprehensive income as a means to fully inform financial statement users of the change in equity from all nonowner transactions. Comprehensive income is one of the 10 accounting elements we began introducing in Chapter 3 (see Exhibit 9–8). As we have with the other nine elements, we will give the actual FASB definition in italics, followed by a less technical explanation.

comprehensive income
The change in equity during a period from nonowner sources.

Comprehensive income is *the change in equity of a business enterprise during a period from transactions and other events and circumstances from non-owner sources. It includes all changes in equity during a period except those resulting from investments by owners and distributions to owners* (Statement of Financial Accounting Concepts No. 6, paragraph 70). Comprehensive income includes all changes in equity during the accounting period *except* for investments by owners and distributions to owners. Comprehensive income not only includes net income from the income statement, but may also include some "gains" and "losses," called *other comprehensive income*, that the income statement doesn't show. There are three types of gains and losses that companies must report as direct adjustments to shareholders' equity, thus bypassing the income statement altogether. Although an understanding of these items is beyond the scope of this text, it may help you to know they are associated with accounting for foreign currency, certain pension liabilities, and unrealized holding gains and losses on certain securities (called available-for-sale securities).

EXHIBIT 9–8 Conceptual Framework with Comprehensive Income Highlighted

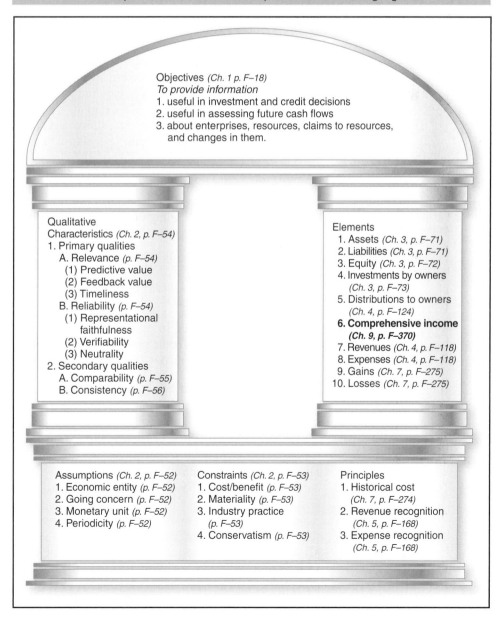

Objectives *(Ch. 1 p. F–18)*
To provide information
1. useful in investment and credit decisions
2. useful in assessing future cash flows
3. about enterprises, resources, claims to resources, and changes in them.

Qualitative
Characteristics *(Ch. 2, p. F–54)*
1. Primary qualities
  A. Relevance *(p. F–54)*
    (1) Predictive value
    (2) Feedback value
    (3) Timeliness
  B. Reliability *(p. F–54)*
    (1) Representational faithfulness
    (2) Verifiability
    (3) Neutrality
2. Secondary qualities
  A. Comparability *(p. F–55)*
  B. Consistency *(p. F–56)*

Elements
1. Assets *(Ch. 3, p. F–71)*
2. Liabilities *(Ch. 3, p. F–71)*
3. Equity *(Ch. 3, p. F–72)*
4. Investments by owners *(Ch. 3, p. F–73)*
5. Distributions to owners *(Ch. 4, p. F–124)*
6. **Comprehensive income (Ch. 9, p. F–370)**
7. Revenues *(Ch. 4, p. F–118)*
8. Expenses *(Ch. 4, p. F–118)*
9. Gains *(Ch. 7, p. F–275)*
10. Losses *(Ch. 7, p. F–275)*

Assumptions *(Ch. 2, p. F–52)*
1. Economic entity *(p. F–52)*
2. Going concern *(p. F–52)*
3. Monetary unit *(p. F–52)*
4. Periodicity *(p. F–52)*

Constraints *(Ch. 2, p. F–53)*
1. Cost/benefit *(p. F–53)*
2. Materiality *(p. F–53)*
3. Industry practice *(p. F–53)*
4. Conservatism *(p. F–53)*

Principles
1. Historical cost *(Ch. 7, p. F–274)*
2. Revenue recognition *(Ch. 5, p. F–168)*
3. Expense recognition *(Ch. 5, p. F–168)*

The FASB allows companies to choose from any one of the following three methods of disclosing comprehensive income:

1. A separate statement of comprehensive income
2. A combined statement of income and comprehensive income
3. Comprehensive income included in the statement of changes in stockholders' equity

Of the 600 companies surveyed by the authors of *Accounting Trends and Techniques* in 2001, 519 reported other comprehensive income for 2000. Of those companies, 65 prepared a separate statement, such as **Chevron Corporation** and **Enesco Group, Inc.** Thirty-two companies, including **Chesapeake Corporation** and **Metro-Goldwyn-Mayer,** combined comprehensive income with the income statement; and 422, like **Armstrong World Industries, Inc.,** and **PE Corporation,** included comprehensive income in the statement of stockholders' equity.

It appears that many firms will continue to select the third option because that has been the practice in recent years. An in-depth understanding of this issue is beyond the scope of this text, but we include the information because most of the annual reports you may examine will include comprehensive income in one of these places in the financial statements.

◆ EARNINGS PER SHARE

earnings per share (EPS)
The amount of a company's total earnings attributable to each share of common stock.

Many investors and other financial statement users rely on one statistic more than any other to measure a company's performance—earnings per share. GAAP require companies to disclose earnings per share on the face of their income statements. **Earnings per share (EPS)** is the amount of a company's earnings attributable to each share of common stock. Note, earnings per share is calculated for *common* stock only. Companies do not calculate earnings per share on preferred stock.

BASIC EARNINGS PER SHARE

basic earnings per share
Earnings per share based on the average number of common shares outstanding.

Basic earnings per share is earnings per common share based on the average number of common shares outstanding during the year. Companies use the following formula to calculate basic earnings per share:

$$\frac{\text{Net income} - \text{Preferred dividends}}{\text{Weighted average number of common shares outstanding}} = \text{Basic earnings per share}$$

Both the numerator and denominator in this calculation require a bit of explanation. In the numerator, dividends paid to preferred shareholders are subtracted from net income, because when a company computes earnings per share, it should only include income that it could possibly use to someday pay dividends to common shareholders. That is, it should only use the earnings available to common shareholders. Because the preferred dividends are paid to preferred shareholders and not available to common shareholders, they are deducted from income in the earnings per share calculation. The resulting amount is divided by the average number of common shares outstanding during the year.

There are a couple of reasons why the average number of shares of common stock is used as the denominator in the basic earnings per share calculation, rather than the number of shares outstanding at the end of the year. The first can be attributed to the desire every company has to show as high an earnings per share amount as possible. If you look back at the calculation, you will note that the way to make earnings per share higher is to either increase the numerator or decrease the denominator. Note also that the shares of stock used in the calculation are shares outstanding. That means shares actually owned by shareholders. If the number of shares outstanding at the end of the year were used in the calculation, a company could go out on the open market and repurchase shares of its own stock (called treasury stock), thereby reducing the number of shares outstanding and making earnings per share greater. Requiring companies to use the average number of shares outstanding for the year lessens a company's ability to manipulate earnings per share.

The second reason for using the average number of shares outstanding is that the net income included in the numerator was earned throughout the year (some in January, some in February, etc.), therefore, it makes sense to use the number of shares outstanding throughout the year. There are a number of ways to calculate the weighted average shares outstanding for the year. Maybe the simplest conceptually is to take the number of shares outstanding on January 1, add the number of shares outstanding on January 2, add those outstanding on January 3, and so on, all the way to December 31. Then divide the total by 365 (the number of days in the year), and the result will be the weighted average number of shares outstanding for the entire year.

We will use Toy Box, Inc., as our example for the earnings per share calculations we present. As you can see, to calculate Toy Box's basic earnings per share, we need three important pieces of information: net income, preferred dividends, and the weighted average number of common shares outstanding. As the income statement in Exhibit 9–6 shows, Toy Box's net income for 2006 was $208,470. Toy Box's partial balance sheet in Exhibit 9–9 shows that for 2005, the company had $500,000 worth of 4 percent preferred stock outstanding all year. In 2005, Toy Box paid preferred dividends of $20,000 ($500,000 × 4 percent).

Next, we determine the weighted average number of common shares outstanding during the year. Assume that during 2005, Toy Box had 85,000 common shares outstanding for three months of the year and 90,000 shares outstanding for the remaining nine months of the year. The weighted average number of common shares outstanding for Toy Box would be 88,750 shares calculated as follows:

Dates	Number of Shares Outstanding		Period of Time	Weighted Amount
January 1 to March 31	85,000	×	3/12	21,250
April 1 to December 31	90,000	×	9/12	67,500
			Weighted average shares	88,750

Now that we know Toy Box's net income, its preferred dividends, and its weighted average common shares outstanding, we can calculate the company's basic earnings per share as follows:

$$\text{Basic earnings per share} = \frac{\text{Net income} - \text{Preferred dividends}}{\text{Weighted average number of common shares oustanding}} = \frac{\$208,4702 - \$20,000}{88,750} = \$2.12 \text{ (Rounded)}$$

For some companies, basic earnings per share adequately informs financial statement users, but there are companies that have securities outstanding that can potentially reduce (dilute) earnings per share.

EXHIBIT 9–9   Stockholders' Equity Section of Toy Box, Inc.'s Balance Sheet

Toy Box, Inc.
Stockholders' Equity Section
December 31, 2005 and 2004

	2005	2004
Contributed capital:		
4% Preferred stock, $100 par value, 5,000 shares authorized, issued, and outstanding	$ 500,000	$ 500,000
Common stock, $10 par value, 100,000 shares authorized, 90,000 for 2005 and 85,000 for 2004 issued and outstanding	900,000	850,000
Additional paid-in capital	450,000	390,000
Total contributed capital	$1,850,000	$1,740,000
Retained earnings	794,050	675,580
Total stockholders' equity	$2,644,050	$2,415,580

DILUTED EARNINGS PER SHARE

Some companies sell securities or enter into contracts that may require the company to issue additional common stock. These securities have the potential to reduce (dilute) earnings per share because, if converted or exercised, they can increase the number of common shares outstanding. Potentially more common shares means potentially lower earnings per share. Securities that have the potential to reduce earnings per share are called **dilutive securities.**

dilutive securities
Securities that have the potential to reduce earnings per share.

diluted earnings per share A calculation of earnings per share that takes into account all potentially dilutive securities.

If a company has dilutive securities, GAAP require the company to report both basic earnings per share and diluted earnings per share. **Diluted earnings per share** is an *as if* calculation, meaning that it is calculated as if the dilutive securities had been converted into shares of common stock. There are two types of potentially dilutive securities:

- Convertible securities are debt and equity securities (generally corporate bonds and preferred stocks) that can be exchanged for specified amounts of common stock. When security holders trade these securities for common shares, we say the securities were *converted*.
- Securities such as stock options and stock warrants permit their holder to purchase shares of common stock from the company at a specified price, within a specified time period. When security holders acquire common shares under the terms of these securities, we say the securities were *exercised*.

The actual calculations for diluted earnings per share can be quite involved, and are beyond the scope of this text. The basic idea, however, is that diluted earnings per share should reflect the earnings per common share as though the dilutive securities had been converted or exercised at the beginning of the year even though in fact, they were not.

When a company calculates diluted earnings per share, it recalculates earnings per share under the *assumption* that dilutive securities were converted or exercised at the very beginning of the accounting period (or on the dilutive security's issue date if it was issued during the current accounting period). Keep in mind that the securities were not really converted or exercised and they are still outstanding on the balance sheet date. So what we do when we calculate diluted earnings per share is to calculate the earnings per share that would have resulted *if* the securities had been converted or exercised. To do this, we adjust preferred dividends and the weighted average number of common shares outstanding as necessary to reflect the situation that *would have existed* had the securities been converted.

As an example, assume that each of the 5,000 shares of Toy Box's 4 percent preferred stock is convertible to six shares of Toy Box common stock, a total of 30,000 shares. To calculate diluted earnings per share, we assume that the preferred stock was converted at the very first day of the year. If it had been converted, the preferred stock dividend would not have been paid. Additionally, the preferred stock would have been converted to 30,000 (5,000 preferred shares × 6) common shares, so the weighted average common shares outstanding would have increased by this amount. Accordingly, we calculate diluted earnings per share for Toy Box, Inc., as follows:

$$\text{Diluted earnings per share} = \frac{\text{Net income} - \text{Adjusted preferred dividends}}{\text{Adjusted weighted average number of common shares outstanding}} = \frac{\$208,470 - 0}{88,750 + (5,000 \times 6)} = \$1.76 \text{ (Rounded)}$$

To better understand the earnings per share calculation, look first to the numerator of the equation. If we assume the preferred stock was converted at the beginning of the year, there would have been no requirement to pay preferred dividends for the year. The denominator changes because, if we assume the preferred stock was converted, there would have been an additional 30,000 shares of common stock outstanding all year. The result lowers (dilutes) the earnings per share by $0.36 per share.

INCOME STATEMENT PRESENTATION

GAAP require that basic and diluted earnings per share be prominently displayed on the income statement for many of the items on the income statement that appear below income tax expense. If a company has nonrecurring items, where applicable, it should prominently present basic and diluted earnings per share amounts for income from continuing operations, income before extraordinary items, income before cumulative effect of changes in accounting principle, and net income on the face of its income statement. The remaining earnings per share amounts are required but can be presented either on the face of the income statement or in the accompanying notes. Exhibit 9–10 shows Toy Box, Inc.'s 2005 income statement with all earnings per share information included.

The income statement provides users with a great deal of information, but having only one year's information may prove inadequate for many of the economic decisions we have to make. For this reason, companies are required to present financial statements for more than one accounting period.

EXHIBIT 9–10   Income Statement for Toy Box, Inc., for the Year Ended December 31, 2005

Toy Box, Inc.
Income Statement
For the Year Ended December 31, 2005

Sales		$858,600
Less: Cost of goods sold		456,800
Gross profit on sales		$401,800
Less: Operating expenses:		
Selling expense	$ 94,450	
General and administrative expense	116,050	
Total operating expenses		(210,500)
Operating income		$191,300
Less: Interest expense		(30,650)
Income from continuing operations before taxes		$160,650
Less: Income taxes		(64,260)
Income from continuing operations		$ 96,390
Discontinued operations:		
Income from discontinued operations ($118,800, less: income taxes of $47,520)	$ 71,280	
Loss on disposal of discontinued operation ($90,000, less: income taxes of $36,000)	(54,000)	17,280
Income before extraordinary item and cumulative effect of a change in accounting principle		$113,670
Extraordinary gain ($220,000, less: income taxes of $88,000)		132,000
Income before cumulative effect of a change in accounting principle		245,670
Cumulative effect of a change in accounting principle ($62,000, less: income taxes of $24,800)		(37,200)
Net income		$208,470

Earnings per Common Share	*Basic*	*Diluted*
Income from continuing operations	$ 0.86	$ 0.81
Income from discontinued operation, net of income tax	0.80	0.60
Loss on disposal of discontinued operation, net of income tax	(0.61)	(0.45)
Gain from discontinued operation, net of income tax	$ 0.19	$ 0.15
Income before extraordinary item and cumulative effect of a change in accounting principle	$ 1.05	$ 0.96
Extraordinary gain, net of income tax	1.49	1.11
Income before cumulative effect of a change in accounting principle	$ 2.54	$ 2.07
Cumulative effect of a change in accounting principle, net of tax	(0.42)	(0.31)
Net income	$ 2.12	$ 1.76

◆ COMPARATIVE FINANCIAL STATEMENTS

comparative financial statements Financial statements showing results from two or more consecutive periods.

Comparative financial statements show results for two or more consecutive periods—usually years or quarters. As we will see in Chapter 11, financial statement users use information from comparative financial statements to apply analytical techniques that will help them develop a sense of the company's performance over time.

Companies registered with the SEC are required to present at least two years' balance sheets and three years' income statements and statements of cash flows plus selected financial information for at least five preceding years. The Committee on Accounting Procedure described the importance of comparative financial statements this way:

> *Such presentation emphasizes the fact that statements for a series of periods are far more significant than those for a single period and that the accounts for one period are but an installment of what is essentially a continuous history.*[8]

To illustrate the comparative financial statements, we provide the financial statements for Norton Tire Company, Inc., in Exhibit 9–11 (earnings per share omitted).

Discussion Questions

9–12. Using the comparative income statements and balance sheets of Norton Tire Company, Inc., presented in Exhibit 9–11, prepare the company's 2003 statement of retained earnings.

9–13. What specific information did this statement of retained earnings provide that was not apparent from Norton's income statements or balance sheets?

Comparative financial statements enhance the user's ability to analyze a company's past performance and present condition. And, as we will see in the next chapter, information from comparative financial statements is needed to prepare the statement of cash flows.

◆ USING FINANCIAL INFORMATION

Next, we will present several measures that economic decision makers use to evaluate items presented on the classified balance sheet and expanded income statement. As an example, we will use the financial statements for Norton Tire Company, Inc., in Exhibit 9–11.

ASSET TURNOVER RATIO

asset turnover ratio A financial ratio that shows the amount of sales produced for a given level of assets used.

The **asset turnover ratio** shows the amount of sales produced for a given level of assets used. It is good when a company can produce high sales with a low investment in assets. Therefore, companies should try to get the most out of every dollar invested in assets. The asset turnover ratio is important because it indicates how efficiently the company uses its total assets to generate sales. The formula for this ratio is:

$$\text{Asset turnover ratio} = \frac{\text{Net sales}}{\text{Average total assets}}$$

The net sales figure in the numerator of this ratio comes from the income statement. The amounts we use to calculate the denominator come from the balance sheet. We use an average amount for the same reason we did in earlier ratios. Since the sales in the numerator occurred throughout 2003, we want to know the amount of assets

---

[8]Accounting Research Bulletin No. 43, Chapter 2, paragraph 1.

employed throughout the year. We determine this by calculating the average of the total assets. This is done by adding the beginning balance of total assets to the ending balance of total assets and then dividing that number by two ($9,032 + $10,725 = $19,757/2 = $9,878.5). We calculate Norton's asset turnover ratio for 2003 as:

$$\frac{\$14,745}{\$9,878.5} = 1.49 \text{ times}$$

Our calculation indicates that Norton Tire Company, Inc., produced $1.49 in sales during 2003 for every dollar it had invested in assets. The higher the multiple, the more efficiently the company is using its assets to produce sales.

EXHIBIT 9–11   Comparative Financial Statements for Norton Tire Company, Inc.

Norton Tire Company, Inc.
Income Statements
For the Years Ended December 31, 2003, 2002, and 2001
(in thousands)

	2003	2002	2001
Sales	$14,745	$12,908	$10,888
Less: cost of goods sold	10,213	8,761	7,661
Gross profit on sales	$ 4,532	$ 4,147	$ 3,227
Selling, general, and administrative expenses	(3,627)	(2,997)	(2,087)
Operating income	$ 905	$ 1,150	$ 1,140
Interest expense	(145)	(138)	(107)
Income before taxes	$ 760	$ 1,012	$ 1,033
Income taxes	(266)	(354)	(362)
Net income	$ 494	$ 658	$ 671

Norton Tire Company, Inc.
Balance Sheets
December 31, 2003, and December 31, 2002
(in thousands)

	2003	2002
ASSETS:		
Current assets:		
Cash	$ 2,240	$ 1,936
Accounts receivable	2,340	2,490
Merchandise inventory	776	693
Prepaid expenses	200	160
Total current assets	$ 5,556	$ 5,279
Property, plant, and equipment:		
Buildings, net	$ 4,046	$ 2,889
Equipment, net	1,123	864
Total plant and equipment	$ 5,169	$ 3,753
Total assets	$10,725	$ 9,032
LIABILITIES:		
Current liabilities:		
Accounts payable	$ 1,616	$ 1,080
Notes payable	2,720	2,920
Total current liabilities	$ 4,336	$ 4,000
Long-term liabilities	2,000	1,600
Total liabilities	$ 6,336	$ 5,600
STOCKHOLDERS' EQUITY:		
Common stock, no-par value	$ 3,000	$ 2,400
Retained earnings	1,389	1,032
Total stockholders' equity	$ 4,389	$ 3,432
Total liabilities and stockholders' equity	$10,725	$ 9,032

RECEIVABLES TURNOVER RATIO

receivables turnover ratio An efficiency ratio that measures how quickly a company collects its accounts receivable.

The **receivables turnover ratio** measures how efficiently a company manages its accounts receivable. Accounts receivable is the amount a company is owed by its customers, and it is often a significant current asset. Companies need to convert accounts receivable to cash as quickly as possible because, for many companies, they represent interest-free loans to customers. The receivables turnover ratio indicates how quickly a company collects its receivables. The formula for this ratio is:

$$\text{Receivables turnover ratio} = \frac{\text{Net sales}}{\text{Average accounts receivable}}$$

The net sales figure in the numerator comes from Norton's 2003 income statement and the denominator is based on the accounts receivable shown on the balance sheet. We use an average amount for the denominator in this calculation for the same reason we did in earlier ratios. Since the sales used in the numerator occurred throughout 2003, we want to know the amount of accounts receivable throughout the year. We determine this by calculating the average of the accounts receivable shown on the 2002 and 2003 balance sheets. Our average accounts receivable calculation is ($2,490 + $2,340 = $4,830/2 = $2,415). We calculate Norton's receivables turnover ratio for 2003 as:

$$\frac{\$14,745}{\$2,415} = 6.11 \text{ times}$$

Our calculation indicates that Norton turns its receivables over an average of 6.11 times per year. A higher number would suggest that the company collects cash from its credit customers more quickly and is apparently managing its receivables better. On the other hand, a lower receivables turnover means the company manages its receivables less efficiently.

The information that Norton turns over its accounts receivable 6.11 times per year becomes easier to interpret if we extend it to determine the average collection period for its accounts receivable. We can do that by dividing the receivables turnover into 365 (the number of days in a year) to determine the average time it takes the company to collect its receivables or the **average accounts receivable collection period in days:**

average accounts receivable collection period in days The average time it takes a company to collect its receivables.

$$\frac{\text{Average accounts receivable}}{\text{collection period in days}} = \frac{365}{\text{Receivables turnover ratio}}$$

$$\frac{365}{6.11} = 59.74 \text{ days}$$

Our calculation shows that it takes Norton an average of 59.74 days from the sale date to collect cash from its customers.

CURRENT RATIO

current ratio A liquidity ratio that measures a company's ability to meet short-term obligations by comparing current assets to current liabilities.

The **current ratio** was probably the most widely used measure of a company's liquidity for much of the 20th century. Its purpose is to gauge a company's current assets relative to its current liabilities, thereby attempting to offer a measure of the company's ability to meet its short-term financial obligations (its current liabilities) with cash generated from current assets. The formula for this ratio is:

$$\text{Current ratio} = \frac{\text{Current assets}}{\text{Current liabilities}}$$

This ratio indicates the amount of current assets a company has for each dollar of current liabilities, and both the numerator and the denominator come directly from the balance sheet. We calculate Norton's current ratio for 2003 as:

$$\frac{\$5,556}{\$4,336} = 1.28 \text{ to } 1, \text{ or simply, } 1.28$$

A current ratio of 1.28 tells us that Norton had $1.28 of current assets for every $1.00 of current liabilities at the end of 2003.

The current ratio is a well-respected indicator of liquidity, but the problem with this measure is that a company does not pay its bills with accounts receivable, inventory, and other noncash items included in current assets. It must pay its bills with cash. For this reason, many financial analysts have begun questioning the importance of the current ratio.

QUICK RATIO

quick ratio   A liquidity ratio that is similar to the current ratio, but a more stringent test of liquidity, because only current assets considered to be highly liquid (quickly converted to cash) are included in the calculation.

acid-test ratio   Another name for the quick ratio.

The **quick ratio** (sometimes called the **acid-test ratio**) is similar to the current ratio. It is a more stringent test of liquidity, however, because it considers only current assets that are highly liquid (quickly convertible into cash) in the numerator. The calculations for this ratio vary because there is some debate as to what assets to include. This stems from the fact that the definition of "highly liquid" is quite subjective. The formula that we are using is one of the more conservative and it is quite popular among financial analysts. The formula for this ratio is:

$$\text{Quick ratio} = \frac{\text{Cash + Short-term investments + Current receivables}}{\text{Current liabilities}}$$

In the numerator of our equation, cash is obviously liquid. We also assume accounts receivable will be quickly converted to cash. However, if an analyst knows that any current receivable will not be quickly converted, it should not include that receivable in the calculation of this ratio. Since Norton shows no short-term investments on its balance sheet, cash and accounts receivable constitute the numerator for the company's quick ratio calculation. As was the case with the current ratio, the denominator of the quick ratio is total current liabilities. We calculate Norton's quick ratio for 2003 as:

$$\frac{\$2,240 + \$2,340}{\$4,336} = 1.06 \text{ to } 1$$

This ratio calculation tells us that Norton had $1.06 of quick assets for each $1.00 of current liabilities at the end of 2003. Note that Norton's quick ratio is lower than its current ratio. That is usually the case because we have removed assets that are not highly liquid from the numerator, while the denominator remains unchanged.

TIMES INTEREST EARNED RATIO

times interest earned ratio   A financial ratio that indicates a company's ability to earn (cover) its periodic interest payments.

coverage ratio   Same as the times interest earned ratio.

EBIT   Earnings before interest and taxes.

The **times interest earned ratio** (often called the **coverage ratio**) indicates a company's ability to earn (cover) its periodic interest payments. It compares the amount of income available for interest payments to the interest requirements. Creditors use this ratio to assess the risk associated with lending money to a business. The formula for this ratio is:

$$\text{Times interest earned ratio} = \frac{\text{Earnings before interest and income taxes}}{\text{Interest expense}}$$

Earnings before interest and taxes, which is often called **EBIT,** is what Norton calls operating income. We calculate Norton's times interest earned ratio for 2003 as:

$$\frac{\$905}{\$145} = 6.23 \text{ times}$$

This ratio calculation tells us Norton's income available to pay interest expense was $6.23 for every $1.00 of interest expense. In other words, the income Norton had available to pay interest expense was 6.23 times the amount of interest the company reported on its income statement.

Many financial analysts believe a times interest earned ratio of at least four provides an appropriate degree of safety for creditors. This means a company's EBIT should be at least four times as great as its interest expense.

Summary •

The two primary financial statements we have explored thus far—the balance sheet and the income statement—provide important information for economic decision makers. The balance sheet provides a picture of a company's financial position on a given day. This statement outlines what the company owns (assets), what it owes (liabilities), and the residual amount that can be claimed by the owner(s) (equity). The income statement provides a report of the result of business activity during a specific period. Its disclosures of revenues, expenses, gains, and losses for the period are used to measure a company's past performance.

Both the balance sheet and income statement are useful tools. By learning more about the construction and organization of these statements, users of balance sheet and income statement information are able to use the information contained in the statements more effectively.

The classified balance sheet separates assets into four major categories: current, long-term, investments, and intangibles. Liabilities on a classified balance sheet are separated into current and long-term. These classifications provide additional information to users of the information.

Income statements often include items that are not part of the company's normal operations and are not expected to recur. Inflows or outflows of this type must be separated from results of activities that are expected to recur as part of the company's normal, ongoing operations. Reporting recurring items and nonrecurring items separately offers financial statement users additional useful information. Three major types of nonrecurring items (discontinued operations, extraordinary items, and changes in accounting principles) are presented below income from continuing operations and are shown net of tax. An item that is unusual or infrequent, but not both, is shown within the section of the income statement related to continuing operations but is identified as a special item.

Comprehensive income represents the change in equity from nonowner sources. GAAP now require that comprehensive income be prominently displayed in the financial statements. GAAP also require that basic and diluted earnings per share be disclosed on the income statement for each item of income from income from continuing operations through net income. Even with the additional detail offered by a classified balance sheet or an expanded format income statement, economic decision makers are not getting the "big picture" if they consider financial statement information from only one period. Comparative financial statements, providing information for two or more consecutive periods, offer a clearer view of a company's performance and financial position than a financial statement from a single period.

Key Terms •

- acid-test ratio, F–379
- asset turnover ratio, F–376
- average accounts receivable collection period in days, F–378
- basic earnings per share, F–372
- business segment, F–366
- classified balance sheet, F–357
- comparative financial statements, F–376
- comprehensive income, F–371
- contributed capital, F–361
- coverage ratio, F–379

- cumulative effect of an accounting change, F–370
- current assets, F–357
- current liabilities, F–360
- current ratio, F–378
- diluted earnings per share, F–374
- dilutive securities, F–374
- discontinued operations, F–365
- earnings per share (EPS), F–372
- EBIT, F–379
- extraordinary item, F–367
- intangible assets, F–359

- long-term assets, F–359
- long-term investments, F–359
- long-term liabilities, F–360
- net of tax, F–365
- nonrecurring item, F–362
- other assets, F–359
- property, plant, and equipment, F–359
- quick ratio, F–379
- receivables turnover ratio, F–378
- retained earnings, F–361
- times interest earned ratio, F–379

Review the Facts

A. What was the original purpose of accounting records?

B. What caused the shift in attention from the balance sheet to the income statement?

C. Explain why a decision maker may prefer a classified balance sheet to one using the simplest possible format.

D. What is the difference between current and long-term assets? Offer two examples of each.

E. In what order are assets presented on a classified balance sheet?

F. Describe investments and intangible assets and provide two examples of each.

G. Describe the difference between current and long-term liabilities and provide two examples of each.

H. Explain the difference between recurring and nonrecurring items on an income statement. Why are these items reported separately from one another?

 I. Identify the three major types of nonrecurring items that are shown net of tax on the income statement.

J. Explain the effect of taxes on gains and on losses.

K. With respect to discontinued operations, what is a business segment?

L. What criteria must be met for an item to be considered extraordinary?

M. What does the cumulative effect of a change in accounting principle represent?

N. What is comprehensive income? How does it differ from net income?

O. What is the difference between basic and diluted earnings per share?

P. Describe comparative financial statements and explain their benefits to economic decision makers.

Q. What is the focus of the asset turnover ratio and the receivables turnover ratio?

R. What can the current and quick ratios reveal about a company?

S. What does the times interest earned ratio indicate?

Apply What You Have Learned

LO 2: BALANCE SHEET TERMINOLOGY

9–14. Below are items related to the organization of the classified balance sheet, followed by the definitions of those items in scrambled order:

a. Liquidity	f. Long-term liabilities
b. Current assets	g. Stockholders' equity
c. Long-term assets	h. Total liabilities and stockholders' equity
d. Current liabilities	i. Plant and equipment, net
e. Intangible asset	j. Investments

1. _____ Obligations not requiring payment within the next year

2. _____ Items controlled by a company that are not expected to become cash within the next year

3. _____ Describes an item's nearness to cash

4. _____ The owners' residual interest in a corporation

5. _____ Long-lived tangible assets less all the depreciation expense ever recognized on those assets

6. _____ Obligations that must be retired within the next year

7. _____ Equal to total assets

8. _____ Items controlled by a company that are expected to become cash within the next year

9. _____ An investment in a contractual arrangement such as a patent

10. _____ A long-term commitment to ownership of other entities

Required: Match the letter next to each item with the appropriate definition. Use each letter only once.

LO 2: BALANCE SHEET ACCOUNTS

9–15. **Required:**

a. What are investments on a balance sheet and how are they classified?

b. Provide three examples of investments and discuss how they would be classified on the balance sheet.

LO 2: BALANCE SHEET ACCOUNTS

9–16. **Required:**

a. Define intangible assets in your own words.

b. Provide three examples of intangible assets and discuss how they would be classified on the balance sheet.

c. What is the term applied to the process of matching the cost of an intangible with the periods of time benefited or with the revenues they help to create?

LO 2: BALANCE SHEET ACCOUNTS

9–17. Below are the major sections of the classified balance sheet, followed by a list of items normally shown on the balance sheet:

a. Current assets
b. Long-term assets
c. Current liabilities
d. Intangible asset

e. Long-term liabilities
f. Contributed capital
g. Retained earnings
h. Investments

1. _____ Accounts payable
2. _____ Common stock
3. _____ Franchise
4. _____ Accounts receivable
5. _____ Notes payable due within one year
6. _____ Prepaid expenses
7. _____ Preferred stock
8. _____ Notes payable due in two years
9. _____ Amounts earned by the company but not yet distributed to the owners of the business
10. _____ Amounts received in excess of par value on the sale of stock
11. _____ Bonds held by the company to earn interest revenue
12. _____ Land
13. _____ Stock of a subsidiary
14. _____ Wages payable
15. _____ Vehicles
16. _____ Copyright
17. _____ Cash
18. _____ Buildings
19. _____ Bonds payable
20. _____ Trademark

Required: Indicate where each item on the list should be shown on the classified balance sheet by placing the letter of the appropriate balance sheet section in the space provided. The letters may be used more than once.

LO 2: SIMPLE CLASSIFIED BALANCE SHEET PREPARATION

9–18. The following items relate to the Carol Strong Company at December 31, 2004:

Cash	$ 124,200
Accounts receivable	315,200
Inventory	864,800
Prepaid expenses	56,000
Land	620,000
Building	1,450,000
Accumulated depreciation—building	685,000
Accounts payable	546,500
Current notes payable	75,000
Long-term bonds payable	350,000
Common stock, $1 par	55,000
Additional paid-in capital—common	866,400
Retained earnings	852,300

Required:

    a. How many shares of Strong Company's common stock are outstanding at December 31, 2004? Explain how you determined your answer.

    b. How much cash did Strong Company receive from the sale of its common stock? Explain how you determined your answer.

    c. Prepare a classified balance sheet for Strong Company at December 31, 2004.

LO 7: CURRENT AND QUICK RATIO CALCULATIONS

9–19. This problem is a continuation of problem 9–18.

Required:

    a. Using information from the balance sheet you prepared for problem 9–18, calculate the following ratios for the company:

        1. The current ratio
        2. The quick ratio

    b. Based on ratios you calculated, what is your impression of the company's liquidity? Explain your answer.

LO 2: CLASSIFIED BALANCE SHEET PREPARATION

9–20. The following items relate to the Dana Corporation at December 31, 2004:

Land	$210,000
Cash	14,600
Accounts receivable	92,300
Accounts payable	74,000
Common stock (75,000 shares outstanding)	300,000
Bonds payable	100,000
Additional paid-in capital—common stock	10,000
Inventory	118,000
Prepaid expenses	11,200
Taxes payable	17,000
Short-term notes payable	50,000
Building	400,000
Accumulated depreciation—building	142,000
Retained earnings	117,300
Wages payable	35,800

Required:

    a. What is the par value of Dana Corporation's common stock? Explain how you determined your answer.

    b. How much cash did Dana Corporation receive from the sale of its common stock? Explain how you determined your answer.

    c. Prepare a classified balance sheet for Dana Corporation at December 31, 2004.

LO 7: CURRENT AND QUICK RATIO CALCULATIONS

9–21. This problem is a continuation of problem 9–20.

Required:

    a. Using information from the balance sheet you prepared for problem 9–20, calculate the following ratios for the company:

        1. The current ratio
        2. The quick ratio

    b. Based on ratios you calculated, what is your impression of the company's liquidity? Explain your answer.

LO 2: CLASSIFIED BALANCE SHEET PREPARATION

9–22. The following items relate to Murphy and Company at December 31, 2005:

Accounts payable	$172,000
Common stock ($2 par value)	400,000
Bonds payable	307,700
Prepaid expenses	9,800
Taxes payable	47,000
Short-term notes payable	70,000
Building	875,000
Accumulated depreciation—building	271,000
Additional paid-in capital—common stock	240,000
Land	490,000
Cash	124,200
Accounts receivable	212,000
Inventory	338,000
Retained earnings	463,700
Wages payable	77,600

Required:

    a. How many shares of Murphy and Company's common stock are outstanding at December 31, 2005? Explain how you determined your answer.

    b. How much cash did Murphy and Company receive from the sale of its common stock? Explain how you determined your answer.

    c. Prepare a classified balance sheet for Murphy and Company at December 31, 2005.

LO 7: CURRENT AND QUICK RATIO CALCULATIONS

9–23. This problem is a continuation of problem 9–22.

Required:

    a. Using information from the balance sheet you prepared for problem 9–22, calculate the following ratios for the company:

        1. The current ratio
        2. The quick ratio

    b. Based on ratios you calculated, what is your impression of the company's liquidity? Explain your answer.

LO 2: BALANCE SHEET CLASSIFICATIONS

9–24. Many of the assets on a classified balance sheet are identified as current assets. Liabilities on the classified balance sheet are also identified as either current or long-term.

Required:

    a. What criterion is used to determine whether an asset or liability is classified as current or long-term?

    b. Explain in your own words why the following parties would be interested in the separation of current and long-term assets and liabilities on a company's balance sheet:

        1. Short-term creditors (other businesses from whom the company buys inventory, supplies, etc.)
        2. Long-term creditors (banks and others from whom the company borrows money on a long-term basis)
        3. The company's stockholders
        4. The company's management

LO 2: CLASSIFIED BALANCE SHEET

9–25. Stockholders' equity on the classified balance sheet of a corporation is divided into two major categories: contributed capital and retained earnings.

Required:

a. Explain in your own words what each of the two major categories under stockholders' equity represents.

b. Explain in your own words why the following parties would be interested in the relative amounts of contributed capital and retained earnings in the stockholders' equity section of a company's balance sheet:

1. Short-term creditors (other businesses from whom the company buys inventory, supplies, etc.)
2. Long-term creditors (banks and others from whom the company borrows money on a long-term basis)
3. The company's stockholders
4. The company's management

LO 3: INCOME STATEMENT TERMINOLOGY

9–26. Below are several sections of the multiple-step income statement, followed by several independent situations or transactions:

a. Sales
b. Cost of goods sold
c. Operating expenses
d. Income from continuing operations
e. Discontinued operation
f. Extraordinary item
g. Change in accounting principle
h. Not shown on income statement

1. _____ A manufacturing company sells a warehouse with a book value of $20,000 for $20,000.
2. _____ A company changed from the FIFO method to the average cost method of accounting for inventory cost flows.
3. _____ A company sells units of inventory in the normal course of its business operation.
4. _____ A company located in San Francisco, California, experiences a loss from earthquake damage. This loss is determined to be a "special" item.
5. _____ A company disposes of a major segment of its business.
6. _____ A company pays wages, rent, utilities, and so forth.
7. _____ A company located in Columbia, South Carolina, experiences a loss from earthquake damage. This loss is determined to be both unusual in nature and infrequent in occurrence.
8. _____ A company adopts a newly required accounting standard for accounting for postretirement benefits other than pensions. As a result, net income for the year is adversely affected.

Required: Indicate where the result of each situation or transaction should be shown on the multiple-step income statement by placing the letter of the appropriate income statement section in the space provided. The letters may be used more than once. *Note*: The results of some situations or transactions may not be shown on the income statement. If so, place the letter h in the space provided.

LO 3: INCOME STATEMENT TERMINOLOGY

9–27. Below are items related to the multiple-step income statement as discussed in this chapter, followed by the definitions of those items in scrambled order:

a. Gross profit on sales
b. Operating expenses
c. Income from continuing operations
d. Discontinued operation
e. Extraordinary item
f. Change in accounting principle
g. Recurring item
h. Nonrecurring item

1. _____ A material gain or loss that is both unusual in nature and infrequent in occurrence
2. _____ Generally, the difference between normal ongoing revenues and normal ongoing expenses
3. _____ The difference between sales and cost of goods sold
4. _____ Any item that should not be considered a normal part of continuing operations because it is not expected to happen again
5. _____ Sacrifices incurred in the normal day-to-day running of a business

6. ____ Any item considered a normal part of continuing operations because it is expected to happen on an ongoing basis
7. ____ A change from a less preferred to a more preferred method of accounting
8. ____ The disposal of a business segment

Required: Match the letter next to each item with the appropriate definition. Use each letter only once.

LO 3: INCOME TAX DISCLOSURE

9–28. **Required:**

a. What is the purpose of reporting discontinued items, extraordinary gains and losses, and the cumulative effect of changes in accounting principle net of income taxes?
b. Discuss the meaning of the phrase "net of tax" and how this is reported on the income statement.

LO 3: DISCONTINUED OPERATIONS

9–29. On March 1, 2005, the board of directors of Photoception approved the disposal of a segment of its business. For the period of January 1 through February 28, 2005, the segment had revenues of $200,000 and expenses of $350,000. The company sold the assets of the segment at a loss of $100,000.

Required: Describe how the corporation should report the previous information on the financial statements. Be as specific as possible.

LO 3: DISCONTINUED OPERATIONS

9–30. On July 1, 2004, the board of directors of Donahue Company approved the sale of a segment of its business. For the period of January 1 through June 30, 2004, the segment had revenues of $1,100,000 and expenses of $1,500,000. The company sold the assets of the segment at a gain of $200,000.

Required: Describe how the corporation should report the previous information on the financial statements. Be as specific as possible.

LO 3: DISCONTINUED OPERATIONS

9–31. On October 1, 2005, the board of directors of Lopez Company approved the disposal of a segment of its business. For the period of January 1 through September 30, 2005, the segment had revenues of $1,500,000 and expenses of $2,500,000. The company sold the assets of the segment at a gain of $300,000.

Required: Describe how the corporation should report the previous information on the financial statements. Be as specific as possible.

LO 4: MULTIPLE-STEP INCOME STATEMENT

9–32. The following items relate to Kim Hahn, Inc., for the year ended December 31, 2004:

- Net sales for the year totaled $665,000.
- Cost of goods sold for the year totaled $271,000.
- Regular operating expenses for the year were $145,000.
- Interest expense for the year was $27,000.
- On February 18, 2004, one of Hahn's warehouses burned to the ground. The company's loss (after the insurance settlement) was $106,000 before any tax effect. This loss was determined to be both unusual in nature and infrequent in occurrence.
- During 2004, Hahn changed the way it depreciated its property, plant, and equipment from an accelerated method to the straight-line method. The cumulative effect of this change was a $93,000 increase in net income before any tax effect.
- Hahn's income tax rate is 40 percent on all items.

Required: Prepare Hahn's income statement for the year ended December 31, 2004, using the expanded multiple-step format presented in this chapter.

LO 7: ASSET TURNOVER, RECEIVABLES TURNOVER, AND TIMES INTEREST EARNED RATIO CALCULATIONS

9–33. This problem is a continuation of problem 9–32.

In addition to the information from the financial statements you prepared for 9–32, the following information is available:

- The average total assets for the company are $950,000.
- Average accounts receivable for the company are $140,000.

Required:

  a. Calculate the following ratios for the company:

  1. The asset turnover ratio
  2. The receivables turnover ratio
  3. The average accounts receivable collection period in days
  4. The times interest earned ratio

  b. Based on the ratios, what is your impression of the company? Explain your answer.

LO 4: MULTIPLE-STEP INCOME STATEMENT

9–34. The following items relate to Linda Jones and Company for the year ended December 31, 2005:

- Net sales for the year totaled $575,000.
- Cost of goods sold for the year totaled $372,500.
- Regular operating expenses for the year were $121,500.
- Interest expense for the year was $16,000.
- On September 5, 2005, Jones sold the only land it owned at a pretax gain of $50,000. The land was acquired in 1996 for future expansion, but shortly thereafter, the company abandoned all plans for expansion and held the land for appreciation.
- During 2005, Jones changed the way it accounted for inventory from the FIFO method to the average cost method. The cumulative effect of this change was an $80,000 decrease in net income before any tax effect.
- Jones's income tax rate is 30 percent on all items.

Required: Prepare Jones's income statement for the year ended December 31, 2005, using the expanded multiple-step format presented in this chapter.

LO 7: ASSET TURNOVER, RECEIVABLES TURNOVER, AND TIMES INTEREST EARNED RATIO CALCULATIONS

9–35. This problem is a continuation of problem 9–34.

In addition to the information from the financial statements you prepared for 9–34, the following information is available:

- The average total assets for the company are $360,000.
- Average accounts receivable for the company are $55,000.

Required:

  a. Calculate the following ratios for the company:

  1. The asset turnover ratio
  2. The receivables turnover ratio
  3. The average accounts receivable collection period in days
  4. The times interest earned ratio

  b. Based on the ratios, what is your impression of the company? Explain your answer.

LO 4: MULTIPLE-STEP INCOME STATEMENT

9–36. The following items relate to Mark Ripley Company for the year ended December 31, 2004:

- Net sales for the year totaled $1,075,000.
- Cost of goods sold for the year totaled $667,000.

- Operating expenses for the year were $102,500.
- Interest expense for the year was $43,000.
- On June 30, 2004, Ripley sold a major segment of its business at a loss of $95,000 before any tax effects. This segment of the company represented a major line of business that was totally separate from the rest of Ripley's operation.
- Prior to being sold, the business segment had sales during 2004 of $150,000, cost of goods sold of $90,000, and operating expenses of $45,000. These amounts are not included in the previous information provided.
- Ripley's income tax rate is 40 percent on all items.

Required: Prepare Ripley's income statement for the year ended December 31, 2004, using the expanded multiple-step format presented in this chapter.

LO 7: ASSET TURNOVER, RECEIVABLES TURNOVER, AND TIMES INTEREST EARNED RATIO CALCULATIONS

9–37. This problem is a continuation of problem 9–36.

In addition to the information from the financial statements you prepared for 9–36, the following information is available:

- The average total assets for the company are $390,000.
- Average accounts receivable for the company are $165,000.

Required:

  a. Calculate the following ratios for the company:

  1. The asset turnover ratio
  2. The receivables turnover ratio
  3. The average accounts receivable collection period in days
  4. The times interest earned ratio

  b. Based on the ratios, what is your impression of the company? Explain your answer.

LO 4: MULTIPLE-STEP INCOME STATEMENT

9–38. The following items relate to Andre Holmes, Inc., for the year ended December 31, 2005:

- Net sales for the year totaled $465,000.
- Cost of goods sold for the year totaled $239,000.
- Operating expenses for the year were $113,200.
- Interest expense for the year was $11,000.
- On July 16, 2005, Holmes sold a major segment of its business at a gain of $50,000 before any tax effects. This segment of the company represented a major line of business that was totally separate from the rest of Holmes's operation.
- Prior to being sold, the business segment had sales during 2005 of $60,000, cost of goods sold of $40,000, and operating expenses of $35,000. These amounts are not included in the previous information provided.
- Holmes's income tax rate is 30 percent on all items.

Required: Prepare Holmes's income statement for the year ended December 31, 2005, using the expanded multiple-step format presented in this chapter.

LO 7: ASSET TURNOVER, RECEIVABLES TURNOVER, AND TIMES INTEREST EARNED RATIO CALCULATIONS

9–39. This problem is a continuation of problem 9–38.

In addition to the information from the financial statements you prepared for 9–38, the following information is available:

- The average total assets for the company are $738,000.
- Average accounts receivable for the company are $47,000.

Required:

    a. Calculate the following ratios for the company:

        1. The asset turnover ratio
        2. The receivables turnover ratio
        3. The average accounts receivable collection period in days
        4. The times interest earned ratio

    b. Based on the ratios, what is your impression of the company? Explain your answer.

LO 4: DISCUSSION OF INCOME STATEMENT

9–40. The multiple-step income statement as presented in this chapter separates recurring items from nonrecurring items. Further, three major types of nonrecurring items are shown on the income statement net of tax.

Required:

    a. Explain in your own words the rationale behind showing recurring and nonrecurring items separately on the multiple-step income statement.
    b. Explain in your own words what the phrase "net of tax" means and why three major types of nonrecurring items are shown in this manner on the income statement.

LO 5: SIMPLE CALCULATION OF BASIC EARNINGS PER SHARE—SIMPLE CAPITAL STRUCTURE

9–41. The Tatum Company reported net income for the year ended December 31, 2005, of $337,600. At the end of the year 2005, the Tatum Company had the following shares of capital stock outstanding:

- Preferred stock, 5 percent, $200 par value, nonconvertible, 10,000 issued and outstanding.
- Common stock, $2 par value, 40,000 shares issued and outstanding.

Required: Assume the preferred dividends were paid and calculate basic earnings per share for 2005.

LO 5: BASIC EARNINGS PER SHARE—SIMPLE CAPITAL STRUCTURE

9–42. The Kreutzer Company reported net income for the year ended December 31, 2005, of $554,800. During the year 2005, the Kreutzer Company had the following shares of capital stock outstanding:

- Preferred stock, 6 percent, $100 par value, nonconvertible, 20,000 issued and outstanding.
- Common stock, $1 par value, 40,000 shares issued and outstanding on January 1, 2005.
- An additional 5,000 shares of common stock were issued on April 1, 2005.

Required: Assume the preferred dividends were paid and calculate basic earnings per share for 2005.

LO 5: BASIC EARNINGS PER SHARE—SIMPLE CAPITAL STRUCTURE

9–43. The Witt Company reported income after taxes for the year ended December 31, 2005, of $775,200. During the year 2005, the Witt Company had the following shares of capital stock outstanding:

- Preferred stock, 5 percent, $100 par value, nonconvertible, 20,000 issued and outstanding.
- Common stock, $3 par value, 80,000 shares issued and outstanding on January 1, 2005.
- An additional 10,000 shares of common stock were issued on July 1, 2005.

Required: Assume the preferred dividends were paid and calculate basic earnings per share for 2005.

LO 1, 2, & 5: INCOME STATEMENT, STATEMENT OF RETAINED EARNINGS, BALANCE SHEET WITH NO NONRECURRING ITEMS (SELECTED CHECK FIGURE PROVIDED)

9–44. The following information is taken from accounting records of Kevin's Toy Store as of the year ended December 31, 2004:

Income tax rate	34%
Net sales	$1,268,000
Cost of goods sold	975,000
Operating expenses	225,000
Rent revenue	6,000
Interest expense	5,000
Check figure—income tax	23,460
Beginning retained earnings balance	114,460
Dividends	10,000
Cash	126,000
Accounts receivable	185,000
Inventory	225,000
Other current assets	38,000
Property, plant, and equipment	875,000
Accumulated depreciation—property, plant, and equipment	350,000
Accounts payable	260,000
Current notes payable	30,000
Long-term notes payable	34,000
Common stock, $2 par, 50,000 shares authorized, 12,500 shares issued and outstanding	25,000
Additional paid-in capital—common	600,000
Check figure—ending retained earnings balance	150,000

Required:

a. Prepare an income statement for the company using a multiple-step format.
b. Calculate basic earnings per share and include it at the bottom of the income statement. Assume that the number of common shares outstanding remained constant all year.
c. Prepare a statement of retained earnings for the company.
d. Prepare a classified balance sheet for the company as of the end of the accounting period.

LO 7: FINANCIAL RATIO CALCULATIONS

9–45. This problem is a continuation of problem 9–44.

In addition to the information from the financial statements you prepared for 9–44, the following information is available:

- The company's assets totaled $1,027,000 at December 31, 2003.
- The company's accounts receivable totaled $165,000 at December 31, 2003.

Required:

a. Calculate the following ratios for the company:

1. The asset turnover ratio
2. The receivables turnover ratio
3. The average accounts receivable collection period in days
4. The current ratio
5. The quick ratio
6. The times interest earned ratio

b. Based on the ratios, what is your impression of the company? Explain your answer.

LO 1, 2, & 5: INCOME STATEMENT, STATEMENT OF RETAINED EARNINGS, BALANCE SHEET WITH NO NONRECURRING ITEMS (SELECTED CHECK FIGURE PROVIDED)

9–46. The following information is taken from accounting records of Kyle's Lawns, Inc., as of the fiscal year ended November 30, 2005:

Income tax rate	30%
Net sales	$3,000,000
Cost of goods sold	2,000,000
Operating expenses	380,000
Interest revenue	2,000
Interest expense	22,000
Income tax	180,000
Beginning retained earnings balance	122,000
Dividends	42,000
Cash	125,000
Accounts receivable	175,000
Merchandise inventory	245,000
Other current assets	25,000
Property, plant, and equipment	965,000
Accumulated depreciation—property, plant, and equipment	335,000
Accounts payable	285,000
Current notes payable	10,000
Wages payable	5,000
Long-term notes payable	50,000
Common stock, $1 par, 150,000 shares authorized,	
95,000 shares issued and outstanding	95,000
Additional paid-in capital—common	255,000
Check figure—ending retained earnings balance	500,000

Required:

a. Prepare an income statement for the company using a multiple-step format.

b. Calculate basic earnings per share and include it at the bottom of the income statement. Assume that the number of common shares outstanding remained constant all year.

c. Prepare a statement of retained earnings for the company.

d. Prepare a classified balance sheet for the company as of the end of the accounting period.

LO 7: FINANCIAL RATIO CALCULATIONS

9–47. This problem is a continuation of problem 9–46.

In addition to the information from the financial statements you prepared for 9–46, the following information is available:

- The company's assets totaled $1,100,000 at November 30, 2004.
- The company's accounts receivable totaled $191,000 at November 30, 2004.

Required:

a. Calculate the following ratios for the company:

1. The asset turnover ratio
2. The receivables turnover ratio
3. The average accounts receivable collection period in days
4. The current ratio
5. The quick ratio
6. The times interest earned ratio

b. Based on the ratios, what is your impression of the company? Explain your answer.

LO 1, 2, & 5: INCOME STATEMENT, STATEMENT OF RETAINED EARNINGS, BALANCE SHEET WITH NO NONRECURRING ITEMS (SELECTED CHECK FIGURE PROVIDED)

9–48. The following information is taken from accounting records of Fashions by Christie as of the year ended December 31, 2004:

Income tax rate	30%
Net sales	$350,000
Cost of goods sold	150,000
Operating expenses	135,000
Interest revenue	1,000

Interest expense	16,000
Income tax	15,000
Beginning retained earnings balance	57,000
Dividends	17,000
Cash	62,000
Inventory	78,000
Property, plant, and equipment	186,000
Accumulated depreciation—property, plant, and equipment	26,000
Accounts payable	90,000
Current notes payable	10,000
Long-term notes payable	25,000
Common stock, $5 par, 10,000 shares authorized,	
1,000 shares issued and outstanding	5,000
Additional paid-in capital—common	95,000
Check figure—ending retained earnings balance	75,000

Required:

  a. Prepare an income statement for the company using a multiple-step format.

  b. Calculate basic earnings per share and include it at the bottom of the income statement. Assume that the number of common shares outstanding remained constant all year.

  c. Prepare a statement of retained earnings for the company.

  d. Prepare a classified balance sheet for the company as of the end of the accounting period.

LO 1, 2, 3, 4, & 5: INCOME STATEMENT, STATEMENT OF RETAINED EARNINGS, BALANCE SHEET WITH EXTRAORDINARY ITEM (SELECTED CHECK FIGURES PROVIDED)

9–49. The following information is taken from accounting records of Art by Nicole as of the year ended December 31, 2004:

Income tax rate	32%
Sales	$427,650
Cost of goods sold	255,340
Operating expenses	119,850
Rent revenue	1,240
Interest expense	3,000
Loss on extinguishment of debt	19,000
Beginning retained earnings balance	215,000
Dividends	2,000
Cash	18,000
Accounts receivable	63,500
Inventory	98,450
Other current assets	26,800
Property, plant, and equipment	230,000
Accumulated depreciation—property, plant, and equipment	40,000
Accounts payable	38,600
Current notes payable	25,000
Long-term bonds payable	50,000
Common stock, $1 par, 50,000 shares authorized,	
3,500 shares issued and outstanding	3,500
Additional paid-in capital—common	45,094
Check figure—ending retained earnings balance	234,556
Check figure—income tax amount for nonrecurring item	6,080
Check figure—income tax on income before extraordinary item	16,224

Required:

  a. Prepare an income statement for the company using a multiple-step format.

  b. Calculate basic earnings per share and include it at the bottom of the income statement. Assume that the number of common shares outstanding remained constant all year.

  c. Prepare a statement of retained earnings for the company.

  d. Prepare a classified balance sheet for the company as of the end of the accounting period.

LO 7: FINANCIAL RATIO CALCULATIONS

9–50. This problem is a continuation of problem 9–49.

In addition to the information from the financial statements you prepared for 9–49, the following information is available:

- The company's assets totaled $374,250 at December 31, 2003.
- The company's accounts receivable totaled $69,250 at December 31, 2003.

Required:

a. Calculate the following ratios for the company:

1. The asset turnover ratio
2. The receivables turnover ratio
3. The average accounts receivable collection period in days
4. The current ratio
5. The quick ratio
6. The times interest earned ratio

b. Based on the ratios, what is your impression of the company? Explain your answer.

LO 1, 2, 3, 4, & 5: INCOME STATEMENT, STATEMENT OF RETAINED EARNINGS, BALANCE SHEET WITH EXTRAORDINARY ITEM (SELECTED CHECK FIGURES PROVIDED)

9–51. The following information is taken from accounting records of Adrienne's Cosmetics as of the year ended December 31, 2004:

Income tax rate	36%
Net sales	$1,525,000
Cost of goods sold	925,000
Operating expenses	386,000
Interest revenue	3,000
Interest expense	15,000
Extraordinary casualty loss—flood damage	36,000
Beginning retained earnings balance	160,000
Dividends	20,000
Cash	126,500
Accounts receivable	186,500
Inventory	225,500
Other current assets	38,000
Property, plant, and equipment	875,000
Accumulated depreciation—property, plant, and equipment	350,000
Accounts payable	260,000
Current notes payable	30,000
Long-term notes payable	37,000
Common stock, $5 par, 100,000 shares authorized, 10,000 shares issued and outstanding	50,000
Additional paid-in capital—common	478,260
Check figure—ending retained earnings balance	246,240
Check figure—income tax amount for nonrecurring item	12,960
Check figure—income tax on income before extraordinary item	72,720

Required:

a. Prepare an income statement for the company using a multiple-step format.
b. Calculate basic earnings per share and include it at the bottom of the income statement. Assume that the number of common shares outstanding remained constant all year.
c. Prepare a statement of retained earnings for the company.
d. Prepare a classified balance sheet for the company as of the end of the accounting period.

LO 1, 2, 3, 4, & 5: INCOME STATEMENT, STATEMENT OF RETAINED EARNINGS, BALANCE SHEET WITH ACCOUNTING CHANGE (SELECTED CHECK FIGURES PROVIDED)

9–52. The following information is taken from accounting records of Jerry's Tile Depot as of the year ended December 31, 2004:

Income tax rate	34%
Sales	$2,300,000
Cost of goods sold	1,450,000
Operating expenses	787,000
Rent revenue	19,000
Interest expense	5,000
Gain from cumulative effect of accounting change	33,000
Beginning retained earnings balance	160,000
Dividends	15,000
Cash	126,500
Accounts receivable	186,500
Inventory	225,500
Other current assets	38,000
Property, plant, and equipment	875,000
Accumulated depreciation—property, plant, and equipment	350,000
Accounts payable	260,000
Current notes payable	25,000
Wages payable	5,000
Long-term notes payable	37,000
Common stock, $1 par, 100,000 shares authorized, 50,000 shares issued and outstanding	50,000
Additional paid-in capital—common	506,900
Check figure—ending retained earnings balance	217,600
Check figure—income tax amount for nonrecurring item	−$11,220
Check figure—income tax on income before cumulative effect of account change	26,180

Required:

a. Prepare an income statement for the company using a multiple-step format.
b. Calculate basic earnings per share and include it at the bottom of the income statement. Assume that the number of common shares outstanding remained constant all year.
c. Prepare a statement of retained earnings for the company.
d. Prepare a classified balance sheet for the company as of the end of the accounting period.

LO 1, 2, 3, 4, & 5: INCOME STATEMENT, STATEMENT OF RETAINED EARNINGS, BALANCE SHEET WITH DISCONTINUED OPERATION (SELECTED CHECK FIGURES PROVIDED)

9–53. The following information is taken from accounting records of Danielle's Shoes as of the year ended December 31, 2004:

Income tax rate	30%
Sales	$960,000
Cost of goods sold	575,600
Operating expenses	276,000
Interest expense	1,500
Discontinued operation	
Loss on operation of discontinued operation	8,500
Loss on disposal of discontinued operation	29,500
Beginning retained earnings balance	98,650
Dividends	4,823
Cash	68,500
Accounts receivable	140,000
Inventory	175,500
Other current assets	2,000
Equipment	185,000

Accumulated depreciation—equipment	32,000
Accounts payable	80,500
Current notes payable	2,000
Long-term notes payable	15,000
Preferred stock, $50 par, 5,000 shares authorized,	
2,400 shares issued and outstanding	120,000
Additional paid-in capital—preferred	3,000
Common stock, $1 par, 100,000 shares authorized,	
27,000 shares issued and outstanding	27,000
Additional paid-in capital—common	149,443
Check figure—ending retained earnings balance	142,057
Check figure—income tax amount for nonrecurring items	11,400
Check figure—income tax on income from continuing operations	32,070

Required:

a. Prepare an income statement for the company using a multiple-step format.
b. Calculate basic earnings per share and include it at the bottom of the income statement. Assume that the number of common shares outstanding remained constant all year.
c. Prepare a statement of retained earnings for the company.
d. Prepare a classified balance sheet for the company as of the end of the accounting period.

LO 1, 2, 3, 4, & 5: COMPLEX DETAILED INCOME STATEMENT, STATEMENT OF RETAINED EARNINGS, BALANCE SHEET WITH DISCONTINUED OPERATION, EXTRAORDINARY ITEM, AND ACCOUNTING CHANGE (SELECTED CHECK FIGURES PROVIDED)

9–54. The following information is taken from accounting records of Mark's Custom Decks and Ponds as of the fiscal year ended November 30, 2005:

Income tax rate	32%
Sales	$2,650,500
Cost of goods sold	1,825,000
Wages and salaries	420,000
Rent	108,000
Electricity	10,200
Telephone	4,200
Interest revenue	1,600
Interest expense	36,000
Discontinued operation	
Loss on operation of discontinued operation	1,000
Loss on disposal of discontinued operation	14,000
Extraordinary loss	22,000
Cumulative effect of accounting change—gain	5,000
Beginning retained earnings balance	43,116
Dividends	20,000
Cash	34,500
Accounts receivable	152,500
Inventory	231,232
Supplies	2,500
Land	100,000
Building	155,000
Accumulated depreciation—building	75,000
Equipment	20,300
Accumulated depreciation—equipment	10,000
Intangible assets—copyrights	15,000
Accounts payable	155,300
Current notes payable	5,000
Current bonds payable	31,000
Long-term bonds payable	150,000
Preferred stock, $100 par, 500 shares authorized,	
issued, and outstanding	50,000
Additional paid-in capital—preferred	5,000

Common stock, $1 par, 10,000 shares authorized, 2,500 shares issued and outstanding	2,500
Additional paid-in capital—common	56,760
Check figure—ending retained earnings balance	170,472
Check figure—income tax on continuing operations	79,584

Required:

a. Prepare an income statement for the company using a multiple-step format.
b. Calculate basic earnings per share and include it at the bottom of the income statement. Assume that the number of common shares outstanding remained constant all year.
c. Prepare a statement of retained earnings for the company.
d. Prepare a classified balance sheet for the company as of the end of the accounting period.

LO 1, 2, 3, 4, & 5: COMPLEX VERY DETAILED INCOME STATEMENT, STATEMENT OF RETAINED EARNINGS, BALANCE SHEET WITH DISCONTINUED OPERATION, EXTRAORDINARY ITEM, AND ACCOUNTING CHANGE (SELECTED CHECK FIGURES PROVIDED)

9–55. The following information is taken from accounting records of Louie's Lumber as of the fiscal year ended June 30, 2005:

Income tax rate	30%
Net sales	$950,000
Cost of goods sold	596,500
Wages and salaries	123,000
Rent	36,000
Electricity	4,200
Telephone	1,800
Advertising	6,000
Interest revenue	1,000
Rent revenue	12,000
Interest expense	16,000
Casualty loss (infrequent but not unusual)	9,500
Discontinued operation	
Loss on operation of discontinued operation	8,000
Gain on disposal of discontinued operation	3,000
Extraordinary loss—storm damage	7,500
Cumulative effect of accounting change—gain	6,300
Beginning retained earnings balance	195,640
Dividends	17,000
Cash	68,520
Accounts receivable	104,640
Inventory	174,020
Supplies	2,500
Prepaid expenses	1,800
Long-term investments	34,000
Land	96,350
Building	128,750
Accumulated depreciation—building	29,000
Equipment	85,000
Accumulated depreciation—equipment	30,000
Intangible asset—copyright	2,400
Accounts payable	77,500
Current notes payable	5,000
Long-term notes payable	15,000
Long-term bonds payable	50,000
Preferred stock, $100 par, 5,000 shares authorized, 500 shares issued and outstanding	50,000
Additional paid-in capital—preferred	2,000
Common stock, $2 par, 20,000 shares authorized, 8,000 shares issued and outstanding	16,000
Additional paid-in capital—common	130,180

Check figure—ending retained earnings balance	293,300
Check figure—income tax amount for nonrecurring items	1,860
Check figure—income tax on income from continuing operations	51,000

Required:

   a. Prepare an income statement for the company using a multiple-step format.

   b. Calculate basic earnings per share and include it at the bottom of the income statement. Assume that the number of common shares outstanding remained constant all year.

   c. Prepare a statement of retained earnings for the company.

   d. Prepare a classified balance sheet for the company as of the end of the accounting period.

LO 7: FINANCIAL RATIO CALCULATIONS

9–56. This problem is a continuation of problem 9–55.

In addition to the information from the financial statements you prepared for 9–55, the following information is available:

- The company's assets totaled $620,000 at June 30, 2004.
- The company's accounts receivable totaled $92,000 at June 30, 2004.

Required:

   a. Calculate the following ratios for the company:

      1. The asset turnover ratio
      2. The receivables turnover ratio
      3. The average accounts receivable collection period in days
      4. The current ratio
      5. The quick ratio
      6. The times interest earned ratio

   b. Based on the ratios, what is your impression of the company? Explain your answer.

LO 7: FINANCIAL RATIO CALCULATIONS

9–57. The following information is available for Carter, Inc.:

Carter, Inc.
Income Statement
For the Year Ended December 31, 2004

Sales	$250,000
Cost of goods sold	130,000
Gross profit	120,000
Operating expenses	87,000
Operating income	33,000
Interest expense	3,000
Income before income tax	30,000
Income tax	6,000
Net income	$ 24,000

Statement of Retained Earnings
For the Year Ended December 31, 2004

Beginning retained earnings balance	$ 38,000
Net income	24,000
Dividends	(2,000)
Ending retained earnings	$ 60,000

Balance Sheet
December 31, 2004

ASSETS:
Current assets:

Cash	$ 14,000

Accounts receivable	48,000
Inventory	39,000
Supplies	1,000
Prepaid expenses	2,000
Total current assets	104,000
Property, plant, and equipment:	79,000
Accumulated depreciation—property, plant, and equipment	(13,000)
Property, plant, and equipment, net	66,000
Total assets	$ 170,000
LIABILITIES:	
Current liabilities:	
Accounts payable	$ 18,000
Current notes payable	27,000
Total current liabilities	45,000
Long-term liabilities:	
Notes payable	11,000
Total liabilities	56,000
EQUITY:	
Contributed capital:	
Common stock, $2 par, 100,000 shares authorized, 2,500 shares issued and outstanding	5,000
Additional paid-in capital—common	49,000
Total contributed capital	54,000
Retained earnings	60,000
Total equity	114,000
Total liabilities and equity	$ 170,000

Required: Assume the following:

- The company's assets totaled $160,000 at December 31, 2003.
- The company's accounts receivable totaled $44,000 at December 31, 2003.

a. Calculate the following ratios for the company:

1. The asset turnover ratio
2. The receivables turnover ratio
3. The average accounts receivable collection period in days
4. The current ratio
5. The quick ratio
6. The times interest earned ratio

b. Do any of the ratios reveal anything that you find troubling about the company?

LO 7: FINANCIAL RATIO CALCULATIONS

9–58. The president of Stacyjohn Industries, Inc., is expanding and would like to obtain additional external financing. The following information is available:

Stacyjohn Industries, Inc.
Income Statement
For the Year Ended December 31, 2004

Net sales	$12,188,720
Cost of goods sold	8,850,400
Gross profit	3,338,320
Operating expenses	(2,158,080)
Operating income	1,180,240
Interest expense	($32,690)
Income before income tax	1,147,550
Income tax	(413,118)
Net Income	$ 734,432

Statement of Retained Earnings
For the Year Ended December 31, 2004

Beginning retained earnings balance	$1,864,900
Net income	734,432
Dividends	0
Ending retained earnings	$2,599,332

Balance Sheet
December 31, 2004

ASSETS:
Current assets:

Cash	$ 236,580
Accounts receivable	1,235,500
Merchandise inventory	1,580,000
Prepaid expenses	56,000
Total current assets	3,108,080

Property, plant, and equipment:

Land	1,684,000
Building	1,968,000
Accumulated depreciation—building	(685,000)
Building, net	1,283,000
Total property, plant, and equipment	2,967,000
Total assets	$6,075,080

LIABILITIES:
Current liabilities:

Accounts payable	$ 546,500
Current portion of notes	50,000
Total current liabilities	596,500
Long-term liabilities—bonds payable	350,000
Total liabilities	946,500

EQUITY:
Contributed capital:

Common stock, $1 par, 200,000 shares authorized, 85,000 shares issued and outstanding	85,000
Additional paid-in capital—common	2,444,248
Total contributed capital	2,529,248
Retained earnings	2,599,332
Total equity	5,128,580
Total liabilities and equity	$6,075,080

Required: Assume the following:

- The company's assets totaled $5,680,000 at December 31, 2003.
- The company's accounts receivable totaled $1,150,250 at December 31, 2003.

a. Calculate the following ratios for the company:

1. The asset turnover ratio
2. The receivables turnover ratio
3. The average accounts receivable collection period in days
4. The current ratio
5. The quick ratio
6. The times interest earned ratio

b. Based on the ratios you calculated, do you feel the company will have difficulty securing additional external financing? Explain your answer.

LO 7: FINANCIAL RATIO CALCULATIONS

9–59. The following information is available for the Fox Company, Inc.:

Fox Company, Inc.
Income Statement
For the Year Ended December 31, 2005

Sales	$6,500,000
Cost of goods sold	4,850,000
Gross profit	1,650,000
Operating expenses	(780,000)
Operating income	870,000
Other expenses—interest expense	(125,000)
Income before income tax	745,000
Income tax	(268,200)
Net income	$ 476,800

Statement of Retained Earnings
For the Year Ended December 31, 2005

Beginning retained earnings balance	$ 950,000
Net income	476,800
Dividends	(47,680)
Ending retained earnings	$1,379,120

Balance Sheet
December 31, 2005

ASSETS:	
Current assets:	
Cash	$ 126,000
Accounts receivable	750,000
Inventory	598,000
Supplies	12,000
Prepaid expenses	36,000
Total current assets	1,522,000
Property, plant, and equipment:	
Land	865,000
Building	2,350,000
Accumulated depreciation—building	(360,000)
Building, net of accumulated depreciation	1,990,000
Total property, plant, and equipment	2,855,000
Total Assets	$4,377,000
LIABILITIES:	
Current liabilities:	
Accounts payable	$ 550,000
Current notes payable	65,000
Total current liabilities	615,000
Long-term liabilities:	
Long-term notes payable	150,000
Long-term bonds payable	1,350,000
Total long-term liabilities	1,500,000
Total liabilities	2,115,000
EQUITY:	
Paid-in capital:	
Common stock, $5 par, 200,000 shares authorized,	
38,000 shares issued and outstanding	190,000
Additional paid-in capital—common	692,880
Total paid-in capital	882,880
Retained earnings	1,379,120
Total equity	2,262,000
Total liabilities and equity	$4,377,000

Required: Assume the following:

- The company's assets totaled $4,290,000 at December 31, 2004.
- The company's accounts receivable totaled $720,000 at December 31, 2004.

a. Calculate the following ratios for the company:

1. The asset turnover ratio
2. The receivables turnover ratio
3. The average accounts receivable collection period in days
4. The current ratio
5. The quick ratio
6. The times interest earned ratio

b. Based on the ratios, what is your impression of the company? Explain your answer.

Financial Reporting Exercises

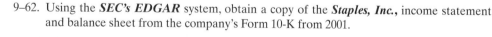

9–60. Using the *SEC's Electronic Data Gathering, Analysis, and Retrieval (EDGAR)* system, obtain a copy of the *Office Depot, Inc.,* income statement and balance sheet from the company's Form 10-K from 2001.

Required:

a. Calculate the following ratios for the company for 2001:

1. The asset turnover ratio
2. The receivables turnover ratio
3. The average accounts receivable collection period in days
4. The current ratio
5. The quick ratio
6. The times interest earned ratio

b. What is the impression you get about the company from these ratios?
c. Look at the ratios calculated for *Office Depot, Inc.,* in problem 4–73. Did these ratios give you the same impression as those did? Why or why not and what do you think this means?

9–61. Using the *SEC's EDGAR* system, obtain a copy of the *OfficeMax, Inc.,* income statement and balance sheet from the company's Form 10-K from 2001.

Required:

a. Calculate the following ratios for the company for 2001:

1. The asset turnover ratio
2. The receivables turnover ratio
3. The average accounts receivable collection period in days
4. The current ratio
5. The quick ratio
6. The times interest earned ratio

b. What is the impression you get about the company from these ratios?
c. Look at the ratios calculated for *OfficeMax, Inc.,* in problem 4–74. Did these ratios give you the same impression as those did? Why or why not and what do you think this means?
d. Compare your impression of *OfficeMax, Inc.,* to that of *Office Depot, Inc.* Now that you have more information, which company would you be more likely to invest in and why? Is this the same as the company you chose in Chapter 4 and why or why not?

9–62. Using the *SEC's EDGAR* system, obtain a copy of the *Staples, Inc.,* income statement and balance sheet from the company's Form 10-K from 2001.

Required:

a. Calculate the following ratios for the company for 2001:

1. The asset turnover ratio
2. The receivables turnover ratio
3. The average accounts receivable collection period in days
4. The current ratio
5. The quick ratio
6. The times interest earned ratio using interest and other expense net for interest expense

  b. What is the impression you get about the company from these ratios?
  c. Look at the ratios calculated for *Staples, Inc.*, in problem 4–75. Did these ratios give you the same impression as those did? Why or why not and what do you think this means?
  d. Compare the impressions of the *Office Depot, Inc., OfficeMax, Inc.,* and *Staples, Inc.* For each of the six ratios, choose which company you believe is most favorable and explain your answer. Now that you have more information, which company would you be most likely to invest in and why? Is this the same as the company you chose in Chapter 4 and why or why not? What does this tell you about using the ratios presented together?

ANNUAL REPORT PROJECT

9–63. Section 9—Financial Statements—A Closer Look

In this assignment, you will prepare a report that further explores information contained in your company's balance sheet and income statement.

Required: Prepare a report that includes the following information:

  a. List your company's major asset classifications.
  b. Describe how your company's asset classifications compare to those of its peer.
  c. Discuss which of your company's assets is most significant? Discuss which is least significant? Does your company's asset holding seem excessive to you? Discuss why it would be risky for your company to hold more assets than it really needs.
  d. List your company's major liability classifications.
  e. Describe how your company's liabilities compare to those of its peer.
  f. Discuss which of your company's liabilities is most significant? Discuss which is least significant? Does your company's liabilities seem excessive to you?
  g. Does your company or the peer company you are using include any nonrecurring items on its income statements? In other words, do the income statements include any discontinued operations, extraordinary items, or cumulative effect of accounting changes? If so, provide information about each of them. Are there items or events mentioned by either your company or its peer's financial reports or that you happen to know about that you feel should give rise to a nonrecurring item, but did not? An example of such a situation would be when a company's annual report mentions major losses due to the massive freight delays in connection with the Longshoreman labor strike that occurred in 2002, and yet does not list the loss as extraordinary.
  h. A schedule that includes the following ratios for your company with those of the peer company you selected:

  • Basic earnings per share for three years (use the amounts from the income statements)
  • Diluted earnings per share for three years (use the amounts from the income statements)
  • Asset turnover ratio for the current year
  • Receivables turnover ratio for the current year
  • Current ratio for two years
  • Quick ratio for two years
  • Times interest earned for three years

  i. Comment in your report on the information that each one of the ratios provides. How does your company compare to its peer? And where applicable, comment on how your company has performed over time relative to the peer company you selected.
  j. Your report should conclude with comments regarding what you think of your company and how you think your company compares to its peer in light of the work you did in connection with this assignment.

CHAPTER 10

The Statement of Cash Flows— A Closer Look

Net income is an opinion; cash is a fact.

—ANONYMOUS

Your best friend Sally recently told about what she says is a "can't miss" investment opportunity. The company she described to you manufactures digital cameras and is extremely successful. It has had compounded sales growth of 25 percent per year since it began five years ago. More importantly, Sally says, profits have increased by 15 percent per year over that same period. "Buy some stock!" she urges. "The future prospects for the company are virtually unlimited. The cameras the company produces sell themselves!"

Even after poring over the income statements and balance sheets your friend provided, you are still not sure what to do. Everything *seems* to make sense. The sales and profits are certainly there, and you know Sally is really smart (she was, after all, an accounting major). Then it hits you—you can ask your Aunt Matilda's advice. She's a bit of a crotchety old goat, and she still pinches your cheek when she sees you, but you know she has made a lot of money in the stock market.

When you arrive at your auntie's mansion, the butler leads you to the den, where you find Aunt Matilda sitting in her easy chair watching a soap opera. Before you can even speak, she pinches your cheek. "What can I do for you, my darling niece?" Aunt Matilda asks. You explain the investment opportunity Sally has recommended. Throughout your lengthy discourse, your aunt sits quietly, her chin in her hand. You tell her all you know about the company—about the sales growth and the profits. "Should I buy some stock, Aunt Matilda?" you ask. With a wry smile on her face, your aunt leans forward, looks you straight in the eye, and says, "Profit schmofit, show me the cash." When you ask what she means by that, she laughs and says, "That you must figure out for yourself, my dear." Then she pinches your cheek and says she must get back to her soap opera.

In the first nine chapters of this text, we focused primarily on three major financial statements: the income statement, the statement of owners' equity, and the balance sheet. Each of these three financial statements developed over time in response to the needs of economic decision makers. Generally, the financial information presented in the financial statements we explored is produced using accrual accounting to measure results of business activity. Recall that we discussed a number of items that affect financial statements that are prepared using accrual accounting, including:

- The difficulties in determining when revenue should be recognized
- The difficulties in matching expenses to the same income statement period as the revenues they helped generate
- The estimates of useful life and residual value required for depreciation of property, plant, and equipment
- Choices of inventory cost flow method (e.g., first-in, first-out [FIFO], last-in, first-out [LIFO]) and depreciation method (e.g., straight-line, double-declining-balance).

These are just a few of the items that make periodic financial measurement under accrual accounting challenging. Although accrual accounting has advantages and it is the acceptable measurement basis under generally accepted accounting principles (GAAP), it is not perfect. Perhaps accrual accounting's most serious weakness is that it takes the financial statement user's eye off cash. To address this problem and bring the user's focus back to cash, a fourth financial statement was developed: the statement of cash flows. When information from the statement of cash flows is combined with the information contained in the other three financial statements, decision makers have a more complete picture of a company's financial health.

You should already be somewhat familiar with the statement of cash flows because we discussed parts of it as appropriate in earlier chapters. In this chapter, we will review some of the concepts introduced previously, introduce new topics relating to the statement of cash flows, and demonstrate how to prepare and use the statement.

Learning Objectives

After completing your work on this chapter, you should be able to do the following:

1. Explain the purpose of the statement of cash flows.
2. Describe the three types of activities that can either generate or use cash in any business.
3. Prepare a statement of cash flows using the indirect method for the operating activities section.
4. Evaluate and use the information the statement of cash flows provides.
5. Prepare a statement of cash flows using the direct method for the operating activities section. (Appendix)

◆ INTRODUCTION TO THE STATEMENT OF CASH FLOWS

In its present format, the statement of cash flows has existed since 1988. However, it existed in other forms for decades before that. These earlier forms were known by such names as the *Where-Got and Where-Gone Statement*, the *Funds Statement*, the *Statement of Sources and Application of Funds*, and the *Statement of Changes in Financial Position*.

All of these earlier versions had the same objectives as today's statement of cash flows. That is, their main purpose was to provide information about a company's cash receipts and cash payments during a specific period, because the balance sheet, income statement, and statement of owners' equity prepared using accrual accounting were not giving economic decision makers all the information they needed.

Discussion Question •

10–1. How do revenue recognition and expense recognition criteria under accrual accounting take the focus off cash?

Unlike the current statement of cash flows, which focuses exclusively on changes in cash, most of the earlier versions of this financial statement included other items as well. A good example of this is the Statement of Changes in Financial Position, which is the form of the statement that immediately preceded the currently used statement of cash flows. When the *Statement of Changes in Financial Position* was adopted as GAAP in 1971, companies had the choice of using either the cash format or the working capital format. The vast majority of companies chose to prepare the statement using the working capital format. This format was based on the assumption that **working capital,** which is defined as current assets less current liabilities, is a good predictor of future cash flows. Some argued that by examining items other than cash, the working capital format presented a broader picture of the changes a company experienced.

working capital The difference between current assets and current liabilities.

By the early 1980s, however, many financial analysts became increasingly concerned about cash flows because some companies with strong working capital positions had weak cash flow. The financial markets, too, became more concerned about companies' cash flows and, therefore, grew steadily more dissatisfied with the working capital format of the *Statement of Changes in Financial Position.* After years of mounting pressure on companies to provide more detailed information about the sources and uses of their cash, the new statement of cash flows was introduced in 1988.

In addition to providing information about a company's cash receipts and cash payments during a specific period, the statement of cash flows helps investors, creditors, and other external parties to:

1. Assess a company's ability to generate positive future net cash flows.
2. Assess a company's need for external financing and its ability to pay its debts and pay dividends.
3. Reconcile the differences between net income and the change in cash.

◆ BASIC ORGANIZATION OF THE STATEMENT OF CASH FLOWS

How does the statement go about fulfilling its purpose? The statement of cash flows begins by disclosing what caused changes in the balance of cash from the beginning of the period to the end. Then the statement reflects the cash balance at the beginning of the period and incorporates the change in cash to arrive at the cash balance at the end of the period. As an example of the statement, Exhibit 10–1 on page F–406 shows the statement of cash flows for *The Rowe Companies,* a major furniture and home furnishings company.

As you recall from our discussions in prior chapters and as you can see in Exhibit 10–1, the statement of cash flows is grouping cash flows by three major business activities: operating activities, investing activities, and financing activities. Therefore, one of the most important tasks when preparing a statement of cash flows is to identify the cash flows associated with each of these activities. We have done a significant amount of work on this process in earlier chapters and we will now review each of the activities in turn.

Discussion Question   •

10–2. Imagine that you are the owner of a bookstore. What would constitute your bookstore's:

   a. operating activities?
   b. investing activities?
   c. financing activities?

Explain your reasons for the classifications you made.

OPERATING ACTIVITIES

operating activities
Activities centered on the day-to-day business transactions of the company.

Operating activities are those centered on the actual day-to-day business transactions of the company. A variety of transactions either generates or uses cash. Cash is received (inflows) from the sale of goods or services. For example, *McDonald's* receives cash when its customers buy hamburgers. *Bank of America* receives cash for interest it earns on loans it has made to individuals and companies, or when it receives dividends on investments it owns. Cash is paid by *Boeing* (outflows) to *Honeywell* and other suppliers for inventory, to employees for wages, to the government for taxes, to lenders for interest on loans, and to other parties for the expenses of running the company. For example, cash flow from operating activities for *The Rowe Companies* includes cash received from customers, cash paid to suppliers and employees, income taxes paid, interest paid, interest received, and other receipts.

When you think about it, all of the items listed in the previous paragraph appear on their company's income statements. Remember that the actual name of the income statement is the *Statement of Results of Operations.* So the operating activities section of the statement of cash flows is related to items presented on the income statement.

The Rowe Companies
Statement of Cash Flows
Year Ended December 31, 2000
(in thousands)
Increase (Decrease) in Cash

Cash flows from operating activities:

Cash received from customers	$379,400
Cash paid to suppliers and employees	(354,570)
Income taxes paid, net of refunds	(6,183)
Interest paid	(5,693)
Interest received	288
Other receipts—net	1,156
Net cash and cash equivalents provided by (used in) operating activities	14,398

Cash flows from investing activities:

Proceeds from sale of property and equipment	21
Capital expenditures	(9,155)
Payments to acquire businesses (Note 2)	(5,160)
Net cash used in investing activities	(14,294)

Cash flows from financing activities:

Net borrowings (payments) under line of credit	(164)
Proceeds from issuance of long-term debt	13,020
Payments to reduce long-term debt	(11,922)
Proceeds from issuance of common stock	51
Dividends paid	(1,849)
Purchase of treasury stock	(951)
Net cash provided by (used in) financing activities	(1,815)
Net increase (decrease) in cash and cash equivalents	(1,711)
Cash at beginning of year	5,104
Cash at end of year	$ 3,393

EXHIBIT 10–1 Statement of Cash Flows for *The Rowe Companies*

Discussion Questions

10–3. Imagine once again that you own a bookstore. If you sold one of your customers several books on account and she had 30 days after she received the books to pay for them, how would this credit sale be reported by your company under the cash basis of accounting? How about under the accrual basis?

10–4. For your bookstore's statement of cash flows, how would you determine the net cash flow from operations on an accrual basis?

Under GAAP, there are two acceptable methods of preparing the operating activities section of the statement of cash flows: the direct method and the indirect method. Both arrive at exactly the same amount of cash flow from operations. The difference lies in how the information is presented.

DIRECT METHOD VERSUS INDIRECT METHOD

direct method The format of a statement of cash flows that provides detail about the individual sources and uses of cash associated with operating activities.

The **direct method** involves a series of calculations to determine the amount of cash inflow and cash outflow from each individual facet of operating activities. For example, under the direct method, accountants determine the cash collections from customers, cash received for interest earned on bank accounts or from making loans, cash received for rents, and so forth. Accountants also determine the cash paid for inventory, for wages, for electricity, for taxes, for interest, and for other expense items. The operating activities section of the statement of cash flows under the direct method consists of a summarized list of these individual cash inflows and outflows. The examples we presented in earlier chapters of this book and the statement of cash flows for **The Rowe Companies** in Exhibit 10–1 use the direct method of presenting cash flows from operating activities.

indirect method The more widely used format of the statement of cash flows. This approach reconciles accrual net income to the cash provided by or used by operating activities.

The **indirect method** is more closely tied to accrual accounting than is the direct method. Unlike the direct method, it does not attempt to provide any detail about the individual inflows and outflows of cash associated with the company's operating activities. When a company uses the indirect method, the statement of cash flows begins with the accrual net income for the period. Remember, though, that if the company uses the accrual basis of accounting, the net income figure must be adjusted for any revenues that did not provide cash during the income statement period. Similarly, net income must be adjusted for any expenses that did not use cash during the period. Therefore, if you are attempting to determine *Microsoft*'s cash flows from operating activities using the indirect method, for example, the place to start is the company's net income as shown on the income statement. Then a series of adjustments are made to convert the accrual net income amount to cash flow from operating activities. In other words, adjustments are made for all items included in the calculation of net income that did not either generate or use cash. If this concept is not totally clear to you at this point, don't fret; we will show you how it works a little later in the chapter.

Now that you have an idea of the difference between the direct method and the indirect method, we should tell you that if a company uses the direct method, it must also include a reconciliation of net income to operating cash flows as a supplementary schedule to the statement of cash flows. Think about it. This reconciliation is the same thing as the indirect method. The Financial Accounting Standards Board (FASB) required this supplementary information because the reconciliation links (articulates) the statement of cash flows to the income statement. However, if a company uses the indirect method (which is the same as the reconciliation), it does not have to include the direct method, *but* it does have to include a supplementary schedule indicating the amount of cash paid for interest and taxes.

The direct method presents an easy-to-understand list of each cash inflow and outflow from operating activities. Many users (including students) find the direct method more logical and intuitive and therefore easier to read and understand than the indirect method. This is why all of our presentations of the operating activities section of the statement of cash flows in previous chapters used the direct method. In actual practice, however, very few companies use the direct method. *Accounting Trends and Techniques* reports that of the 600 companies it surveyed in 2001, only seven (slightly more than 1 percent of companies) used the direct method in preparing the statement of cash flows for 2000 (Exhibit 10–2 on page F–408).

As you have seen in prior chapters, the operating activities section of a statement of cash flows using the direct method is not overly challenging to prepare as long as you have a detailed list containing each of the operating cash flows. Since the vast majority of firms use the indirect method, however, this is the method we will concentrate on in this chapter. We have included an appendix to the chapter presenting calculation specifics for preparing the operating activities section of the statement using the direct method.

INVESTING ACTIVITIES

investing activities Activities associated with buying and selling the investments used to support the operation of the business.

Investing activities are those associated with buying and selling the investments used to support the operation of the business. For many companies, the vast majority of this investment is in the assets required to operate the company. As with operating activities, investing activities include both outflows and inflows of cash. As examples of cash outflow, **Campbell Soup Company** uses cash to invest in the machinery it needs to can its soup, and **American Express** uses cash when it builds a transactions processing center. As we have discussed in previous chapters, the long-lived assets used in a company's operations are usually reported on the balance sheet in a category called *property, plant, and equipment* and include the buildings, vehicles, furniture, machinery, and other items a business uses to run its operations. The cash paid when a company buys this type of asset is an outflow from investing activities.

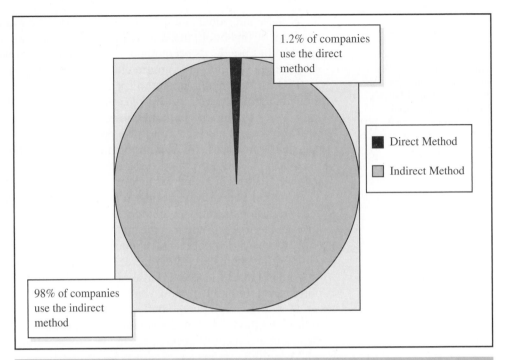

1.2% of companies use the direct method

■ Direct Method
□ Indirect Method

98% of companies use the indirect method

EXHIBIT 10–2 Direct Method versus Indirect Method of Preparing the Statement of Cash Flows

As we discussed in Chapter 7, companies sell long-lived assets from time to time when they are no longer needed. For example, *Campbell Soup* might sell a soup canning machine that it is no longer using, and *American Express* might sell one of its processing centers because it needs a bigger facility. The cash received when a company sells this type of asset is an inflow from investing activities.

While the cash received from selling property, plant, and equipment is a legitimate source of cash, a company cannot sell off assets it needs to run its operations because before long the cash generated through operating activities would be adversely affected. *American Airlines,* for example, could generate cash by selling all its airplanes, but if it did so, it would no longer be able to transport passengers and would go out of business. Instead of selling its property, plant, and equipment to generate cash, a growing and healthy company will likely use cash to acquire additional assets it can use in its operations. Therefore, the net cash flow from investing activities may very well be negative (net outflow) for companies that are experiencing healthy growth. For example, the statement of cash flows in Exhibit 10–1 for *The Rowe Companies* shows that the company received $21,000 from selling property and equipment while it spent $9,155,000 for capital expenditures (property and equipment) and $5,160,000 to acquire a business during the same year. Other companies, such as *Boeing, Procter & Gamble,* and *Target,* all very different kinds of companies, show significant investing activities related to their acquisition and disposal of property, plant, and equipment.

Besides investing in property, plant, and equipment, investments in stocks, bonds, and other financial investments are included as part of investing activities. For example, *Navistar International*'s cash flow associated with the purchase and sale of marketable securities would be included in the investing activities section of its statement of cash flows. A company receives cash (inflow) from investing activities when it sells equity or debt investments (stocks or bonds of other companies) it owns.

Logically, companies might classify the interest they earn on loans to others and the dividends they receive from investments in the stock of other companies as inflows in the investing activities section. However, because interest earned and dividends received are reported on the income statement of the period, *the cash a company receives from interest and dividends is almost always reported in the operating activities section.*

Think about the examples of investing activities we just mentioned. Notice that they involve items that are reported in the long-term asset section of the balance sheet. Therefore, if you are attempting to determine the cash flows from investing activities, you should analyze the long-term section of the company's balance sheets, paying particular attention to the changes in account balances from the beginning of the period to the end. Once again, do not be concerned if this is not totally clear to you at this point. We will demonstrate the process a little later in the chapter.

FINANCING ACTIVITIES

financing activities
Business activities, such as the issuance of debt or equity and the payment of dividends, that focus on the external financing of the company.

Recall from our discussion in Chapter 3 that the financing options available to any business are broadly classified as either internal or external. *Internal financing* comes from a company's profitable operation, that is, from income. The statement of cash flows reports the cash flows from internal financing in the operating activities section discussed earlier. Therefore, the **financing activities** section of the statement deals only with external financing. A company's *external financing* comes from either selling shares of the company's stock (common or preferred) or borrowing (from banks or by selling corporate bonds). ***Verizon Communications*** or ***International Paper,*** for example, can obtain cash (inflow) from selling shares of their stock or from borrowing.

Companies also report the cash outflows to repay loans and retire bonds, to pay dividends to shareholders, and to reacquire shares of common or preferred stock from their stockholders in the financing activities section of the statement of cash flows. Logically, you might think that companies classify the interest they pay as outflows in the financing activities section. However, because interest expense is reported on the income statement, the *cash payments (outflows) for interest are almost always reported in the operating activities section of the statement of cash flows*. Unlike interest expense, dividends paid to shareholders are not reported on the income statement. So dividends paid *are* included in financing activities.

Think about the examples of financing activities mentioned in the previous two paragraphs. Notice that they involve items that are reported in the long-term liabilities and owners' equity sections of the balance sheet. Therefore, when you are attempting to determine the cash flow from financing activities, analyze the long-term liabilities and equity sections of the balance sheets and pay particular attention to the changes in the accounts' balances that took place during the year. Once again, do not be concerned if this is not totally clear to you at this point. We will demonstrate the process a little later in the chapter.

Exhibit 10–3 on page F–410 lists examples of the cash flows associated with the three types of business activities reported in the statement of cash flows. Refer to this exhibit often as we discuss how to prepare and use the statement.

In practice, the inflows and outflows a particular company shows on its statement of cash flows may be more or less extensive than the list we have included in Exhibit 10–3. However, regardless of a company's complexity, we can classify every cash inflow and outflow as an operating activity, an investing activity, or a financing activity in the statement of cash flows.

◆ GATHERING INFORMATION TO PREPARE THE STATEMENT OF CASH FLOWS

In order to prepare a company's statement of cash flows for a particular income statement period, we need information from three important sources:

1. That period's income statement.
2. A set of comparative balance sheets (a balance from the current period and one from the previous period).
3. Additional information about transactions that is not explained by the income statement or comparative balance sheets mentioned above. For example, we would need information about the purchase and sale of investments and property, plant, and equipment that is too detailed to find on financial statements.

Operating Activities

Cash Inflows
From customers as a result of the sale of goods or services or rent received
From interest earned on loans to others
From dividends received from investment in the stock of other companies

Cash Outflows
To suppliers for the purchase of inventory
To employees for salaries and wages
To governments for taxes
To creditors for interest on loans
To others for operating expenses

Investing Activities

Cash Inflows
From the sale of property, plant, and equipment
From the sale of investments in debt or equity securities of other companies
From collecting on loans made to other companies

Cash Outflows
To purchase property, plant, and equipment
To purchase debt and equity investments in other companies
Making loans to other companies

Financing Activities

Cash Inflows
From selling shares of the company's own common or preferred stock
From bank loans or the sale of corporate bonds

Cash Outflows
To pay dividends to stockholders
To reacquire shares of the company's own stock from stockholders
To repay loans or redeem corporate bonds

EXHIBIT 10–3 Summary of the Three Business Activities Reported on the Statement of Cash Flows

For our example, we will gather information for Tsujimoto's Oriental Rug Factory, a rug manufacturer. We begin with Tsujimoto's income statement. Remember, in our discussion in this chapter, we will use the indirect method of preparing the operating activities section, which uses net income as its starting point. Exhibit 10–4 shows Tsujimoto's income statement for the year ended December 31, 2004.

EXHIBIT 10–4 Tsujimoto's Oriental Rug Factory's Income Statement for 2004

Tsujimoto's Oriental Rug Factory
Income Statement
For the Year Ended December 31, 2004
(in thousands)

Sales		$15,158
Cost of goods sold		11,151
Gross margin		4,007
Operating expenses:		
Depreciation expense	$ 231	
Selling and administration	3,047	
Total operating expenses		(3,278)
Operating income		729
Gain on sale of long-term investments		31
Less: Interest expense		(160)
Income before income taxes		600
Income tax expense		(180)
Net income		$ 420

In addition to the income statement, we also need information from the balance sheet. Exhibit 10–5 shows Tsujimoto's comparative balance sheets for 2004 and 2003. Keep in mind that the asset, liability, and stockholders' equity balances at the end of one period become the beginning balances in the next period. Thus, Exhibit 10–5 provides beginning and ending balances for Tsujimoto's balance sheet amounts for 2004—necessary information for preparing the company's statement of cash flows for that year.

EXHIBIT 10–5 Tsujimoto's Oriental Rug Factory's Comparative Balance Sheets for 2004 and 2003

Tsujimoto's Oriental Rug Factory
Balance Sheet
December 31, 2004, and December 31, 2003
(in thousands)

ASSETS:	2004	2003
Current assets:		
Cash	$ 981	$ 419
Accounts receivable	1,925	2,112
Merchandise inventory	1,022	858
Prepaid expenses	192	132
Total current assets	4,120	3,521
Long-term investments	21	73
Plant and equipment:		
Equipment	1,155	1,045
LESS: Accumulated depreciation	(851)	(620)
Equipment, net	304	425
Total assets	$4,445	$4,019
LIABILITIES:		
Current liabilities:		
Accounts payable	$ 820	$ 710
Accrued expenses	17	28
Income tax payable	25	10
Total current liabilities	862	748
Long-term liabilities:		
Notes payable	425	700
Bonds payable	1,100	900
Total long-term liabilities	1,525	1,600
Total liabilities	2,387	2,348
STOCKHOLDERS' EQUITY:		
Common stock, no-par value	1,332	1,228
Retained earnings	726	443
Total stockholders' equity	2,058	1,671
Total liabilities and stockholders' equity	$4,445	$4,019

Discussion Questions

Refer to Exhibit 10–5 to answer the following questions:

10–5. What was Tsujimoto's Oriental Rug Factory's balance in accounts receivable on January 1, 2004? Did accounts receivable increase or decrease during 2004?

10–6. What was Tsujimoto's balance in retained earnings on January 1, 2004?

10–7. What do you think caused retained earnings to increase during 2004?

Before we tackle the preparation of the statement of cash flows, there are a couple of things you should understand about Tsujimoto's income statement and balance sheet. First, look at the cash balances on the two balance sheets in Exhibit 10–5, and you will see that cash increased from the start of 2004 to the end of 2004 by $562 ($981 − $419). Note that Tsujimoto's Oriental Rug Factory's financial statements are presented "in thousands." This means that the $562 increase in cash is really $562,000. But what caused the increase? It was not the company's net income, because if you look at Tsujimoto's income statement in Exhibit 10–4, you will see that net income for the year ended December 31, 2004, was $420,000. Tsujimoto's Oriental Rug Factory uses accrual accounting, so it is no surprise that the company's net income for the year does not equal the change in cash. So, we ask again: What caused the $562,000 increase in cash in 2004? Well, the statement of cash flows we are about to prepare will answer this question. If properly prepared and analyzed, the statement of cash flows will tell us the amount by which cash changed, and what caused the change. Plus, it will reconcile the company's net income figure to the change in cash.

In addition to Tsujimoto's income statement and its balance sheet, we need some information that cannot be found on financial statements. For Tsujimoto's, three bits of additional information will be helpful as we create the company's statement of cash flows:

- During 2004, Tsujimoto's sold some of its long-term investments for $83,000 but did not purchase any.
- During 2004, Tsujimoto's purchased equipment for cash of $110,000.
- During 2004, Tsujimoto's paid $137,000 cash dividends to its stockholders.

We now have all the information necessary to prepare Tsujimoto's Oriental Rug Factory's statement of cash flows for 2004. The detailed presentation that follows is not intended to make you an expert preparer, but rather to help you become a wiser user of this financial tool. Knowing how the amounts on a statement of cash flows were determined will help you to assess their usefulness and impact on your decision making process.

◆ PREPARING THE STATEMENT OF CASH FLOWS

To give you an idea of what we will be doing as we prepare the statement of cash flows, we will begin by showing you the basic format of Tsujimoto's statement of cash flows (Exhibit 10–6).

EXHIBIT 10–6   Basic Format of the Statement of Cash Flows for Tsujimoto's Oriental Rug Factory

Tsujimoto's Oriental Rug Factory
Statement of Cash Flows
For the Year Ended December 31, 2004
(in thousands)

Cash Flows from Operating Activities:	
Net income	$420
Adjustments to reconcile net income to net cash provided by operating activities	
Net cash provided (used) by operating activities	?
Cash Flows from Investing Activities:	___
Net cash provided (used) by investing activities	?
Cash Flows from Financing Activities:	___
Net cash provided (used) by financing activities	?
Net increase (decrease) in cash during 2004	**$562**
Beginning cash balance, January 1, 2004	419
Ending cash balance, December 31, 2004	$981

There are two things to note about the statement's format. First, it is divided into the three broad types of activities that generate or use cash (operating, investing, and financing). Second, we have already put four amounts into the statement. Net income came directly from Tsujimoto's income statement in Exhibit 10–4. The beginning and ending cash balances came directly from Tsujimoto's balance sheets in Exhibit 10–5. We determined the change in cash by subtracting the beginning cash balance from the ending cash balance. Remember, the purpose of the statement of cash flows is not to disclose what the change in cash was, but to show what caused the change and also to reconcile the change in cash to the net income.

DETERMINING CASH FLOW FROM OPERATING ACTIVITIES

As we said earlier, we are going to use the indirect method of determining cash flow from operations because the vast majority of the statements of cash flows you will see are prepared using this method. The direct method is presented in an appendix to this chapter using the same Tsujimoto's Oriental Rug Factory example. Remember, the net cash flow from operating activities is the same using either the indirect method or the direct method. It's only the approach that is different.

When we determine cash flows from operating activities using the indirect method, we begin with net income because most items involved in net income either already affected cash (inflow or outflow) or will eventually affect cash (inflow or outflow). Because of the way accrual accounting recognizes revenues and expenses, however, net income for a particular income statement period does not equate to the change in cash for that same period. Remember from our discussion of revenue recognition in Chapter 5 that a company using accrual accounting may receive the cash associated with revenue before the revenue is recognized, at the time the revenue is recognized, or after the revenue is recognized. The same is true for expenses. A company using accrual accounting may pay the cash associated with expense before the expense is recognized, at the time the expense is recognized, or after the expense is recognized. For this reason, in determining net cash flow from operating activities for this period, we must adjust the net income figure for any revenues that did not generate cash during this period and any expenses that did not use cash during this period. This is a crucial concept, so before you proceed, read it again if you don't fully understand it.

Discussion Question ●

10–8. Why are retained earnings not equal to cash?

To determine cash flow from operating activities using the indirect method, we make three basic adjustments to net income:

1. Add back depreciation expense and amortization expense if any exist.
2. Add back losses and subtract gains associated with the sale of investments or property, plant, and equipment.
3. Adjust for the changes in current assets and current liabilities that are associated with operating activities.

The information we need to make these adjustments is found in the income statement and the current assets and current liabilities sections of the balance sheet.

1. *Depreciation.* The first adjustment we will make to Tsujimoto's net income is for depreciation expense, because as we mentioned in Chapter 7, depreciation is a noncash expense. When we say *noncash*, we don't mean to imply that there never is cash paid for this expense, because there was (or will be); it just wasn't paid during this income statement period. To fully grasp this concept, you must remember just what depreciation is. It is an accrual accounting process of converting the cost of long-lived items (buildings and equipment in Tsujimoto's case) from asset to expense. It is completely unrelated to when the buildings and equipment were paid for (cash outflow). Therefore, to determine the cash flow

from Tsujimoto's operating activities, one of the things we must do is add the depreciation expense for the period to net income. We do this because depreciation is an expense that did not use cash in 2004, but which was included in the expenses subtracted from revenue to arrive at net income for 2004. If you look at Tsujimoto's income statement in Exhibit 10–4, you will see that the company had depreciation expense for 2004 of $231,000. The adjustment for depreciation expense for Tsujimoto's statement of cash flows is shown in Exhibit 10–7.

EXHIBIT 10–7	Statement of Cash Flows Adjustment for Depreciation Expense

Tsujimoto's Oriental Rug Factory
Partial Statement of Cash Flows
For the Year Ended December 31, 2004
(in thousands)

Cash Flows from Operating Activities:

Net income		$449
Adjustments to reconcile net income to net cash provided by operating activities:		
Depreciation expense	$231	
Net cash provided (used) by operating activities		?

2. *Gains and losses from disposal of long-lived assets.* Companies normally have a gain or a loss when they sell investments or property, plant, and equipment. This is because companies almost never sell an asset for an amount that exactly equals the asset's book value. Recall from Chapter 7 that if a company sells an asset for more than its book value, there is a gain. If the company sells the asset for less than its book value, there is a loss. The amount of the gain or loss is the *difference* between the amount of cash received for the sale and the book value of the asset sold. It is *not* the amount of cash received. For example, if a company were to sell an asset that had a book value of $1 million for cash of $990,000, the company would have a whopping $990,000 cash inflow, but its income statement would actually reflect a $10,000 loss. This example makes it easy to see that the gain or loss on the sale of assets does not equal cash flow from the sale. These gains and losses are included in the calculation of net income because gains are treated similarly to revenues, and losses are treated similarly to expenses. Because the gains and losses are not equal to cash flow and because the cash flow for such transactions should be in investing activities anyway, we adjust net income to remove the effect of gains and losses associated with the sale of investments and property, plant, and equipment. Since a gain shown on the accrual income statement served to increase net income, we must subtract the gain from net income. Since a loss shown on the accrual income statement served to decrease net income, we must add the loss to net income. The cash a company receives from selling a long-lived asset is reported in the investing activities section of the statement of cash flows, so if we don't adjust for the gain or loss in the operating activities section, we will effectively show the amount twice on the statement of cash flows. Tsujimoto had a gain of $31,000 for the sale of long-term investments. The adjustment for the gain for Tsujimoto's statement of cash flows is as shown in Exhibit 10–8.

3. *Changes in current assets and current liabilities.* Since most current assets and current liabilities are associated with the day-to-day operation of the company, they are related to the revenues and expenses that make up the income statement. The current asset and current liability sections from Tsujimoto's comparative balance sheets are shown in Exhibit 10–9. We have added a column that calculates the change in the balance of each item.

We will not consider the change in cash as an adjustment to net income because cash is the object of the entire statement of cash flows. In addition, if current liabilities included general borrowing such as notes payable or bonds payable, changes in such

Tsujimoto's Oriental Rug Factory
Partial Statement of Cash Flows
For the Year Ended December 31, 2004
(in thousands)

Cash Flows from Operating Activities:		
Net income		$449
Adjustments to reconcile net income to net cash provided by operating activities:		
Depreciation expense	$231	
Gain on sale of long-term investments	(31)	
Net cash provided (used) by operating activities		?

EXHIBIT 10–8   Adjustment for Gain on Sale of Investments for Tsujimoto's Oriental Rug Factory's Statement of Cash Flows

items would be treated as financing activities and not as adjustments to net income to calculate cash flows from operating activities. In our example, Tsujimoto's does not include any general borrowing in current liabilities.

A change in any of the other items listed in Exhibit 10–9 will require an adjustment to net income in determining the net cash provided by operating activities. The adjustments, however, will be exactly opposite of what you probably think they should be.

- Adjustments for current assets—An increase in a current asset item (except cash) is considered a use of cash, and a decrease in a current asset item (except cash) is considered a source of cash.
- Adjustments for current liabilities—An increase in a current liability item is considered a source of cash, and a decrease in a current liability item is considered a use of cash.

This adjustment process makes sense if you really ponder it. Consider accounts receivable, for example. Where do they come from? They come from selling to customers on a credit basis (i.e., customers pay some time after they purchase whatever they purchase). Now answer this question: What does a company *not have* when it sells on credit that it *would have had* if it had sold for cash instead? The answer, of course, is cash! We consider credit sales as revenue under accrual accounting and, therefore, use them in the calculation of net income. But remember, we are trying to determine the amount of cash

EXHIBIT 10–9   Current Assets and Current Liabilities Sections of Balance Sheets for Tsujimoto's Oriental Rug Factory for 2004 and 2003

Tsujimoto's Oriental Rug Factory
Partial Balance Sheets
December 31, 2004, and December 31, 2003
(in thousands)

ASSETS:	2004	2003	Increase/Decrease
Current assets:			
Cash	$ 981	$ 419	$562
Accounts receivable	1,925	2,112	(187)
Merchandise inventory	1,022	858	164
Prepaid expenses	192	132	60
Total current assets	$4,120	$3,521	
LIABILITIES:			
Current liabilities:			
Accounts payable	$ 820	$ 710	$110
Accrued expenses	17	28	(11)
Income tax payable	25	10	15
Total current liabilities	$ 862	$ 748	

generated by operating activities. Any increase in accounts receivable must be deducted from net income because such an increase represents the credit sales that have not been collected as of the end of the year. Accounts receivable decrease when customers pay the cash they owe, so a decrease in accounts receivable is a source of cash.

Now think about accounts payable. Where do they come from? They are created when a company buys merchandise inventory on a credit basis (it pays some time after the purchase). Now answer this question: What does a company *have* when it buys on credit that it *would not have* if it paid cash? The answer, again, is cash! Therefore, we consider an increase in accounts payable a source of cash. Accounts payable decrease as the company pays the cash it owes, so a decrease in accounts payable is a use of cash.

Now let's go through the specifics of the adjustments to net income caused by the changes in Tsujimoto's current assets and current liabilities:

a. *Accounts receivable*—According to Exhibit 10–9, accounts receivable decreased by $187,000 during 2004. Accounts receivable decrease when customers' payments during the income statement period are greater than the sales during that period. This means that the cash Tsujimoto's collected from its customers during 2004 was $187,000 *more* than the $15,158,000 revenue the accrual income statement used to calculate net income. Therefore, we must add $187,000 to net income.

b. *Merchandise inventory*—According to Exhibit 10–9, merchandise inventory increased by $164,000 during 2004. Inventory increases when a company buys more inventory than it sells. This means that during 2004, Tsujimoto's purchased $164,000 *more* inventory than the $11,151,000 cost of goods the accrual income statement used to calculate net income. It is possible, of course, that at least part of this $164,000 increase has not yet been paid for. If so, it will be reflected in accounts payable, which we will analyze a little later. For now, we will consider the increase in inventory as a use of cash. Therefore, we must deduct $164,000 from net income.

c. *Prepaid expenses*—According to Exhibit 10–9, prepaid expenses increased by $60,000 during 2004. Prepaid expenses, as you recall, are items that are not recognized as expense until some time after they are paid for. They are classified as assets at the time of purchase and then recognized as expense in a later income statement period as they are used up. Tsujimoto's classifies this expense as *selling and administration*. Undoubtedly, some of the prepaid expenses shown on Tsujimoto's 2003 balance sheet were recognized as selling and administration expense in 2004, which would cause the balance in prepaid expenses to decrease. The balance in prepaid expenses, however, increased by $60,000 from the end of 2003 to the end of 2004. Prepaid expenses increase during an income statement period when a company purchases more of them during that period than it recognizes as expense. This means that during 2004, Tsujimoto's purchased and paid cash for $60,000 *more* prepaid expense than it recognized as expense, so we must deduct $60,000 from net income.

d. *Accounts payable*—According to Exhibit 10–9, accounts payable increased by $110,000 during 2004. Accounts payable increase when a company's payments to suppliers during the income statement period are less than the purchases during that period. This means that the cash Tsujimoto's paid to its suppliers during 2004 was $110,000 *less* than the amount of its purchases. Therefore, we must add $110,000 to net income. This adjustment, coupled with the one we made for merchandise inventory, adjusts cost of goods sold on the income statement to the amount of cash Tsujimoto's actually paid to suppliers during 2004.

e. *Accrued expenses*—According to Exhibit 10–9, accrued expenses decreased by $11,000 during 2004. Accrued expenses is a liability amount that accountants use to reflect liabilities for expenses that they record at the last minute as they prepare company financial statements. For practical purposes, accrued expenses are the same as accounts payable. (Please refer to Chapter 6 to see a more detailed discussion of accrued expenses.) When accrued expenses increase, it means that the company's cash payments for expenses are less than the expense amount shown on the income statement. On the other hand, when accrued expenses decrease as they did for the Tsujimoto's Oriental Rug Factory, it means that the company's cash payments for expenses are more than the expense amount shown on the income statement. This means that the cash Tsujimoto's paid for operating expenses in 2004 was $11,000 *more* than the amount shown on its income statement. Therefore, we must subtract $11,000 from net income. Tsujimoto's actually paid this money to suppliers during 2004.

f. *Income taxes payable*—According to Exhibit 10–9, income taxes payable increased by $15,000 during 2004. Income taxes payable increase when a company's payments for income tax are less than the tax expense shown on the income statement for that period. Therefore, we must add $15,000 to net income.

Exhibit 10–10 shows the completed operating activities section of Tsujimoto's statement of cash flows after we include the adjustments for the changes in the current assets and current liabilities.

EXHIBIT 10–10   Partial Statement of Cash Flows for Tsujimoto's Oriental Rug Factory: Operating Activities Section

Tsujimoto's Oriental Rug Factory
Partial Statement of Cash Flows
For the Year Ended December 31, 2004
(in thousands)

Cash Flows from Operating Activities:		
Net income		$420
Adjustments to reconcile net income to net cash provided by operating activities:		
Depreciation expense	$231	
Gain on sale of long-term investments	(31)	
Decrease in accounts receivable	187	
Increase in merchandise inventory	(164)	
Increase in prepaid expense	(60)	
Increase in accounts payable	110	
Decrease in accrued expenses	(11)	
Increase in income taxes payable	15	277
Net cash provided by operating activities		$697

We have now determined that Tsujimoto's Oriental Rug Factory generated a positive cash flow of $697,000 through its operating activities during 2004. Since cash increased during 2004 by only $562,000, there must have been cash outflow in one or both of the other types of activities (investing and financing). We will look at investing activities next.

DETERMINING CASH FLOW FROM INVESTING ACTIVITIES

Determining cash flow from investing activities requires an analysis of the noncurrent asset section of the balance sheet. Tsujimoto's Oriental Rug Factory has two classifications of assets that are noncurrent: long-term investments and property, plant, and equipment. Exhibit 10–11 on page F–418 shows that section of Tsujimoto's comparative balance sheets with a column added that calculates the change in each item from the end of 2003 to the end of 2004. If there were any investments in the current assets section of Tsujimoto's balance sheet, we would also list them here as they would be part of investing activities rather than operating activities.

We already know from the additional information provided about the company's activities earlier in the chapter that Tsujimoto's sold long-term investments for $83,000 and purchased equipment for $110,000 during 2004. But even if these details are not

Tsujimoto's Oriental Rug Factory
Partial Balance Sheets
December 31, 2004, and December 31, 2003
(in thousands)

	2004	2003	Increase/Decrease
Long-term investments	21	73	$ (52)
Plant and equipment:			
Equipment	1,155	1,045	110
LESS: Accumulated depreciation	(851)	(620)	231
Equipment, net	304	425	
Total noncurrent assets	$4,445	$4,019	

EXHIBIT 10–11   Noncurrent Asset Section of Balance Sheets for Tsujimoto's Oriental Rug Factory for 2004 and 2003

disclosed, it is sometimes possible to determine these amounts by noting the change in the account balances. An increase in a noncurrent asset balance would most likely be the result of a purchase of assets. For example, the balance shown on Tsujimoto's balance sheet for equipment increased by $110,000 as a result of the company's equipment purchase. On the other hand, a decrease in a noncurrent asset balance would likely be the result of a sale. To determine the resulting cash inflow when there is a sale of an investment activities item, we must combine the amount of the decrease in the item's balance with the gain or loss on the sale of that item. For example, Tsujimoto's long-term investments decreased by $52,000. This $52,000 decrease combined with the $31,000 gain equals the $83,000 cash inflow Tsujimoto's received when it sold the investments. However, determining the cash flows for investing activities by examining the changes in a balance sheet amount works only if the change is the result of a single transaction such as either a purchase or a sale. It would not work if the change in the balance were composed of multiple transactions such as a sale and a purchase together. In such a case, you would be forced to use additional information, which is not included in the financial statements themselves.

Aside from the long-term investments and equipment, there are no other items listed as noncurrent assets on Tsujimoto's balance sheets, so we know that the sale of the long-term investment securities and the purchase of equipment are the only items that will be in the investing activities section of the statement of cash flows. After including the investing activities section, Tsujimoto's Oriental Rug Factory's statement of cash flows is shaping up as shown in Exhibit 10–12.

If we combine the cash provided by operating activities and the cash used by investing activities, we arrive at a net cash inflow for 2004 of $670,000 (697,000 inflow − 27,000 outflow). This means there must have been cash outflow from financing activities, because we know that overall cash increased by $562,000 during 2004.

DETERMINING CASH FLOW FROM FINANCING ACTIVITIES

Determining cash flow from financing activities generally requires an analysis of the long-term liabilities and stockholders' equity sections of the balance sheet. Exhibit 10–13 shows those sections from Tsujimoto's Oriental Rug Factory's comparative balance sheets with a column added that calculates the change in each item from the end of 2003 to the end of 2004. If there was any general borrowing in the current liabilities section of Tsujimoto's balance sheet, we would have also listed it here as it would be part of financing activities.

Tsujimoto's cash flow from financing activities is made up of several elements. By examining the company's comparative balance sheets, we determine that notes payable decreased substantially. This is due to the company making principal payments on its promissory notes totaling $275,000. These payments are a cash outflow from financing activities. The increase in bonds payable is due to the company selling an

Tsujimoto's Oriental Rug Factory
Partial Statement of Cash Flows
For the Year Ended December 31, 2004
(in thousands)

Cash Flows from Operating Activities:

Net income		$420
Adjustments to reconcile net income to net cash provided by operating activities:		
Depreciation expense	$231	
Gain on sale of long-term investments	(31)	
Decrease in accounts receivable	187	
Increase in merchandise inventory	(164)	
Increase in prepaid expense	(60)	
Increase in accounts payable	110	
Decrease in accrued expenses	(11)	
Increase in income taxes payable	15	277
Net cash provided by operating activities		697
Cash Flows from Investing Activities:		
Sale of long-term investments	83	
Purchase of equipment	(110)	
Net cash used by investing activities		(27)

EXHIBIT 10–12 Partial Statement of Cash Flows for Tsujimoto's Oriental Rug Factory: Operating Activities and Investing Activities Sections

additional $200,000 in bonds. The sale of bonds results in a cash inflow from financing activities. Likewise, the $104,000 increase in common stock stems from the company selling additional shares of stock, a cash inflow from financing activities. All of these amounts can be determined simply by looking at the changes in those three items in Exhibit 10–13. In addition, there was a cash outflow from cash dividends paid during 2004 totaling $137,000. We know this amount because it was included in the additional information provided earlier in the chapter. But if we didn't already know the amount of dividends, we could determine it from information in Tsujimoto's income statement and balance sheets (Exhibits 10–4 and 10–5).

We know the balance in retained earnings at the end of 2003 is $443,000. We also know that the balance in retained earnings at the end of 2004 is $726,000. As discussed in earlier chapters, we know that the balance of retained earnings is increased by net income and decreased by dividends. We know from Tsujimoto's income statement that

EXHIBIT 10–13 Long-Term Liabilities and Stockholders' Equity Sections of Tsujimoto's Oriental Rug Factory's Balance Sheets for 2004 and 2003

Tsujimoto's Oriental Rug Factory
Partial Balance Sheets
December 31, 2004, and December 31, 2003
(in thousands)

	2004	2003	Increase/Decrease
Long-term liabilities:			
Notes payable	$ 425	$ 700	$(275)
Bonds payable	1,100	900	200
Total long-term liabilities	$1,525	$1,600	
Stockholders' equity:			
Common stock, no-par value	$1,332	$1,228	$ 104
Retained earnings	726	443	283
Total stockholders' equity	$2,058	$1,671	

the net income was \$420,000, so the only amount we are missing is dividends. Therefore:

Retained earnings at 12/31/03	\$443,000
PLUS: 2004 net income	420,000
LESS: Dividends paid during 2004	(?)
Equals retained earnings at 12/31/04	\$726,000

The unknown amount of dividends must be \$137,000. This calculation is based on the relationships we already know from the statement of retained earnings:

Beginning retained earnings + Net income − Dividends = Ending retained earnings

The net cash flow from financing activities, then, is \$108,000. It is composed of the \$275,000 outflow for the loan payments, the \$200,000 inflow from the sale of bonds, the \$104,000 inflow from the sale of Tsujimoto's common stock, and the outflow of \$137,000 for the payment of dividends. If we have considered everything we were supposed to, the cash provided by operating activities combined with the cash used by investing activities and the cash used by financing activities should equal the change in cash from the end of 2003 to the end of 2004. Exhibit 10–14 shows the completed statement.

Tsujimoto's Oriental Rug Factory's statement of cash flows was a fairly simple one to prepare because there were relatively few things to consider. But whether simple or complex, all statements of cash flows assume the basic format we used for Tsujimoto's Oriental Rug Factory.

EXHIBIT 10–14 Tsujimoto's Oriental Rug Factory's Complete Statement of Cash Flows for 2004

Tsujimoto's Oriental Rug Factory
Statement of Cash Flows
For the Year Ended December 31, 2004
(in thousands)

Cash Flows from Operating Activities:

Net income		\$420
Adjustments to reconcile net income to net cash provided by operating activities:		
Depreciation expense	\$231	
Gain on sale of long-term investments	(31)	
Decrease in accounts receivable	187	
Increase in merchandise inventory	(164)	
Increase in prepaid expense	(60)	
Increase in accounts payable	110	
Decrease in accrued expenses	(11)	
Increase in income taxes payable	15	277
Net cash provided by operating activities		697
Cash Flows from Investing Activities:		
Sale of long-term investments	83	
Purchase of equipment	(110)	
Net cash used by investing activities		(27)
Cash Flows from Financing Activities:		
Payments on long-term notes payable	(275)	
Proceeds from sale of bonds	200	
Proceeds from sale of common stock	104	
Payment of cash dividends	(137)	
Net cash used by financing activities		(108)
Net increase in cash during 2004		562
Cash balance at January 1, 2004		419
Cash balance at December 31, 2004		\$981

SUPPLEMENTAL SCHEDULE

To complete the statement of cash flows disclosures for users, companies are required to include a supplemental schedule that outlines any significant noncash investing and financing activities during the period. Examples of such transactions include purchasing an asset by signing a promissory note instead of paying cash, using an asset other than cash to retire a loan, or trading one asset for another. In such transactions, no cash changes hands, but the transaction may have future cash consequences. If a company pays off a bond issue with common stock, that removes the future cash outflow required to repay the bond, because common stock has no maturity date or amount. On the other hand, dividend requirements will be increased in the future.

◆ HOW TO USE THE STATEMENT OF CASH FLOWS

One of the two main purposes of the statement of cash flows is to disclose a company's sources of cash during a specific time period and what it used the cash for (the other being to reconcile accrual net income to the change in cash). One of the most important things the statement shows is a company's investment during the period and how that investment was financed. We are talking here mostly about a company's investment in long-lived assets that will be used to produce future revenues and, eventually, cash. The things the company invested in during the period are presented in the middle section of the statement (investing activities). How that investment was financed is presented in the top section of the statement (operating activities) and the bottom section of the statement (financing activities). To demonstrate this concept, we have extracted the cash flow totals for the three types of activities from Tsujimoto's Oriental Rug Factory's statement of cash flows from Exhibit 10–14:

Net cash provided by operating activities	$ 697,000
Net cash used by investing activities	$ (27,000)
Net cash provided by financing activities	$ (108,000)

Tsujimoto's Oriental Rug Factory has a net cash investment of $27,000 during 2004. This total is a bit misleading, because the company's actual investment in new equipment was $110,000. The total is reduced by the sale of long-term investments for $83,000. The company invested cash in the equipment to enhance the way it conducts its business by upgrading manufacturing facilities, entering into new markets, or developing new products. The point is there had to be a reason for Tsujimoto's to make this investment. We can't assess whether this investment was good or bad because we don't have enough information, but we can determine where the cash came from to finance it.

Aside from selling off investments, there are only two sources of cash available to any company, and Tsujimoto is no exception. A company either generates cash internally (from profitable operations) or it obtains it from external sources (borrowing or selling stock). In our example, virtually all of Tsujimoto's needed cash was generated internally through operating activities. In fact, the company's operations generated enough cash to pay down loans and to pay dividends, thus resulting in a net cash outflow for financing activities. With that in mind, focus on this important concept: *In the long run, all investment (disclosed in the middle section of the statement of cash flows) must be financed through operations (disclosed in the top section of the statement).* If a company wants or needs to invest, but does not generate enough cash from operations to pay for it, the only alternative is to go outside the company for the financing, by either borrowing or by selling shares of stock (disclosed in the bottom section of the statement). On the other hand, if a company does not generate enough cash from operations to pay for its investment, but either can't or doesn't want to go outside the company for financing, the only alternative is to cut back on the investment. However, this may not be a smart business decision. Remember why companies make these investments. The purpose of the investment is to generate cash from operations. If a company decides to cut back on its investment because it is not generating sufficient cash from operations to pay for it (and won't or can't finance the investment externally), the company may reduce its cash flow even further. We said earlier that Tsujimoto's invested $27,000 in 2004 to enhance the way the company conducts its business by upgrading manufacturing facilities, entering into new markets, or developing new products. If it hadn't made the investment, perhaps it couldn't upgrade its manufacturing facilities, enter new markets, or develop any new products. What might be the result of this decision? Well, the result may very well be declining cash flows from operations in subsequent years. This can cause an even more dramatic cutback in investment, which will likely lead to a further decline in cash generated by operations. Finally, the company may go bankrupt. Exhibit 10–15 illustrates this downward spiral using information extracted from the statements of cash flow for the years 1998 through 2003 for the Weiser Company, a videotape manufacturing firm.

EXHIBIT 10–15   The Downward Spiral of the Weiser Company

	2003	2002	2001	2000	1999	1998
Net cash provided by operating activities	$150	300	700	800	1,200	1,000
Net cash used by investing activities	(125)	(450)	(450)	(900)	(900)	(900)
Net cash provided by financing activities	(25)	60	(275)	150	(250)	(300)

Discussion Question

10–9. From what you see in Exhibit 10–15, what do you think Weiser Company's cash flow prospects are for 2004?

There are a couple of things we should note about the presentation in Exhibit 10–15. First, the *amount* of cash Weiser Company invests is not nearly as important as the *quality* of what it invests in. There is no information in the exhibit about the quality of any of this company's investments. The rapid decline in net cash provided by operating activities could be a result of the company investing in the wrong things in 1998 and 1999 (or even earlier years). If Weiser's investment in 1998 and 1999 was to upgrade its tape manufacturing equipment, the company may be in real trouble. Perhaps the investment in those years should have been in digital video disc (DVD) manufacturing equipment, because the DVD market is rapidly replacing the video tape market.

The second thing we should note about the presentation in Exhibit 10–15 is that the investing activities in a given year likely did not generate the cash from operating activities in that year. In other words, the $900 Weiser invested in 1998 probably did not generate the $1,000 cash from operating activities in 1998. The cash provided by operating activities in 1998 likely was a result of investments the company made in earlier years. What this means, of course, is that the rapid decline in Weiser's cash flows from operating activities in 2002 and 2003 may be due to the company's cutback in its investing activities in 2001 and 2002.

As you can see, the statement of cash flows provides valuable information to financial statement users. In and of itself, however, it cannot answer all an economic decision maker's questions about a company's past performance, present condition, or future prospects. As is the case with the other three financial statements we have discussed in this text, the statement of cash flows is best utilized in conjunction with the other statements and other pertinent information about the company.

◆ USING FINANCIAL INFORMATION

At the beginning of the chapter, we posed the hypothetical situation in which you were trying to decide whether to buy stock in the company your friend Sally has recommended. When you asked your Aunt Matilda's advice, her response was, "Profit, schmofit. Show me the cash." The statement of cash flows we have presented in this chapter provides you with solid information about a company's ability to generate positive cash flow. Additionally, analysts have developed certain ratios in recent years that focus on cash. In the remainder of this chapter, we will present two of them: the operating cash flow to current debt ratio and the operating cash flow coverage ratio. We will use the information from Tsujimoto's Oriental Rug Factory's financial statements to calculate these ratios for 2004.

Operating Cash Flow to Current Debt Ratio

operating cash flow to current debt ratio A financial ratio that measures the sufficiency of cash flows from operating activities to meet current obligations.

The **operating cash flow to current debt ratio** measures the sufficiency of cash flows from operating activities to meet current obligations. In other words, it measures the company's ability to generate enough cash from operating activities to meet its current obligations. Whereas the current and quick ratios measure a firm's liquidity based on the financial resources the company has on hand (its assets), the operating cash flow to current debt ratio measures a company's ability to maintain liquidity by generating sufficient cash inflows from its operations. The formula for this ratio is:

$$\text{Operating cash flow to current debt ratio} = \frac{\text{Cash provided by operating activities}}{\text{Average current liabilities}}$$

The numerator for this ratio is cash provided by operating activities from the statement of cash flows. For Tsujimoto's, that amount is $697,000 as shown in Exhibit 10–14. The denominator is based on current liabilities from the balance sheet. We use an average for current liabilities for the same reason we used average amounts for ratios presented in earlier chapters. Since the cash provided by operating activities in the numerator occurred throughout 2004, we should use an approximation of the current liabilities outstanding throughout the year. We determine this by calculating the average of the current liabilities shown on the 2003 and 2004 balance sheets shown in Exhibit 10–5 ($748,000 + $862,000 = $1,610,000/2 = $805,000). We calculate Tsujimoto's operating cash flow to current debt ratio for 2004 as:

$$\frac{\$697,000}{\$805,000} = 0.87 \text{ to } 1$$

This ratio calculation tells us that Tsujimoto's operating activities generated $0.87 of cash in 2004 for each $1.00 of its average current liabilities. Generally speaking, generating a high amount of cash inflow from operating activities relative to current liabilities is a positive indication. Averages vary from company to company and industry to industry, but many analysts get a bit nervous if this ratio falls below $0.90 cash flow from operating activities to every $1.00 of average current liabilities.

Operating Cash Flow Coverage Ratio

operating cash flow coverage ratio A financial ratio that indicates a company's capacity to repay its liabilities from the net cash generated by its operating activities.

The **operating cash flow coverage ratio** indicates a company's capacity to repay its liabilities from the net cash generated by its operating activities. The formula for this ratio is:

$$\text{Operating cash flow coverage ratio} = \frac{\text{Cash provided by operating activities}}{\text{Average total liabilities}}$$

As you can see, the numerator for this ratio is the same as for the operating cash flow to current liabilities ratio—cash provided by operating activities shown on the statement of cash flows. For Tsujimoto's, that amount is $697,000 as shown in Exhibit 10–14. The denominator is based on the total liabilities shown on the balance sheet. We use an average amount for the same reason we have in earlier ratios. Since the cash provided by operating activities in the numerator occurred throughout 2004, we want to know the total liabilities throughout the year. We determine this by calculating the average of the total liabilities shown on the 2003 and 2004 balance sheets as shown in

Exhibit 10–5 ($2,348,000 + $2,387,000 = $4,735,000/2 = $2,367,500). We calculate Tsujimoto's operating cash flow coverage ratio for 2004 as:

$$\frac{\$697,000}{\$2,367,500} = 0.29 \text{ to } 1$$

This ratio tells us that Tsujimoto's generated $0.29 of cash through its operation in 2004 for every $1.00 of its average total liabilities for 2004. The higher this ratio is, the more likely a company is to be able to service its debt without going outside the company for financing (by either borrowing additional funds or selling additional shares of its stock). Averages vary from company to company and industry to industry, but many analysts get a bit nervous if this ratio falls below $0.40 cash flow from operating activities to every $1.00 of average current liabilities.

Based on these two ratios, Tsujimoto's Oriental Rug Factory's cash position relative to its liabilities does not appear to be exceptionally good. In order to assess this, however, we must compare its ratios (and other financial information) to its industry, peer companies within that industry, and how these ratios have changed over time. This analysis is the subject of the next chapter.

Summary

One of the disadvantages of accrual basis accounting is that it takes the financial statement reader's eye off cash. Over the past several decades, economic decision makers' interest in the cash flows of companies has risen. The accounting profession developed the statement of cash flows to give financial statement users information about the cash flows of companies during a particular period. This financial statement provides information about cash flows used by or provided by three major types of business activities: operating, investing, and financing. Information necessary for the development of a statement of cash flows can be found on a company's comparative balance sheets and the income statement of the period.

Cash flows provided or used by operating activities can be presented using either of two acceptable approaches—the indirect method or the direct method. The indirect method begins with net income. Adjustments to this figure are made for any revenue items not producing cash this period and expense items not using cash this period. The direct method provides detail about the individual sources and uses of cash associated with operating activities. Because the indirect method is the more widely used format, we presented this method in the chapter. A presentation of the direct method is found in an appendix to the chapter.

Results of investing activities can be found in the long-term asset section of the balance sheet. Typical transactions that are classified as investing activities are the purchase and sale of property, plant, and equipment.

The financing activities section of the statement of cash flows shows what types of external financing the company used to provide funds. Information showing the results of financing activities can be found in the long-term liability section and the owners' equity section of the balance sheet.

The statement of cash flows furnishes valuable information about the cash inflows and outflows of a business during a particular period. It provides an explanation of the changes in cash from the beginning to the end of a period. Therefore, the statement of cash flows can be considered a financial statement analysis tool as well as a financial statement.

Determining Cash Flows from Operating Activities—Direct Method

When the FASB introduced the statement of cash flows as one of the required financial statements in 1988, it recommended that companies use the direct method and include a supplemental schedule reconciling net income to the change in cash from operating activities. Recall that this reconciliation is the indirect method we presented in this chapter.

Many people (the authors of this text included) think it is unfortunate that the vast majority of companies use the indirect method. While the indirect method is every bit as logical as the direct method, it does not provide information regarding individual operating activity cash flows.

The direct method involves a series of calculations to determine the individual cash inflows from customers, interest earned on loans, dividends received from stock investments in other companies, and the like, and individual cash outflow for payments to suppliers, employees, creditors, and others. Remember, both the direct and the indirect methods deal only with the operating activities section of the statement of cash flows. The investing activities section and the financing activities section are the same, regardless of whether the direct or the indirect method is used for the operating activities section.

To determine net cash flow from operating activities using the direct method, we will, in effect, convert the accrual basis income statement into a cash basis income statement in order to get the focus back onto cash. To accomplish this, we examine the income statement along with the current assets and current liabilities on the comparative balance sheets. We will use Tsujimoto's Oriental Rug Factory as our example, so we have duplicated its 2004 income statement and the current assets and current liabilities sections of its balance sheets at the end of 2003 and 2004 as Exhibit 10A–1 on page F–426.

Exhibit 10A–2 on page F–427 shows the basic format of the cash flows from operating activities section of the statement of cash flows using the direct method.

As you can see from Exhibit 10A–2, we must determine five amounts to complete the operating activities section of Tsujimoto's statement of cash flows.

1. *Cash received from customers*. Credit sales increase accounts receivable, and cash received from customers that previously bought on account decreases accounts receivable. To determine the cash Tsujimoto's received from its customers during 2004, we combine the beginning balance in accounts receivable with sales to arrive at the total amount the company could have collected. Next, we subtract the amount they *did not* collect, namely the ending balance of accounts receivable to determine the total cash collected from customers.

Beginning accounts receivable balance (from the 2003 balance sheet)	$ 2,112
+ Sales during 2004 (from the 2004 income statement)	15,158
= Amount Tsujimoto's could have collected from customers in 2004	$17,270
− Ending accounts receivable balance (from the 2004 balance sheet)	(1,925)
= Total cash received from customers during 2004	$15,345

2. *Cash paid for merchandise inventory*. As it happens, rather than paying cash for the merchandise it sells, a company may sell the merchandise it has on hand. And, if it does buy merchandise, instead of paying for it, the company may buy some or all of the merchandise on account. Therefore, to determine the cash paid for merchandise during a period, we must examine cost of goods sold, merchandise inventory, and accounts payable together. Determining the cash Tsujimoto's paid its suppliers during 2004 is a two-step calculation. First, we must determine the cost of the merchandise the company purchased during the year. To do this, we take the company's cost of goods sold, reduce it by the amount of the beginning inventory, and then we add the ending balance in merchandise inventory. Second, we must determine the amount the company actually paid for the merchandise it purchased. To do this, we must consider the amount of merchandise purchased calculated in step one, in light of the beginning and ending balances in accounts payable. This two-step calculation is as follows:

Tsujimoto's Oriental Rug Factory
Income Statement
For the Year Ended December 31, 2004
(in thousands)

Sales		$15,158
Cost of goods sold		11,151
Gross margin		$ 4,007
Operating expenses:		
Depreciation expense	231	
Selling and administration	3,047	
Total operating expenses		(3,278)
Operating income		$ 729
Gain on sale of long-term investments		31
Less: Interest expense		(160)
Income before income taxes		$ 600
Income tax expense		(180)
Net income		$ 420

Tsujimoto's Oriental Rug Factory
Partial Balance Sheets
December 31, 2003, and December 31, 2003
(in thousands)

ASSETS:	2004	2003	Increase/Decrease
Current assets:			
Cash	$ 981	$ 419	$ 562
Accounts receivable	1,925	2,112	(187)
Merchandise inventory	1,022	858	164
Prepaid expenses	192	132	60
Total current assets	$4,120	$3,521	
LIABILITIES:			
Current liabilities:			
Accounts payable	$ 820	$ 710	$ 110
Accrued expenses	17	28	(11)
Income tax payable	25	10	15
Total current liabilities	$ 862	$ 748	

EXHIBIT 10A–1   Tsujimoto's Oriental Rug Factory's Income Statement for 2004 and Partial Balance Sheets for 2003 and 2004

Step One—Determine the amount of merchandise inventory purchased in 2004:

Cost of goods sold (from the 2004 income statement)	$11,151
− Beginning merchandise inventory balance (from the 2003 balance sheet)	(858)
= Amount of cost of goods sold purchased in 2004	10,293
+ Ending merchandise inventory balance (from the 2004 balance sheet)	1,022
= Merchandise inventory purchased in 2004	$11,315

Step Two—Determine the amount of merchandise inventory paid for in 2004:

Beginning accounts payable balance (from the 2003 balance sheet)	$ 710
+ Merchandise inventory purchased in 2004 (calculated in step one)	11,315
= Amount Tsujimoto's could have paid to suppliers in 2004	$12,025
− Ending accounts payable balance (from the 2004 balance sheet)	(820)
= Total cash paid for merchandise inventory in 2004	$11,205

3. *Cash paid for operating expenses.* Some of the operating expenses in Tsujimoto's 2004 income statement were not paid in 2004. Some were paid before 2004 and some might be paid after 2004. A company classifies operating expenses it pays for in advance (such as insurance or rent) as assets (prepaid expenses) on the balance sheet until they are subsequently recognized as expenses on the income statement. Conversely, when a company

Tsujimoto's Oriental Rug Factory
Partial Statement of Cash Flows
For the Year Ended December 31, 2004
(in thousands)

Cash Flows from Operating Activities:

Cash received from customers	$?
Cash paid for:	
Merchandise inventory	?
Operating expenses	?
Interest	?
Income taxes	?
Net cash provided (used) by operating activities	$?

EXHIBIT 10A–2 Basic Format of Cash Flow from Operating Activities Section of the Statement of Cash Flows Using the Direct Method

recognizes operating expenses on its income statement (such as supplies, utilities, and wages) but has not paid for them by the end of the period, it classifies the amount owed for those expenses as a liability (accrued expenses) on the balance sheet. Accrued expenses is a liability very similar to accounts payable. To determine the cash Tsujimoto's paid for operating expenses in 2004, then, we must consider not only the operating expenses from the income statement, but prepaid expenses and accrued expenses from the balance sheets, as well.

One last thing we should mention before we demonstrate the calculation of cash paid for operating expenses is depreciation. Recall from our discussion in Chapter 7 that depreciation is a noncash expense. When we say *noncash*, we don't mean to imply that cash was never paid for this expense, because it was; it just wasn't paid during this income statement period. In fact, depreciation is associated with a very special prepaid expense, called property, plant, and equipment. The cash flow associated with property, plant, and equipment is reported in the investing activities section of the statement of cash flows so we exclude any treatment here. The calculation of Tsujimoto's Oriental Rug Factory's cash paid for operating expenses is as follows:

Operating expenses other than depreciation (from the 2004 income statement)	$3,047
− Beginning prepaid expenses balance (from the 2003 balance sheet)	(132)
+ Ending prepaid expenses balance (from the 2004 balance sheet)	192
+ Beginning accrued expenses balance (from the 2003 balance sheet)	28
− Ending accrued expenses balance (from the 2004 balance sheet)	(17)
= Total cash paid for operating expenses in 2004	$3,118

4. *Cash paid for interest.* To determine the amount of cash Tsujimoto's Oriental Rug Factory paid for interest in 2004, we must examine the beginning balance of accrued interest (from the 2003 balance sheet), interest expense (from the 2004 income statement), and the ending balance of accrued interest (from the 2004 balance sheet). Since there is no balance for accrued interest on either the 2003 or 2004 balance sheet, we can conclude that the cash Tsujimoto's paid for interest in 2004 is exactly the $160,000 shown as interest expense on the 2004 income statement. If there had been a balance in either the beginning or ending balance of accrued interest, we would need to do a calculation similar to the one we did for cash collected from customers.

5. *Cash paid for income taxes.* To calculate the amount of cash Tsujimoto's paid for income taxes in 2004, we must examine the beginning balance of taxes payable (from the 2003 balance sheet), income tax expense (from the 2004 income statement), and the ending balance of income taxes payable (from the 2004 balance sheet). The calculation of Tsujimoto's Oriental Rug Factory's cash paid for income taxes follows:

Income tax expenses (from the 2004 income statement)	$180
+ Beginning taxes payable (from the 2003 balance sheet)	10
− Ending taxes payable (from the 2004 balance sheet)	(25)
= Cash paid for income taxes	$165

Tsujimoto's Oriental Rug Factory
Statement of Cash Flows
For the Year Ended December 31, 2004
(in thousands)

Cash Flows from Operating Activities:

Cash received from customers	$15,345	
Cash paid for:		
Merchandise inventory	(11,205)	
Operating expenses	(3,118)	
Interest	(160)	
Income taxes	(165)	
Net cash provided (used) by operating activities		$697
Cash Flows from Investing Activities:		
Sale of long-term investments	83	
Purchase of equipment	(110)	
Net cash used by investing activities		(27)
Cash Flows from Financing Activities:		
Payments on long-term notes payable	(275)	
Proceeds from sale of bonds	200	
Proceeds from sale of common stock	104	
Payment of cash dividends	(137)	
Net cash used by financing activities		(108)
Net increase in cash during 2004		562
Cash balance at January 1, 2004		419
Cash balance at December 31, 2004		$981

EXHIBIT 10A–3 Statement of Cash Flows for Tsujimoto's Oriental Rug Factory: Operating Activities Section—Direct Method

With these five calculations, we can now complete the operating activities section of Tsujimoto's Oriental Rug Factory's statement of cash flows as shown in Exhibit 10A–3.

So you can more easily compare the operating activities section using the direct method with the operating activities section using the indirect method, Exhibit 10A–4 duplicates the indirect method statement of cash flows we presented earlier in the chapter.

As you can see by examining the two exhibits, the statements are exactly the same except for the operating activities sections. And even the operating activities sections are similar in that the net cash flows from operating activities is the same regardless of whether the indirect method or direct method was used. Remember, however, that the FASB requires that the reconciliation of net income to cash flow from operating activities (essentially, a presentation of the indirect method) also be presented when the direct method is employed.

Tsujimoto's Oriental Rug Factory
Statement of Cash Flows
For the Year Ended December 31, 2004
(in thousands)

Cash Flows from Operating Activities:

Net income		$420
Adjustments to reconcile net income to net cash provided by operating activities:		
Depreciation expense	$231	
Gain on sale of long-term investments	(31)	
Decrease in accounts receivable	187	
Increase in merchandise inventory	(164)	
Increase in prepaid expense	(60)	
Increase in accounts payable	110	
Decrease in accrued expenses	(11)	
Increase in income taxes payable	15	277
Net cash provided by operating activities		697
Cash Flows from Investing Activities:		
Sale of long-term investments	83	
Purchase of equipment	(110)	
Net cash used by investing activities		(27)
Cash Flows from Financing Activities:		
Payments on long-term notes payable	(275)	
Proceeds from sale of bonds	200	
Proceeds from sale of common stock	104	
Payment of cash dividends	(137)	
Net cash used by financing activities		(108)
Net increase in cash during 2004		562
Cash balance at January 1, 2004		419
Cash balance at December 31, 2004		$981

EXHIBIT 10A–4 Statement of Cash Flows for Tsujimoto's Oriental Rug Factory: Operating Activities Section—Indirect Method

Key Terms

- direct method, F–406
- financing activities, F–409
- indirect method, F–407
- investing activities, F–407
- operating activities, F–405
- operating cash flow coverage ratio, F–423
- operating cash flow to current debt ratio, F–423
- working capital, F–404

Review the Facts

A. When did the present format of the statement of cash flows come into existence?
B. What is the main purpose of the statement of cash flows?
C. Name the two methods of presenting the operating activities section of statement of cash flows. Which method is more commonly used by publicly traded companies?
D. What are the three activity classifications presented on the statement of cash flows?
E. Which category includes the cash inflows for interest received?
F. Which category includes the cash outflows for interest paid?
G. Which category includes the cash inflows for dividends received?
H. Which category includes the cash outflows for dividends paid?
I. Provide three examples of cash flows for each of the three activities shown on the statement of cash flows.

J. What is the starting point for calculating cash flows from operating activities under the indirect method?

K. When gathering information to prepare the operating activities section, where on the financial statements would you likely find most of the information you need?

L. Where would you find information to prepare the investing activities section?

M. Where would you find information to prepare the financing activities section?

N. Which section of the statement of cash flows shows cash outflows to acquire the property, plant, and equipment the company will use in its business operations?

O. According to the chapter, what ratios help financial statement users evaluate a company's operating cash flows? What do the ratios measure?

Apply What You Have Learned ●

LO 1 & 2: STATEMENT OF CASH FLOWS TERMINOLOGY

10–10. Below is a list of items relating to the concepts discussed in this chapter, followed by definitions of those items in scrambled order:

a. Operating activities   e. Financing activities
b. Indirect method   f. Working capital
c. Depreciation expense   g. Direct method
d. Comparative financial statements   h. Investing activities

1. _____ Provides a reconciliation of accrual net income to the cash provided by or used by operating activities

2. _____ Accounting reports providing information from two or more consecutive periods at once

3. _____ Activities centered around the actual day-to-day business transactions of a company

4. _____ Current assets less current liabilities

5. _____ Business activities related to long-term assets

6. _____ Provides detail as to the individual sources and uses of cash associated with operating activities

7. _____ An item that reduces reported net income, but does not require the use of cash

8. _____ Activities such as the issuance of debt or equity and the payment of dividends

Required: Match the letter next to each item on the list with the appropriate definition. Use each letter only once.

LO 2: IDENTIFICATION OF ACTIVITIES

10–11. Listed below are the three broad types of activities that can either generate or use cash in any business, followed by descriptions of various items:

a. Operating activities
b. Investing activities
c. Financing activities

1. _____ Payment of dividends
2. _____ Adjustment for depreciation
3. _____ Purchase of merchandise inventory
4. _____ Purchase of vehicles
5. _____ Repayment of loan principal
6. _____ Payment of loan interest
7. _____ Issuing capital stock
8. _____ Payment of wages to employees
9. _____ Payment of taxes
10. _____ Cash received from sale of property and equipment
11. _____ Cash paid for loans made to other companies
12. _____ Interest received on loans to other companies
13. _____ Adjustments for changes in most current asset and current liability items
14. _____ Cash from selling investments in other companies

Required: Classify each of the items listed above by placing the letter of the appropriate activity category in the space provided.

LO 2: IDENTIFICATION OF ACTIVITIES

10–12. Listed below are the three broad types of activities that can either generate or use cash in any business, followed by descriptions of various items:

a. Operating activities
b. Investing activities
c. Financing activities

1. _____ Adjustment to income for depreciation or amortization expense
2. _____ Cash received for sale of merchandise inventory
3. _____ Cash paid for merchandise inventory
4. _____ Principal part of loan payments
5. _____ Interest part of loan payments
6. _____ Cash paid when a company buys common stock in another company
7. _____ Cash paid when a company buys back its own common stock
8. _____ Payment of rent on office space
9. _____ Cash received for dividends
10. _____ Cash paid for dividends
11. _____ Cash paid for wages
12. _____ Cash paid for income taxes
13. _____ Cash paid for insurance on factory equipment
14. _____ Cash paid to buy factory equipment
15. _____ Cash received for the sale of factory equipment
16. _____ Cash received from sale of treasury stock
17. _____ Cash received when a company sells bonds of other companies, which were held for investment
18. _____ Cash received when a company sells its own company bonds
19. _____ Cash from the collection of accounts receivable

Required: Classify each of the items listed above by placing the letter of the appropriate activity category in the space provided.

LO 2: IDENTIFICATION OF SOURCES AND USES—INDIRECT METHOD

10–13. Following are the changes in some of George R. Violette Company's assets, liabilities, and equities from December 31, 2004, to December 31, 2005:

1. _____ Accounts payable decreased.
2. _____ Property and equipment increased.
3. _____ Accounts receivable increased.
4. _____ Long-term notes payable decreased.
5. _____ Prepaid expenses decreased.
6. _____ Notes payable increased.
7. _____ Taxes payable decreased.
8. _____ Common stock increased.
9. _____ Wages payable increased.
10. _____ Accrued expenses decreased.
11. _____ Merchandise inventory decreased.

Violette is in the process of preparing the operating activities section of its statement of cash flows using the indirect method. Some of the items above will be included and others will not.

Required: Designate each of the items listed above as follows:

S Place the letter S in the space next to each item that should be considered a source of cash in the operating activities section.
U Place the letter U in the space next to each item that should be considered a use of cash in the operating activities section.
N Place the letter N next to any item not included in the indirect method operating activities section.

LO 3: SIMPLE OPERATING ACTIVITIES SECTION PREPARATION

10–14. The Doran Company gathered the following information from its accounting records:

Collections from customers	$450,000
Payments to suppliers	150,000
Payments for income taxes	75,000
Interest received on investments	5,000
Payments to employees for wages	64,000
Payments for interest	85,000
Depreciation expense	50,000

Required: Prepare the operating activities section of the statement of cash flows for the Doran Company. (Use a format similar to the one in Exhibit 10–1.)

LO 3: SIMPLE OPERATING ACTIVITIES SECTION PREPARATION

10–15. The McDaniel Company gathered the following information from its accounting records:

Collections of accounts receivable	$350,000
Cash sales	85,000
Payments for merchandise	260,000
Payments for income taxes	45,000
Payments of electricity	40,000
Interest received on investments	15,000
Wage payments to employees	55,000
Interest payments	68,000
Depreciation expense	25,000

Required: Prepare the operating activities section of the statement of cash flows for the McDaniel Company. (Use a format similar to the one in Exhibit 10–1.)

LO 3: SIMPLE OPERATING ACTIVITIES SECTION PREPARATION

10–16. The PJ Boardman Company gathered the following information from its accounting records:

Payment for treasury stock	$200,000
Payments for dividends	100,000
Collections of accounts receivable	870,000
Cash sales	385,000
Payments to suppliers on account	738,000
Cash purchases of merchandise inventory	250,000
Payments for income taxes	245,000
Interest received on investments	95,000
Payments to employees for salaries	460,000
Payments for interest	35,000
Depreciation expense	125,000

Required: Prepare the operating activities section of the statement of cash flows for the PJ Boardman Company. (Use a format similar to the one in Exhibit 10–1.)

LO 3: SIMPLE INVESTING ACTIVITIES SECTION PREPARATION

10–17. In preparing its statement of cash flows for the year ended December 31, 2003, Debbie Hoffman Company gathered the following data:

Gain on sale of machinery	$ 18,000
Proceeds from sale of machinery	60,000
Purchase of new machinery	420,000
Purchase of Fred, Inc., bonds (face value $100,000)	80,000
Dividends declared and paid	40,000
Proceeds from the sale of common stock	50,000

Required: Prepare the investing activities section of the statement of cash flows for Debbie Hoffman Company. (Use a format similar to the one in Exhibit 10–1.)

LO 3: SIMPLE INVESTING ACTIVITIES SECTION PREPARATION

10–18. In preparing its statement of cash flows for the year ended December 31, 2004, Imelda Company gathered the following data:

Purchased new production equipment for cash	$128,000
Loss on sale of machinery	24,000
Proceeds from sale of old machinery	40,000
Purchase of *Eastman Kodak* bonds (face value $8,000)	9,000
Sold half of the Aka, Inc., bonds	5,000
Imelda Company dividends paid	96,000
Sold Imelda Company bonds	80,000

Required: Prepare the investing activities section of the statement of cash flows for Imelda Company. (Use a format similar to the one in Exhibit 10–1.)

LO 3: SIMPLE INVESTING ACTIVITIES SECTION

10–19. In preparing its statement of cash flows for the year ended December 31, 2004, Juliany Company gathered the following data:

Purchased *IBM* stock	$ 45,000
Purchased back some Juliany common stock	6,000
Received cash dividends from *IBM*	3,000
Paid Juliany cash dividends	28,000
Loss on sale of equipment	4,000
Proceeds from sale of equipment	20,000
Purchase of equipment	980,000

Required: Prepare the investing activities section of the statement of cash flows for Juliany Company. (Use a format similar to the one in Exhibit 10–1.)

LO 3: SIMPLE FINANCING ACTIVITIES SECTION PREPARATION

10–20. In preparing its statement of cash flows for the year ended December 31, 2004, Pat Van Liu Company gathered the following data:

Gain on sale of equipment	$ 4,000
Proceeds from sale of equipment	30,000
Cash paid to purchase equipment	280,000
Purchased *Dow Chemical* stock	32,000
Received cash dividends from *Dow Chemical*	2,000
Sold some of the *Dow Chemical* stock	15,000
Paid Pat Van Liu cash dividends	28,000
Sold Pat Van Liu common stock	60,000
Borrowed cash from *Bank Atlantic*	120,000

Required: Prepare the financing activities section of the statement of cash flows for Pat Van Liu Company. (Use a format similar to the one in Exhibit 10–1.)

LO 3: SIMPLE FINANCING ACTIVITIES SECTION PREPARATION

10–21. In preparing its statement of cash flows for the year ended December 31, 2004, Lori Beloff Company gathered the following data:

Loss on sale of equipment	$ 54,000
Proceeds from sale of equipment	230,000
Cash paid for *Eastman Kodak* stock	23,000
Proceeds from sale of Lori Beloff preferred stock	200,000
Paid Lori Beloff dividends	80,000
Proceeds from sale of Lori Beloff common stock	160,000
Proceeds from sale of part of the *Kodak* stock	9,000

Borrowed cash from *Ocean Bank*	300,000
Payment of interest on *Ocean Bank* loan	20,000
Repayment of principal on *Ocean Bank* loan	120,000

Required: Prepare the financing activities section of the statement of cash flows for Lori Beloff Company. (Use a format similar to the one in Exhibit 10–1.)

LO 3: SIMPLE FINANCING ACTIVITIES SECTION PREPARATION

10–22. In preparing its statement of cash flows for the year ended December 31, 2005, Marc Oliver Company gathered the following data:

Proceeds from sale of equipment	$115,000
Proceeds from sale of Oliver preferred stock	100,000
Paid Oliver dividends	75,000
Proceeds from sale of Oliver common stock	500,000
Proceeds from bank loan	200,000
Payment of interest on bank loan	14,000
Repayment of bank loan principal	100,000

Required: Prepare the financing activities section of the statement of cash flows for Marc Oliver Company. (Use a format similar to the one in Exhibit 10–1.)

LO 3: SIMPLE STATEMENT OF CASH FLOWS PREPARATION

10–23. The following information is from the records of the Greenfield Company for the year ended December 31, 2004:

Loaned $2,000 to Adams Company
Sold Greenfield Company stock for cash of $10,000
Purchased equipment for cash of $20,000
Cash sales to customers were $95,000
Sold equipment for cash of $4,000
Paid cash to employees for wages, $9,500
Paid cash for merchandise, $29,000
Paid a $2,000 cash dividend
Borrowed $6,000 from Friendly National Bank
Purchased *Ford Motor Company* stock, $5,000
Received a cash dividend from *Ford* of $200
Paid cash for other expenses, $8,000
Made a loan payment to Friendly Bank of $2,200, which included $200 interest
Cash balance at December 31, 2003, is $15,000

Required: Prepare a statement of cash flows for Greenfield Company for the year ended December 31, 2004. (Use a format similar to the one in Exhibit 10–1.)

LO 3: SIMPLE STATEMENT OF CASH FLOWS PREPARATION

10–24. The following information is from the records of the Jane Avery Company for the year ended December 31, 2005:

Purchased equipment for cash of $8,000
Cash sales to customers were $75,000
Sold Jane Avery Company stock for cash of $6,000
Loaned $1,000 to Denson Company
Sold equipment for cash of $1,000
Paid cash to employees for wages, $4,500
Borrowed $5,000 from Peoples National Bank
Paid cash for merchandise, $32,000
Paid a $500 cash dividend
Made a loan payment to Peoples Bank of $1,500, which included $100 interest
Purchased *DuPont Company* stock, $2,000
Received a cash dividend from *DuPont,* $100
Paid cash for other expenses, $3,000
Cash balance at December 31, 2004, is $7,500

Required: Prepare a statement of cash flows for Jane Avery Company for the year ended December 31, 2005. (Use a format similar to the one in Exhibit 10–1.)

LO 3: SIMPLE STATEMENT OF CASH FLOWS PREPARATION

10–25. The following information is from the records of the Beth Toland Company for the year ended December 31, 2005:

Paid cash to employees for wages, $7,000
Purchased equipment for cash of $3,000
Cash sales to customers were $80,000
Sold Beth Toland Company stock for cash of $9,000
Loaned $2,000 to Furman Company
Paid cash for merchandise, $24,000
Sold equipment for cash of $2,000
Borrowed $8,000 from Central National Bank
Paid a $100 cash dividend
Made a loan payment to Central Bank of $3,000, which included $500 interest
Purchased Lucent stock, $1,000
Received a cash dividend from Lucent, $50
Paid cash for other expenses, $2,000
Cash balance at December 31, 2004, is $4,500

Required: Prepare a statement of cash flows for Beth Toland Company for the year ended December 31, 2005. (Use a format similar to the one in Exhibit 10–1.)

LO 3: OPERATING ACTIVITIES SECTION PREPARATION—INDIRECT METHOD

10–26. Below are partial comparative balance sheets for Zhang Chinese Trading Company as of December 31, 2004, and 2003:

Zhang Chinese Trading Company
Partial Balance Sheets
December 31, 2004, and December 31, 2003
Current Assets and Current Liabilities Only
(in thousands)

	2004	**2003**	**Increase (Decrease)**
Current assets:			
Cash	$ 110	$ 150	$(40)
Accounts receivable	750	670	80
Merchandise inventory	620	680	(60)
Total current assets	$1,480	$1,500	$(20)
Current liabilities:			
Accounts payable	$ 550	$ 460	$ 90
Wages payable	28	38	(10)
Total current liabilities	$ 578	$ 498	$ 80

Additional Information: Net income for 2004 was $120,000. Included in the operating expenses for the year was depreciation expense of $30,000.

Required: Prepare the operating activities section of Zhang Chinese Trading Company's statement of cash flows for 2004 using the indirect method.

LO 3: OPERATING ACTIVITIES SECTION PREPARATION—INDIRECT METHOD

10–27. Following are partial comparative balance sheets for Sheridan Company as of December 31, 2005, and 2004:

Sheridan Company
Partial Balance Sheets
December 31, 2005, and December 31, 2004
Current Assets and Current Liabilities Only
(in thousands)

	2005	2004	Increase (Decrease)
Current assets:			
Cash	$3,400	$2,920	$480
Accounts receivable	1,825	2,212	(387)
Merchandise inventory	1,170	966	204
Prepaid expenses	240	270	(30)
Total current assets	$6,635	$6,368	$267
Current liabilities:	—	—	
Accounts payable	$2,321	$1,740	$581
Interest payable	0	200	(200)
Total current liabilities	$2,321	$1,940	$381

Additional Information: Net income for 2005 was $406,000. Included in the operating expenses for the year was depreciation expense of $175,000.

Required: Prepare the operating activities section of Sheridan Company's statement of cash flows for 2005 using the indirect method.

LO 3: OPERATING ACTIVITIES SECTION PREPARATION—INDIRECT METHOD

10–28. Below are partial comparative balance sheets for Vincent Scelta Company as of December 31, 2004, and 2003:

Vincent Scelta Company
Partial Balance Sheets
December 31, 2004, and December 31, 2003
Current Assets and Current Liabilities Only
(in thousands)

	2004	2003	Increase (Decrease)
Current assets:			
Cash	$2,110	$2,650	$(540)
Accounts receivable	1,254	977	277
Merchandise inventory	730	856	(126)
Prepaid expenses	127	114	13
Total current assets	$4,221	$4,597	$(376)
Current liabilities:	—	—	
Accounts payable	$1,054	$1,330	$(276)
Wages payable	125	75	50
Total current liabilities	$1,179	$1,405	$(226)

Additional Information: Net income for 2004 was $185,000. Included in the operating expenses for the year was depreciation expense of $102,000.

Required: Prepare the operating activities section of Scelta Company's statement of cash flows for 2004 using the indirect method.

LO 3: OPERATING ACTIVITIES SECTION PREPARATION—INDIRECT METHOD

10–29. Steven Hunter Corporation's worksheet for the preparation of its 2005 statement of cash flows included the following:

	January 1	December 31
Accounts receivable	$78,000	$71,000
Prepaid insurance	48,000	36,000
Inventory	56,000	75,000
Accounts payable	64,000	57,000

Steven Hunter Corporation reported net income of $450,000 for the year, and depreciation expense was $39,000.

Required: Prepare the operating activities section of Hunter Corporation's statement of cash flows for 2005 using the indirect method.

LO 3: INDIRECT METHOD PREPARATION OF THE STATEMENT OF CASH FLOWS

10–30. Use the balance sheets, income statement, and the additional information provided below to complete this problem.

Jim Boyd Company
Balance Sheets
As of December 31, 2005, and December 31, 2004
(in thousands)

	2005	2004
ASSETS:		
Current assets:		
Cash	$ 1,618	$1,220
Accounts receivable	1,925	2,112
Merchandise inventory	1,070	966
Prepaid expenses	188	149
Total current assets	$ 4,801	$4,447
Plant and equipment:		
Buildings	$4,818	$3,292
LESS: Accumulated depreciation	(361)	(300)
Buildings, net	$ 4,457	$2,992
Equipment	$1,434	$1,145
LESS: Accumulated depreciation	(141)	(100)
Equipment, net	$ 1,293	$1,045
Total plant and equipment	$ 5,750	$4,037
Total assets	$10,551	$8,484
LIABILITIES:		
Current liabilities:		
Accounts payable	$ 1,818	$ 1,686
Wages payable	900	1,100
Total current liabilities	$ 2,718	$ 2,786
Long-term liabilities	2,500	2,000
Total liabilities	$ 5,218	$4,786
STOCKHOLDERS' EQUITY:		
Common stock, no-par value	$ 3,390	$ 2,041
Retained earnings	1,943	1,657
Total stockholders' equity	$ 5,333	$3,698
Total liabilities and stockholders' equity	$10,551	$8,484

Jim Boyd Company
Income Statement
For the Year Ended December 31, 2005
(in thousands)

Net sales		$11,228
LESS: Cost of goods sold		7,751
Gross profit on sales		$ 3,477
Operating expenses:		
Depreciation—buildings and equipment	$ 102	
Other selling and administrative	2,667	
Total operating expenses		(2,769)
Operating income		$ 708
Interest expense		(168)
Income before taxes		$ 540
Income taxes		(114)
Net income		$ 426

Additional Information: There were no sales of plant and equipment during the year, and the company paid dividends to stockholders during the year of $140,000.

Required:

  a. Prepare Boyd Company's statement of cash flows for the year ended December 31, 2005, using the indirect method for operating activities.
  b. In which of the three categories of activities did Boyd use the majority of its cash during 2005?
  c. What does your answer to the previous question tell you about Boyd Company?
  d. From which of the three types of activities did Boyd obtain the majority of its cash during 2005?
  e. Is the activity you identified in the previous requirement an appropriate source of cash in the long run? Explain your reasoning.

LO 5: APPENDIX—DIRECT METHOD PREPARATION OF THE STATEMENT OF CASH FLOWS

10–31. Use the Boyd financial statements in 10–30 to complete the following requirements.

Required:

  a. Prepare Boyd Company's statement of cash flows for the year ended December 31, 2005, using the direct method for operating activities.
  b. In which of the three categories of activities did Boyd use the majority of its cash during 2005?
  c. What does your answer to the previous question tell you about Boyd Company?
  d. From which of the three types of activities did Boyd obtain the majority of its cash during 2005?
  e. Is the activity you identified in the previous requirement an appropriate source of cash in the long run? Explain your reasoning.

LO 4: FINANCIAL RATIO CALCULATIONS

10–32. This problem is a continuation of either problem 10–30 or 10–31. Use the financial statements in 10–30 and the statement of cash flows you prepared for problem 10–30 or 10–31 to complete the following requirements.

Required:

  a. Calculate operating cash flow to current debt ratio.
  b. Calculate the operating cash flow coverage ratio.
  c. What do these ratios tell you about the company? Explain your answer.

LO 4: INDIRECT METHOD PREPARATION OF THE STATEMENT OF CASH FLOWS

10–33. Use the balance sheets, income statement, and the additional information presented below to complete this problem.

Thomas Greco Company
Balance Sheets
As of December 31, 2005, and December 31, 2004
(in thousands)

	2005	**2004**
ASSETS:		
Current assets:		
Cash	$ 529	$ 660
Accounts receivable	1,006	1,011
Merchandise inventory	396	452
Prepaid expenses	38	62
Total current assets	$ 1,969	$ 2,185

Property, plant, and equipment:

Buildings	$2,000	$1,681
LESS: Accumulated depreciation	(176)	(146)
Buildings, net	$1,824	$1,535
Equipment	$ 809	$ 609
LESS: Accumulated depreciation	(76)	(61)
Equipment, net	733	548
Total plant and equipment	$2,557	$2,083
Total assets	$4,526	$4,268

LIABILITIES:

Current liabilities:

Accounts payable	$726	$ 809
Total current liabilities	$ 726	$ 809
Long-term liabilities		
Notes payable	2,250	1,800
Total long-term liabilities	2,250	1,800
Total liabilities	$2,976	$2,609

STOCKHOLDERS' EQUITY:

Common stock, no-par value	$1,300	$1,000
Retained earnings	250	659
Total stockholders' equity	$1,550	$1,659
Total liabilities and stockholders' equity	$4,526	$4,268

Thomas Greco Company
Income Statement
For the Year Ended December 31, 2005
(in thousands)

Sales		$6,391
LESS: Cost of goods sold		4,474
Gross profit on sales		$1,917
LESS: Operating expenses:		
Depreciation—buildings and equipment	$ 45	
Other selling and administrative	2,066	
Total operating expenses		(2,111)
Operating income		$ (194)
LESS: Interest expense		(145)
Income before taxes		$ (339)
Income taxes		0
Net loss		$ (339)

Additional Information: There were no sales of plant and equipment during the year, and the company paid dividends to stockholders during the year of $70,000.

Required:

a. Prepare Greco Company's statement of cash flows for the year ended December 31, 2005, using the indirect method for operating activities.

b. In which of the three broad activities did Greco use the majority of its cash during 2005?

c. What does your answer to the previous question tell you about Greco Company?

d. In which of the three broad activities did Greco obtain the majority of its cash during 2005?

e. Is the activity you identified in the previous requirement an appropriate source of cash in the long run? Explain your reasoning.

LO 5: APPENDIX—DIRECT METHOD PREPARATION OF THE STATEMENT OF CASH FLOWS

10–34. Use the Greco financial statements in 10–33 to complete the following requirements.

Required:

    a. Prepare Greco Company's statement of cash flows for the year ended December 31, 2005, using the direct method for operating activities.

    b. In which of the three broad activities did Greco use the majority of its cash during 2005?

    c. What does your answer to the previous question tell you about Greco Company?

    d. In which of the three broad activities did Greco obtain the majority of its cash during 2005?

    e. Is the activity you identified in the previous requirement an appropriate source of cash in the long run? Explain your reasoning.

LO 3: INDIRECT METHOD PREPARATION OF THE STATEMENT OF CASH FLOWS

10–35. Use the balance sheets, income statement, and the additional information provided below to complete this problem.

Walton Imports
Balance Sheets
As of December 31, 2004, and December 31, 2003

	2004		2003	
ASSETS:				
Current assets:				
Cash		$ 14,000		$ 26,400
Accounts receivable		48,000		38,000
Inventory		39,000		42,000
Prepaid expenses		10,000		15,000
Total current assets		$111,000		$121,400
Long-term investment		0		60,000
Property, plant, and equipment	$109,000		$53,000	
LESS: Accumulated depreciation	(13,000)		(6,000)	
Property, plant, and equipment, net		$ 96,000		$ 47,000
Total assets		$207,000		$228,400
LIABILITIES:				
Current liabilities:				
Accounts payable		$ 18,000		$ 49,000
Accrued expenses		11,650		10,650
Income taxes payable		3,750		5,750
Total current liabilities		$ 33,400		$ 65,400
Long-term liabilities:				
Notes payable		7,000		0
Bonds payable		30,000		110,000
Total long-term liabilities		37,000		110,000
Total liabilities		$ 70,400		$175,400
STOCKHOLDERS' EQUITY:				
Preferred stock, no par		10,000		8,000
Common stock, $1 par		$ 4,500		$ 3,500
Additional paid-in capital—common		17,500		13,500
Retained earnings		104,600		28,000
Total stockholders' equity		$136,600		$ 53,000
Total liabilities and stockholders' equity		$207,000		$228,400

Walton Imports
Income Statement
For the Year Ended December 31, 2004

Net sales		$585,000
Cost of goods sold		328,000
Gross profit on sales		$257,000
Operating expenses:		
Depreciation—buildings and equipment	$ 7,000	
Other selling and administrative	109,000	
Total operating expenses		(116,000)

Operating income	$141,000
Interest expense	(3,000)
Loss on sale of long-term investments	(20,000)
Income before taxes	$118,000
Income taxes	(35,400)
Net income	$ 82,600

Additional Information: Walton sold the long-term investments for cash of $40,000. There were no sales of property, plant, and equipment during the year. Walton paid cash dividends to stockholders during the year of $6,000.

Required:

a. Prepare a statement of cash flows for Walton Imports for the year ended December 31, 2004, using the indirect method for operating activities.
b. In which of the three categories of activities did Walton use the majority of its cash during 2004?
c. What does your answer to the previous question tell you about Walton Imports?
d. From which of the three types of activities did Walton obtain the majority of its cash during 2004?
e. Is the activity you identified in the previous requirement an appropriate source of cash in the long run? Explain your reasoning.

LO 5: APPENDIX—DIRECT METHOD PREPARATION OF THE STATEMENT OF CASH FLOWS

10–36. Use the Walton Imports financial statements in 10–35 to complete the following requirements.

Required:

a. Prepare a statement of cash flows for Walton Imports for the year ended December 31, 2004, using the direct method for operating activities.
b. In which of the three categories of activities did Walton use the majority of its cash during 2004?
c. What does your answer to the previous question tell you about Walton Imports?
d. From which of the three types of activities did Walton obtain the majority of its cash during 2004?
e. Is the activity you identified in the previous requirement an appropriate source of cash in the long run? Explain your reasoning.

LO 4: FINANCIAL RATIO CALCULATIONS

10–37. This problem is a continuation of either problem 10–35 or 10–36. Use the Walton Imports financial statements in 10–35 and the statement of cash flows you prepared for problem 10–35 or 10–36 to complete the following requirements.

Required:

a. Calculate operating cash flow to current debt ratio.
b. Calculate the operating cash flow coverage ratio.
c. What do these ratios tell you about the company? Explain your answer.

LO 4: STATEMENT OF CASH FLOWS CONCEPTS

10–38. Below is Steve Frim Company's statement of cash flows for the year ended December 31, 2005:

Steve Frim Company
Statement of Cash Flows
For the Year Ended December 31, 2005
(in thousands)

Cash Flows from Operating Activities:

Net income		$ 389
Adjustments to reconcile net income		
to net cash provided by operating activities:		
Depreciation expense	$ 131	
Increase in accounts receivable	(287)	

Increase in merchandise inventory	(104)	
Increase in prepaid expense	(70)	
Decrease in accounts payable	(4)	(334)
Net cash provided by operating activities		$ 55

Cash Flows from Investing Activities:

Purchase of building	$(1,255)	
Purchase of equipment	(304)	
Net cash used by investing activities		(1,559)

Cash Flows from Financing Activities:

Proceeds from long-term loan	$ 800	
Proceeds from sale of common stock	300	
Payment of cash dividends	(100)	
Net cash provided by financing activities		1,000
Net decrease in cash during 2005		$ (504)
Cash balance, January 1, 2005		1,200
Cash balance, December 31, 2005		$ 696

Required: Respond to the following questions:

  a. For which of the three broad types of activities did Frim use the majority of its cash during 2005?
  b. What does your answer to the previous question tell you about Frim Company?
  c. From which of the three broad types of activities did Frim obtain the majority of its cash during 2005?
  d. Is the activity you identified in the previous requirement an appropriate source of cash in the long run? Explain your reasoning.

LO 4: FINANCIAL RATIO CALCULATIONS

10–39. Refer to problem 10–38. Use the statement of cash flows in problem 10–38 to complete the following requirements.

Required: Assume that average current liabilities total $338,000 and average total liabilities total $1,180,000.

  a. Calculate operating cash flow to current debt ratio.
  b. Calculate the operating cash flow coverage ratio.
  c. What do these ratios tell you about the company? Explain your answer.

LO 4: STATEMENT OF CASH FLOWS CONCEPTS

10–40. Below is Flaherty Company's statement of cash flows for the year ended December 31, 2005:

Flaherty Company
Statement of Cash Flows
For the Year Ended December 31, 2005
(in thousands)

Cash Flows from Operating Activities:

Net income		$ 1,608
Adjustments to reconcile net income to net cash provided by operating activities:		
Depreciation expense	$ 218	
Increase in accounts receivable	(341)	
Decrease in merchandise inventory	81	
Increase in prepaid expense	(100)	
Increase in accounts payable	154	12
Net cash provided by operating activities		$ 1,620

Cash Flows from Investing Activities:

Purchase of building	$(1,000)	
Purchase of equipment	(200)	
Net cash used by investing activities		(1,200)

Cash Flows from Financing Activities:

Repayment of long-term loan	$ (350)	
Proceeds from sale of common stock	350	
Payment of cash dividends	(100)	
Net cash used by financing activities		(100)
Net increase in cash during 2005		$ 320
Cash balance, January 1, 2005		430
Cash balance, December 31, 2005		$ 750

Required: Respond to the following questions:

a. For which of the three types of activities did Flaherty use the majority of its cash during 2005?

b. What does your answer to the previous question tell you about Flaherty Company?

c. From which of the three types of activities did Flaherty obtain the majority of its cash during 2005?

d. Is the activity you identified in the previous requirement an appropriate source of cash in the long run? Explain your reasoning.

LO 4: FINANCIAL RATIO CALCULATIONS

10–41. Refer to problem 10–40. Use the statement of cash flows in problem 10–40 to complete the following requirements.

Required: Assume that average current liabilities total $680,000 and average total liabilities total $1,790,000.

a. Calculate operating cash flow to current debt ratio.

b. Calculate the operating cash flow coverage ratio.

c. What do these ratios tell you about the company? Explain your answer.

LO 4: ANALYSIS OF CASH FLOW INFORMATION

10–42. Below are the totals from the main three sections of Kay Carnes and Company's most recent statement of cash flows:

Net cash provided by operating activities	$ 1,812,000
Net cash used by investing activities	$(1,280,000)
Net cash used by financing activities	$ (153,000)

Required:

a. What do these totals tell you about Carnes and Company?

b. What additional information would you want to see before you analyze Carnes and Company's ability to generate positive cash flow in the future?

c. Did Carnes and Company have a net income or loss for the period? What additional information would you want before trying to predict the company's net income for the next period?

LO 4: ANALYSIS OF CASH FLOW INFORMATION

10–43. Below are the totals from the main three sections of Mary D. Maury and Company's most recent statement of cash flows:

Net cash used by operating activities	$ (835,000)
Net cash used by investing activities	$(1,280,000)
Net cash provided by financing activities	$ 2,153,000

Required:

a. What do these totals tell you about Maury and Company?

b. What additional information would you want to see before you analyze Maury and Company's ability to generate positive cash flow in the future?

c. Did Maury and Company have a net income or loss for the period? What additional information would you want before trying to predict the company's net income for the next period?

LO 4: ANALYSIS OF CASH FLOW INFORMATION

10–44. Below are the totals from the main three sections of Paul Smolenski and Company's most recent statement of cash flows:

Net cash used by operating activities	$(1,409,000)
Net cash provided by investing activities	$ 1,980,000
Net cash used by financing activities	$ (303,000)

Required:

    a. What do these totals tell you about Smolenski and Company?

    b. What additional information would you want to see before you analyze Smolenski and Company's ability to generate positive cash flow in the future?

LO 4: DISCUSSION

10–45. One of the main purposes of the statement of cash flows is to disclose a company's sources of cash during a specific time period and what it used the cash for. From this standpoint, the statement of cash flows is considered a tool of accounting. Such tools are developed to solve problems.

Required:

    a. Explain in your own words how the income statement and balance sheet using accrual accounting take the focus off cash.

    b. Describe how the statement of cash flows serves as a tool to bring the focus of economic decision makers back to cash.

LO 4: DISCUSSION—DIRECT METHOD VERSUS INDIRECT METHOD

10–46. Compare the two methods for preparing the statement of cash flows, the direct method and the indirect method. Which sections are different and which sections are the same?

LO 3: COMPLEX EQUIPMENT SALE AND PURCHASE CALCULATIONS

10–47. The Calvert Company is preparing a statement of cash flows for the year ended December 31, 2004. Selected beginning and ending account balances are as follows:

	Beginning	Ending
Machinery	$450,000	$475,500
Accumulated depreciation—machinery	(95,000)	(129,000)
Loss on sale of machinery		(2,000)

During the year, the company received $44,500 for a machine that cost $49,500 and purchased other items of equipment.

Required:

    a. Compute the depreciation on machinery for the year.

    b. Compute the amount of machinery purchases for the year.

LO 3: COMPLEX EQUIPMENT SALE AND PURCHASE CALCULATIONS

10–48. Charles Lewis Company is preparing a statement of cash flows for the year ended December 31, 2005. Selected beginning and ending account balances are as follows:

	Beginning	Ending
Machinery	$250,000	$280,000
Accumulated depreciation—machinery	(65,000)	(89,000)
Gain on sale of machinery		2,000

During the year, the company received $50,000 for a machine that cost $65,000 and purchased some other items of equipment.

Required:

    a. Compute the depreciation on machinery for the year.

    b. Compute the amount of machinery purchases for the year.

LO 3: COMPLEX EQUIPMENT SALE AND PURCHASE CALCULATIONS

10–49. The Morrissey Company is preparing a statement of cash flows for the year ended December 31, 2004. Selected beginning and ending account balances are as follows:

	Beginning	Ending
Computers	$300,000	$390,000
Accumulated depreciation—computers	165,000	215,000
Gain on sale of computers		12,000

During the year, the company received $20,000 for a computer that cost $40,000 and purchased other items of equipment.

Required:

    a. Compute the depreciation on computers for the year.
    b. Compute the amount of computer purchases for the year.

Financial Reporting Exercises ●

10–50. Using the **Securities and Exchange Commission**'s (**SEC**'s) Electronic Data Gathering, Analysis, and Retrieval (EDGAR) system, obtain a copy of the **Guess, Inc.,** income statement and balance sheet for 2001 and 2000 from the company's Form 10-K from 2001.

Required:

    a. Does this company use the direct or indirect method for their operating cash flows?
    b. List the total cash flows for the operating, investing, and financing activities sections for 2001 and state whether you think the number is favorable or not.
    c. Calculate the operating cash flow to current debt ratio for 2001.
    d. Calculate the operating cash flow coverage ratio for 2001.
    e. Based on this information, what impression do you get about this company as an investment possibility?

10–51. Using the SEC's EDGAR system, obtain a copy of the **Liz Claiborne, Inc.,** income statement and balance sheet for 2001 and 2000 from the company's Form 10-K from 2001.

Required:

    a. Does this company use the direct or indirect method for their operating cash flows?
    b. List the total cash flows for the operating, investing, and financing activities sections for 2001 and state whether you think the number is favorable or not.
    c. Calculate the operating cash flow to current debt ratio for 2001.
    d. Calculate the operating cash flow coverage ratio for 2001.
    e. Based on the information about these two companies (**Guess, Inc.,** and **Liz Claiborne, Inc.**), circle for each ratio which number you think is more favorable. Which company would you be more likely to invest in?

10–52. Visit the PHLIP Web site for this book at *www.prenhall.com/werner* to locate the **Walt Disney Company** link. Find **Disney**'s statement of cash flows to answer the following questions.

Required:

    a. List the total cash flows for operating, investing, and financing activities for each of the years shown in the report's statement of cash flows.
    b. Does the company use the direct or indirect method of preparing the statement of cash flows?
    c. Have the operating cash flows been positive?
    d. List the transactions that affect the cash flow for investing activities.
    e. List the transactions that affect the cash flow for financing activities.
    f. Write a brief report that summarizes your feelings regarding information provided by **Disney**'s statements of cash flows.

10–53. Visit the PHLIP Web site for this book at *www.prenhall.com/werner* to find the **Coca-Cola Company** link. Find **Coke**'s statement of cash flows to answer the following questions.

Required:

 a. List the total cash flows for operating, investing, and financing activities for each of the years shown in the report's statement of cash flows.

 b. Does the company use the direct or indirect method of preparing the statement of cash flows?

 c. Have the operating cash flows been positive?

 d. List the transactions that affect the cash flow for investing activities.

 e. List the transactions that affect the cash flow for financing activities.

 f. Write a brief report that summarizes your feelings regarding information provided by *Coca-Cola*'s statements of cash flows.

ANNUAL REPORT PROJECT

10–54. Section 10—The Statement of Cash Flows

In this assignment, you will prepare a report based on your company's statement of cash flows.

Required: Prepare a report that includes the following information:

 a. A schedule that presents the cash flows from operating, investing, and financing activities for your company and that of its peer for the past three years.

 b. Examine the operating cash flows. Have the operating cash flows been positive? Have the operating cash flows increased or decreased in the years presented? Are the operating cash flows sufficient to pay principal and interest on debt and meet other cash requirements? What method is used to prepare the operating activities section of the statement of cash flows, direct or indirect?

 c. Examine investing cash flows. For each line presented in the investing section, discuss how it impacts the other financial statements and other parts of the annual report. Include the page number where you found the information. The management discussion and analysis may be a very good place to find this information.

 d. Examine the financing cash flows. For each line presented in this section, discuss how it impacts other financial statements. The balance sheet and statement of stockholders' equity may be an excellent place to look.

 e. Also comment on significant changes that have occurred over time regarding each company's sources and uses of cash. For example, have cash flows from operating activities been increasing or decreasing? Have cash flows from investing activities been increasing or decreasing? Have cash flows from financing activities been increasing or decreasing? Provide an explanation of the significance of the changes or the lack of change.

 f. A schedule that presents the following ratios for your company with those of the peer company you selected:

  • Operating cash flows to current debt ratio for the current year
  • Operating cash flow coverage ratio for the current year

 g. Comment in your report on the information that the comparison of each one of the ratios provides. How does your company compare to its peer?

 h. Your report should conclude with a summary of what you think of your company's sources and uses of cash and your thoughts regarding how your company's statement of cash flows information compares to that of its peer.

CHAPTER 11

Financial Statement Analysis—A Closer Look

During lunch one day, your classmate Marcus tells you all about a company that has net income of $250,000. It's a small company owned by a mutual acquaintance, and you are both quite impressed with the profits the company has generated. You begin to dream about how wonderful it would be to own a company with that amount of income. It's a lot of money, and you think of all the nice things you could do with it.

A company that has a net income of $250,000 must be successful, stable, and profitable, right? Well, not necessarily. Even though income of $250,000 could be a sign of exceptional business performance, it could just as easily be the result of a dismal year of underachievement. For example, if the company had sales of $3 million and assets totaling $2 million, income of a quarter of a million dollars might be fine, but what if sales were a whopping $200 million or the investment in assets was a huge $100 million? In that case, an income of $250,000 would be unacceptably low. What's more, it's possible that the company's debt is so high and it generates so little cash that the owner will never get a dime of the company's profits.

In order to properly evaluate a company, we must not be tempted to use just one or two financial statement amounts to form our opinion. In fact, even if we examine every amount on an entire set of financial statements, it is unlikely that this alone will enable us to make a well-informed judgment regarding the company's potential for future success. Financial statements alone simply do not provide enough information to enable us to do this. We must consider other important factors such as general business conditions, the outlook for the company's industry, and the economic and political conditions that impact the business.

As we mentioned in previous chapters, the *Securities and Exchange Commission (SEC)* requires publicly traded companies to publish an annual report. It also requires companies to file other reports, such as an annual Form 10-K. These reports contain general information about the company and its business, at least five years of key financial information, income statements and statements of cash flows for three years, and balance sheets for two years. While these resources provide a wealth of information, gathering and reading it is just the first step in using the information to make a sound economic decision. For one thing, we need to look beyond the numbers. In other words, we can't just look at the financial statements—we must analyze them.

Financial statement analysis means looking beyond the face of the financial statements to gain additional insight into a company. In this chapter, we will focus primarily on ratio analysis—the most comprehensive form of financial statement analysis. Most of the material in this chapter will already be familiar to you. This is because in earlier chapters we introduced the computations of all the ratios we present in this chapter. In this chapter, we will show you something more important—how to use their results in proper combination with other information to make economic decisions.

Learning Objectives

After completing your work on this chapter, you should be able to do the following:

1. Identify the three major categories of users of financial statement analysis and describe the objectives of each.

2. Gather information to evaluate the political climate and general economic conditions and describe the ways each of them can affect business.

3. Locate sources of information about specific industries.

4. Describe the two industry classification systems and explain what a NAICS code or an SIC code indicates.

5. Describe the purpose of ratio analysis and the four aspects of business it helps users evaluate.

6. Calculate and use financial ratios designed to measure a company's profitability, efficiency, liquidity, and solvency, and evaluate a company's ratios compared to those of peer companies and industry averages.

7. Describe the limitations of financial statement analysis.

◆ FINANCIAL STATEMENT ANALYSIS—WHO DOES IT AND WHY

Why would someone take the time to analyze a company's financial statements? Well, usually because they are making an economic decision, and understanding the company's current position and what has happened to a company in the past can make that decision easier. The decision maker could be a potential creditor trying to decide whether to lend money to a company, a potential investor trying to decide whether to buy stock in the company, or a manager trying to select the best course of action for the company. Other decision makers include current and prospective employees, internal and external auditors, customers, suppliers, and government agencies. By providing additional insight, financial statement analysis helps decision makers reduce the risk of making poor choices. This is because financial statement analysis often uncovers financial strengths and weaknesses that would otherwise go unnoticed. Because there is an array of decision makers that might analyze financial statements, and because the objectives of each vary, their perspectives on the results of the analysis will differ.

In this chapter, we will focus on just three types of decision makers:

1. Creditors (short-term and long-term)
2. Equity investors (present and potential)
3. Company managers

Let's examine objectives of each of these economic decision makers.

OBJECTIVES OF CREDITORS

Some creditors make loans to companies for a relatively short period of time while others lend on a long-term basis. There are two major types of short-term creditors. One type, called *trade creditors*, provides goods and services to a business on credit and expects payment within whatever time period is customary in the industry (in most industries somewhere between 10 and 90 days). Normally, trade creditors don't charge interest, so the credit they extend to companies amounts to interest-free financing. Trade creditors analyze financial statements to determine whether they should grant or continue to grant credit to a particular customer. Their goal is to determine the likelihood that the customer will pay them promptly in the future.

Banks and other lending institutions also extend short-term credit to businesses. That is, they make short-term loans to companies, often in the form of credit lines that support the day-to-day operations of businesses. Unlike trade creditors, banks do charge interest. The objectives of both trade creditors and lending institutions, however, are quite similar. Both want to be assured that they will receive prompt payment for the credit they extend.

Long-term creditors have a very different perspective than short-term creditors. These creditors—generally banks and corporate bondholders—lend money to companies for relatively long time periods. Therefore, their principal objective in analyzing a company's financial statements is to acquire information to help them determine whether the company is likely to be financially healthy over the long haul. These creditors are trying to assure themselves that, in addition to making interest payments, their borrowers will be able to pay back loans when they finally come due.

OBJECTIVES OF EQUITY INVESTORS

In this context, equity investors are those who have purchased or might purchase an ownership interest in a company, meaning those that have already invested (current equity investors) and those that might invest in the future (potential equity investors). Equity investors expect a reasonable return *on* their investment and, ultimately, the return *of* their investment. As we mentioned in Chapter 3, the return for a corporate equity investor has two components:

1. Dividends—the distribution of corporate earnings to stockholders
2. Stock appreciation—the increase in the market value of stock between the time it is purchased and the time it is sold

Therefore, when analyzing financial statements, the principal objective of present and potential equity investors is to determine whether it is likely that the combination of dividends and stock appreciation will provide an adequate return. The return depends on the company's ability to generate income and cash in the future. This is because dividends can only be paid if a company has sufficient retained earnings and cash, both of which depend on a company's ability to generate earnings in the future. Further, many experts consider a company's ability to generate earnings to be the single most important factor affecting the value of its stock over time.

Both creditors and equity investors are external decision makers. However, financial statement analysis is also a useful tool for internal decision makers—namely, a company's management.

OBJECTIVES OF MANAGEMENT

management accounting The branch of accounting developed to meet the informational needs of internal decision makers.

financial accounting The branch of accounting developed to meet the informational needs of external decision makers.

Corporate managers are responsible for operating the company for the benefit of its owners. To make decisions on behalf of the company that maximize the use of company assets and to earn profits, managers rely on two types of information. Primarily, they use **management accounting** information—the information available only to insiders. Management accounting information also helps managers evaluate their company's performance. Corporate managers also use **financial accounting** information—the accounting information available to outsiders.

You may study management accounting as part of your later coursework, but for now, we will limit our discussion in this chapter to financial accounting information.

A corporate manager's performance is evaluated in large part by the financial success of his or her company as reflected in the company's financial statements. Therefore, these managers have a personal stake in seeing the company appear as successful as possible in the financial statements.

It is a legitimate objective to present the company in its best light, since a company's relationship with creditors, stockholders, and other outsiders is vital. However, a corporate manager's own self-interest combined with his or her justifiable desire to analyze the company's financial statements in a way that favorably impresses external parties can lead to managing the financial statements rather than managing the business. *Enron, WorldCom,* and *Global Crossing* quickly come to mind as examples of companies in which corporate managers ceased to manage the business and, instead, managed the numbers.

Some corporate executives have yielded to the pressure to show a strong financial picture by falsifying amounts that appear on their company's financial statements. This devastating practice not only compromises the managers' own personal integrity, but also the integrity of all accounting information. These unscrupulous managers have allowed greed and their desire for power, prestige, and wealth to damage part of the very fabric on which our economic markets are based—reliable financial information. If economic decision makers cannot rely on the information companies provide, they lose faith in the information and they also lose faith in the companies themselves.

Unfortunately, this loss of faith is not limited to the companies that have been implicated in such falsifications. It extends to other companies as suspicions grow and the integrity of all financial reporting comes into question. This is because decision makers who need to use the information are unable to tell the difference between information that includes falsifications and information that doesn't. The result is that everyone loses faith in all financial information as more and more cases of "aggressive accounting" and outright falsification of financial information surface.

Discussion Questions ●

11–1. What do you think the phrase "managing the financial statements rather than managing the business" means?

11–2. Assume you have invested $10,000 in Company A and $10,000 in Company B. Both are solid companies according to their financial statements. In fact, their financial statements look quite similar to one another. Then, Company A goes bankrupt, shocking the financial community. The value of your investment in Company A plummets to a fraction of what it once was. It turns out that the company's financial statements had been doctored in some way to conceal huge financial weaknesses. In light of what happened to your investment in Company A, how do you feel about your investment in Company B?

Now that we have discussed the basic objectives of three primary financial information users, we will explore how to gather the background information you will need for financial statement analysis.

◆ GATHERING BACKGROUND INFORMATION—AN IMPORTANT FIRST STEP

In the appendix to Chapter 1, we discussed how you could find background information on virtually any publicly traded company. If you want to do a thorough analysis of a company's financial statements, use the sources in that chapter's appendix to gather enough information to put the company's financial statement information in proper context. Businesses do not operate in a vacuum, so it is important to also gather background information about a company's external environment. In its *Conceptual Framework of Accounting*, the Financial Accounting Standards Board (FASB) warns that external factors can seriously affect a company's performance:

> *Those who use financial information for business and economic decisions need to combine information provided by financial reporting with pertinent information from other sources, for example, information about general economic conditions or expectations, political events and political climate, or industry outlook.*[1]

When we are analyzing data from financial statements, we should also consider the three factors mentioned by the FASB: general economic conditions, political events and the political climate, and the industry outlook.

GENERAL ECONOMIC CONDITIONS AND EXPECTATIONS

The general economic environment in which a company operates affects its business activity and therefore its financial results. For a company producing goods bought by the general public, bright economic conditions generally enhance sales. For a company manufacturing and selling equipment to other companies, an economy that encourages business growth is an important positive factor. So we must first consider general economic conditions and expectations when evaluating the performance and overall financial position of a business.

---

[1]Statement of Financial Accounting Concepts No. 1, paragraph 22.

The health of the American economy and information about anticipated changes in economic conditions receives widespread daily news coverage. Popular business periodicals such as *BusinessWeek*, the *Wall Street Journal*, and *Fortune* inform their readers about current economic conditions. Business analysts, economists, and politicians often voice their views on television and radio. Additionally, statistical data on measures of economic health (e.g., gross domestic product, consumer price index) are available in such books as *The Economic Indicators Handbook*. The U.S. Department of Commerce, in a monthly publication called *Survey of Current Business*, provides data from dozens of general economic and business cycle indicators. Remember, though, all of these "expert" predictions of the future of the United States and world economies are, in fact, nothing more than educated guesses. Use this information carefully!

Although general economic conditions certainly affect a company's performance, we should not totally excuse poor company performance because the economy is in a downturn. Neither should a company's exceptional performance be dismissed as simply the product of a healthy economy. **Kmart** declared bankruptcy at the same time business was booming at **Target** and **Wal-Mart. Lowe's Home Improvement** has been expanding rapidly over the past decade, while **Home Base** went out of business. And no one believes that **Enron**'s collapse was due totally to what was happening in the economy. Economic conditions provide *one context* within which we evaluate the results of business activity. We must also consider other external factors.

POLITICAL EVENTS AND POLITICAL CLIMATE

Politics is the second external factor mentioned by the FASB. The terms *political events* and *political climate* are closely related, yet they are different. A political event is an action that has already taken place, whereas a political climate is a situation that can lead to an action.

Each political party takes credit when the general economy improves and blames the others when it declines. That's the nature of politics. The truth is that both improvement and decline in the general economy result from many interrelated and complex factors. Indeed, the factors affecting the general economy are so complicated and intertwined that no political party can control it enough to take credit or blame. Still, there is no question that what goes on in politics, both domestic and foreign, has a significant influence on the general economy as well as on the world of business. The actions taken by Congress and the president on such matters as the amount of government regulation, income taxes, health care, and welfare reform have an enormous impact on the general economy. And we know that changes in the general economy will affect the level of business activity.

In the last decade of the 20th century, the collapse of the Soviet Union, the reunification of Germany, and other world political events that marked the end of the Cold War had strong repercussions in the U.S. economy. These foreign political events changed the entire defense industry, which created a ripple effect on many other industries and the communities that depend on them. Reduced purchases by the Pentagon of items used for national defense, for example, forced such companies as **Motorola, Lockheed,** and **Rockwell International** to make major adjustments in their businesses.

Certainly no one would question the impact the terrorist attack on the World Trade Center on September 11, 2001, had on the United States economy, and indeed, on that of the rest of the world. When President Bush announced the war on terrorism shortly after the attack, the implication for companies in the defense industry was enormous.

In the United States, the political climate is generally reflected in public opinion. For the past three decades, the public has scrutinized companies' positions on social and environmental issues. The concept of being "politically correct" arose from such public scrutiny. As we discussed in Chapter 1, a wise firm pays close attention to its social responsibility and frequently describes its corporate citizenship in its annual report. A growing number of investors have resolved to invest their money only in companies that have a genuine commitment to responsible behavior. This trend has generated a broader sense of social responsibility in American corporations.

Where, then, can you find accurate, objective information about a company's corporate citizenship? Your library most likely has publications intended to give you this information, but the evaluations you read will reflect the writer's views of corporate social responsibility, which may not coincide with your own. We suggest that instead of naively accepting such appraisals, you carefully consider the perspective of each author.

INDUSTRY OUTLOOK

The third factor to consider when using financial information is the industry in which a company operates, because industry affiliation may define the company's prospects for future growth. As Roy Taub, vice president of Standard and Poor's, once pointed out:

> *The industry is the environment in which the company operates and it defines both the opportunities the company may seize and the challenges it must face.*[2]

Industry opportunities and challenges are key considerations in evaluating a company's outlook. For example, a company in an industry that is facing an overall decline in demand may be powerless to take any action to ensure its own future growth. As we mentioned earlier, cuts in the federal defense budget resulted in reduced demand for such items as military aircraft and tanks, affecting the entire industry producing these goods. Certainly, this type of industry-wide trend touches all companies within the industry.

Government action is not the only force that produces industry-wide effects. Technological change often spurs spectacular growth within an industry. The field of telecommunications, for instance, has undergone a revolution in the past two decades. Just a few years ago, the fax machine was an expensive luxury—a form of communication reserved for "big business." Today, most personal computers come from the factory with internal fax capabilities.

Often, a technological change that opens the doors of opportunity in one industry closes them in another. For example, the development of personal computers has virtually wiped out opportunities for expansion among companies producing typewriters. But remember that each threat produces opportunity. Adaptable companies change their product mix to seize upon new opportunities and discontinue product lines that no longer have markets. So when considering a company's outlook for the future, it is important to learn what likely lies ahead for the entire industry.

Discussion Question ●

11–3. Changes in society, family structures, and the way people behave and interact have always had dramatic impact on business. Cite two examples of such changes in your lifetime, identify industries they have affected, and describe how they did so.

Not only does a company's industry affiliation affect its opportunities, but it may also define the challenges ahead. For example, a few decades ago, companies did not have to consider the environmental impact of their actions. After the Environmental Protection Agency (EPA) was established, however, many companies were forced to spend significant amounts of money to comply with EPA regulations. These regulations cost some industries more than others. For example, when the EPA banned the use of DDT as a pesticide, companies that manufactured this product either had to convert their factories to produce other products or they went out of business. The impact of this ban was also felt in agriculture, as farmers who had depended on DDT as their primary pesticide were forced to switch to less effective, sometimes more expensive, products.

The flip side of government regulation is deregulation. When the government suddenly discontinues its regulation and frees the market, this has an impact on all companies operating within the deregulated industry. For example, when the federal government deregulated the commercial airline industry in the early 1980s, all airlines were affected. Prior to deregulation, the federal government set standard airfares. All airlines flying passengers from one specific destination to another were required to charge the

---

[2]*S&P*, 1983, p. 2.

same fare. Companies competed on amenities (in-flight movies, food, drink, and the like), not on price. The government also required airlines to operate unprofitable flights for the convenience of customers in underpopulated areas. Fares of profitable flights were set high enough to offset the companies' losses from these unprofitable flights.

With deregulation came competition. Forced to make every flight profitable, airlines canceled many routes and began scrambling to attract customers. The result was a price war that forced several legendary carriers such as ***Pan American Airlines*** and ***Eastern Airlines*** out of business. Deregulation was seen by newer "upstart" companies such as ***Southwest Airlines*** and ***America West Airlines*** as an opportunity. Unregulated competition became an environment of survival of the fittest, and many companies— both new and old—did not survive.

Discussion Questions ●

11–4. Identify two industries and describe their similarities and their differences.
11–5. If two companies offered you upper-level management positions—one from each of the industries you identified in your response to question 11–4—which would you take? Why?
11–6. If you had $2,000 to invest and your only option was to invest it all in one of two companies—one from each of the industries you identified in your response to question 11–4—which would you choose? Explain your reasoning.

Where do you look for information about a particular industry? Several sources are available. *Standard and Poor's Industry Surveys* is composed of numerous sections with various types of information. One section offers recent articles about each industry written by professional business analysts or drawn from business publications. Another good source is the *U.S. Industry & Trade Outlook*, which offers background information and projections for the 10 fastest-growing and 10 slowest-growing industries, 40 service industries, and over 150 manufacturing industries. This book includes references to sources that contain more detailed information about each industry. *Mergent's Industry Review* provides comparative statistics on specific industries. These are three good examples available in your library.

Heeding the warning of the FASB, economic decision makers should gather background information regarding general economic conditions and expectations, political climate and events, and industry outlook. Anyone analyzing financial statements must consider the impact of each of these factors on a company's past performance and its future prospects, for they provide the context within which financial data should be evaluated.

Now we turn to actually analyzing financial statement information.

◆ ANALYZING FINANCIAL STATEMENTS—*PIER 1 IMPORTS*

In the sections that follow, we will analyze the financial statements of ***Pier 1 Imports, Inc.*** As you may know, ***Pier 1 Imports*** is an international specialty retailer of decorative home furnishings, furniture, and gifts. The company was established in 1962 and now has over 900 stores and more than 17,500 employees. A copy of ***Pier 1***'s 2002 annual report (on page F–503) is included as an appendix to this text. Since the computation of each ratio will be illustrated using the ***Pier 1*** financial statements presented in the company's 2002 annual report, take a look at it before you try to follow the ratio calculations and the way we analyze them. Be certain you understand how we determine which items from the balance sheet, income statement, and statement of cash flows we use for each ratio.

We will calculate 17 financial ratios using ***Pier 1 Imports***' 2002 financial statements as an example. As you recall, we included ratio calculations near the end of several earlier chapters. Because of this, you should have no difficulty understanding the calculations we present. In fact, the calculations are exactly the same as those in earlier chapters. Exhibit 11–1 on page F–454 presents a list of the 17 ratios we will use as we analyze ***Pier 1***'s financial statements.

EXHIBIT 11–1 Summary of Key Ratios

Ratio	Calculation	Purpose of Ratio	Reference
Profitability Ratios			
1. Gross profit margin ratio	$\dfrac{\text{Gross profit}}{\text{Net sales}}$	Measures the percentage gross profit generated by each sales dollar	Chapter 4, page F–134
2. Net profit margin ratio	$\dfrac{\text{Net income}}{\text{Net sales}}$	Measures the percentage profit generated by each sales dollar	Chapter 4, page F–134
3. Rate of return on assets ratio	$\dfrac{\text{Net income} + \text{Interest expense}}{\text{Average total assets}}$	Measures the rate of return earned on investment in assets	Chapter 4, page F–135
4. Rate of return on common equity ratio	$\dfrac{\text{Net income} - \text{Preferred dividend}}{\text{Average common stockholders' equity}}$	Measures the rate of return earned on investment in equity	Chapter 4, page F–135
5. Dividend payout ratio	$\dfrac{\text{Cash dividends}}{\text{Net income}}$	Indicates the proportion of net income paid out in dividends	Chapter 4, page F–136
6. Earnings per share	$\dfrac{\text{Net income} - \text{Preferred dividend}}{\text{Average common shares outstanding}}$	Measures the earning per common share of stock	Chapter 4, page F–136, and Chapter 9, page F–372
7. Price-to-earnings ratio	$\dfrac{\text{Average market price per share of stock}}{\text{Earnings per share}}$	A measure of the market price per common share compared to the earnings per share	Chapter 4, page F–137
Efficiency Ratios			
8. Asset turnover ratio	$\dfrac{\text{Net sales}}{\text{Average total assets}}$	Indicates a firm's ability to generate revenues from a given level of assets	Chapter 9, page F–376
9. Receivables turnover ratio	$\dfrac{\text{Net sales}}{\text{Average accounts receivable}}$	An indication of the quality of a company's accounts receivable; indicates how quickly a company collects its accounts receivable	Chapter 9, page F–378
10. Inventory turnover ratio	$\dfrac{\text{Cost of goods sold}}{\text{Average inventory}}$	An indication of the quality of a company's inventory; indicates how long a company holds inventory	Chapter 8, page F–328
Liquidity Ratios			
11. Current ratio	$\dfrac{\text{Current assets}}{\text{Current liabilities}}$	Indicates a company's ability to meet short-term obligation	Chapter 9, page F–378
12. Quick ratio	$\dfrac{\text{Cash} + \text{Short-term investments} + \text{Current receivables}}{\text{Current liabilities}}$	Measures short-term liquidity more stringently than the current ratio does	Chapter 9, page F–379
13. Operating cash flow to current debt ratio	$\dfrac{\text{Cash provided by operating activities}}{\text{Average current liabilities}}$	A measure of the sufficiency of cash provided by operating activities relative to current liabilities	Chapter 10, page F–423

Solvency Ratios			
14. Debt ratio	Total liabilities / Total assets	Measures the proportion of assets financed by debt	Chapter 3, page F–92
15. Debt-to-equity ratio	Total liabilities / Total equity	Compares the amount of debt financing to the amount of equity financing	Chapter 3, page F–93
16. Times interest earned ratio	Earnings before interest and income taxes / Interest expense	Indicates a company's ability to make its periodic interest payments	Chapter 9, page F–379
17. Operating cash flow coverage ratio	Cash provided by operating activities / Average total liabilities	A measure of the sufficiency of cash provided by operating activities relative to total liabilities	Chapter 10, page F–423

EXHIBIT 11–1 *Continued*

A particular ratio for just one company for a single year doesn't tell you very much. Let's think of it this way. Suppose your friend Mark tells you that he walked from one end of Duval Street to the other in 20 minutes. Would you be impressed? You might be if you knew something about Duval Street. What if he told you that the first time he walked the length of Duval Street it took him over an hour, or what if you knew that it took three of your other friends 45 minutes to walk it? Once you had this additional information for comparison, you would probably be impressed that Mark was able to improve his time so much and that he could walk the distance so much faster than his peers. For information to really take on life, we need a basis for judgment.

Once we calculate these 17 ratios for ***Pier 1 Imports,*** how will we use them to evaluate the business? Financial ratios are bits of data that only become valuable information when they are used in comparison to prior years' ratios, to peer companies, or to industry averages. This kind of interpretation is what we would call the "art of ratio analysis."

After we show how to calculate each ratio, we will present a chart that depicts that ratio for as many years as we have data. Since we are using only the information included in ***Pier 1***'s annual report published in 2002, we have enough data to calculate many ratios for five years. For other ratios, we will be forced to present fewer years due to the lack of data.

In addition to presenting ***Pier 1***'s ratios, we will compare the results with the ratios of two peer companies. **Peer companies** are companies that are similar to one another, usually in the same industry and of similar size, which analysts use for financial comparisons.

peer companies
Companies that are similar to one another, usually in the industry and of similar size.

It would be best if the peer companies we use are in the same industry as ***Pier 1.*** Therefore, before we discuss the selection of peer companies, you need to understand something about the systems that are used to classify companies into industry groupings.

INDUSTRY CLASSIFICATIONS

Industry classifications are a key component of selecting peer companies. In the United States, there are two widely used industry classification systems: the ***North American Industry Classification System (NAICS),*** and the ***Standard Industrial Classification (SIC)*** system.

NAICS (pronounced Nakes) is rapidly becoming the most widely accepted industry classification system in the United States. NAICS was developed by representatives of the governments of the United States, Canada, and Mexico (hence the name North American Industry Classification System) in 1997 to replace the Standard Industrial

Classification (SIC) system. The SIC system was established by the United States Office of Management and Budget in 1987.

NAICS uses six-digit codes to specify the industry in which a company operates. In developing NAICS, the United States, Canada, and Mexico agreed that the first five digits of the code would be universal and useful for comparing industry information among the three countries. They further agreed that the sixth digit would allow each country to further subdivide the industries specified in the five-digit categories. In the United States, all NAICS codes have six digits, and if there is no subdivision of a particular industry, the sixth digit is a zero.

You might think that as soon as NAICS was put in place the SIC system (which uses four-digit codes) would quickly go by the wayside. Such has not been the case. Many financial institutions, publications, and government agencies continue to use the four-digit SIC system. For example, federal agencies such as the Occupational Safety and Health Administration (OSHA) and the SEC still use the SIC system. Further, even though NAICS has been in existence since 1997, many business publications either have not yet switched to NAICS or have done so only recently. For example, the *Almanac of Business and Industrial Financial Ratios*, a leading annual business publication, did not switch from the SIC system to NAICS until its 2002 edition.

Any business can be classified by industry using the NAICS or SIC system. If you would like to find the industry classification for a publicly traded company, all you have to do is visit the SEC's Web site at *www.sec.gov*. This Web site can provide the SIC code for a particular company, and in addition, it can provide a list of companies within the same SIC classification. For example, *Pier 1 Imports*' SIC code on the SEC's Electronic Data Gathering, Analysis, and Retrieval (EDGAR) system is 5700.

But what if the company we are analyzing is not registered with the SEC? You can visit the NAICS Web site. As long as you have some knowledge regarding the company's line of business, you can determine an appropriate industry classification code for any company. To find *Pier 1*'s classification code, let's begin with the assumption that we know *Pier 1* is a retailer and that it sells household furnishings, furniture, and gifts. Type in the address, *www.census.gov/epcd/www/naicstab.htm*, or type "NAICS" into almost any Internet browser. For *Pier 1,* the closest NAICS code description is *Retail Trade, Furniture and Home Furnishings Stores*, which corresponds to NAICS code 442000. If you know a company's SIC code and wish to find the corresponding NAICS code, visit the NAICS Web site and click on *Correspondence between NAICS and SIC*. Then, follow the prompts until you find the corresponding NAICS code.

By now, you probably know more about industry classification systems than you ever wanted to know, but if you still want to learn more about the background and development of NAICS, or want more information about the differences between NAICS and the SIC, visit the U.S. Census Web site at *www.census.gov/epcd/www/naicsdev.htm*.

FINDING PEER COMPANIES

Once we know a company's NAICS code or SIC, how can we find peer companies to use as comparisons in our financial analysis? There are several ways, and we are going to show you how to find peer companies using the SEC's Web site. It's really quite simple. First, visit the SEC's Web site at *www.sec.gov*, and use the EDGAR system to look up the company you are analyzing. Then all you have to do is to click on the company's SIC code, 5700 for *Pier 1,* and a list of all the companies in that industry classification will appear. You can use that list to find peer companies for financial comparisons.

We looked at the 10-Ks (which include annual financial statements) for several companies listed by the SEC for SIC 5700. We were trying to find companies that were about the same size as *Pier 1* and that had a fairly similar business style. After eliminating many of the companies because they were too small or their line of business didn't seem close enough, we chose *Bed Bath & Beyond* and *Williams-Sonoma* as the peer companies we would use as comparisons to evaluate *Pier 1 Imports.* These two companies are classified along with *Pier 1* under SIC 5700. Although they do not sell the exact same products as *Pier 1 Imports,* they are of similar size. Like *Pier 1,* their products cover a limited spectrum (as opposed to a department store that sells just about every kind of product), and like *Pier 1,* they compete with independent businesses and selected departments of major department stores. In addition, all three companies have assets and sales in the billions of dollars.

INDUSTRY AVERAGES

We can also compare the company we are analyzing to the ratios for its entire industry. The *Almanac of Business and Industrial Financial Ratios* (hereafter referred to simply as "the Almanac") is a book published annually that lists selected key ratios for over 190 industries and is the publication we will use for industry comparisons in this chapter. Other widely used sources of industry averages include the **Risk Management Association**'s (**RMA**'s) *Annual Statement Studies* and **Dunn & Bradstreet**'s *Industry Norms and Key Business Ratios.*

Regardless of the source, your first step in making an industry comparison is to determine the company's NAICS code or SIC. Although the Almanac began using NAICS in its 2002 edition, it includes an appendix that cross-references the SIC system to NAICS.

Data in the Almanac are compiled from approximately 4.8 million corporate federal income tax returns. Gathering data from the **IRS** rather than other publicly available sources of financial information has two distinct advantages: (1) Information about all active corporations is included (other sources include only large or publicly held corporations); and (2) because of substantial penalties for misreporting, corporate data submitted to the **IRS** are generally more reliable than that from other sources.

Information provided in the Almanac for each industry is reported in two tables. Table I provides an analysis of all companies in the particular industry, regardless of whether they had any net income or a net loss. Table II provides the same information items as Table I, but it considers only companies that showed a net income. Exhibit 11–2 on page F–458 shows a portion of Table II for industry classification 442000, the NAICS code for *Pier 1 Imports,* from the 2002 edition of the Almanac.

Note that Table II in Exhibit 11–2 arranges the ratios in 13 columns. The first column ("Total") provides industry averages for all companies in the industry. The other columns provide averages for companies based on their total assets. When we compare *Pier 1*'s ratios to industry averages, we will use the first column (the total column) and the last column (for companies with assets in excess of $250 million). This is because we would like to see how *Pier 1* compares with the entire industry and to companies of somewhat similar size.

Now that we have selected our peer companies and we know something about industry averages, we are ready to present the calculations and interpretations of the financial ratios we will use to evaluate *Pier 1 Imports, Inc.*

◆   CALCULATING FINANCIAL RATIOS AND INTERPRETING THEIR RESULTS

Ratio analysis, as we explained earlier, is a method of analyzing the relationship between two items from a company's financial statements. We said important relationships may exist between two items on the same financial statement or between two items from different financial statements. All the ratios we calculate here are based on information from the balance sheets, income statements, and statements of cash flows for *Pier 1 Imports, Inc., Bed Bath & Beyond,* and *Williams-Sonoma* published in 2002.

Understand that the absolute numbers resulting from the calculations are of little value in themselves. It's like the friend telling you that he walked the length of Duval Street in 20 minutes. So what! It is the *analysis* and *interpretation* of the numbers—the art of ratio analysis—that provides the usefulness. For the ratios to be truly useful to economic decision makers, an analyst must compare those ratios to other information, such as the company's ratios in past years, the ratios of peer companies, or industry averages. So, in addition to calculating the ratios for just a single year, we will present a

Table II
Corporations with Net Income
Furniture and Home Furnishings Stores
Money Amounts and Size of Assets in Thousands of Dollars

Item Description for Accounting Period 7/98 Through 6/99		Total	Zero Assets	Under 100	100 to 250	251 to 500	501 to 1,000	1,001 to 5,000	5,001 to 10,000	10,001 to 25,000	25,001 to 50,000	50,001 to 100,000	100,001 to 250,000	250,001 and over
Number of Enterprises	1	23738	132	6982	6338	3840	3523	2509	250	107	25	0	0	11
Revenues ($ in Thousands)														
Net Sales	2	56154823	434489	2525522	4771410	5055847	6555770	13112347	5018841	4406253	2563686	0	0	7861403
Interest	3	191413	691	60	23	2630	22699	48531	12025	7076	1731	0	0	60554
Rents	4	20227	0	0	0	0	431	2826	1	3316	2	0	0	7076
Royalties	5	21163	0	0	0	0	0	0	16395	4	0	0	0	2856
Other Portfolio Income	6	136135	1203	40	398	3111	10442	2661	5127	27783	303	0	0	68422
Other Receipts	7	519773	1183	2998	3390	16228	27008	110639	52879	83083	47852	0	0	99952
Total Receipts	8	57043534	437566	2528620	4776221	5077816	6616350	13277004	5105267	4527515	2613574	0	0	8100263
Average Total Receipts	9	2403	3315	362	753	1322	1878	5292	2041	42313	104543	•	•	736388
Operating Costs/Operating Income (%)														
Cost of Operations	10	62.6	63.3	62.0	64.7	61.5	63.6	63.0	67.0	66.6	69.2	•	•	55.0
Salaries and Wages	11	10.9	8.3	5.4	5.6	9.7	10.5	11.8	11.8	12.0	11.9	•	•	13.3
Taxes Paid	12	2.2	1.9	2.8	2.5	2.5	2.4	2.0	1.6	1.7	1.4	•	•	2.6
Interest Paid	13	0.8	0.5	0.2	0.5	0.4	0.8	0.7	0.4	0.6	0.9	•	•	1.5
Depreciation	14	1.0	0.3	0.9	0.9	0.6	0.9	0.8	0.7	1.0	0.8	•	•	2.3
Amortization and Depletion	15	0.1	0.1	0.0	0.1	0.0	0.0	0.0	0.0	0.0	0.0	•	•	0.4
Pensions and Other Deferred Comp.	16	0.2	•	0.1	0.0	0.2	0.5	0.2	0.3	0.3	0.1	•	•	0.2
Employee Benefits	17	0.6	0.1	0.4	0.3	0.5	0.6	0.5	0.0	0.5	0.0	•	•	1.1
Advertising	18	3.5	4.2	2.3	2.4	2.9	3.2	3.4	3.8	3.6	2.6	•	•	4.1
Other Expenses	19	12.4	10.4	15.0	15.2	14.2	10.9	11.2	10.4	10.1	10.4	•	•	14.6

EXHIBIT 11-2 Continued

#	Item												
20	Officers' Compensation	3.0	1.8	6.0	3.5	4.6	4.7	3.7	2.1	2.0	1.0	●	0.9
21	Operating Margin	2.7	9.1	4.9	4.3	3.0	2.1	2.7	1.3	1.7	1.1	●	4.1
22	Operating Margin Before Officers' Comp.	5.7	10.9	10.9	7.8	7.6	6.8	6.3	3.4	3.6	2.1	●	5.0
	Selected Average Balance Sheet ($ in Thousands)												
23	Net Receivables	175	0	7	35	59	136	446	1871	3795	10154	●	53893
24	Inventories	352	0	9	76	183	292	880	2413	5197	12879	●	174356
25	Net Property, Plant, and Equipment	105	0	14	20	41	112	316	301	2907	6020	●	148291
26	Total Assets	944	0	48	165	357	724	2063	6702	15125	35076	●	542318
27	Notes and Loans Payable	210	0	18	48	75	160	495	1131	3065	10587	●	105336
28	All Other Liabilities	311	0	16	59	115	196	668	2331	5746	14278	●	181895
29	Net Worth	423	0	15	59	168	368	900	3240	6314	10212	●	255087
	Selected Financial Ratios (Times to 1)												
30	Current Ratio	1.8	●	1.9	1.8	2.6	2.6	1.9	1.8	1.6	1.5	●	1.4
31	Quick Ratio	0.8	●	1.3	0.7	1.0	1.1	0.8	1.0	0.8	0.7	●	0.5
32	Net Sales to Working Capital	8.0	●	23.4	13.3	7.1	5.4	6.6	8.1	9.6	12.9	●	8.9
33	Coverage Ratio	6.7	21.4	21.4	9.3	10.2	4.9	6.5	8.4	8.4	4.5	●	5.6
34	Total Asset Turnover	2.5	●	7.5	4.6	3.7	2.6	2.5	3.0	2.7	2.9	●	1.3
35	Inventory Turnover	4.2	●	23.8	6.4	4.4	4.1	3.7	5.6	5.3	5.5	●	2.3
36	Receivables Turnover	●	●	●	●	●	●	●	●	●	●	●	●
37	Total Liabilities to Net Worth	1.2	●	2.2	1.8	1.1	1.0	1.3	1.1	1.4	2.4	●	1.1
38	Current Assets to Working Capital	2.2	●	2.2	2.3	1.6	1.6	2.1	2.2	2.6	3.2	●	3.6
39	Current Liabilities to Working Capital	1.2	●	1.2	1.3	0.6	0.6	1.1	1.2	1.6	2.2	●	2.6

EXHIBIT 11-2 | Continued

Item Description for Accounting Period 7/98 Through 6/99		Total	Zero Assets	Under 100	100 to 250	251 to 500	501 to 1,000	1,001 to 5,000	5,001 to 10,000	10,001 to 25,000	25,001 to 50,000	50,001 to 100,000	100,001 to 250,000	250,001 and over
Working Capital to Net Sales	40	0.1	•	0.0	0.1	0.1	0.2	0.2	0.1	0.1	0.1	•	•	0.1
Inventory to Working Capital	41	1.2	•	0.6	1.3	1.0	0.8	1.1	1.0	1.2	1.6	•	•	2.2
Total Receipts to Cash Flow	42	8.4	6.4	6.6	7.8	8.1	9.6	9.5	10.2	9.2	9.6	•	•	6.6
Cost of Goods to Cash Flow	43	5.2	4.0	4.1	5.1	5.0	6.1	6.0	6.9	6.2	6.7	•	•	3.6
Cash Flow to Total Debt	44	0.5	•	1.6	0.9	0.9	0.5	0.5	0.6	0.5	0.4	•	•	0.4
Selected Financial Factors (in Percentages)														
Debt Ratio	45	55.2	•	69.1	64.5	53.0	49.2	56.4	51.7	58.3	70.9	•	•	53.0
Return on Total Assets	46	12.7	•	39.6	22.3	14.1	9.7	11.8	10.2	13.6	11.5	•	•	11.4
Return on Equity Before Income Taxes	47	24.1	•	122.0	56.1	27.0	15.3	22.9	18.7	28.8	30.7	•	•	19.9
Return on Equity After Income Taxes	48	20.8	•	120.6	55.4	26.1	13.8	20.8	15.5	26.9	27.9	•	•	13.4
Profit Margin (Before Income Tax)	49	4.3	9.8	5.0	4.4	3.4	3.0	3.9	3.0	4.4	3.1	•	•	7.1
Profit Margin (After Income Tax)	50	3.7	8.3	5.0	4.3	3.3	2.7	3.6	2.5	4.1	2.8	•	•	4.8

series of charts depicting *Pier 1*'s ratios for several years along with the ratios of the two peer companies we selected. Then we will briefly discuss the implications of the information presented in the chart. Seeing the charted ratios for three peer companies, for several years when possible, will bring meaning to the ratios and help you readily comprehend their implications.

Using the resources available over the internet, we could calculate ratios for each company going back 10 years or even more. However, for this introduction to financial statement analysis, we will limit our presentation to ratios that can be calculated using data from the annual reports published in 2002. In annual reports, the SEC requires companies to present selected financial information for five years, income statements and statements of cash flows for three years, and balance sheets for only two years. What this means is that we will be able to present five years of information for some ratios, three or four years for others, and only one year for still others. As we will see, if a ratio requires an average balance sheet amount, such as average inventory, with only two years of balance sheets available, we can calculate the average for only one year. You can track each of the ratios we present for *Pier 1 Imports* back to the annual report included with this text.

Let's address two more items before we begin computing the ratios:

- First, there is a lack of consistency among analysts in the way they calculate various ratios. Even when two analysts use the same name for a particular ratio, the calculations they use for the ratios may be different from one another. This inconsistency often makes it difficult to compare ratios calculated by different analysts or financial publications.

  One popular difference in the way ratios are calculated has to do with using average amounts for certain balance sheet items. In practice, many analysts use year-end amounts instead of averages when they calculate their ratios. For example, the analyst will use the year-end amount for total assets instead of average total assets. This way, the ratio calculations are simpler and the results are generally adequate. When completing the exercises in this text, use averages unless instructed otherwise.

- Second, virtually all ratios were developed by financial analysts, not accountants. What this means is that some of the ratio language (from analysts) does not match exactly with financial statement language (from accountants). For example, financial analysts may use the word *profit* in the ratios, whereas accountants may use the words *net income* in the financial statements. The two terms are synonymous but can cause confusion. As we proceed through the ratios, we will make certain to reconcile the descriptive terms used in the ratios with what they represent in the financial statement information.

Decision makers calculate a variety of ratios to gain meaningful insight into a company's past performance and current financial position. Don't get the idea that the 17 ratios we present represent a complete list of the financial ratios analysts use. In fact, there are so many useful and revealing financial ratios that it was difficult to limit our presentation to just 17 of them.

To fully assess a company's well-being, it is critically important that the analyst evaluate four important characteristics of the business: profitability, efficiency, liquidity, and solvency. The 17 ratios we present will provide you with a solid overview of *Pier 1*'s performance in each of those areas.

MEASURING PROFITABILITY

profitability The ease with which a company generates income.

Profitability is the ease with which a company generates income. If a company generates a high level of income very easily, it is said to have high profitability. All companies must maintain at least a minimum level of profitability to meet their obligations, such as servicing long-term debt and paying dividends to stockholders. Profitability ratios measure a firm's past performance. This past performance is generally helpful in predicting a company's future profitability level. Present stockholders, potential stockholders, and long-term creditors, therefore, use these ratios to evaluate investments.

Company managers use profitability ratios to monitor and evaluate their company's performance. A growing concern, however, is that some managers may be trying too desperately to improve their company's apparent performance and, thus, their profitability ratios. There are two potential reasons for this. First, managers may want to make the company's financial results look more appealing to external decision makers. Second, at least a portion of their own compensation may be directly tied to these profitability ratios, for often managers receive bonuses based on the level of profitability achieved by the company.

Stockholders and creditors also want the company to be profitable, but profitability ratios are based on short-term results (usually one year), and the only way to boost them is to attain the highest possible profit for any given year. That doesn't sound so bad, does it? Well, profits are not bad, but remember this:

A Preoccupation with Short-Term Profits is Detrimental to the Long-Term Value of a Business!

Stockholders and creditors, then, generally take a longer-term view of the company's health than can be measured by profitability alone.

As you look at the profitability ratios in this section, focus both on what they should reveal about a company and on how they might encourage shortsighted behavior by management. It is quite common for managers to slant business decisions toward that which makes the ratios "look better" to the decision makers who are using their company's financial statements. In 2001, for example, *WorldCom* made itself appear more profitable by not including $3.8 billion of expenses in its income statement.

Discussion Question

11–7. Give an example of a management decision that would be made differently depending on whether the manager is concerned with short-term profits versus the long-term well-being of the company. Explain the impact of the two different perspectives on the outcome of the decision.

Gross Profit Margin Ratio

gross profit margin ratio
A profitability ratio that expresses a company's gross profit (often called gross margin on the financial statements) as a percentage of sales revenue.

net sales
Total sales less any discounts or reductions due to returns or sales allowances.

Introduced in Chapter 4, the **gross profit margin ratio** expresses a company's gross profit (often called gross margin on the financial statements) as a percentage of net sales. **Net sales** is total sales less any discounts or reductions due to returns or sales allowances. The formula for this ratio is:

$$\text{Gross profit margin ratio} = \frac{\text{Gross profit}}{\text{Net sales}}$$

Both the numerator and denominator for this ratio come from the income statement information in *Pier 1*'s annual report. Recall that we calculate gross margin (gross profit) by subtracting cost of goods sold (cost of sales) from net sales. Unfortunately, *Pier 1* does not include gross margin as a subtotal on its income statement on page 34 of the annual report. In fact, the company has lumped cost of sales with the other operating expenses, including the cost of buying merchandise and store occupancy. The notes to *Pier 1*'s financial statements fail to provide enough information for us to distinguish the company's cost of sales from its other costs. Even the gross profit figure of $649.8 million that *Pier 1* presents in its Financial Summary on page 21 is calculated using cost of sales *including* the buying and store occupancy costs ($1,548,556 − $898,795 = $649,761 rounded to $649.8 million). Returning to the income statement on page 34, we have no choice but to calculate gross profit by subtracting cost of sales *including* the buying and store occupancy costs from net sales ($1,548,556 − $898,795 = $649,761). Using this amount and the net sales figure from the income statement, we calculate *Pier 1*'s gross profit margin ratio for 2002 as:

$$\frac{\$649,761}{\$1,548,556} = .4196 \text{ or } 41.96\%$$

This ratio calculation tells us that after covering the cost of product sold during 2002, *Pier 1* had 41.96 percent of each sales dollar remaining to cover all the company's operating expenses, interest cost, and income taxes. You can also look at it this way: For every one dollar of sales, the company had about 42 cents remaining after it paid for the merchandise it sold. The 42 cents is what ***Pier 1*** has left to pay all its other costs. Gross profit margin ratios vary from industry to industry, but, clearly, the higher the gross profit margin percentage, the better.

As we mentioned earlier in this chapter, where possible, we will compare ***Pier 1***'s ratios to industry averages taken from the 2002 edition of the Almanac. Unfortunately, we can't compare ***Pier 1***'s gross profit margin to industry averages because the Almanac does not include this ratio in the industry statistics it publishes. Frankly, this is not uncommon because different publications present different ratios. If we really wanted to see how ***Pier 1***'s gross profit margin ratio compares to its industry average, we would need to refer to one of the other publications.

So the question remains, how does ***Pier 1***'s gross profit margin ratio measure up when compared to other large specialty retailers? And what has happened to ***Pier 1***'s gross profit margin over time? Has it been increasing, staying the same, or is it declining? To answer these important questions, we calculated the gross profit margins for ***Pier 1, Bed Bath & Beyond,*** and ***Williams-Sonoma*** for each of the five years ending with their financial statements published in 2002. We then created a bar chart graph to illustrate our findings. Exhibit 11–3 shows the chart we created for the gross profit margin ratio for the three companies.

EXHIBIT 11–3	Gross Profit Margin Ratio for 1998 Through 2002

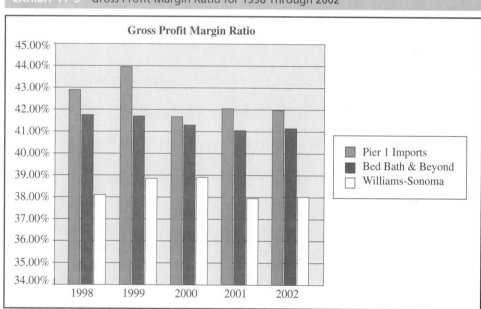

As the chart in Exhibit 11–3 shows, all three companies have consistently high gross profit margin ratios. All of them seem to be performing well by this measure; however, ***Pier 1***'s gross profit margin ratio is consistently higher than those of ***Bed Bath & Beyond*** and ***Williams-Sonoma.*** The chart in Exhibit 11–3 also shows that ***Pier 1***'s gross profit percentage has been fairly constant—between about 42 and 44 percent.

Net Profit Margin Ratio

net profit margin ratio
A profitability ratio that expresses a company's net profit (almost always called either net income or net earnings on the financial statements) as a percentage of sales revenue. It indicates the amount of net income generated by a dollar of sales.

Introduced in Chapter 4, the **net profit margin ratio** expresses a company's net profit (almost always called either net income or net earnings on the financial statements) as a percentage of sales revenue. It indicates the amount of net income generated by a dollar of sales. The formula for this ratio is:

$$\text{Net profit margin ratio} = \frac{\text{Net profit}}{\text{Net sales}}$$

Both the numerator and denominator for this ratio come from the income statement on page 34 of ***Pier 1***'s annual report. We calculate ***Pier 1***'s net profit margin ratio for 2002 as:

$$\frac{\$100,209}{\$1,548,556} = .0647 \text{ or } 6.47\%$$

This ratio tells us that during 2002, ***Pier 1*** had 6.47 percent of each sales dollar remaining as profit after covering the cost of products sold, all operating expenses, interest cost, and income taxes. In other words, it reveals the percentage of each sales dollar remaining after *all* the costs of running the business for the year. So for every one dollar of sales, ***Pier 1*** had about 6.5 cents (of each sales dollar) remaining after it paid its costs for the year. Net profit margin ratios vary from industry to industry, but clearly, the higher the net profit margin percentage, the better. As Dennis E. Logue suggests in the *Handbook of Modern Finance*:

> *The profit margin percentage measures a firm's ability to (1) obtain higher prices for its products relative to competitors and (2) control the level of operating costs, or expenses, relative to revenues generated. By holding down costs, a firm increases the profits from a given amount of revenue and thereby improves its profit margin percentage.*[3]

Compared to the industry averages for furniture and home furnishings stores published in the Almanac for 2002, ***Pier 1***'s net profit margin ratio is quite strong. The industry's average net profit margin ratio (called the "profit margin after tax" in the Almanac) for all companies in Table II is 3.7 percent, and the industry average for companies with assets in excess of $250 million is 4.8 percent. Clearly ***Pier 1***'s 6.47 percent net profit margin ratio is substantially higher than the industry averages.

We will next see how ***Pier 1***'s net profit margin ratio compares to our peer companies and how it has changed over time. To do this, we calculated the net profit margins for ***Pier 1, Bed Bath & Beyond,*** and ***Williams-Sonoma*** for each of the five years ending with information from their financial statements published in 2002. Then we created a bar chart to summarize the information, shown in Exhibit 11–4.

As you can see by the chart in Exhibit 11–4, ***Pier 1***'s net profit margin ratio is consistently between about 6 and 7 percent. It is clearly higher than ***Williams-Sonoma***'s net profit margin, but in the last three years, ***Bed Bath & Beyond***'s ratio has edged out ***Pier 1***'s. All in all, the graph shows that ***Pier 1*** has a strong and consistent net profit compared to its peer companies.

EXHIBIT 11–4   Net Profit Margin Ratio for 1998 Through 2002

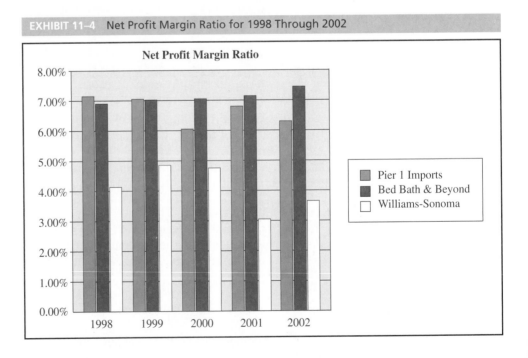

---

[3]Dennis E. Logue, *Handbook of Modern Finance.*

Rate of Return on Assets Ratio

rate of return on assets ratio A profitability ratio that shows the amount of profit (net income) produced for a given level of assets.

Introduced in Chapter 4, the **rate of return on assets ratio** shows the amount of profit (net income) produced for a given level of assets. This is an important ratio because it indicates how effectively the company uses its total assets to generate net income. The formula for this ratio is:

$$\text{Rate of return on assets ratio} = \frac{\text{Net income}}{\text{Average total assets}}$$

The net income amount we use in the numerator of this ratio comes directly from the income statement. The amount we use as the denominator requires a bit of explanation. Since the net income in the numerator was earned throughout 2002 (some in January, some in February, etc.), we want to know the amount of assets employed throughout the year. We determine this by calculating the average of the total assets shown on the 2001 and 2002 balance sheets on page 35 of the annual report ($735,710 + $862,672 = $1,598,382/2 = $799,191). We calculate ***Pier 1***'s rate of return on assets for 2002 as:

$$\frac{\$100{,}209}{\$799{,}191} = .1254 \text{ or } 12.54\%$$

This ratio calculation tells us that during 2002, ***Pier 1*** had a 12.54 percent return on its investment in assets. This is an important measure because, after all, the reason companies invest in assets is to produce revenue and ultimately profit (net income).

Compared to the industry averages for furniture and home furnishings stores published in the Almanac for 2002, ***Pier 1***'s rate of return on assets ratio is stronger than the industry average for companies with assets over $250 million, but slightly less than the average of all companies in Table II. The industry average for the rate of return on assets ratio for all companies in Table II is 12.7 percent and the industry average for companies with assets in excess of $250 million is 11.4 percent. ***Pier 1***'s 12.54 percent return on assets ratio is on par with the industry averages.

Next we will examine how ***Pier 1***'s rate of return on assets ratio compares to the peer companies. The chart in Exhibit 11–5 shows how ***Pier 1, Bed Bath & Beyond,*** and ***Williams-Sonoma***'s rate of return on assets has faired from 1999 to 2002.

Although ***Pier 1***'s rate of return on assets has been somewhat lower than that of ***Bed Bath & Beyond,*** it has been quite stable, if not increasing. In contrast, even though their rates of return on assets are still strong, the other two company's rates have been declining somewhat.

EXHIBIT 11–5 Rate of Return on Assets Ratio for 1999 Through 2002

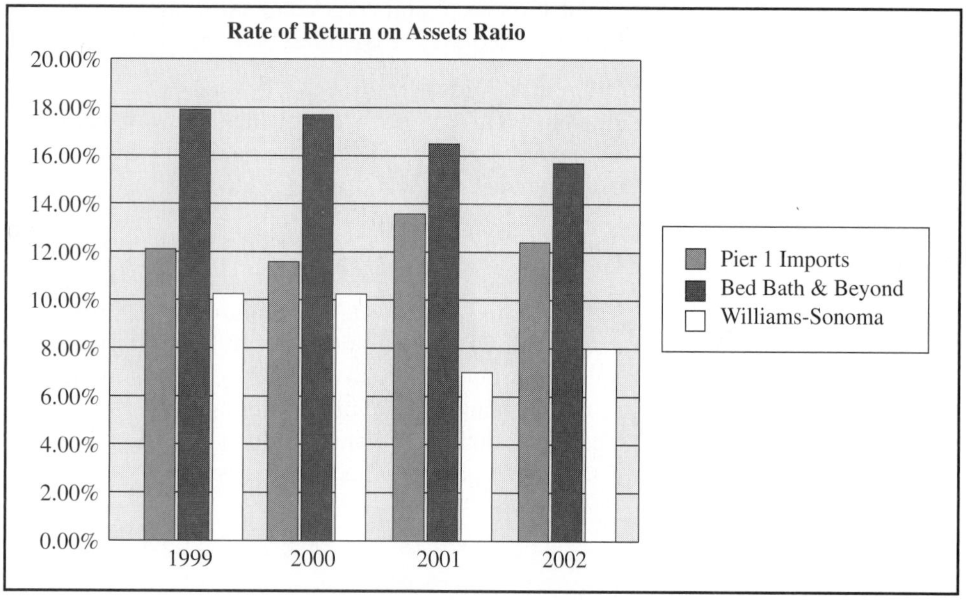

rate of return on common equity ratio   A profitability ratio that shows the amount of profit (net income) in relation to the amount of investment by the company's owners.

Rate of Return on Common Equity Ratio

Introduced in Chapter 4, the **rate of return on common equity ratio** shows the amount of profit (net income) in relation to the amount of investment by the company's owners. The purpose of this ratio is similar to that of the rate of return on assets ratio except that it focuses on the assets provided by the owners, rather than total assets. The formula for this ratio is:

$$\text{Rate of return on common equity ratio} = \frac{\text{Net income} - \text{Preferred dividends}}{\text{Average common stockholders' equity}}$$

The net income used in the numerator of this ratio comes from the income statement, but it must be adjusted for any preferred stock dividend requirement, because that amount is not available to common stockholders. Since *Pier 1* has no preferred stock (we determine this by looking at the shareholder' equity section of the balance sheet), there are no preferred stock dividends to deduct in our calculation. We use an average amount for the denominator in this calculation for the same reason we did in the rate of return on assets ratio. Since the net income in the numerator was earned throughout 2002, we want to know the amount of common equity throughout the year. We determine this by calculating the average of the common stockholders' equity shown on the 2001 and 2002 balance sheets ($581,879 + $585,656 = $1,167,535 /2 = $583,767.5). We calculate *Pier 1*'s rate of return on common equity ratio for 2002 as:

$$\frac{\$100,209}{\$583,767.5} = .1717 \text{ or } 17.17\%$$

This ratio tells us that during 2002, *Pier 1* had a 17.17 percent return on the owners holdings in the company. Do not confuse this with what the owners themselves earned on their investment. The owners' return is a combination of the dividends they receive and appreciation of the stock's price in the marketplace. The company's rate of return on common equity does, however, greatly influence the market price of the company's stock and, therefore, the stockholders' return on their investment.

Compared to the industry averages for furniture and home furnishings stores published in the Almanac for 2002, *Pier 1*'s 17.17 percent rate of return on common equity ratio is substantially higher than the 13.4 percent industry average for companies with assets over $250 million, but somewhat less than the 20.8 percent industry average of all companies in Table II.

Now let's look at the rate of return on common equity ratio for *Pier 1 Imports, Bed Bath & Beyond,* and *Williams-Sonoma.* Exhibit 11–6 shows the rates of return on equity for our peer companies for 1999 to 2002.

Pier 1 Imports' rate of return on common equity ratio is consistently between about 17 percent and 20 percent. Although it is below that of *Bed Bath & Beyond*, it has surpassed that of *Williams-Sonoma* and is holding steady.

dividend payout ratio   A financial ratio that shows what portion of a company's net income for a given year was paid to its owners as cash dividends during that year.

Dividend Payout Ratio

Introduced in Chapter 4, the **dividend payout ratio** shows what portion of a company's net income for a given year was paid to its owners as cash dividends during that year. The formula for this ratio is:

$$\text{Dividend payout ratio} = \frac{\text{Cash dividends}}{\text{Net income}}$$

We could determine the amount of cash dividends to use in the numerator by examining the stockholders' equity section of the balance sheet and calculating the amount. A better way, however, is to simply look for the amount of cash dividends paid in the financing section of the statement of cash flows on page 36 of the annual report. The denominator is simply net income from the income statement. We calculate *Pier 1*'s dividend payout ratio for 2002 as:

$$\frac{\$15,134}{\$100,209} = .1510 \text{ or } 15.10\%$$

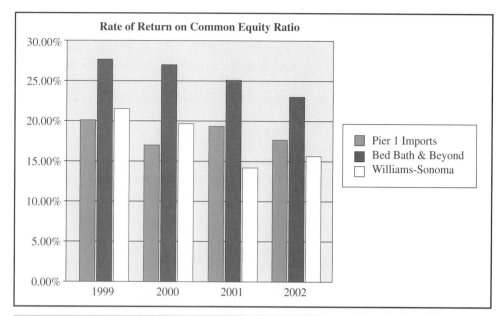

EXHIBIT 11–6   Rate of Return on Common Equity Ratio for 1999 Through 2002

This ratio tells us that during 2002, ***Pier 1*** paid out 15.10 percent of its net income to its stockholders as dividends. On the surface, it might seem that a high dividend payout ratio is better than a low one, and for some investors this is true (those who count on dividends as a significant portion of their yearly income). Many investors and analysts, however, believe a low dividend payout ratio is superior to a high one. The reason is actually pretty simple. Remember that a company can do only two things with the profits it earns. It can either distribute them to the stockholders as dividends or it can reinvest them in the business in the form of property, plant, and equipment or new products and processes. A high dividend payout ratio may indicate that a company is not investing sufficiently for the future.

The Almanac does not publish industry averages for the dividend payout ratio, but we will compare ***Pier 1***'s dividend payout to our peer companies. Exhibit 11–7 shows ***Pier 1, Bed Bath & Beyond,*** and ***Williams-Sonoma***'s dividend payout ratio for 2000 through 2002.

EXHIBIT 11–7   Dividend Payout Ratio for 2000 Through 2002

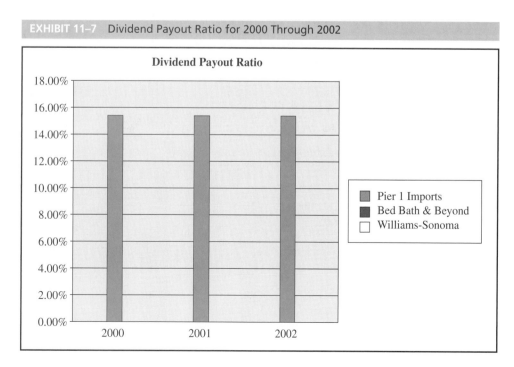

It is likely that the comparison of *Pier 1*'s dividend payout ratio with those of *Bed Bath & Beyond* and *Williams-Sonoma* yields results that may look quite strange to you. This is because *Pier 1* pays a dividend of about 15 percent of net income and neither *Bed Bath & Beyond* nor *Williams-Sonoma* pays a dividend at all. Now, we must caution you that paying no dividend is not a sign of financial weakness. Both *Bed Bath & Beyond* and *Williams-Sonoma* are reinvesting earnings instead of distributing them. You may ask which is better, a company that pays dividends or one that doesn't. Well, there is no one correct answer to that question because some investors desire a greater distribution of profits than others. Those who want a greater distribution view a high dividend payout ratio as good. Other investors prefer to see a company reinvest a higher percentage of its profits so the company can continue to grow. These folks view a low dividend payout ratio as good.

Earnings per Share

earnings per share ratio
The amount of a company's total earnings attributable to each share of common stock.

Introduced in Chapter 4 and discussed further in Chapter 9, the **earnings per share ratio** expresses a company's net income as a per common share amount. The formula for this ratio is:

$$\text{Earnings per share} = \frac{\text{Net income} - \text{Preferred dividend}}{\text{Average common shares}}$$

We demonstrated very simple earnings per share (EPS) calculations in Chapter 4 and more complicated basic and diluted earnings per share calculations in Chapter 9. When you are evaluating a company whose stock is publicly traded, however, you will *never* have to calculate earnings per share, because the SEC requires that the company calculate it for you and include it in the annual report. *Pier 1*'s basic and diluted earnings per share for 2002 were:

Basic earnings per share = $1.06
Diluted earnings per share = $1.04

Clearly, all interested parties desire a company's earnings per share to be as high as possible. The Almanac does not publish industry averages for earnings per share, but we will compare *Pier 1*'s earnings per share to that of *Bed Bath & Beyond* and *Williams-Sonoma.* When we look at the annual reports for *Pier 1 Imports, Bed Bath & Beyond,* and *Williams-Sonoma,* we find that all three companies disclose diluted earnings per share information for the past five years (see Exhibit 11–8).

EXHIBIT 11–8   Diluted Earnings per Share for 1998 Through 2002

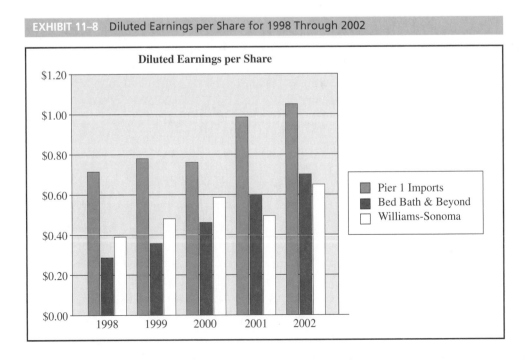

The chart in Exhibit 11–8 shows that ***Pier 1***'s earnings per share is clearly the highest, but the earnings per share for each of our three companies has generally increased over time.

Price-to-Earnings Ratio

Introduced in Chapter 9, the **price-to-earnings ratio** (often referred to as simply the PE ratio) expresses the relationship between a company's earnings per share and the market value of the company's stock. Financial analysts use this measure to decide whether a company's stock is *under*valued or *over*valued. The formula for this ratio is:

$$\text{Price-to-earnings ratio} = \frac{\text{Average market price per share of stock}}{\text{Earnings per share}}$$

The numerator for this ratio is not found in any of a company's financial statements. We can, however, calculate it from the market price and dividend information found on page 51 of the annual report. Analysts can use the current market price per share or they can use an average price to calculate the PE ratio. We will use an average price per share from amounts for the fourth quarter only. We calculate the average the same way we did in previous ratios, except this time we will use the high and low market prices, rather than the beginning and ending market prices ($20.24 high + $14.50 low = $34.74/2 = $17.37). The denominator is earnings per share from the income statement. We calculate ***Pier 1***'s PE ratio for 2002 as:

$$\frac{\$17.37}{\$1.06} = 16.39 \text{ times}$$

This ratio calculation tells us that ***Pier 1***'s stock was selling for 16.39 times its earnings per share in 2002 (at least during the fourth quarter). The Almanac does not include industry averages for earnings per share, but Exhibit 11–9 shows the price-to-earnings ratios for ***Pier 1 Imports, Bed Bath & Beyond,*** and ***Williams-Sonoma*** for 2001 and 2002.

This is a difficult ratio to interpret because it means different things to different analysts. A high PE ratio may indicate that the stock is overvalued (and may be an unwise investment), whereas a low PE ratio may indicate that is undervalued (and may be a wise investment). Since the market value of a stock is not directly related to earn-

EXHIBIT 11–9 Price-to-Earnings Ratios for 2001 and 2002

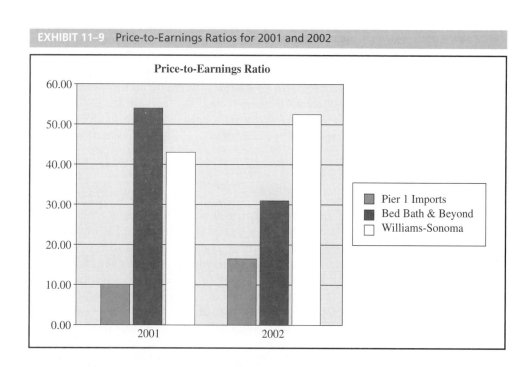

price-to-earnings ratio
A profitability ratio that is often called simply the PE ratio that expresses the relationship between a company's earnings per share and the market value of the company's stock.

ings per share, smart analysts evaluate this ratio in conjunction with many other factors. In any case, *Pier 1*'s PE ratio is clearly much lower than those of *Bed Bath & Beyond* and *Williams-Sonoma.*

MEASURING EFFICIENCY

efficiency ratios Financial ratios that measure the investment in assets relative to business activity.

Companies use resources (assets) to conduct business. The more business a company can generate with a given amount of assets, the better. For example, when a company can generate a tremendous amount of revenue with a relatively small amount of assets, the company must be using those assets efficiently. **Efficiency ratios** measure the investment in assets relative to business activity. For example, assume that Custom Ride Inc., plans to sell 5,200 hydraulic cylinders during the next year. If we assume that each cylinder costs $100, Custom Ride would have to invest $520,000 (5,200 × $100) in inventory if the company purchases all 5,200 cylinders on January 1. Although the company would have the cylinders in stock and ready to sell throughout the year, this plan would result in a very inefficient use of company assets. Instead of buying all of the cylinders at the very beginning of the year, Custom Ride could buy just a two-week supply at a time. On average, the company sells about 100 cylinders per week (5,200/52 weeks), so buying a two-week supply (200 cylinders) rather than a one-year supply would reduce the company's investment in inventory from $520,000 to $20,000 (200 × $100). The idea here is that the company will buy 200 cylinders, sell the 200 cylinders, then buy 200 more cylinders, and sell those 200 cylinders. In other words, their inventory of cylinders would *turn over* every two weeks, or 26 times per year. The higher the asset turnover, the more efficiently the company is using its investment in assets. This is because high asset turnover signifies that the company is doing more business with a smaller investment in assets. We will examine the efficiency ratios for total assets, accounts receivable, and inventory.

Asset Turnover Ratio

asset turnover ratio An efficiency ratio that shows the amount of sales produced for a given level of assets used.

Introduced in Chapter 9, the **asset turnover ratio** shows the amount of sales produced for a given level of assets used. It is good when a company can produce high sales with a low investment in assets. Therefore, companies should try to get the most out of every dollar invested in assets. In considering *Pier 1,* we are talking about getting the most sales. The asset turnover ratio is important because it indicates how efficiently the company uses its total assets to generate sales. The formula for this ratio is:

$$\text{Asset turnover ratio} = \frac{\text{Net sales}}{\text{Average total assets}}$$

The net sales figure in the numerator of this ratio comes from the income statement. The amounts we use to calculate the denominator come from the balance sheet. We use an average amount for the same reason we did in earlier ratios. Since the sales in the numerator occurred throughout 2002, we want to know the amount of total assets employed throughout the year. We determine this by calculating the average of the total assets shown on the 2001 and 2002 balance sheets ($735,710 + $862,672 = $1,598,382/2 = $799,191). We calculate *Pier 1*'s asset turnover ratio for 2002 as:

$$\frac{\$1,548,556}{\$799,191} = 1.94 \text{ times}$$

Our calculation indicates that *Pier 1* produced 1.94 times as many dollars in sales during 2002 as it had invested in assets. The higher the multiple, the more efficiently the company is using its assets to produce sales.

Compared to the industry averages for furniture and home furnishings stores published in the Almanac for 2002, *Pier 1*'s asset turnover ratio of 1.94 times is higher than the industry average of 1.3 times for companies with assets over $250 million, but less than the industry average of 2.5 times for all companies in Table II. *Pier 1* is doing better than companies with assets in excess of $250 million, but not as well as the industry as a whole.

Now let's look at the asset turnover ratio for ***Pier 1 Imports, Bed Bath & Beyond,*** and ***Williams-Sonoma.*** The chart in Exhibit 11–10 depicts the asset turnover ratios for the three peer companies for 1999 through 2002.

EXHIBIT 11–10 Asset Turnover Ratios for 1999 Through 2002

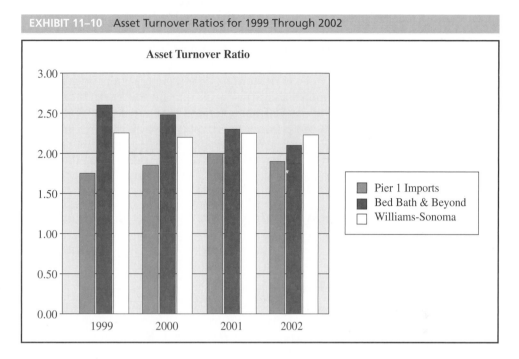

Over the past four years, ***Pier 1***'s asset turnover ratio has improved steadily. Currently, the asset turnover ratio of all three companies is around two, which indicates that ***Pier 1*** compares favorably with the peer companies we are using.

Receivables Turnover Ratio

receivables turnover ratio An efficiency ratio that measures how quickly a company collects its accounts receivable.

Introduced in Chapter 9, the **receivables turnover ratio** measures how efficiently a company manages its accounts receivable. Accounts receivable is the amount a company is owed by its customers, and it is often a significant current asset. Companies need to convert accounts receivable to cash as quickly as possible because, for many companies, they represent interest-free loans to customers. The receivables turnover ratio indicates how quickly a company collects its receivables. The formula for this ratio is:

$$\text{Receivables turnover ratio} = \frac{\text{Net sales}}{\text{Average accounts receivable}}$$

The net sales figure in the numerator comes from the income statement, and the denominator is based on the accounts receivable shown on the balance sheet. We use an average amount for the denominator in this calculation for the same reason we did in earlier ratios. Since the sales used in the numerator occurred throughout 2002, we want to know the amount of accounts receivable throughout the year. We determine this by calculating the average of the accounts receivable shown on the 2001 and 2002 balance sheets. ***Pier 1*** shows two classifications of its accounts receivable on the balance sheets (beneficial interest in securitized receivables and other accounts receivable). If we look in the notes to the financial statements on page 39 of the annual report, we find three paragraphs explaining what the securitized receivables represent. After reading each of the three paragraphs several times to try and figure out what they are talking about, we are satisfied that these receivables should be included in our calculation. Our average accounts receivable calculation, then, is ($75,403 + $8,370 + $44,620 + $6,205 = $134,598/2 = $67,299). We calculate ***Pier 1***'s receivables turnover ratio for 2002 as:

$$\frac{\$1,548,556}{\$67,299} = 23.01 \text{ times}$$

Our calculation indicates that ***Pier 1*** turns its receivables over an average of 23.01 times per year. A higher number would suggest that the company collects cash from its credit customers more quickly and is apparently managing its receivables better. On the other hand, a lower receivables turnover means the company manages its receivables less efficiently.

Although the Almanac publishes industry averages for receivables turnover, it does not calculate the ratio for furniture and home furnishings stores. This is probably because the credit sales these businesses make are generally through credit card companies. Therefore, companies in this industry generally collect their receivables almost immediately. This would explain why ***Pier 1***'s receivables turnover is so high.

The information that ***Pier 1*** turns over its accounts receivable 23.01 times per year becomes easier to interpret if we extend it to determine the average collection period for its accounts receivable. We can do that by dividing the receivables turnover into 365 (the number of days in a year) to determine the average time it takes the company to collect its receivables:

$$\text{Average accounts receivable collection period in days} = \frac{365}{\text{Receivables turnover ratio}}$$

$$\frac{365}{23.01} = 15.86 \text{ days}$$

Our calculation shows that it takes ***Pier 1*** an average of 15.86 days from the sale date to collect cash from its customers. In addition to our calculations for ***Pier 1***, we also calculated the average accounts receivable collection period in days for ***Williams-Sonoma*** for 2002. ***Bed Bath & Beyond*** shows no accounts receivable on their balance sheet, so the company either has no current receivables or they are insignificant and included in other current assets. Exhibit 11–11 shows a chart for the average accounts receivable collection period in days for ***Pier 1*** and ***Williams-Sonoma*** for 2002.

EXHIBIT 11–11   Average Accounts Receivable Collection Period in Days for 2002

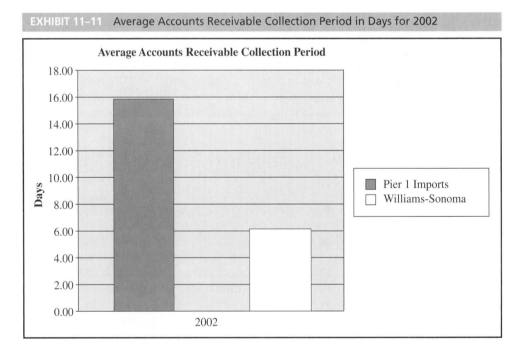

This ratio tells us that the average collection period for receivables is quite short for both ***Pier 1 Imports*** and ***Williams-Sonoma.*** The reason for this is that most of the credit sales for the two companies are done through credit card companies such as ***American Express, MasterCard,*** and ***VISA.*** We can tell from the chart in Exhibit 11–11 that both of the companies are collecting their receivables very quickly, so it appears that neither is having difficulties with collections.

Inventory Turnover Ratio

inventory turnover ratio
An efficiency ratio that indicates how long a company holds its inventory.

Introduced in Chapter 8, the **inventory turnover ratio** measures how efficiently a company uses its investment in inventory. Inventory is often a sizable current asset, and every dollar tied up in inventory is a dollar that can't be used for some other purpose. A company should strive to keep its investment in inventory as low as possible by, for example, purchasing a one-month supply instead of a year's worth of inventory at a time. This way, the company would have to make inventory purchases more often, but the investment in inventory would be substantially less. The inventory turnover ratio indicates the number of times total merchandise inventory is purchased and sold during a period. If a company keeps a one-year supply of inventory on hand, the inventory would turn over once a year. On the other hand, if a company keeps only a one-month supply on hand, the inventory would turn over 12 times per year. The formula for this ratio is:

$$\text{Inventory turnover ratio} = \frac{\text{Cost of goods sold}}{\text{Average inventory}}$$

The cost of goods sold (cost of sales) figure in the numerator comes from the income statement. Remember that *Pier 1* has lumped cost of sales with its buying and store occupancy costs. However, since that is the best amount we have for cost of goods sold—the only amount really—we will use it as this ratio's numerator. The denominator is based on the inventory shown on the balance sheet. We use an average amount for this ratio for the same reason we used an average amount in earlier ratios. Since the cost of sales in the numerator occurred throughout 2002, we should use the amount of inventory throughout the year. We determine this by calculating the average of the inventory shown on the 2001 and 2002 balance sheets ($310,704 + $275,433 = $586,137/2 = $293,068.5). We calculate *Pier 1*'s inventory turnover ratio for 2002 as:

$$\frac{\$898,795}{\$293,068.5} = 3.07 \text{ times}$$

This ratio calculation tells us that *Pier 1* turns its inventory an average of 3.07 times per year. A higher ratio suggests the company requires a lower investment in inventory and is, therefore, using its inventory more efficiently. On the other hand, a lower inventory turnover means the company is using its inventory less efficiently.

Compared to the industry averages for furniture and home furnishings stores published in the Almanac for 2002, *Pier 1*'s inventory turnover ratio of 3.07 times is higher than the industry average of 2.3 times for companies with assets over $250 million, but less than the industry average of 4.2 times for all companies in Table II. *Pier 1* is doing better than companies with assets in excess of $250 million, but not as well as the industry as a whole.

Pier 1's inventory turnover of 3.07 times per year becomes easier to comprehend if we extend the calculation to determine average length of time a product is held in inventory before it is sold. To calculate the average inventory holding period, we divide the inventory turnover ratio into 365 (the number of days in a year). *Pier 1*'s average inventory holding period is:

$$\text{Average inventory holding period in days} = \frac{365}{\text{Inventory turnover ratio}}$$

$$\frac{365}{3.07} = 118.89 \text{ days}$$

This ratio tells us that, on average, 118.89 days pass between the time *Pier 1* purchases inventory and the time it sells that inventory. Exhibit 11–12 on page F–474 shows the average inventory holding period in days for *Pier 1 Imports, Bed Bath & Beyond,* and *Williams-Sonoma* for 2002.

Exhibit 11–12 shows that *Pier 1*'s average inventory holding period is in line with the two peer companies we are using. All three companies have substantial inventories relative to their sales, but *Pier 1*'s average inventory holding period falls between that of *Williams-Sonoma* (about 70 days) and *Bed Bath & Beyond* (just over 140 days).

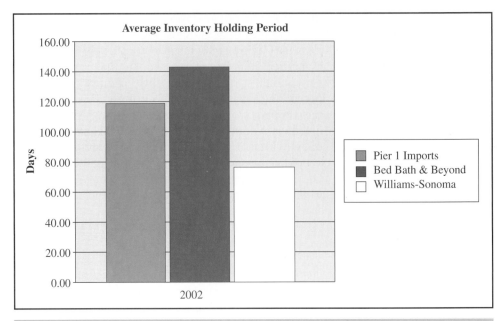

EXHIBIT 11–12   Average Inventory Holding Period in Days for 2002

MEASURING LIQUIDITY

liquidity   An item's nearness to cash.

Cash is the lifeblood that flows through every business. **Liquidity** refers to a company's ability to generate the cash needed to meet its short-term obligations. If a company is very liquid, it means that the company has or can generate enough cash to meet its short-term requirements for cash—it can easily pay its bills on time. If a company is not liquid, it means that the company has difficulty generating enough cash to pay its bills. The bills we are talking about here are those due in the near term, primarily the company's current liabilities. Clearly, all economic decision makers must consider a firm's liquidity, because if a company can't meet its current obligations, it may not be around long enough to prove whether or not it will be profitable in the long run. Short-term creditors and a company's management, however, tend to be those who pay most careful attention to liquidity.

Current Ratio

current ratio   A liquidity ratio that measures a company's ability to meet short-term obligations by comparing current assets to current liabilities.

Introduced in Chapter 9, the **current ratio** was probably the most widely used measure of a company's liquidity for much of the 20th century. Its purpose is to gauge a company's current assets relative to its current liabilities, thereby attempting to offer a measure of the company's ability to meet its short-term financial obligations (its current liabilities) with cash generated from current assets. The formula for this ratio is:

$$\text{Current ratio} = \frac{\text{Current assets}}{\text{Current liabilities}}$$

This ratio indicates the amount of current assets a company has for each dollar of current liabilities, and both the numerator and the denominator come directly from the balance sheet. We calculate *Pier 1*'s current ratio for 2002 as:

$$\frac{\$605,153}{\$208,396} = 2.90 \text{ to } 1, \text{ or simply, } 2.9$$

A current ratio of 2.9 tells us that *Pier 1* had $2.90 of current assets for every $1.00 of current liabilities at the end of 2002.

Compared to the industry averages for furniture and home furnishings stores published in the Almanac for 2002, *Pier 1*'s current ratio of 2.9 to 1 is higher than both the industry average of 1.4 to 1 for companies with assets over $250 million and the industry average of 1.8 to 1 for all companies in Table II. Analysts that are focusing on *Pier 1*'s ability to pay its short-term obligations would be pleased that *Pier 1*'s current ratio is outpacing the industry by so much. On the other hand, analysts focusing on efficient use of assets might argue that a current ratio that is too high is a sign of inefficiency and that the company has too much invested in current assets.

Exhibit 11–13 shows a chart of the current ratios for *Pier 1, Bed Bath & Beyond,* and *Williams-Sonoma* for 2001 and 2002.

EXHIBIT 11–13 Current Ratio Chart for 2001 and 2002

Current Ratio

Legend:
- Pier 1 Imports
- Bed Bath & Beyond
- Williams-Sonoma

It is clear from the chart in Exhibit 11–13 that *Pier 1* has a higher current ratio and, therefore, more current assets relative to their liabilities than the other two companies. This is an indication that *Pier 1* is probably in a stronger position when it comes to their ability to pay current debt. The question then becomes, does the company have *too much* invested in current assets. Analysts use the efficiency ratios we calculated in the previous section to evaluate how efficiently a company uses its assets. If a company has too much invested in current assets, the current ratio looks better, but the company's efficiency ratios suffer.

The current ratio is a well-respected indicator of liquidity, but the problem with this measure is that a company does not pay its bills with accounts receivable, inventory, and other noncash items included in current assets. It must pay its bills with cash. Recall our discussion in Chapter 10 of the renewed focus on cash flow in the 1980s. Part of that renewed focus was that many financial analysts began questioning the importance of the current ratio.

Discussion Question •

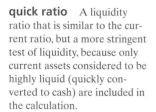

11–8. If *Pier 1* was to borrow money to pay its current liabilities, it would have to pay interest on the borrowed funds. What effect (if any) would the additional interest expense have on the following ratios:

   a. Gross profit margin?
   b. Net profit margin?
   c. Rate of return on assets?
   d. Rate of return on common equity?
   e. Asset turnover?

Quick Ratio

Introduced in Chapter 9, the **quick ratio** (sometimes called the **acid-test ratio**) is similar to the current ratio. It is a more stringent test of liquidity, however, because it considers only current assets that are highly liquid (quickly convertible into cash) in the numerator. The calculations for this ratio vary because there is some debate as to what assets to include. This stems from the fact that the definition of "highly liquid" is quite

quick ratio A liquidity ratio that is similar to the current ratio, but a more stringent test of liquidity, because only current assets considered to be highly liquid (quickly converted to cash) are included in the calculation.

acid-test ratio Another name for the quick ratio.

subjective. The formula that we are using is one of the more conservative, and it is quite popular among financial analysts. The formula for this ratio is:

$$\text{Quick ratio} = \frac{\text{Cash} + \text{Short-term investments} + \text{Current receivables}}{\text{Current liabilities}}$$

In the numerator of our equation, cash is obviously liquid. We also assume accounts receivable will be quickly converted to cash. However, if an analyst knows that any account receivable will not be quickly converted, it should not include that receivable in the calculation of this ratio. For our calculation, *Pier 1* has two classifications of accounts receivable, both of which are included. Marketable securities (temporary investments) held in a company's trading portfolio are usually highly liquid and often represent excess cash that the company plans to use in the near future. As was the case with the current ratio, the denominator of the quick ratio is total current liabilities. We calculate *Pier 1*'s quick ratio for 2002 as:

$$\frac{\$235,609 + \$44,620 + \$6,205}{\$208,396} = 1.37 \text{ to } 1$$

This ratio calculation tells us that *Pier 1* had $1.37 of quick assets for each $1.00 of current liabilities at the end of 2002. Note that *Pier 1*'s quick ratio is lower than its current ratio. That is usually the case because we have removed assets that are not highly liquid from the numerator, while the denominator remains unchanged.

Compared to the industry averages for furniture and home furnishings stores published in the 2002 edition of the Almanac, *Pier 1*'s quick ratio of 1.37 to 1 is higher than both the industry average of 0.5 to 1 for companies with assets over $250 million and the industry average of 0.8 to 1 for all companies in Table II. *Pier 1*'s high quick ratio relative to the industry is a positive indication regarding the company's ability to pay its short-term obligations. But again, some analysts would argue that a quick ratio that is too high is a sign of inefficiency and that the company has too much invested in current assets.

Exhibit 11–14 shows a chart for the quick ratios for *Pier 1, Bed Bath & Beyond,* and *Williams-Sonoma* for 2001 and 2002.

EXHIBIT 11–14 Quick Ratio Chart for 2001 and 2002

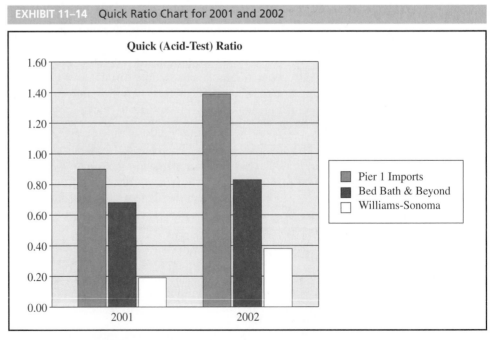

As was the case with the current ratio, *Pier 1 Imports* has a very strong showing for the quick ratio. The fact that *Pier 1*'s quick ratio is higher than those of *Bed Bath & Beyond* and *Williams-Sonoma* is an indication that *Pier 1* is in a better position to pay its short-term liabilities using quick assets.

Discussion Questions

11–9. Besides the three assets—cash, accounts receivable, and notes receivable—considered in our version of the quick ratio, what other quick assets might a company have?

11–10. How would holding an excessive amount of inventory affect the following ratios:

    a. Gross profit margin?
    b. Net profit margin?
    c. Rate of return on assets?
    d. Rate of return on common equity?
    e. Asset turnover?
    f. Current ratio?
    g. Quick ratio?

Operating Cash Flow to Current Debt Ratio

operating cash flow to current debt ratio A financial ratio that measures the sufficiency of cash flows from operating activities to meet current obligations.

Introduced in Chapter 10, the **operating cash flow to current debt ratio** measures the sufficiency of cash flows from operating activities to meet current obligations. In other words, it measures the company's ability to generate enough cash from operating activities to meet its current obligations. Whereas the current and quick ratios measure liquidity based on the financial resources the company has on hand (its assets), the operating cash flow to current debt ratio measures a company's ability to maintain liquidity by generating sufficient cash inflows from its operations. The formula for this ratio is:

$$\text{Operating cash flow to current debt ratio} = \frac{\text{Cash provided by operating activities}}{\text{Average current liabilities}}$$

As you can see, the numerator is cash provided by operating activities from the statement of cash flows and the denominator is based on current liabilities from the balance sheet. We use an average for current liabilities for the same reason we used average amounts for earlier ratios. Since the cash provided by operating activities in the numerator occurred throughout 2002, we should use an approximation of the current liabilities outstanding throughout the year. We determine this by calculating the average of the current liabilities shown on the 2001 and 2002 balance sheets ($144,110 + $208,396 = $352,506/2 = $176,253). We calculate *Pier 1*'s operating cash flow to current debt ratio for 2002 as:

$$\frac{\$244,324}{\$176,253} = 1.39 \text{ to } 1$$

This ratio calculation tells us that *Pier 1*'s operating activities generated $1.39 of cash in 2002 for each $1.00 of its average current liabilities. Generally speaking, generating a high amount of cash inflow from operating activities relative to current liabilities is a positive indication. But, how does *Pier 1*'s operating cash flow to current debt ratio of 1.39 stack up compared to other companies? Unfortunately, the Almanac does not publish industry averages for this ratio, so we will have to rely solely on our peer company comparison. Exhibit 11–15 on page F–478 shows a chart for the operating cash flow to current debt for *Pier 1 Imports, Bed Bath & Beyond,* and *Williams-Sonoma.*

As Exhibit 11–15 shows, *Pier 1*'s operating cash flows to current debt is consistently above that of the peer companies we are using. This means that *Pier 1*'s cash inflow from operating activities relative to current liabilities is higher than those of *Bed Bath & Beyond* and *Williams-Sonoma.*

MEASURING SOLVENCY

solvency A company's ability to meet the obligations created by its long-term debt obligations.

Solvency refers to a company's ability to meet its long-term financial obligations. Debt obligations include both paying back the amount borrowed and paying interest on the debt. Over time, analysts have developed a set of solvency ratios, some focusing on the

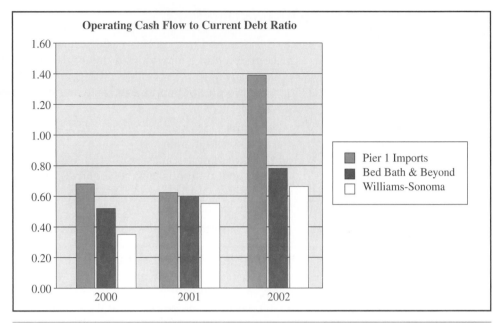

Operating Cash Flow to Current Debt Ratio

Pier 1 Imports
Bed Bath & Beyond
Williams-Sonoma

EXHIBIT 11–15   Operating Cash Flow to Current Debt Chart for 2000 Through 2002

overall level of debt a company carries, while others measure a company's ability to make interest payments. Solvency ratios are of most importance to economic decision makers interested in the long-term outlook for the company. These decision makers include stockholders, long-term creditors, and, of course, company management.

Debt Ratio

debt ratio   A solvency ratio that indicates what proportion of a company's assets is financed by debt.

Introduced in Chapter 3, the **debt ratio** measures the proportion of a company's assets financed by debt. All of a company's assets are financed by either creditors (debt) or by the owners (equity). This can be demonstrated by looking once again at the accounting (business) equation:

$$\text{Assets} \;=\; \text{Liabilities} \;+\; \text{Owners' equity}$$
$$100 \text{ percent} = \text{Some percent} + \text{ Some percent}$$

Or:

$$\text{Assets} \;=\; \text{Liabilities} \;+\; \text{Owners' equity}$$
$$100\% \;=\; \text{Some \%} \;+\; \text{Some \%}$$

The debt ratio calculates the percentage of a company's assets that are financed by debt. Like other ratios, the exact formula for the debt ratio varies somewhat depending on the analyst. Some analysts exclude interest-free financing from liabilities, for example. In our example, we will include all liabilities so the formula is:

$$\text{Debt ratio} = \frac{\text{Total liabilities}}{\text{Total assets}}$$

As you know, both assets and liabilities are found on the balance sheet; however, in *Pier 1*'s case, the balance sheet does not show a total liabilities amount. We can calculate it two ways: One way is to add up all the liabilities (current liabilities of \$208,396 + long-term debt of \$25,356 + other noncurrent liabilities of \$43,264 = \$277,016). A second, simpler way to calculate total liabilities is to subtract the shareholders' equity amount from total liabilities and shareholders' equity (total liabilities and shareholders' equity of \$862,672 − shareholders' equity of \$585,656 = \$277,016). As you can see, either approach yields the same amount for total liabilities. We calculate *Pier 1*'s debt ratio for 2002 as:

$$\frac{\$277,016}{\$862,672} = 0.3211 \text{ or } 32.11\%$$

This ratio calculation tells us that as of the end of 2002, 32.11 percent of *Pier 1*'s assets are financed by debt. By extension then, 67.89 percent of the company's assets are financed by equity.

Compared to the industry averages for furniture and home furnishings stores published in the Almanac for 2002, *Pier 1*'s debt ratio of 32.11 percent is lower than both the industry average of 53.0 percent for companies with assets over $250 million and the industry average of 55.2 percent for all companies in Table II. Analysts that are focusing on *Pier 1*'s ability to meet its obligations would be pleased that *Pier 1*'s debt ratio is so low relative to the industry.

Now let's see how *Pier 1*'s debt ratio compares to our two peer companies. Exhibit 11–16 shows how *Pier 1*'s debt ratio compares to those of *Bed Bath & Beyond* and *Williams-Sonoma.*

EXHIBIT 11–16   Debt Ratio Chart for 1998 Through 2002

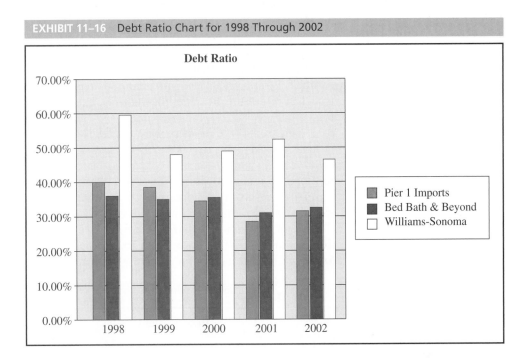

Pier 1 Imports has less of its assets financed through debt than the two peer companies we are using. It is also interesting to note the *Pier 1*'s debt ratio has generally decreased over the past five years. There is no hard-and-fast rule concerning what amount of a company's assets should be financed through debt. Creditors tend to feel better when a company's debt ratio is on the low, more conservative side. Equity investors may feel the same way, but in some situations, the equity investors would like more debt. Remember, the company pays a certain amount, a certain interest rate for its debt financing. For example, if a company borrows funds at 8 percent, say, it pays the 8 percent and no more. If the company uses the funds it has borrowed and earns a return of say, 20 percent, 12 percent of the return (20% − 8%) is available to equity investors. This situation, called *financial leverage,* is a very interesting phenomenon because the equity investors are earning a return on funds they did not even invest. That is, by virtue of owning stock in the company, the shareholders are able to earn a return on not only their equity investment, but also on the investment made by creditors. Of course, if the company earns a return that is less than the fixed interest rate it must pay on borrowed funds, any shortfall comes from the return that would otherwise be available to equity investors. Most analysts would agree that less debt is more conservative and in many cases the best approach. Although all of the companies in Exhibit 11–16 are all within a reasonably close range, *Pier 1 Imports* is in the most conservative debt position of the three. A company's debt ratio must be evaluated in light of peer companies in the industry, the maturity of the company (new businesses tend to have more debt relative to equity), and management's philosophy concerning the appropriate balance between debt financing and equity financing.

debt-to-equity ratio A solvency ratio that expresses the proportional relationship between liabilities and equity.

Debt-to-Equity Ratio

Introduced in Chapter 3, the **debt-to-equity ratio** expresses the proportional relationship between liabilities and equity. Many financial publications call this ratio the *total liabilities to net worth ratio*. You must remember this, because many of these publications do not include a ratio called the debt-to-equity ratio. They have the ratio, but call it something else. The formula for this ratio is:

$$\text{Dept-to-equity ratio} = \frac{\text{Total liabilities}}{\text{Total equity}}$$

Both the items necessary to calculate the debt-to-equity ratio come from the balance sheet. As you can see, the numerator, total liabilities, is the same as it is for the debt ratio, and for the denominator, we use total shareholders' equity. We calculate *Pier 1*'s debt-to-equity ratio for 2002 as:

$$\frac{\$277,016}{\$585,656} = .4730 \text{ to } 1$$

This ratio tells us that at the end of 2002, *Pier 1* had $0.47 of debt for every $1.00 of equity. This ratio reveals essentially the same information as the debt ratio but presents it slightly different. The lower the debt-to-equity ratio, the lower total debt is relative to total equity.

Compared to the industry averages for furniture and home furnishings stores published in the Almanac for 2002, *Pier 1*'s debt-to-equity ratio (called the *total liabilities to net worth ratio* in the Almanac) of .4730 to 1 is lower than both the industry average of 1.1 to 1 for companies with assets over $250 million and the industry average of 1.2 to 1 for all companies in Table II. Analysts that are focusing on *Pier 1*'s ability to meet its obligations would be pleased that *Pier 1*'s debt-to-equity is so low relative to the industry.

Now let's see how *Pier 1*'s debt-to-equity ratio compares to our two peer companies. Exhibit 11–17 shows a chart for *Pier 1, Bed Bath & Beyond,* and *Williams-Sonoma*'s debt-to-equity ratios for 1998 through 2002.

EXHIBIT 11–17   Debt-to-Equity Ratio for 1998 Through 2002

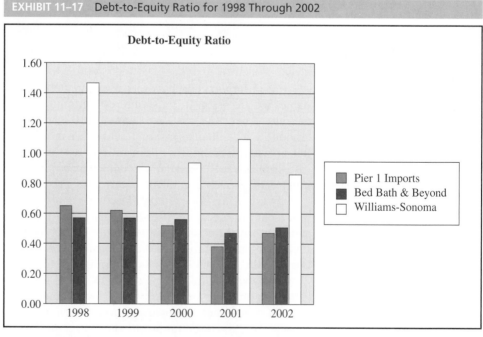

As we would expect after looking at the debt ratio for the three companies, we see that *Pier 1*'s debt is lower in proportion to equity than that of *Bed Bath & Beyond* or *Williams-Sonoma.* And, once again, there is no hard-and-fast rule concerning what a company's debt should be relative to its equity. A company's debt-to-equity ratio must be evaluated in light of peer companies in the industry, the maturity of the company (new businesses tend to have more debt relative to equity), and management's philosophy concerning the appropriate balance between debt financing and equity financing.

times interest earned ratio A financial ratio that indicates a company's ability to earn (cover) its periodic interest payments.

coverage ratio Same as the times interest earned ratio.

Times Interest Earned Ratio

Introduced in Chapter 9, the times interest earned ratio (often called the **coverage ratio**) indicates a company's ability to earn (cover) its periodic interest payments. It compares the amount of income available for interest payments to the interest requirements. Creditors use this ratio to assess the risk associated with lending money to a business. The formula for this ratio is:

$$\text{Times interest earned ratio} = \frac{\text{Earnings before interest and income taxes}}{\text{Interest expense}}$$

Earnings before interest and taxes, which is often called *EBIT*, can be calculated by taking net income and adding back income taxes and interest. In the case of *Pier 1,* EBIT is $161,297 (net income of $100,209 + income taxes of $58,788 and interest expense of $2,300). We calculate *Pier 1*'s times interest earned ratio for 2002 as:

$$\frac{\$161,297}{\$2,300} = 70.13 \text{ times}$$

This ratio calculation tells us *Pier 1*'s income available to pay interest expense was a whopping $70.13 for every $1.00 of interest expense. In other words, the income *Pier 1* had available to pay interest expense was 70.13 times the amount of interest the company reported on its income statement.

Compared to the industry averages for furniture and home furnishings stores published in the Almanac for 2002, *Pier 1*'s times interest earned ratio (called the *coverage ratio* in the Almanac) of 70.13 times is much higher than both the industry average of 5.6 times for companies with assets over $250 million and the industry average of 6.7 times for all companies in Table II. This is because *Pier 1*'s debt is almost entirely comprised of interest-free financing through short-term creditors. Analysts that are focusing on *Pier 1*'s ability to pay interest would have no concern whatsoever that *Pier 1* could meet this obligation.

Now let's see how *Pier 1*'s times interest earned ratio compares to our two peer companies. Exhibit 11–18 shows a chart depicting the times interest earned for *Pier 1 Imports, Bed Bath & Beyond,* and *Williams-Sonoma* for 2000 through 2002.

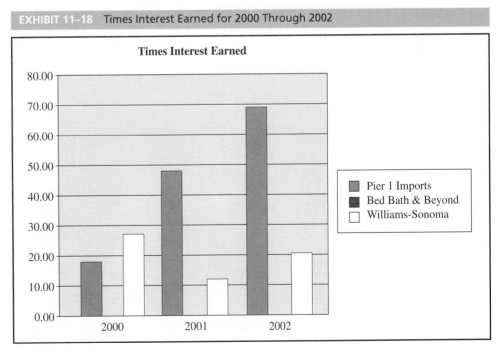

EXHIBIT 11–18 Times Interest Earned for 2000 Through 2002

Many financial analysts believe a times interest earned ratio of at least four provides an appropriate degree of safety for creditors. This means a company's EBIT should be at least four times as great as its interest expense. The chart in Exhibit 11–18 reveals that both *Pier 1* and *Williams-Sonoma* far exceed that level. *Bed Bath &*

Beyond does not even appear on the chart because the company has virtually no interest expense.

Operating Cash Flow Coverage Ratio

operating cash flow coverage ratio A financial ratio that indicates a company's capacity to repay its liabilities from the net cash generated by its operating activities.

Introduced in Chapter 10, the **operating cash flow coverage ratio** indicates a company's capacity to repay its liabilities from the net cash generated by its operating activities. The formula for this ratio is:

$$\text{Operating cash flow coverage ratio} = \frac{\text{Cash provided by operating activities}}{\text{Average total liabilities}}$$

As you can see, the numerator is cash provided by operating activities shown on the statement of cash flows. The denominator is based on the total liabilities shown on the balance sheet. We use an average amount for the same reason we did in earlier ratios. Since the cash provided by operating activities in the numerator occurred throughout 2002, we want to know the total liabilities throughout the year. We determine this by calculating the average of the total liabilities shown on the 2001 and 2002 balance sheets ($203,831 + $277,016 = $480,847/2 = $240,423.5). We calculate *Pier 1*'s operating cash flow coverage ratio for 2002 as:

$$\frac{\$244,324}{\$240,423.5} = 1.02 \text{ to } 1$$

This ratio tells us that *Pier 1* generated $1.02 of cash through its operation in 2002 for every $1.00 of its average total liabilities for 2002. The higher this ratio is, the more likely a company is to be able to service its debt without going outside the company for financing (by either borrowing additional funds or selling additional shares of its stock).

Although the Almanac publishes some industry averages for cash flow ratios, it defines cash flows as *the difference between cash receipts and cash disbursements*. Unlike the ratio we are using, the Almanac does not focus specifically on cash flow from operating activities. Therefore, we will have to rely on our peer companies as comparisons to evaluate *Pier 1*'s operating cash flow coverage ratio. A chart depicting the operating cash flow coverage ratio for *Pier 1 Imports, Bed Bath & Beyond,* and *Williams-Sonoma* appears in Exhibit 11–19.

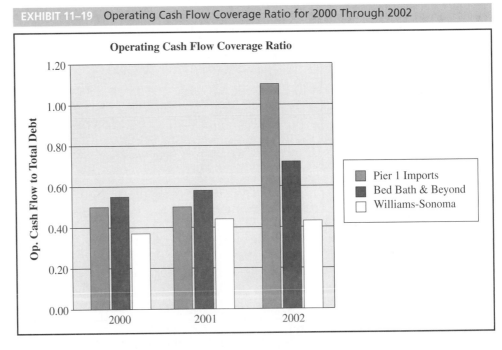

EXHIBIT 11–19 Operating Cash Flow Coverage Ratio for 2000 Through 2002

Pier 1's operating cash flow coverage ratio has been improving, and it compares favorably to the ratios of the peer companies we have been examining. As Exhibit 11–19 shows, *Pier 1*'s operating cash flow coverage ratio is currently above that of the peer companies we are using. This means that *Pier 1*'s cash inflow from operating activities relative to total debt is higher than those of *Bed Bath & Beyond* and *Williams-Sonoma.*

Discussion Questions

11–11. Assume you had to decide to invest in one of two companies with no information other than values of four of their financial ratios. Which four would you want to know? Explain the reasons for your choices.

11–12. Carol Company and Cindy Corporation are in the same line of business. However, Carol uses straight-line depreciation, whereas Cindy uses an accelerated depreciation method. If this is the only difference in the business activity of the two companies, how should their financial ratios compare at the end of their first year of operations? Explain the effect of the difference in depreciation methods on each of the 17 ratios described in this chapter.

Analysts use ratio analysis to evaluate the company's current levels of profitability, efficiency, liquidity, and solvency. Ratios can send up red flags that warn management, creditors, and investors of trouble ahead. An unprofitable company becomes illiquid because it cannot generate profits and cash, which eventually leads to insolvency. Insolvency leads to bankruptcy. When red flags appear, management can initiate corrective action to prevent future troubles. Next, we will summarize our findings concerning *Pier 1*'s profitability, efficiency, liquidity, and solvency.

SUMMARIZING *PIER 1*'S RATIO ANALYSIS

In the following section, we summarize the results of our ratio analysis and try to rate *Pier 1*'s performance relative to the furniture and home furnishings stores industry and the two peer companies we used as comparisons. Where appropriate, to make the summaries a little easier to follow, we will use the following performance descriptions:

Very strong
Strong
Fairly strong
Average
Fairly weak
Weak
Very weak

We are only using these descriptions to help you understand the explanations that follow. They are not official financial analysis rankings of any kind.

Profitability

Gross profit margin ratio — Very strong. *Pier 1*'s gross profit margin ratio is consistently higher than those of *Bed Bath & Beyond* and *Williams-Sonoma. Pier 1*'s gross profit percentage has been fairly constant between about 42 and 44 percent. Note that the Almanac does not publish industry averages for this ratio.

Net profit margin ratio — Strong. Clearly, *Pier 1*'s 6.47 percent net profit margin ratio is substantially higher than the industry averages of 3.7 percent for all companies and 4.8 percent for companies with assets in excess of $250 million. *Pier 1*'s net profit margin ratio is consistently between about 6 and 7 percent. This is higher than *Williams-Sonoma*'s net profit margin but, in the last three years, *Bed Bath & Beyond*'s ratio has edged out *Pier 1*'s.

Rate of return on assets ratio — Strong. *Pier 1*'s 12.54 percent rate of return on assets ratio is on par with the industry averages of 12.7 percent for all companies and 11.4 percent for companies with assets in excess of $250 million. *Pier 1*'s rate of return on assets is clearly higher than that of *Williams-Sonoma* but somewhat lower than that of *Bed Bath & Beyond. Pier 1*'s return on assets ratio has been quite stable, if not increasing. This contrasts to those of the two peer company's rates, which have been declining somewhat.

Rate of return on common equity ratio—Strong. **Pier 1**'s 17.17 percent rate of return on common equity ratio is less than the industry average of 20.8 percent for all companies, but much stronger than the 13.4 percent for companies with assets in excess of $250 million. **Pier 1**'s rate of return on common equity is consistently between about 17 and 20 percent. Although it is below that of **Bed Bath & Beyond,** it has surpassed that of **Williams-Sonoma,** and it is holding steady.

Dividend payout ratio—Strong. **Pier 1** consistently pays a dividend of about 15 percent of net income, while neither **Bed Bath & Beyond** nor **Williams-Sonoma** pays a dividend at all. Note that the Almanac does not publish industry averages for this ratio.

Earnings per share—Very strong. **Pier 1**'s earnings per share is clearly the highest of the three peer companies, and the earnings per share for each of our three companies has generally increased over time. Note that the Almanac does not publish industry averages for earnings per share.

Price-to-earnings ratio—Rating not possible because it is too subjective. **Pier 1**'s PE ratio is clearly lower than those of **Bed Bath & Beyond** and **Williams-Sonoma.** Although it is not always the case, a high PE ratio *may* indicate that the stock is overvalued, whereas a low PE ratio may indicate that it is undervalued. Note that the Almanac does not publish industry averages for this ratio.

Efficiency

Asset turnover ratio—Fairly strong. Compared to the industry averages, **Pier 1**'s asset turnover ratio of 1.94 times is higher than the industry average of 1.3 times for companies with assets over $250 million, but less than the industry average of 2.5 times for all companies. **Pier 1** is doing better than companies with assets in excess of $250 million, but not as well as the industry as a whole. Over the past five years, **Pier 1**'s asset turnover ratio has improved steadily. Currently, the asset turnover ratio of all three companies is around two, which indicates that **Pier 1** compares favorably with the peer companies we are using.

Receivables turnover ratio—Very strong. This ratio tells us that the average collection period for receivables is quite short for both **Pier 1 Imports** and **Williams-Sonoma.** Both of the companies are collecting their receivables so quickly that it appears that neither is having difficulties with collections. Note that there were no receivables listed in **Bed Bath & Beyond**'s annual report. Due to the lack of data for this industry, the Almanac does not publish industry averages for this ratio for furniture and home furnishings stores.

Inventory turnover ratio—Fairly strong. Compared to the industry averages published in the 2002 edition of the Almanac, **Pier 1**'s inventory turnover ratio of 3.07 times is higher than the industry average of 2.3 times for companies with assets over $250 million, but less than the industry average of 4.2 times for all companies in Table II. This is an indication that **Pier 1** is doing better than the industry average for companies with assets in excess of $250 million, but not as well as the industry as a whole. With respect to the peer company comparison, all three companies have substantial inventories relative to their sales, and **Pier 1**'s average inventory holding period of 118.89 days falls between that of **Williams-Sonoma** (about 70 days) and **Bed Bath & Beyond** (just over 140 days).

Liquidity

Current ratio—Very strong. Compared to the industry, **Pier 1**'s current ratio of 2.9 to 1 is higher than both the industry average of 1.4 to 1 for companies with assets over $250 million and the industry average of 1.8 to 1 for all companies in Table II. In the peer company comparison, it is also clear that **Pier 1 Imports** has a higher current ratio than the other two companies. This is an indication that **Pier 1** is probably in a stronger position when it comes to its ability to pay current debt. However, if a company has too much invested in current assets, the current ratio looks better, but the company's efficiency ratios suffer.

Quick ratio—Very strong. Compared to the industry averages, *Pier 1*'s quick ratio of 1.37 to 1 is higher than both the industry average of 0.5 to 1 for companies with assets over $250 million and the industry average of 0.8 to 1 for all companies in Table II. *Pier 1*'s high quick ratio relative to the industry is a positive indication regarding the company's ability to pay its short-term obligations. With respect to the peer company comparison, *Pier 1 Imports* has a very strong showing for the quick ratio. The fact that *Pier 1*'s quick ratio is higher than those of *Bed Bath & Beyond* and *Williams-Sonoma* is an indication that *Pier 1* is in a better position to pay its short-term liabilities using quick assets. Some analysts would argue, however, that a quick ratio that is too high is a sign of inefficiency and that the company has too much invested in current assets.

Operating cash flows to current debt ratio—Very strong. The Almanac does not publish industry averages for this ratio, so we will have to rely solely on our peer company comparison. *Pier 1*'s operating cash flows to current debt ratio is consistently above those of *Bed Bath & Beyond* and *Williams-Sonoma,* indicating that *Pier 1*'s cash inflow from operating activities relative to current liabilities is higher than that of the two peer companies.

Solvency

Debt ratio—Very strong. Compared to the industry averages, *Pier 1*'s debt ratio of 32.11 percent is lower than both the industry average of 53.0 percent for companies with assets over $250 million and the industry average of 55.2 percent for all companies in Table II. With respect to our peer company comparison, *Pier 1* has less of its assets financed through debt than *Bed Bath & Beyond* and *Williams-Sonoma.* Also, *Pier 1*'s debt ratio has generally decreased over the past five years. Although there is no hard-and-fast rule concerning what amount of a company's assets should be financed through debt, analysts that are focusing on *Pier 1*'s ability to meet its obligations would be pleased that *Pier 1*'s debt ratio is so low relative to the industry and its peer companies.

Debt-to-equity ratio—Very strong. Compared to the industry averages, *Pier 1*'s debt-to-equity ratio (called the *total liabilities to net worth ratio* in the Almanac) of .4730 to 1 is lower than both the industry average of 1.1 to 1 for companies with assets over $250 million and the industry average of 1.2 to 1 for all companies in Table II. With respect to our peer company comparison, *Pier 1*'s debt is lower in proportion to equity than that of *Bed Bath & Beyond* or *Williams-Sonoma.* Once again, there is no hard-and-fast rule concerning what a company's debt should be relative to its equity; however, analysts that are focusing on *Pier 1*'s ability to meet its obligations would be pleased that *Pier 1*'s debt-to-equity ratio is so low relative to the industry and its peer companies.

Times interest earned ratio—Very strong. Compared to the industry averages, *Pier 1*'s times interest earned ratio (called the *coverage ratio* in the Almanac) of 70.13 times is much higher than both the industry average of 5.6 times for companies with assets over $250 million and the industry average of 6.7 times for all companies in Table II. With respect to our peer comparisons, *Bed Bath & Beyond* has virtually no interest expense, but *Pier 1*'s times interest earned ratio compared favorably with that of *Williams-Sonoma.* Additionally, *Pier 1*'s times interest earned ratio has increased substantially over the past three years. All of this indicates that *Pier 1* is in a very strong position when it comes to its ability to meet its obligation to pay interest.

Operating cash flow coverage ratio—Very strong. The Almanac does not publish industry averages for this ratio, so we will have to rely solely on our peer company comparison. *Pier 1*'s operating cash flow coverage ratio has been improving, and it compares favorably to the ratios of the peer companies we have been examining. At 1.02 to 1, *Pier 1*'s operating cash flow coverage ratio is currently above that of the peer companies we are using. This means that *Pier 1*'s cash inflow from operating activities relative to total debt is higher than those of *Bed Bath & Beyond* and *Williams-Sonoma.*

CONSIDERING THE INDUSTRY ENVIRONMENT—A CRUCIAL STEP IN FINANCIAL ANALYSIS

Any change in political or economic forecasts will have a ripple effect and impact most industries. *Pier 1 Imports Inc.,* is a specialty retailer operating three store chains under the names *Pier 1 Imports, The Pier,* and *Cargo,* selling furniture, decorative home furnishings, dining and kitchen goods, and bath and bedding accessories. When researching the industry outlook, we find the outlook for SIC 5700 in Chapter 42 of the *U.S. Industry & Trade Outlook 2000* (a Standard & Poor's publication). This chapter includes the outlook for retail trade covering SIC codes 5200 through 5999. It predicts moderate growth for retailers through the year 2004 with a 4.5 percent average growth rate. This growth rate is due to a slight slowdown in spending on new homes and related durable and nondurable home furnishings. Standard & Poor's suggests that a successful retailer will have to increase its market share by offering fair prices, creating value for its customers, being convenient for busy shoppers, and emphasizing customer service.

Standard & Poor's produces another publication, *Industry Surveys*, which is more specific to individual industry groups. It contains weekly and monthly updates in a loose leaf publication format. In the July 2002 issue ("Monthly Investment Review," p. 64), S&P discusses that the retail specialty stores industry has outperformed the total stock market with a stock price increase of 7.6 percent contrasted with the 9.3 percent decrease in the S&P 1500 stocks. The companies' stocks, which are classified in this industry, have risen 7.6 percent, while their home furnishing sales during the same time period have increased only 1 percent. Since consumers are spending more time at home, *Industry Surveys* predicts neutral to slightly favorable short-term results for home furnishing retailers and forecasts that internet sales will become increasingly important for future growth. It suggests that firms with value, a strong brand name, aggressive brand support, and internet sales market will prosper in the long run.

Industry Surveys focuses on one area in each publication, such as the January 31, 2002, issue that focused on specialty retailing. Specialty stores increased slightly in the market share of home furnishings. More consumers are precision shoppers who go after what they want and are less likely to make impulse purchases.

Now that we have analyzed *Pier 1*'s financial information and we have reviewed the outlook for the company's industry, we can draw some conclusions.

FINANCIAL ANALYSIS CONCLUSIONS

The conclusions that an analyst draws depends largely on individual perceptions and the analysts objectives. Remember, the objectives of financial analysts differ. But, generally, we can draw the flowing conclusions from our analysis of *Pier 1 Imports, Inc.*

1. *Pier 1* is an industry leader with strong profitability and liquidity and a very strong solvency picture.
2. If *Pier 1* can maintain its leadership position and hold down its debt, it might be a survivor in the tough competitive industry in which it operates.
3. We expect the furniture and home furnishings stores industry to continue to be at least neutral or perhaps slightly positive.
4. If we choose to invest in a specialty retail company, *Pier 1* is one to consider.

◆ LIMITATIONS OF FINANCIAL STATEMENT ANALYSIS

Ratio analysis is an excellent tool for gathering additional information about a company, but it does have its limitations.

1. Attempting to predict the future using past results depends on the predictive value of the information we use. Changes in the general economy, in the economy of the particular industry being studied, and in the company's management present some of the uncertainties that can cause past results to be an unreliable predictor of the future.

2. The financial statements used to compute the ratios are based on historical cost. In a time of rapidly changing prices, comparison between years might be difficult.

3. Figures from the balance sheet (i.e., assets, liabilities) used to calculate the ratios are year-end numbers. Because most businesses have their fiscal year-end in the slowest part of the year, the balances in such accounts as receivables, payables, and inventory at year-end may not be representative of the rest of the year. Even when averages are used instead of year-end amounts, the problem is not eliminated, for averages are typically based on year-end numbers from two consecutive years.

4. Industry peculiarities create difficulty in comparing the ratios of a company in one industry with those of a company in another industry. Even comparison of companies within an industry may not be reasonable at times because different companies use different accounting methods (e.g., depreciation methods).

5. Lack of uniformity concerning what is to be included in the numerators and denominators of specific ratios makes comparison to published industry averages extremely difficult.

Perhaps the greatest single limitation of ratio analysis is that people tend to place too much reliance on the ratios. Financial ratios should not be viewed as a magical checklist in the evaluation process. Ratio analysis only enriches all the other information decision makers should consider when making credit, investment, and similar types of decisions.

Summary ●

In response to the need to reduce uncertainty in the decision making process, analysts developed several techniques to assist economic decision makers as they evaluate financial statement information. Creditors (short-term and long-term), equity investors (present and potential), and company management comprise the three major categories of financial statement users. Because their objectives vary, their perspectives on the results of financial statement analysis will differ.

Three external factors—general economic conditions and expectations, political events and political climate, and industry outlook—affect business performance and should be considered when evaluating results of any type of financial statement analysis.

One important method of financial statement analysis is ratio analysis, a technique for analyzing the relationship between two items from a company's financial statements for a given period. We compute ratios by dividing the dollar amount of one item from the financial statements by the dollar amount of the other item from the statements.

Analysts have developed a great many ratios over time to help economic decision makers assess a company's financial health. Because not all ratios are relevant in a given decision situation, decision makers must take care to select appropriate ratios to analyze. Ratio values, in and of themselves, have very little meaning and become meaningful only when compared to other relevant information, such as industry averages or the company's ratio values from other years.

We broadly classify financial ratios as profitability ratios, efficiency ratios, liquidity ratios, and solvency ratios. Profitability ratios measure the ease with which companies generate income. Efficiency ratios measure the investment in assets relative to business activity. Liquidity ratios measure a company's ability to generate positive cash flow in the short run to pay off short-term liabilities. Solvency ratios measure a company's ability to meet the obligations created by its long-term debt.

Each of the profitability, efficiency, liquidity, and solvency ratios provides valuable information for both internal and external decision makers. Ratio analysis does have its limitations, however. Placing too much reliance on the financial statements and the ratios derived from them without putting the information in the proper political, economic, and industry perspective can lead to poor decisions. Ratio analysis is an important financial analysis tool, but as with the other tools we have discussed throughout this book, it must be used wisely and in the proper context.

Key Terms ●●

- acid-test ratio, F–475
- asset turnover ratio, F–470
- coverage ratio, F–481
- current ratio, F–474
- debt ratio, F–478
- debt-to-equity ratio, F–480
- dividend payout ratio, F–466
- earnings per share ratio, F–468
- efficiency ratios, F–470
- financial accounting, F–449

- gross profit margin ratio, F–462
- inventory turnover ratio, F–473
- liquidity, F–474
- management accounting, F–449
- net profit margin ratio, F–463
- net sales, F–462
- operating cash flow coverage ratio, F–482
- operating cash flow to current debt ratio, F–477

- peer companies, F–455
- price-to-earnings ratio, F–469
- profitability, F–461
- quick ratio, F–475
- rate of return on assets ratio, F–465
- rate of return on common equity ratio, F–466
- receivables turnover ratio, F–471
- solvency, F–477
- times interest earned ratio, F–481

Review the Facts ●●●●●●●●●●●●●●●●●●●●●●●●●●●●●●●●●●●●

A. What is the purpose of financial statement analysis?
B. List the three financial statement user groups discussed in the chapter and describe what each group hopes to learn from financial statement analysis.
C. Describe the three types of external factors the Financial Accounting Standards Board (FASB) warns users of financial information to consider, and explain how each factor can impact a company's performance.
D. Briefly describe the purpose and meaning of NAICS.
E. How does NAICS relate to the SIC code system?
F. Describe how you could find publicly traded peer companies to use for financial comparisons.
G. Name three sources of financial industry averages.
H. Define profitability.
I. List the seven profitability ratios discussed in the chapter. Describe the calculation and the purpose of each.
J. Describe the calculation and the purpose of each of the three efficiency ratios mentioned in the chapter.
K. Define liquidity.
L. List the three liquidity ratios discussed in the chapter. For each one, describe the calculation used and the purpose of the ratio.
M. What is the difference between the current ratio and the quick ratio? What is the purpose in examining both?
N. Define solvency.
O. List the four solvency ratios discussed in the chapter. For each one, describe the calculation used and the purpose of the ratio.
P. How are the debt ratio and debt-to-equity ratio related?
Q. What information can be learned from a company's times interest earned ratio?
R. Describe five limitations of ratio analysis discussed in the chapter.

Apply What You Have Learned ●●●●●●●●●●●●●●●●●●●●●●●●●

LO 1: IDENTIFY FINANCIAL STATEMENT ANALYSIS USERS

11–13. Identify the three major categories of financial statement analysis users and describe the basic objectives of each group.

LO 2: GATHERING BACKGROUND INFORMATION

11–14. Discuss how one goes about gathering background information on a company.

LO 1 & 4: MATCHING

11–15. Listed below are items relating to the concepts presented in this chapter, followed by definitions of those items in scrambled order:

a. Financial statement analysis
b. Ratio analysis
c. Short-term creditors
d. Long-term creditors
e. Stockholders
f. Management
g. Profitability

h. Profitability ratios
i. Liquidity
j. Liquidity ratios
k. Solvency
l. Solvency ratios
m. Standard Industrial Classification
n. NAICS

1. _____ Designed to measure a firm's ability to generate sufficient cash to meet its short-term obligations.
2. _____ A method for analyzing the relationship between two items from a company's financial statements for a given period.
3. _____ Designed to measure the ease with which a company generates income.
4. _____ Focus on interest payments and the overall debt load a company carries.
5. _____ The old system to indicate a company's industry.
6. _____ The new system to indicate a company's industry.
7. _____ Looking beyond the face of the financial statements to gather additional information.
8. _____ Those who own an equity interest in a corporation.
9. _____ The ease with which an item, such as an asset, can be converted into cash.
10. _____ Trade creditors and lending institutions such as banks.
11. _____ A company's ability to meet the obligations created by its long-term debt.
12. _____ Bondholders and lending institutions such as banks.
13. _____ The ease with which companies generate income.
14. _____ Responsible for a company's day-to-day operations.

Required: Match the letter next to each item on the list with the appropriate definition. Each letter will be used only once.

LO 5: MATCHING

11–16. Listed below are all the ratios discussed in this chapter, followed by explanations of what the ratios are designed to measure in scrambled order:

a. Gross profit margin ratio
b. Net profit margin ratio
c. Rate of return on assets ratio
d. Rate of return on common equity
e. Dividend payout ratio
f. Earnings per share
g. Price-to-earnings ratio
h. Asset turnover ratio
i. Receivables turnover ratio

j. Inventory turnover ratio
k. Current ratio
l. Quick ratio
m. Operating cash flow to current debt ratio
n. Debt ratio
o. Debt-to-equity ratio
p. Times interest earned
q. Operating cash flow coverage ratio

1. _____ Most common ratio used to measure a company's ability to meet short-term obligations.
2. _____ Measures a company's ability to make periodic interest payments.
3. _____ Measures the return earned on investment in assets.
4. _____ A more stringent test of short-term liquidity than the current ratio.
5. _____ Measures the amount of after-tax net income generated by a dollar of sales.
6. _____ Indicates the proportion of assets financed by debt.
7. _____ Measures a company's ability to generate revenues from a given level of assets.
8. _____ Compares the amount of debt financing with the amount of equity financing.
9. _____ Indicates how long a company holds its inventory.
10. _____ Measures how quickly a company collects amounts owed to it by its customers.
11. _____ Measures operating cash flow relative to current debt.
12. _____ Measures operating cash flow relative to total debt.
13. _____ Expresses the relationship between per share earnings and stock price.

Required: Match the letter next to each item on the list with the appropriate explanation. Use a letter only once. Not all letters will be used.

LO 5: MATCHING

11–17. Listed below are all the ratios discussed in this chapter:

    1. _____ Debt ratio
    2. _____ Rate of return on common equity ratio
    3. _____ Quick ratio
    4. _____ Dividend payout ratio
    5. _____ Operating cash flow coverage ratio
    6. _____ Price-to-earnings ratio
    7. _____ Gross profit margin ratio
    8. _____ Asset turnover ratio
    9. _____ Times interest earned ratio
    10. _____ Inventory turnover ratio
    11. _____ Net profit margin ratio
    12. _____ Current ratio
    13. _____ Rate of return on assets ratio
    14. _____ Operating cash flow to current debt ratio
    15. _____ Earnings per share
    16. _____ Debt-to-equity ratio
    17. _____ Receivables turnover ratio

Required: Identify each of the 17 ratios as a profitability ratio (P), efficiency ratio (E), a liquidity ratio (L), or a solvency ratio (S) by assigning it the appropriate letter.

LO 6: FINANCIAL RATIO CALCULATIONS

11–18. Below are partial comparative balance sheets of P.J. Boardman Company at December 31, 2005, and 2004:

P.J. Boardman Company
Partial Balance Sheets
December 31, 2005, and December 31, 2004
Current Assets and Current Liabilities Only
(in thousands)

	2005	*2004*
Current assets:		
Cash	$3,400	$2,920
Accounts receivable	1,825	2,212
Merchandise inventory	1,170	966
Supplies	240	270
Total current assets	$6,635	$6,368
Current liabilities:		
Accounts payable	$2,321	$1,740
Notes payable	3,100	3,300
Total current liabilities	$5,421	$5,040

Required:

    a. Calculate Boardman's current ratios for 2005 and 2004.
    b. Calculate Boardman's quick ratios for 2005 and 2004.
    c. Which financial statement users are most interested in these two sets of ratios? Explain why the ratios are considered important to these users.
    d. Assume that the average company in Boardman's industry has a current ratio of 2:1 and a quick ratio of 1.25:1. If you were evaluating Boardman's liquidity, what could you learn from comparing Boardman's ratios to the industry averages?

LO 6: CURRENT AND QUICK RATIO CALCULATIONS

11–19. Following are partial comparative balance sheets of Stephen Deitmer Company at December 31, 2005, and 2004:

Stephen Deitmer Company
Partial Balance Sheets
December 31, 2005, and December 31, 2004
Current Assets and Current Liabilities Only
(in thousands)

	2005	2004
Current assets:		
Cash	$2,110	$2,650
Accounts receivable	1,254	977
Merchandise inventory	730	856
Prepaid insurance	127	114
Total current assets	$4,221	$4,597
Current liabilities:		
Accounts payable	$1,054	$1,330
Notes payable	2,100	1,750
Total current liabilities	$3,154	$3,080

Required:

a. Calculate Deitmer's current ratios for 2005 and 2004.
b. Calculate Deitmer's quick ratios for 2005 and 2004.
c. Which financial statement users are most interested in these two sets of ratios? Explain why the ratios are considered important to these users.
d. Assume that the average company in Deitmer's industry has a current ratio of 2.5:1 and a quick ratio of 1:1. If you were evaluating Deitmer's liquidity, what could you learn by comparing Deitmer's ratios to those of the industry averages?
e. What, if anything, could you determine by comparing Deitmer's current ratio and quick ratio for 2004 with the same ratios for 2005? Explain your reasoning.

LO 6: LIQUIDITY EVALUATION

11–20. A five-year comparative analysis of the Amy Whitaker Company's current ratio and quick ratio is as follows:

	2000	2001	2002	2003	2004
Current ratio	1.24	1.95	2.55	3.68	4.13
Quick ratio	1.20	1.06	0.96	0.77	0.51

Required:

a. What does this analysis tell you about the overall liquidity of the Amy Whitaker Company over the five-year period?
b. What does this analysis tell you about what has happened to the composition of Whitaker's current assets over the five-year period?

LO 6: LIQUIDITY EVALUATION

11–21. A five-year comparative analysis of the Margaret Elsea Company's current ratio and quick ratio is as follows:

	2000	2001	2002	2003	2004
Current ratio	4.24	3.95	2.95	2.68	1.93
Quick ratio	0.51	0.86	1.03	1.33	1.68

Required:

a. What does this analysis tell you about the overall liquidity of the Margaret Elsea Company over the five-year period?
b. What does this analysis tell you about what has happened to the composition of Elsea's current assets over the five-year period?

LO 6: PROFITABILITY EVALUATION

11–22. A five-year comparative analysis of the Annie Todd Company's gross profit margin ratio and net profit margin ratio is as follows:

	2000	2001	2002	2003	2004
Gross profit margin ratio	13.83	13.65	13.34	12.75	12.53
Net profit margin ratio	2.22	2.95	3.41	3.77	4.12

Required:

a. What does this analysis indicate about the company's performance over the five-year period?

b. Which of the following groups would be interested in this analysis? Include in your answer a brief discussion of how you think each of them would interpret this analysis.

1. Trade creditors
2. Long-term creditors
3. Stockholders
4. Company managers

LO 6: PROFITABILITY EVALUATION

11–23. A five-year comparative analysis of Juan Rodriguez Company's gross profit margin ratio and net profit margin ratio is as follows:

	2000	2001	2002	2003	2004
Gross profit margin ratio	11.28	9.16	8.48	7.01	5.78
Net profit margin ratio	9.33	8.59	6.14	5.72	3.89

Required:

a. What does this analysis indicate about Rodriguez's performance over the five-year period?

b. Which of the following groups would be interested in this analysis? Include in your answer a brief discussion of how you think each of them would interpret this analysis.

1. Trade creditors
2. Long-term creditors
3. Stockholders
4. Company managers

LO 6: SOLVENCY EVALUATION

11–24. A five-year comparative analysis of the Kasey Sheehan Company's debt-to-equity ratio and debt ratio is as follows:

	2000	2001	2002	2003	2004
Debt-to-equity ratio	2.75	2.50	2.25	1.50	1.00
Debt ratio	73.33	71.43	69.23	60.00	50.00

Required:

a. What does this analysis indicate about Kasey Sheehan Company's capital structure over the five-year period?

b. Which of the following groups would be interested in this analysis? Include in your answer a brief discussion of how you think each of them would interpret this analysis.

1. Trade creditors
2. Long-term creditors
3. Stockholders
4. Company managers

LO 6: SOLVENCY EVALUATION

11–25. A five-year comparative analysis of the Jane Avery Company's debt-to-equity and debt ratio is as follows:

	2000	2001	2002	2003	2004
Debt-to-equity ratio	1.50	1.15	2.65	2.25	1.90
Debt ratio	60.00	53.49	72.60	69.23	65.52

Required:

a. What does this analysis indicate about Avery's capital structure over the five-year period?

b. Which of the following groups would be interested in this analysis? Include in your answer a brief discussion of how you think each of them would interpret this analysis.

1. Trade creditors
2. Long-term creditors
3. Stockholders
4. Company managers

LO 6: FINANCIAL RATIO CALCULATIONS

11–26. Below are the comparative balance sheets for Oscar Holzmann Company at December 31, 2005, and 2004. Also included is Oscar Holzmann's income statement for the year ended December 31, 2005:

Oscar Holzmann Company
Balance Sheets
December 31, 2005, and December 31, 2004
(in thousands)

	2005	2004
ASSETS:		
Current assets:		
Cash	$ 1,618	$1,220
Accounts receivable	1,925	2,112
Merchandise inventory	1,070	966
Prepaid expenses	188	149
Total current assets	$ 4,801	$4,447
Property, plant, and equipment:		
Buildings, net	$ 4,457	$2,992
Equipment, net	1,293	1,045
Total property, plant, and equipment	$5,750	$4,037
Total assets	$10,551	$8,484
LIABILITIES:		
Current liabilities:		
Accounts payable	$ 1,818	$1,686
Notes payable	900	1,100
Total current liabilities	$ 2,718	$2,786
Long-term liabilities	2,500	2,000
Total liabilities	$ 5,218	$4,786
STOCKHOLDERS' EQUITY:		
Common stock, no-par value	$ 3,390	$2,041
Retained earnings	1,943	1,657
Total stockholders' equity	$5,333	$3,698
Total liabilities and stockholders' equity	$10,551	$8,484

Oscar Holzmann Company
Income Statement
For the Year Ended December 31, 2005
(in thousands)

Sales revenue	$11,228
LESS: Cost of goods sold	7,751
Gross profit on sales	$ 3,477

LESS: Operating expenses:		
Depreciation—buildings and equipment	$ 102	
Other selling and administrative	2,667	
Total operating expenses		2,769
Income from operations		$ 708
LESS: Interest expense		168
Income before taxes		$ 540
Income taxes		114
Net income		$ 426

Additional Information:

Dividends paid during 2005 totaled $140,000.
Cash flows from operating activities for 2005 totaled $504,000.
Average number of common shares outstanding for 2005 was 3,550,000 shares.
Average market price per common share for 2005 was $1.02.

Required: Compute the following ratios for 2005:

1. Gross profit margin ratio
2. Net profit margin ratio
3. Rate of return on assets ratio
4. Rate of return on common equity ratio
5. Dividend payout ratio
6. Earnings per share
7. Price-to-earnings ratio
8. Asset turnover ratio
9. Receivables turnover ratio
10. Inventory turnover ratio
11. Current ratio
12. Quick ratio
13. Operating cash flow to current debt ratio
14. Debt ratio
15. Debt-to-equity ratio
16. Times interest earned ratio
17. Operating cash flow coverage ratio

LO 6: FINANCIAL RATIO CALCULATIONS

11–27. Below are the comparative balance sheets for the Tom Robinson Company at December 31, 2005, and 2004, and the income statements for the years ended December 31, 2005, and 2004.

Tom Robinson Company
Balance Sheets
December 31, 2005, and December 31, 2004
(in thousands)

	2005	2004
ASSETS:		
Current assets:		
Cash	$1,292	$ 980
Accounts receivable	1,068	1,112
Merchandise inventory	970	906
Supplies	40	59
Prepaid expenses	48	50
Total current assets	$3,418	$3,107
Property, plant, and equipment:		
Buildings, net	$3,457	$2,442
Equipment, net	993	945
Total property, plant, and equipment	$4,450	$3,387
Total assets	$7,868	$6,494

LIABILITIES:
Current liabilities:

Accounts payable	$ 998	$ 786
Notes payable	600	500
Total current liabilities	$1,598	$1,286
Long-term liabilities	837	467
Total liabilities	$2,435	$1,753
STOCKHOLDERS' EQUITY:		
Common stock, no-par value	$2,490	$2,000
Retained earnings	2,943	2,741
Total stockholders' equity	$5,433	$4,741
Total liabilities and stockholders' equity	$7,868	$6,494

Tom Robinson Company
Income Statements
For the Years Ended
December 31, 2005, and 2004
(in thousands)

	2005	*2004*
Net sales	$9,228	$8,765
LESS: Cost of goods sold	6,751	6,097
Gross profit on sales	$2,477	$2,668
LESS: Operating expenses:		
Depreciation—buildings and equipment	$ 80	$ 56
Other selling and administrative	1,667	1,442
Total operating expenses	$1,747	$1,498
Operating income	$ 730	$1,170
LESS: Interest expense	98	89
Income before taxes	$ 632	$1,081
Income taxes	190	357
Net income	$ 442	$ 724

Additional Information:
Dividends paid during 2005 totaled $240,000.
Average number of common shares outstanding for 2005 was 2,600,000 shares.
Cash flows from operating activities for 2005 totaled $835,000.
Average market price per common share for 2005 was $1.55.

Required:

a. Calculate the following ratios for 2005:

1. Gross profit margin ratio
2. Net profit margin ratio
3. Rate of return on assets ratio
4. Rate of return on common equity ratio
5. Dividend payout ratio
6. Earnings per share
7. Price-to-earnings ratio
8. Asset turnover ratio
9. Receivables turnover ratio
10. Inventory turnover ratio
11. Current ratio
12. Quick ratio
13. Operating cash flow to current debt ratio
14. Debt ratio
15. Debt-to-equity ratio
16. Times interest earned ratio
17. Operating cash flow coverage ratio

b. Using the ratios you calculated in the previous requirement, complete the following comparison of Tom Robinson's ratios to those of its entire industry and companies of comparable asset size for 2005. Note that industry averages are not available for all the ratios you calculated previously. Accordingly, some of the ratios will not appear in your comparison.

	Total Industry	Assets Between $5 Million and $10 Million	Tom Robinson Company
Gross profit margin ratio			
Net profit margin ratio	4.99	4.61	
Rate of return on assets ratio	9.30	10.40	
Rate of return on common equity ratio	6.12	5.85	
Asset turnover ratio	1.76	1.42	
Receivables turnover ratio	7.83	6.54	
Inventory turnover ratio	5.73	5.47	
Current ratio	1.46	1.95	
Quick ratio	0.93	1.11	
Debt ratio	65.99	65.87	
Debt-to-equity ratio	1.94	1.93	
Times interest earned ratio	5.63	5.16	

c. Analyze the industry comparison you completed in the previous requirement as follows:

1. Identify any ratios you think do not warrant further analysis. Be sure to explain why any particular ratio is not going to be analyzed further.
2. For those ratios you felt deserved further analysis, assess whether Tom Robinson's ratios are better or worse relative to both the entire industry and companies of comparable asset size.

LO 6: RATIO ANALYSIS

11–28. Below is a comparison of certain ratios for the Paul Munter Company for the years 2000 through 2004:

	2000	2001	2002	2003	2004
Gross profit margin ratio	32.25%	31.04%	30.42%	29.22%	28.67%
Net profit margin ratio	8.66%	7.90%	7.14%	6.52%	2.28%
Rate of return on assets ratio	9.28%	8.44%	8.20%	7.68%	6.21%
Rate of return on common equity	8.31%	8.06%	7.22%	6.38%	4.77%
Asset turnover ratio	1.46	1.40	1.17	1.08	0.99
Receivables turnover ratio	8.93	7.41	6.52	5.87	5.34
Inventory turnover ratio	8.88	8.24	8.11	6.46	4.45
Current ratio	1.77	1.91	2.93	2.41	3.12
Quick ratio	1.40	1.26	1.08	0.94	0.79
Debt ratio	48.97%	54.95%	66.33%	68.85%	71.75%
Debt-to-equity ratio	0.96	1.22	1.97	2.21	2.54
Times interest earned ratio	6.90	6.91	5.76	5.24	3.49

Required: Analyze the five-year company comparison as follows:

a. Identify any ratios you think do not warrant further analysis. Be sure to explain why any particular ratio is not going to be analyzed further.
b. For each ratio you felt deserved further analysis, assess whether it has improved or worsened over the five-year period.
c. Based on your analysis of the five-year company comparison, comment briefly on the trend of Paul Munter Company's performance over the five-year period.

Problems 11–29 through 11–33 are based on the following comparative financial statements of Debbie Hoffman and Company:

Debbie Hoffman and Company
Balance Sheets
As of December 31, 2004, 2003, and 2002
(in thousands)

	2004	2003	2002
ASSETS:			
Current assets:			
Cash	$ 2,240	$1,936	$1,836
Accounts receivable	2,340	2,490	2,530

Merchandise inventory	776	693	520
Prepaid expenses	200	160	145
Total current assets	$ 5,556	$5,279	$5,031
Property, plant, and equipment	10,410	8,810	8,480
Accumulated depreciation	(5,241)	(5,057)	(4,810)
Property, plant, and equipment, net	$5,169	$3,753	$3,670
Total assets	$10,725	$9,032	$8,701
LIABILITIES:			
Current liabilities—accounts payable	$ 4,336	$4,000	$3,843
Long-term liabilities—notes payable	2,000	1,600	1,900
Total liabilities	$6,336	$5,600	$5,743
STOCKHOLDERS' EQUITY:			
Common stock, no-par value	$ 3,000	$2,400	$2,400
Retained earnings	1,389	1,032	558
Total stockholders' equity	$ 4,389	$3,432	$2,958
Total liabilities and stockholders' equity	$10,725	$9,032	$8,701

Debbie Hoffman and Company
Income Statements
For the Years Ended December 31, 2004, 2003, and 2002
(in thousands)

	2004	*2003*	*2002*
Net sales revenue	$14,745	$12,908	$11,800
LESS: Cost of goods sold	10,213	8,761	7,810
Gross profit on sales	$ 4,532	$ 4,147	$ 3,990
LESS: Operating expenses:			
Selling expense	$ 1,022	$ 546	$ 523
General and administrative	2,721	2,451	2,390
Total operating expenses	3,743	2,997	2,913
Operating income	789	$ 1,150	$ 1,077
Interest expense	172	137	127
Income before income taxes	$ 617	$ 1,013	$ 950
Income taxes	123	355	323
Net income	$ 494	$ 658	$ 627

Additional Information:

	2004	*2003*	*2002*
Dividends paid	$ 137,000	$184,000	$ 176,000
Cash flow from operating activities	$1,041,000	$914,000	$1,200,000
Average market price per common share	$1.41	$1.83	$1.62
Average number of common shares outstanding	2,470,000	2,350,000	2,160,000

LO 6: FINANCIAL RATIO CALCULATIONS

11–29. Using the Hoffman and Company financial statements, calculate the following ratios for 2004 and 2003:

1. Gross profit margin ratio
2. Net profit margin ratio
3. Rate of return on assets ratio
4. Rate of return on common equity ratio
5. Dividend payout ratio
6. Earnings per share
7. Price-to-earnings ratio
8. Asset turnover ratio
9. Receivables turnover ratio
10. Inventory turnover ratio

11. Current ratio
12. Quick ratio
13. Operating cash flow to current debt ratio
14. Debt ratio
15. Debt-to-equity ratio
16. Times interest earned ratio
17. Operating cash flow coverage ratio

LO 6: COMPARING RATIOS TO INDUSTRY AVERAGES

11–30. Below is a partially completed comparison of Hoffman's ratios to those of its entire industry and companies of comparable asset size for 2004:

	Total Industry	Assets Between $10 Million and $25 Million	Hoffman
Gross profit margin ratio			
Net profit margin ratio	4.49	2.61	
Rate of return on assets ratio	9.30	10.40	
Rate of return on common equity ratio	16.12	15.85	
Dividend payout ratio			
Earnings per share			
Price-to-earnings ratio			
Asset turnover ratio	1.76	1.42	
Receivables turnover ratio	7.83	6.54	
Inventory turnover ratio	5.78	5.77	
Current ratio	2.24	1.95	
Quick ratio	1.33	1.31	
Operating cash flow to current debt ratio			
Debt ratio	69.51	65.99	
Debt-to-equity ratio	2.28	1.94	
Times interest earned ratio	5.43	3.16	
Operating cash flow coverage ratio			

Required:

a. Complete the industry comparison by calculating each of Hoffman and Company's ratios for 2004 and recording them in the space provided. (*Note*: If you have completed problem 11–29, you have already done the calculations. Just use the ratios you have already calculated.)

b. Analyze the industry comparison you completed in the previous requirement as follows:

1. Identify any ratios you think do not warrant further analysis. Be sure to explain why any particular ratio is not going to be analyzed further.
2. For those ratios you felt deserved further analysis, assess whether Hoffman's ratios are better or worse relative to both the entire industry and companies of comparable asset size.
3. Based on your analysis of the industry comparison, comment briefly on how you think Hoffman and Company compares to other companies in its industry.

LO 6: FINANCIAL RATIO ANALYSIS

11–31. Below is a partially completed comparison of Hoffman's ratios for the years 2000 through 2004:

	2000	2001	2002	2003	2004
Gross profit margin ratio	34.16%	34.11%	33.81%		
Net profit margin ratio	5.35%	5.33%	5.31%		
Rate of return on assets ratio	5.22%	6.11%	8.67%		
Rate of return on common equity ratio	23.18%	22.62%	21.20%		
Dividend payout ratio	27.98%	28.02%	28.08%		
Earnings per share	$.32	$.30	$.29		

Price-to-earnings ratio	9.43	8.72	5.58
Asset turnover ratio	1.11	1.86	1.36
Receivables turnover ratio	4.80	4.99	4.66
Inventory turnover ratio	10.88	11.37	15.02
Current ratio	2.07	2.62	1.31
Quick ratio	1.00	1.09	1.14
Operating cash flow to current debt ratio	.45	.39	.31
Debt ratio	54.95%	62.26%	66.00%
Debt-to-equity ratio	1.22	1.65	1.94
Times interest earned ratio	6.31	5.44	8.48
Operating cash flow coverage ratio	.30	.26	.21

Required:

    a. Complete the five-year company comparison by calculating each of Hoffman's ratios for 2003 and 2004 and recording them in the space provided. (*Note*: If you have completed problem 11–29, you have already done the calculations. Just use the ratios you have already calculated.)

    b. Analyze the five-year company comparison you completed in the previous requirement as follows:

        1. Identify any ratios you think do not warrant further analysis. Be sure to explain why any particular ratio is not going to be analyzed further.

        2. For each ratio you felt deserved further analysis, assess whether it has improved or gotten worse over the five-year period.

        3. Based on your analysis of the five-year company comparison, comment briefly on the trend of Hoffman and Company's performance over the five-year period.

COMPREHENSIVE

11–32. The financial statements for Debbie Hoffman and Company do not include a statement of cash flows. To assess the company's overall performance in 2004, however, you should also look at its statement of cash flows.

Required:

    a. Using the 2003 and 2004 comparative balance sheets and the income statement for 2004, prepare Hoffman's 2004 statement of cash flows.

    b. Which of the three broad activities (operating, investing, and financing) provided Hoffman with the majority of its cash during 2004?

    c. Briefly discuss whether the activity you identified in the previous requirement is an appropriate source of cash in the long run.

    d. In which of the three broad activities (operating, investing, and financing) did Hoffman use most of its cash during 2004?

    e. Briefly discuss what your answer to the previous requirement reveals about Hoffman.

COMPREHENSIVE

11–33. The financial statements for Debbie Hoffman and Company did not include a statement of stockholders' equity. To assess the company's overall performance in 2004, however, you should also look at the company's statement of stockholders' equity.

Required:

    a. Using the 2003 and 2004 comparative balance sheets and the income statement for 2004, prepare Hoffman's 2004 statement of stockholders' equity.

    b. Briefly discuss how the statement of stockholders' equity demonstrates articulation among Hoffman's financial statements.

LO 7: LIMITATIONS OF RATIO ANALYSIS

11–34. The chapter discussed several limitations of ratio analysis, namely:

    1. Using past results to predict future performance

    2. Using historical cost as a basis for ratios

3. Using year-end balances as either the numerator or denominator for many ratios
4. Industry peculiarities
5. Lack of uniformity in defining the numerators and denominators used in calculating ratios
6. Giving too much credence to ratio analysis

Required: Explain why each of the six items listed limit the usefulness of ratio analysis.

Financial Reporting Exercises •

LO 6: FINANCIAL RATIO CALCULATIONS AND EVALUATION

11–35. Using the *SEC's EDGAR* system, obtain a copy of the *Nautica, Inc.*, income statement, balance sheet, and statement of cash flows from the company's Form 10-K for 2001.

Required:

a. Using *Nautica*'s financial statements, calculate the 17 ratios presented in the chapter for the latest year presented.
b. Based on the ratios, write a summary of your impression of the company's profitability, efficiency, liquidity, and solvency.

LO 6: FINANCIAL RATIO CALCULATIONS AND EVALUATION

11–36. Using the *SEC's EDGAR* system, obtain a copy of the *Tommy Hilfiger, Inc.*, income statement, balance sheet, and statement of cash flows from the company's Form 10-K for 2001.

Required:

a. Using *Hilfiger*'s financial statements, calculate the 17 ratios presented in the chapter for the latest year presented.
b. Based on the ratios, write a summary of your impression of the company's profitability, efficiency, liquidity, and solvency?

LO 6: PEER COMPANY COMPARISON

11–37. Requires completion of problems 11–35 and 11–36.

Required:

a. For each of the two companies (*Nautica, Inc.*, and *Tommy Hilfiger, Inc.*), circle the ratio you think is more favorable.
b. Write a brief report that compares the two company's profitability, efficiency, liquidity, and solvency.
c. In which company would you rather invest? Explain.

LO 6: FINANCIAL RATIO CALCULATIONS AND EVALUATION (PART B REQUIRES A LIBRARY SOURCE FOR INDUSTRY AVERAGES.)

11–38. Visit the PHLIP Web site for this book at *www.prenhall.com/werner* to find the link for two companies in the same industry. Select an industry in which you are interested.

Required:

a. Calculate the 17 basic ratios presented in the chapter for the most current year for each of the companies.
b. Based on the ratios that you have computed, and the information presented in the chapter, how do these companies compare with each other and the industry averages on the basis of the ratios that you have computed. Industry averages may be obtained from the sources identified in the text, which are usually found in the reference section of the library.

LO 6: FINANCIAL RATIO CALCULATIONS AND EVALUATION

11–39. Visit the PHLIP Web site for this book at *www.prenhall.com/werner* and locate the links for *Ford Motor Company* and for *General Motors Corporation*.

Required:

a. Using the corporations' financial statements, calculate the following ratios for the latest year presented. (Assume minority interest is part of stockholders' equity.) Compute the following ratios:

   1. Gross profit margin ratio
   2. Net profit margin ratio
   3. Rate of return on assets ratio
   4. Rate of return on common equity ratio
   5. Dividend payout ratio
   6. Earnings per share
   7. Price-to-earnings ratio
   8. Asset turnover ratio
   9. Receivables turnover ratio
   10. Inventory turnover ratio
   11. Current ratio
   12. Quick ratio
   13. Operating cash flow to current debt ratio
   14. Debt ratio
   15. Debt-to-equity ratio
   16. Times interest earned ratio
   17. Operating cash flow coverage ratio

b. Write a report comparing the two companies' profitability, efficiency, liquidity, and solvency. In your report's summary, indicate which company you feel is the stronger investment. Explain the reasons for your choice, or, the difficulty you had making a choice.

LO 6: FINANCIAL RATIO CALCULATIONS AND EVALUATION

11–40. Visit the PHLIP Web site for this book at *www.prenhall.com/werner* and locate the link for **Ford Motor Company.**

Required:

a. Using the financial statements and the financial summary of **Ford Motor Company,** prepare a five-year ratio analysis. For several ratios, there will not be enough information provided for all five years. In such cases, write a brief explanation and place it at the end of your response to this requirement. (Assume any minority interest is part of stockholders' equity.)

b. Based on the ratios you prepared for the previous requirement:

   1. Identify any ratios you think are improving.
   2. Identify any ratios you think are getting worse.
   3. Comment briefly on the trend of **Ford's** performance over the five-year period.

ANNUAL REPORT PROJECT

11–41. Section 11—Summary, Conclusions, and Recommendations

In the first 10 sections of this annual report project, you gathered and reported on a variety of information. In addition, you calculated 17 ratios, compared those ratios to a peer company, and commented on each ratio and its comparison. Now it's time to bring all this information together for a final report on the company you selected.

Required:

a. Prepare a schedule that lists all of the ratios you calculated for your company and its peer. Your report should be arranged in the following order, which is the same arrangement as they appear in Chapter 11 and in Exhibit 11–1:

Profitability ratios:

   • Gross profit margin ratio
   • Net profit margin ratio
   • Rate of return on assets ratio

- Rate of return on common equity ratio
- Dividend payout ratio
- Earnings per share
- Price-to-earnings ratio

Efficiency ratios:

- Asset turnover ratio
- Receivables turnover ratio
- Inventory turnover ratio

Liquidity ratios:

- Current ratio
- Quick ratio
- Operating cash flow to current debt ratio

Solvency ratios:

- Debt ratio
- Debt-to-equity ratio
- Times interest earned ratio
- Operating cash flow coverage ratio

b. Review Sections 1 through 10 of your annual report project. Based on the schedule of ratios you prepared and your review of your annual report project, prepare a report that summarizes what you have learned about your company. Your report should include a section with your overall conclusion. Be sure to mention your company's strengths, weaknesses, opportunities, and threats. What is your opinion regarding whether your company is a good investment candidate? Based on what you have learned about the company, do you think the company would be a good prospect for employment?

Pier 1 imports®

annual report 2002

Financial Highlights

For the three years ended March 2, 2002

Pier 1 Imports, as one of North America's largest specialty retailers of unique decorative home furnishings, gifts and related items, achieved record sales of over $1.5 billion and record net income of over $100 million in fiscal 2002. Pier 1 directly imports from over 40 countries around the world, displaying merchandise in a visually appealing setting in stores throughout the United States, Canada, Puerto Rico, the United Kingdom and Mexico.

	2002	2001	2000
	($ in millions except per share amounts)		
For the year:			
Net sales	$ 1,548.6	$1,411.5	$1,231.1
Gross profit	649.8	594.5	512.5
Operating expenses	490.9	442.9	389.4
Operating income	158.8	151.5	123.2
Nonoperating (income) and expenses, net	(0.2)	1.3	4.6
Income before income taxes	159.0	150.2	118.6
Net income	$ 100.2	$ 94.7	$ 74.7
Basic earnings per share	$ 1.06	$ .98	$ .78
Diluted earnings per share	$ 1.04	$ .97	$ .75
Weighted average diluted shares outstanding (millions)	96.2	98.0	103.3
Increase in same-store sales (1)	4.5%	7.8%	2.7%
At year-end:			
Number of stores worldwide (2)	974	899	834
North American retail square feet (millions)(3)	6.9	6.2	5.9

(1) Stores included in the same-store sales calculation are those stores opened prior to the beginning of the preceding fiscal year and that are still open, including qualifying relocated stores. For further explanation regarding the calculation of same-store sales, see Critical Accounting Policies in Management's Discussion and Analysis of Financial Condition and Results of Operations. Same-store sales amounts reflect a 52-week comparison for all periods presented. All other fiscal 2001 data includes 53 weeks of operations. For an explanation regarding the fluctuation in same-store sales increases from year to year, refer to Management's Discussion and Analysis of Financial Condition and Results of Operations for those years.

(2) Worldwide store count at fiscal 2001 year-end includes the acquisition of Cargo Furniture, Inc. on February 21, 2001. Results of operations for fiscal 2001 were not affected by this acquisition. By fiscal 2002 year-end, all Japan locations had been closed. Results of operations for all years presented include Japan's operations.

(3) North American retail square footage includes Pier 1 Imports' locations throughout the United States and Canada, along with Cargo stores.

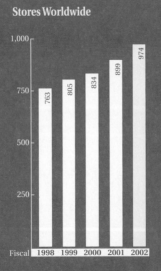

Stores Worldwide

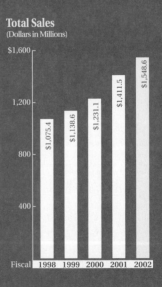

Total Sales
(Dollars in Millions)

Table of contents

Making ourselves at home.

The things that make up a home are simple. Whether they're family, friends or a favorite chair, they fill empty spaces with warmth and love. When someone brings home an armoire or rug from one of our stores, we understand just how big a compliment that is. Invitations home aren't given to casual acquaintances. They're reserved for those you're most comfortable with. It's a statement from our customers that they're at home with us and we're at home with them.

Pier 1 imports®

Fiscal year 2002 was a unique and exceptional year for Pier 1 Imports. The first half of the year was difficult, affected by soft economic conditions. Then the events of September 11th changed our nation forever. During that second half of the year, the influences of "cocooning" took hold in America. Individuals chose to retreat to the security and comfort of their homes. As a company, we moved ahead with even more compassion toward our associates, friends, family and customers. Pier 1 Imports has been a known and trusted brand for 40 years. I believe that we understand the importance of providing customers with value, quality and style that is found in a friendly and relaxing shopping experience.

We are proud that fiscal year 2002, notwithstanding the difficult first half, was a record year for the Company. Net income was over $100 million for the first time in Pier 1's history. Sales were $1.55 billion, an increase of 9.7% over last year's $1.4 billion. All-important same-store sales grew by 4.5%. Diluted earnings per share for the year was $1.04 compared to $.97 a year ago. The increases in traffic, transactions and average ticket for the year were supported by positive customer response to new merchandise assortments during the year and a very successful advertising campaign.

We continue to strengthen the Company's balance sheet, as evidenced by cash of $235.6 million at the end of fiscal 2002. Net income plus depreciation was $143 million, and working capital was a source of funds so that cash generated from operations was $244 million. We repurchased four million shares of the Company's stock during the year, and the Board of Directors recently authorized up to a total of $150 million of additional share repurchases. In keeping with our conservative financial strategy, we will continue to be prudent in our infrastructure investments and in funding the future growth of the Company.

The acceleration of new store growth continued in fiscal 2002, with 104 new Pier 1 stores opening and 20 closing or relocating to stronger trading areas. This year, fiscal 2003, we plan to open 115 to 120 Pier 1 stores and will close 30. Our research has identified more than 500 additional potential sites for Pier 1 stores throughout North America, which we plan to develop over the next eight to ten years. This represents a 65% increase in our current base of store locations at the end of fiscal 2002.

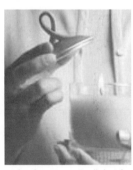

Sales of our Komen Candle benefit breast cancer research.

We ended fiscal 2002 with 910 Pier 1 stores in North America, 16 in Mexico, 7 in Puerto Rico, 23 stores in the United Kingdom operating as "The Pier" and 18 Cargo stores, for a total of 974 stores worldwide. In addition, we are prepared to begin the Cargo store rollout. During fiscal 2003, we plan to open eight to twelve new Cargo stores and have aggressive growth plans for over 300 Cargo stores in North America during the next ten years.

Pier 1 continued its successful national marketing campaign this year with television and print advertising. We increased the use of direct marketing by growing our proprietary database to over 7.5 million customers. Special incentives targeted to our most valued customers were used to increase shopping frequency and average ticket. The Pier 1 preferred card continued to be widely accepted among our most loyal shoppers. Sales from the preferred card represent 30% of Pier 1 and Cargo's store sales, and the average amount spent on the card is more than three times that of a typical Pier 1 or Cargo customer. We continue to see growth from our e-commerce business. Pier1.com has become a valuable source for our customers in gaining product information, receiving promotional and sale event notifications, and for finding store locations throughout North America. Additionally, our e-marketing efforts are beginning to generate very positive results with the acquisition of more than 250,000 e-mail subscribers. As a whole, these integrated marketing initiatives have raised brand awareness for our unique selling proposition, resulting in a significant increase in customer traffic in Pier 1 stores.

Our charitable efforts extend internationally from the countries where we source merchandise, to national causes and local initiatives in our hometown that our associates and customers believe in and support. This year our philanthropic work took on a whole new meaning, as our Pier 1 associates, as well as our customers, reached out with added enthusiasm. Sales of 2001 UNICEF greeting cards generated almost $2 million, all of which was donated to help families, and especially children, that needed food, medicine and supplies in Third-World countries. Pier 1 also was a national box distributor for "Trick-or-Treat" for UNICEF, which raised an estimated $3.5 million for emergency relief for the children of Afghanistan. In November

Our support for UNICEF helps impoverished children and families.

2001, we donated an additional $100,000 to UNICEF to help save the lives of Afghan women and children.

Nationally, we also sell a specially designed candle in October, Breast Cancer Awareness Month, to help fund the Susan G. Komen Breast Cancer Foundation. In 2001, our contribution from the sale of these candles to the Komen foundation was over $144,000, which strengthens our belief that our customers share in our passion to help those in need. This is in addition to sponsoring thousands of Pier 1 associates to participate in Race for the Cure® events across the U.S. and Canada. In our headquarters city of Fort Worth, Texas, we continued to donate time and gifts to the United Way, Daggett Elementary (our Adopt-A-School) and other various organizations that support the community.

Since accepting my position as Chairman and CEO in 1998, I have worked very hard to enhance Pier 1's culture of unquestionable integrity and responsibility, expressed in both written codes and living example. Our retail business is simple and straightforward, and so are our financials. Many public companies, including ours, have reviewed current board and company policies. Your Board of Directors will continue to oversee the corporate governance and ethical principles of the Company in order to serve the interests of our shareholders and associates.

Tomorrow's successful retailers must be customer-centered with a focus on increasing *value*. Value means not only price, but quality, selection and an engaging shopping experience. This defines the Pier 1 Imports brand

and is the promise we will keep in satisfying our loyal and passionate customers. As we reflect on our 40 successful years in the retail business, I am pleased with our accomplishments ... but I believe the best is yet to come as we implement plans to grow in totally new ways and directions. To our customers, suppliers, associates, Board of Directors and shareholders who make it all possible: Thank you for your support.

Marvin J. Girouard
Chairman and Chief Executive Officer

Coming home to Pier 1 Imports. To an ever-broadening spectrum of consumers – including baby boomers and Gen-X and -Yers – there's no place like home.

A decade ago, business author/trend consultant Faith Popcorn dubbed this trend *cocooning*, defined as "the need to protect oneself from the unpredictable realities of the outside world." In this scenario, consumer spending focuses on safety, security … and comfort.

If there was ever any question about Popcorn's theory, all doubt seems to have been erased in the last year, as the "trend" has become a full-blown cultural phenomenon. Goods and services that responded to this lifestyle shift have experienced a strong market – a conclusion borne out by the fact that during the slumping economy in 2001, Pier 1 Imports and other retailers that addressed these needs performed quite well.

Pier 1's answers to the trend? An ever-changing mix of products that stimulates the senses, making homes not just warm and inviting, but also a reflection of individual style. A value proposition that promises a decorating resource that fits any budget. And refocused store location metrics that prove while we're already established and well-entrenched, there's still plenty of room for growth.

Our marketing campaign also meshes with this stay-at-home trend, conveying our brand position of casual comfort, style and fun. We have achieved success through marketing our preferred card, a national TV campaign, print advertising and database marketing, plus national programs for interior designers and bridal and gift registries. E-commerce initiatives are also growing, with online sales and e-mail marketing to a database that already includes 250,000 subscribers.

The proof of our efforts? Our customers have rewarded us by making Pier 1 Imports a part of their homes – resulting in record sales of $1.55 billion during fiscal 2002.

The marketplace has undergone a paradigm shift most evident in the past several months – a shift accelerated by recent econom events, terrorism and other uncertainties. People seem to be looking deeper inside to find what they really value. For Pier this shift places us not just at the right place at the right time … but the right place for the future as well.

It was an uncomfortably hot Saturday in July when Darrell learned of Lisa's new love.

Well-built, good-looking. She said it would last. Darrell was generous in his response, even understanding. After all, the cabinet was perfect – like everything she'd fallen for from Pier 1.

A world of value. The success of the Pier 1 Imports brand is built upon offering unique and exclusive merchandise at a value. The brand is known for being casual, eclectic and culturally inspired.

Just as unique as our products are the people behind them. Stocking America's best-known chain of imported home fashions is no simple task – but it is a labor of love. Our merchandising team consists of some of the most-traveled people on the planet. Our buyers spend many a week far from home. Expertise and a sense of style are required to develop and select merchandise that will delight our customers' demanding tastes. Some items are created with designers abroad, others with our experienced in-house product development team.

Equally vital to our success is our exceptional network of 600+ suppliers in 40 countries worldwide. After all, not just any artisan can craft the captivating beauty of our wicker collections, or create the memorable fragrances of our popular candles. In many cases, our relationships with these suppliers have been built over the past 40 years. The longevity of these relationships helps us deliver consistent quality, value and results.

Of course, styles and trends are a moving target. Our merchandise assortment remains in a state of perpetual motion, with seasonal transitions that keep our product offerings fresh. As much as 65% of Pier 1's merchandise changes each year.

A typical Pier 1 store inventory forms multiple tiers. Broad-appeal items at entry-level price points break the ice with younger customers and those on a budget. A mid-level assortment of furniture and accessories includes our best-known products and is at the core of the Pier 1 brand. And to test new ideas and satisfy the cravings of trendier tastes, we devote a portion of our assortment to the more fashion-forward. Cash-and-carry convenience is a key strategy – the merchandise must be on hand in the store to close the sale when the customer is ready to buy.

Stroll through a Pier 1 store and you'll see a world of craftsmanship on display. Our wicker isn't produced by machines, but by the age-old art of weaving by hand. Many of our dinnerware patterns are original pieces painted by artisans. Delivering one-of-a-kind products of this caliber could mean pricing most customers out of the picture. But our product development and merchandising teams consider all aspects of design, manufacturing and country of origin for every item we sell. The result is uncommon craftsmanship and quality at a surprisingly affordable value.

A lot has changed since Stan and Linda's kids left home.

Family vacations and Saturday soccer games have been replaced by a strange quiet in the house. And the odd group of chipped plates and bowls that screamed "tater tot casserole" has been replaced with a set of understated, beautiful dinnerware that whispers, "Maybe this empty nest isn't so bad, after all."

Growth in store. Merchandising a store might seem easy when you have such an exquisite array of countries and cultures on display. The product is key, of course, but our team of visual merchandisers continuously refines our store presentations with meticulous care to create a pleasing environment that sparks ideas and results in add-on sales.

Pier 1 Imports operates almost 1,000 stores, including the 18-store Cargo chain, in 48 states, Canada, Mexico, Puerto Rico and the United Kingdom. The store network is supported by six distribution centers that provide efficient access to the greatest concentrations of stores and major ports of entry. Enhanced warehouse management systems enable smarter inventory control that makes us more responsive to our customers and, ultimately, more profitable.

New store growth continues to sustain our momentum. Research has pointed to a compelling prospect: Thanks to residential development, as well as economic and demographic factors, markets once thought to be saturated plus undiscovered new markets are capable of supporting additional stores – adding sales volume and creating economies of scale for our distribution and marketing.

The implication is significant, with current projections calling for us to reach 1,500 Pier 1 stores by the end of the decade. Moving toward that goal, we added 84 net new stores in fiscal 2002 and project 85 to 90 more in fiscal 2003. Beyond 2003, we hope to average 70 to 80 net new Pier 1 stores and 15 to 20 new Cargo stores per year through 2010.

An average Pier 1 store is 8,000 to 12,000 square feet and produces approximately $1.6 million in annual sales. We are testing a new large-store format for product introductions and for offering merchandise designed for larger homes. We now have five of these new stores, which, at 12,000 to 17,000 square feet, are significantly larger than a typical Pier 1. Located in highly targeted areas, these stores are producing beyond expected results. An average Cargo store is 4,500 square feet and produces annual sales volume of approximately $1 million.

Over the last five years, Pier 1 Imports has enjoyed a compound annual growth rate in sales and diluted earnings per share of almost 10%. Continued growth potential is promising, as younger consumers earn more buying power and our store base grows.

Brad saw the vase, and it said "Holly."

It spoke to everything he loves about his wife. Which is why Brad felt compelled to take it home, and Holly felt compelled to ask what got into Brad. We think it might have been the unique craftsmanship.

Traditional strengths, uncommon potential. Pier 1 got its start 40 years ago with one small store in San Mateo, California. During the '60s, it became a haven for the "flower children" of the baby-boom generation. We've moved way beyond beads and incense, but some products, like our famous Papasan chair, still help define us, thanks to their timeless appeal. It is promising for us to know that we've been embraced by baby-boomer children, and now their children, too.

Research tells us that these baby boomers have settled down and now appreciate the fundamental pleasures of family and home life. Gen-Xers are establishing homes at an earlier age. And college students are taking dorm décor to a new level – in fact, we've seen a marked increase in sales to these younger customers.

It's quite simple: We sell home furnishings. Success is predicated on our ability to source products that people want at prices that will make Pier 1 profitable. Our steady growth may not have seemed exciting during the days of skyrocketing tech stocks. In retrospect, we're pleased that our beliefs about the business and our strategies have been confirmed.

Putting customers first enables us to return value to our shareholders and employees, and to practice good corporate citizenship. We never lose sight of what got us where we are and where we want to go. Outstanding customer service, convenient locations and ever-changing merchandise at a value are our commitments to our customers.

Pier 1's corporate-giving activities are meant to touch the sensibilities of the customers we serve. Internationally, our suppo for UNICEF, now 19 years strong, has raised over $16 million for children's charities. Nationally, sales of our Komen Cano have raised over $250,000 for breast cancer research since 2000, and nearly 17,000 Pier 1 employees have participate in Race for the Cure® events since 1991. And since 1985, in our headquarters city of Fort Worth, Texas, Pier 1 and employees have donated over $3.7 million to the United Way of Metropolitan Tarrant County.

It was the one dorm room everyone gravitated to at the end of the day.

Sure, Cindy Parker was popular, and her roommate was tolerable. But for most of the girls in Livingston Hall, it was the classic comfort of their rattan furniture that had the most appeal.

Key Financial Statistics
For the five years ended March 2, 2002

Total Sales
(Dollars in Millions)

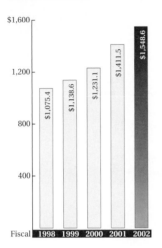

Fiscal	1998	1999	2000	2001	2002
	$1,075.4	$1,138.6	$1,231.1	$1,411.5	$1,548.6

Net Income
(Dollars in Millions)

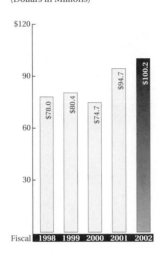

Fiscal	1998	1999	2000	2001	2002
	$78.0	$80.4	$74.7	$94.7	$100.2

Preferred Credit Card Sales
(Dollars in Millions)

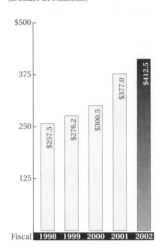

Fiscal	1998	1999	2000	2001	2002
	$257.5	$276.2	$300.5	$377.0	$412.5

Diluted Earnings Per Share
(Dollars)

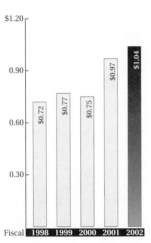

Fiscal	1998	1999	2000	2001	2002
	$0.72	$0.77	$0.75	$0.97	$1.04

Stores Worldwide

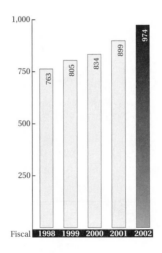

Fiscal	1998	1999	2000	2001	2002
	763	805	834	899	974

Shareholders' Equity Per Share
(Dollars)

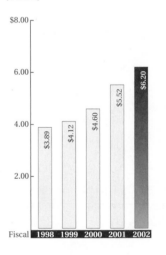

Fiscal	1998	1999	2000	2001	2002
	$3.89	$4.12	$4.60	$5.52	$6.20

Merchandise Sales Mix
For fiscal year 2002

Furniture 39%
Seasonal 8%
Housewares 12%
Bed & Bath 18%
Decorative Accessories 23%

Pier 1 Imports, Inc.

FINANCIAL SUMMARY
($ in millions except per share amounts)

	4-Year Compound Annual Growth Rate	2002	2001(1)	2000	1999	1998
SUMMARY OF OPERATIONS:						
Net sales	9.5%	$ 1,548.6	1,411.5	1,231.1	1,138.6	1,075.4
Gross profit	8.9%	$ 649.8	594.5	512.5	500.4	461.5
Selling, general and administrative expenses	9.1%	$ 448.1	399.8	349.4	334.6	315.8
Depreciation and amortization	15.7%	$ 42.8	43.2	40.0	31.1	23.9
Operating income	6.9%	$ 158.8	151.5	123.2	134.7	121.7
Nonoperating (income) and expenses, net (2)		$ (0.2)	1.3	4.6	5.0	(2.3)
Income before income taxes	6.4%	$ 159.0	150.2	118.6	129.6	124.0
Net income	6.5%	$ 100.2	94.7	74.7	80.4	78.0
PER SHARE AMOUNTS (ADJUSTED FOR STOCK SPLITS AND DIVIDENDS):						
Basic earnings	8.3%	$ 1.06	.98	.78	.82	.77
Diluted earnings	9.6%	$ 1.04	.97	.75	.77	.72
Cash dividends declared	15.5%	$ .16	.15	.12	.12	.09
Shareholders' equity	12.4%	$ 6.20	5.52	4.60	4.12	3.89
OTHER FINANCIAL DATA:						
Working capital (3)	9.0%	$ 396.8	333.0	239.3	252.1	280.8
Current ratio (3)	(3.2%)	2.9	3.3	2.4	2.9	3.3
Total assets	7.2%	$ 862.7	735.7	670.7	654.0	653.4
Long-term debt (3)	(31.4%)	$ 25.4	25.0	25.0	96.0	114.9
Shareholders' equity	10.5%	$ 585.7	531.9	440.7	403.9	392.7
Weighted average diluted shares outstanding (millions)		96.2	98.0	103.3	108.9	112.9
Effective tax rate		37.0%	37.0	37.0	38.0	37.1
Return on average shareholders' equity		17.9%	19.5	17.7	20.2	21.8
Return on average total assets		12.5%	13.5	11.3	12.3	12.8
Pre-tax return on sales		10.3%	10.6	9.6	11.4	11.5

(1) Fiscal 2001 consisted of a 53-week year. All other fiscal years presented reflect 52-week years.
(2) Nonoperating (income) and expenses, net, were comprised of interest expense and interest and investment income in each fiscal year presented, and in addition, included net recoveries associated with trading activities in fiscal 1998.
(3) The reduction in fiscal 2000 working capital, current ratio and long-term debt was the result of the Company's call of its outstanding 5¾% convertible subordinated notes. The notes were primarily converted into shares of the Company's common stock in March 2000. Excluding the reclassification of the 5¾% notes from long-term to short-term, working capital would have been $278.5 million with a current ratio of 3.0 to 1 at fiscal 2000 year-end.

Pier 1 Imports, Inc.
MANAGEMENT'S DISCUSSION AND ANALYSIS OF FINANCIAL CONDITION AND RESULTS OF OPERATIONS

Pier 1 Imports, Inc. and its consolidated subsidiaries (the "Company") is one of North America's largest specialty retailers of unique decorative home furnishings, gifts and related items, with over 950 stores in 48 states, Canada, Puerto Rico, the United Kingdom and Mexico as of fiscal 2002 year-end. The Company directly imports merchandise from over 40 countries around the world and designs offerings that are proprietary to Pier 1 Imports. During fiscal 2002, the Company reported record sales of $1,548.6 million and record net income of $100.2 million, or $1.04 per diluted share. In February 2001, the Company acquired certain assets and assumed certain liabilities of Cargo Furniture, Inc. and formed New Cargo Furniture, Inc. ("Cargo"). Cargo, an 18-store retailer and wholesaler of casual lifestyle furniture, gifts and home décor, had no impact on the Company's fiscal 2001 operations due to the timing of the acquisition, but is reflected in the Company's fiscal 2002 and 2001 year-end balance sheets and fiscal 2002 results of operations.

FISCAL YEARS ENDED MARCH 2, 2002
AND MARCH 3, 2001

During the 52-week period of fiscal 2002, net sales increased $137.1 million, or 9.7%, to $1,548.6 million. Net sales for the 53-week period of fiscal 2001 were $1,411.5 million. Same-store sales for fiscal 2002 improved 4.5% over the prior year, excluding the 53rd week of sales in fiscal 2001. Despite a slow start in sales growth during the first half of the fiscal year, the Company began to see improvements in customer traffic, average ticket and customer conversion in the third quarter. These sales trends began after the events of September 11th when consumers shifted their spending away from travel and entertainment and began making purchases for their homes. In addition to this change in consumer behavior, the Company believes that its value-oriented merchandising efforts and the success of its marketing campaign contributed to the sales increases experienced during fiscal 2002.

The Company's accelerated new store growth plans in North America also contributed to sales growth during fiscal 2002. The Company opened 104 and closed 20 North American Pier 1 stores during the fiscal year. The North American Pier 1 store count totaled 910 at the end of fiscal 2002 compared to 826 a year ago. Including Cargo and all other worldwide locations, the Company's store count totaled 974 at the end of fiscal year 2002 compared to 899 at the end of fiscal year 2001. Prior to the close of fiscal year 2002, the franchise agreement with Akatsuki Printing Co., Ltd. and Skylark Co., Ltd. expired without any additional costs or further obligations to the Company. As a result, the Company no longer has stores in Japan.

A summary reconciliation of the Company's stores open at the beginning of fiscal 2002, 2001 and 2000 to the number open at the end of each period follows:

	Pier 1 North American	International (1)	Cargo (2)	Total
Open at February 27, 1999	752	54	–	806
Openings (3)	63	5	–	68
Closings (3)	(30)	(10)	–	(40)
Open at February 26, 2000	785	49	–	834
Openings (3)	65	3	–	68
Closings (3)	(24)	–	–	(24)
Acquisition (February 2001)	–	–	21	21
Open at March 3, 2001	826	52	21	899
Openings (3)	104	3	3	110
Closings (3)	(20)	(9)	(6)	(35)
Open at March 2, 2002	910	46	18	974

(1) International stores were located in Puerto Rico, the United Kingdom, Mexico and Japan for fiscal 2000 and 2001. All Japan locations were closed by fiscal 2002 year-end.
(2) The Company's results of operations for fiscal 2001 were not affected by the acquisition of Cargo.
(3) Openings and closings include stores which were relocated.

Pier 1 Imports, Inc.

MANAGEMENT'S DISCUSSION AND ANALYSIS OF FINANCIAL CONDITION AND RESULTS OF OPERATIONS
(continued)

Sales on the Company's proprietary credit card for fiscal 2002 were $412.5 million compared to $377.0 million last year and accounted for 28.9% of U.S. store sales for both fiscal periods. Proprietary credit card customers spent an average of $153 per transaction, which was comparable to last year. The Company continues to encourage sales on its proprietary credit card by opening new accounts, including accounts on Cargo's new proprietary credit card, and developing customer loyalty through marketing promotions specifically targeted to cardholders, including deferred payment options on larger purchases. Although the proprietary credit card generates income, it primarily serves as a marketing and communication tool for the Company's most loyal customers.

Gross profit, after related buying and store occupancy costs, expressed as a percentage of sales, was 42.0% for fiscal 2002 compared to 42.1% a year ago. Merchandise margins for fiscal year 2002 remained unchanged at 54.2% of sales when compared to last fiscal year. Although the first half of fiscal 2002 was more promotional as a result of soft economic conditions, the second half of fiscal 2002 yielded sales with a more favorable blend of regular-priced merchandise and promotional items and merchandise margins rebounded accordingly. Store occupancy costs were 12.3% of sales in fiscal 2002 versus 12.1% of sales last fiscal year. This increase was primarily attributable to the effect of leveraging occupancy costs over an additional week of sales in fiscal year 2001 versus fiscal year 2002. This increase was also the result of additional store rental expense due to the sale and subsequent leaseback of six store properties previously owned by the Company. These sale-leaseback transactions also resulted, although to a lesser extent, in a reduction of depreciation expense, which is not classified as a component of store occupancy costs.

As a percentage of sales, selling, general and administrative expenses, including marketing, increased 60 basis points to 28.9% of sales for fiscal year 2002 from 28.3% of sales a year ago. Expenses that normally increase proportionately with sales and number of stores, such as store payroll, equipment rental, supplies and marketing expenses, were well controlled and declined 50 basis points to 19.7% of sales. Store payroll decreased 20 basis points as a percentage of sales, which was largely the result of a decrease in store

bonuses that are awarded based on sales gains over the prior year. Marketing as a percentage of sales decreased 10 basis points, to 4.5% of sales, due to lower television advertising rates negotiated by the Company. All other selling, general and administrative expenses increased 110 basis points to 9.3% of sales for the fiscal year. These increases were largely the result of increases in non-store payroll, medical, workers' compensation, and general insurance expenses, and the impact of Cargo's expenditures this year with no corresponding expense last year. The increases in non-store payroll resulted primarily from an enhancement to the field management structure in the first quarter of fiscal 2002 to provide for future growth.

Depreciation and amortization expense for fiscal 2002 was $42.8 million, or 2.8% of sales, compared to $43.2 million, or 3.1% of sales, last fiscal year. The decrease was primarily the result of store point of sale equipment, which became fully depreciated in March 2001, along with the sale of eight store properties previously owned, six of which were subsequently leased back by the Company.

Operating income improved to $158.8 million, or 10.3% of sales, in fiscal 2002 from $151.5 million, or 10.7% of sales, in fiscal 2001.

Interest income increased $0.6 million, or 10 basis points as a percentage of sales, to $2.5 million due to considerably higher average cash and investment balances during the current fiscal year compared to last fiscal year, partially offset by a decrease in interest rates. Interest expense was $2.3 million in fiscal year 2002 compared to $3.1 million in fiscal year 2001, a 10 basis point reduction. The decline in interest expense was due to lower average interest rates on a relatively fixed long-term debt balance along with no borrowings under the Company's revolving credit facility during fiscal 2002 compared to several months of outstanding balances on the revolver during fiscal 2001.

The Company's effective tax rate remained constant at 37% of income before income taxes for both fiscal 2002 and 2001.

Fiscal 2002 net income totaled $100.2 million, representing 6.5% of sales, or $1.04 per share on a diluted basis. In fiscal 2001, net income was 6.7% of sales and totaled $94.7 million, or $.97 per share on a diluted basis.

Pier 1 Imports, Inc.

MANAGEMENT'S DISCUSSION AND ANALYSIS OF FINANCIAL CONDITION AND RESULTS OF OPERATIONS
(continued)

FISCAL YEARS ENDED MARCH 3, 2001
AND FEBRUARY 26, 2000

During fiscal 2001, the Company recorded net sales of $1,411.5 million, an increase of $180.4 million, or 14.7%, over net sales of $1,231.1 million for the prior fiscal year. Fiscal 2001 consisted of a 53-week year, while fiscal 2000 and 1999 were 52-week years. Same-store sales for fiscal 2001 improved 7.8%, excluding the 53rd week of sales. The Company believes that its new advertising campaign, proprietary credit card and other promotions, and continued focus on a value pricing initiative, which began in fiscal 2000, resulted in higher customer traffic, average purchases per customer and conversion ratios during fiscal 2001.

The Company's continued efforts to expand by opening new stores also contributed to sales growth during fiscal 2001. The Company opened 65 new stores and closed 24 stores in North America during fiscal 2001, bringing the Pier 1 North American store count up to 826 at year-end. With the addition of Cargo, the store count worldwide, including North America, Puerto Rico, the United Kingdom, Mexico and Japan, totaled 899 at the end of fiscal 2001 compared to 834 at the end of fiscal 2000. A summary reconciliation of the Company's stores open at the beginning of fiscal 2001, 2000 and 1999 to the number open at the end of each period follows:

	Pier 1 North American	International (1)	Cargo (2)	Total
Open at February 28, 1998	719	45	–	764
Openings (3)	63	11	–	74
Closings (3)	(30)	(2)	–	(32)
Open at February 27, 1999	752	54	–	806
Openings (3)	63	5	–	68
Closings (3)	(30)	(10)	–	(40)
Open at February 26, 2000	785	49	–	834
Openings (3)	65	3	–	68
Closings (3)	(24)	–	–	(24)
Acquisition (February 2001)	–	–	21	21
Open at March 3, 2001	826	52	21	899

(1) International stores were located in Puerto Rico, the United Kingdom, Mexico and Japan.
(2) The Company's results of operations for fiscal 2001 were not affected by the acquisition of Cargo.
(3) Openings and closings include stores which were relocated.

Pier 1 Imports, Inc.
MANAGEMENT'S DISCUSSION AND ANALYSIS OF FINANCIAL CONDITION AND RESULTS OF OPERATIONS
(continued)

Increased use of the Company's proprietary credit card added to the Company's sales growth during fiscal 2001. Sales on the proprietary credit card were $377.0 million and accounted for 28.9% of U.S. store sales during fiscal 2001, an increase of $76.5 million over proprietary credit card sales in the prior year of $300.5 million, which represented 26.3% of U.S. store sales during that year. Proprietary credit card customers spent an average of $152 per transaction in fiscal 2001 compared to $142 per transaction in fiscal 2000. The Company attributed the growth in sales on the card to continued efforts to open new accounts, deferred payment options offered to cardholders during furniture promotions, and enhanced customer loyalty through targeted promotions.

Gross profit, after related buying and store occupancy costs, expressed as a percentage of sales, increased 50 basis points in fiscal 2001 to 42.1% from 41.6% in fiscal 2000. Merchandise margins, as a percentage of sales, declined from 54.6% in fiscal 2000 to 54.2% in fiscal 2001, a decrease of 40 basis points. The decrease was a result of management's concerted decision to continue to give value back to customers by offering unique merchandise at affordable prices. In addition, the effect of a full year of price reductions taken as a result of the value pricing initiative started in May 1999 which continued throughout fiscal 2000 created downward pressure on fiscal 2001 merchandise margins. This decline was also due in part to higher freight rates during the first half of fiscal 2001 as compared to the same period in fiscal 2000. The decreases in merchandise margins were more than offset by the leveraging of relatively fixed rental costs over a higher sales base, which included an additional week of sales in fiscal 2001. Store occupancy costs improved 90 basis points as a percentage of sales from 13.0% in fiscal 2000 to 12.1% in fiscal 2001.

As a percentage of sales, selling, general and administrative expenses, including marketing, improved 10 basis points to 28.3% in fiscal 2001 from 28.4% in fiscal 2000. In total dollars, selling, general and administrative expenses for fiscal 2001

increased $50.4 million over the prior fiscal year. Expenses that normally increase proportionately with sales and number of stores, such as marketing, store payroll, supplies and equipment rental, increased by $34.3 million, but as a percentage of sales declined nearly 20 basis points to 20.2% this fiscal year. Marketing as a percentage of sales decreased 20 basis points as a result of reduced spending on newspaper and magazine advertisements, along with leveraging marketing expenditures over a higher sales base. As a percentage of sales, the decrease in marketing expenses was offset by a 10 basis point increase in store payroll when comparing the two fiscal years. This increase was largely attributable to store bonuses awarded based on sales gains. All other selling, general and administrative expenses increased by $16.0 million, and increased 10 basis points as a percentage of sales. This increase was primarily due to an increase in information technology and other non-store salaries, partially offset by effective management of other administrative expenses and a reduction in net credit card costs.

Depreciation and amortization increased by $3.2 million to $43.2 million in fiscal 2001 primarily because of the Company's increased capital expenditures throughout fiscal 2001 and 2000, especially expenditures on technology-related assets which tend to have relatively short useful lives.

In fiscal 2001, operating income for the year improved to $151.5 million or 10.7% of sales, from $123.2 million or 10.0% of sales in fiscal 2000, an increase of 23.0% or $28.3 million.

Interest income decreased slightly to $1.9 million in fiscal 2001 from $2.3 million in fiscal 2000 due to lower average cash balances during the current fiscal year. Interest expense was $3.1 million in fiscal 2001 compared to $6.9 million in fiscal 2000, a decline of $3.8 million. The decrease in interest expense was primarily due to the repurchase of $28.6 million of the Company's 5¾% convertible subordinated notes during fiscal 2000 and the retirement of the remaining $39.2 million of these notes during the first quarter of fiscal 2001. *See Note 5 of the Notes to Consolidated Financial Statements.*

Pier 1 Imports, Inc.

MANAGEMENT'S DISCUSSION AND ANALYSIS OF FINANCIAL CONDITION AND RESULTS OF OPERATIONS
(continued)

The Company's effective tax rate remained constant at 37% of income before income taxes for both fiscal 2001 and 2000.

Net income in fiscal 2001 was $94.7 million, or $.97 per share on a diluted basis, an increase of $20.0 million, or 26.7%, as compared to fiscal 2000's net income of $74.7 million, or $.75 per share on a diluted basis. Net income, as a percentage of sales, improved from 6.1% in fiscal 2000 to 6.7% in fiscal 2001.

LIQUIDITY AND CAPITAL RESOURCES

The Company ended fiscal year 2002 with $235.6 million of cash compared to $46.8 million a year ago. Total cash generated from operations was $244.3 million compared to $107.5 million last year. Net income, adjusted for non-cash and non-operating related items, was $147.0 million and served as the Company's primary source of operating cash for the fiscal year. The Company's reduction in inventory levels provided cash of $34.8 million compared to a use of cash in the prior fiscal year of $39.1 million. The Company's ability to better manage inventory levels resulted in higher inventory turns and lower overall inventories this year compared to last year, with only a slight decline in average inventory per store. After a successful January clearance event, inventory levels were well positioned at the end of fiscal 2002, enabling a smooth transition into the spring selling season. Increases in accounts payable and accrued liabilities provided cash of $66.0 million. These increases were primarily the result of an increase in merchandise-related accounts payable, increased sales of the Company's gift cards and increases in federal and state income taxes payable resulting from a change in the timing of tax payments.

During fiscal 2002, the Company spent a net of $10.5 million on investing activities. Capital expenditures were $57.9 million, a majority of which was used for new and existing store development and investments in the Company's information systems. The Company opened a record 104 new Pier 1 stores in North America, as well as three international stores, and relocated three existing Cargo stores, which together

accounted for $27.9 million of the total amount expended for capital purchases. The Company remodeled five stores in fiscal 2002 at a cost of $5.1 million. Continuing with its commitment to invest in current store locations, the Company spent an additional $4.5 million to improve floor plans and upgrade fixtures on existing stores. The Company also spent $16.7 million on computer software and other system enhancements, including a new financial system, warehouse management system and customer relations management system. Proceeds from disposition of properties totaled $16.7 million, which included $12.6 million in proceeds from the sale-leaseback of six Company-owned properties throughout fiscal 2002. *See Note 9 of the Notes to Consolidated Financial Statements for additional discussion of the sale-leaseback transactions.*

As of March 2, 2002, the Company's beneficial interest in securitized receivables decreased $30.8 million from the balance at fiscal 2001 year-end. During the third quarter of fiscal 2002, the Company completed a new credit card securitization transaction through the Pier 1 Imports Credit Card Master Trust (the "Master Trust"). The Master Trust is not consolidated by the Company as it is a qualifying special-purpose entity under Statement of Financial Accounting Standards ("SFAS") No. 140, "Accounting for Transfers and Servicing of Financial Assets and Extinguishments of Liabilities." The Master Trust issued $100 million in trust certificates to a third party, which bear interest at a floating rate equal to the rate on commercial paper issued by the third party. As of the end of fiscal year 2002, this rate was 1.81%. In conjunction with this transaction, the Master Trust retired $50 million in previously issued certificates, which bore interest at a fixed rate of 6.74% and were scheduled to mature in May 2002. After the retirement of these certificates, the new transaction provided the Company with net proceeds of approximately $49 million. The sale of the additional $50 million of retained interest contributed to this decrease in beneficial interest in securitized receivables, but was partially offset by increases subsequent to the sale of the retained interest due to

Pier 1 Imports, Inc.

MANAGEMENT'S DISCUSSION AND ANALYSIS OF FINANCIAL CONDITION AND RESULTS OF OPERATIONS
(continued)

increased sales on the Company's proprietary credit card. The Company has continued to experience payment rates comparable to last fiscal year on its proprietary credit card receivables. *See Note 2 of the Notes to Consolidated Financial Statements.*

During fiscal 2002, the Company paid $44.1 million to repurchase 4,020,500 common shares under the Board of Directors-approved stock buyback program at an average price of $10.98, including fees. Subsequent to the end of fiscal 2002, the Company announced that its Board of Directors authorized share repurchases of up to $150 million of the Company's common stock. This authorization replaced the previously authorized 2.8 million shares that were remaining for repurchase at the end of fiscal 2002. These repurchases will be made in open market or private transactions over the next two to three years depending on prevailing market conditions, the Company's available cash, loan covenant restrictions and consideration of its corporate credit ratings. During the year, the Company continued to pay dividends and $15.1 million of cash was expended for dividend payments during fiscal 2002. Also, subsequent to the end of the fiscal year, the Company declared an increased quarterly cash dividend of $.05 per share payable on May 22, 2002 to shareholders of record on May 8, 2002. The Company expects to continue to pay cash dividends in fiscal 2003, but to retain most of its future earnings for expansion of the Company's business. Other financing activities, primarily the exercise of stock options, provided cash of $14.2 million during fiscal 2002.

At fiscal 2002 year-end, the Company's sources of working capital were cash flow from operations, sales of proprietary credit card receivables and bank lines of credit. The bank facilities include a $125 million credit facility, which expires in November 2003, all of which was available at fiscal 2002 year-end. The Company had no borrowings on this facility during fiscal 2002. Additionally, the Company has a $120 million short-term line of credit, which is primarily used to issue merchandise letters of credit. At fiscal 2002 year-end, approximately $64.6 million had been utilized, leaving $55.4 million available. The Company also has $28.7 million in credit lines used to issue other special-

purpose letters of credit, all of which were fully utilized at fiscal 2002 year-end. Of the $28.7 million in special-purpose letters of credit, $25.6 million related to the Company's industrial revenue bonds. *See Note 5 of the Notes to Consolidated Financial Statements.* Most of the Company's loan agreements require the Company to maintain certain financial ratios and limit certain investments and distributions to shareholders, including cash dividends and repurchases of common stock. The Company's current ratio was 2.9 to 1 at fiscal 2002 year-end compared to 3.3 to 1 at fiscal 2001 year-end.

A summary of the Company's other commercial commitments as of March 2, 2002 is listed below (in thousands):

	Total Amounts Committed	Amount of Commitment Expiration per Period	
		Less Than 1 Year	1 to 3 Years
Merchandise letters of credit	$ 64,640	$ 64,640	$ –
Standby letters of credit	28,740	3,175	25,565
Total other commercial commitments	$ 93,380	$ 67,815	$ 25,565

A summary of the Company's contractual cash commitments as of March 2, 2002 is listed below (in thousands):

Fiscal Year	Long-term Debt	Operating Leases
2003	$ 356	$ 162,315
2004	356	158,525
2005	–	145,608
2006	–	132,855
2007	–	118,102
Thereafter	25,000	426,946
Total contractual cash commitments	$ 25,712	$ 1,144,351

The present value of total existing minimum operating lease commitments discounted at 10% was $751.9 million at fiscal 2002 year-end. The Company plans to continue to fund these commitments from operating cash flow.

Pier 1 Imports, Inc.
MANAGEMENT'S DISCUSSION AND ANALYSIS OF FINANCIAL CONDITION AND RESULTS OF OPERATIONS
(continued)

The Company's securitization transaction accounts for a significant source of its funding, with a face amount of outstanding debt securities (the Class A Certificates) assumed by third parties of $100 million. The Company does not provide recourse to third-party investors that purchase the debt securities issued by the Master Trust. However, should the performance of the underlying credit card receivables held by the Master Trust deteriorate to a level that the Company's retained subordinated interests were insufficient to collateralize the Class A Certificates, the Master Trust would be contractually required to begin repayment of the Class A Certificates, thereby limiting the amount of receivables that could be sold to the Master Trust and limiting the securitization as a source of funding. However, this repayment would only be required to the extent that the Master Trust was out of compliance with its required performance measures. The performance measures that could trigger this repayment, such as payment rate, returns and fraud, portfolio yield and minimum transferor's interest, would have to decline significantly to result in such an early amortization event. In addition, if the Company was required to consolidate the Master Trust due to a change in accounting rules, the Company's operations for fiscal 2002 would not have been materially different than its reported results and both its assets and liabilities would have increased by approximately $100 million as of March 2, 2002.

The Company plans to open approximately 115 to 120 new Pier 1 stores during fiscal year 2003 and plans to close approximately 30 stores as their leases expire or otherwise end. A majority of the store closings are planned relocations within the same markets. In addition, the Company will begin its expansion plans for Cargo and will open eight to ten locations during fiscal 2003. New store buildings and land will be financed primarily through operating leases. Total capital expenditures for fiscal 2003 are expected to

be approximately $85 million. Of this amount, the Company expects to spend approximately $43 million on store development, $15 million on the replacement of its Savannah distribution facility, net of estimated proceeds from the disposal of the current facility, $15 million on information systems and $12 million on the land and other costs related to construction of the Company's new headquarters.

In summary, the Company's primary uses of cash in fiscal 2002 were to fund operating expenses, provide for new and existing store development and repurchase common stock of the Company. Historically, the Company has financed its operations primarily from internally generated funds and borrowings under the Company's credit facilities. The Company believes that the funds provided from operations, available lines of credit and sales of its proprietary credit card receivables will be sufficient to finance working capital and capital expenditure requirements throughout fiscal year 2003.

CRITICAL ACCOUNTING POLICIES

The preparation of the Company's consolidated financial statements in accordance with accounting principles generally accepted in the United States requires the use of estimates that affect the reported value of assets, liabilities, revenues and expenses. These estimates are based on historical experience and various other factors that are believed to be reasonable under the circumstances, the results of which form the basis for the Company's conclusions. The Company continually evaluates the information used to make these estimates as the business and the economic environment changes. Actual results may differ from these estimates under different assumptions or conditions. The use of estimates is pervasive throughout the consolidated financial statements, but the accounting policies and estimates considered most critical are as follows:

Pier 1 Imports, Inc.

MANAGEMENT'S DISCUSSION AND ANALYSIS OF FINANCIAL CONDITION AND RESULTS OF OPERATIONS
(continued)

Beneficial interest in securitized receivables - In February 1997, the Company sold all of its proprietary credit card receivables to a special-purpose wholly-owned subsidiary, Pier 1 Funding, Inc., predecessor to Pier 1 Funding, LLC ("Funding"), which transferred the receivables to the Pier 1 Imports Credit Card Master Trust (the "Master Trust"). The Master Trust is not consolidated by the Company as it meets the requirements of a qualifying special-purpose entity under SFAS No. 140. The Master Trust issues beneficial interests that represent undivided interests in the assets of the Master Trust consisting of the transferred receivables and all cash flows from collections of such receivables. The beneficial interests include certain interests retained by Funding, which are represented by Class B Certificates, and the residual interest in the Master Trust (the excess of the principal amount of receivables held in the Master Trust over the portion represented by the certificates sold to investors and the Class B Certificates). Gain or loss on the sale of receivables depends in part on the previous carrying amount of the financial assets involved in the transfer, allocated between the assets sold and the retained interests based on their relative fair value at the date of transfer. The beneficial interest in the Master Trust is accounted for as an available-for-sale security. The Company estimates the fair value of its beneficial interest in the Master Trust, both upon initial securitization and thereafter, based on the present value of future expected cash flows estimated using management's best estimates of key assumptions including credit losses and timeliness of payments. Although not anticipated by the Company, a significant deterioration in the financial condition of the Company's credit card holders, interest rates, or other economic conditions could result in other than temporary losses on the beneficial interest in future periods.

Inventories - The Company's inventory is comprised of finished merchandise and is stated at the lower of average cost or market; cost is determined on a weighted average method. Calculations of the carrying value of inventory are made on an item-by-item basis. The Company reviews its inventory levels in order to identify slow-moving merchandise and uses merchandise markdowns to clear such merchandise. Reserves are established to reduce the value of such slow-moving merchandise. The Company records inventory shrink expense based upon known inventory losses plus unknown losses estimated by reviewing historical experience of the results of its physical inventories. Although inventory shrink rates have not fluctuated significantly in recent years, should actual inventory shrink rates differ from the Company's estimates, revisions to the inventory shrink expense may be required. Most inventory purchases and commitments are made in U.S. dollars.

Income taxes - The Company records income tax expense using the liability method for taxes. The Company is subject to income tax in many jurisdictions, including the United States, various states and localities, and foreign countries. The process of determining tax expense by jurisdiction involves the calculation of actual current tax expense, together with the assessment of deferred tax expense resulting from differing treatment of items for tax and financial accounting purposes. Deferred tax assets and liabilities are recorded in the Company's consolidated balance sheets.

In accordance with Accounting Principles Board ("APB") Opinion No. 23, deferred federal income taxes, net of applicable foreign tax credits, are not provided on the undistributed earnings of foreign subsidiaries to the extent the Company intends to permanently reinvest such earnings abroad. The Company intends these earnings to be indefinitely reinvested in international operations. If future events require that certain assets associated with these earnings be repatriated to the United States, an additional tax provision will be required. Determination of the amount of additional taxes that would be payable if such earnings were not considered indefinitely reinvested is not practical due to the complexities in tax laws and the assumptions that would have to be made.

Pier 1 Imports, Inc.

MANAGEMENT'S DISCUSSION AND ANALYSIS OF FINANCIAL CONDITION AND RESULTS OF OPERATIONS
(continued)

Revenue recognition - The Company recognizes revenue upon customer receipt or delivery for retail sales, including sales under deferred payment promotions on its proprietary credit card. Credit card receivable deferrals are for approximately 90 days and have historically resulted in no significant increases in bad debt losses arising from such receivables. Revenue from gift cards, gift certificates and merchandise credits is deferred until redemption. The Company records an allowance for estimated merchandise returns based on historical experience and other known factors. Should actual returns differ from the Company's estimates and current provision for merchandise returns, revisions to the estimated merchandise returns may be required.

Same-store sales - Stores included in the same-store sales calculation are those stores opened prior to the beginning of the preceding fiscal year and that are still open. Also included are stores that are relocated during the year within a specified distance serving the same market, where there is not a significant change in store size and where there is not a significant overlap between the opening of one store and the closing of the existing store. Stores that are expanded or renovated are excluded from the same-store sales calculation during the period they are closed for such remodeling. When these stores re-open for business, they are included in the same-store sales calculation in the first full month after the re-opening if there is no significant change in store size. If there is a significant change in store size, the store continues to be excluded from the calculation until it meets the Company's established definition of a same-store. Sales over the internet are included, but clearance stores are omitted from the same-store sales calculation. Also, Cargo was not included in the operations of the Company for fiscal 2001 and was not included in the same-store sales calculation for fiscal 2002.

MARKET RISK DISCLOSURES

Market risks relating to the Company's operations result primarily from changes in foreign exchange rates and interest rates. The Company has only limited involvement with derivative financial instruments, does not use them for trading purposes and is not a party to any leveraged derivatives.

The Company periodically enters into forward foreign currency exchange contracts to hedge some of its foreign currency exposure. The Company uses such contracts to hedge exposures to changes in foreign currency exchange rates, primarily the EMU euro and British pounds, associated with purchases denominated in foreign currencies. The Company also uses contracts to hedge its exposure associated with repatriation of funds from its Canadian operations. Changes in the fair value of the derivatives are included in the Company's consolidated statements of operations. Forward contracts, which hedge merchandise purchases, generally have maturities not exceeding six months, and contracts which hedge the repatriation of Canadian funds have maturities not exceeding eighteen months. At March 2, 2002, the notional amount of the Company's forward foreign currency exchange contracts and contracts to hedge its exposure associated with repatriation of Canadian funds totaled approximately $3.9 and $12.2 million, respectively.

The Company manages its exposure to changes in interest rates by optimizing the use of variable and fixed rate debt. The Company had $25.0 million of variable rate borrowings at March 2, 2002. A hypothetical 10% adverse change in interest rates would have a negligible impact on the Company's earnings and cash flows.

Collectively, the Company's exposure to these market risk factors was not significant and did not materially change from March 3, 2001.

Pier 1 Imports, Inc.

MANAGEMENT'S DISCUSSION AND ANALYSIS OF FINANCIAL CONDITION AND RESULTS OF OPERATIONS
(continued)

IMPACT OF INFLATION AND CHANGING PRICES

Inflation has not had a significant impact on the operations of the Company during the preceding three years.

IMPACT OF NEW ACCOUNTING STANDARDS

In the first quarter of fiscal 2002, the Company adopted SFAS No. 133, "Accounting for Derivative Instruments and Hedging Activities," which was amended by SFAS No. 137 and SFAS No. 138. This statement establishes accounting and reporting guidelines for derivatives and requires the Company to record all derivatives as assets or liabilities on the balance sheet at fair value. The Company's use of derivatives is primarily limited to forward foreign currency exchange contracts, which the Company uses to mitigate exposures to changes in foreign currency exchange rates. The Company also uses contracts which hedge the repatriation of Canadian funds. Upon adoption of SFAS No. 133, the Company did not designate such derivatives as hedging instruments; thus, the changes in the fair value of the derivatives have been included in the consolidated statements of operations. Prior to adoption, the Company deferred all gains and losses on its derivative contracts and recognized such gains and losses as an adjustment to the transaction price. The adoption of SFAS No. 133 has not had a material impact on the Company's consolidated balance sheets or its statements of operations, shareholders' equity and cash flows.

The Company adopted SFAS No. 140, "Accounting for Transfers and Servicing of Financial Assets and Extinguishments of Liabilities," in the first quarter of fiscal 2002. This statement established new conditions for a securitization to be accounted for as a sale of receivables, changed the requirements for an entity to be a qualifying special-purpose entity, and modified the conditions for determining whether a transferor has relinquished control over transferred assets. SFAS No. 140 also requires additional disclosures related to securitized financial assets and retained interests in securitized financial assets.

See Note 2 of the Notes to Consolidated Financial Statements. Prior to adoption, the Company made the necessary amendments to its securitization agreements and continues to receive sale treatment for its securitized proprietary credit card receivables. The implementation of SFAS No. 140 did not have a material impact on the Company's consolidated balance sheets or its statements of operations, shareholders' equity and cash flows.

In June 2001, the Financial Accounting Standards Board ("FASB") issued SFAS No. 141, "Business Combinations," which supersedes APB Opinion No. 16, "Business Combinations," and SFAS No. 38, "Accounting for Preacquisition Contingencies of Purchased Enterprises." Statement No. 141 eliminates the pooling-of-interests method of accounting for business combinations and requires all such transactions to be accounted for under the purchase method. This statement also addresses the initial recognition and measurement of goodwill and other intangible assets acquired in a business combination and is effective for all business combinations initiated after June 30, 2001. The adoption of SFAS No. 141 did not have a material impact on the Company's consolidated balance sheets or its statements of operations, shareholders' equity and cash flows.

In June 2001, the FASB also issued SFAS No. 142, "Goodwill and Other Intangible Assets," which supersedes APB Opinion No. 17, "Intangible Assets." This statement addresses the initial recognition and measurement of intangible assets acquired outside of a business combination and the accounting for goodwill and other intangible assets subsequent to their acquisition. SFAS No. 142 also provides that intangible assets with finite useful lives be amortized and that goodwill and intangible assets with indefinite lives will not be amortized, but will rather be tested on an annual basis for impairment. The Company is required to adopt SFAS No. 142 for its fiscal year beginning March 3, 2002. The Company has analyzed the implementation requirements

Pier 1 Imports, Inc.

MANAGEMENT'S DISCUSSION AND ANALYSIS OF FINANCIAL CONDITION AND RESULTS OF OPERATIONS
(continued)

and does not anticipate that the adoption of SFAS No. 142 will have a material impact on the Company's consolidated balance sheets or its statements of operations, shareholders' equity and cash flows.

In October 2001, the FASB issued SFAS No. 144, "Accounting for the Impairment or Disposal of Long-Lived Assets," which replaces SFAS No. 121, "Accounting for the Impairment of Long-Lived Assets and for Long-Lived Assets to Be Disposed Of." Statement No. 144 retains the fundamental provisions of SFAS No. 121 with additional guidance on estimating cash flows when performing a recoverability test, requires that a long-lived asset to be disposed of, other than by sale, be classified as "held and used" until it is disposed of, and establishes more restrictive criteria to classify an asset as "held for sale." SFAS No. 144 also supersedes APB Opinion No. 30, "Reporting the Results of Operations – Reporting the Effects of Disposal of a Segment of a Business, and Extraordinary, Unusual and Infrequently Occurring Events and Transactions" regarding the disposal of a segment of a business and would extend the reporting of a discontinued operation to a "component of an entity" and requires the operating losses thereon to be recognized in the period in which they occur. The Company is required to adopt SFAS No. 144 for its fiscal year beginning March 3, 2002. The Company has analyzed the implementation requirements and does not anticipate that the adoption of SFAS No. 144 will have a material impact on the Company's consolidated balance sheets or its statements of operations, shareholders' equity and cash flows.

FORWARD-LOOKING STATEMENTS

Certain matters discussed in this annual report, other than historical information, may constitute "forward-looking statements" that are subject to certain risks and uncertainties that could cause actual results to differ materially from those described in the forward-looking statements. The Company may also make forward-looking statements in other reports filed with the Securities and Exchange Commission and in material delivered to the Company's shareholders. Forward-looking statements provide current expectations of future events based on certain assumptions. These statements encompass information that does not directly relate to any historical or current fact and often may be identified with words such as "anticipates," "believes," "expects," "estimates," "intends," "plans," "projects" and other similar expressions. Management's expectations and assumptions regarding planned store openings, financing of Company obligations from operations and other future results are subject to risks, uncertainties and other factors that could cause actual results to differ materially from the anticipated results or other expectations expressed in the forward-looking statements. Risks and uncertainties that may affect Company operations and performance include, among others, the effects of terrorist attacks or other acts of war, weather conditions that may affect sales, the general strength of the economy and levels of consumer spending, the availability of new sites for expansion along with sufficient labor to facilitate growth, the strength of new home construction and sales of existing homes, the ability of the Company to import merchandise from foreign countries without significantly restrictive tariffs, duties or quotas and the ability of the Company to ship items from foreign countries at reasonable rates in timely fashion. The foregoing risks and uncertainties are in addition to others discussed elsewhere in this annual report. The Company assumes no obligation to update or otherwise revise its forward-looking statements even if experience or future changes make it clear that any projected results expressed or implied will not be realized.

Pier 1 Imports, Inc.

REPORT OF INDEPENDENT AUDITORS

To the Board of Directors of Pier 1 Imports, Inc.

We have audited the accompanying consolidated balance sheets of Pier 1 Imports, Inc. as of March 2, 2002 and March 3, 2001, and the related consolidated statements of operations, shareholders' equity and cash flows for each of the three years in the period ended March 2, 2002. These financial statements are the responsibility of the Company's management. Our responsibility is to express an opinion on these financial statements based on our audits.

We conducted our audits in accordance with auditing standards generally accepted in the United States. Those standards require that we plan and perform the audit to obtain reasonable assurance about whether the financial statements are free of material misstatement. An audit includes examining, on a test basis, evidence supporting the amounts and disclosures in the financial statements. An audit also includes assessing the accounting principles used and significant estimates made by management, as well as evaluating the overall financial statement presentation. We believe that our audits provide a reasonable basis for our opinion.

In our opinion, the financial statements referred to above present fairly, in all material respects, the consolidated financial position of Pier 1 Imports, Inc. at March 2, 2002 and March 3, 2001, and the consolidated results of its operations and its cash flows for each of the three years in the period ended March 2, 2002, in conformity with accounting principles generally accepted in the United States.

Ernst & Young LLP

Fort Worth, Texas
April 8, 2002

REPORT OF MANAGEMENT

To our shareholders:

Management is responsible for the preparation and the integrity of the accompanying consolidated financial statements and related notes, which have been prepared in accordance with accounting principles generally accepted in the United States and include amounts based upon our estimates and judgments, as required. The consolidated financial statements have been audited by Ernst & Young LLP, independent certified public accountants. The accompanying independent auditors' report expresses an independent professional opinion on the fairness of presentation of management's financial statements.

The Company maintains a system of internal controls over financial reporting. We believe this system provides reasonable assurance that transactions are executed in accordance with management authorization and that such transactions are properly recorded and reported in the financial statements, that assets are properly safeguarded and accounted for, and that records are maintained so as to permit preparation of financial statements in accordance with accounting principles generally accepted in the United States. The Company also has instituted policies and guidelines, which require employees to maintain a high level of ethical standards.

In addition, the Board of Directors exercises its oversight role with respect to the Company's internal control systems primarily through its Audit Committee. The Audit Committee consists solely of outside directors and meets periodically with management, the Company's internal auditors and the Company's independent auditors to review internal accounting controls, audit results, financial reporting, and accounting principles and practices. The Company's independent and internal auditors have full and free access to the Audit Committee with and without management's presence. Although no cost-effective internal control system will preclude all errors and irregularities, we believe our controls as of and for the year ended March 2, 2002 provide reasonable assurance that the consolidated financial statements are reliable.

Marvin J. Girouard
Chairman of the Board
and Chief Executive Officer

Charles H. Turner
Executive Vice President,
Chief Financial Officer
and Treasurer

Pier 1 Imports, Inc.

CONSOLIDATED STATEMENTS OF OPERATIONS
(in thousands except per share amounts)

| | Year Ended | | |
	2002	2001	2000
Net sales	$ 1,548,556	$ 1,411,498	$ 1,231,095
Operating costs and expenses:			
Cost of sales (including buying and store occupancy costs)	898,795	817,043	718,547
Selling, general and administrative expenses	448,127	399,755	349,394
Depreciation and amortization	42,821	43,184	39,973
	1,389,743	1,259,982	1,107,914
Operating income	158,813	151,516	123,181
Nonoperating (income) and expenses:			
Interest and investment income	(2,484)	(1,854)	(2,349)
Interest expense	2,300	3,130	6,918
	(184)	1,276	4,569
Income before income taxes	158,997	150,240	118,612
Provision for income taxes	58,788	55,590	43,887
Net income	$ 100,209	$ 94,650	$ 74,725
Earnings per share:			
Basic	$ 1.06	$ .98	$ .78
Diluted	$ 1.04	$ .97	$ .75
Dividends declared per share	$ .16	$ .15	$ .12
Average shares outstanding during period:			
Basic	94,414	96,306	95,766
Diluted	96,185	97,952	103,297

The accompanying notes are an integral part of these financial statements.

Pier 1 Imports, Inc.

CONSOLIDATED BALANCE SHEETS
(in thousands except share amounts)

	2002	2001
ASSETS		
Current assets:		
Cash, including temporary investments of $213,488 and $31,142, respectively	$ 235,609	$ 46,841
Beneficial interest in securitized receivables	44,620	75,403
Other accounts receivable, net of allowance for doubtful accounts		
of $275 and $295, respectively	6,205	8,370
Inventories	275,433	310,704
Prepaid expenses and other current assets	43,286	35,748
Total current assets	605,153	477,066
Properties, net	209,954	212,066
Other noncurrent assets	47,565	46,578
	$ 862,672	$ 735,710
LIABILITIES AND SHAREHOLDERS' EQUITY		
Current liabilities:		
Current portion of long-term debt	$ 356	$ –
Accounts payable and accrued liabilities	208,040	144,110
Total current liabilities	208,396	144,110
Long-term debt	25,356	25,000
Other noncurrent liabilities	43,264	34,721
Shareholders' equity:		
Common stock, $1.00 par, 500,000,000 shares authorized, 100,779,000 issued	100,779	100,779
Paid-in capital	140,190	139,424
Retained earnings	429,910	344,809
Cumulative other comprehensive income	(4,702)	(3,115)
Less – 7,362,000 and 4,619,000 common shares in treasury, at cost, respectively	(80,521)	(49,933)
Less – unearned compensation	–	(85)
	585,656	531,879
Commitments and contingencies	–	–
	$ 862,672	$ 735,710

The accompanying notes are an integral part of these financial statements.

Pier 1 Imports, Inc.

CONSOLIDATED STATEMENTS OF CASH FLOWS
(in thousands except share amounts)

	Year Ended		
	2002	**2001**	**2000**
CASH FLOW FROM OPERATING ACTIVITIES:			
Net income	$ 100,209	$ 94,650	$ 74,725
Adjustments to reconcile to net cash provided by operating activities:			
Depreciation and amortization	42,821	43,184	39,973
Loss on disposal of fixed assets	4,205	6,514	5,828
Deferred compensation	3,697	2,072	1,543
Deferred taxes	(2,238)	735	1,724
Other	(1,707)	(184)	1,938
Change in cash from:			
Inventories	34,804	(39,127)	(10,133)
Other accounts receivable and other current assets	(2,983)	(5,847)	586
Accounts payable and accrued expenses	66,048	6,280	8,962
Other noncurrent assets	(32)	(378)	(2,382)
Other noncurrent liabilities	(500)	(390)	(911)
Net cash provided by operating activities	244,324	107,509	121,853
CASH FLOW FROM INVESTING ACTIVITIES:			
Capital expenditures	(57,925)	(42,745)	(48,219)
Proceeds from disposition of properties	16,682	353	19,425
Net cost from disposition of Sunbelt Nursery Group, Inc. properties	–	–	(439)
Acquisitions, net of cash acquired	–	(3,917)	–
Beneficial interest in securitized receivables	30,783	(21,583)	(12,820)
Net cash used in investing activities	(10,460)	(67,892)	(42,053)
CASH FLOW FROM FINANCING ACTIVITIES:			
Cash dividends	(15,134)	(14,494)	(11,504)
Purchases of treasury stock	(44,137)	(34,270)	(31,806)
Proceeds from stock options exercised, stock purchase plan and other, net	13,463	5,627	4,148
Borrowings under long-term debt	712	82,500	4,035
Repayments of long-term debt	–	(82,515)	(36,242)
Net cash used in financing activities	(45,096)	(43,152)	(71,369)
Change in cash and cash equivalents	188,768	(3,535)	8,431
Cash and cash equivalents at beginning of year	46,841	50,376	41,945
Cash and cash equivalents at end of year	$ 235,609	$ 46,841	$ 50,376
Supplemental cash flow information:			
Interest paid	$ 2,493	$ 3,171	$ 7,137
Income taxes paid	$ 35,951	$ 58,302	$ 40,883

During fiscal 2001, the Company issued 4,764,450 shares of its common stock upon the conversion of $39,164,000 principal amount of 5¾% convertible subordinated notes.

The accompanying notes are an integral part of these financial statements.

Pier 1 Imports, Inc.

CONSOLIDATED STATEMENTS OF SHAREHOLDERS' EQUITY
(in thousands except per share amounts)

	Common Stock Shares	Common Stock Amount	Paid-in Capital	Retained Earnings	Cumulative Other Comprehensive Income	Treasury Stock	Unearned Compensation	Total Shareholders' Equity
Balance February 27, 1999	97,672	$ 100,779	$ 159,631	$ 201,457	$ (1,850)	$ (54,654)	$ (1,469)	$ 403,894
Comprehensive income:								
Net income	–	–	–	74,725	–	–	–	74,725
Other comprehensive income, net of tax:								
Currency translation adjustments	–	–	–	–	314	–	–	314
Comprehensive income								75,039
Purchases of treasury stock	(4,393)	–	–	–	–	(31,806)	–	(31,806)
Restricted stock forfeits and amortization	(83)	–	709	–	–	(1,392)	1,168	485
Exercise of stock options, stock purchase								
plan and other	625	–	(4,629)	–	–	9,184	–	4,555
Cash dividends ($.12 per share)	–	–	–	(11,504)	–	–	–	(11,504)
Balance February 26, 2000	93,821	100,779	155,711	264,678	(1,536)	(78,668)	(301)	440,663
Comprehensive income:								
Net income	–	–	–	94,650	–	–	–	94,650
Other comprehensive income, net of tax:								
Currency translation adjustments	–	–	–	–	(1,579)	–	–	(1,579)
Comprehensive income								93,071
Purchases of treasury stock	(3,269)	–	–	–	–	(34,270)	–	(34,270)
Restricted stock amortization	–	–	–	–	–	–	216	216
Exercise of stock options, stock purchase								
plan and other	825	–	(1,774)	(25)	–	9,119	–	7,320
Cash dividends ($.15 per share)	–	–	–	(14,494)	–	–	–	(14,494)
Conversion of 5¾% convertible debt	4,764	–	(14,513)	–	–	53,886	–	39,373
Balance March 3, 2001	96,141	100,779	139,424	344,809	(3,115)	(49,933)	(85)	531,879
Comprehensive income:								
Net income	–	–	–	100,209	–	–	–	100,209
Other comprehensive income, net of tax:								
Currency translation adjustments	–	–	–	–	(1,587)	–	–	(1,587)
Comprehensive income								98,622
Purchases of treasury stock	(4,021)	–	–	–	–	(44,137)	–	(44,137)
Restricted stock amortization	–	–	–	–	–	–	85	85
Exercise of stock options, stock purchase								
plan and other	1,269	–	766	26	–	13,549	–	14,341
Cash dividends ($.16 per share)	–	–	–	(15,134)	–	–	–	(15,134)
Balance March 2, 2002	93,389	$100,779	$140,190	$429,910	$ (4,702)	$ (80,521)	$ –	$ 585,656

The accompanying notes are an integral part of these financial statements.

Pier 1 Imports, Inc.
NOTES TO CONSOLIDATED FINANCIAL STATEMENTS

NOTE 1 - SUMMARY OF SIGNIFICANT ACCOUNTING POLICIES

Organization - Pier 1 Imports, Inc. is one of North America's largest specialty retailers of imported decorative home furnishings, gifts and related items, with retail stores located in the United States, Canada, Puerto Rico, the United Kingdom and Mexico. Concentrations of risk with respect to sourcing the Company's inventory purchases are limited due to the large number of vendors or suppliers and their geographic dispersion around the world. The Company sells merchandise imported from over 40 different countries, with 35% of its sales derived from merchandise produced in China, 11% derived from merchandise produced in India and 29% derived from merchandise produced in Indonesia, Thailand, Brazil, Italy, the Philippines and Mexico. The remaining 25% of sales was from merchandise produced in various Asian, European, Central American, South American and African countries or was obtained from U.S. manufacturers.

Basis of consolidation - The consolidated financial statements of Pier 1 Imports, Inc. and its consolidated subsidiaries (the "Company") include the accounts of all subsidiary companies except Pier 1 Funding, LLC, which is a non-consolidated, bankruptcy remote, securitization subsidiary. *See Note 2 of the Notes to Consolidated Financial Statements.* Material intercompany transactions and balances have been eliminated.

Acquisitions - The Company completed its acquisition of certain assets and assumption of certain liabilities of Cargo Furniture, Inc. and formed New Cargo Furniture, Inc. ("Cargo") for $3,931,000, including cash acquired, on February 21, 2001. These assets and liabilities were included in the Company's consolidated balance sheet as of March 3, 2001; however, this acquisition had no effect on the Company's fiscal 2001 operations. Cargo is a retailer and wholesaler of casual lifestyle furniture, gifts and home décor with a focus on children's furniture. This acquisition was accounted for under the purchase method of accounting, and ultimately resulted in goodwill of $4,386,000, which has been amortized using the straight-line method over 20 years through fiscal 2002, at which time amortization ceases due to the adoption of Statement of Financial Accounting Standards ("SFAS") No. 142. The pro forma effect on the Company's results of operations, as if the acquisition had been completed at the beginning of fiscal 2001, was not significant. Cargo's operations for fiscal 2002 are fully consolidated with the Company's results.

Use of estimates - Preparation of the financial statements in conformity with accounting principles generally accepted in the United States requires management to make estimates and assumptions that affect the amounts reported in the financial statements and accompanying notes. Actual results could differ from those estimates.

Reclassifications - Certain reclassifications have been made in the prior years' consolidated financial statements to conform to the fiscal 2002 presentation.

Fiscal periods - The Company utilizes 5-4-4 (week) quarterly accounting periods with the fiscal year ending on the Saturday nearest the last day of February. Fiscal 2002 and 2000 consisted of 52-week years and fiscal 2001 was a 53-week year. Fiscal 2002 ended March 2, 2002, fiscal 2001 ended March 3, 2001 and fiscal 2000 ended February 26, 2000.

Cash and cash equivalents - The Company considers all highly liquid investments with an original maturity date of three months or less to be cash equivalents. The effect of foreign currency exchange rate fluctuations on cash is not material.

Translation of foreign currencies - Assets and liabilities of foreign operations are translated into U.S. dollars at fiscal year-end exchange rates. Income and expense items are translated at average exchange rates prevailing during the year. Translation adjustments arising from differences in exchange rates from period to period are included as a separate component of shareholders' equity and are included in comprehensive income.

Financial instruments - The fair value of financial instruments is determined by reference to various market data and other valuation techniques as appropriate. There were no significant assets or liabilities with a fair value different from the recorded value as of March 2, 2002 and March 3, 2001.

Risk management instruments: The Company may utilize various financial instruments to manage interest rate and market risk associated with its on- and off-balance sheet commitments.

The Company hedges certain commitments denominated in foreign currencies through the purchase of forward contracts. The forward contracts are purchased only to cover specific commitments to buy merchandise for resale. The Company also uses contracts to hedge its exposure associated with the repatriation of funds from its Canadian

Pier 1 Imports, Inc.
NOTES TO CONSOLIDATED FINANCIAL STATEMENTS
(continued)

operations. At March 2, 2002, the notional amount of the Company's forward foreign currency exchange contracts and contracts to hedge its exposure associated with repatriation of Canadian funds totaled approximately $3.9 million and $12.2 million, respectively. For financial accounting purposes, the Company has not designated such contracts as hedges. Thus, changes in the fair value of both of these forward contracts are included in the Company's consolidated statements of operations.

The Company enters into forward foreign currency exchange contracts with major financial institutions and continually monitors its positions with, and the credit quality of, these counterparties to such financial instruments. The Company does not expect non-performance by any of the counterparties, and any losses incurred in the event of non-performance would not be material.

Beneficial interest in securitized receivables - In February 1997, the Company sold all of its proprietary credit card receivables to a special-purpose wholly-owned subsidiary, Pier 1 Funding, Inc., predecessor to Pier 1 Funding, LLC ("Funding"), which transferred the receivables to the Pier 1 Imports Credit Card Master Trust (the "Master Trust"). The Master Trust is not consolidated by the Company as it meets the requirements of a qualifying special-purpose entity under SFAS No. 140. The Master Trust issues beneficial interests that represent undivided interests in the assets of the Master Trust consisting of the transferred receivables and all cash flows from collections of such receivables. The beneficial interests include certain interests retained by Funding, which are represented by Class B Certificates, and the residual interest in the Master Trust (the excess of the principal amount of receivables held in the Master Trust over the portion represented by the certificates sold to investors and the Class B Certificates).

Gain or loss on the sale of receivables depends in part on the previous carrying amount of the financial assets involved in the transfer, allocated between the assets sold and the retained interests based on their relative fair value at the date of transfer. A servicing asset or liability was not recognized in the Company's credit card securitizations (and thus was not considered in the gain or loss computation) since the Company received adequate compensation relative to current market servicing prices to service the receivables sold. Initial transaction costs for credit card securitizations were deferred and are being amortized over the expected life of the securitization.

The beneficial interest in the Master Trust is accounted for as an available-for-sale security. The Company estimates fair value of its beneficial interest in the Master Trust, both upon initial securitization and thereafter, based on the present value of future expected cash flows estimated using management's best estimates of key assumptions including credit losses and timeliness of payments. As of March 2, 2002, the Company's assumptions included credit losses of 5% of the outstanding balance and expected payment within a six-month period using a discount rate of 15% to calculate the present value of the future cash flows. A sensitivity analysis was performed assuming a hypothetical 20% adverse change in both interest rates and credit losses, which had an immaterial impact on the fair value of the Company's beneficial interest.

Inventories - Inventories are comprised of finished merchandise and are stated at the lower of average cost or market; cost is determined on a weighted average method.

Properties, maintenance and repairs - Buildings, equipment, furniture and fixtures, and leasehold interests and improvements are carried at cost less accumulated depreciation. Depreciation is computed using the straight-line method over estimated remaining useful lives of the assets, generally thirty years for buildings and three to seven years for equipment, furniture and fixtures. Amortization of improvements to leased properties is based upon the shorter of the remaining primary lease term or the estimated useful lives of such assets. Depreciation costs were $41,047,000, $41,882,000 and $38,672,000 in fiscal 2002, 2001 and 2000, respectively.

Expenditures for maintenance, repairs and renewals, which do not materially prolong the original useful lives of the assets, are charged to expense as incurred. In the case of disposals, assets and the related depreciation are removed from the accounts and the net amount, less proceeds from disposal, is credited or charged to income.

Revenue recognition - Revenue is recognized upon customer receipt or delivery for retail sales, including sales under deferred payment promotions on the Company's proprietary credit card. An allowance has been established to provide for estimated merchandise returns. Revenue from gift cards, gift certificates and merchandise credits is deferred until redemption.

Pier 1 Imports, Inc.
NOTES TO CONSOLIDATED FINANCIAL STATEMENTS
(continued)

Advertising costs - Advertising costs are expensed the first time the advertising takes place. Advertising costs were $64,414,000, $59,721,000 and $54,970,000 in fiscal 2002, 2001 and 2000, respectively. Prepaid advertising at the end of fiscal years 2002 and 2001 was $2,303,000 and $2,086,000, respectively, consisting primarily of production costs for advertisements not yet run.

Income taxes - The Company records income tax expense using the liability method for taxes. Under this method, deferred tax assets and liabilities are recognized based on differences between financial statement and tax bases of assets and liabilities using presently enacted tax rates. Deferred federal income taxes, net of applicable foreign tax credits, are not provided on the undistributed earnings of foreign subsidiaries to the extent the Company intends to permanently reinvest such earnings abroad.

Stock-based compensation - The Company grants stock options and restricted stock for a fixed number of shares to employees with stock option exercise prices equal to the fair market value of the shares on the date of grant. The Company accounts for stock option grants and restricted stock grants in accordance with Accounting Principles Board ("APB") Opinion No. 25, "Accounting for Stock Issued to Employees," and, accordingly, recognizes no compensation expense for the stock option grants.

Earnings per share - Basic earnings per share amounts were determined by dividing net income by the weighted average number of common shares outstanding for the period. Diluted earnings per share amounts were similarly computed, but included the effect, when dilutive, of the Company's weighted average number of stock options outstanding and the average number of common shares that would be issuable upon conversion of the Company's convertible securities. To determine diluted earnings per share, interest and amortization of debt issue costs related to the subordinated notes, net of any applicable taxes, have been added back to net income to reflect assumed conversions.

The following earnings per share calculations reflect the effect of the Company's conversion of its 5¾% convertible subordinated notes, which were primarily converted, without interest, on or before March 23, 2000. Earnings per share amounts are calculated as follows (in thousands except per share amounts):

	2002	2001	2000
Net income	$ 100,209	$ 94,650	$ 74,725
Plus interest and debt issue costs, net of tax, on the assumed conversion of the 5¾% subordinated notes	–	–	2,237
Diluted net income	$100,209	$ 94,650	$ 76,962
Average shares outstanding:			
Basic.....................	94,414	96,306	95,766
Plus assumed exercise of stock options	1,771	1,325	644
Plus assumed conversion of the 5¾% subordinated notes ...	–	321	6,887
Diluted	96,185	97,952	103,297
Earnings per share:			
Basic.....................	$ 1.06	$ .98	$ .78
Diluted	$ 1.04	$ .97	$ .75

Stock options for which the exercise price was greater than the average market price of common shares were not included in the computation of diluted earnings per share as the effect would be antidilutive. At the end of fiscal years 2002, 2001 and 2000, there were 433,800, 1,078,200 and 1,157,025, respectively, stock options outstanding with exercise prices greater than the average market price of the Company's common shares.

Impact of recently issued accounting standards - In the first quarter of fiscal 2002, the Company adopted SFAS No. 133, "Accounting for Derivative Instruments and Hedging Activities," which was amended by SFAS No. 137 and SFAS No. 138. This statement establishes accounting and reporting guidelines for derivatives and requires the Company to record all derivatives as assets or liabilities on the balance sheet at fair value. The Company's use of derivatives is primarily limited to forward foreign currency exchange contracts, which the Company uses to mitigate exposures to changes in foreign currency exchange rates. The Company also uses contracts which hedge the repatriation of Canadian funds. Upon adoption of SFAS No. 133, the Company did not designate such derivatives as hedging instruments; thus, the changes in the fair value of the derivatives have been included in the consolidated statements of operations. Prior

Pier 1 Imports, Inc.

NOTES TO CONSOLIDATED FINANCIAL STATEMENTS
(continued)

to adoption, the Company deferred all gains and losses on its derivative contracts and recognized such gains and losses as an adjustment to the transaction price. The adoption of SFAS No. 133 has not had a material impact on the Company's consolidated balance sheets or its statements of operations, shareholders' equity and cash flows.

The Company adopted SFAS No. 140, "Accounting for Transfers and Servicing of Financial Assets and Extinguishments of Liabilities," in the first quarter of fiscal 2002. This statement established new conditions for a securitization to be accounted for as a sale of receivables, changed the requirements for an entity to be a qualifying special-purpose entity, and modified the conditions for determining whether a transferor has relinquished control over transferred assets. SFAS No. 140 also requires additional disclosures related to securitized financial assets and retained interests in securitized financial assets. *See Note 2 of the Notes to Consolidated Financial Statements.* Prior to adoption, the Company made the necessary amendments to its securitization agreements and continues to receive sale treatment for its securitized proprietary credit card receivables. The implementation of SFAS No. 140 did not have a material impact on the Company's consolidated balance sheets or its statements of operations, shareholders' equity and cash flows.

In June 2001, the Financial Accounting Standards Board ("FASB") issued SFAS No. 141, "Business Combinations," which supersedes Accounting Principles Board ("APB") Opinion No. 16, "Business Combinations," and SFAS No. 38, "Accounting for Preacquisition Contingencies of Purchased Enterprises." Statement No. 141 eliminates the pooling-of-interests method of accounting for business combinations and requires all such transactions to be accounted for under the purchase method. This statement also addresses the initial recognition and measurement of goodwill and other intangible assets acquired in a business combination and is effective for all business combinations initiated after June 30, 2001. The adoption of SFAS No. 141 did not have a material impact on the Company's consolidated balance sheets or its statements of operations, shareholders' equity and cash flows.

In June 2001, the FASB also issued SFAS No. 142, "Goodwill and Other Intangible Assets," which supersedes APB Opinion No. 17, "Intangible Assets." This statement addresses the initial recognition and measurement of intangible assets acquired outside of a business combination and the accounting for goodwill and other intangible assets subsequent to their acquisition. SFAS No. 142 also provides that intangible assets with finite useful lives be amortized and that goodwill and intangible assets with indefinite lives will not be amortized, but will rather be tested on an annual basis for impairment. The Company is required to adopt SFAS No. 142 for its fiscal year beginning March 3, 2002. The Company has analyzed the implementation requirements and does not anticipate that the adoption of SFAS No. 142 will have a material impact on the Company's consolidated balance sheets or its statements of operations, shareholders' equity and cash flows.

In October 2001, the FASB issued SFAS No. 144, "Accounting for the Impairment or Disposal of Long-Lived Assets," which replaces SFAS No. 121, "Accounting for the Impairment of Long-Lived Assets and for Long-Lived Assets to Be Disposed Of." Statement No. 144 retains the fundamental provisions of SFAS No. 121 with additional guidance on estimating cash flows when performing a recoverability test, requires that a long-lived asset to be disposed of, other than by sale, be classified as "held and used" until it is disposed of and establishes more restrictive criteria to classify an asset as "held for sale." SFAS No. 144 also supersedes APB Opinion No. 30, "Reporting the Results of Operations – Reporting the Effects of Disposal of a Segment of a Business, and Extraordinary, Unusual and Infrequently Occurring Events and Transactions," regarding the disposal of a segment of a business and would extend the reporting of a discontinued operation to a "component of an entity" and requires the operating losses thereon to be recognized in the period in which they occur. The Company is required to adopt SFAS No. 144 for its fiscal year beginning March 3, 2002. The Company has analyzed the implementation requirements and does not anticipate that the adoption of SFAS No. 144 will have a material impact on the Company's consolidated balance sheets or its statements of operations, shareholders' equity and cash flows.

NOTE 2 - PROPRIETARY CREDIT CARD INFORMATION

The proprietary credit card receivables, securitized as discussed below, arise primarily under open-end revolving credit accounts issued by the Company's subsidiary, Pier 1 National Bank, to finance purchases of merchandise and services offered by the Company. These accounts have various billing and payment structures, including varying

Pier 1 Imports, Inc.

NOTES TO CONSOLIDATED FINANCIAL STATEMENTS
(continued)

minimum payment levels. The Company has an agreement with a third party to provide certain credit card processing and related credit services, while the Company maintains control over credit policy decisions and customer service standards.

As of fiscal 2002 year-end, the Company had approximately 5,178,000 proprietary cardholders and approximately 1,205,000 customer credit accounts considered active (accounts with a purchase within the previous 12 months). The Company's proprietary credit card sales accounted for 28.9% of total U.S. store sales in fiscal 2002. Net proprietary credit card income is included in selling, general and administrative expenses on the Company's statements of operations. The Company has sold virtually all of its proprietary credit card receivables. The following information presents a summary of the Company's proprietary credit card results for each of the last three fiscal years on a managed basis (in thousands):

	2002	2001	2000
Income:			
Finance charge income, net of debt service costs..........	$ 24,124	$ 21,759	$ 16,780
Insurance and other income	231	253	287
	24,355	22,012	17,067
Costs:			
Processing fees..........	14,197	13,608	10,763
Bad debts..............	6,977	5,285	4,664
	21,174	18,893	15,427
Net proprietary credit card income..........	$ 3,181	$ 3,119	$ 1,640
Proprietary credit card sales...................	$412,469	$377,045	$300,462
Costs as a percent of proprietary credit card sales..............	5.13%	5.01%	5.13%
Gross proprietary credit card receivables at year-end................	$ 140,713	$ 122,876	$ 100,095
Proprietary credit card sales as a percent of total U.S. store sales	28.9%	28.9%	26.3%

In February 1997, the Company securitized its entire portfolio of proprietary credit card receivables (the "Receivables"). The Company sold all existing Receivables to a special-purpose wholly-owned subsidiary, Pier 1 Funding, Inc., predecessor to Pier 1 Funding, LLC ("Funding"), which transferred the Receivables to the Pier 1 Imports Credit Card Master Trust (the "Master Trust"). The Master Trust issues beneficial interests that represent undivided interests in the assets of the Master Trust consisting of the Receivables and all cash flows from collections of the Receivables. On a daily basis, the Company sells to Funding and Funding transfers to the Master Trust all newly generated Receivables, except those failing certain eligibility criteria, and receives as the purchase price payments of cash (funded from previously undistributed principal collections from the Receivables in the Master Trust) and retains residual interests in the Master Trust. Cash flows received from the Master Trust for each of the last three fiscal years are as follows (in thousands):

	2002	2001	2000
Proceeds from collections reinvested in revolving securitizations	$ 366,228	$ 347,404	$ 303,340
Proceeds from new securitizations	$ 49,226	$ –	$ –
Servicing fees received	$ 2,381	$ 2,189	$ 1,820
Cash flows received on retained interests.....	$ 172,473	$ 199,619	$ 147,314

Gains or losses resulting from the sales of the Company's proprietary credit card receivables were not material in any of the periods presented. The Company's exposure to deterioration in the performance of the receivables is limited to its retained beneficial interest in the Master Trust. As such, the Company has no corporate obligation to reimburse Funding, the Master Trust or purchasers of any certificates issued by the Master Trust for credit losses from the Receivables.

Funding was capitalized by the Company as a special-purpose wholly-owned subsidiary that is subject to certain covenants and restrictions, including a restriction from engaging in any business or activity unrelated to acquiring and selling interests in receivables. The Master Trust is not consolidated with the Company.

Pier 1 Imports, Inc.

NOTES TO CONSOLIDATED FINANCIAL STATEMENTS
(continued)

In the initial sale of the Receivables, the Company sold all of its Receivables and received cash and beneficial interests in the Master Trust. The Master Trust sold to third parties $50.0 million of Series 1997-1 Class A Certificates, which bore interest at 6.74% and were scheduled to mature in May 2002. Funding retained $14.1 million of Series 1997-1 Class B Certificates, which were subordinated to the Class A Certificates. Funding also retained the residual interest in the Master Trust.

In September 2001, the Master Trust negotiated the purchase of all of the Series 1997-1 Class A Certificates from their holders. Subsequently the Master Trust retired both the Series 1997-1 Class A and Class B Certificates in connection with the issuance of $100 million in 2001-1 Class A Certificates to a third party. The 2001-1 Class A Certificates bear interest at a floating rate equal to the rate on commercial paper issued by the third party. As of March 2, 2002, this rate was 1.81%. Funding continued to retain the residual interest in the Master Trust and $9.3 million in 2001-1 Class B Certificates, which are subordinated to the 2001-1 Class A Certificates. As a result of this securitization transaction, the Company effectively sold a portion of its beneficial interest for net proceeds of $49.2 million. As of March 2, 2002 and March 3, 2001, the Company had $44.6 million and $75.4 million, respectively, in beneficial interests (comprised primarily of principal and interest related to the underlying Receivables) in the Master Trust.

Under generally accepted accounting principles, if the structure of the securitization meets certain requirements, these transactions are accounted for as sales of receivables. As the Company's securitizations met such requirements as discussed above, they were accounted for as sales. Gains or losses from sales of these receivables were not material during fiscal 2002, 2001 and 2000. The Company expects no material impact on net income in future years as a result of the sales of receivables, although the precise amounts will be dependent on a number of factors such as interest rates and levels of securitization.

NOTE 3 - PROPERTIES

Properties are summarized as follows at March 2, 2002 and March 3, 2001 (in thousands):

	2002	2001
Land	$ 16,458	$ 22,353
Buildings	51,747	59,716
Equipment, furniture and fixtures	238,454	207,956
Leasehold interests and improvements	183,676	171,021
	490,335	461,046
Less accumulated depreciation and amortization	280,381	248,980
Properties, net	$209,954	$212,066

NOTE 4 - ACCOUNTS PAYABLE AND ACCRUED LIABILITIES/OTHER NONCURRENT LIABILITIES

The following is a summary of accounts payable and accrued liabilities and other noncurrent liabilities at March 2, 2002 and March 3, 2001 (in thousands):

	2002	2001
Trade accounts payable	$ 78,961	$ 52,637
Accrued payroll and other employee-related liabilities	36,999	33,685
Accrued taxes, other than income	16,815	15,576
Gift cards, gift certificates and merchandise credits outstanding	29,288	18,989
Accrued income taxes payable	29,738	7,786
Other	16,239	15,437
Accounts payable and accrued liabilities	$208,040	$144,110
Accrued average rent	$ 19,230	$ 17,590
Other	24,034	17,131
Other noncurrent liabilities	$ 43,264	$ 34,721

NOTE 5 - LONG-TERM DEBT AND AVAILABLE CREDIT

Long-term debt is summarized as follows at March 2, 2002 and March 3, 2001 (in thousands):

	2002	2001
Industrial revenue bonds	$ 25,000	$ 25,000
Other	712	–
	25,712	25,000
Less – portion due within one year	356	–
Long-term debt	$ 25,356	$ 25,000

Pier 1 Imports, Inc.
NOTES TO CONSOLIDATED FINANCIAL STATEMENTS
(continued)

In fiscal 1987, the Company entered into industrial revenue development bond loan agreements aggregating $25 million. Proceeds were used to construct three warehouse distribution facilities. The loan agreements and related tax-exempt bonds mature in the year 2026. The Company's interest rates on the loans are based on the bond interest rates, which are market driven, reset weekly and are similar to other tax-exempt municipal debt issues. The Company's weighted average interest rates were 3.8% and 5.7% for fiscal 2002 and 2001, respectively.

In September 1996, the Company issued $86.3 million principal amount of $5\frac{3}{4}$% convertible subordinated notes due October 1, 2003. The notes were convertible at any time prior to maturity, unless previously redeemed or repurchased, into shares of common stock of the Company at a conversion price of $8.22 per share, adjusted for stock splits. The Company had the option to redeem the notes, in whole or in part, on or after October 2, 1999, at a redemption price (expressed as a percentage of principal amount) of 103% of par value which was scheduled to decline annually to 100% of par value at the maturity date. Interest on the notes was payable semiannually on April 1 and October 1 of each year. In February 2000, the Company announced its intention to call the remaining $39.2 million outstanding principal amount of these notes for redemption on March 23, 2000. The notes were convertible into common stock of the Company at any time prior to the close of business on March 22, 2000, at a conversion price of $8.22 per share. During March 2000, the Company converted $39,164,000 of the notes into 4,764,450 shares of the Company's common stock and redeemed $15,000 of the notes for cash at a redemption price of 103% of par value. The conversion and redemption of these notes during fiscal 2001 reduced the Company's debt by $39.2 million and increased its capitalization by $39.4 million. Accordingly, these notes are not detailed in the above schedule as the notes were fully redeemed at fiscal 2001 year-end.

In November 2001, the Company executed a note payable in the original principal amount of £500,000. The note bears interest at 4.0% per annum and has a maturity date of April 2003. Interest is payable in semiannual installments and principle is payable in two installments, June 2002 and April 2003. At March 2, 2002, this note was valued at $712,000.

Long-term debt matures as follows (in thousands):

Fiscal Year	Long-term Debt
2003	$ 356
2004	356
2005	–
2006	–
2007	–
Thereafter	25,000
Total long-term debt	$ 25,712

The Company has a $125 million unsecured credit facility available, which expires in November 2003. The interest rate on borrowings against this facility is determined based upon a spread from LIBOR that varies depending upon either the Company's senior debt rating or leverage ratio. All of the $125 million revolving credit facility was available at fiscal 2002 year-end. The Company had no borrowings under this facility during fiscal 2002. The weighted average interest rate on borrowings outstanding for fiscal 2001 was 7.2%.

The Company has a $120 million short-term line of credit, which is primarily used to issue merchandise letters of credit. At fiscal 2002 year-end, approximately $64.6 million had been utilized for letters of credit, leaving $55.4 million available. The Company also has $28.7 million in credit lines used to issue other special-purpose letters of credit, all of which were fully utilized at fiscal 2002 year-end. Of the $28.7 million in special-purpose letters of credit, $25.6 milllion related to the Company's industrial revenue bonds.

Most of the Company's loan agreements require that the Company maintain certain financial ratios and limit specific payments and equity distributions including cash dividends, loans to shareholders and repurchases of common stock. The Company is in compliance with all debt covenants.

NOTE 6 - EMPLOYEE BENEFIT PLANS

The Company offers a qualified, defined contribution employee retirement plan to all its full- and part-time personnel who are at least 18 years old and have been employed for a minimum of six months. Employees contributing 1% to 5% of their compensation receive a matching Company contribution of up to 3%. Company contributions to the plan were $1,734,000, $1,790,000 and $1,753,000 in fiscal 2002, 2001 and 2000, respectively.

Pier 1 Imports, Inc.
NOTES TO CONSOLIDATED FINANCIAL STATEMENTS
(continued)

In addition, a non-qualified retirement savings plan is available for the purpose of providing deferred compensation for certain employees whose benefits under the qualified plan are limited under Section 401(k) of the Internal Revenue Code. The Company's expense for this non-qualified plan was not significant for fiscal 2002, 2001 and 2000.

The Company maintains supplemental retirement plans (the "Plans") for certain of its executive officers. The Plans provide that upon death, disability or reaching retirement age, a participant will receive benefits based on highest compensation and years of service. The Company recorded expenses related to the Plans of $2,488,000, $1,850,000 and $1,409,000 in fiscal 2002, 2001 and 2000, respectively.

Measurement of plan assets and obligations for the Plans are calculated as of each fiscal year-end. The discount rates used to determine the actuarial present value of projected benefit obligations under such plans were 7.25% and 7.50% as of March 2, 2002 and March 3, 2001, respectively. The assumed weighted average rate increase in future compensation levels under such plans was 5.0% as of both March 2, 2002 and March 3, 2001. The following provides a reconciliation of benefit obligations and funded status of the Plans as of March 2, 2002 and March 3, 2001 (in thousands):

	2002	2001
Change in projected benefit obligation:		
Projected benefit obligation, beginning of year	$ 12,962	$ 8,944
Service cost	569	434
Interest cost	1,055	779
Actuarial loss	1,278	–
Plan amendments	–	2,805
Projected benefit obligation, end of year	$ 15,864	$ 12,962
Reconciliation of funded status:		
Funded status	$ (15,864)	$ (12,962)
Unrecognized net loss	1,338	60
Unrecognized net transitional obligation	–	2
Unrecognized prior service cost	7,086	7,948
Accrued pension cost	(7,440)	(4,952)
Additional minimum liability	(3,980)	(5,663)
Accrued benefit liability	$ (11,420)	$ (10,615)
Amounts recognized in the balance sheets:		
Accrued benefit liability	$ (11,420)	$ (10,615)
Intangible asset	3,980	5,663
Net amount recognized	$ (7,440)	$ (4,952)

Net periodic benefit cost included the following actuarially determined components during fiscal 2002, 2001 and 2000 (in thousands):

	2002	2001	2000
Service cost	$ 569	$ 434	$ 459
Interest cost	1,055	779	543
Amortization of unrecognized prior service cost	862	635	374
Amortization of net obligation at transition	2	2	2
Recognized net actuarial loss	–	–	31
	$ 2,488	$ 1,850	$ 1,409

NOTE 7 - MATTERS CONCERNING SHAREHOLDERS' EQUITY

Stock purchase plan - Substantially all employees and directors are eligible to participate in the Pier 1 Imports, Inc. Stock Purchase Plan under which the Company's common stock is purchased on behalf of employees at market prices through regular payroll deductions. Each employee participant may contribute up to 10% of the eligible portions of compensation and directors may contribute part or all of their directors' fees. The Company contributes from 10% to 100% of the participants' contributions, depending upon length of participation and date of entry into the plan. Company contributions to the plan were $985,000, $921,000 and $954,000 in fiscal years 2002, 2001 and 2000, respectively.

Restricted stock grant plans - In fiscal 1998, the Company issued 238,500 shares of its common stock to key officers pursuant to a Management Restricted Stock Plan, which provides for the issuance of up to 415,600 shares. The fiscal 1998 restricted stock grant vested over a four-year period of continued employment. The fair value at the date of grant of these restricted stock shares was expensed over the afore-mentioned vesting period. The fair value at the date of grant of the restricted shares granted in fiscal 1998 was $3,000,000. Shares not vested were returned to the plan if employment was terminated for any reason. To date, 107,184 shares have been returned to the plan.

In fiscal 1991, the Company issued 726,804 shares of its common stock to key officers pursuant to a Restricted Stock

Pier 1 Imports, Inc.

NOTES TO CONSOLIDATED FINANCIAL STATEMENTS
(continued)

Grant Plan, which provided for the issuance of up to 1,037,214 shares. These shares vested, and the fair value at the date of grant was expensed, over a ten-year period of continued employment. Unvested shares are returned to the plan upon employment termination. As of March 2, 2002, 407,742 shares have been returned to the plan. In fiscal 2000, the Restricted Stock Grant Plan was terminated by the Board of Directors and is no longer available for issuance of common stock to key officers. The final vesting period was March 2000.

Total compensation expense for both of the restricted stock grant plans was $85,000, $216,000 and $485,000 for fiscal 2002, 2001 and 2000, respectively.

Stock option plans - In June 1999, the Company adopted the Pier 1 Imports, Inc. 1999 Stock Plan (the "Plan"). The Plan will ultimately replace the Company's two previous stock option plans, which were the 1989 Employee Stock Option Plan (the "Employee Plan") and the 1989 Non-Employee Director Stock Option Plan (the "Director Plan").

The Plan provides for the granting of options to directors and employees with an exercise price not less than the fair market value of the common stock on the date of the grant. Options may be either Incentive Stock Options authorized under Section 422 of the Internal Revenue Code or non-qualified options, which do not qualify as Incentive Stock Options. Current director compensation provides for non-qualified options covering 6,000 shares to be granted once each year to each non-employee director. Additionally, the Plan authorizes a Director Deferred Stock Program. As the program is currently implemented by the Board of Directors, each director must defer a minimum of 50% and may defer up to 100% of the director's cash fees into a deferred stock account. The amount deferred receives a 50% matching contribution from the Company. The Plan provides that a maximum of 7,000,000 shares of common

stock may be issued under the Plan, of which not more than 250,000 may be issued in exchange for deferred stock units. Options issued to non-director employees vest equally over a period of four years while directors' options are fully vested at the date of issuance. Additionally, employee options will fully vest upon retirement or, under certain conditions, a change in control of the Company. As of March 2, 2002 and March 3, 2001, respectively, there were 1,026,978 and 3,520,887 shares available for grant under the Plan, of which 171,673 and 200,381 may be used for deferred stock issuance. Additionally, outstanding options covering 894,200 and 429,600 shares were exercisable and 78,327 and 49,619 shares were issuable in exchange for deferred stock units at fiscal years ended 2002 and 2001, respectively. The Plan will expire in June 2009, and the Board of Directors may at any time suspend or terminate the Plan or amend the Plan, subject to certain limitations.

Under the Employee Plan, options may be granted to qualify as Incentive Stock Options under Section 422 of the Internal Revenue Code or as non-qualified options. Most options issued under the Employee Plan vest over a period of four to five years. As of March 2, 2002 and March 3, 2001, outstanding options covering 2,303,198 and 2,318,042 shares were exercisable and 932,684 and 878,059 shares were available for grant, respectively. The Employee Plan expires in June 2004. The Director Plan expired in fiscal 2000. As of March 2, 2002 and March 3, 2001, outstanding options covering 48,264 and 61,764 shares, respectively, were exercisable under the Director Plan. Due to the expiration of the Director Plan during fiscal 2000, no shares are available for future grants. Both plans were subject to adjustments for stock dividends and certain other changes to the Company's capitalization.

A summary of stock option translations related to the stock option plans during the three fiscal years ended March 2, 2002 is as follows:

Pier 1 Imports, Inc.

NOTES TO CONSOLIDATED FINANCIAL STATEMENTS
(continued)

	Shares	Weighted Average Exercise Price	Weighted Average Fair Value at Date of Grant	Exercisable Shares Number of Shares	Weighted Average Exercise Price
Outstanding at February 27, 1999	4,597,830	$ 9.20		1,810,819	$ 6.66
Options granted	2,379,500	6.20	$ 3.18		
Options exercised	(134,936)	4.63			
Options cancelled or expired	(793,187)	10.63			
Outstanding at February 26, 2000	6,049,207	7.94		2,214,717	7.28
Options granted	1,589,000	10.49	5.31		
Options exercised	(569,326)	5.38			
Options cancelled or expired	(351,900)	8.47			
Outstanding at March 3, 2001	6,716,981	8.73		2,809,406	8.07
Options granted	2,711,500	8.32	4.59		
Options exercised	(937,619)	7.06			
Options cancelled or expired	(314,125)	9.90			
Outstanding at March 2, 2002	8,176,737	8.74		3,245,662	8.81

For shares outstanding at March 2, 2002:

Ranges of Exercise Prices	Total Shares	Weighted Average Exercise Price	Weighted Average Remaining Contractual Life	Shares Currently Exercisable	Weighted Average Exercise Price – Exercisable Shares
$2.85 - $ 8.19	2,732,912	$ 5.96	5.82	1,794,112	$ 5.89
$8.26 - $ 8.50	3,026,475	8.29	9.15	289,600	8.49
$9.08 - $18.50	2,417,350	12.45	7.51	1,161,950	13.39

The Company accounts for its stock options using the intrinsic value-based method of accounting prescribed by APB Opinion No. 25, but is required to disclose the pro forma effect on net income and earnings per share as if the options were accounted for using a fair value-based method of accounting. The fair values for options issued in fiscal 2002, 2001 and 2000 have been estimated as of the date of grant using the Black-Scholes or a similar option pricing model with the following weighted average assumptions for 2002, 2001 and 2000, respectively: risk-free interest rates of 3.75%, 5.68% and 5.79%, expected stock price volatility of 60.25%, 55.86% and 51.50%, expected dividend yields of 0.8%, 1.0% and 1.0% and weighted average expected lives of six years from date of grant to date of exercise for all options. For purposes of computing pro forma net income and earnings per share, the fair value of the stock options is amortized on a straight-line basis as compensation expense over the vesting periods of the options. The pro forma effects on net

Pier 1 Imports, Inc.

NOTES TO CONSOLIDATED FINANCIAL STATEMENTS
(continued)

income and earnings per share are as follows (in thousands except per share amounts):

	2002	2001	2000
Pro forma net income	$ 95,863	$ 91,573	$ 72,317
Pro forma basic earnings per share	$ 1.02	$ .95	$ .76
Pro forma diluted earnings per share	$ 1.00	$ .93	$ .72

Option valuation models are used in estimating the fair value of traded options that have no vesting restrictions and are fully transferable. In addition, option valuation models require the input of highly subjective assumptions, including the expected stock price volatility and the average life of options. Because the Company's stock options have characteristics significantly different from those of traded options, and because changes in the subjective input assumptions can materially affect the fair value estimate, in management's opinion, the existing models do not necessarily provide a reliable single measure of the fair value of its stock options. In addition, the pro forma net income and earnings per share amounts shown above for fiscal 2002, 2001 and 2000 do not include the effect of any grants made prior to fiscal 1996.

Share purchase rights plan - On December 9, 1994, the Board of Directors adopted a Share Purchase Rights Plan and declared a dividend of one common stock purchase right (a "Right") payable on each outstanding share of the Company's common stock on December 21, 1994, and authorized the issuance of Rights for subsequently issued shares of common stock. The Rights, which will expire on December 21, 2004, are initially not exercisable, and until becoming exercisable will trade only with the associated common stock. After the Rights become exercisable, each Right entitles the holder to purchase at a specified exercise price one share of common stock. The Rights will become exercisable after the earlier to occur of (i) ten days following a public announcement that a person or group of affiliated or associated persons have acquired beneficial ownership of 15% or more of the outstanding common stock or (ii) ten business days (or such later date as determined by the Board of Directors) following the commencement of, or announcement of an intention to make, a tender or exchange offer the consummation of which would result in beneficial ownership by a person or group of 15% or more of the outstanding common stock. If the Company were acquired in a merger or other business combination transaction or 50% or more of its consolidated assets or earning power were sold, proper provision would be made so that each Right would entitle its holder to purchase, upon the exercise of the Right at the then current exercise price (currently the exercise price is $14.81), that number of shares of common stock of the acquiring company having a market value of twice the exercise price of the Right. If any person or group were to acquire beneficial ownership of 15% or more of the Company's outstanding common stock, each Right would entitle its holder (other than such acquiring person whose Rights would become void) to purchase, upon the exercise of the Right at the then current exercise price, that number of shares of the Company's common stock having a market value on the date of such 15% acquisition of twice the exercise price of the Right. The Board of Directors may at its option, at any time after such 15% acquisition but prior to the acquisition of more than 50% of the Company's outstanding common stock, exchange all or part of the then outstanding and exercisable Rights (other than those held by such acquiring person whose Rights would become void) for common stock at an exchange rate per Right of one-half the number of shares of common stock receivable upon exercise of a Right. The Board of Directors may, at any time prior to such 15% acquisition, redeem all the Rights at a redemption price of $.01 per Right.

Shares reserved for future issuances - As of March 2, 2002, the Company had approximately 114,416,000 shares reserved for future issuances under the stock plans and the share purchase rights plan.

Pier 1 Imports, Inc.

NOTES TO CONSOLIDATED FINANCIAL STATEMENTS
(continued)

NOTE 8 - INCOME TAXES

The provision for income taxes for each of the last three fiscal years consists of (in thousands):

	2002	2001	2000
Federal:			
Current.................	$ 56,207	$ 50,455	$ 39,463
Deferred...............	(2,110)	583	355
State:			
Current.................	3,909	3,368	1,890
Deferred...............	(128)	152	1,370
Foreign:			
Current.................	910	1,032	809
	$ 58,788	$ 55,590	$ 43,887

Deferred tax assets and liabilities at March 2, 2002 and March 3, 2001 are comprised of the following (in thousands):

	2002	2001
Deferred tax assets:		
Inventory	$ 2,166	$ 1,727
Deferred compensation...............	9,129	7,292
Accrued average rent	8,476	7,784
Losses on a foreign subsidiary	3,948	3,301
Self insurance reserves...............	2,408	910
Fixed assets, net	–	795
Other	2,470	2,326
	28,597	24,135
Valuation allowance....................	(3,948)	(3,301)
Total deferred tax assets..............	24,649	20,834
Deferred tax liabilities:		
Fixed assets, net	(1,577)	–
Total deferred tax liabilities............	(1,577)	–
Net deferred tax assets..................	$ 23,072	$ 20,834

The Company has settled and closed all Internal Revenue Service ("IRS") examinations of the Company's tax returns for all years through fiscal 1999. An IRS audit of fiscal years 2000 and 2001 is expected to begin in the first quarter of fiscal year 2003. For financial reporting purposes, a valuation allowance exists at March 2, 2002 to offset the deferred tax asset relating to the losses of a foreign subsidiary.

Undistributed earnings of the Company's non-U.S. subsidiaries amounted to approximately $22.6 million at March 2, 2002. These earnings are considered to be indefinitely reinvested and, accordingly, no additional U.S. income taxes or non-U.S. withholding taxes have been provided. Determination of the amount of additional taxes that would be payable if such earnings were not considered indefinitely reinvested is not practical.

The difference between income taxes at the statutory federal income tax rate of 35% in fiscal 2002, 2001 and 2000, and income tax reported in the consolidated statements of operations is as follows (in thousands):

	2002	2001	2000
Tax at statutory federal			
income tax rate	$ 55,649	$ 52,584	$ 41,514
State income taxes,			
net of federal benefit	3,387	3,200	2,526
Work opportunity tax			
credit, foreign tax			
credit and R&E credit....	(202)	(207)	(283)
Net foreign income taxed			
at lower rates...........	(101)	(1,048)	(960)
Other, net	55	1,061	1,090
	$ 58,788	$ 55,590	$ 43,887

NOTE 9 - COMMITMENTS AND CONTINGENCIES

Leases - The Company leases certain property consisting principally of retail stores, warehouses and material handling and office equipment under leases expiring through the year 2021. Most retail store locations are leased for initial terms of 10 to 15 years with varying renewal options and rent escalation clauses. Certain leases provide for additional rental payments based on a percentage of sales in excess of a specified base. The Company's lease obligations are considered operating leases, and all payments are reflected in the accompanying consolidated statements of operations.

During fiscal 2002, the Company sold certain store properties for $12.6 million. These stores were leased back from unaffiliated third parties for periods of approximately ten years. The resulting leases are being accounted for as operating leases. The Company deferred gains of $5.1 million

Pier 1 Imports, Inc.

NOTES TO CONSOLIDATED FINANCIAL STATEMENTS
(continued)

in fiscal 2002 on these sale-leaseback transactions; the gains are being amortized over the initial lives of the leases. Future minimum lease commitments of these operating leases are included in the summary below of the Company's operating leases. The Company had no sale-leaseback transactions in fiscal 2001.

At March 2, 2002, the Company had the following minimum lease commitments in the years indicated (in thousands):

Fiscal Year	Operating Leases
2003	$ 162,315
2004	158,525
2005	145,608
2006	132,855
2007	118,102
Thereafter	426,946
Total lease commitments	$ 1,144,351
Present value of total operating lease commitments at 10%	$ 751,919

Rental expense incurred was $159,461,000, $144,035,000 and $131,835,000, including contingent rentals of $921,000, $979,000 and $794,000, based upon a percentage of sales, and net of sublease incomes totaling $1,191,000, $2,650,000 and $2,141,000 in fiscal 2002, 2001 and 2000, respectively.

Legal matters - There are various claims, lawsuits, investigations and pending actions against the Company and its subsidiaries incident to the operations of its business. Liability, if any, associated with these matters is not determinable at March 2, 2002; however, the Company considers them to be ordinary and routine in nature. The Company maintains liability insurance against most of these claims. While certain of the lawsuits involve substantial amounts, it is the opinion of management, after consultation with counsel, that the ultimate resolution of such litigation will not have a material adverse effect on the Company's financial position, results of operations or liquidity.

NOTE 10 - SELECTED QUARTERLY FINANCIAL DATA (UNAUDITED)

Summarized quarterly financial data for the years ended March 2, 2002 and March 3, 2001 are set forth below (in thousands except per share amounts):

	Three Months Ended			
Fiscal 2002	6/2/01	9/1/01	12/1/01	3/2/02
Net sales	$ 325,387	357,248	387,360	478,561
Gross profit	$ 134,914	137,539	165,408	211,900
Net income	$ 12,345	13,802	25,046	49,016
Basic earnings per share	$ .13	.15	.27	.53
Diluted earnings per share	$ .13	.14	.26	.51

	Three Months Ended			
Fiscal 2001	5/27/00	8/26/00	11/25/00	3/3/01
Net sales	$ 299,528	337,991	343,493	430,486
Gross profit	$ 126,646	135,616	147,160	185,033
Net income	$ 16,877	17,715	23,569	36,489
Basic earnings per share	$ .17	.18	.25	.38
Diluted earnings per share	$ .17	.18	.24	.38

Pier 1 Imports, Inc.
SHAREHOLDER INFORMATION

EXECUTIVE OFFICES

Suite 600

301 Commerce Street

Fort Worth, Texas 76102

(817) 252-8000

www.pier1.com

COMMON STOCK

Approximately 40,000 shareholders of record

Traded on the New York Stock Exchange

Symbol: PIR

INVESTOR RELATIONS AND FORM 10-K REPORT

A copy of the Pier 1 Imports, Inc. Form 10-K report filed with
the Securities and Exchange Commission is available by
writing the Investor Relations Department at:

Pier 1 Imports, Inc.

P.O. Box 961020

Fort Worth, Texas 76161-0020

or by calling (817) 252-7835

Toll Free (888) 80-PIER1

    (888) 807-4371

Investor inquiries also may be directed to that department.

INDEPENDENT AUDITORS

Ernst & Young LLP

Fort Worth, Texas

TRANSFER AGENT

Mellon Investor Services

85 Challenger Road

Ridgefield Park, New Jersey 07660

Shareholder Line Toll Free (888) 884-8086

ANNUAL MEETING

The annual meeting of shareholders will be held at
10 a.m. Central Daylight Time, Thursday, June 27, 2002,
in the Brazos Room at the Renaissance Worthington Hotel,
Fort Worth, Texas.

MARKET PRICE AND DIVIDEND INFORMATION

The Company's common stock is traded on the New York Stock Exchange. The following tables show the high and low closing sale
prices on such Exchange, as reported in the consolidated transaction reporting system, and the dividends paid per share, for each
quarter of fiscal 2002 and 2001.

Fiscal 2002	Market Price		Cash Dividends Per Share (1)	Fiscal 2001	Market Price		Cash Dividends Per Share (1)
	High	Low			High	Low	
First quarter	$ 14.5500	$ 11.1000	$ .04	First quarter	$ 11.8750	$ 7.8750	$ .03
Second quarter	12.6500	10.3000	.04	Second quarter	12.7500	8.5000	.04
Third quarter	14.7000	8.1300	.04	Third quarter	14.0000	10.4375	.04
Fourth quarter	20.2400	14.5000	.04	Fourth quarter	13.8750	8.1875	.04

*(1) For restrictions on the payments of dividends, see Management's Discussion and Analysis of Financial Condition and Results of Operations – Liquidity and
Capital Resources.*

Pier 1 Imports, Inc.
DIRECTORS AND OFFICERS

BOARD OF DIRECTORS

Marvin J. Girouard
Chairman and
Chief Executive Officer

John H. Burgoyne
Principal
Burgoyne and Associates

James D. Carreker
Owner
JDC Holdings

Dr. Michael R. Ferrari
Chancellor
Texas Christian University

James M. Hoak, Jr.
Chairman
Hoak Capital Corporation

Karen W. Katz
President and Chief Executive Officer
Neiman Marcus Direct

Tom M. Thomas
Senior Partner
Kolodey, Thomas & Blackwood, LLP

EXECUTIVE OFFICERS

Marvin J. Girouard
Chairman and
Chief Executive Officer

Charles H. Turner
Executive Vice President, Chief
Financial Officer and Treasurer

Robert A. Arlauskas
Executive Vice President,
Stores

Jay R. Jacobs
Executive Vice President,
Merchandising

J. Rodney Lawrence
Executive Vice President, Legal
Affairs and Corporate Secretary

Phil E. Schneider
Executive Vice President,
Marketing

David A. Walker
Executive Vice President,
Logistics and Allocations

E. Mitchell Weatherly
Executive Vice President,
Human Resources

Pier 1 imports

Suite 600
301 Commerce Street
Fort Worth, Texas 76102
www.pier1.com

Glossary

accelerated depreciation methods   Those methods that record more depreciation expense in the early years of an asset's life and less in the later years.

accounting   A service activity that has the function of providing quantitative information, primarily financial in nature, about economic entities that is intended to be useful in making economic decisions.

accounting information   Raw data concerning transactions that have been transformed into financial numbers that can be used by economic decision makers.

accounts   Subclassifications used to classify and record economic events and transactions. For example, some accounts that may be found under assets are accounts receivable, office supplies, and property, plant, and equipment. Under expenses, we may find wages, rent, and advertising.

accrual basis accounting   A method of accounting in which revenues are recognized when they are earned, regardless of when the associated cash is collected. The expenses incurred in generating the revenue are recognized when the benefit is derived rather than when the associated cash is paid.

accruals   Adjustments made to record items that should be included on the income statement but have not yet been recorded.

accrue   As used in accounting, to come into being as a legally enforceable claim.

accrued expenses   Expenses appropriately recognized under accrual accounting in one income statement period although the associated cash will be paid in a later income statement period.

accrued revenues   Revenues appropriately recognized under accrual accounting in one income statement period although the associated cash will be received in a later income statement period.

accumulated depreciation   The total amount of cost that has been systematically converted to expense since a long-lived asset was first purchased.

acid-test ratio   Another name for the quick ratio.

additional paid-in capital   The amount in excess of the stock's par value received by the corporation when par value stock is issued.

adjusted trial balance   A trial balance that is prepared after all of the adjusting entries have been made.

adjusting entries   The entries to modify account balances so that all revenue earned and all expenses incurred are recorded and all asset, liability, and equity accounts are properly stated as of the balance sheet date.

adjustments   Changes made in recorded amounts of revenues and expenses in order to follow the guidelines of accrual accounting.

annual report   A corporate document that provides interested parties with a variety of information including financial statements and a host of general information about the company and its management.

articulation   The links among the financial statements.

asset turnover ratio   A financial ratio that shows the amount of sales produced for a given level of assets used.

assets   An accounting element that is one of the three components of a balance sheet. Assets are probable future economic benefits controlled by an entity as a result of previous transactions or events—that is, what a company has.

authorized shares   The maximum number of shares of stock a corporation has been given permission to issue under its corporate charter.

average accounts receivable collection period in days   The average time it takes a company to collect its receivables.

average cost method   The inventory cost flow method that assigns an average cost to the units of inventory on hand at the time of each sale.

average inventory holding period   The average length of time product is held in inventory.

balance sheet   The financial tool that focuses on the present condition of a business.

basic earnings per share   Earnings per share based on the average number of common shares outstanding.

beginning inventory   The amount of merchandise inventory (units or dollars) on hand at the beginning of the income statement period.

bond   An interest-bearing debt instrument that allows corporations to borrow large amounts of funds for long periods of time and creates a liability for the borrower.

book inventory   The amount of ending inventory (units and dollars) resulting from transactions recorded by a perpetual inventory system.

book of original entry   The same thing as a journal.

book value   The original cost of a long-lived asset less its accumulated depreciation. This item is often shown on the balance sheet.

business   Depending on the context, the area of commerce or trade, an individual company, or the process of producing and distributing goods and services.

business segment   A portion of an entity representing either a separate major line of business or a class of customer.

capital   A factor of production that includes the buildings, machinery, and tools used to produce goods and services. Also, sometimes used to refer to the money used to buy those items.

capitalism   An example of a market economy. A *market economy* is one that relies on competition to determine the most efficient way to allocate the economy's resources.

cash basis accounting   A basis of accounting in which cash is the major criterion used in measuring revenue and expense for a given income statement period. Revenue is recognized when the associated cash is received, and expense is recognized when the associated cash is paid.

chart of accounts   A list of all the accounts used by a business entity. The list usually contains the name of the account and the account number.

classified balance sheet   A balance sheet that provides a breakdown of the composition of the items the balance sheet includes.

closing entries   A series of entries to reset revenues, expenses, and dividends to zero in preparation for a new accounting year.

collateral   Something of value that will be forfeited if a borrower fails to make payments as agreed.

commercial borrowing   The process that businesses go through to obtain financing.

common stock   A share of ownership in a corporation. Each share represents one vote in the election of the board of directors and other pertinent corporate matters.

communism   An example of a planned economy. A *planned economy* is one with a strong centralized government that controls all or most of the natural resources, labor, and capital used to produce goods and services.

comparability   A quality needed to meaningfully assess the relative performance on *two different entities*. The requirement that every company provide accounting information in conformity with a fairly uniform structure enables decision makers to compare one company to another.

comparative financial statements   Financial statements showing results from two or more consecutive periods.

compound entries   Entries recorded in the general journal that contain more than two accounts.

comprehensive income   The change in equity during a period from nonowner sources.

computerized accounting system   An accounting system in which the accountants and bookkeepers make entries in a computer system where the journals and ledgers consist of listings of transactions on computer printouts or in files in the computer's memory.

Conceptual Framework of Accounting   A framework created by the FASB to establish the objectives of financial reporting and the qualitative characteristics of useful accounting information, and to define the accounting elements, assumptions, principles, and constraints.

conservatism   Provides a guideline in difficult valuation or measurement situations. Accountants should guard against accounting treatments that unjustly overstate financial position or earnings.

consistency   A quality that is needed to meaningfully assess the performance of a *single entity* over time. Consistent application of accounting rules enables us to track a single company's performance over time.

consumer borrowing   Loans obtained by individuals to buy homes, cars, or other personal property.

contra-account   An account that carries a normal balance that decreases the accounting element in which it is classified.

contract rate   *See* nominal interest rate.

contributed capital   Total amount invested in a corporation by its shareholders. Also called paid-in capital.

corporation   A business that is a separate legal entity from its stockholders (owners).

cost of goods sold   The cost of the product sold as the primary business activity of a company.

cost of products sold   *See* cost of goods sold.

cost of sales   *See* cost of goods sold.

cost/benefit   Deals with the trade-off between the rewards of selecting a given alternative and the sacrifices required to obtain those rewards.

coupon rate   *See* nominal interest rate.

coverage ratio   Same as the times interest earned ratio.

cumulative effect of an accounting change   Result of adopting a new accounting standard or changing from one acceptable method of accounting to another. One of the nonrecurring items shown net of tax on the income statement.

current assets   Assets that are cash, will become cash, or will be consumed within the longer of one year or the current operating cycle.

current liabilities   Liabilities that require settlement (payment) within one year or the current operating cycle, whichever is longer.

current ratio   A liquidity ratio that measures a company's ability to meet short-term obligations by comparing current assets to current liabilities.

data   The raw results of transactions. Facts and figures that are not organized enough to be useful to decision makers.

date of declaration   The date upon which a corporation announces plans to distribute a dividend. At this point, the corporation becomes legally obligated to make the distribution: A liability is created.

date of payment   The date a corporate dividend is actually paid. The payment date is generally announced on the date of declaration.

date of record   Owners of the shares of stock on this day are the ones who will receive the dividend announced on the date of declaration.

debenture bond   An unsecured bond payable.

debt financing   Acquiring funds for business operations by borrowing. Debt financing is one type of external financing.

debt ratio   A solvency ratio that indicates what proportion of a company's assets is financed by debt.

debt-to-equity ratio   A financial ratio that expresses the proportional relationship between liabilities and equity.

deferrals   Situations in which cash is either received or paid, but the income statement effect is delayed until some later period. Deferred revenues are recorded as liabilities, and deferred expenses are recorded as assets.

deferred expenses   Expenses created when cash is paid before any benefit is received. Because the benefit to be derived is in the future, the item is recorded as an asset. Later, when the benefit is received from the item, it will be recognized as an expense.

deferred revenues   Revenues created when cash is received before the revenue is earned. Because the cash received has not yet been earned, an obligation is created and a liability is recorded. Later, when the cash is deemed to have been earned, it will be recognized as a revenue.

depreciable base   The total amount of depreciation expense that is allowed to be claimed for an asset during its useful life. The depreciable base is the cost of the asset less its residual value.

depreciation   The systematic and rational conversion of a long-lived asset's cost from asset to expense in the income statement periods benefited.

diluted earnings per share   A calculation of earnings per share that takes into account all potentially dilutive securities.

dilutive securities   Securities that have the potential to reduce earnings per share.

direct method   The format of a statement of cash flows that provides detail about the individual sources and uses of cash associated with operating activities.

discontinued operations   The disposal of a business segment. One of the nonrecurring items shown net of tax on the income statement.

discount   If a bond's selling price is below its par value, the bond is being sold at a discount.

distributions to owners   Decreases in equity resulting from transferring assets to the owners of an enterprise.

dividend payout ratio   A financial ratio that shows what portion of a company's net income for a given year was paid to its owners as cash dividends during that year.

dividends   A distribution of earnings from a corporation to its owners. Dividends are most commonly distributed in the form of cash.

double-declining-balance method An accelerated depreciation method in which depreciation expense is twice the straight-line percentage multiplied by the book value of the asset.

drawings Distributions to the owners of proprietorships and partnerships. Also called withdrawals.

earned equity The total amount a company has earned since its beginning, less any amounts distributed to the owner(s). In a corporation, this amount is called retained earnings.

earnings per share A calculation indicating how much of a company's total earnings is attributable to each share of common stock.

earnings per share (EPS) The amount of a company's total earnings attributable to each share of common stock.

EBIT Earnings before interest and taxes.

economic entity The assumption that economic activities can be identified with a particular enterprise.

effective interest rate The rate of interest actually earned by a lender. This amount will be different from the nominal interest rate if a bond is bought at a discount or premium, or a note is discounted. Also called yield rate or market interest rate.

efficiency ratios Financial ratios that measure the investment in assets relative to business activity.

Electronic Data Gathering, Analysis, and Retrieval (EDGAR) A system operated by the SEC to facilitate the collection and, more importantly, the dissemination of corporate information to all interested parties. Access to EDGAR is available over the Internet at *www.sec.gov.*

entrepreneurship The factor of production that brings the other three factors—natural resources, labor, and capital—together to form a business.

equity An accounting element that is one of the three components of a balance sheet. Equity is the residual interest in the assets of an entity that remains after deducting liabilities. Also called net assets.

equity financing Acquiring funds for business operations by giving up ownership interest in the company. For a corporation, this means issuing capital stock. Equity financing is one type of external financing.

expense An accounting element representing the outflow of assets resulting from an entity's ongoing major or central operations. These are the sacrifices required to attain the rewards (revenues) of doing business.

exports Goods produced in a country but sold outside that country.

external decision makers Economic decision makers outside a company who make decisions about the company. The accounting information they use to make those decisions is limited to what the company provides them.

external financing Acquiring funds from outside the company. Equity and debt financing are the two major types of external financing.

extraordinary item A gain or loss that is both unusual in nature and infrequent in occurrence. One of the nonrecurring items shown net of tax on the income statement.

factors of production The four major items needed to support economic activity: natural resources, labor, capital, and entrepreneurship.

feedback value A primary characteristic of relevance. To be useful, accounting must provide decision makers with information that allows them to assess the progress of an investment.

financial accounting The branch of accounting developed to meet the informational needs of external decision makers.

Financial Accounting Standards Board (FASB) The organization that is principally responsible for establishing accounting guidelines and rules in the United States at the present time.

financial statement analysis The process of looking beyond the face of the financial statements to gather more information.

financing activities Business activities, such as the issuance of debt or equity and the payment of dividends, that focus on the external financing of the company.

first-in, first-out (FIFO) The inventory flow concept based on the assumption that the first units of inventory purchased are the first ones sold.

Form 10-K Less glamorous than the annual report, this corporate document includes additional financial and nonfinancial details that are invaluable to external decision makers.

fully depreciated When all of the allowable depreciation expense has been recognized for an asset's entire useful life.

gains Net inflows resulting from peripheral activities of a company. An example is the sale of an asset for more than its book value.

general journal A book of original entry in which is recorded all transactions not otherwise recorded in special journals.

general ledger A book of final entry that contains a page for each account listed in the chart of accounts.

general ledger accounts The same thing as accounts.

generally accepted accounting principles (GAAP) Guidelines for presentation of financial accounting information designed to serve external decision makers' need for consistent and comparable information.

going concern The assumption that unless there is persuasive evidence otherwise, a particular business enterprise will stay in business indefinitely.

goods available for sale The total amount of merchandise inventory a company has available to sell in a given income statement period.

gross margin An item shown on a multiple-step income statement, calculated as: Sales − Cost of goods sold.

gross profit *See* gross margin.

gross profit margin ratio A financial ratio that expresses a company's gross profit (often called gross margin on the financial statements) as a percentage of sales revenue.

historical cost principal The accounting principle that requires balance sheet amounts generally to be shown at acquisition price rather than fair value.

hybrid companies Those companies involved in more than one type of activity (manufacturing, merchandising, service).

imports Foreign products brought into a country.

income from operations *See* operating income.

income statement A financial statement providing information about an entity's past performance. Its purpose is to measure the results of the entity's operations for some specific time period.

income tax A tax based on the amount of income a company has earned.

indenture The legal agreement made between a bond issuer and a bondholder that states repayment terms and other details.

indirect method The more widely used format of the statement of cash flows. This approach provides accrual net income to the cash provided by or used by operating activities.

industry practice The notion that the peculiar nature of some industries actually causes adherence to GAAP to have misleading results, and therefore, these industries have developed accounting treatments for certain items that depart from GAAP.

information Facts and figures that are sorted, arranged, and summarized and otherwise put into a form that is useful to decision makers.

intangible assets Things that have future value but lack physical presence such as patents, copyrights, trademarks, and purchased goodwill.

internal decision makers Economic decision makers within a company who make decisions for the company. They have access to much or all of the accounting information generated within the company.

internal financing Providing funds for the operation of a company through the earnings process of that company.

inventory The stockpile of tangible product that a company has on hand to sell.

inventory turnover ratio A liquidity ratio that indicates how long a company holds its inventory.

investing activities Business activities related to long-term assets. Examples are the purchase and sale of property, plant, and equipment.

investments by owners That part of owners' equity generated by the receipt of cash (or other assets) from the owners.

issued shares Stock that has been distributed to the owners of the corporation in exchange for cash or other assets.

journal A book of original entry used to record the economic events and transactions that affect the accounts of a company.

labor The mental and physical efforts of all workers performing tasks required to produce and sell goods and services. This factor of production is also called the human resource factor.

last-in, first-out (LIFO) The inventory flow concept based on the assumption that the last units of inventory purchased are the first ones sold.

liabilities An accounting element that is one of the three components of a balance sheet. Liabilities are probable future sacrifices of assets arising from present obligations of an entity as a result of past transactions or events—that is, what a company owes.

liquidity An item's nearness to cash.

long-term assets Assets that are expected to benefit the company for longer than one year.

long-term investments Sometimes called *investments*. Investments in securities such as stocks, bonds, and long-term notes receivable; investments in fixed assets that are not currently being used in operations; special funds established to set aside financial resources.

long-term liabilities Liabilities that will not require settlement within one year or the current operating cycle.

losses Net outflows resulting from peripheral activities of a company. An example is the sale of an asset for less than its book value.

management accounting The branch of accounting developed to meet the informational needs of internal decision makers.

manual accounting system An accounting system in which the accountants and bookkeepers write all of the entries by hand in pen and ink.

manufacturing The business activity that converts purchased raw materials into some tangible, physical product.

market interest rate *See* effective interest rate.

market price (of bonds) The amount that investors are actually willing to pay for a bond. A bond's selling price.

matching Accounting principle that relates the expenses to the revenues of a particular income statement period. Once it is determined in which period a revenue should be recognized, the expenses that helped to generate the revenue are matched to that same period.

materiality Something that will influence the judgment of a reasonable person.

merchandise inventory The physical units (goods) a company buys to resell as part of its business operation. Also called inventory.

merchandising The business activity involving the selling of finished goods produced by other businesses.

Modified Accelerated Cost Recovery System (MACRS) Depreciation method taxpayers use to calculate depreciation expense for tax purposes.

monetary unit The assumption that all economic transactions and events can be measured by some monetary unit. In the United States, for example, the dollar is used.

mortgage A document that states the agreement between a lender and a borrower who has secured the loan by offering something of value as collateral.

multiple-step income statement An income statement format that highlights gross margin and operating income.

natural resources Land and the materials that come from the land, such as timber, mineral deposits, oil deposits, and water. One of the factors of production.

net assets *See* equity.

net cash flow The difference between cash inflows and cash outflows; it can be either positive or negative.

net earnings *See* net income.

net income The amount of profit that remains after all costs have been considered. The net reward of doing business for a specific time period.

net loss The difference between revenues and expenses of a period in which expenses are greater than revenues.

net of tax The amount remaining for an item after income tax has been deducted.

net profit *See* net income.

net profit margin ratio A financial ratio that expresses a company's net profit (almost always called either net income or net earnings on the financial statements) as a percentage of sales revenue. It indicates the amount of net income generated by a dollar of sales.

net sales Total sales less any discounts or reductions due to returns or sales allowances..

net worth *See* equity.

neutrality A primary characteristic of reliability. To be useful, accounting information must be free of bias.

nominal interest rate The interest rate set by the issuers of bonds, stated as a percentage of the par value of the bonds. Also called the contract rate.

nonrecurring item Results of activities that are not expected to occur again and, therefore, should not be used to predict future performance.

normal balance The balance of the account derived from the type of entry (debit or credit) that increases the account.

operating activities Activities that result in cash inflows and outflows generated from the normal course of business.

operating cash flow coverage ratio A financial ratio that indicates a company's capacity to repay its liabilities from the net cash generated by its operating activities.

operating cash flow to current debt ratio A financial ratio that measures the sufficiency of cash flows from operating activities to meet current obligations.

operating income Income produced by the major business activity of the company. An item shown on the multiple-step income statement.

opportunity cost The benefit or benefits forgone by not selecting a particular alternative. Once an alternative is selected in a decision situation, the benefits of all rejected alternatives become part of the opportunity cost of the alternative selected.

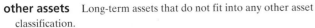

other assets Long-term assets that do not fit into any other asset classification.

outstanding shares Shares of stock actually held by shareholders. The number may be different than that for issued shares because a corporation may reacquire its own stock (treasury stock).

paid-in capital Total amount invested in a corporation by its shareholders.

paid-in capital in excess of par Same thing as additional paid-in capital.

par value (bonds) The amount that must be paid back upon maturity of a bond. Also called face value or maturity value.

par value (stock) An arbitrary amount assigned to each share of stock by the incorporators at the time of incorporation.

partnership A business form similar to a proprietorship, but having two or more owners.

peer companies Companies that are similar to one another, usually in the same industry and of similar size.

periodic inventory system An inventory system in which all inventory and cost of goods sold calculations are done at the end of the income statement period.

periodicity The assumption that the economic activities of an entity can be traced to some specific time period and results of those activities can be reported for any arbitrary time period chosen.

permanent (real) accounts The general ledger accounts that are never closed. The permanent accounts include assets, liabilities, and equity accounts except for owner withdrawals.

perpetual inventory system An inventory system in which both the physical count of inventory units and the cost classification (asset or expense) are updated when a transaction involves inventory.

post-closing trial balance A trial balance prepared after all closing entries have been posted, which proves that the only accounts remaining in the general ledger are the permanent accounts and that the accounting equation remains in balance.

posting The process of transcribing information from journals to the ledger.

predictive value A primary characteristic of relevance. To be useful, accounting must provide information to decision makers that can be used to predict the future and timing of cash flows.

preferred stock A share of ownership in a corporation that has preference over common stock as to dividends and as to assets upon liquidation of the corporation. Usually nonvoting stock.

premium If a bond's selling price is above its par value, the bond is being sold at a premium.

price-to-earnings ratio A financial ratio that is often called simply the PE ratio that expresses the relationship between a company's earnings per share and the market value of the company's stock.

principal In the case of notes and mortgages, the amount of funds actually borrowed.

profit The excess of benefit over sacrifice. A less formal name for net income or net profit.

profitability The ease with which a company generates income.

promissory note A written promise to repay a loan.

property, plant, and equipment Physical long-lived assets used by the business including land, buildings, equipment, machinery, vehicles, and furniture.

proprietorship Same thing as a sole proprietorship.

purchases The amount of merchandise inventory bought during the income statement period.

quick ratio A liquidity ratio that is similar to the current ratio, but a more stringent test of liquidity, because only current assets considered to be highly liquid (quickly converted to cash) are included in the calculation.

quotas A limit on the quantities of particular items that can be imported.

rate of return on assets ratio A financial ratio that shows the amount of profit (net income) produced for a given level of assets.

rate of return on common equity ratio A financial ratio that shows the amount of profit (net income) in relation to the amount of investment by the company's owners.

ratio analysis A technique for analyzing the relationship between two items from a company's financial statements for a given period.

receivables turnover ratio An efficiency ratio that measures how quickly a company collects its accounts receivable.

recognition The process of recording an event in your records and reporting it on your financial statements.

reconciling items Items that are causing the difference between a bank's cash balance and the balance shown on a company's records. These items are listed in the appropriate places on the company's bank reconciliation form.

relevance Pertinent to the decision at hand. The capability of making a difference in a decision by helping users to form predictions or to adjust their expectations.

reliability A characteristic of information whereby decision makers can depend on information actually depicting the reality of a given situation.

representational faithfulness A primary characteristic of reliability. To be useful, accounting information must reasonably report what actually happened.

retained earnings Constitutes the earnings reinvested by the corporation and not distributed to owners in the form of dividends.

revenue An accounting element representing the inflows of assets as a result of an entity's ongoing major or central operations. These are the rewards of doing business.

risk/reward trade-off The relationship between uncertainty and reward. It indicates that the higher the risk, the higher the reward required to induce the risk taking.

sales revenue The revenue generated from the sale of a tangible product as a major business activity.

Securities and Exchange Commission (SEC) The government agency empowered to regulate the buying and selling of stocks and bonds and to establish accounting rules, standards, and procedures, and the form and content of published financial reporting.

selling price (of bonds) See market price (of bonds).

separate entity assumption The assumption that economic activity can be identified with a particular economic entity and that the results of activities for each entity will be recorded separately.

service company A business that performs a service as its major business activity.

single-step income statement A format of the income statement that gathers all revenues into "total revenues" and all expenses into "total expenses." Net income is calculated as a subtraction of total expenses from total revenues.

sole proprietorship An unincorporated business that is owned by one person. Also called a proprietorship.

solvency A company's ability to meet the obligations created by its long-term debt obligations.

special journal A book of original entry designed to record a specific type of transaction.

specific identification method The method of inventory cost flow that identifies each item sold by a company.

stakeholder Anyone who is affected by the way a company conducts its business.

stated rate *See* nominal interest rate.

statement of capital   A statement of owner's equity for a proprietorship.

statement of cash flows   A financial statement that provides information about the causes of a change in the company's cash balance from the beginning to the end of a specific period.

statement of owners' equity   The financial statement that reports activity in the capital accounts of proprietorships and partnerships and in the stockholders' equity accounts of corporations. The statement of owners' equity serves as a bridge between the income statement and the balance sheet.

statement of partners' capital   A statement of owners' equity for a partnership.

statement of results of operations   *See* income statement.

statement of retained earnings   A corporate financial statement that shows the changes in retained earnings during a particular period.

statement of stockholders' equity   The financial statement that shows the changes in owners' equity for a corporation for a given time period.

straight-line depreciation   A method of calculating periodic depreciation. The depreciable base of an asset is divided by its estimated useful life. The result is the amount of depreciation expense to be recognized in each year of the item's useful life: (Cost − Residual Value)/N = Annual Depreciation Expense.

tariffs   Taxes that raise the price of imported products to about the same as similar domestic products.

temporary (nominal) accounts   The general ledger accounts that are closed to a zero balance at the end of the fiscal year as the net income or net loss is transferred to the appropriate equity account. Temporary accounts include revenues, expenses, gains, losses, owner withdrawal, and dividend accounts.

timeliness   A primary characteristic of relevance. To be useful, accounting information must be provided in time to influence a particular decision.

times interest earned ratio   A financial ratio that indicates a company's ability to earn (cover) its periodic interest payments.

title   Legal ownership of something.

treasury stock   Corporate stock that has been issued and then reacquired by the corporation.

trial balance   The listing of the general ledger account balances, which proves that the general ledger and therefore the accounting equation is in balance.

unearned revenue   A liability account used to record a company's liability to provide goods or services, which customers have paid for but have not yet received.

units-of-production depreciation method   A straight-line depreciation method that uses production activity as the basis of allocating depreciation expense. Instead of using an amount of depreciation per year, an amount of depreciation per unit produced is used.

verifiability   A primary characteristic of reliability. Information is considered verifiable if several individuals, working independently, would arrive at similar conclusions using the same data.

withdrawals   *See* drawings.

working capital   The difference between current assets and current liabilities.

worksheet   A tool used by the accountant to accumulate the necessary information used to prepare the financial statements.

yield rate   *See* effective interest rate.

Company Index

Real company names are in bold type.

A

Accelerated Movers, F-265, 266, 280–283
Ace Company, F-347
Ace Corporation, F-111
A&C Enterprises, F-103
Adrienne's Cosmetics, F-393
Alana Bradley Company, F-352–353
Alberto Pons, F-191
Alex's Baseball Card Shop, F-141–142
Allen Corporation, F-300
Al's Boating Supplies, F-142
Alto Corporation, F-110–111
Alvarez Company, F-256
Alvin Smith Company, F-144–145
Amanda's Cooking Supplies, F-100
AMC Entertainment, F-275
American Airlines, F-264, 408
American Express, F-37, 407, 408
American Home Products, F-367
America West Airlines, F-453
Amy Whitaker Company, F-491
Andersen, F-20
Andre Holmes, Inc., F-388–389
Andrew D. Company, F-336
Annie Todd Company, F-492
AOL Time Warner, F-359
A.R. Oddo Leasing Corporation, F-211, 212
Armstrong World Industries, F-372
Art by Nicole, F-392–393
Arthur Johnson Enterprises, F-103
AT&T, F-1
Avonia's Clothes, F-192

B

Baker Company, F-338
Banana Republic, F-11
Bank of America, F-11, 41, 117, 405
Barlow Paving Corporation, F-269–273, 277–280, 288–291
Barnes & Nobles, F-114–115
Bassett Furniture Company, F-304
Bea's Pet Shop, F-144
Bed Bath & Beyond, F-301, 302, 456–485
Belski & Miglio, F-192
Ben Jones Company, F-145
Bennett Corporation, F-108–109
Benny Blades Company, F-347
Best Buy, F-74–75, 78, 89–91, 121
Best Home Improvement Center, F-259–260
Beth Toland Company, F-435
Betty Hart Company, F-293
Big Company, F-109
Bill Carter Company, F-336
Bill Matheis and Company, F-337
Bill Simon Computer Repair, F-246–247
Bishop Company, F-251
Bishop Corporation, F-148
Blockbuster, F-115–116
Blues Brothers Consulting, F-263
Bob Franks and Company, F-189–190
Boeing, F-10, 405, 408
Boston Brothers, F-83
Brad Sanders Auto Repair Shop, F-248

Brandess-Kalt-Aetna Corporation, F-11
Brown Company, F-251–252
BusinessWeek, F-26, 451
Butler Company, F-249
Butterfield Wholesale Company, F-351

C

Calvert Company, F-444
Campbell Soup Company, F-407, 408
Cam's Sportswear, F-297–298
Cargo, F-486
Carlos Garcia Company, F-249
Carl Smythe Company, F-145
Carlson Company, F-345–346
Carl Young Publishing Company, F-293
Carnival Cruise Lines, F-197
Carole's Delivery Service, F-194
Carol Levine Company, F-255–256
Carol Strong Company, F-382–383
Carter, Inc., F-397–398
Casey's Computer Supply, F-340
Chang's Gift Shop, F-339
Charles Company, F-352
Charles Lewis Company, F-444
Chesapeake Corporation, F-372
Chevron, F-268, 372
Chevy, F-65
Chris Scott Corporation, F-299–300
Citibank, F-82
Clarke Company, F-252
Clifford Company, F-252–253
Coca-Cola, F-72, 81, 445, 446
Cohen Company, F-250, 297
Coke, F-445
Collins Container Corporation, F-201, 202, 213–240
Colton Company, F-297
Computer Center of America, F-31
Computer Exchange, Inc., F-306–311
Cooke Company, F-300
Cooking with Penny, F-298
Corning Company, F-347
Cox Company, F-344–345
Cramer Company, F-295
Cronin Corporation, F-162–163
Cunningham Corporation, F-299
Cupcake's Specialty Bakery, F-154

D

Daisy Trading Company, F-351
Dale's Computer Center, F-111
Dana Corporation, F-383
Danielle Company, F-295–296
Danielle's Shoes, F-394–395
Davenport Corporation, F-192
David Brown, Inc., F-296
David Harris Company, F-346
David Luza Corporation, F-105
David Watts and Company, F-62
Debbie Hoffman and Company, F-432–433, 496–499
Delta, F-268
Dennis Lee Company, F-346–347
Dillard's, Inc., F-370

Dillon Corporation, F-62
Dobbs Motor Company, F-313–314
Doran Company, F-432
Dow Chemical, F-81
Dowers Company, F-352
Dunn & Bradstreet, F-457
DuPont, F-9

E

Eastern Airlines, F-453
Eastman Kodak, F-265, 330
Eaton Corporation, F-367
Edwards Company, F-349
Einstein Corporation, F-148
Eliason and Company, F-357–363
Elizabeth Arden, F-116
Elsea Computer Component Company, F-345
Elsea Corporation, F-110
Emerson Radio Corporation, F-115
Enesco Group, F-372
Enron, F-16, 20, 449, 451
Ericsson, F-1
Esposito, Inc., F-300
ExxonMobil, F-368

F

Fashions by Christie, F-391–392
Fineries, F-261–262
First Union, F-41
Fisher, Inc., F-193
Flaherty Company, F-442–443
Flemming Real Estate Company, F-193
Florence Company, F-350
Ford Motor Company, F-11, 500, 501
Fowks Company, F-194
Fox Company, F-156, 399–401
Foxmore Company, F-111
Frank Collins Two Mile High Flight School, F-247
Fred Berfel Enterprises, F-103
Freeport-McMoran Copper & Gold, F-284
Friedman Corporation, F-196–197

G

Gap, F-9, 11, 24
Gaylord Corporation, F-98
General Electric, F-353
General Mills, F-48
General Motors, F-11, 304, 500
Gene's Pool Supply, F-339–340
George R. Violette Company, F-431
Gerner Enterprises, F-112
Gina's Nail Salon, F-142–143
Glenna Corporation, F-196
Global Crossing, F-16, 449
Goodyear, F-10, 81
Gourmet Outlets, F-359
Grand Oil Company, F-109
Green Corporation, F-196
Greenfield Company, F-434
Greif Brothers, F-370
Gruber Company, F-348
Guess, F-445

Snow and Ice Company, F-189
SOBE Entertainment, F-159
South Beach Dive Center, F-113–114
Southwest Airlines, F-267, 453
Speace Electrical Company, F-342
Spring Sales Company, F-343
Sprint, F-1, 265
Stacy Corporation, F-107
Stacyjohn Industries, F-398–399
Stacy Sexton Industries, F-161–162
Stacy's Giftware, F-101
Standard & Poor's, F-26, 486
Staples, F-164, 402
Starbucks, F-138
Steinmann Industries, F-110
Stephen Deitmer Company, F-490–491
Steve Frim Company, F-441–442
Steven Hunter Corporation, F-436–437
Stevens Company, F-250
Steve's Retailing Company, F-351
Straight-Line Movers, F-265, 266, 280–283
Strickland, F-298
Sunny Corporation, F-194–195
Susan Drake and Associates, F-112
Suzanne, Inc., F-301

T

Target, F-8, 265, 408, 451
Tatum Company, F-389
Tatum Sales, Inc., F-350
Texaco, F-8
Thomas Greco Company, F-438–440
Thomas Wholesale Company, F-157
Thompson Company, F-255

3Com, F-267, 270
Tide, F-115
Tiffany & Company, F-120
Todd's Toppers, F-193
Tom Dunn and Company, F-190–191
Tomlin Company, F-338
Tommy Hilfiger, F-500
Tom Robinson Company, F-159–160, 494–496
Toy Box, Inc., F-363–367, 369, 375
Tressa's Treasures, F-152
Tsujimoto's Oriental Rug Factory, F-410–429

U

UAL Corporation, F-267–268
Union Carbide, F-9
United Air Lines, F-264, 267–268
United Stationers, F-368
UPS, F-36–37, 274

V

Ventura Corporation, F-111
Venture Company, F-63–64
Verizon, F-1, 408
Vincent Scelta Company, F-436
Virgin Record Store, F-305
Visa, F-11

W

Walker Company, F-344
Wall Street Journal, F-24, 26, 451

Wal-Mart, F-90, 138, 304, 353, 451
Walt Disney, F-8, 198, 445
Walton Imports, F-440–441
Wayne Cox Enterprises, F-247
Wayne Industries, F-160–161
Weiser Company, F-422
Weiss Company, F-251
Wendy's, F-5
Whitaker Company, F-253–254
Williams Sonoma, F-66, 301, 302, 456–485
William's Wholesale Supply, F-340
Winch Company, F-295
Winter Company, F-338–339
Witt Company, F-389
World Book Encylopedias, F-45
WorldCom, F-16, 20, 449
W.W. Grainger, F-11
Wynn Corporation, F-147–148

X

XXX Pest Control, F-248

Y

Young Company, F-348

Z

Zeus Grocery Store, F-339
Zhang Chinese Trading Company, F-435
Zhang Company, F-100, 105

Subject Index

A

Accelerated depreciation methods, F-268
Accounting Evolution to 1900 (Littleton), F-356
Accounting system
  changes in accounting principles, F-364, 369–370
  classification structure, F-201
  cycle, the accounting
    adjusted trial balance, F-206, 235–237
    adjusting general ledger accounts, F-205–206, 226–235
    analyzing economic events and transactions, F-203, 213–221
    closing entries, preparing/posting, F-207, 237, 239
    financial statements, preparing, F-206, 237, 238
    journalizing transactions, F-203, 213–221
    overview, F-201–202
    post-closing trial balance, F-207, 239–240
    posting transactions to general ledger, F-204–205, 221–225
    trial balance, preparing a, F-205, 226
  debits and credits
    double-entry system of bookkeeping, F-209
    equation, accounting, F-208–209
    normal balance, F-209
    overview, F-208
    revenues/expenses/dividends, F-210–211
    T-account, F-209–210
  general journal, F-212
  learning objectives, F-200–201, 208
  review exercises/questions and key terms, F-241–264
  summary, chapter, F-240–241
  useful information provided by recording/classifying/reporting economic activities, F-1, 12–13
  See also accounting information *under* Decision making, economic; *individual subject headings*
Accounting Trends and Techniques
  comprehensive income, F-372
  depreciation, F-268
  discontinued operations, F-367
  extraordinary items, F-368
  headings of financial statements, F-120
  Income Statement, F-120, 121
  inventory, F-326
  Statement of Stockholders' Equity, F-131
Accounts, definition of, F-201
Accounts payable
  accrual basis accounting, F-183
  adjusting general ledger account balances, F-232
  Statement of Cash Flows, F-416
Accounts receivable
  accrual basis accounting, F-183
  adjusting general ledger account balances, F-229
  Statement of Cash Flows, F-416
  turnover ratio, receivables, F-378, 471–472, 484

Accrual basis accounting, F-173, 303
  See also under Measurement, economic
Accumulated depreciation, F-183, 269
Acid-test ratio, F-379, 475–477
Additional paid-in capital, F-80, 130
Adjusted trial balance as step in accounting cycle, F-206, 235–238
Adjusting general ledger accounts as step in accounting cycle, F-205–206, 226–235
Adjustments and accrual basis accounting, F-178–180
Adverse opinion and audits/auditors, F-22
American Institute of Certified Public Accountants (AICPA), F-19
Analysis, financial statement
  background information, gathering
    economic conditions/expectations, F-450–451
    industry outlook, F-452–453
    political events/climate, F-451–452
  comparative financial statements, F-376, 377
  defining terms, F-92
  learning objectives, F-447–448
  limitations of, F-486–487
  overview, F-16
  peer companies, F-455–460
  profitability ratios
    defining terms, F-461
    dividend payout ratio, F-136, 466–468
    earnings per share, F-136–137, 468–469
    gross profit margin ratio, F-134, 462–463
    net profit margin ratio, F-134–135, 463–464
    price-to-earnings ratio, F-137, 469–470
    rate of return on assets ratio, F-135, 465
    rate of return on common equity ratio, F-135–136, 466
    review exercises/questions and key terms, F-139, 158–164
    summary, chapter, F-483–484
  ratio analysis. *See also* profitability ratios *above*
    debt ratio, F-92–93
    debt-to-equity ratio, F-93
    defining terms, F-92
    efficiency, measuring, F-470–474
    key ratios, summary of, F-454–455
    liquidity, measuring, F-474–477
    overview, F-457, 461
    review exercises/questions and key terms, F-112–114
    solvency ratios, F-477–483
    summary, chapter, F-94, 483–486
  review exercises/questions and key terms, F-488–502
  Statement of Cash Flows, F-137–138
  summary, chapter, F-139, 487
  who does it and why
    creditors, objectives of, F-448–449
    equity investors, objectives of, F-449
    management, objectives of, F-449–450
  See also evaluating items presented on *under* Income Statement; Measurement, economic

Analyzing transactions as step in accounting cycle, F-203, 213–221
Annual Report
  additional information about a company, gathering, F-26, 27–28
  Balance Sheet, F-116
  depreciation, F-302
  equity and debt information, F-114–116
  financial statements, F-402
  general information, F-37, 67–68
  how to get an, F-24–25, 38
  Income Statement, F-165
  information provided in, F-25
  inventory and cost of goods sold, F-353–354
  peer companies, F-264
  Pier 1 Imports, F-505–558
    auditors, report of independent, F-539
    Balance Sheets (2001-2002), consolidated, F-541
    CEO's statements, F-508–509
    charitable contributions, F-522
    directors and officers, F-558
    growth projections, F-518
    highlights (2000-2002), financial, F-506
    key financial statistics (1998-2002), F-526
    management's discussion/analysis of financial condition/results of operations, F-528–539
    notes to consolidated financial statements, F-544–556
    operations (2000-2002), consolidated statements of, F-540
    review exercises/questions and key terms, F-34–35
    shareholder information, F-557
    Statements of Cash Flows (2000-2002), consolidated, F-542
    Statements of Stockholders' Equity (1999-2002), consolidated, F-543
    summary (1998-2002), financial, F-527
  Securities and Exchange Commission, F-447
  Statement of Cash Flows, F-446
  Statement of Owner's Equity, F-165
  strengths/weaknesses/opportunities/threats, F-198–199
  summary, conclusions and recommendations, F-501–502
Articles of incorporation, F-77
Articulation as link among the financial statements, F-131–132
Assets
  Balance Sheet, F-14, 71, 357–360
  cash used to acquire, F-86–87
  current, F-357–359
  debt ratio, F-92–93, 478–479, 485
  equation, accounting/business, F-73–75, 208–209, 211, 357
  intangible, F-359
  long-term, F-359
  rate of return on assets ratio, F-135, 465
  turnover ratio, F-376–377, 470–471, 484
  See also Cash; Depreciation
Audits/auditors, F-20–22
Authorized shares, F-78
Average cost inventory method, F-322–324